Moholy-Nagy: Mentor to Modernism

by

Lloyd C. Engelbrecht

with essays by Hattula Moholy-Nagy
and Regan Brown

volume two

Cincinnati: Flying Trapeze Press, 2009

DVD design by Regan Brown

graphic design by Lloyd C. Engelbrecht

printed on acid-free paper by
Corporate Printing, Cincinnati

ISBN: 978-0-615-32366-4

Table of Contents, Volumes One and Two

Chapter Three: the Bauhaus Years, 1923-1928   196

DVD Tutorial, by Regan Brown

Table of Contents, Volumes One and Two

Chapter Four: Berlin, Amsterdam and London; Essays on the Life and Work of a Versatile Creative Man, 1928-1937

Film Clip 3, excerpt from *Exhibition of Student Work*, a color film of 1942 showing László Moholy-Nagy looking at student work in progress

Illustrated Selected Bibliography of Works Cited, in Adobe PDF format

Moholy-Nagy: Mentor to Modernism in Adobe PDF format, including the entire text with all figures, sound clips and film clips

Video Tutorial, filmed by Regan Brown

Chapter Four: Berlin, Amsterdam and London; Essays on the Life and Work of a Versatile Creative Man, 1928-1937

"By 1929 Germany had become the world's second industrial power behind the United States."
—Paul Bookbinder, 1996

"What once had been the most progressive capital in Europe had become a provincial town of gigantic proportions."
—Franz Schulz (Spencer), 1934

"[The strategy of England's Unit One is] to form a point in the forward thrust of modernism in architecture, painting and sculpture, and to harden this point in the fires of criticism and controversy."
—Herbert Read, 1934

WITHOUT THE DEMANDS on his energy that his intensive involvement in teaching required, Moholy's activities became so diverse as to become mind-boggling. These activities, centered in Berlin, Amsterdam and London, included designs for the spoken theatre as well as for grand opera, graphic design, exhibition design, interior design, photography in black-and-white and color, movies, sound experiments, continued exploration of the interaction of painting with new materials on which to paint, increasing productivity as a lecturer and writer, and speculation about new media such as light shows on natural and artificial mists. His social life continued to center on avant-garde artists and writers, and his personal life became fluid as his marriage (but not his friendship) with Lucia disintegrated as he developed close relationships with Ellen Frank, sister-in-law of Walter Gropius, and then with Sibyl Pietzsch, who became his second wife in 1935. His move to London later in the same year enabled him to enjoy a home life that included Sibyl and their two daughters, one born in Berlin and the other in London. In addition to his participation in group exhibitions, single-artist showings were staged in Paris, Amsterdam, Utrecht, Rotterdam, Brno, Bratislava, London and New York. Because Moholy's activities were so diverse from 1928 to 1937, I have not opened this chapter with a summary. In effect, this chapter is a series of long and short essays putting aspects of Moholy's life and work into a context of time and place.

Berlin beckoned as Moholy prepared to leave Dessau in April, 1928. The German capital had become a different city from the one he had known just five years earlier; the "dance on the edge of the volcano," as Peter Gay so memorably termed it, continued, for Berlin had retained its lively theatrical, literary, artistic and musical culture, along with its bustling cafés and cabarets, but Germany's metropolis had also become more prosperous and had thus become a good base for an innovative design practice and, indeed, proved to be such fertile ground for design reform that Moholy emerged as a cultural star.

After settling in Berlin, László and Lucia worked closely together on design commissions. Although, as noted in the previous chapter, their marriage had begun to break up as early as May, 1928,[1] Moholy recalled that they stopped living together about a year after that; nevertheless as late as the end of October, 1931, they still saw each other very often.[2] They not only continued to be friends, but maintained a close professional relationship, as will be seen throughout this chapter.

Moholy's Design Studio in Berlin

The transition from Dessau to Berlin was eased for László and Lucia by a number of Bauhäusler who worked with them in their design studio in the German capital. These included Max Gebhard (1906-1990), who had studied with Moholy at the Bauhaus and worked in the Berlin studio in 1928 and 1929; he provided some revealing information about his experiences in the studio.[3]

Hannes Neuner (born 1906), worked with Herbert Bayer in the Dorland studio in Berlin before working in Moholy's studio during the years 1933 through 1935; from 1929 to 1931 he had been at the Bauhaus, where he studied advertising design with Joost Schmidt and photography with Walter Peterhans.[4] Another member of Moholy's Berlin

---

[1] As noted in Chapter Three, the simple note, "anfang mai: berlin moholy—ellen frank," appears on a page dating from 1928 in Lucia Moholy's diary, Bauhaus-Archiv, Berlin, Inv. Nr. 11782/18. Divorces were not easy to obtain, and, as noted in Chapter Two, the divorce of László and Lucia did not become legally valid until March 3, 1934.

[2] László Moholy-Nagy to Matthew Josephson, October 26, 1931, TLS, Matthew Josephson Papers, Box 8, folder 200, Beinecke Rare Book and Manuscript Library, Yale University, New Haven, Connecticut.

[3] Max Gebhard, "Erinnerungen des Bauhäuslers Max Gebhard an Moholy-Nagy," in: Irene-Charlotte Lusk, *Montagen ins Blaue; Laszlo Moholy-Nagy Fotomontagen und-collagen 1922-1943* (Giessen: Anabas-Verlag Günter Kämpf KG, 1980), 181-182; and Bogomil J. Helm, "Produktive Begegnungen: Gespräch mit Max Gebhard," in: Klaus Kändler, Helga Karolewski and Ilse Siebert, editors, *Berliner Begegnungen: ausländische Künstler in Berlin 1918 bis 1933* (Berlin: Dietz Verlag, 1987), 301-310, here 305-308.

[4] On Hannes Neuner, see: Sabine Hartmann and Karsten Hinz, "Hannes Neuner," in: Jeanine Fiedler, editor, *Photography at the Bauhaus* (Cambridge, Massachusetts: The MIT Press, 1990), 351; Max Bense, *Hannes Neuner: Kugelplastiken* (Darmstadt: Eduard Roether Verlag, 1973), 59; and Hans M. Wingler, editor, *Hannes Neuner und seine Grundlehre: eine Weiterentwicklung des Bauhaus-Vorkurses* (Berlin: Bauhaus-Archiv, 1973), unpaginated (third page after title page).

studio was Hein Neuner (1910-1984), brother of Hannes;[5] he also had studied at the Bauhaus.[6]

Other Bauhäusler working for Moholy in Berlin included Hajo (Hans-Joachim) Rose (1910-1989),[7] in the studio in 1933 and 1934;[8] and Erich Comeriner (1907-1978),[9] in the studio from 1929 to 1933.[10] Hin Bredendieck (1904-1995), who had studied with Moholy at the Bauhaus,[11] was in the studio in 1930 and 1931.[12] Still another Bauhäusler in Moholy's studio was Gyula Pap, who worked in the studio in 1932, when he helped with designs for *die neue linie*,[13] for which he recalled working on the *Karneval* [*i.e., Fasching*] issue, [volume II, number 5 (January, 1931)]. (DVD figure 276)

---

[5]Walter Scheiffele, "Typofoto und Jenaer Haushaltglas: László Moholy-Nagys Reklame für Schott & Gen.," in: Gottfried Jäger and Gudrun Wessing, editors, *über moholy-nagy* (Bielefeld: Kerber Verlag, 1997), 225-233, here 225.

[6]Ute Brüning and Magdalene Droste, editors, *Das A und O des Bauhauses; Bauhauswerbung: Schriftbilder, Drucksachen, Austellungsdesign* (Leipzig: Ed. Leipzig; Berlin: Bauhaus-Archiv, 1995), 325.

[7]On Hajo Rose, see: Sabine Hartmann and Karsten Hinz, "Hajo Rose," in: Fiedler, editor, *Photography at the Bauhaus*, 342-353; Kurt Schmidt, editor, *Marianne Brandt, Hajo Rose, Kurt Schmidt: drei Künstler am Bauhaus; Ausstellung im Kupferstich-Kabinett . . . vom 15. März bis 26. Mai 1978* (Dresden: Kupferstich-Kabinett des Staatlichen Kunstsammlungen Dresden, 1978), 1 and 4-[9]; and Amanda Hochensmith, "Hajo (Hans-Joachim) Rose," in: Matthew Witkovsky, editor, *Foto: Modernity in Central Europe, 1918-1945* (New York: Thames & Hudson Inc., 2007), 244.

[8]Schmidt, editor, *Marianne Brandt, Hajo Rose, Kurt Schmidt*, 4; Hochensmith, "Hajo (Hans-Joachim) Rose," 244; Scheiffele, "Typofoto und Jenaer Haushaltglas," 225-227; and Brüning and Droste, editors, *Das A und O des Bauhauses*, 326.

[9]On Erich Comeriner see: Sabine Hartmann and Karsten Hinz, "Erich Comeriner," in: Fiedler, editor, *Photography at the Bauhaus*, 343-344; Gerd Fleischmann, editor, *Bauhaus Drucksachen, Typografie, Reklame* [from the collection of Grete and Walter Dexel, now in the Getty Research Center, Los Angeles] (Dusseldorf: Edition Marzona, 1984), 290-295; Elizabeth Cronin, "Erich Comeriner," in: Witkovsky, editor, *Foto: Modernity in Central Europe*, 223; and Brüning and Droste, editors, *Das A und O des Bauhauses*, 195 and 269.

[10]Scheiffele, "Typofoto und Jenaer Haushaltglas," 226; and Brüning and Droste, editors, *Das A und O des Bauhauses*, 321.

[11]László Moholy-Nagy, *The New Vision: Fundamentals of Bauhaus Design, Painting, Sculpture, and Architecture, with Abstract of an Artist* (Mineola, New York: Dover Publications, Inc., 2005), 128.

[12]Jeannine Fiedler, "Kurzbiografien," in: Peter Hahn and Lloyd C. Engelbrecht, editors, *50 Jahre New Bauhaus; Bauhausnachfolge in Chicago,* (Berlin: Argon Verlag, 1987), 249-269, here 251.

[13]Gyula Pap, "Moholy-Nagy László Kiállitása Ürügyén," *Ars Hungarica*, volume V, number 1 (1977), 147-150.

T HESE ASSISTANTS, in effect, demonstrated that the Bauhaus had prepared its students to work creatively and effectively on a wide variety of design commissions. Also contributing to a Bauhaus ambience in Berlin was the circumstance that former Bauhaus students working in Berlin for Moholy, Breuer, Bayer and Gropius interacted and communicated with each other, as described by Bayer's assistant, Kurt Kranz (born 1910).[14] Among the Bauhäusler on Gropius's staff was Marianne Brandt, who worked there from July to December, 1929.[15] Although she and Moholy were in contact with each other several times after they had left the Bauhaus,[16] they never worked together. Most of these contacts can not be documented, but Sibyl Moholy-Nagy, who met her future husband in 1931, had gotten to know her well, which would have been through Moholy.[17] Just as Moholy was about to move to London, he received a letter from Brandt reporting that she was feeling sad and isolated,[18] as he and Gropius were trying, without success, to get her some work in England.[19]

Not all of Moholy's Berlin studio staff had been associated with the Bauhaus: György Kepes (1906-2001), who was in the studio from 1930 to 1935, had studied art in Hungary;[20] Werner Bürger, in the studio about 1931, had studied in the *Staatliche*

---

[14]Kurt Kranz, "Bauhaus Pedagogy and Thereafter," in: Eckhard Neumann, editor, *Bauhaus and Bauhaus People: Personal Opinions and Recollections of Former Bauhaus Members and Their Contemporaries*, revised edition (New York: Van Nostrand Reinhold, 1993), 268-282, here 277.

[15]Hans Brockhage and Reinhold Lindner, *Marianne Brandt; "Hab ich je an Kunst gedacht"* (Chemnitz: Chemnitzer Verlag, 2001), 220.

[16]*E.g.*, László Moholy-Nagy to Marianne Brandt, TLS, September 13, 1932, Bauhaus-Archiv, Berlin.

[17]Sibyl Moholy-Nagy to Ise Gropius, photographic copy of TLS, October 27, 1947, Bauhaus-Archiv, Berlin.

[18]László Moholy-Nagy to Ise and Walter Gropius, TLS, April 10, 1935, Bauhaus-Archiv, Berlin. In the lettler, Mohoy described Brandt's letter, which cannot now be located.

[19]László Moholy-Nagy to Ise and Walter Gropius, MLS, April 4, 1935; László Moholy-Nagy to Ise and Walter Gropius, MLS, April 10, 1935; and Walter Gropius to László Moholy-Nagy, April 6, 1935; all three letters are in the Bauhaus-Archiv, Berlin.

One of the firms Gropius had in mind for Brandt was Best & Lloyd, a lighting firm in Manchester.

[20]György Kepes, interviewed by Robert Brown, March 7 and Aug. 30, 1972, and Jan. 11, 1973, pages 4-8 in a typescript in the Archives of American Art, Washington, D.C.; and Hattula Moholy-Nagy interviewing György Kepes, May 11, 1981, xerox copies of two pages of notes are in my files. See also: Sibyl Moholy-Nagy, *Laszlo Moholy-Nagy: Experiment in Totality*, second edition (Cambridge: M.I.T. Press, 1969) , 62-63.

On Kepes, see: Lloyd C. Engelbrecht, "Kepes, Gyorgy," in: Colin Naylor, editor, *Contemporary Designers*, second edition (Chicago: St. James Press, 1990), 293-294.

Akademie für graphische Künste und Buchgewerbe zu Leipzig (now *Die Hochschule für Grafik und Buchkunst Leipzig*);[21] and Stefan Sebök (1901-1942), in the studio in 1929 and 1930, had studied architecture in the *Sächsische technische Hochschule Dresden.*[22]

Architect Rudolf Luderer also worked for Moholy, but not much could be found about him. As discussed below, he worked as a draftsman with Moholy and Sebök in connection with exhibition spaces in Paris and Hanover.

The studio staff often worked very independently, sometimes with minimal contact with Moholy, who was frequently away from the studio for most of the day.[23]

Gebhard, himself a Communist activist, remembered Moholy as one who chose to refrain from any active role in day-to-day politics, although he had very strong social feelings.[24] Moholy himself described his views on politics to an American friend late in 1931; these views were discernibly less inclined toward an activist position than they had seemed to be in the period just before he moved to Weimar, as discussed in Chapter Two, and constitute an important and perceptive statement:

> inzwischen kam in deutschland eine ganz aussergewöhnliche depression, eine unerhört starke rechtsradikalisierung breiter volksschichten und augenblicklich ist die lage so, dass kein mensch aus und ein weiss.
>
> es scheint mir, dass die intellektuellen und liberalen bürgerlichen von dem unabwendbaren sieg des kommunismus überzeugt sind, aber die arbeiterschaft selbst nicht genügend vertrauen in dieser, in eigenen lösung hat.
>
> das beispiel russlands begeistert die leute, aber gleichzeitig stösst sie ab, weil sie oft falsch informiert, angst haben, dass eine proletar-diktatur oder ein kommunismus das individuum zu sehr nivellieren würde.
>
> es existiert auch unter den intellektuellen und der arbeiterschaft eine kleine gruppe von syndikalisten (anarchitsten), die scharfe gegner der kommunisten sind, die alles autotiäre ablehnen und die organisation einer zukünftigen gesellschaft von der arbeit der räte von unten hinauf erwarten.
>
> ich selbst bin der meinung, dass der kommunismus evenso ein schrittmacher des sozialistischen anarchismus ist, wie die sozialdemokratie ein schrittmacher des kommunismus gewesen war. ich bin selbst in keiner partei drin und wenn ich manche verbindung zu den parteileuten habe, brüte ich meist über eigene

---

[21]Scheiffele, "Typofoto und Jenaer Haushaltglas," 226.

[22]Hubertus Gaßner, editor, *!Avantgarden! in Mitteleuropa 1910-1930* (Munich: Haus der Kunst, 2002), 25-26; and Karin Wilhelm, Stefan Sebök e l'Idea di 'Totaltheater'," *Casabella*, number 551, volume LII), number 551 (November, 1988), 34-45, here 34.

[23]According to Werner Bürger, quoted in: Scheiffele, "Typofoto und Jenaer Haushaltglas," 225.

[24]Gebhard, "Erinnerungen," 182.

probleme und ich glaube, dass die wirkliche revolution eines metiers nicht von den politischen lösungen, sondern aus revolutionierung des metiers selbst kommen kann.

ich bin noch immer der meinung, dass meine aufgabe wäre, aus der pigmentmalerei eine lichtgestaltung zu machen und ich beschäftige mich mit filmideen fast mehr als mit malerei.[25]

[Meanwhile there is in Germany an extraordinary economic Depression, an unheard-of strong right-oriented radicalization among a wide range of people, and at the moment the situation is that no one knows what is happening.

It seems to me that the intellectuals and the liberal middle class are convinced of the ultimate victory of Communism, but the proletariat themselves do not have sufficient trust in this as an intrinsic solution.

The example of Russia inspires people, but at the same time repels them, because they are often misled, and fear a dictatorship of the proletariat or a Communism that would put all individuals at the same level.

There is also among the intellectuals and the proletariat a small group of syndicalists (anarchists), who are strong opponents of Communism, who abhor all authority, and await the organization of a future society from within their own ranks.

I myself am of the opinion that socialist anarchy leads to Communism, as Communism has led to social democracy. I myself am in no party and while I have many ties to party activists, I am concerned with my own problems and, I believe, the true revolution of a profession does not have a political solution, but can come out of the particular profession itself.

It is also my opinion that my task would be to replace pigment painting with creating with light, and I am involved with film ideas almost more than with painting.]

This was summarized more succinctly by Moholy late in his life:

The so-called "unpolitical" approach to art is a fallacy. Politics is taken here, not in its party connotation, but as a way of realizing ideas for the benefit of the community.[26]

Although some studio activities took place in the dwelling Lucia and László shared on Spichernstraße, as described below, László's most visible Berlin studio was located atop an apartment building in the *Bezirk* [borough] of Charlottenburg; it is now considered a modernist landmark, albeit one that had no direct connection with the Bauhaus. Opened in 1929, it has imaginative white façades on Kaiserdamm, Königin

---

[25]László Moholy-Nagy to Matthew Josephson, October 26, 1931.

[26]László Moholy-Nagy, *The New Vision* (2005), 220.

Elisabeth Straße and Fredericiastraße designed by Hans Scharoun (1893-1972) to enclose interior spaces devised by Georg Jacobowitz to appeal to young professionals.[27] (DVD figures 219and 220) On the ground level were a restaurant and retail shops, above which are four storeys of single-room units as well as two-room suites with small kitchens,[28] each unit having its own bath. The building is served by an underground garage and the top level consists of roof areas enlivened by studios and roof gardens. Moholy's studio was on this top level, served by an elevator, and Fredericiastraße 27, Atelier, was the address. (DVD figures 221 and 222)

The building is unusual in that, while the longest portion of the building, facing Königin Elisabeth Straße, has a flat roof, parts of the southern and northern portions have gabled roofs. The north surface of the gable over the space that was Moholy's studio is a skylight. (DVD figures 221 and 222) Attached to the studio was a bedroom,[29] but the "kitchen" facilities consisted only of a small cupboard.[30] Nevertheless Moholy used this as his living quarters for an undetermined length of time after breaking up with Lucia and before moving into an apartment on Lietzenseeufer, as described below. During the early years of the Nazi era, Xanti Schawinsky recalled, "Moholy helped people who were persecuted and in the most dangerous situations sheltered them in the room adjoining his studio."[31]

The Berlin studio remained in operation until Moholy moved to London in May of 1935, even after Amsterdam had become the center of his own activities.

Out of the Studio and Into the Lecture Hall

Punctuating all of the activities described below were Moholy's frequent appearances as an invited lecturer. He summed these up late in 1930 as taking place in almost all of the larger cities of Germany as well as in numerous cities in other countries, some but not all presented in connection with exhibitions. Not enough information is available to discuss all of these lectures in detail, but what stands out in Moholy's summary is a semester-long series of guest lectures in *Die Hochschule für Grafik und Buchkunst Leipzig* [Leipzig Institute for Graphic and Book Arts] on the topic "die optische

---

[27]Peter Blundell Jones, *Hans Scharoun* (London: Phaidon Press, Ltd., 1995), 63-64.

[28]Rolf Rave and Hans-Joachim Knöfel, *Bauen seit 1900 in Berlin* (Berlin: Verlag Kiepert, 1968), column 162.

[29]Hattula Moholy-Nagy interviewing György Kepes, May 11th, 1981; xerox copies of two pages of notes are in my files. See also: Sibyl Moholy-Nagy, *Moholy-Nagy: Experiment in Totality*, 69.

[30]Sibyl Moholy-Nagy, *Moholy-Nagy, Experiment in Totality*, 63.

[31]Xanti Schawinsky to Sibyl Moholy-Nagy, August 25th, 1948, quoted in English translation in: Krisztina Passuth, *Moholy-Nagy* (New York: Thames and Hudson, 1985), 410-412, here 411.

gestaltung" [optical form-giving].[32] In his summary, Moholy was evidently referring to the summer semester of 1928, which in Germany meant a term beginning about April 1st and running until about the end of July; whether he had agreed to the lecture series before resigning from the Bauhaus cannot now be ascertained, but it is possible that he had originally planned a series of round trips from Dessau to nearby Leipzig and had to adjust his plans to accommodate the much longer distance from Leipzig to Berlin after he moved there.

What appears to be an indication of his approach to his lecture series in Leipzig was published in 1928 as "elementare buchtechnik," discussed below, evidently written before the lectures because it appeared in a catalogue connected with an exhibition that opened May 11th, 1928.[33]

Another text provided further details of his approach to typography in his lectures in Leipzig; this text appeared on eight panels at a traveling exhibition, that opened May 20th, 1929, in Berlin; that exhibition, and the text on these panels, are discussed below; see pages 385 and 386.

Some of Moholy's other lectures are discussed in appropriate places below.

Opera on the Barricades: Moholy
and the Einsteins at the Kroll

A LEADING GERMAN MUSIC CRITIC, Adolf Weißmann (1873-1929), pointed out in the 1920s that Germany ". . . has the best-organized operatic system in the world."[34] He added: "No other country does for opera what Germany is doing." John Rockwell put this into historical context by explaining that opera was ". . . central to most Germans' self-image as a cultured people. At least since the time of Richard Wagner, opera had seemed to them an inherently German art form."[35] The importance of opera to the cultural life of Germany during the Weimar period is also evident from the fact that Germany then had about one-hundred separate opera companies, three of them

---

[32] László Moholy-Nagy, "für die darmstädter-sammlung," December 5, 1930 [three-page handwritten manuscript of answers to a questionnaire]. The copy in the Bauhaus-Archiv, Berlin, is labeled: "Orig. in der Staatsbibliothek Handschriftenabt.."

[33] László Moholy-Nagy, "elementare buchtechnik," in: Verein deutsche Buchkünstler, *Europäische Buchkunst der Gegenwart* (Leipzig: Verlag Rudolf Schick & Co., 1928), 60-64.

[34] Adolf Weissmann, *Music Come to Earth*, translated by Eric Blom (London: J.M. Dent and Sons, Ltd., 1930), 93. Germans spelled Weismann's last name as Weißman; two German editions of the book appeared in 1926 and 1930.

[35] John Sargent Rockwell, "The Prussian Ministry of Culture and the Berlin State Opera, 1918-1931" (Ph.D. dissertation, University of California, Berkeley, 1972), xiii.

in Berlin.[36] Hence it is not surprising that Moholy's standing as a cultural star in Germany stemmed in large part from his brief but widely-noted career as an opera designer.

Moholy designed for the Kroll Opera, or *Kroll-Oper*, officially known as the *Staatsoper am Platz der Republik* [{Prussian} State Opera on the Plaza of the Republic], a branch of the State Opera which operated its main theatre on *Unter den Linden*. The Kroll Opera, formed in 1927, presented innovative performances that were frequented by such notables as physicist and humanitarian Albert Einstein, Minister of Foreign Affairs Gustav Stresemann, writer Thomas Mann, and philosopher and cultural critic Walter Benjamin.[37]

The site of the Kroll Opera, near the Spree River and the large park known as the *Tiergarten*, was part of an elegant and fashionable indoor-and-outdoor entertainment complex dating well back into the nineteenth century. Its founder was restaurateur Joseph Kroll, who died in 1848, but the name "Kroll" had retained, for Berliners, an air of good times in festive surroundings.[38] The well-equipped theatre that dominated the site had recently been extensively remodeled and modernized by Oskar Kaufmann (1873-1956), a specialist in theatre design.[39] (DVD figure 223)

Otto Klemperer (1875-1973), the founder of the Kroll Opera, explained what had made it special:

> At the Kroll we were in the fortunate position of only having to give a limited number of operas. . . . Each year we had only to offer, at the most, seven to ten operas, which were then repeated very often. What I wanted to achieve at the Kroll was a good opera house that would be untouched by the bad practices of the repertory system and illuminated by the light of a new direction.[40]

---

[36]Weissmann, *Music Come to Earth*, 88; and Susan C. Cook, *Opera for a New Republic: the Zeitopern of Krenek, Weill and Hindemith* (Ann Arbor, Michigan: UMI Research Press, 1988), [1]-3.

[37]Peter Heyworth, editor, *Conversations with Klemperer*, revised edition (London: Faber and Faber, 1985), 80; Hans Heinz Stuckenschmidt, quoted in: Rockwell, *op. cit.,* 217; and Hans Curjel, *Experiment Krolloper, 1927-1931* [edited by] Eigel Kruttge (Munich: Prestel Verlag, 1975), 70, 74 and 353-355.

[38]Curjel, *Experiment Krolloper*, 157-160; Hans J. Reichhardt, *. . . bei Kroll 1844 bis 1957: Etablissement, Ausstellungen, Theater, Konzerte, Oper, Reichstag, Gartenlokal* (Berlin: Transit Buchverlag, 1988), 7-84; and Thomas Wieke, *Vom Etablissement zur Oper; die Geschichte der Kroll-Oper* (Berlin: Haude & Spener, 1993).

[39]Curjel, *Experiment Krolloper*, 160-166. A plan and illustrations of the Kroll Opera House can be found in: *Der Architect Oskar Kaufmann*, Vorwort von Oscar Bie (Berlin: Ernst Pollak Verlag, 1928), pages 74-82, unnumbered pages facing page 74 and following page 79.

[40]Heyworth, editor, *Conversations with Klemperer*, 68-69.

One of the Kroll singers, Jarmila Novotna (1907-1994; she is discussed below for her role in *Madama Butterfly*), later recalled of Klemperer, "He was a very stern conductor who worked incessantly to obtain a homogeneous ensemble."[41]

Another view of Klemperer during his Kroll years came from Otto Wertheimer:

> In Klemperer, Berlin has a wide-awake, enthusiastic spirit, who as a follower of modern music accomplishes great things. He even understands how to embellish old operas and make them interesting.

As an example of the latter accomplishment, Wertheimer cited a contribution by Moholy, which I have discussed in detail below:

> At the presentation of *Tales of Hoffmann* one encountered something as new, for the stylization of the performance through the arrangement of the scenery by Professor Moholy-Nagy from the Bauhaus in Dessau made possible a uniform presentation.[42]

The limited number of operas presented per year was made possible by the help of several theatre clubs, the largest of which dated back to 1890. There was a mutually beneficial arrangement that provided a measure of financial stability to the Kroll Opera, while a large number of seats were sold at reduced prices to the members of the theatre clubs.[43]

Klemperer recognized that: "The two other opera houses [in Berlin] had better voices than we did. Our singers were limited, though some of them were very good."[44] But since all of the Kroll productions were rehearsed with exceptional care and thereafter

---

[41] Jarmila Novotna, interviewed in 1979, quoted in: Lanfranco Rasponi, *The Last Prima Donnas* (New York: Alfred A. Knopf, 1982), 320.

[42] Otto Wertheimer, "Recent Art Activities in Berlin," *Parnassus*, volume I, number 7 (November, 1929), 32-36 and 44, here 35 and 36. *Parnassus* was published by the influential College Art Association, based in New York.

[43] Rockwell, *op. cit*, 3, 207-208, 266-274 *et passim*; Cecil Davies, *The Volksbühne Movement: a History* (Amsterdam: Harwood Academic Publishers, 2000), 15-47 *passim* and 102; Peter Heyworth, *Otto Klemperer, His Life and Times* (Cambridge, England: Cambridge University Press, 1983), 1:186-187 and 1:276-277; Antony Beaumont, *Zemlinsky* (London: Faber and Faber, 2000), 351; Harold H. Punke, "Subsidized Opera, Concerts and Related Agencies in German Adult Education for Leisure Time," *School and Society*, volume XXXVI, number 916 (July 16, 1932), 86-88, here 87; and John Willett, *Art and Politics in the Weimar Period: the New Sobriety, 1917-1933* (New York: Pantheon Books, 1978), 160-161 and 210-211.

[44] Heyworth, editor, *Conversations with Klemperer*, 80.

In his *Experiment Krolloper*, Curjel discussed the singers ("Die Sängerfrage," 33-36), and listed the casts for every production (219-314).

maintained in quality by follow-up rehearsals,[45] one can presume that Kroll patrons enjoyed accomplished acting and ensemble singing; in any case, the result, according to Hans Heinz Stuckenschmidt, was:

> In every performance and even in every rehearsal of the Kroll Opera, there was an atmosphere of spiritual tension. . . . This theater was in some magical way more than a temple of art. One felt that its artistic efforts were part of some larger task.[46]

The reaction of the audience, typically a mix of a few proletarian and many petit-bourgeois theatre-club members, along with some well-to-do opera-lovers and intellectuals from various fields, was described thus by Stuckenschmidt: "Some applauded wildly, some protested with whistles and shouts, but nobody kept silent. People were concerned."[47]

Moholy was probably recruited to work for the Kroll Opera by Hans Curjel (1896-1974), who, like him, was a bit of a polymath. Curjel was not only an art historian but also was an orchestra conductor who worked as a theatre producer and director, and in addition was active as a dramaturge. Curjel had visited the Bauhaus in Weimar in 1923 to see its summer exhibition;[48] he had also visited the school in Dessau in 1925 in an unsuccessful attempt to get a teaching position in theatre there.[49] There is no documentation proving that he met Moholy at that time, but Curjel was a friend of Sigfried Giedion,[50] who was also one of Moholy's friends, so a meeting with Moholy in Dessau during Curjel's visit there was likely. At the time Moholy began work on his first opera at the Kroll, Curjel was an adviser to Otto Klemperer, its principal conductor and Gropius-like guiding spirit, who also shared administrative duties with Ernst Legal (1881-1955), one of its stage directors. In 1931 Curjel became deputy director.

---

[45]Rockwell, *op. cit*, 207.

[46]Hans Heinz Stuckenschmidt, quoted in: Rockwell, *op. cit.*, 219; and in: Curjel, *Experiment Krolloper*, 73-74.

[47]Stuckenschmidt, quoted in: Rockwell, *op. cit.*, 219; and in: Curjel, *Experiment Krolloper*, 74.

[48]Curjel described his 1923 visit to Weimar in a letter to a newspaper editor: *Allgemeine Thüringische Landeszeitung Deutschland*, April 29, 1924, [1]. A copy is in: Theo van Doesburg files, Rijksbureau voor Kunsthistorische Dokumentie, The Hague, also available on microfiche (*Theo van Doesburg Archive*, Leiden: IDC, 1991), sheet 270.

[49]Day-book entry by Ise Gropius for September 21, 1925.

[50]*Ibid.*

Several designers from Moholy's studio worked with him at the Kroll Opera, including Gebhard,[51] Kepes[52] and Sebök.[53] Lucia Moholy documented her estranged husband's Kroll settings with skillful and appealing photographs that still are widely esteemed and have appeared frequently in publications. (DVD figures 225, 228, 232, 233, 240, 241, 243 and 244).

Working with Moholy from the Kroll Opera staff was Teo Otto (1904-1968). He later recalled the experience in a radio broadcast interview:

> Ich erinnere mich, daß Moholy . . . eine faszinierende Mischung war von Liebenswürdigkeit und unerbittlicher Zähigkeit. Ich meine, er machte nicht die geringste Konzession. Das war auch sehr gut und steuerte zum Experiment hin. Sie erinerre sich eine besondere Weise "Hoffmanns Erzählungen" in der damalig doch sensationallen Aufführung—viel kritiziert.[54] [I remember that Moholy . . . was a fascinating blend of amiability and pitiless toughness. I mean, he did not make the slightest concession. That was also very good and guided the experiment forward. One remembers in a special way "The Tales of Hoffmann" although at the time a sensational production—much criticized.]

Indeed Teo Otto's assertion was justified: the most spectacular setting Moholy devised for the Kroll Opera was *The Tales of Hoffmann* (originally known as *Les Contes d'Hoffmann*; also known as *Hoffmanns Erzählungen*), of 1929.[55] And none of his other works of art or design evoked more critical comment.[56] (Reviewers of his gallery exhibitions rarely commented on individual works.)

---

[51]Gebhard, "Erinnerungen," 181; and Eckhard Neumann, editor, *Bauhaus und Bauhäusler; Erinnerungen und Bekenntnisse*, erweiterte Neuausgabe (Cologne: DuMont Buchverlag, 1985), 196.

[52][Elizabeth Siegel and Julie Stone (née Kepes)], biographical outline of György Kepes, seven-page word-processing computer printout, Photography Department files, Art Institute of Chicago.

[53]Gebhard, "Erinerungen," 181.

[54]Teo Otto, radio interview as part of a presentation, "Die Berliner Krolloper," broadcast November 24 and December 1, 1962; transcription included in: Curjel, *Experiment Krolloper*, [15]-84, quotation on pages 50-51.

[55]Many of the drawings made for the production are in the Theatre Collection of the University of Cologne Institute of Theatre-, Film- and Television Studies. Three of these are illustrated in: Elmar Buck, *Vision Raum Szene: Gemälde, Graphik, Skulptur, Plakat, Foto, Film in der Theaterwissentlischaftlichen Sammlung Schloß Wahn, Universität Köln* (Kassel: Verlag M. Faste, 2001), 248-251. Six are illustrated in: Hannelore Kersting and Bernd Vogelsang, editors, *Raumkonzepte; konstruktivische Tendenzen in Bühnen- und Bildkunst, 1910-1930* (Frankfurt am Main: Städtische Galerie im Städelschen Kunstinstitut, 1986), 351-352 and 354-355. Additional drawings are in a private collection.

[56]Some of the Kroll reviews are reprinted in: Curjel, *Experiment Krolloper*, 259-267. The critics are described in *ibid.*, 215-218.

ORIGINALLY PERFORMED in 1881 at the *Opéra Comique* in Paris, *The Tales of Hoffmann* had been composed by Jacques Offenbach (1819-1880). Offenbach had made his reputation with lighter theatrical fare, and *The Tales of Hoffmann* was his only successful stage work with sufficient *gravitas* to be considered grand opera.[57] He provided glorious but highly entertaining music that highlighted themes of mystery and magic in the libretto; what emerges from the opera's combination of lyrical and literary elements is an underlying sense of engagement with some vital and profound aspects of human experience. The libretto was written by Jules Barbier and Michel Carré, as an adaptation of their stage play, which had been loosely based on the writings of E.T.A. (Ernst Theodor Amadeus) Hoffmann (1776-1822).[58] The heart of the drama is the eponymous protagonist's hopeless pursuit of attractive women, each of whom proves unobtainable. Among them are Olympia, a singing mechanical doll (DVD figure 276), seemingly human before being dismantled in front of Hoffmann; and Antonia, another singer, this one actually human but dying of tuberculosis.

A sense of engagement with an opera based on the tales written by E.T.A. Hoffmann may have been easy for Berliners in the 1920s because Hoffmann's tales were again popular in Germany after fifty years of neglect. An American critic, Edwin Muir, argued that: ". . . improbable as it may seem at first glance, there is no doubt some connexion between the birth of psychoanalysis in the German countries and the re-emergence of Hoffmann's name." Muir further argued that psychoanalysis had: ". . . a value for the artist, for it reveals to him, if he is alert enough, a whole new world of beauty and terror. Hoffmann apprehended that world a century ago and found expression for it in art."[59] I have already noted Moholy's early interest in psychoanalysis. This continued into his later years when he wrote, in his last book, that Freud's discoveries ". . . would be justification enough for a new literary form."[60]

It should also be pointed out that Offenbach had died several months before the opening of *The Tales of Hoffmann*, and the *Opéra Comique*, left without any continuing guidance from the composer, took many obvious liberties in its presentation (*e.g.*, most

---

[57]An earlier attempt by Offenbach at creating a grand opera was *Die Rheinnixen* [The Water Sprites of the Rhine] of 1864, composed for Vienna. This attempt was not successful and has nearly been forgotten, except that one brief excerpt was re-worked for *The Tales of Hoffmann*, as noted below.

[58]Some of the sources from Hoffmann utilized for the libretto are discussed in: Enid Rhodes Peschel and Richard Peschel, "Medicine, Music and Literature: the Figure of Dr. Miracle in Offenbach's *Les Contes d'Hoffmann*," *Opera Quarterly*, volume III, number 2 (Summer, 1985), [59]-65 and 70.

[59]Edwin Muir, "The Tales of Hoffmann," *The Freeman* [New York], volume VIII, number 203 (January 30, 1924), 499.

[60]The quoted words are part of a summary of Freud's writings and his impact; see: László Moholy-Nagy, *Vision in Motion* (Chicago: Paul Theobald, 1947), 340-341.

of the Venetian scene was eliminated). As one result, there was no reliable tradition for those working on later productions to fall back on.[61]

For all these reasons many Kroll patrons expected a creatively imaginative production of *The Tales of Hoffmann*, an unspoken challenge that inspired Moholy and his collaborators. The opera was staged by Ernst Legal, and Alexander Zemlinsky (1871-1942) conducted the first performance on February 12th, 1929. There were a total of sixty-one performances,[62] most conducted by Zemlinsky, a well-known composer and a veteran conductor of this opera,[63] but some were conducted by Klemperer, who was very fond of Offenbach.[64] Few, if any, of these performances were on consecutive days,[65] and Moholy's production of *The Tales of Hoffmann* was available to Berliners off and on through June 8th, 1931.[66]

Moholy devised and presented to the Kroll designs for highly abstract stage settings, as Klemperer's biographer noted, in the form of ". . . coloured geometrical drawings of astonishing beauty."[67] (DVD figures 224 and 227) Some of the elements of these

---

[61] On the history of the various versions of the score and libretto used over the years, see: A[ndrew] L[amb], "Contes d'Hoffmann, Les," in: Stanley Sadie, editor, *The New Grove Book of Operas* (New York: St. Martin's Press, 1997), 132-135; Richard Bonynge, "Notes," in: Jacques Offenbach, *The Tales of Hoffmann* (New York: London Records, 1972), 7 [issued and re-issued to accompany various physical formats of a sound recording of a performance of *The Tales of Hoffmann* conducted by Bonynge]; Fritz Oeser, "Preface," in: Jacques Offenbach, *The Tales of Hoffmann (Les Contes d'Hoffmann)*, new critical edition, based on original sources, by Fritz Oeser; English translation by Walter Ducloux (Kassel: Alkor-Edition, 1982), ix-xx; and Mary Dibbern, *The Tales of Hoffmann: a Performance Guide*, with a foreword by Thomas Grubb (Hillsdale, New York: Pendragon Press, 2002).

[62] Georg Droescher, editor, *Die vormals Königlichen, jetzt Preußischen Staatstheater zu Berlin: statistischer Rückblick auf die künstlerische Tätigkeit und die Personalverhältnisse während der Zeit vom 1. Januar 1886 bis 31. Dezember 1935* (Berlin: Otto Elsner Verlagsgesellschaft, 1936), 8 and 80.

[63] Beaumont, *Zemlinsky*, 129-130 and [250]; and Theodor W. Adorno, "Berlin Opernmemorial: am Platz der Republik," *Musikblätter des Anbruch*, volume 11, number 6 (June, 1929), 261-266, here 261.

[64] Heyworth, *Otto Klemperer, His Life and Times*, 1:285.

[65] Rockwell, *op. cit.*, note 1 on page 207.

[66] Droescher, editor, *Die vormals Königlichen, jetzt Preußischen Staatstheater zu Berlin*, 8 and 80; and *Vorwärts, Berliner Volksblatt; Centralorgan der sozialdemokratischen Partei Deutschlands*, June 8, 1931, advertisement on unnumbered page.

[67] Heyworth, *Otto Klemperer, His Life and Times*, 1:285. As noted above, these designs were illustrated in: Curjel, *Experiment Krolloper*, [293] and 301; and in: Kersting and Vogelsang, editors, *Raumkonzepte*, 351-352.

settings could be re-arranged for more than one scene, thus facilitating changes of scenery. Moreover, a revolving stage was used.[68]

THE SETTING FOR THE DRAWING ROOM of inventor Spalanzani (Kroll act one; there is no universally agreed-on sequence or numbering of the acts of *The Tales of Hoffmann*) was described by one critic as *ein weißer Seziersaal* [a white dissection room].[69] Nevertheless, the opera had fired Moholy's imagination, as some critics recognized,[70] and what transpired in this act was, in a general way, like some of his own work around 1921 in which modern technology was ridiculed by depicting machine elements that were put together without regard to mechanical function but rather to provide wry comment on such ideas as *The Peace Machine Devouring Itself* (text figure 9, DVD figures 83 and 84), *The Machine of Emotional Discharge* (DVD figure 85)*, and *The Large Emotion Meter* (DVD figure 81), as discussed in Chapter Two on pages 132-134. Olympia, that mechanical doll created by Spalanzani, stuns party guests with her beauty and her engaging, if somewhat mechanical, singing. She appears to be especially lifelike to Hoffmann, who views her through magic spectacles and immediately falls in love with her. After Spalanzani's angry unpaid creditor smashes her into her mechanical components Hoffmann is forced to realize that he has fallen in love with clockworks. It could be added that although there is an ancient tradition of using mechanical human figures on stage,[71] there would have been little or no precedent for Offenbach and his librettists to utilize a real person to play an automaton. Coincidentally, it was precisely during the run of *The Tales of Hoffmann* at the Kroll that the human voice was first synthesized and presented to a mass public as part of the sound-track of a film starring Constance Bennett.[72]

---

[68]Curjel, *Experiment Krolloper*, photographs 53-60 following page 84.

[69]Bernhard Diebold, "Opernzauber 1929," *Frankfurter Zeitung*, February 17, 1929; this review was reprinted in: Curjel, *Experiment Krolloper*, 264-267.

[70]E.g., Adolf Weißmann wrote: "Er ist Bauhäusler, aber einer mit schöpferischer Phantasie" [He is a Bauhäusler, but one with creative imagination]. Quoted from Adolf Weißmann, [review], *B.Z. am Mittag,* February 13, 1929, in: Curjel, *Experiment Krolloper*, 262.

[71]Alfred Chapuis and Edmond Droz, *Automata; a Historical and Technological Study*, translated by Elec Reid (Neuchatel, Switzerland: Editions du Griffon; New York: Central Book Company, Inc., 1958), 355-360.

Moholy was clearly fascinated by the history of automata; in 1944 he told a Chicago reporter: "At the start of the 17th century a great many automatons began to appear—automatic chess players, automatic draftsmen. They were used to amuse the royalty. Well, very few people know about it, but those automatons, regarded as toys, had already solved the problem of mechanization. They were predecessors of our modern weaving machines and dial telephones." See: Emery Hutchison, "Stories of the Day," *Chicago Daily News*, June 28, 1944, 10.

[72]Thomas Y. Levin, "'Tones from out of Nowhere': Rudolf Pfenninger and the Archaeology of Sound," *Grey Room 12* (Summer, 2003), 32-79, here 33.

The upper part of Moholy's setting for Spalanzani's drawing room was dominated by hanging objects that illustrated aspects of the action. One of these was a mechanical copper cockerel, reflecting a reference in the libretto to *"un petit coq en cuivre"* [a little copper cockerel].[73] (One thinks here of Moholy's experience heading the Metal Workshop at the Bauhaus.) Behind the hanging objects dramatic, shifting shadows were projected onto the cyclorama. (DVD figure 228)

Moholy usually managed to avoid any suggestions of stylistic revival. Nevertheless, for the act set in Venice there is just a hint of the Venetian Gothic that in the mid-nineteenth century had inspired John Ruskin, the most persuasive writer on design-reform of all time. (DVD figure 229) But what captured the attention of the newspaper critics, and amused Moholy's old friend, Hannah Höch,[74] was a brothel orgy that took place on severe hospital-like beds, designed by Marcel Breuer.[75] The beds folded down from the wall like Murphy beds, one by one, on signals from the conductor.

Whether these plain, austere beds provided a suitably erotic setting for an orgy could be debated, but Curjel wrote of the charming appearance on stage of Breuer's chromium-plated steel furniture: ". . . Chromglanz magisch im farbigen Licht aufleuchtete,"[76] [Flashing magical reflections of colored lights on the chromium-plated surfaces].

More directly erotic than any furniture were three girls, remembered by Klemperer as "nearly naked,"[77] but described by one critic as wearing just enough costume to evoke parrots,[78] swinging high over the audience on trapezes, in time with the *Barcarolle*, a sensuous duet sung by two women. (DVD sound clip 1; film clip 1) These girls on

---

[73]Offenbach, *The Tales of Hoffmann (Les Contes d'Hoffmann)*, new critical edition, 81.

[74]Hannah Höch, "Die Freunde," in: Heinz Ohff, *Hannah Höch* (Berlin: Gebr, Mann Verlag, 1968), 22-29, here 28.

[75]Hans Curjel, "Moholy-Nagy und das Theater," *Du Atlantis: Culturelle Monatschrift*, volume XXIV, number 285 (November, 1964), 11-[14], here 12.

[76]Hans Curjel,"Moholy Arbeiten für Berliner Bühnen," quoted in: Hubertus Gaßner, editor, "Dok. 111," in: *Wechsel Wirkungen: ungarische Avantgarde in der Weimarer Republik* [exhibition catalogue] (Marburg, Germany: Jonas Verlag für Kunst und Literatur GmbH, 1986), 446-449, here 447-448.

[77]Heyworth, editor, *Conversations with Klemperer*, 80; see also: Curjel, "Moholy-Nagy und das Theater," 12.

In film clip 1 on the DVD disk accompanying *Moholy-Nagy: Mentor to Modernism*, Klemperer's voice is heard in a sequence of a 1970s television documentary, *Otto Klemperers lange Reise durch seine Zeit* [*Otto Klemperer's Long Journey Through His Times*], as he recalls working with Moholy.

[78]Max Marschalk, "'Hoffmanns Erzählungen,' 'Absage' an Jacques Offenbach," *Vossische Zeitung: Berlinische Zeitung von Staats- und gelehrten Sachen*, Post Ausgabe, February 14, 1929, [11].

trapezes were ignored by most of the critics, but one hostile critic denounced the use of swinging girls as ". . . ein ganz gewöhnlicher Varieté-Trick!" [A common variety-show trick!],[79] and another critic, Max Marschalk, also made reference to a variety show in this regard, as quoted below. Surely Moholy was pleased (no matter how much the rest of these two reviews might have displeased him), for this was no doubt the effect he had been aiming at.

SINCE THE TRAPEZE ARTISTS appeared in the act set in Venice (act two at the Kroll), it is tempting to think of the lilting and sensuous rhythms of the *Barcarolle* as describing the swaying of a gondola in the currents of that city's fabled canals, but this part of *The Tales of Hoffmann* was re-fashioned by the composer from an earlier work and was originally written with the Rhine River in mind.[80] Of course one has to wonder how successfully Moholy's grand gesture was co-ordinated by Zemlinsky and the singers, musicians and trapeze artists. And it would be hard for anyone to avoid a mental construct of the presence of an ardent Kroll Opera fan and master theoretician of time and motion, namely Albert Einstein; he surely witnessed at least one of the sixty-one performances of the opera, listening to the music and watching Zemlinsky co-ordinating the trapeze artists with the musical performers. Moreover, one hostile critic, Bernhard Diebold, actually did mention Einstein at the time. He complained that Moholy's settings lacked a necessary sense of enchantment, and that this was clearly a kind of charlatanism: "Klare Zauberei. Wie von Einstein. Oder: Verstehen Sie etwa die Relavitätstheorie? Ich nicht." [Transparent charlatanism. As from Einstein. Or: Do you perhaps understand the Theory of Relativity? Neither do I.][81] The comparison is a bit strained, with Moholy criticized for not offering enough mystery, and Einstein criticized for not offering enough enlightenment, but it nevertheless remains a fascinating conjunction of science and art.

While there is no record that Albert Einstein commented on the trapeze artists, his friend, Alfred Einstein (1880-1952),[82] clearly found them alluring:

---

[79]Paul Zschorlich, [review], *Deutsche Zeitung*, February 13, 1929; the review was reprinted in: Curjel, *Experiment Krolloper,* 263-264.

[80]See note 57.

[81]Diebold, as cited in note 69.

It should be borne in mind that by 1929 there had been numerous book-length attempts to make the theory of relativity intelligible to the general public; these books were written by Albert Einstein himself and by others and sold very well. See: Ronald W. Clark, *Einstein: the Life and Times* (New York: The World Publishing Company, 1971), 313-315.

[82]Though sometimes identified as a cousin, his near namesake Albert was not closely related but did sometimes address Alfred as his cousin (and probably actually *was* a very distant cousin, as noted by Bess and Hieronymus, cited in the following paragraph of this note), evidently in order to establish a relationship that could allow him to help Alfred emigrate from Germany. Albert did rent a home in Ostend, Belgium, where Alfred and his family lived briefly after fleeing Germany in

(continued...)

> There were . . . three pretty girls on swings, who were pushed far out over the orchestra and audience by three servants. Surely, many a pair of eyes was strained upward; I was always hoping that one of them would fall onto my lap (my seat was in an advantageous position), but the wish was never fulfilled—something like the erotic dream experiences of poor E.T.A. Hoffmann.[83]

As is now well known, by the time he had reached his fiftieth birthday, Albert Einstein was engaged in actually living out any erotic dream experiences he might have had. At the height of his fame, the photogenic mustachioed scientist, with his distinctive mane of thick, unruly, leonine hair, was described as affecting women "as a magnet acts on iron filings."[84] With no effective opposition from his second wife, Elsa, he spent

---

[82](...continued)

July, 1933. Alfred and Albert jokingly referred to themselves as "Die Zweistein"; see: Catherine Dower, *Alfred Einstein on Music* (New York: Greenwood Press, 1991), fifth illustration following page 36.

The two Einsteins had been schoolmates in the Luitpold Gymnasium in Munich about 1894 or 1895, where they sang in the chorus together (*ibid.*, note 22 on page 22). See also: Michael Fink and Bess Hieronymus, "The Autobiography and Early Diary of Alfred Einstein (1880-1952)," *Musical Quarterly*, volume LXVI, number 3 (July, 1980), 361- 377, here 371.

As the best-known luminary of the Weimar era, Albert Einstein, physicist and humanitarian, returned to Berlin in 1923, the year he presented his Nobel Prize acceptance speech, and lived there until 1932. His return to Berlin followed extensive visits abroad to Paris, Pasadena, Tokyo, and other cities, visits that augmented his international reputation.

Upon moving to Berlin in 1927, Alfred wrote a letter to Albert reminding him of their schooldays together; see: Albrecht Fölsing, *Albert Einstein: a Biography*, translated from the German by Ewald Osers (New York: Viking, 1997), 25. As it happened, the Einsteins ended up living around the corner from each other in Berlin, a circumstance that often led to their mail being mixed up because of the similarity in their names (Dower, *Alfred Einstein on Music*, note 38 on page 22).

In Berlin, Alfred Einstein served as music critic for the *Berliner Tageblatt*, a newspaper the famous physicist sometimes read; see: Friedrich Herneck, *Einstein Privat: Herta W. [i.e., Waldow] Erinnert Sich an die Jahre 1927 bis 1933* (Berlin: Buchverlag Der Morgen, 1978), 93-94. Alfred Einstein was also a well-known musicologist who was the most accomplished Mozart scholar of the twentieth century.

[83]Alfred Einstein, "Offenbach Restaged; 'Tales of Hoffmann' Revived in Berlin with Modernist Settings," by Alfred Einstein, Berlin, March 2, *New York Times*, March 17, 1929, X 9. The same observation was made in his Berlin review: "'Hoffmanns Erzählungen,' Staatsoper am Platz der Republik," *Berliner Tageblatt und Handels-Zeitung*, Abend-Ausgabe, February 13, 1929, [10].

[84]Konrad Wachsmann, quoted in: Michael Grüning, editor, *Ein Haus für Albert Einstein; Erinnerungen, Briefe, Dokumente* (Berlin: Verlag der Nation, 1990), 158; and Fölsing, *Albert Einstein*, 616.

much time in the company of beautiful women,[85] including Else (Toni) Mendel, an attractive widow, perhaps just a bit younger than Albert, who often picked him up in her chauffeur-driven limousine for an evening at a concert or at the opera.[86] Sometimes he spent the night in her elegant lakeside mansion in the neighborhood of Wannsee, on the southwestern outskirts of Berlin.[87]

Although he might not have commented on the settings for *The Tales of Hoffmann*, Albert Einstein did comment on Breuer's furniture, and this took place during the run of the opera at the Kroll. For his lakeside summer house in Caputh, near Potsdam, completed in October, 1929,[88] his Modernist architect, Konrad Wachsmann, had arranged for bent-steel tubing furniture to be designed for the house by Breuer, but Albert and Elsa would have none of it.[89] When shown Breuer's sketches, Elsa would not even consider installing the proposed furniture, nor would her husband, who declared: "Ich will doch nicht auf Möbeln sitzen, die mich unentwegt an eine Maschinenhalle oder einen Operationssaal erinnern"[90] [I will surely not sit on furniture that so strongly reminds me of a machine hall or an operating room]. A photograph of Einstein's study in Caputh shows an ordinary armchair, in the current petit-bourgeois taste, contrasted with Wachsmann's functional built-in bookshelves and Modernist wooden-slat walls.[91]

Moholy also had direct experience with Albert Einstein's antipathy to modernism. As we have seen in Chapter Three, Einstein had a few connections with the Bauhaus. He was a member of the *Kuratorium* [Board of Trustees] of the *Kreis der Freunde des Bauhauses* [Circle of the Friends of the Bauhaus][92] and in 1924 joined the (unsuccessful)

---

[85]Dennis Brian, *Einstein: a Life* (New York: John Wiley & Sons, Inc., 1996), 180-181; and Thomas Levenson, *Einstein in Berlin* (New York: Bantam Books, 2003), 307-310.

[86]Fölsing, *Albert Einstein*, 616-617; Herneck, *Einstein Privat*, 146; and Roger Highfield and Paul Carter, *The Private Lives of Albert Einstein* (New York: St. Martin's Press, 1995), 207 and 326.

[87]Herneck, *Einstein Privat*, 146-147; Highfield and Carter, *The Private Lives of Albert Einstein*, 207.

[88]Herneck, *Einstein Privat*, 112.

[89]Grüning, editor, *Ein Haus für Albert Einstein*, 129-130.

[90]Grüning, editor, *Ein Haus für Albert Einstein*, 130.

[91]Grüning, editor, *Ein Haus für Albert Einstein*, 135.

[92]Hans M. Wingler, editor, *The Bauhaus: Weimar, Dessau, Berlin, Chicago,* translated by Wolfgang Jabs and Basil Gilbert (Cambridge, Massachusetts: The MIT Press, 1978), 78; Gerd Fleischmann, editor, *Bauhaus Drucksachen, Typografie, Reklame* [from the collection of Grete and Walter Dexel, now in the Getty Research Center, Los Angeles] (Dusseldorf: Edition Marzona, 1984), 136-[137]; and "Sitzung des Bauhausrates am 24. April 1924," in: Volker Wahl and Ute Ackermann, editors, *Die Meisterprotokolle des Stattlichen Bauhauses Weimar 1919 bis 1925* (Weimar: Verlag Hermann Böhlaus Nachfolger, 2001), 342 and note on page 532.

effort to prevent its closing in Weimar.[93] (It was after this effort failed that the school was forced to move to Dessau). But possibly Einstein was supporting this bastion of Modernism mainly because it was under attack by supporters of Germany's far-right political parties that he was so strongly opposed to.

Also, as described in Chapter Three, Moholy and Gropius co-edited a series called Bauhaus Books. Although, in the end, no scientific texts were brought out, Moholy had wanted to include some volumes on recent trends in science to signify that the Bauhäusler were part of a common Modernist impulse that included the efforts of scientists,[94] and thus a book to be written by Einstein was discussed with him. But in a conference with Einstein that lasted about an hour, Moholy found that Einstein had displayed "naiveté" about the Modernist efforts that he and Theo van Doesburg, the leader of the Dutch De Stijl movement (and, as discussed in Chapter Three, author of one of the Bauhaus Books), were engaged in.[95] Although Einstein in the end was persuaded of the desirability of working together, he maintained that he was not able to write in a "popular" manner, and instead suggested that he might recommend someone who could write the kind of book Moholy had in mind.

Einstein may not have placed a high priority on joint efforts with Moholy, but surely he was not averse to writing for the general public. In fact, his *Relativity, the Special and the General Theory*, first published in book form in 1916, was republished in German in 1917 and in English in 1920 with the word "popular" in the subtitle,[96] and it sold so well in both languages that it was obvious that many non-scientists had purchased it.[97] Moreover, in his preface, originally written in 1916, Einstein had maintained that:

> The present book is intended, as far as possible, to give an exact insight in the
> theory of Relativity to those readers who, from a general scientific and

---

[93] *Pressestimmen für das Staatliche Bauhaus Weimar; Auszüge, Nachtrag, Kundegebungen, 1924,* mit einem Nachwort zur Reprintausgabe von Peter Hahn (Munich: Kraus Reprint, 1980), 106-109 and 117-119.

[94] László Moholy-Nagy to Theo van Doesburg, July 26, 1924, MLS in: Theo van Doesburg files, Rijksbureau voor Kunsthistorische Dokumentie, The Hague; available on microfiche (Leiden: IDC, 1991), microfiche sheet 33. A photocopy of the letter is in the Bauhaus-Archiv, Berlin; a transcription appeared in: Theo van Doesburg, *Grondbegrippen der nieuwe beeldende Kunst* (Nijmegen: SUN Socialistiese Uitgeverij Nijmegen, 1983), 107-110.

[95] László Moholy-Nagy to Theo van Doesburg, July 26, 1924.

[96] Albert Einstein, *Über die spezielle und die allgemeine Relativitätstheorie (Gemeinverständlich)* (Braunschweig: F. Vieweg, 1917); and *idem, Relativity, the Special & the General Theory: a Popular Exposition* (London: Methuen & Co., Ltd., 1920). See also note 81.

[97] Clark, *Einstein: the Life and Times,* 314.

philosophical point of view, are interested in the theory, but who are not conversant with the mathematical apparatus of theoretical physics.[98]

Albert Einstein was an avid amateur violinist who also played the piano, and it is worth noting here that the physicist's son, Hans Albert Einstein, recalled:

> He often told me that one of the most important things in his life was music. Whenever he felt that he had come to the end of the road or into a difficult situation in his work he would take refuge in music, and that would usually resolve all his difficulties.[99]

His father explained that turning to music allowed the subconscious to solve particularly tricky problems.[100] Thus it is tempting to conclude that Moholy and his colleagues at the Kroll made some modest contribution to modern physics!

Alfred Einstein made a fascinating comment on an aspect of the Venetian scene of *The Tales of Hoffmann* (act two at the Kroll) not mentioned by other critics (DVD figure 230):

> . . . there stands a decorative piece, the Venus of Medicis, as a symbol of the mise en scène. The statue is made of wire, thus being presented only in outline and lacking all the pleasing curves which the scenic director of the Bauhaus, L. Moholy-Nagy, would surely not want to forego in real life.[101]

Hoffmann's costume for that scene stood outside a definable period style, with its white-trimmed asymmetrical lapels, turned-up sleeve cuffs and tapered pant-legs, predominantly black but with red and pink accents. (DVD figures 230 and 231).

The act set in the house of Crespel in Munich (act three at the Kroll) consisted of simple furniture and a severely-simple mock-up of a harpsichord, which was central to the action (Alfred Enstein called it "the aquarium that is supposed to be a piano").[102] Three stairs at stage rear led to overscaled windows created with strikingly exaggerated perspective and back-projected muntins that were reconfigured during the performance. These windows were dominated by an even more overscaled, half-drawn window shade, on which still images and some short movie sequences were projected. Framed on stage right was an elongated rendering of the late mother of Hoffmann's beloved, Antonia; this

---

[98] Albert Einstein, *Relativity, the Special & the General Theory*, v.

[99] Hans Albert Einstein, quoted in: G. J. Withrow, editor, *Einstein: the Man and His Achievement; a Series of Broadcast Talks under the General Editorship of G. J. Withrow* (London: British Broadcasting Corporation, 1967), 21.

[100] Clark, *Einstein: the Life and Times*, 106.

[101] Alfred Einstein, "Offenbach Restaged," X 9.

[102] Alfred Einstein, "Offenbach Restaged," X 9; *idem*, "'Hoffmanns Erzählungen,' Staatsoper am Platz der Republik," February 13, 1929, [10].

rendering was designed to glow when the otherwise dead woman, an opera singer, sang mysteriously.[103] (DVD figures 232 and 233)

One incident in this act that Moholy used in a film sequence concerns Dr. Mirakel, who presents himself as a healer but who nevertheless seems sinister and somehow threatening.[104] His patient, Antonia, suffers from a severe case of tuberculosis. He carries remedies in a cluster of bottles, which he manipulates like castanets ("*Il tire plusiers flacons de sa poche et les fait sonner comme des castagnettes*").[105] This detail was based on a disturbing experience that Offenbach himself had recently undergone. His son was seriously ill, and his doctor had carried some bottles of medicine that kept clinking into each other, greatly adding to the sense of anxiety that Offenbach already felt.[106]

Framing the three acts were the scenes known at the Kroll as *Vorspiel* [prelude] and *Nachspiel* [postlude], set in an elegant Weinkeller, or basement wine-café, with its below-street-grade location emphasized by a serpentine stairway. This stairway, along with the circular metal bar and stools, suggested a fashionable modern version of the kind of Berlin establishment that the real E.T.A. Hoffmann, sometimes described as a bit of an imbiber, might have himself frequented while living in Berlin. (DVD figures 224. 225 and 226) A rendering of the scene, although signed by Moholy,[107] was likely made by his assistant Stefan Sebök. DVD figure 224)

The cellar café in *Hoffmann* resembles a design for a similar establishment in Walter Mehring's *The Merchant of Berlin*, a play that, as discussed below on pages 369-377, opened in Berlin's *Theater am Nollendorfplatz* on September 6, 1929, with scenery designed by Moholy, assisted by Sebök.[108] It also resembles a signed rendering by Sebök of a social room in a high-rise apartment house for the 1930 Werkbund Exhibition in

---

[103] The set was illustrated with a photograph (with added collage elements) by Lucia Moholy in: Buck, *Vision Raum Szene*, 250-251.

[104] See: Peschel and Peschel, "Medicine, Music and Literature," [59]-71.

[105] Offenbach, *The Tales of Hoffmann (Les Contes d'Hoffmann)*, new critical edition, 261.

[106] Siegfried Kracauer, *Orpheus in Paris: Offenbach and the Paris of His Time*, translated from the German by Gwenda David and Eric Mosbacher (New York: Alfred A. Knopf, 1938), 346 and 355.

[107] Curjel, *Experiment Krolloper*, figure VII on page [293]; the drawing is in the Theatre Collection of the University of Cologne Institute of Theatre-, Film- and Television Studies.

[108] Illustrated with a rendering and a photograph in: John Willett, *The Theatre of Erwin Piscator* (New York: Holmes & Meier Publishers, Inc., 1979), 99. The rendering and the photograph also appear in: Marianne Mildenberger, *Film und Projektion auf der Bühne* (Emsdetten, Germany: Verlag Lechte, 1961), illustrations 79 and 81.

Paris,[109] discussed below on page 475. (DVD figure 332) Thus it is possible that Sebök's work on *The Tales of Hoffmann* involved more than the making of drawing; moreover, Gebhard recalled that during the work on the settings: "Es gab zwischen den beiden endlose und heftige Diskussionen, natürlich auf Ungarisch; Sebök war noch temperamentvoller als Moholy-Nagy"[110] [There were endless and vigorous discussions between the two, of course in Hungarian; Sebök was just as temperamental as Moholy-Nagy].

It should be added that the sixty-one performances of *The Tales of Hoffmann* were presented in one of Germany's largest opera houses, which had about 2,200 seats.[111] Even though not all seats were filled for every performance, particularly after the stock-market crash of October, 1929, it is obvious that Moholy's work was seen by a mass audience of well beyond 100,000 persons.

This production of *The Tales of Hoffmann*, which, as noted, had opened February 12th, 1929, was denounced on February 20th in the Prussian State Legislature (*Preußischer Landtag*) as cultural Bolshevist experimentation.[112] Cultural Bolshevism (*Kultur Bolschevismus*) was a vague term, and can best be described as what was hated by those whose sympathies were with the far-right political parties; in nearly all cases whatever was denounced had nothing at all to do with any kind of real Bolshevism.[113]

The Modernist critic Alfred Behne exaggerated when he wrote, "With rare unanimity the Berlin music critics excoriated the new production . . ." ["Mit seltener Einmüitgkeit verriß die Berliner Musikkritik die neue Inszenierung

---

[109] Winfried Nerdinger, *Walter Gropius* "Mit einem kritischen Werkverzeichnis/With Complete Project Catalog" (Berlin: Gebr. Mann Verlag, 1985), figure 34b on page [143]; the drawing is in the Bauhaus-Archiv in Berlin; and *idem*, editor, *The Walter Gropius Archive: an Illustrated Catalogue of the Drawings, Prints and Photographs in the Walter Gropius Archive at the Busch-Reisinger Museum, Harvard University* (New York: Garland Publishing, Inc., 1990), 2:71-79.

[110] Helm, "Produktive Begegnungen: Gespräch mit Max Gebhard," 306; see also: Gebhard, "Erinnerungen," 181.

[111] Curjel, *Experiment Krolloper,* 18.

[112] Heyworth, *Otto Klemperer, His Life and Times*, 1:287.

[113] For a more detailed look at "cultural Bolshevism," see: Istvan Deák, *Weimar Germany's Left-Wing Intellectuals: a Political History of the* Weltbühne *and Its Circle* (Berkeley: University of California Press, 1968), 1-3; see also pages 295 and 296 in my Chapter Three.

. . .".[114] Nevertheless Paul Zschorlich (born 1876), writing for the *Deutsche Zeitung*, was an especially hostile critic. His comments on the production of *The Tales of Hoffmann* and its audience were tainted with xenophobia and anti-Semitism. He claimed that three-quarters of the audience was Jewish (unlikely, given the subscription arrangements referred to above), but this was evidently his perception, perhaps because well-known Jewish intellectuals, such as Albert Einstein, were in frequent attendance. Zschorlich objected that both Jews and foreigners were associated with the production, placing Moholy in the latter category (he was evidently unaware of Moholy's Jewish background). Ironically, Zschorlich wrote that Offenbach had been ill served by the production,[115] rather than objecting to the composer's Jewish background or the choice of this Cologne native to spend much of his youth and all of his adult life in Paris. But, as will be seen below, Zschorlich was only warming up for more general attacks on the Kroll Opera and on key officials of the *Preußische Kultusministerium* [Prussian Ministry of Culture], which had jurisdiction over the state's opera companies.

The most sympathetic review of *The Tales of Hoffmann* was written by Adolf Weißmann (1873-1929). This veteran critic, not always an admirer of Kroll productions,[116] nevertheless wrote that the première performance belonged to one of the most interesting nights at the opera he could remember.[117] Although he had not liked the Venetian scene, he found the motion-picture sequences in the third act (DVD figure 234) to be very effective, providing compelling drama that matched compelling music.[118]

Another critic, Oscar Bie, did not object to the use of modern dress and settings on principle, but questioned whether Constructivism was the necessary expression of our time. He nevertheless was fascinated by the lighting effects, and he made it clear that he

---

[114]Adolf Behne, "Berlin, Moholy-Nagy Inszeniert 'Hoffmanns Erzählungen'," *Das neue Frankfurt; Monatsschrift für die Probleme moderner Gestaltung*, volume III, number 3 (March, 1929), 61; reprinted in: Heinz Hirdina, editor, *Neues Bauen, neues Gestaltung; das neue Frankfurt/die neue Stadt, eine Zeitschrift zwischen 1926 und 1933* (Berlin: Elefanten Press, 1984), 347.

Another review by Behne contained a similar assertion; see: *idem*, "Neu-Inszenierung von Hoffmanns Erzählungen in der Kroll-Oper," *Das Neue Berlin: Großstadtprobleme*, volume I, number 2 (February, 1929), 44-45.

Each review was illustrated by three photographs made by Lucia Moholy.

[115]Paul Zschorlich, [review], 263-264. Portions quoted in English in: Heyworth, *Otto Klemperer, His Life and Times*, 1:286.

[116]Rockwell, *op. cit.*, 203.

[117]Adolf Weißmann, [review], 260.

[118]*Ibid.*

favored a problematic experiment over idle stagnation ["Besser ein problematisches Experiment, als eine leere Stagnation"].[119]

Bernhard Diebold, in a generally unsympathetic review for a newspaper in Frankfurt am Main, was nevertheless fascinated by the movies in act three. Referring to Moholy as "Dessau," he rhetorically asked how he would treat this act: "Was soll nun Dessau machen?" and replied, "Dessau macht bestenfalls ein Atelier mit Glasbedachung, durch deren weiße Fläche Doktor Mabuses (oder Mirakels?) Film: Teufelsaugen riesengroß blinkern und seine krampfige Geisterhand nach der Seele der sterbenden Antonia hascht." [What shall Dessau do? Dessau makes at best a glass-roofed studio, through the white walls of which permeates Doctor Mabuses's (or Miracle's?) film: huge, blinking devilish eyes and his convulsing, ghostly hands grasping at the soul of the dying Antonia.][120] (DVD figure 234)

Very telling is Diebold's comparison of Miracle with Mabuse. In a once-famous 1922 film directed by Fritz Lang, *Dr. Mabuse der Spieler* [*Dr. Mabuse the Gambler*], very effective use is made of hands in a famous "table-turning" seance, in which eleven pairs of hands, some seemingly disembodied, lie flat on a table. Moholy had illustrated this scene with a still from the movie in his *Painting, Photography, Film*.[121] Also, as noted in Chapter Two, the rendering of hands was a fascinating challenge for Moholy as a young artist.

In his review Weißmann referred to the issue devoted to *The Tales of Hoffmann* of the *Blätter der Staatsoper und der Städtischen Oper* for February, 1929, edited by Curjel,.[122] The *Blätter* constituted a kind of informative souvenir program book available in all of Berlin's opera houses including the Municipal Opera [*Städtische Oper*], the fore-runner of the present-day *Deutsche Oper Berlin*. (DVD figure 235) Curjel included an article by Moholy, "Theater der Totalität," which was a three-page condensation of the theater-of-totality section of his article in the *Theater of the Bauhaus*.[123] This

---

[119] Oscar Bie, [review], *Berlin Börsen-Courier: Tageszeitung für alle Gebiete*, February 13, 1929; reprinted in: Curjel, *Experiment Krolloper*, 262-263.

[120] Diebold, [review], 266.

[121] László Moholy-Nagy, *Painting, Photography, Film*, with a note by Hans M. Wingler and a postscript by Otto Stelzer; translated by Janet Seligman (Cambridge: The MIT Press, [1969]), 89.

[122] *Blätter der Staatsoper und der Städtischen Oper*, volume IX, number 19 (February, 1929).

[123] *Ibid.*, 14-[16]; the sections included in the *Blätter* appeared on page 57-62, 62-64 and 68-70 in: Oskar Schlemmer, László Moholy-Nagy and Farkas Molnár, *The Theater of the Bauhaus*, edited and with an introduction by Walter Gropius, translated by Arthur S. Wensinger (Middletown, Connecticut: Wesleyan University Press, 1961). A few paragraphs on the cited pages were omitted, as were all of the illustrations.

Moholy's article as it appeared in the *Blätter* was re-printed in: Curjel, *Experiment Krolloper*,

(continued...)

condensed version, read in the context of what Moholy provided in his designs for *The Tales of Hoffmann*, was better received than it had been in its original context (discussed in the previous chapter).

STILL ONE MORE mostly negative review was written by Rudolf Kastner for the *Berliner Morgenpost*, this one reporting a strong Bauhaus connection to Moholy's designs.[124] Basically Kastner was fascinated by what Moholy offered, but thought it unsuitable for *The Tales of Hoffmann*. He did credit Moholy with being ". . . einem der ernstesten und ideenreichsten aus der Schar um Gropius, Kandinsky, Feininger" [. . . one of the most ernest and full of ideas of the band around Gropius, Kandinsky, Feininger], and he clearly was fascinated by ". . . die drei Schaukelmädchen" [the three girls on trapezes]. He summed up: "Es war also großenteils Moholy-Nagys an sich vielleicht fruchtbar Stil an dem ganz untauglichen Object demonstriert" [It was thus in large part Moholy's perhaps fruitful style demonstrated on an entirely unsuitable object]. Kastner went on to praise some of the singers but he wrote that tenor Artur Cavara as Hoffmann was vocally gifted but was still quite unfinished (". . . noch ganz unfertig der gewiß stimmbegabte lettisch [Latvian] Tenor Cavara"), in line with the comments of Max Marschalk quoted below. If these comments were justified and the character of Hoffmann was not adequately cast, that would have been one more hurdle Moholy and his Kroll colleagues had to overcome to make the production a success, at least initially (*i.e.*, it is possible that Carava improved with repeated performances and follow-up rehearsals, and theatre critics rarely review repeat performances).

JUST HOW CONTROVERSIAL the Kroll production of *The Tales of Hoffmann* was can be seen in the review of Max Marschalk (1863-1940), music critic of the *Vossische Zeitung* from 1895 to 1934. As a composer he is best known for his theatrical collaborations with his brother-in-law, Nobel-Prize-winning author Gerhart Hauptmann.[125] Marschalk was not sympathetic with right-wing politics and indeed the *Vossische Zeitung* was the newspaper of the German Democratic Party, the party of Fritz Hesse who, as mayor of Dessau, had invited the Bauhaus to move there. Marschalk's entire review,[126] never previously re-printed or translated, appears below in translation and the original German text appears in Appendix G, pages 739-741.

---

[123](...continued)
374-376.

[124]Rudolf Kastner, "Offenbachs 'Hoffmann' im — Bauhausstil!", *Berliner Morgenpost,* February 14, 1929, 11.

[125]Curjel, *Experiment Krolloper*, 216.

[126]Max Marschalk, "'Hoffmanns Erzählungen,' 'Absage' an Jacques Offenbach,*"* [11]. (Ewald Dülberg had designed several productions for the Kroll Opera; see: Curjel, *Experiment Krolloper,* plates I-V and XVI *et passim*.)

"The Tales of Hoffmann," a "Renunciation" [of] Jacques Offenbach

As I left the State Opera on the Plaza of the Republic, I asked myself: was what I witnessed the fantastic opera of Jacques Offenbach? And I asked myself further: if in this instance the production designer and the director behaved themselves so absurdly, so untrue to the proper style, when they put on such a frivolous performance of an illustrious work of art: why not commission a new text to be written and new music to go with the new text? Might they not wait for the "upcoming authors" if they see as their duty "the creative release of the new and not the (apparently) imagined necessities"? Might they touch the old not irreverently and thoroughly "understand" it? It mustn't happen that one after the other of our monumental masterworks decays through a murky fantasy of theatrical instincts.

All the fantasy in this fantastic opera was basically destroyed by the "production designer" L. Moholy-Nagy. He wants everything new at any price; as if the advance into new territory would come about through will and not, rather, through needs; the needs of truly creative spirits.

But is what emerges here truly an advance? Have not the productive ones long ago abandoned that which this painter-mathematician has invented, practices of abandoned art from yesterday and the day before yesterday? Must we suffer from the obstinate ones who cannot give up or abandon anything? Shouldn't the intendant Ernst Legal have left the craft of the director Ernst Legal alone? Or, if the intendant failed: isn't there a general intendant to speak with authority to prevent the beginning of the end from coming so dangerously near?

I will not go further into the vexing details of this production. At first I thought that through the denial of everything that up until now we considered as fantasy, a new kind of fantasy could emerge. But the not-unfavorable impression rapidly diminished, and finally the awful realization of the stage sets and the stage action and the not less awful obtrusiveness, that scorned the "true requirements" of the work and snubbed its admirers, left behind a very bad feeling; and, what was almost worse, I was bored.

What more is there to say? The work disappeared behind the bustle of the production — what a Venetian scene; a ridiculous variety-show scene with three women dressed like parrots, who sat on trapezes and were catapulted from the background over the orchestra, with Murphy beds, five moons and other unfathomable detail — and it remains to say that Alexander von Zemlinsky, the musical director, handled affairs very well, although he tried in vain to draw attention to the everlastingly beautiful music. In general it seems to me that the lust for experimentation also extends to the singers. There was a perhaps talented tenor [Artur Cavara], but with a not completely developed technique, a not entirely developed tenor of very small calibre, who should first learn stage routines in a small provincial theatre. Also not untalented is the portrayer of Olympia [Valentine Wischnevskaja], but she gave no more than a conservatory performance: by this judgement I do not mean to offend the conservatories. Karl Hammes projected through captivating thespian ability a strong impersonation as Lindorf and as Coppelius-Dapertutto-Miracle. Käthe Heidersbach attracted attention as Antonia, although she seemed too healthy [the character of Antonia is deathly ill in the opera's libretto]. Otherwise there were —unfortunately —

only mediocre performances. There was much organized applause, but it
seemed to me that most of the audience was not exactly edified.

One could imagine that our entire heritage of classic and romantic operas will be
staged in the accustomed matter-of-fact and abstract manner of Moholy-Nagy in
"The Tales of Hoffmann" — Ewald Dülberg is a tame reactionary compared to
this Bauhäusler! It would be unbearable. But this manner is an illness that will
play itself out. For the present, the official house philosopher of the Plaza of the
Republic [Hans Curjel] philosophizes in the "Blätter der Staats und der
Städtischen Oper" about a "renunciation of falsely naturalistic theatre, a
renunciation of false beauty and accuracy of costumes, a renunciation of a false
pathos of gestures"; and what the philosophizing and experimenting in this case
really amounts to is nothing other than a renunciation of Jacques Offenbach.

In stark contrast with Marschalk's sternly negative verdict, the brilliant philosopher,
composer and critic, Theodor W. Adorno (1903-1969), wrote very sympathetically of the
Kroll Opera's *The Tales of Hoffmann* in a Viennese monthly publication.[127] He lauded it
in general, and among the things he singled out was Moholy's use of shadows:

Sein spezifisches Vermögen mag besonders in der Lichtbehandlung sich
erweisen. Das ist nicht mehr das alte illusionäre und zauberische Bühnenlicht,
aber auch nicht das impressionistische der feuchten und nicht die raumlosen
Symbolkegel des Expressionismus: das Licht wird vielmehr selber zur
Raumkonstruktion verwandt, der Raum aus Lichtkomplexen strengen Sinnes
komponiert. [His specific talent may especially lie in his handling of light. That
is no longer the old illusionist and magical stage lighting, but also not the
Impressionist dampness and not the symbolic flat bowling pins of
Expressionism: the light becomes much more itself, related to the construction of
space, the space vividly sensed as composed of light elements.]

In addition to this public praise, Adorno went on to laud Moholy's work in a letter to
his friend and teacher, the composer Alban Berg (1885-1935), writing that the
production ". . . made an extraordinary impression on me."[128]

In a caption to an illustration of the Venetian scene in his *The New Vision*, Moholy
provided his own description and assessment of the settings for *The Tales of Hoffmann*.
He wrote:

An experiment with the problem of creating space from light and shadow.
Among other devices, the wings are employed here to create shadows.
Everything is transparent, and all the transparent surfaces work together to make
an organized and well perceptible space arrangement. It seems that from all this

---

[127] Adorno, "Berlin Opernmemorial: am Platz der Republik," 261-262; reprinted in: *idem*,
Gesammelte Scriften, herausgegeben von Rolf Tiedemann, Band 19: *Musikalische Schriften VI*
(Frankfurt am Main: Suhrkamp Verlag, 2003) as "Berliner Opernmemorial," [267]-275, here 268.

[128] Theodor W. Adorno to Alban Berg, October 9, 1929, in: Theodor W. Adorno and Alban Berg,
Correspondence, 1925-1935, edited by Henri Lonitz, translated by Wieland Hoban (Cambridge,
England: Polity Press, 2005), 162.

study of material, volume and space, the stage will, first among all the fields of expression, gain the most in the very near future. As soon as it leaves the blind alley of the purely literary—the co-ordination of all the elements will take a decisive step forward.[129]

One more point about Moholy's production of *The Tales of Hoffmann*: it is among the most widely illustrated and exhibited opera productions of all time.[130] Part of the reason is that illustrations of it appear in the literature of opera, theatre, photography and art, as well as in biographies of both Lucia and her husband. Moreover, while the production was still being presented in Berlin, a photograph of one of the settings was shown in 1930 at the Grand Palais des Champs-Elysées in Paris.[131] Also numerous color renderings for and three photographs of the production were shown in an exhibition, *Das Problemtheater,* seen in 1930 at the Kunstgewerbemuseum in Cologne and at the Folkwang Museum in Essen, and seen in 1931 at the Gewerbemuseum in Basel;[132] in 1932 it was seen in the Städtisches Kunstmuseum in Duisburg.[133]

The Tales of Hoffmann used movies overtly,[134] and, incidently, the film shown in act three was Moholy's first completed film. (DVD figure 234) Movies figured in another

---

[129]László Moholy-Nagy, *The New Vision* (2005), [197].

[130]Hennig Rischbieter, editor, *Art and the Stage in the 20th Century: Painters and Sculptors Work for the Theater,* documented by Wolfgang Storch, texts translated by Michael Bullock, catalogue translated by Andreas Schroeder (Greenwich, Connecticut: The New York Graphic Society, 1968), 289.

[131]*Neue Dekoration; Schaufenster, Ladenfront, Beschriftung, Werbelicht,* volume III, number 11 (1931 [?]), 117.

Lucia's photograph of the setting for the first act was shown in the theater portion of the "Section Allemande" at the *Salon des Artistes Décorateurs,* seen from May 14 through July 13, 1930, as discussed below.

[132]Carl Niessen, editor, *Das Problemtheater, Gewerbemuseum Basel, 15. Februar bis 15. März 1931* [exhibition catalogue] (Basel: Gewerbemuseum, 1931), 29; and Günter Hansen, editor, *Bibliographie Carl Niessen* (Emsdetten, Germany: Verlag Lechte, 1965), 40-41.

It was explained on page 3 of *Das Problemtheater* that: "Die Ausstellung 'Das Problemtheater' wurde vom Institut für Theaterwissenschaft der Universität Köln, verbunden mit dem Theatermuseum i.E., 1930 zum erstenmal im Kunstgewerbemuseum Köln gezeigt, dann im Folkwang-Museum Essen." Interestingly, as noted above, a number of renderings and photographs of the Kroll production of *The Tales of Hoffmann* are now in the Theatre Collection of the University of Cologne Institute of Theatre-, Film- and Television Studies; see: Rischbieter, editor, *Art and the Stage,* 289. These items were listed by Niessen as owned by the artist as of 1931.

[133]Buck, *Vision Raum Szene,* 538.

[134]Thirty-six frames from the film *Mirakel* from *Hoffmanns Erzählungen* were reproduced in: Theo van Doesburg, "Film als reine Gestaltung," *Die Form; Zeitschrift für gestaltende Arbeit,* volume IV, number 10 (May 15, 1929), 241-249, here 247. I could find no other visual trace of the film.

Moholy production for the Kroll Opera less overtly. This was *Hin und Zurück, Sketch mit Musik*, also known as *Here and There*, with music by Paul Hindemith (1895-1963) and libretto by Marcellus Schiffer, a short opera that had premiered in Baden-Baden in 1927.[135] It was first presented at the Kroll Opera on November 29th, 1930,[136] where it was staged by Curjel and conducted by Klemperer. Presented as part of a quadruple bill, it was last seen on February 7th, 1931.[137]

David Ewen has succinctly described *Here and There*:

> This amusing little opera, described by its authors as a "film sketch," exploits a trick. After the murder of an adulteress by her husband, the plot is put in reverse; the adulteress comes back to life, the husband puts his revolver back in his pocket, the physician backs out the front door, and so forth.[138]

Although *Here and There* is a very short opera. Moholy made about thirty sketches that are preserved in a private collection; some of these have been published. On the other hand, there are no surviving photographs of the opera as staged. Two sketches show variations on a parlor with a tea table set for two. (DVD figures 236 and 237) One sketch is dominated by a rendering of the old-fashioned floor-length Wilhelmine gown worn by the tall, bespectacled deaf aunt of the adulteress, who is present throughout the action but comprehends nothing and stays busy with her knitting; two images on this sheet suggest oppressively claustrophobic domestic interiors, and one also shows the mechanical birds that fly over the stage.[139] (DVD figure 238) Another costume sketch shows the jealous husband, offending gun in hand, in an idiosyncratic suit of clothes, and again with two images on the sheet suggesting oppressively claustrophobic domestic interiors. (DVD figure 239)

A newspaper review by Alfred Einstein had praise for the production of "... *Hin und Zurück* mit einem ulkigen Bühnenbild Moholy-Nagys von lapidarer Einfachheit" [... *Here and There* with funny settings of concise simplicity by Moholy-Nagy].[140] A reviewer for *Vossische Zeitung* found Moholy's work on *Here and There* to be "*witzig und anschaulich*" [witty and with graphic clarity], and went on to note that he was "nicht

---

[135] On *Hin und Zurück*, see: Cook, *Opera for a New Republic*, 154-157; and Curjel, "Moholy-Nagy und das Theater," 12.

[136] *Vossische Zeitung: Berlinische Zeitung von Staats- und gelehrten Sachen*, Abend-Ausgabe, November 29, 1930, 3. Beilage, [3] (advertisement).

[137] Droescher, editor, *Die vormals Königlichen, jetzt Preußischen Staatstheater zu Berlin*, 8 and 80.

[138] David Ewen, *Encyclopedia of the Opera* (New York: A.A. Wyn, Inc., 1955), 209.

[139] Curjel, "Moholy-Nagy und das Theater," 12.

[140] Alfred Einstein, [review], *Berliner Tageblatt*, December 1, 1930; reprinted in Curjel, *Experiment Krolloper*, 302-303.

mehr konstruktiv ausstattendem Dekorateur" [no longer a Constructivist scene-painter].[141]

BY THE TIME MOHOLY BEGAN WORKING on *Here and There* the Kroll Opera was in its final months, its fate already sealed. Although the poisoning of the artistic atmosphere by critics such as Zschorlich,[142] and the machinations within the political arena of the Prussian state government that forced the Kroll's closing, are beyond the scope of this book,[143] it is nevertheless tempting to look for similarities in the fate of the Kroll and the Bauhaus in Weimar. John Rockwell, the leading expert on the Kroll and Prussian politics, concluded that although "the artistic achievement of opera in Weimar Berlin was of extraordinary quality . . . the story [of the Kroll Opera] ends in failure, in the most despairing sense of that word," because "in fighting for its projects in the real world of Weimar politics, the men of the Ministry [of Culture, responsible for the Kroll Opera] revealed a fatal naiveté and lack of nerve."[144] But it could be argued that Gropius and his circle in Thuringia did not share this naiveté and lack of nerve and nevertheless the closing of the Bauhaus there was seemingly inevitable anyway. Or, to return to Peter Gay's memorable metaphor, although the supporters of the Kroll may have made a few missteps, these did not really matter since they were dancing on the edge of a volcano that was soon to erupt anyway.

One difference between Prussia around 1930 and Thuringia in the mid-1920s is that anti-Semitism was more overt in Prussia. Zschorlich wrote that: "Klemperer and Legal would do well . . . to declare their cultural Bolshevist undertaking a 'Jewish Opera.' What goes on has nothing to do with German artistic spirit."[145] Although Klemperer was basically non-political and was a practicing Roman Catholic during the Kroll years, anti-Semites hated him for his Jewish background anyway.[146]

In any case, as Rockwell reported,

> The last months of activity at Kroll proceeded under a cloud of gathering oppression and gloom. The game was lost, and everyone knew it. A sign of the times came when Klemperer, six feet, four inches tall, was attacked and beaten

---

[141] E.M., "Festlicher Abend bei Kroll; Music," *Vossische Zeitung: Berlinische Zeitung von Staats- und gelehrten Sachen*, Post Ausgabe, December 2, 1930, erste Beilage, [7].

[142] Zschorlich opened a lengthy denunciation with the words: "Schluß mit Kroll!" [Close the Kroll!] This diatribe originally appeared in *Deutsche Zeitung*, February 9, 1930; reprinted in: Curjel, *Experiment Krolloper*, 477-479.

[143] The reader interested in this topic should consult: Rockwell, *op. cit.*, 201-294 *et passim*.

[144] Rockwell, *op. cit.*, viii-ix.

[145] Heyworth, *Otto Klemperer, His Life and Times*, 1:286; and Paul Zschorlich, [review], 264.

[146] Heyworth, *Otto Klemperer, His Life and Times*, 1:1-3, 7, 136-138, 261 and 412-415

up by a Nazi gang in broad daylight as he was walking in the Tiergarten near
Kroll. . . . Yet, indefatigueably, Klemperer and his associates pushed on. . . . [147]

Madama Butterfly by Giacomo Puccini (1858-1924), premiered in 1904 in Milan,
was first presented at the Kroll Opera on February 23rd, 1931.[148] It would seem to be, at
first glance, just the kind of theatrical production Moholy would try to avoid. He was
firmly committed to a stage esthetic that had emerged early in the twentieth century
based on opposition to the old-fashioned sentimental scenes that had been dominating
theatrical expression. Cio-Cio-San, a young Nagasaki beauty known as Madame
Butterfly, undergoes just the kind of emotional experience that Moholy would have
regarded as grist for overly sentimental theatrics. Perhaps by 1931 he felt a sense of
loyalty to the embattled opera company that had been very good to him, and the choice
of a popular Puccini masterpiece, presented in German[149] (foreign-language operas were
presented in German at the Kroll, a practice common in Germany at the time), was part
of an (unsuccessful) attempt to soothe the feelings of some of its critics.[150]

Actually two other circumstances may have made *Madama Butterfly* an attractive
challenge for Moholy. One is that the time of day revealed by changes in light is a key
element in the action and, as usual, Moholy was fascinated by the expressive possibilities
of manipulating light. Cio-Cio-San waits overnight at her house for her American
husband, naval Lieutenant B.F. Pinkerton,[151] with their son, Trouble [*Dolore*], and her
servant, Suzuki, at her side, having observed, with her telescope, her husband's naval
vessel entering Nagasaki harbor. Her hopes fade as the daylight dims into dusk and
eventually into darkness, accompanied by a muted humming chorus, superbly eloquent in
spite of being wordless. The listener is left to wonder whether Cio-Cio-San is beginning
to sense that her husband, unaware of the depth of her feelings toward him, has been
unfaithful and has abandoned her.

The other appealing factor for Moholy is that Puccini's librettists, Luigi Illica and
Giuseppe Giacosa, had expected that the Bay of Nagasaki be visible behind Cio-Cio-
San's house, a challenge Moholy seemed to welcome. (These librettists made much use

---

[147]Rockwell, *op. cit.*, 290-291; the incident was also discussed in: Curjel, *Experiment Krolloper,*
82.

[148]Curjel, *Experiment Krolloper*, 308.

[149]The German translation was by A. Brüggemann; see: *Blätter der Staatsoper und der Städtischen
Oper*, volume XI, number 14 (February, 1931), unnumbered page preceding page 1.

[150]Heyworth, *Otto Klemperer, His Life and Times*, 1:359-360.

[151]On the origins of Pinkerton's first and middle names, see: William Ashbrook, *The Operas of
Puccini*, with a new foreword by Roger Parker (Ithaca, New York: Cornell University Press,
1985), 112. Curiously, at the Kroll the role was called "Linkerton."

of a play by David Belasco, an earlier short story by John Luther Long, and a still earlier novel by Pierre Loti.)[152]

T HE ACTION TAKES PLACE in Nagasaki, in the house Pinkerton has leased for Cio-Cio-San, and in the garden beside the house. Moholy represented the Bay of Nagasaki as seen from her house, (DVD figures 240 and 243) and the city of Nagasaki as seen from her garden, (DVD figure 244) by creating theatrical flats that had the appearance of large-scale black-and-white photocollages.[153]

There are inherent similarities between traditional Japanese domestic architecture and Constructivism. Moholy emphasized these similarities by simplifying the house to a skeletal core that allowed him to speed up scene changes by simply sliding elements within each other (like *shoji* screens themselves) while making changes in light and color.[154] (DVD figure 241) He also made effective use of shadows. (DVD figures 242 and 244) The bright, primary colors of the costume for Prince Yamadori, unsuccessful suitor of Madame Butterfly, seen in a rendering (DVD figure 246), make clear that the black-and-white photographs of the settings miss the stunning colors that Kroll patrons enjoyed. A bit more restrained are the colors in a rendering of the garden but the colors do not seem naturalistic. (DVD figure 245)

The Japanese characters, *e.g.*, the Bonze, Cio-Cio-San's uncle, wear traditional Japanese dress (DVD figure 247), while Sharpless, the American consul in Nagasaki, appears (to judge from an available photograph)[155] to be wearing a business suit of the kind that would have changed very little from 1904, the year of the opera's première. No photographs or drawings of Moholy's Pinkerton have been found, but he would have been wearing an American naval dress uniform of the period.

---

[152] A full account of the blending of fictional and real-life characters portrayed in Puccini's opera is beyond the scope of this book; interested readers should consult: Jan van Rij, *Madame Butterfly, Japonisme, Puccini & the Search for the Real Cho-Cho-San* (Berkeley, California: Stone Bridge Press, 2001). Van Rij provides some startling information about one of the consequences of the dropping of an atom bomb on Nagasaki on August 9, 1945; see his pages 155, 156, 168 and his note 3 on page 181.

[153] Curjel, "Moholy-Nagy und das Theater," 12.

[154] Curjel, "Moholy-Nagy und das Theater," 12.

[155] Curjel, *Experiment Krolloper*, figure 95 following page 84.

There were twenty-six Kroll performances of *Madama Butterfly*, staged by Curjel;[156] the last on July 2nd, 1931.[157] Zemlinsky conducted the first performance, and at least one performance was conducted by Kroll chorus-master Karl Rankl (1898-1968).[158]

Moholy's settings for *Madama Butterfly* were not so controversial as his settings for *The Tales of Hoffmann*. While there were criticisms, they were moderate in tone, as in a newspaper review by Alfred Einstein:

> Das Szenenbild von L. Moholy-Nagy zeigt Nagasaki aus der Vogelperspektive, es wirkt wie ein Ausschnitt aus einer unkolorierten Ansichtspostkarte; ein Bambusgehänge belebt den Bühnenrahmen, man sieht den Pfahlrost des Häuschens; das Nebeneinander von Naturalismus und Konstruktion ist fast gespenstisch. Aber es stört ebensowenig wie ein eifrige Tätigkeit der Schiebebühne wenig hilft.[159] [The set by L. Moholy-Nagy shows Nagasaki from a bird's-eye perspective and gives the impression of a portion of a panoramic postcard. A bamboo festoon enlivens the stage space, and one sees the framework of the little house; the juxtaposition of naturalism and Constructivism is almost spooky. But this detracts as little as the energetic activity of the sliding stage elements help.]

In another newspaper review Oscar Bie denounced the use of a soft-contoured silhouette of the waiting Butterfly as "überflussig und nicht sehr geschmackvoll" [unnecessary and not very tasteful]. This silhouette was shown as a projection during the orchestral intermezzo that introduced the third act, evoking the night-long vigil begun at the end of act two; in any case, it was based on a photograph by Lucia Moholy.

Bie went on to write:[160]

> The scene with Butterfly's vigil was not successful because the space lacked privacy, which Moholy-Nagy was unable to express with his scenic system. The Bauhaus master, with his bent toward the abstract and Constructivist, found inspiration for his imagination in the design of the Japanese house. He set the house as an isolated object, let the walls be shoved back and forth, turned it only a little to the other side between the first and second acts, everywhere emphasized the pure mathematics of his constructions, let a row of Japanese

---

[156]Curjel, *Experiment Krolloper,* 308 and 500.

[157]*Vorwärts, Berliner Volksblatt; Centralorgan der sozialdemokratischen Partei Deutschlands,* July 2, 1931, advertisement on unnumbered page.

[158]*Blätter der Staatsoper und der Städtischen Oper*, volume XI, number 14 (February, 1931), unnumbered page preceding page 1.

[159]Alfred Einstein, [review], *Berliner Tageblatt*, February 24, 1931; reprinted in Curjel, *Experiment Krolloper*, 308-309.

[160]Oscar Bie, [review], *Berlin Börsen-Courier; Tagezeitung für alle Gebiete*, February 24, 1931; reprinted in Curjel, *Experiment Krolloper*, 309-310. The full German text appear in Appendix G, page 741.

staffs hang down over half of the stage to heighten the decorative effect, had the sliding stage deploy parts of the house and its environment in different juxtapositions, designed a charming mountain landscape as a background, with spits of land extending far into the sea somewhat in the manner that we recognize as Japanese art. [This is] a unique form of stage backdrop that is far removed from the familiar showy kind of Japanese landscape, at the same time keeping a realistic opera from dissolving into pure abstraction.

There was also a brief reference to Moholy's work on *Madama Butterfly* in an article summarizing recent musical events in *Die Musik*, a monthly magazine:

Moholy-Nagys Bühnenbild wurde diesmal der gewohnten kubistischen Sachlichkeit untreu und schwelgte in landschaftlichen Aspekt, ein ganzes Panorama der Japanischen Stadt, des Meeres, der Küste aufrolleng, in einer seltsamen, wohl als japanisch geabsichtigten Perspektive, bildlich jedoch nicht ohne Reiz.[161] [Moholy-Nagy's settings were not faithful to the usual cubistic soberness and reveled in the landscape aspect, unrolling an entire panorama of the Japanese city, the ocean and the coast, in a curious perspective, probably intended as Japanese, realistic but not without charm.]

Moholy's settings for *Madama Butterfly* shared a distinction with those for *The Tales of Hoffmann*: they are among the most frequently illustrated opera productions of all time.

AS THE READER WILL GUESS, in view of Klemperer's general comments on the singers at the Kroll, with very few exceptions they were not stars of the operatic world at the time.[162] That was an advantage, however: since the Kroll singers were not in great demand in other venues they were, as Klemperer wished them to be, available for extended repeat performances in their operatic roles. Actually Alfred Einstein did not mention any singers in his review of *The Tales of Hoffmann* for *The New York Times*, and replaced the discussion of the singers that had appeared in his Berlin review with background material on the Bauhaus, little known at the time to most Americans. Nevertheless, two of the cast members of *Madama Butterfly* later became well known in the United States and, unlike most of their former colleagues at the Kroll, are known to later generations through recordings, transcriptions of radio broadcasts, and films; hence their names might be familiar to some readers of these pages. One, Charles Kullman (1903-1983), sang Pinkerton, and the other, Jarmila Novotna, sang the title role. Kullman, an American, was in Berlin as an exchange student;[163] his casting might have been due, in part, to the traditional German craving for authenticity, since he was an American singer playing the part of an American naval lieutenant. Alfred Einstein, referring to him as "*ein echter amerikanischer Tenor*," praised his singing but found his acting awkward; on the other hand, he had high praise for Novotna as singer and

---

[161]Hugo Leichtentritt, "Das Musikleben der Gegenwart, Berlin, Oper," *Die Musik,* volume XXIII, number 7 (April, 1931), 521.

[162]Curjel, *Experiment Krolloper*, 33.

[163]Alfred Einstein, [review], *Berliner Tageblatt*, February 24, 1931.

actress.[164] The American consul was sung by Mathieu Ahlersmeyer (1896-1979), known through the media of recordings and film, while Suzuki was sung by Else Ruziczka, who also made recordings, among them excerpts from her Kroll roles as Niklaus in *The Tales of Hoffmann* and Suzuki in *Madama Butterfly*.

Moholy had begun design work on another opera, Mozart's *Das Hochzeit des Figaro* [*Le Nozze di Figaro*, or *The Marriage of Figaro*],[165] but withdrew and Teo Otto replaced him.[166] That production was first presented on January 25th, 1931. Its performance on July 3rd, 1931, marked the closing of the Kroll Opera.

It is likely that all of Moholy's sets, props and costumes, along with the movies for *The Tales of Hoffmann*, were thrown out. After the Kroll Opera was discontinued by its parent company, nearly all productions were presented at the opera house on *Unter den Linden*. A few productions were transferred from the Kroll to that opera house, but none Moholy had worked on. It is possible that anything not needed in the productions transferred to the opera house on *Unter den Linden* was simply discarded.

In one of history's ironies, after the nearby *Reichstag Bau* (Germany's national parliament building) was heavily damaged by fire early in 1933, the Nazi-era *Reichstag* met in the Kroll Opera building.[167] Meanwhile, for a brief time during the war it served again as an opera house (while continuing to serve as a parliament building), this time for the *Staatsoper* on *Unter den Linden,* after the opera house there was severely damaged and before it was rebuilt (while the war still waged on).[168] The Kroll Opera building itself later suffered military damage and was demolished in the 1950s.[169] Any sets or costumes that might by chance have remained in the damaged building would have been destroyed at that time.

Another irony concerning Berlin's Kroll Opera is that during the Weimar era there was a good deal of daring innovation in opera houses in other German cities, but, with only a few exceptions, these were outside Prussia and hence not under the control of the besieged Prussian Ministry of Culture.[170]

---

[164]Alfred Einstein, [review], *Berliner Tageblatt*, February 24, 1931.

[165]Unused costume sketches by Moholy are in a private collection.

[166]Heyworth, *Otto Klemperer, His Life and Times*, 1:352.

[167]Reichhardt, *op. cit.*, 117-136 *et passim*.

[168]Reichhardt, *op. cit.*, 149-152.

[169]Reichhardt, *op. cit.*, 153-164.

[170]Walter Panofsky, *Protest in der Oper; das provokative Musiktheater der zwanziger Jahre* (Munich: Laokoon Verlag GmbH, 1966), *passim*.

And, to turn once more to Albert Einstein, in still another irony he became one of the tiny number of real persons whose name appears in the title of an opera, or, in fact, two. *Einstein*, written by Paul Dessau (1894-1979), with a libretto by Karl Mickel (1935-2000), was first presented at the Berlin State Opera [*Staatsoper*] on *Unter den Linden* in 1974. Dessau and Mickel's Einstein is one of the characters in an opera only loosely fitted around historical events.[171]

By way of contrast, *Einstein on the Beach*, by Philip Glass and Robert Wilson, first presented at a festival in Avignon, France, July 25th, 1976, has no narrative elements, but rather presents metaphorical references to Einstein's Theory of Relativity. For example, the railroad train that he so memorably used to describe relative motion[172] was represented.

To sum up, the Kroll Opera was the scene not only of attempts to rejuvenate traditional arts with modern points of view, but of an unusual coming together of science, visual and theatre arts, and music. The reader is left to imagine a time warp in which Einstein's famous but humdrum railroad train might have been a set of trapezes bearing beautiful young women dressed as parrots.

Moholy and Piscator, Together Again

NOT LONG AFTER HIS DEBUT as an opera designer, Moholy returned to work for the spoken theatre on a production of *The Merchant of Berlin*. He was re-united with a director with whom, as discussed in Chapter Two, he had worked shortly after arriving in Berlin in 1920: Erwin Piscator (1893-1966). Piscator had been born into a family famous for rebelliousness as reflected in his name. According to a family tradition, a sixteenth-century ancestor, Johannes Fischer, Latinized the family name literally to Piscator to "hide himself from the wrath of Rome" because of his meticulous and scholarly but unauthorized Bible translation.[173]

Although Piscator described himself as a Communist, he was not a party official, and he did not always get along well with those who did serve as party officials. Nevertheless, as he once wrote, " . . . I have placed the total apparatus of the theater in the service of the revolutionary [Communist] movement and adapted it to the aims of the

---

[171] M.A. Orthofer, "Humanistic Failings: Karl Mickel's *Einstein*," *The Complete Review Quarterly*, volume II, number 1 (February, 2001). Available on the internet, http://www.complete-review.com/quarterly/vol2/issue1/mickele.htm, accessed January 18, 2007.

[172] Albert Einstein, *Relativity; the Special & the General Theory*, 9-10.

[173] Maria Ley-Piscator, *The Piscator Experiment: the Political Theatre* (New York: James H. Heineman, Inc., 1967), 61.

movement."[174] Thus, he insisted, ". . . technical innovations were never an end in themselves for me."[175] By the time *The Merchant of Berlin* opened, Piscator had given up all hope of building the total theatre had been designed for him in 1927 by Gropius and Sebök, discussed on page 263 in Chapter Three, but he had not given up his hopes for achieving a technically innovative political theatre that had motivated him to seek to build his total theatre.

Piscator had recently received financial backing for continuing his theatrical work as *Die Piscator Bühne*, most importantly from Felix Weil, one of the principal patrons of George Grosz (1893-1959).[176] Piscator was thus able to return to a large theatre he had used previously, the *Neues Schauspielhaus*. With 1,100 seats, it was part of the building known as the *Theater am Nollendorf Platz* (Albert Fröhlich, 1906; the part of the building containing the *Neues Schauspielhaus* was destroyed in World War II). (DVD figure 248) The only new production of the second Piscator Buehne at Nollendorf Platz was Walter Mehring's drama, *Der Kaufmann von Berlin* [*The Merchant of Berlin*]. Moholy had probably met Mehring during the Dada-Constructivist Congress of 1922 in Weimar and Jena, discussed in Chapter Two.

There were three principal reasons why Piscator would want to turn to Moholy: one was the latter's daring work on *The Tales of Hoffmann* for the Kroll Opera; another was that Moholy had been a sympathetic observer of, and an inspiration for, that attempt of Piscator and Gropius to build a total theatre in Berlin; the third was that Stefan Sebök, Moholy's assistant, had played a key role in the 1927 design of Piscator's total-theatre project. In addition, as noted below on pages 378-380, Ellen Frank (1904-1999) had acted in Piscator productions in 1924 and 1928.

The *Merchant of Berlin* was originally scheduled to open on August 30th, 1929,[177] but due to the complexity of the production the opening was delayed.[178] It finally opened on September 6th and ran for six weeks, closing on October 15th.

---

[174]*Erwin Piscator, Das Politische Theater* (Berlin: Adalbert Schultz Verlag, 1929), 74; *idem, Das politische Theater*, Faksimiledruck der Erstausgabe 1929 (Berlin: Henschelverlag Kunst und Gesellschaft, 1968), 74; and *idem, The Political Theatre*, translations and introductions to each section by Hugh Rorrison (New York: Avon Books, 1978), 102.

[175]Piscator, *The Political Theatre* , 188; and *idem, Das Politische Theatre*, 132.

[176]Willett, *The Theatre of Erwin Piscator*, 78; and Piscator, *The Political Theatre*, 312.

[177]Alfred Joseph Loup, *The Theatrical Productions of Erwin Piscator in Weimar Germany: 1920-1931* (Ann Arbor, Michigan: Xerox University Microfilms, 1975), 251.

[178]Paul Fechter, "Das neue Piscator-Theater, 'Der Kaufmann von Berlin' am Nollendorfplatz," *Deutsche Allgemeine Zeitung* (Berlin), Abendausgabe, September 7, 1929; reprinted in: Günther Rühle, *Theater für die Republik, 1917-1933, im Spiegel der Kritik* (Frankfurt am Main: S. Fischer Verlag, 1967), 967.

The full title of the play is: *Der Kaufmann von Berlin, ein historisches Schauspiel aus der deutschen Inflation*[179] [The Merchant of Berlin, a Historical Drama about the German Inflation]. The action centered on the inflation of 1922 and 1923, with which Moholy himself had had to struggle, and which virtually all of the audience members had themselves recently experienced.

Moholy played a role in planning the production from an early stage. Key decisions were made, and later carried out as planned, in creative sessions attended by Piscator, Mehring, Wolfgang Roth, Bauhäusler Johan Niegeman (1902-1977), and Moholy (and evidently Sebök as well), along with some technicians. Numerous ideas were considered, some of which were abandoned as too impractical or too expensive. Preliminary sketches were made; none of these were signed, but some, utilizing mechanical instruments such as a straight-edge, were probably drawn by Sebök. (DVD figures 253 and 254) Notes were written on some sketches, but none of them in Moholy's hand.[180]

SIMON CHAIM KAFTAN, the play's merchant of Berlin, speaks Yiddish, a language Mehring was familiar with through his Jewish parents. Although Yiddish is closely related to German, speakers of standard German cannot readily understand Yiddish unless they also grew up with that language, or had made a study of it as adults. One critic, Bernard Diebold, wrote of the play's "kaum verständlich Jiddisch" [barely understandable Yiddish].[181] A 1995 German-language reprint of the play even has a Yiddish glossary.[182] Moreover, in an attempt to get a pure version of Yiddish, a Yiddish-speaking actor from New York who had been born in Russia, Paul Baratoff (1872-1951), was cast as Kaftan. In addition to

---

[179] Walter Mehring, *Der Kaufmann von Berlin, ein historisches Schauspiel aus der deutschen Inflation* (Berlin: S. Fischer Verlag, 1929).

[180] These planning sessions were described by Johan Niegeman in an unpublished typewritten essay dated June, 1973, "Der Kaufmann von Berlin," VFM 27, Special Collections Research Center, Southern Illinois University at Carbondale; another copy is in the *Akademie der Künste*, Berlin.

Niegeman's essay is bound with thirty-four preliminary sketches in ink and pencil in an unidentified hand, but probably that of Stefan Sebök, along with Niegeman's own diagrams and explanatory comments, presumably dating from 1973.

On Niegeman, see: Brüning and Droste, editors, *Das A und O des Bauhauses*, 325; and Cor de Wit, *Johan Niegeman 1902-1977* (Amsterdam: Van Gennep, 1979), 41-51.

[181] Bernhard Diebold, [review], *Frankfurter Zeitung*, September 11, 1929; reprinted in: Rühle, *Theater für die Republik*, 964.

[182] Hans-J. Weitz, editor, *Drei jüdische Dramen: Herman Ungar: Der rote General; Walter Mehring: Der Kaufmann von Berlin; Paul Kornfeld: Jud Süß; mit Dokumenten zur Rezeption* (Göttingen: Wallstein Verlag, 1995), [177]-188.

Yiddish, local Berlin dialects, not readily understandable by some Germans, were also used.[183]

The German inflation of 1922 and 1923 is represented through a parable based on Kaftan's experiences in Berlin and nearby Potsdam. He arrives from the East by rail with one-hundred American dollars, a huge sum of money in inflation-ridden Germany. He is manipulated by a crooked right-wing lawyer, Müller, and eventually becomes penniless. Before his luck runs out Kaftan acquires a retail establishment on fashionable Kurfürstendamm, as well as a bank, but he also engages in illegal arms-dealing. The parable is punctuated with a series of brief slice-of-life episodes based on Kaftan's wanderings through various neighborhoods of the big city, delineated by signs and symbols as well as props such as an entrance to an underground railway. Except for the Kaftan and Müller roles, the other characters appear briefly, and include black-marketeers, porters, prostitutes, police officers and ghetto Jews. A reconstruction of the list of the scenes and a brief summary of each was made in 1961 by Marianne Mildenberger,[184] based in part on sketches by Moholy.[185]

Piscator had begun to use movies in his stage productions at least as early as 1925, when he incorporated newsreel footage into *Trotz Alledem* [Despite All], written by Piscator with his dramaturge, Felix Gasbarra. The movies used in *The Merchant of*

---

[183] *E.g.*, Mehring, *Der Kaufmann von Berlin*, 26-28; see also: Erwin Piscator, *The Political Theatre*, 315.

[184] Mildenberger, *Film und Projection*, 194-199.

[185] Moholy's notes and sketches for the first half of the production are in the Theatre Collection of the University of Cologne Institute of Theatre-, Film- and Television Studies. About one-hundred sketches are in the Akademie der Künste in Berlin; one is reproduced in: Walther Huder, editor, *Erwin Piscator, 1893-1966* (Berlin: Akademie der Künste, 1971), [117].

PISCATORBÜHNE

Ludwig Klopfer
Im Theater am Nollendorfplatz

Anfang 7½ Uhr

Der Kaufmann von Berlin
ein historisches Schauspiel aus der deutschen Inflation
von
Walter Mehring
Inszenierung: Erwin Piscator

Gesamtausstattung: L. Moholy-Nagy

Bühnentechnik: Herbert Selinger

Film:

  Regie: Moholy-Nagy
  Aufnahmen: Alex Strasser
  Zeichentricks: Elwitz-Schönfeld

Musik: Hanns Eisler
Assistenz:
  Herbert Breth-Mildner
Orchester:
  Weintraub Syncopaters
  (m. Genehm. d. „Wintergarten")
Rhythmik: Claire Bauroff

P e r s o n e n :

Kaftan	Paul Baratoff	Kneifer	Erich Bartels
Lodenrock	Hermann Speelmans	Arbeiter	Albert Venohr
		Schreiber	E. Bornträger
Bauersfrau	Edith Angold	Schaffner	Fritz Erpenbeck

Gepäckträger: Karl Hannemann, Leopold Lindtberg, Friedrich Gnas
Huren: Ilva Günten, Lotte Loebinger, Felicitas Niedermayer,
Marta John, Frieda Bohm, Hella Bialer

Greise Männerstimme	Jacob Schöps	2. Polizist	Kurt Lieck
Heisere Männerstimme	Friedrich Gnas	Alter Mann	Ernst Busch
Wurstmaxe	W. Bernhardy	Arme Frau	Ilva Günten
1. Polizist	Erich O. Peters	Kleines Kind	Grete Merory

Frauen: Edith Angold, Bertl Eisenberg, Felicitas Niedermayer, F. Bohm, Kaethe de Neuf

---

program for Walter Mehring's
The Merchant of Berlin, 1929

text figure 12, DVD figure 251

Berlin were directed by Moholy and shot by Alex Strasser (1898-1974).[186] (text figure 12, DVD figure 251) Strasser had already directed a film, *Berlin from Below* (1928),[187] which probably meant that he had some relevant experience in putting cityscapes onto film. Some of the film footage for *The Merchant of Berlin*, as described by John Willett, was:

> . . . not so much used for comment as knitted ingeniously into the stage action projecting it on the gauze [drop curtains], then lighting up the stage behind as the gauze was raised, thus smoothly transferring the action to the stage. . . . To [critic Bernhard] Diebold the beginning with Kaftan's wanderings through the East End of Berlin, first on the screen, then on the stage, was unforgettable.[188]

Moholy himself noted: "It is possible to enrich our spacial experience by projecting light on to a succession of semitransparent planes (nets, trellis-work, etc.). I did this in my scenic experiments for the 'Kaufmann von Berlin' . . ."[189]

Strasser described using a theatre lobby as a film-studio for reasons of cost and convenience,[190] and one of his friends, the Hungarian writer János Reismann (1905-1976), witnessed some of the filming that was done by Strasser during September, 1929, when he was completing some scenes using the lobby of the theatre at Nollendorf Platz as his studio; Reismann reported that clips from the scenes Strasser shot were shown

---

[186]Marion Beckers and Elisabeth Moortgat, *Atelier Lotte Jacobi, Berlin, New York* [English-language edition] (Berlin: Nicolai, 1998), 85; and Alex Strasser, "Film auf der Bühne," *Film Technik; Zeitschrift für alle künstlerischen, technischen und wirtschaftlichen Fragen des Filmwesens*, volume V, number 20 (September 28, 1929), 417-419; reprinted, without the illustrations, in: *Erwin Piscator, eine Arbeitsbiographie in 2 Bänden*, edited by Knut Boeser and Renata Vatková (Berlin: Frölich & Kaufmann, 1986), 1:253-258.

Not much can be learned about Strasser. He directed three short films during 1931 for the Berlin sound-film studio Tonbild-Sindikat A.G., also known as Tobis; see: Hans-Michael Bock, Wiebke Annkatrin Mosel and Ingrun Spazier, editors, *Die Tobis 1928-1945; eine kommentierte Filmografie* (Munich: Edition Text + Kritik, 2003), 74-75.

Strasser later emigrated to England where he worked with Len Lye on the short 1935 color film *The Birth of a Robot*. Strasser went on to become a director of documentary films.

[187]Jan-Christopher Horak, *Making Images Move: Photographers and Avant-Garde Cinema* (Washington: Smithsonian Institution Press, 1997), 119.

[188]Willett, *The Theatre of Erwin Piscator*, 100.

[189]"Az Űj Film Problémái," *Korunk*, number 10 (1930), 712-719; re-printed in English translation as "Problems of the Modern Film," in: Passuth, *Moholy-Nagy*, 311-315, here 315.

[190]Alex Strasser, "Film auf der Bühne" (1929) 419; *idem* (1986), 256-257.

during the performance of *The Merchant of Berlin*.[191] Since the play opened on September 6, at least some of Strasser's filming would have been accomplished at the last minute, evidently in order to co-ordinate his footage with the stage action and settings. This is borne out by Strasser's own account, in which he wrote about the difficulties of co-ordinating film with live stage action; problems were created when there were alterations in some scenes while others were dropped, sometimes while rehearsals were going on and sometimes even just before public performances were begun.[192] These difficulties went beyond what Moholy had to deal with in his film for *The Tales of Hoffmann*, because at the Kroll Opera last-minute changes in score or libretto would have been unlikely.

In addition to using a gauze curtain (*i.e.*, a scrim) as a projection surface, numerous film sequences and still images were projected onto three screens, including colored still images by George Grosz for a scene set in Alexanderplatz, the site of Kaftan's arrival in Berlin. The Grosz images evidently have not survived, but this was the only time Moholy and Grosz were associated in Europe.[193] Many other images were projected as well, included documentary photographs,[194] and enlarged Hebrew letters.[195] At the top of the stage opening a running account of the value of the German mark to the American dollar was projected; this was created by Max Gebhard, who also ran the film projector for these titles from the third tier of the theatre auditorium.[196] There were also sound effects.[197]

The production was the most elaborate Piscator had thus far put on, and the theatre at his disposal on Nollendorf Platz was enhanced with even more technical resources to supplement those already installed earlier.[198] No curtain was used so that scene changes could be more fluid. Much flexibility was made possible by varying the size and shape of the stage opening and by the selective use of lighting. On a revolving stage there had been constructed two long treadmills, whose relative positions could be altered. There

---

[191]János Reismann, "Memoiren" as "Dok. 112," in: Gaßner, editor, *Wechsel Wirkungen*, 449-451, here 450.

[192]Strasser, "Film auf der Bühne" (1929), 417; *idem* (1986), 254.

[193]Except for *Buch neuer Künstler*, which illustrated one work by Grosz; *Buch neuer Künstler* was the 1922 book co-edited by Moholy, as discussed in Chapter Two.

[194]Willett, *The Theatre of Erwin Piscator,* 98; Piscator, *The Political Theatre*, 316.

[195]*Erwin Piscator, Das Politische Theater*, frontispiece; *idem*, *The Political Theatre*, illustration preceding page 341.

[196]Gebhard, "Erinnerungen," 182; and Helm, "Produktive Begegnungen: Gespräch mit Max Gebhard," 306.

[197]Willett, *The Theatre of Erwin Piscator,* 100.

[198]Willett, *The Theatre of Erwin Piscator*, 78.

were also three expansive but narrow bridges, which could be raised and lowered independently using elevators, with the actors and sets remaining on them. The bridges were sometimes connected with each other by means of stairs.[199] (DVD figure 254) A high rigging-loft allowed the bridges to be stored when not needed. Not all of the mechanics worked well. The elevators were not always on cue, for example, and the opening-night performance lasted from 7:30 until after midnight.[200] There was evidently some danger involved,[201] but no writers have described any actual injuries to cast or crew. One writer, however, did describe a near miss:

> . . . in *The Merchant of Berlin* the complex machinery malfunctioned during the first scene, when the chorus who stood on steps leading down to the stalls (the steps were supposed to sink into the pit after the prologue while the stage-floor closed above them and an iron construction was lowered from the flies) were almost crushed when the lift jammed on the first night. This was a mistake that could not be disguised. Frantic cries brought the machinery to a halt, the actors scrambled up into the wings and stage-hands appeared to do repairs.[202]

It is noteworthy that Moholy had written about using suspended bridges in the theatre as early as 1924, when he wrote of "suspended bridges and drawbridges running horizontally, diagonally, and vertically within the space of the theatre."[203]

Piscator wrote that: "We saw from the beginning that the proletariat was almost entirely absent from Mehring's play." He explained that one means of representing the proletariat was ". . . with long, interpolated songs, such as 'The Cantata of War, Peace and Inflation.' In these songs the proletariat was to appear as an active factor."[204] The text of the Cantata was written for the production by Mehring;[205] music was written by Hanns Eisler (1898-1962).

Piscator described how the proletariat was also represented through the use of the bridges:

---

[199]Loup, *The Theatrical Productions of Erwin Piscator*, 254-255.

[200]Monty Jacobs, "Piscators Anfang und Ende? Der Kaufmann von Berlin im Theater am Nollendorfplatz," *Vossische Zeitung: Berlinische Zeitung von Staats- und gelehrten Sachen*, Post-Ausgabe, September 8, 1929, vierte Beilage [fourth supplement], [1]. A curtain time of 8:00 was given in an advertisement in the *Vossische Zeitung: Berlinische Zeitung von Staats- und gelehrten Sachen*, September 6, 1929, [6].

[201]Willett, *The Theatre of Erwin Piscator*, 113-114.

[202]C.D. Innes, *Erwin Piscator's Political Theatre: the Development of Modern German Drama* (London: Cambridge University Press, 1972), 71.

[203]Schlemmer, Moholy-Nagy and Molnár, *The Theater of the Bauhaus*, 68.

[204]Piscator, *The Political Theatre*, 332; *idem, Das Politische Theater*, 253.

[205]Mehring, *Der Kaufmann von Berlin*, 163-165.

. . . I saw the play from the start in three stages: a tragic stage (proletariat), a tragicomic stage (middle class), and a grotesque stage (upper classes and military). This sociological system produced the three-tier system of staging, which we constructed with the aid of elevators and bridges. Each of these social classes was to have a stage of its own—upper, middle, lower—and the classes were to meet from time to time whenever the focus of the dramatic action demanded it. The movement of the various levels toward and away from one another created a dramatic stage space.[206]

Although his approach to theatre grew directly out of his political beliefs, Piscator was very careful in choosing plays:

Besides being sharp and logical in its convictions, a play must also be a likely stage success. A mere editorial in dialogue is not enough. The theater needs theatricality. This is what makes it effective. Only then can it claim to be real propaganda.[207]

Piscator's success at presenting riveting dramatic experiences, mostly in venues in upscale neighborhoods such as Nollendorf Platz, may lead many to agree with Willett's conclusion that "Piscator's political theatre . . . was essentially a bourgeois theatre dependent on attracting an experiment-conscious audience, even though the bourgeoisie was what it was out to overthrow."[208]

There were extensive reviews in Berlin and out-of-town newspapers of a play and production that proved to be very controversial, with severe criticism originating from across the political spectrum.[209] However, most reviews of *The Merchant of Berlin* did not mention Moholy. One exception was Bernhard Diebold, who had already reviewed *The Tales of Hoffmann* at the Kroll Opera, and thus was familiar with Moholy's work in the theatre; he wrote of the Dessau architect [sic] who collaborated with Piscator on the settings.[210] Another was Bertolt Brecht (1898-1956), the equal of Mehring as a controversial playwright, who wrote: ". . für ein Inflationsstück Moholy-Nagy eine Nickel- und Glaskonstruktion verwendete, was die unerwünschte Assoziation eines

---

[206]Piscator, *The Political Theatre*, 331; *idem, Das Politische Theater*, 253.

[207]Piscator, *The Political Theatre*, 328; *idem, Das Politische Theater*, 249.

[208]Willett, *The Theatre of Erwin Piscator,* 191.

[209]Since most of the controversy did not involve Moholy, it lies outside the scope of this book. Readers interested in the controversy should consult: Piscator, *The Political Theatre,* 335-340; *idem, Das Politische Theater*, 257-262; Loup, *The Theatrical Productions of Erwin Piscator,* 256-259; Willett, *The Theatre of Erwin Piscator*, 78-79; Rühle, *Theater für die Republik,* 961-968; and Wietz, editor, *Drei jüdische Dramen,* 297-357 and 402-404.

[210]Bernard Diebold, "Piscator-Premiere," *Franfurter Zeitung*, Abend-Blatt, September 7, 1929, 1; reprinted in: Rühle, *Theater für die Republik*, 962-965.

chirurgischen Bestecks erweckte."[211] [. . . for a theatre piece on inflation Moholy-Nagy used nickel-and-glass construction that evoked an unwished-for association with a set of surgical instruments.] Still another, Paul Fechter, described in some detail what he saw as the difficulties and absurdities of the extensive use of stage machinery, *e.g.*, "Alles knarrte, knackte, brummte" [everything creaked, cracked and rumbled], but went on to write that: "Gelegentlich gab's ein hübsches Bild (Moholy-Nagy hat da die Verantwortung), gelegentlich gab's ein Raumwirkung mit Reizen . . ."[212] [By the way the setting was attractive (Moholy-Nagy was responsible), and also, by the way, there was a fascinating use of space].

NO OTHER PRODUCTION of *The Merchant of Berlin* seems to have taken place on stage or screen. Whether this was because of the difficulties of staging or filming it or that Mehring's text began to seem dated can only be guessed at. What is clear, however, from the vast literature about it created over the years, is that Piscator's production of the play has become legendary. In fact the first retrospective consideration of Piscator's production of the play was in 1930, 1931 and 1932 when its settings were featured in a traveling theatre exhibition seen in Cologne, Essen, Basel and Duisburg.[213]

Piscator's only book, *Das Politische Theater,* came out in 1929;[214] most of the text was written before the end of August, but a few passages and the choice of illustrations were completed during the run of *The Merchant of Berlin.* The frontispiece was a photocollage of scenes from Mehring's play.[215] Moholy designed the dust jacket and the binding; one of the type faces he used had been designed by Josef Albers. The dust jacket included a photocollage extending across the front and back covers and the spine. Moholy utilized three images from Traugott Müller's globular setting for Piscator's 1927 production of *Rasputin*[216] (written by Piscator himself with Gasbarra) for his own collage; this setting dominated the jacket illustration, which represented a stage-setting that was penetrated by a photograph of a huge political demonstration with figures small in scale compared with the setting, and placed so that the demonstration seemed to

---

[211]Bertolt Brecht, "Über den Bühnenbau der nichtaristotelischen Dramatik" [About the theatrical presentation of non-Aristotlean drama], in his: *Gesammelte Werke in 20 Bänden: Band 15* [edited by] Elisabeth Hauptmann (Frankfurt am Main: Suhrkamp Verlag, 1967), note 1 on page 445. Neither Brecht nor his editor made it clear when the quoted passage, or a comparable one, was first written.

[212]Fechter, "Das neue Piscator-Theater, 'Der Kaufmann von Berlin' am Nollendorfplatz"; reprinted in: Rühle, *Theater für die Republik,* 967-968.

[213]Shown were twenty-nine drawings and nine photographs; see: Niessen, editor, *Das Problemtheater*, 40 and photograph following page 43.

[214]Cited fully in note 174.

[215]It is not clear who made the photocollage; it does not resemble the work of Moholy in that medium.

[216]Piscator, *Das politische Theater*, facing page 145; see also: Lusk, *Montagen ins Blaue*, 164-165.

extend from the street and into the setting itself. The stage-setting on the jacket was
made to appear massive because the figures of the demonstrators seemed so small
compared to it (DVD figures 249 and 250).[217]

It is possible that Moholy taught stage design in *Die Schule der Piscatorbühne*, the
school that Piscator operated at the Theatre on Nollendorf Platz. The only
documentation on this was published in an article that appeared with a November 2,
1929, dateline,[218] which was after *The Merchant of Berlin* had already closed and just
before a production Piscator was directing in Mannheim opened on November 23. So it
is likely that Moholy taught for Piscator but only briefly.

Ellen Frank's role in Piscator's theatrical efforts, noted above, was relatively minor.
In 1926 she took part in a production of Friedrich Schiller's *Die Räuber* [The Robbers],
written in 1781, directed by Piscator.[219] Later Ellen Frank was part of the Piscator-
Bühne Studio, basically an educational effort, and appeared in its 1928 world-première
production of Upton Sinclair's *Singing Jailbirds*,[220] written in 1924,[221] presented by the
Studio at the Lessing Theatre[222] (no longer extant). The director was Ernst Löhner.[223]

---

[217] Concerning this jacket see: Helm, "Produktive Begegnungen: Gespräch mit Max Gebhard," 307.

[218] *Deutsche Bühne: amtliches Blatt des deutsches Bühnenvereins*, November 2, 1929, 309.

[219] The only female role in Schiller's play is Amelia von Edelreich, a role played by Maria
Koppenhöfer, as documented in: Piscator, *The Political Theatre*, page facing 164 and page 358;
and *idem*, *Das Politische Theater*, page facing page 96.

The only source that I found connecting Ellen Frank with the production is an Internet web
site. Perhaps Ellen Frank was an understudy, or perhaps alterations in the text made by Piscator
opened up another female role, perhaps one in which she did not speak. On these alterations see:
Innes, *Erwin Piscator's Political Theatre*, 67-68 and 166-169; and Davies, *The Volksbühne
Movement*, 114-115.

[220] "Sinclair über die 'Singende Galgenvögel;' die heutigen Erstaufführung bei Piscator," *Die Rote
Fahne*, March 1, 1928, 2. Beilage, [3]. The documentation of the production as a world première
is in: John Ahouse, *Upton Sinclair: a Descriptive, Annotated Bibliography* (Los Angeles: Mercer
& Aitchison, 1994), 55.

[221] Upton Sinclair, *Singing Jailbirds: a Drama in Four Acts* (Pasadena: published by the author,
1924).

[222] Mildenburger, *Film und Projektion*, 192-193 and figure 78 following page 315; and Willett, *The
Theatre of Erwin Piscator*, 75-76.

[223] Piscator, *The Political Theatre*, 176-177, 293 and 360; *idem*, *Das Politische Theater*, 221; and
Herms, "The German Reception of Upton Sinclair," 243, as in note 229.

The role of Nell Adams was played by Renée Stobrawa,[224] and thus Ellen Frank would have been cast in the other principal female role, Muriel, an attractive young stenographer.[225]

Singing Jailbirds, known in Germany as *Singende Galgenvögel*,[226] is about the struggles of the Industrial Workers of the World ("Wobblies") in a California harbor city. The Piscator-Bühne Studio production, which opened on March 1st, 1928, and played only two weeks,[227] included the singing of a number of rousing American labor-union songs (in German translations by Wieland Herzfelde) called for by the playwright,[228] but nevertheless it was not considered a success.[229] The play is seldom seen anywhere, but Sinclair's well-crafted text provides a compelling reading experience and is the principal literary treatment of the I.W.W., a once lively sector of the American labor movement that was nearly obliterated as a (well-documented) victim of severe, and at times clearly illegal, political oppression by public authorities.[230]

Of course the reader will wonder whether Moholy saw Ellen Frank in *The Singing Jailbirds* in a role in which she was supposed to look very attractive. But for most of March he would have been in Dessau. Perhaps he and Lucia made a short trip to Berlin as part of a search for living quarters there; it is known that Ise Gropius went to Berlin for that purpose on March 7,[231] while *The Singing Jailbirds* was still playing. Naturally

---

[224]Piscator, *The Political Theatre*, unnumbered page facing page 201; *idem, Das Politische Theater*, unnumbered page facing page 209; and Peter [the author used only one name], "Upton Sinclair: Singende Galgenvögel, Die neue Inszenierung der Piscator-Bühne," *Die Rote Fahne*, March 3, 1928, 1. Beilage, [3-4]; reprinted in: Manfred Brauneck, editor, *Die Rote Fahne: Kritik, Theorie, Feuilleton, 1918-1933* (Munich: Wilhelm Fink Verlag, 1973), 330-338, here 335.

[225]In one review Ellen Frank's character, Muriel, is mentioned but she is not: Harry Kahn, "Singende Galgenvögel," *Die Weltbühne: Wochenschrift für Politik, Kunst, Wirtschaft*, volume XXIV, number 10 (March 6, 1928), 373-375.

[226]Upton Sinclair, *Singende Galgenvögel: Drama in vier Aufzügen*, autorisierte Übertragung aus dem amerikanischen Manuskript von Hermynia zur Mühlen; Nachdichtung der Lieder von Wieland Herzfelde (Berlin: Malik-Verlag, 1927).

[227]Piscator, *Das Politische Theater*, 229; *idem, The Political Theatre*, 304.

[228]Willett, *The Theatre of Erwin Piscator*, 77; and Peter, "Upton Sinclair: Singende Galgenvögel," in: Brauneck, editor, *Die Rote Fahne: Kritik, Theorie, Feuilleton, 1918-1933*, 332 and 335.

[229]Willett, *The Theatre of Erwin Piscator*, 77; Mildenberger, *Film und Projektion*, 192-193; and Gerhard Probst, "Erwin Piscator and Upton Sinclair," in: Dieter Herms, editor, *Upton Sinclair: Literature and Social Reform* (Frankfort am Main: Peter Lang, 1990), 234-241, here 237. See also: Dieter Herms, "The German Reception of Upton Sinclair," in: *ibid.*, 242-248, here 243.

[230]Sinclair, *Singing Jailbirds*, "Postscript," 87-95.

[231]Day-book entry by Ise Gropius for March 7, 1928.

Ise would have been expected to attend her sister's performance, and, if the Moholy-Nagys were also in the city at that time, they probably went with her.

Although Piscator moved to New York in 1938, there is no record that he and Moholy ever met in the U.S.[232] Nevertheless their American careers were parallel in that both wielded strong influence, personally and through the schools they each founded. Piscator and his Dramatic Workshop at the New School for Social Research (now New School University) were influential in the early careers of actors such as Marlon Brando and Harry Belafonte, as well as playwrights Tennessee Williams and Arthur Miller, and producer, director and actress Judith Malina.[233] Thus Piscator's years in America help to illustrate my observation in Chapter Two that sometimes Germany's Weimar era seems to be part of America's cultural past.

Meanwhile, Outside the Theatre: Rumblings of an Unsettling Future

It was during the run of *The Merchant of Berlin* that two events took place that led to profound changes in the economic and political life of Germany. On October 3rd, 1929, a serious decline began in the New York stock market, a decline that led to a crash a few weeks later. And also on October 3rd, German Foreign Minister (and former Chancellor) Gustav Stresemann died of a brain stroke.

One reason Germany was hit so hard by the stock-market crash is that, although it had become the world's second-largest industrial power,[234] it was heavily dependent on foreign capital. In a population of about sixty-five million, unemployment rose from 1,368,000 in 1929 to 3,144,000 in 1930; the figure was 5,668,000 in 1931 and 6,014,000 in 1932.[235] Clearly the economic recovery, begun in 1924, had come to an end.

---

[232]While resident in Chicago Moholy frequently visited New York, and might have met with Piscator there. One likely time would have been on May 20, 1946, when, as described in Chapter Five, Moholy attended an organizational meeting for a New York chapter of the *CIAM* held at the New School for Social Research, where Piscator was a member of the faculty. See: Eric Mumford, *The CIAM Discourse on Urbanism, 1928-1960* (Cambridge: The MIT Press, 2000), 145-147.

[233]Willett, *The Theatre of Erwin Piscator*, 155 and 166; Thomas George Evans, "Piscator in the American Theatre, New York, 1939-1951" (Ann Arbor, Michigan: University Microfilms, 1968), 265-266; Huder, editor, *Erwin Piscator*, 39 and [74]; Juergen Stein and Katharine Lockwood, editors, *Erwin Piscator Exhibit* (Carbondale, Illinois: Friends of Morris Library, 1974), 12-14; and Maria Ley-Piscator, *The Piscator Experiment*, 99-100, 112-116 and 236-239.

[234] Paul Bookbinder, *Weimar Germany: the Republic of the Reasonable* (Manchester: Manchester University Press, 1996), 169.

[235]Koppel S. Pinson, *Modern Germany, Its History and Civilization* (New York: The Macmillan Company, 1955), 452-453.

Many Germans, among them some political moderates, had been critical of a few of Gustav Stresemann's policies and actions, including, as noted in Chapter Three, the unseating of the Thuringian government in 1923. Still, by 1929 the fifty-one year old Nobel Peace laureate[236] had emerged as a statesman whom many regarded, correctly as it turned out, to be the last hope that moderation rather than Fascism would prevail in Germany. Count Harry Kessler's immediate reaction to his death was: "It is an irreparable loss whose consequences cannot be foreseen."[237] As one result of this loss, as Lucia Moholy's brother, Franz (né Schulz) Spencer, lamented in1934 about the city from which she had fled the previous year, "What once had been the most progressive capital in Europe had become a provincial town of gigantic proportions." He added: "The reason for this provincialization was clear. The people of integrity, initiative and culture had been killed, jailed or exiled [by the Nazi regime]."[238]

Summer at Schwarzerden and a Summer Adventure in Greece

ONE MORE COLLABORATION between Moholy and Sebök was in connection with a gymnastics hall for Schwarzerden, a school mentioned on page 285 in Chapter Three. One of the directors was Elisabeth Vogler (1892-1975), who had spent some time at the Loheland school in the Rhön Mountains[239] before deciding to help set up *Die Schule Schwarzerden* nearby. She was the sister of Paul Vogler, a Berlin medical doctor and social hygienist for whom Moholy had designed offices in 1928.[240] When the school's directors wanted to build a new building, they turned to Moholy for advice and he suggested Gropius. Gropius turned to Sebök, then working in his office, and asked him to work out some suggestions. A commission followed, and Sebök designed the building in July, 1930.[241] The project was not built because of the economic crisis, but before it was scrapped Moholy and Sebök collaborated on a design for the interior of the part of the building that was to be devoted to a two-storey gymnastics hall; they also designed a wide burlap awning that would have shielded the hall's large opening

---

[236] The Nobel Peace Prize for 1926 was shared by Gustav Stresemann and Aristide Briand.

[237] Harry Kessler, *Berlin in Lights; the Diaries of Count Harry Kessler (1918-1937)*, translated and edited by Charles Kessler, with an introduction by Ian Buruma (New York: Grove Press, 2000), 368.

[238] Franz Spencer, *Battles of a Bystander* (New York: Liveright Publishing Corporation, 1941), 249.

[239] Ortrud Wörner-Heil, *Von der Utopie zur Sozialreform; Jugendsiedlung Frankenfeld im hessischen Ried und Frauensiedlung Schwarze Erde in der Rhön, 1915 bis zur 1933* (Darmstadt and Marburg: Selbstverlag der Hessischen Kommission Darmstadt und der Historischen Kommission für Hessen, 1996), 188-191.

[240] Rolf Sachsse, *Lucia Moholy* (Dusseldorf: Edition Marzona, 1985), 164-165.

[241] Nerdinger, *Walter Gropius*, 148, 149, 151 and 254; and *idem*, editor, *The Walter Gropius Archive*, 2:93 and 95-107.

overlooking a valley.[242] One report noted that the project would have been carried out "in schönen hellen Farben, grau und gelb, mit heller Rupfenbespannung" [in beautiful bright colors, gray and yellow, with a brightly-colored burlap awning].[243] (DVD figures 256 and 257) Lucia Moholy was also involved in the Schwarzerden project when she made a site photograph of the planned location.[244]

A considerable summer adventure for Moholy occurred in connection with the fourth *CIAM* (*Congrès internationaux d'architecture moderne*) dedicated to "The Functional City" and held from July 29th to August through August 14th, 1933.[245] The meetings were on board the S S Patria II as it sailed from Marseille to Athens and back, and in Athens. Meetings on board the S S Patria II took place on July 30th, 31st, August 12th and 13th and in Athens on August 3rd and 9th.[246] The S S Patria arrived in Athens on August 2nd and departed on August 11th, so ample free time was available. The film made by Moholy of the fourth meeting of the *CIAM* is discussed below, and also below is a more general description of the group.

For the fourth *CIAM*, plans to the same scale had been prepared of thirty-three European and American cities[247] (the plan of the county of London was more than twelve feet tall!)[248] and these plans and their implications were carefully discussed by an attentive assemblage of more than one-hundred people, including some of the best-known architects and artists of the early twentieth century. Moholy, of course, was especially busy making his film. Nevertheless, this was his first (and only) trip to Greece, and his *gimnázium* education evoked in him a feeling of awe at being in Athens. He wrote to Sibyl about the fantastic experience of being on the same ground as his *schulhelden* or, literally, school heroes, as he strolled around the Acropolis; specifically named were Themistocles, Socrates, Plato, Pericles and Aristophanes. He was also impressed by the extraordinary talents of the designers of the Parthenon and the other buildings of the Acropolis complex, and marveled at the sense of proportion they

---

[242]Nerdinger, *Walter Gropius Archive*, 2:93.

[243]*Mitteilungen des Bundes für sozialangewandte Gymnastik und Körperpflege e.V.*, number 1 (July, 1930), 5; portions quoted in: Wörner-Heil, *Von der Utopie zur Sozialreform*, 507.

[244]Nerdinger, *Walter Gropius Archive*, 2:102.

[245]Mumford, *The CIAM Discourse on Urbanism*, 73-92; Auke van der Woud, *Het Nieuwe Bouwen Internationaal/International [and] CIAM Volkshuisvesting. Stedebouw/Housing, Town Planning* [text in Dutch and English] (Delft: Delft University Press, 1983), 70-72; and Martin Steinmann, editor, *CIAM = Internationale Kongresse für Neues Bauen = Congrès internationaux d'architecture moderne: Dokumente 1928-1939* (Basel: Birkhäuser Verlag, 1979), 113-171.

[246]Steinmann. editor, *CIAM*, 128 and 130-131.

[247]Mumford, *The CIAM Discourse on Urbanism*, 77; and Woud, *Het Nieuwe Bouwen*, 70-71.

[248]Sigfried Giedion, "CIAM at Sea: the Background of the Fourth (Athens) Congress," *Architects' Yearbook: 3* (London: Paul Elek, 1949), 36-39, here 37.

displayed.[249] (DVD figure 258) To his friend Sigfried Giedion he said, as they stood together on the hill of the Acropolis, "Never since my school days have I been so conscious of how directly the Greek world speaks to us—though in a very different sense to what the nineteenth century understood by this."[250] For the August 11th showing of a preliminary version of his film that would come to be known as *Architekturkongres Athen*, he was careful to include, along with sequences showing the conferees hard at work, shots of Athens as well as the passage of the S S Patria II through the picturesque narrow canal across the Isthmus of Corinth, with its steep and high rock walls.[251]

THE ATTEMPT to see some of the architectural monuments of the Greek islands provided some unexpected high adventure. Moholy and a small group of Congress participants engaged a small ship and explored architectural monuments at Aegina and other sites. But the ship was actually a former coal barge, and had only room for a few passengers to sleep inside; the others, including Moholy, slept in cots on the deck. This proved to be a problem at Santorini when a storm assaulted the ship, which became helpless because any attempt to steer it would have risked capsizing it. Those sleeping on deck were tied to their cots and subjected to wind and waves; nearly everyone became seasick (Moholy was not one of the exceptions). When the storm broke, the voyage continued to Ios, then Sunnion and back to Piraeus and Athens. Those on board included Le Corbusier, his brother and colleague Pierre Jeanneret and Fernand Léger, as well as Moholy and Giedion.[252] As Giedion summed it up: "If the former coal barge had sunk during the storm that night, a decisive chapter in contemporary art history would have come to a close."[253]

Innovations in Graphic Design

After leaving the Bauhaus, Moholy quickly established himself as a leading figure in graphic design. His stature was already evident at the huge *Internationale Pressa-Ausstellung* [International Press Exhibition], usually known as *Pressa*. Devoted to all aspects of the modern press, including advertising, it was shown from May 11th through October, 1928, in a series of structures on the Cologne exhibition grounds on the right

---

[249]László Moholy-Nagy to Sibyl Moholy-Nagy, ALS, August 2, 1933, microfilm reel 951, frames 0076-0081, Archives of American Art, Washington, D.C.

[250]Giedion, "CIAM at Sea," 37.

[251]László Moholy-Nagy to Sibyl Moholy-Nagy, ALS, August 13, 1933, microfilm reel 951, frames 0076-0081, Archives of American Art, Washington, D.C.

[252]László Moholy-Nagy to Sibyl Moholy-Nagy, August 13, 1933; Giedion, "CIAM at Sea," 39; and Sibyl Moholy-Nagy, *Moholy-Nagy: Experiment in Totality*, 95.

[253]Sigfried Giedion, quoted in: Sibyl Moholy-Nagy, *Experiment in Totality*, 95.

bank of the Rhine River.[254] Moholy showed some work (presumably examples of the Bauhaus Books)[255] in the German section of *Europäische Buchkunst der Gegenwart* [European Book Art of the Present Day],[256] set up by the *Verein deutsche Buchkünstler* of Leipzig as part of *Pressa*; more importantly, it was he who wrote the essay discussing new methods of book production for a catalogue containing essays that were otherwise devoted to summaries of book production in individual countries. His essay, "elementare buchtechnik," was the only section of the catalogue set in lower-case type, and in it he declared that: "das buch von gestern ist so sehr festgelegt in seiner form: es ist auch in seiner maschinellen herstellung noch abhängig von alten handtechniken."[257] [The book of the immediate past is very fixed in its form: even in its machine production it is still dependent on the old manual techniques.] He lamented that there was no special room in Cologne for demonstrating new methods of book production.[258] As one example of new methods he pointed to the possibility of printing by X-ray on multiple sheets of photosensitive paper,[259] a fascinating idea that probably would be impractical if only because of the necessary precautions to prevent radiation exposure. He concluded with a call for removing the shackles of the past from book design by proclaiming ". . . entsteht die klare form des neuen buches von seinen eigenen geistigen und technischen mitteln aus als selbstverständliches resultat"[260] [the clear form of the new book arises from its own spirit and technical means as a self-evident outcome].

   His reputation as a leading figure in graphic design was enhanced through Moholy's participation in an exhibition, *Neue Typographie*, held from April 20th through May 20th, 1929, in the light court of the *Kunstgewerbemuseum* in Berlin,

---

[254]Jeremy Anysley, "Pressa, Cologne, 1928: Exhibitions and Publication Design in the Weimar Era," *Design Issues*, volume X, number 3 (Autumn, 1994), [52]-76.

The showing of modern European books is described in: Verein deutsche Buchkünstler, *Europäische Buchkunst der Gegenwart*, 5-93; *Pressa, Internationale Presse-Ausstellung, Köln, 1928: amtlicher Katalog* (Berlin: Rudolf Mosse, 1928), 203-206; and Internationale Presse-Ausstellung, *Pressa: Kulturschau am Rhein* (Cologne: Verlag Max Schröder, 1928), 78-80 and 142-144.

[255]In any case, a review of the first eleven Bauhaus Books appeared in an American Magazine in the autum of 1928; see: Louis Lozowick, "Modern Art in Germany," *The Nation*, November 7, 1928, 494. Lozowick had been in Europe while the exhibition was on view; see: *idem, Survivor from a Dead Age; the Memoirs of Louis Lozowick*, edited by Virginia Hagelstein Marquardt (Washington: Smithsonian Institution Press, 1997), 305.

[256]Verein deutsche Buchkünstler, *Europäische Buchkunst der Gegenwart*, 70.

[257]Moholy-Nagy, "elemenare buchtechnik," in: Verein deutsche Buchkünstler, *Europäische Buchkunst der Gegenwart*, 61-64, here 61.

[258]*Ibid.*, 61.

[259]*Ibid.*, 62.

[260]*Ibid.*, 64.

sponsored by the *Staatliche Kunstbibliothek* in Berlin and the *Ring neuer Werbegestalter*. Shown was current work by twenty-three European graphic designers along with seventy-eight panels with the collective title: *Wohin Geht die typografische Entwicklung?* [where is typographic development heading?], set up by Moholy to illustrate the origins and the aims of the new typography by means of explanatory texts, reproductions, and original typographic examples.[261] The text panels consisted of enlarged typewritten text, with white letters on a black background.[262] The exhibition was later seen August 3rd through 19th at an exhibition hall in Magdeburg located on Adolf-Mittag-See, an artificial lake on an island in the Elbe River,[263] as well as in other venues.

Eight of the panels were devoted to a didactic text Moholy wrote outlining the origins and aims of the new typography in order to elucidate the examples seen on the other seventy panels.[264] Among the twenty-three designers showing, in addition to Moholy himself, were Herbert Bayer, Walter Dexel, Lajos Kassák, Johannes Molzahn and Jan Tschichold. (DVD figure 259)

The text that appeared on the eight panels exists in an English-language version, "Some Principles of Typography." with a date of 1928, virtually identical to the German text except for a comment on the differing practices in capitalization in German and English; the date can probably be explained by the circumstance that the basis for the text was his 1928 lectures in Leipzig, discussed above. Two variants of the English-language text exist: one with Moholy's London address of 7 Farm Walk included;[265] the

---

[261] Claudia Müller, *Typofoto: Wege der Typografie zur Foto-Text-Montage bei Laszlo Moholy-Nagy* (Berlin: Gebr. Mann Verlag, 1994), 91-93 and 107-108; and Christine Kühn, editor, *Neues Sehen in Berlin: Fotografie der Zwanziger Jahre* (Berlin: Kunstbibliothek, 2005), 169-170.

The original seventy-eight panels are in the *Gebrauchsgraphische Sammlung* of the *Kunstbibliothek* in Berlin (Kästen 4830-4832, Inventar-Nummern 4830.1-4832.33 and 4832-33a).

[262] "Neue Typographie in der Staatlichen Bibliothek," *Das Neue Berlin: Großstadtprobleme*, volume I, number 6 (June, 1929), 128.

[263] Theo van Doesburg files, Rijksbureau voor Kunsthistorische Dokumentie, The Hague, also available on microfiche (Theo van Doesburg Archive, Leiden: IDC, 1991), sheet 189; and Kühn, editor, *Neues Sehen in Berlin*, 169.

[264] The texts of these eight panels was reprinted in: Müller, *Typofoto*, 107-108; and in: Stedelijk van Abbemuseum, Eindhoven, *Moholy-Nagy*, [Tentoonstelling], inleiding door [introduction by] Hannah Weitemeier Steckel (Eindhoven: Stedelijk van Abbemuseum, 1967), 24-25.

[265] "Some Principles of Typography" appears in Senter, "Moholy-Nagy in England," 334-336; Senter did not give his source for the text.

other, without the address, was formerly owned by Harry Blacker, who is discussed below.[266]

In his text Moholy hailed ". . . the french poet guillaume apollinaire and the futurist leader f.t. marinetti," because "they burst the bounds of the old limitations [in typography] . . ." He went on to summarize other early modern innovations in typography and concluded:

> the new typographer, "typographic model-maker" will in future be led
> only by the law innate in the typographic task before him. this alone will
> guide him in his choice of means to end.

One of the early productions of Moholy's Berlin studio involved the Bauhaus; this was the design of his *von material zu architektur* of 1929, the fourteenth and last of the Bauhaus Books, and its dust jacket. (DVD figure 260) Moholy worked on the book's jacket with Lucia and with Max Gebhard. The latter recalled it as reaching a new level of achievement compared to the jackets for the thirteen other Bauhaus Books, and described his and Lucia's role in producing it:

> Ich habe die Titelzeilen auf eine Glasplatte übertragen. Moholy-Nagy baute
> damit eine plastische "Komposition" vor eine rote Fläche. Durch
> Schattenwirkung und Transparenz entstand eine erstaunliche räumliche Wirkung;
> die Typografie stand nicht mehr für sich, sondern ging mit dem Raum eine
> verbindung ein. Seine Frau Lucia machte davon die Farbaufnahme.[267] [I
> transferred the lines of the title to a glass plate. Moholy built with it a sculptural
> "composition" in front of a red plane. Through transparency and the play of
> shadows an astounding spatial effect emerged; the typography no longer stood
> apart but entered into a union with space. His wife Lucia made the color
> photograph.]

One of the most striking interior pages is devoted to a view of an airshaft looking upward from the bottom of an engine room on an ocean steamer. (DVD figure 261) Reyner Banham took note of this photograph as "a view up an airshaft, in which the stairs and landings are all pierced to promote better airflow," thus creating "quite accidentally" a play of space. Obtained from the monthly magazine *Uhu* [eagle-owl (an onomatopoeic German word based on the bird's call)], this photograph is also a good example of what Banham referred to as Moholy's "phenomenal command of the non-

---

[266] The Stephen Daiter Gallery obtained the copy of the text that belonged to Harry Blacker from his son, Michael Blacker; it is typed on eight sheets, like the German-language panels. A xerox copy is in the Hattula Moholy-Nagy files.

[267] Helm, "Produktive Begegnungen: Gespräch mit Max Gebhard," 305.

Jeannine Fiedler was skeptical of Gebhardt's account when we discussed it with Hattula Moholy-Nagy in Ann Arbor in 2007, since the book jacket preceded the earliest known color photograph by László, and Lucia herself never did develop an interest in color photography. Moreover, Gebhardt's account was written many years after leaving Moholy's studio. Thus it seems likely that another photographer was brought in for the book-jacket photograph.

artistic visual experiences of his time." Banham went on to write: "Words cannot convey the impact made on the eye by the original edition of this book, its emphatic typography, its businesslike layout, and the range of its illustrations . . . "[268]

There were now fourteen Bauhaus Books, and for the eight-page brochure describing the series, Moholy designed a striking cover with a blue accent, along with a variation with a red accent.[269] (DVD figures 262 and 263)

Moholy's work as a graphic designer very often involved his friends. As an example, in 1928 he designed a cover and jacket for Sigfried Giedion's *Bauen in Frankreich: Bauen in Eisen, Bauen in Eisenbeton.*[270] (DVD figures 264 and 265) Another example was a small catalogue (sixteen pages, 15 by 22 centimeters) for a Walter Gropius exhibition held in the Schinkelsaal of the Architektenhaus in Berlin, April 8th through 23rd, 1930; included was a four-page text by Max Osborn. The cover utilized a photograph of the Bauhaus by Klaus Hertig.[271] (DVD figure 266) A variation was designed for the *Kunstverein* in Frankfurt am Main, for a showing of the exhibition there during June 6th through 18th, 1930.[272]

One of Moholy's more curious graphic designs appeared in 1931: this was a linen book cover and its dust jacket (DVD figures 267 and 268) for a coming-of-age war novel written from a pacifist point of view by Rudolf Frank, assisted by Georg Lichey: *Der Schädel des Negerhäuptlings Makaua, Kriegsroman für die junge Generation*[273] [The Skull of the Sultan of Mkwawa, a War Novel for the New Generation]. It appeared in English as *No Hero for the Kaiser.*[274] The skull in question is not really the focus of the

---

[268] Reyner Banham, *Theory and Design in the First Machine Age*, second edition (New York: Praeger Publishers, Inc., 1967), 315 and 317.

[269] Brüning and Droste, editors, *Das A und O des Bauhauses*, 114.

[270] Sigfried Giedion, *Bauen in Frankreich: Bauen in Eisen, Bauen in Eisenbeton* (Leipzig: Klinkhardt & Biermann, 1928).

Reyner Banham made some fascinating comments about the intellectual relationship between Giedion's *Bauen in Frankreich* and Moholy's *von material zu architektur*: see: Banham, *Theory and Design,* 309-312.

[271] Walter Gropius, *Ausstellung Walter Gropius; Zeichnungen, Fotos, Modelle in der ständigen Bauwelt-Musterschau* (Berlin: Architektenhaus, 1930). The cover is illustrated in: Fiedler, editor, *Photography at the Bauhaus*, 234 and 331.

[272] Fleischmann, editor, *Bauhaus Drucksachen, Typografie, Reklame*, 302.

[273] Rudolf Frank and Georg Lichey, *Der Schädel des Negerhäuptlings Makaua, Kriegsroman für die junge Generation* (Potsdam: Müller & I. Kiepenheuer G. m. b. H. Verlag, 1931).

[274] Rudolf Frank, *No Hero for the Kaiser*, translated from the German by Patricia Crampton (New York: Lothrop, Lee & Shepard, 1983).

(continued...)

novel, but rather is meant to demonstrate the elusiveness of war aims, even rather specific ones. Since the collage Moholy created for the jacket[275] (DVD figure 267) is based on the original German title it cannot be understood without a little background. The Treaty of Versailles contains some very specific demands of Germany; article 246 contains this sentence:

> Within the same period [i.e., within six months of the coming into force of the present Treaty] Germany will hand over to His Britannic Majesty's Government the skull of the Sultan Mkwawa which was removed from the Protectorate of German East Africa and taken to Germany.

The same passage in the German-language version of the Treaty reads:

> Binnen der gleichen Frist ist der Schädel des Sultan Makaua, der aus dem deutschen Schutzgebiet Ostafrika entfernt und nach Deutschland gebracht worden ist, von Deutschland der Regierung Seiner Britischen Majestät zu überbringen.

The phrase "der Schädel des Sultan Makaua" in the Treaty is similar to but slightly different from a phrase in the title of the book, the latter being the wording first used in the book by a German soldier who had served in German East Africa.

GERMAN EAST AFRICA existed from 1885 to 1920, and included the territory of what is now the mainland portion of Tanzania, plus the countries of Ruanda and Burundi. Sultan Mkwawa (1855-1898), part of a dynasty of *HeHe* rulers and the leader of a long-sustained uprising by indigenous East Africans, was beheaded posthumously in 1898. His skull was sent to Berlin but could not be located at the time the Treaty of Versailles went into force in 1920. It should be emphasized again that the skull of Mkwawa was used by Rudolf Frank solely to illustrate the elusiveness of war aims. The skull had been promised by the French as a reward for East African natives fighting in the French army. Nevertheless, as noted, when the war ended the skull could not be found.[276]

The principal character of Frank's novel is Jan Kubitzky, a German-speaking Pole who was fourteen-years old when the War broke out, and who becomes a kind of mascot and good omen for a German artillery company.

---

[274](...continued)

Georg Lichey is not listed on the title page of the English-language edition; on the verso of the title page he is listed as: military-technical advisor.

[275]Discussed, and illustrated in black-and-white in: Lusk, *Montagen ins Blaue*, 170-171.

[276]Although Moholy was dead before the matter could be resolved, the skull was eventually found in a museum in Bremen and turned over to a representative of the British government in 1954; it is now in a small museum in Kalenga, Tanzania. See: Edward Twining, "A Chief's Skull Returned to His People," *The Times British Colonies Review*, number 15 (Autumn, 1954), 11-12.

On the front of the dust jacket a model representing the fictional Jan is seen in profile, separated from a photograph of an enormous cannon by a curvilinear red mass that covers part of the front, the back and the spine of the jacket. On the back a symbolic rendering of the skull in question is juxtaposed over a portion of the last page of the novel, showing the passage in German from the Treaty of Versailles, quoted above, but printed with red ink. The symbolic rendering is based on royal Kuba Makenga masks from Tanzania's neighbor, Congo. By 1931, Moholy could well have become familiar with examples of these masks from visits to museums or from illustrations in publications. His rendering incorporates cowrie shells, used to denote royalty in Kuba Makenga masks. A pair of eyes appear behind the eye-holes in the mask, an idiosyncracy of Moholy's, quite evident in a number of his photocollages. The back of the dust-jacket includes Moholy's name, as does the verso of the title page.

Rudolf Frank (not related to Ellen Frank) fondly recalled his brief collaboration with Moholy in his 1960 autobiography,[277] but it is not known how Moholy and Frank got together. One possibility is through Sibyl's connection with the movie studio Tobis, since Rudolf Frank had begun working there in 1930 as a writer of German scripts for replacement sound-tracks for American films.[278]

Der Schädel des Negerhäuptlings Makaua was banned by the Nazis,[279] but recently the original text has been re-issued,[280] along with an English translation.[281] (These editions have not alluded to the once-elusive skull in their titles.)

Moholy's first British commission came in 1931; this was for a jacket for *An Outline of the Universe* by James Gerald Crowther (1899–1983),[282] (DVD figure 269) a jacket discussed below because of its similarity to the opening sequence of one of Moholy's films. The author, usually known as J.G. Crowther, was a pioneer in science journalism as a writer for the *Manchester Guardian*; he was also one of Moholy's earliest English friends.

During the same year, 1931, another indication that Moholy was beginning to gain some international recognition for his graphic design accomplishments came on March 3rd, 1931, when it was announced that he had received honorable mention for his work shown in New York at the *Exhibition of Foreign Advertising Photography*, assembled by

---

[277]Rudolf Frank, *Spielzeit meines Lebens* (Heidelberg: Verlag Lambert Schneider, 1960), 319.

[278]Rudolf Frank, *Der Junge, der seinen Geburtstag Vergass; ein Roman gegen den Krieg* (Ravensburg: Otto Maier Verlag, 1983), 224.

[279]Frank, *Der Junge, der seinen Geburtstag Vergass*, [5] and 226.

[280]*Idem.*

[281]Frank, *No Hero for the Kaiser*.

[282]James Gerald Crowther, *An Outline of the Universe* (London: K. Paul, Trench, Trubner, & Co., 1931).

Abbott Kimball and shown at The Art Centre, 65 East 56th Street.[283] The panel of judges included pioneer Modernist designer Joseph Sinel and famed motion-picture director D.W. Griffith. It was Moholy's jacket for the 1929 Bauhaus Book *von marerial zu architektur*, (DVD figure 260) discussed above, that was honored; first prize went to Herbert Bayer for a cover for *bauhaus*, the magazine published by the Bauhaus. Man Ray and Florence Henri also won honorable mention. Work by Bauhäusler Andreas Feininger and Walter Peterhans was included in the exhibition but was not premiated.[284]

The 1931 *Exhibition of Foreign Advertising Photography* included at least one of Moholy's photographs: *Portrait*, a study of the face of a toothy smiling man that had been published in in 1930 in a German photographic annual[285] and that he was to use (in slightly altered form) in an advertisement.[286] (DVD figure 277) Evidently some of his designs involving photograms, and the photograms themselves, also aroused interest, as noted in a New York newspaper:

> It is interesting to know how many different techniques account for the highly
> varied effects in this fascinating exhibit. According to Mr. Abbott Kimball, who
> assembled the group, the techniques include the "photogram" or camera-less
> photography, which involves the exposure of the objects to sensitized paper
> without the use of a lens. The principal exponents of this unusual procedure are
> Moholy-Nagy, in Germany and Man Ray in France.[287]

Meanwhile, Moholy had some presence as a designer in Hungary. He showed in a group exhibition of Hungarian book and advertising design, *Könyv-és Reklám Kiállitás*, seen from April 12th to 27th, 1930, in the light court of the *Iparművészeti Múzeum* [Museum of Applied Arts], Üllői ut 33 in Budapest. Included was work of Sándor Bortnyik, Róbert Berény (who designed the poster for the exhibition), Lajos Kassák, and other designers; Moholy showed at least four photomontages. The exhibition was set up by the *Magyar Könyv- és Reklámművészek Társasága* (Society of Hungarian Book-and-

---

[283]"Eight Nations Show Ad Photographs Here; Berlin Man Wins First Award at Exhibition of European Commercial Art," *The New York Times*, March 3, 1931, 5.

[284]A copy of the three-page mimeographed announcement, and a xerox copy of Moholy's award, is in the Hattula Moholy-Nagy archives; a xerox copy is in the author's collection.

[285]As in note 693.

[286]"Photographs from the First Comprehensive Exhibition of Foreign Commercial Photographers, on View at the Art Centre Beginning This Week," *The New York Times,* March 1, 1931, Rotogravure Picture Section, [22].

[287]Margaret Breuning, "Exhibitions Continue to Tumble over Each Other in Week's Events, Foreign Commercial Photographers Make Brilliant Showing," *The New York Evening Post*, March 7, 1931, D 5.

Poster Artists).[288] By 1928 Moholy, Bortnyik, Kassák and Farkas Molnár had become members of the group.[289]

   Still another book jacket design of the period, this one from 1930, was for *Arbeitsuntersuchung* published by the *Allgemeiner Deutscher Gewerkschaftsbund (ADGB)*, or General German Trade Union Federation.[290] The title can be translated as "operations analysis," and what the book aims at is the improvement of building practices to benefit both the worker and his employer, through better construction-management and more efficient work on the construction-site. Hence Moholy's design superimposes a technical management document over a construction work-site where a crane is being utilized. (DVD figure 271) This design shows his rapport with, and interest in, organized labor.

   Moholy's work on *Arbeitsuntersuchung* makes a vivid contrast with his most visible graphic-design presence in Germany: his work on the elegant monthly fashion magazine, *die neue linie*, the first issue of which was dated September, 1929. (DVD figure 272) The founding editor, Bruno Erich Werner (1896-1964), thought of the magazine as the German counterpart to the venerable New York magazine *Vanity Fair*,[291] which by the 1920s had become fascinated with the avant-garde; *e.g.*, it commissioned essays by Tristan Tzara, as noted in Chapter Two. In the pages of *die neue linie* Werner sought to promote an attractive modern lifestyle with coverage of female fashion, travel and domestic interiors as well as literature, dance and movies.

   Ellen's open Fiat automobile is discussed below. She was presented, in winter clothes and behind the Fiat's characteristically large steering wheel, on the cover of the December, 1930, issue of *die neue linie*, along with some Christmas motifs..[292] (DVD figure 274) Another holiday was presented by Moholy in the pages of *die neue linie* for its *Karneval*, or *Fasching*, pre-Lenten holiday issue (January, 1931). For this issue Moholy was aided by Giula Pap, but on the inside page reproduced on DVD figure 276

---

[288]Toshino Iguchi, [Hungarian Avant-Garde: MA and Moholy-Nagy], ISBN: 88202-684-8 (Tokyo: Sairyusha, 2000), 248-249; and Heidrun Schröder-Kehler, "Künstler Erobern die Warenwelt," in: Gaßner, editor, *Wechsel Wirkungen*, 388-412, here 401.

[289]Katalin Bakos, "Az első magyar Gebrauchsraphiker: Bortnyik Sándor műhelye és 'Műhely' -e," *Új Művészet*, volume 4, number 11 (November, 1993), 9-12 and 78-79, here 10; and *idem*, "The First Hungarian Gebrauchsgrafiker: Sándor Bortnyik's Workshop and 'Workshop'," *ibid*, 79-81 here 80 (additional title on cover: "ART TODAY").

[290]*Arbeitsuntersuchung*, edited by Verband sozialer Baubetriebe (Berlin: Verlagsgesellschaft des Allgemeinen deutschen gewerkschaftsbundes, 1930); the jacket is discussed and illustrated in: Lusk, *Montagen ins Blaue*, 166-167. Moholy is credited on the lower left of the back cover of the jacket.

[291]Bruno E. Werner, *Die zwanziger Jahre; von Morgens bis Mitternachts* (Munich: F. Bruckmann KG, 1962), 84.

[292]*die neue linie*, volume xx, number yy (December, 1930), front cover.

left, some characteristic Moholy touches dominate: two uncoiled springs from a photogram (DVD figure 276 right), the upper of which form a necklace of a festively-clad woman. On the left of the page is a drawing for the costume for Olympia in *The Tales of Hoffmann*, then still showing at the Kroll Opera.[293]

Werner engaged Moholy and Bayer,[294] who jointly set the design tone for the magazine. Werner also worked closely with Gropius[295] and featured illustrations of his work as well as articles he wrote for the magazine.[296] Another direct link with the Bauhaus came through Irmgard Popitz (née Sörensen; born 1896),[297] who, beginning in 1929, served as art director for the magazine's Leipzig-based publisher, Beyer-Verlag,[298] a leading fashion publishing house that had a branch office in Berlin. Sörensen-Popitz had been Moholy's student at the Bauhaus.[299]

For *die neue linie* Moholy did interior layouts, as noted above, as well as ten covers,[300] making use of the newest avant-garde techniques, including not only photocollage but also photograms.[301] (DVD figure 276 left) The use of the latter in graphic design was an idea he tried out during his earliest work in the medium, as described in Chapter Two concerning his photogram studies for a cover for the magazine *Broom*. One of the ironies of *die neue linie* is that this elegant journal first appeared just before the stock-market crash in New York. It was aimed at people who were fortunate enough to enjoy some disposable income, a group that steadily diminished in Germany because many suffered

---

[293]Note the similarity of the costume of Olympia as it appears in a performance photograph in: Curjel, *Experiment Krolloper*, illustration 56 on page [103].

[294]Herbert Bayer to Eckhard Neumann, June 7, 1979, portions quoted in: Patrick Rössler, *die neue linie, 1929-1943: das Bauhaus am Kiosk*, Begleitpublikation zur gleichnamigen Ausstellung (Bielefeld: Kerber, 2007), [32].

[295]Werner, *Die zwanziger Jahre*, 84.

[296]"Deutscher Geist in Paris," *die neue linie*, volume I, number 11 (July, 1930), 12-13; "Das Haus Gropius in Dessau," *ibid*, volume II, number 5 (January, 1931), 20-21; Walter Gropius, "Wie sollte der Großstädter Wohnen?," *ibid*., volume II, number 12 (August, 1931), 22; and "Das Haus der neuen Linie," *ibid*., volume IV, number 5 (January, 1933), 11.

[297]Also known professionally as Söre Popitz and Irmgard Sörensen-Popitz.

[298]Rössler, *die neue linie, 1929-1943*, 31-[32].

[299]László Moholy-Nagy, *The New Vision* (2005), 127.

[300]For examples of Moholy's interior layouts see: *die neue linie*, volume I, number 1 (September, 1929), table-of-contents page; *ibid.*, volume II, number 5 (January, 1931), 11; and *ibid.*, volume III, number 8 (April, 1932), 24-25. For reproductions of his covers and interior layouts see: Rössler, *die neue linie, 1929-1943*, 36-[37], 38-42, 48-49 and 150-153; and Lusk, *Montagen ins Blaue*, 186-189

[301]Rössler, *die neue linie, 1929-1943*, 48; and Lusk, *Montagen ins Blaue*, 186-189.

from unemployment and other adverse results of the crash. Nevertheless, the magazine did manage to survive through some tough economic years.

EVEN THOUGH there were 50,000 subscribers within a year of its founding,[302] copies of *die neue linie* are no longer readily available, although published reproductions of some covers and interior pages can give an idea of what Moholy's work for the magazine looked like. Ellen Frank was a frequent model for Moholy in his work for the magazine; in the very first issue she is seen from behind, dressed for the coming winter, staring from behind a window wall at a glacier from the Rhône Mountains. (DVD figures 272 and 273). Daring spatial ambiguity was used in presenting the name of the new magazine: the lower-case title, in a Bayer-designed type face, seems to be both inside and outside the window wall. Another striking cover for May, 1931, also featured Ellen. (DVD figure 275)[303] She appears, smartly dressed and with her engaging smile, posed against a modern blue-hued interior punctuated by bright colors and dominated by bent-metal-tubing furniture. The openness of the furniture prevents it from marring the view of the brightly-colored rya rug on the floor; the rya rug itself presents an example of a traditional Scandinavian craft object brought up to date with bright colors and a simple geometric design.

Ellen, a redhead with freckles, usually appeared in Moholy's photographs without the freckles being evident; nevertheless see DVD figure 293 right, where the freckles can be clearly seen. While Moholy obviously admired Ellen's slender beauty and made good use of it in *die neue linie*, he did feel that her hair was too red! But by the spring of 1935, after seeing her after evidently not having seen her for an extended period, he remarked in a letter to Walter and Ise Gropius: "sie sieht unverändert gut aus, ihr haar ist gott sei dank nicht mehr so rot." [Her marvellous good looks are unchanged, her hair is not so red as before, thank goodness.] And Moholy was careful to ask Ise not to tell her he had written that.[304]

In contrast to the upscale lifestyle, for those who could afford it, featured in *die neue linie*, a chain of men's clothing stores, *s.s. kettenläden* [s.s. chain stores], with locations in Berlin, Breslau, Hamburg and Leipzig,[305] offered "superior" merchandise for cost-conscious shoppers. The chain had twelve stores as of March 21st, 1931, when a Moholy-designed announcement marked the opening of the newest of its nine stores located in

---

[302] Gretel Wagner, "Zeietschriften à la mode," in: Lutz S. Malke, editor, *Europäische Moderne : Buch und Graphik aus Berliner Kunstverlagen 1890-1933;* [exhibition catalogue for the] *Kunstbibliothek Berlin, Staatliche Museen Preussischer Kulturbesitz* (Berlin, Dietrich Riemer Verlag, 1989), 191-205, here 201.

[303] Staatliche Museen Preußischer Kulterbesitz, Lipperheidesche Kostümbibliothek (36.5 by 26.7 cm.); illustrated in: Brüning and Droste, editors, *Das A und O des Bauhauses*, 279; and in: Rössler, *die neue linie, 1929-1943*, 41.

[304] László Moholy-Nagy to Walter Gropius, TLS, March 31, 1935, Bauhaus-Archiv, Berlin; an English translation is in: Senter, "Moholy-Nagy in England," 326.

[305] Scheiffele, "Typofoto und Jenaer Haushaltglas," 226 (note 6).

Berlin, this one near the zoo on Joachimsthaler at the corner of Kantstraße.[306] The stores were operated by *schroeder special gmbh*, with headquarters at 91-92 Friedrichstraße in Berlin.[307] Their less-than-full-page advertisements were evidently designed to appear in a variety of publications, but the modest means used are eye-catching and easy to read, set entirely in lower-case letters. Sometimes Moholy re-used his earlier images, in this case a portrait of a smiling man with nicer (though not quite correctly placed) teeth, thanks to the magic of photocollage; (DVD figure 277) other available images were used, such as an X-ray of a fish to echo the herringbone-twill pattern from which the letters on the upper right were cut. (DVD figure 278) Moholy also designed price-labels for the stores.[308]

One of the most intriguing of Moholy's garment-related designs was his foldout device rendering the inside and outside of the jacket of a man's double-breasted suit.[309] (DVD figures 279 and 280)

His work on *die neue linie* and for the *s.s. kettenläden* constituted factors that led to Moholy's role as artistic director for *Der Konfektionär* (the title refers to "ready-to-wear" or *prêt-à-porter* clothing), beginning about 1931. *Der Konfektionär* was a Berlin semi-weekly magazine aimed at garment manufacturers and marketers and well as retail customers. Two pages in a brochure designed by Moholy show intensive work by designers on page setup; the text points out that the publication had its own design studio but sometimes free-lance designers were utilized.[310] (DVD figure 281)

The best account of *Der Konfektionär*, founded in 1886, was provided by Eleonore ("Lore") Hertzberger (née Katz, born 1917), the daughter of Ludwig Katz, its *Werbefachmann* and *Verleger*, or advertising director and publisher. She described her father as one who had a gift for bringing together aesthetic and commercial considerations, and also as one who utilized established professionals while also providing a chance for younger artists to begin their careers. The prime example of the

---

[306]Catherine David and Corinne Diserens, editors, *László Moholy-Nagy* (Marseille: Musées de Marseille, Réunion des Musées Nationaux, 1991), advertisement at center of page 350; and *idem*, *László Moholy-Nagy* (Valencia: IVAM Centre Julio González, 1991), advertisement at center of page 332. Twelve of s.s. kettenläden's advertisements are illustrated in David and Diserens, editors, *László Moholy-Nagy* (Marseille), 380-383, and in: *idem*, *László Moholy-Nagy* (Valencia), 332-335; all are from examples in the Bauhaus-Archiv, Berlin.

[307]Stationery designed by Moholy for the firm is illustrated in: David and Diserens, editors, *László Moholy-Nagy* (Marseille), 388; and *idem*, *László Moholy-Nagy* (Valencia), [340].

[308]Sibyl Moholy-Nagy, *Moholy-Nagy, Experiment in Totality*, 64; and Richard Kostelanetz, *Moholy-Nagy* (New York: Praeger Publishers, 1970), illustration 29.

[309]Moholy-Nagy files, reel 951, frames 0389-0392, Archives of American Art, Washington, D.C.

[310]Illustrated in: Terence A. Senter, "Moholy-Nagy in England: May 1935-July 1937" (Master of Philosophy thesis, University of Nottingham, 1975), illustration 7; and in: Arts Council of Great Britain, *l. moholy-nagy* (London: Arts Council of Great Britain, 1980), 61.

former was Moholy, and her father took special pains to lure him as artistic director.[311] Other established professionals who worked with Katz in Berlin (and later in Amsterdam) included photographer Gerhard Badrian[312] and a veteran illustrator, costume designer and writer known as "Dryden" (né Ernst Deutsch, 1887-1938), whose work was considered by Hertzberger to be "sensationally elegant."[313] From 1926 until 1933, Dryden had been a Paris-based illustrator and writer for *Die Dame*, published in Berlin by Ullstein.[314] Another well-known illustrator, Theo Matejko (1893-1944), worked in Berlin for Katz.[315]

When Eleonore Katz, at age sixteen, joined the staff of *Der Konfektionär* as a kind of apprentice, she became a part-time student, on Moholy's advice, at Johannes Itten's Berlin school, at the time known officially as *Ittenschule*. Although Itten had left the Bauhaus in 1923 after disagreements with Gropius, he nevertheless was aiming at attracting the kind of student who might be interested in the Bauhaus, and placed an advertisement for his school in its official publication.[316] Among his faculty was Lucia Moholy.

Among Eleonore Katz's duties at *Der Konfektionär* was to serve as a model for photographic experiments by Badrian and Moholy.[317]

Meanwhile, Ludwig Katz began planning a new, quadri-lingual international magazine that would stimulate commerce between Berlin, the major center for ready-to-

---

[311]Eleonore Hertzberger, *Durch die Maschen des Netzes; ein jüdisches Ehepaar in Kampf gegen die Nazis* (Munich: Wilhelm Heyne Verlag, 1996), 20.

[312]Hertzberger, *Durch die Maschen des Netzes*, 21 and 32.

[313]Hertzberger, *Durch die Maschen des Netzes*, 21 and 32-33.

On Dryden, see: Anthony Lipmann, *Divinely Elegant: the World of Ernst Dryden* (London: Pavilion Books, Limited, 1989); Angele Zobl, editor, *Von Wien bis Hollywood: die Blüte der Mode-Illustration und Werbegrafik: Ernst Deutsch-Dryden (1887-1938) und Max H. Lang (1901-1984)* (Salzburg: Verlag für Kunst und Kultur, 1990), 3-31 and 80; and Peter Noever, editor, *Ernst Deutsche-Dryden en Vogue!* (Vienna: MAK, Österreiches Museum für angewandte Kunst, 2002).

[314]Zobl, editor, *Von Wien bis Hollywood*, 6-8, 12-14, 20 and 29; and Anthony Lipmann, "Piecing Together the Biography of Ernst Deutsch . . . /Fragmente einer Biografie Ernst Deutsch . . .," and Kathrin Pokorny-Nagel, "Art as a Trend, Ernst Deutsch-Dryden's Advertising Illustrations/Kunst als Trend, Werbeillustrationen von Ernst Deutsch-Dryden," both in: Noever, editor, *Ernst Deutsch-Dryden*, 24-29 and 72-77, respectively.

[315]Hertzberger, *Durch die Maschen des Netzes*, 21.

[316]*bauhaus; vierteljahr-zeitschrift für gestaltung*, volume III, number 4 (October-December, 1929), 31.

[317]Hertzberger, *Durch die Maschen des Netzes*, 26.

wear clothing,[318] and various textile-and-clothing centers throughout Europe that were more specialized (e.g., *haut couture* in Paris, lace in St. Gall).[319]

On March 1st, 1933, *Der Konfektionär* was "*arisiert*" (Aryanized, or removed from Jewish control, as Katz and the magazine's *Chefredakteur* and *Direktor*, or editor-in-chief and manager, Erich Greiffenhagen, each had a Jewish background).[320] Greiffenhagen moved to Paris and eventually to the United States,[321] but ostensibly Katz could remain with the magazine in a subsidiary role. Katz chose to stay with friends in secret while his wife, Klara, and daughter went to Baden-Baden.[322] After about six weeks the family lived a bit less cautiously, but a Dutch clothing manufacturer who frequently traveled to Berlin, Jacques Kattenburg, urged Katz to move to Holland and paved the way for him economically by interesting the large publishing firm of Spaarnestad in his plans for an international magazine. Even though Katz was unable to finance the magazine himself because he was allowed to bring only two-hundred marks with him, he was poised to utilize important contacts. And so in October, 1933, Katz moved to Amsterdam with his wife and daughter.[323]

Canal-enhanced Amsterdam, with a population of more than 700,000 people in 1930, is a seaside, cosmopolitan city with a long history of printing in languages other than Dutch and Flemish (which are nearly identical with each other). Dating back to the early days of printing, this practice was partially due to the relative lack of censorship throughout the history of the Netherlands, since authors and publishers in other European countries sometimes found it simpler and safer to avoid local censorship by having their books printed in the Netherlands. Hence *International Textiles*, the quadri-lingual magazine set up by Katz shortly after he arrived in Amsterdam, seemed like a natural fit.

International Textiles was published twice a month, and its first issue appeared December 15, 1933, with layout by Moholy, a frontispiece by Dryden and photographs of

---

[318]On Berlin as a center for the design, manufacture and distribution of ready-to-wear clothing, see: Mila Ganeva, *Women in Weimar Fashion: Discourses and Displays in German Culture* (Rochester, New York: Camden House, 2008), 4-5.

[319]Hertzberger, *Durch die Maschen des Netzes*, 20-21.

[320]Hertzberger, *Durch die Maschen des Netzes*, 26; and Uwe Westphal, *Berliner Konfektion und Mode; die Zerstörung einer Tradition, 1936-1939,* 2. Auflage (Berlin: Edition Hentrich, 1992), 139-140.

[321]Westphal, *Berliner Konfektion*, 139

[322]Hertzberger, *Durch die Maschen des Netzes*, 26-27.

[323]Hertzberger, *Durch die Maschen des Netzes*, 27.

fabrics by Badrian. It was published by Amsterdam-based Pallas Studio, set up as a subsidiary of Spaarnestad, which provided funding.[324]

S PAARNESTAD MAINTAINED ITS ART DEPARTMENT in Haarlem, but *International Textiles* was published from Nieuwe Zijds Voorburgwal 326-328 in Amsterdam; thus Moholy had to spend time in both Haarlem, where he designed other magazines as well as book covers for Spaarnestad, and in Amsterdam (about fifteen minutes from Haarlem by rail). Paul Hartland (1910-1991), a graduate of the *Koninklijke Academie van Beeldende Kunsten* [Royal Academy of Fine Arts] in The Hague, worked as Moholy's assistant.[325] By the end of 1934 Pallas Studio, "in co-operation with *International Textiles*," also had an office in London at 167 on The Strand, an office Moholy used as his first London address, even before he moved there.[326]

Moholy's temporary living quarters in Amsterdam were at a residential hotel, now known as the Apollo, at 123 on fashionable Apollolaan, a wide leafy street with planted strips separating the two lanes of traffic. However, during his work in Holland he continued to maintain his studio and apartment in Berlin, and Sibyl and their daughter, Hattula (born 1933), primarily lived there (except when Sibyl was with him in Amsterdam or Utrecht, leaving Hattula behind in Berlin with a nanny).

Holland's most famous artist of modern times, of course, is Piet Mondrian, who had lived in Paris since 1919. While he was living in Germany, Moholy had visited with Mondrian from time to time, as described in Chapter Three and below in this chapter, but

---

[324]Hertzberger, *Durch die Maschen des Netzes*, 32; and Terence A. Senter, "Moholy-Nagy: the Transitional Years," in: Achim Borchardt-Hume, editor, *Albers and Moholy-Nagy: from the Bauhaus to the New World* (London: Tate Publishing, 2006), 85-91, here 85-86.

[325]Senter, "Moholy-Nagy in England," 13-16; and Jeannine Fiedler and Hattula Moholy-Nagy, editors, *Laszlo Moholy-Nagy: Color in Transparency; Photographic Experiments in Color, 1934-1946 =Fotografische Experimente in Farbe, 1934-1946* [exhibition catalogue, Bauhaus-Archiv, Berlin, June 21 to September 4, 2006] (Göttingen: Steidl Publishers, 2006), 50-51.

[326]László Moholy-Nagy to Walter Gropius, December 23, 1934, Bauhaus-Archiv, Berlin; English translation by Karen Duckworth in: Senter, "Moholy-Nagy in England," 323-324. See also: advertisement, *International Textiles*, October 27, 1934, 38, reproduced in Senter, "Moholy-Nagy in England," illustration 116.

it was during his residence in Amsterdam that Moholy made regular visits to see him in Paris.[327] In later years Sibyl accompanied him on one of these visits to Mondrian's studio.[328]

In order to update his knowledge of new developments in color printing, Moholy visited London,[329] arriving about November 13th, 1933, staying at the Regent Palace Hotel, off Piccadilly Circus.[330] A side trip was made to confer with Katz in Amsterdam, and from there he planned to travel to Basel.[331] He was back in London by November 30, and planned to leave early in December.[332] The London visit was evidently made after no changes were possible in the initial (December 15) issue of *International Textiles*, but he wanted to make sure he was abreast of new developments in color printing for the benefit of future issues.

No evidence survives as to what photographic color process or processes Moholy studied in London.[333] What is known is that he worked very hard there and he did his own darkroom work, unlike his practice in his black-and-white photography when others did his darkroom work for him:

> gestern anstregend arbeit in der dunkelkammer und später beim tageslicht. der farbige kopierprozess ist unerhört interessant. ein hohes handwerk. aber man

---

[327]The visits to Mondrian were recalled by Paul Hartland, when he was interviewed by Terence Senter in 1973. See: Senter, "Moholy-Nagy in England," 17, 267 and 371.

See also: László Moholy-Nagy to Sigfried Giedion and Carola Giedion-Welcker, July 2, 1934, Giedion Family archives, Zurich. In this letter Moholy wrote of visits to Mondrian as well as to Nelly van Doesburg, Jacques Lipchitz, Robert and Sonia Delaunay, Albert Gleizes, George Vantongerloo and Mme. Hélène de Mandrot.

[328]Sibyl Moholy-Nagy. *Moholy-Nagy, Experiment in Totality*, 113-116.

[329]Senter, "Moholy-Nagy in England," 12-16.

[330]László Moholy-Nagy to Sibyl Moholy-Nagy, ALS, November 13, 1933, roll 951, frames 0096-0099, Moholy-Nagy files, Archives of American Art, Washington, D.C.

[331]László Moholy-Nagy to Sibyl Moholy-Nagy, ALS, November 22, 1933, roll 951, frames 0094 and 0095, Moholy-Nagy files, Archives of American Art, Washington, D.C.

[332]László Moholy-Nagy to Sibyl Moholy-Nagy, ALS, November 30, 1933, roll 951, frames 0100-0101 Moholy-Nagy files, Archives of American Art, Washington, D.C.

[333]Jeannine Fiedler has speculated that it could have been the recently introduced Vivex process, to which the portrait and advertising photographer Yvonne Middleton (née Cumbers; 1893-1975), known professionally as Madame Yevonde, had already begun to draw attention with her imaginative color portraits. See: Jeannine Fiedler, "A Pioneer of Color Photography: Moholy-Nagy's Color Camera Works/Ein Pioneer der Farbfotografie: Moholy-Nagys farbige Kamerafotografien," in: Jeannine Fiedler and Hattula Moholy-Nagy, editors, *Laszlo Moholy-Nagy: Color in Transparency*, [15]-33, here 17-18 and 26-27.

muss ihn selbst praktiziert haben, um überhaupt was zu können. dazu wird es
heute kommen. Ich muss zwei Pfund Kehrgeld pro tag zahlen . . . [334] [Strenuous
work in the darkroom yesterday and later in daylight. The color copying process
is incredibly interesting. A high craft. But one must have done it oneself in order
to be able to do anything at all. That is what I will do today. I must pay two
pounds tuition per day.]

Lucia Moholy was already living in London and she aided László in his studies by
serving as interpreter and through her technical knowledge, and she was also able to learn
about whatever process László was learning.[335]

WHILE IN LONDON Moholy attended the display of furniture designed by Aino and
Alvar Aalto, set up as part of an exhibition of Finnish furniture, textiles,
hardware and decoration that opened in November, 1933, at the galleries at
Fortnum and Mason.[336] Located at 181 Piccadilly, the firm supplied groceries, furniture
and other items to the British upper class, the royal family and wealthy Americans. Philip
Morton Shand (1888-1960; usually known as P. Morton Shand) set up the exhibition for
The Architectural Review; that he was part of the milieu to which the store appealed is
evident from the fact that he was grandfather to Camilla Parker-Bowles, Duchess of
Cornwall, who married Prince Charles on April 8th, 2005. In setting up the exhibition
Shand was aided by fellow *Architectural Review* writer John Betjeman.[337] At the time the
Aaltos were just emerging as leading designers of innovative Modernist wooden
furniture.[338] In Finland they had been influenced by furniture produced by Luterma,[339] a
plywood firm that later became affiliated with Isokon, a British furniture company for
which Moholy would serve as graphic designer. Moholy also has been cited by one of
Aalto's biographers as a major influence on him; they had first met at the *CIAM* meeting
in Frankfort in 1929, and in the years following Moholy himself, and his book, *von*

---

[334]László Moholy-Nagy to Sibyl Moholy-Nagy, [exact date not given but from context is would be
November, 1933], microfilm roll 951, frames 0046 and 0047, Moholy-Nagy files, Archives of
American Art, Washington, D.C.; portions quoted, in English translation and in German, in:
Fiedler, "A Pioneer of Color Photography/Ein Pioneer der Farbfotografie," 20 and 29,
respectively.

[335]*Ibid.*

[336]"Standard Wooden Furniture at the Finnish Exhibition, Alvar Aalto, Designer," *The
Architectural Review: a Magazine of Architecture & Decoration*, volume LXXIV, number 446
(December, 1933), 220-221; László Moholy-Nagy to Sibyl Moholy-Nagy, November 22, 1933;
and Göran Schildt, *Alvar Aalto: the Decisive Years*, translated from the Swedish by Timothy
Binham (New York: Rizzoli, 1986), 103-106.

[337]Schildt, *Alvar Aalto,* 104.

[338]Lloyd C. Engelbrecht, "Aalto, Alvar," in: Naylor, editor, *Contemporary Designers*, second
edition, [xvi] and [1]-2, here 2.

[339]Engelbrecht, "Aalto, Alvar," 2.

material zu architektur, had helped to change the direction of the furniture he and Aino were designing.[340]

In Amsterdam, Moholy explored the possibilities of the various color processes then in use. When Sibyl visited him in April, 1934, she reported on the appearance of his room:

> Our hotel room in Amsterdam changed into a laboratory. Strips of colored paper were tacked to the wall, and strewn on the bedspread were samples of colored gelatine, cellophane, glass, and plastics. I remember two nights when we slept on the floor because the arrangement on the bed couldn't be disturbed. With a battery of lights and borrowed cameras the same colors were photographed according to the Finlay color process, in Agfa color, Dufay color, and other systems I have forgotten. Then he went back to the laboratory of the printing firm, comparing the results.[341]

It was during this visit by Sibyl that Moholy made the experiments to test Goethe's color theory mentioned in Chapter Three.[342] Although he did not discover anything useful for his own work, he did develop a better understanding of Goethe's color theories than did his contemporaries.[343]

What Moholy explored during his second visit to England in August, 1934, was an experimental Kodak system that he found to be ineffectual, partly because of difficulties with registration. Lucia Moholy, as a resident in London, again helped him with his investigation.[344] Moholy continued to find London to be a fruitful place to study innovations in color photography and film after he took up residence there.[345]

---

[340]Schildt, *Alvar Aalto*, 62, 70-73 and 77-79.

[341]Sibyl Moholy-Nagy, *Moholy-Nagy; Experiment in Totality*, 105.

Two of the Dufay experiments appeared in: László Moholy-Nagy, *Vision in Motion*, 170, [171]-172 (original, 1947, printing). One of these also appeared in the second printing, 170 and [171].

[342]Sibyl Moholy-Nagy, *Moholy-Nagy; Experiment in Totality*, 105.

[343]Marilyn Torbruegge, "Goethe's Theory of Color and Practicing Artists," *The Germanic Review*, volume XLIX, number 3 (May, 1974), [189]-199, here 199.

[344]Senter, "Moholy-Nagy in England," 15-16, 267 and 371-372; *idem*, Moholy-Nagy: the Transitional Years," 87. See also: Lászlô Moholy-Nagy to Sibyl Moholy-Nagy, MLS, August 16, 1934, microfilm reel 951, frames 0130 and 0131; and Sibyl Moholy-Nagy to Lászlô Moholy-Nagy, TLS, August 22, 1934, microfilm reel 951, frame 0136, Moholy-Nagy files, Archives of American Art. Washington, D.C.

[345]Senter, "Moholy-Nagy in England," 121-125.

Sibyl complained that Moholy's efforts were not sufficiently appreciated by Spaarnestad.[346] Moholy, nevertheless, had continued to make the use of color in the pages of *International Textiles* more sophisticated.[347] Also, the firm asked Moholy to work on *De Katholieke Illustratie*, a venerable Roman Catholic-oriented publication dating back to 1867, that originally appeared with the subtitle *Zondags-Lektuur voor het Katholieke Nederlandsche Volk*.[348] It had come under the Spaarnestad wing in 1910,[349] and Moholy was asked to work on it just during the time when advertisements in color began to appear in its pages.[350] He also worked on another Sparnestaad magazine utilizing color, the weekly *Panorama*, beginning with its Christmas issue of 1934.[351]

In Amsterdam, probably in 1934, Moholy made at least three color photographs for advertisements for the Swiss producer of jams, Hero, available (then and now) in Holland and internationally.[352] The liveliest of the three appears in DVD figure 270.

Moholy continued his work for *International Textiles* after he moved to London in 1935, and one of the highlights of his work for the magazine during his London years was a series of advertisements for Trubenising, a proprietary term at the time, referring to a process used to make durably stiff shirt collars.[353] Although these advertisements might otherwise be considered classics of modern advertising, they are currently little known because copies of older issues of *International Textiles* are scarce, known mostly through reproductions in Senter's unpublished master's thesis.[354] (DVD figure 282) Senter analyzed Moholy's work for *International Textiles* and demonstrated that it provides

---

[346]Sibyl Moholy-Nagy, *Moholy-Nagy; Experiment in Totality*, 106.

[347]Senter, "Moholy-Nagy in England," 16 and illustrations 2 and 90.

[348]Tijn Hottinja, *De Katholieke Illustratie: de Verkochte Bruid; Honderd Jaar Tijdschriftgecheidenis* (Baarn, The Netherlands: Tirion, 2000), 19; and Leonard Jentjens, *Van Strijdorgaan tot Familienblad*; *De tijdschirftjournalistiek van de Katholieke Illustratie, 1867-1968* (Amsterdam: Otto Cramwinkel, 1995), [20].

[349]Hottinja, *De Katholieke Illustratie,* 27; and Jentjens, *Van Strijdorgaan tot Familienblad*, 65.

[350]Sibyl Moholy-Nagy, *Moholy-Nagy, Experiment in Totality*, 106; Senter, "Moholy-Nagy in England," 14; Hottinja, *De Katholieke Illustratie,* 108 and 111-114; and Leonard Jentjens, *Van Strijdorgaan tot Familienblad*, 106-107.

[351]Senter, "Moholy-Nagy in England," 16 and illustration 2.

[352]Jeannine Fiedler and Hattula Moholy-Nagy, editors, *Laszlo Moholy-Nagy: Color in Transparency*, 126-127.

[353]Senter, "Moholy-Nagy in England," 169-171 and 297.

[354]Senter, "Moholy-Nagy in England," plates 100-106.

perfect examples of the approach that Moholy outlined in his 1928 text, "Some Principles of Typography" that was discussed above.[355]

Spaarnestad did not forget his contributions to the company; in an obituary in *International Textiles* the writer stressed not only that the magazine had "offered him the ideal opportunity to develop his typographical designs," but also his role as an educator: "In conferences with our editorial staff, often lasting late into the night, he showed his admirable vitality; many of his suggestions for the set-up of our paper have become classic," and went on recall his "lectures on his favourite topic: the use of modern materials in art."[356]

In a discussion with Terence Senter in 1973, Hartland remembered "that Moholy dictated the whole form and distinctive style of the periodical from its very first issue."[357]

Eleonore Hertzberger is also important to this narrative because she commented on Moholy's near-sightedness and on his spectacles and a related gesture:

> Obwohl er erst Mitte Dreißig war, hatte Moholy-Nagy schon graue Haare, und wegen seiner extremen Kurzsichtigheit trug er Gläser, die so dick wie Lupen waren. Ich erinnere mich gut an die charakterische Bewegung, mit der er seine Brille ins Haar schob, um sich ales, was er begutachtete, ganz ducht vor der Augen zu halten.[358] [Even though he was in his middle thirties, Moholy-Nagy already had some gray hairs, and because of his extreme short-sightedness he wore spectacles that were as thick as magnifying glasses. I remember well a characteristic gesture as he shoved his glasses into his hair so that whatever he needed to get a good look at he held very close to his eyes.]

Moholy's work for Jenaer Glaswerk was foreshadowed not only by the use of glass from the firm in the famous lamp designed by his student, Wilhelm Wagenfeld, described in Chapter Three, but also by a proposal made by Gropius, dating from 1924, that Moholy would be among the Bauhaus masters who might serve as consultants for Jenaer Glaswerk. There is, however, no evidence that there was any resulting contact with Moholy at the time.[359] That changed when, early in 1933, he began work as advisor on marketing at Schott & Genossen's Jenaer Glas division, formed in 1919 to manufacture and market household glass, and received commissions for work in his studio. His work for the firm was highlighted by advertisements and prospectuses that emerged from his

---

[355] Senter, "Moholy-Nagy in England,"154-161 and illustrations 60-63, 66-78, 80-89, 91 and 92. Moholy's text appears in *ibid.*, 334-336.

[356] Senter, "Moholy-Nagy in England," 15 (exact citation not given by Senter).

[357] Senter, "Moholy-Nagy in England," 14-15 and 371.

[358] Hertzberger, *Durch die Maschen des Netzes*, 20.

[359] Walter Scheiffele, *Wilhelm Wagenfeld und die moderne Glasindustrie* (Stuttgart: Verlag Gerd Hatje, 1994), 53 and 57.

studio featuring innovative kitchen glassware, including its heat-resistant ovenware. Moholy continued his relationship with Jenaer Glas during the entire time of his residence in England.[360]

It is ironic that one of Moholy's most important collaborations with German industry began at about the time the Nazis came into power and continued while he was spending most of his time outside Germany. Schott, the parent company of Jenaer Glas, had been set up in 1878, and was an innovator in glass technology. Jenaer Glas had suffered some setbacks with the onset of the economic depression, but by the 1933-1934 fiscal year their work force was back to pre-depression levels,[361] so Moholy became involved with the firm at an economically opportune time.

DURING MOST OF THE PERIOD Moholy was involved with Jenaer Glas, he himself was working in Amsterdam and London, but he made use of the designers in his Berlin studio, still operating when he himself was in Amsterdam, and he continued his involvement with the firm after he had closed his Berlin studio and moved to London. While he lived in Amsterdam and Sibyl lived in Berlin, she aided in the work for Jenaer Glas, as documented in a series of her letters to him. In his work for Jenaer Glas, Moholy demonstrated his ability to provide overall direction while delegating specific tasks to Sibyl and to the designers in his studio. The unifying factor in the graphic design that he created or co-ordinated for Jenaer Glas was the creative and skillful integration of photographs and type. (DVD figure 283)

It was at the urging of his former student, Wilhelm Wagenfeld, that Jenaer Glas engaged modern artists and designers in designing and marketing its products.[362] Moholy advised the firm on a broad array of matters and developed a close relationship with Erich Schott (1891-1989), son of the company's founder, a member of its board and beginning in 1933, its marketing manager.[363] This close relationship is comparable to the relationship Moholy had with some of the other executives in other firms for which he worked.

---

[360] See: Scheiffele, "Typofoto und Jenaer Haushaltglas," 225-233; Senter, "Moholy-Nagy in England," 162-164, 295, 369 and 371, and illustrations 93-97; and Sibyl Moholy-Nagy to László Moholy-Nagy, TLS, July 18, 1937, microfilm reel 951, frames 0232 and 0233, Moholy-Nagy files, Archives of American Art, Washington, D.C.

[361] Jürgen Steiner and Uta Hoff, "Vom Versuchslaboratorium zum Weltunternehmen das Jenaer Glaswerk 1884-1934," in: Jürgen John and Volker Wahl, editors, *Zwischen Konvention und Avantgarde: Doppelstadt Jena - Weimar* (Weimar: Böhlau Verlag, 1995), 209-232, here 231-232.

[362] Walter Scheiffele, "The Experiment: Schott & Gen. in Jena," in: Beate Manske, editor, *Wilhelm Wagenfeld (1900-1990)* (Ostfildern-Ruit, Germany: Hatje Cantz Publishers, 2000), 38-45, here 38 and 42.

[363] Senter," Moholy-Nagy in England," 162; and Scheiffele, "Typofoto und Jenaer Haushaltsglas," 226-227 and 232-233..

Otto Schott (1851-1935), Erich's father, was the founder of modern glass technology, and one of his achievements was the development of heat-resistant borosilicate glass, first marketed in 1891.[364] He had initiated contacts with the Corning Glass Works in Corning, New York, as early as 1909.[365] Perhaps his interest was aroused by its research laboratory, set up in 1908 as one of the earliest corporate research laboratories in the United States.[366]

IN MANY WAYS Corning's research into and production of heat-resistant glass paralleled that of Jenaer Glas, and the interaction between the two firms cannot now be ascertained in detail.[367] It is known that the scientists in Corning's research laboratory tried to replicate the successes of the borosilicate glass developed in Jena.[368] Both firms began making heat-resistant glass for household use at about the same time, but Corning's household glass was first marketed around 1916,[369] while Jenaer Glas was not set up until 1919. In any case, Erich Schott wrote a letter of recommendation for Moholy to Corning on August 3, 1938,[370] but there is no record of any resulting work Moholy might have been asked to do by Corning.

Moholy and his studio provided designs for Jenaer Glas for advertisements for magazines, prospectuses, subway cards, etc., as well as for show windows in retail stores. In addition Moholy and Wagenfeld engaged authors for advertising copy and for magazine and newspaper articles about cooking with Jenaer Glas kitchenware and use of their nursing bottles for babies.

One of the writers engaged, with the help of Sibyl, was Ilse Molzahn (née Schwollmann; born 1895), who in 1919 had become the first wife of Johannes Molzahn.[371] (As noted in Chapter Three and further discussed in Chapter Five, Johannes Molzahn taught with Moholy at the School of Design in Chicago.) Molzahn had been dismissed for political reasons from his professorship at the *Stattliche Akademie für*

---

[364] Jürgen Steiner, "Otto Schott (1851-1935)—Founder of Modern Glass Science and Glass Technology," *Glass Science and Technology/Glastechnische Berichte*, volume LXXIV, number 10 (October, 2001), 292-302, here 297-298.

[365] Scheiffele, *Wilhelm Wagenfeld und die moderne Glasindustrie*, 49.

[366] Margaret B.W. Graham and Alec T. Schuldner, *Corning and the Craft of Innovation* (New York: Oxford University Press, 2001), 40-43.

[367] Scheiffele, *Wilhelm Wagenfeld und die moderne Glasindustrie*, 50-51.

[368] Graham and Schuldner, *Corning and the Craft of Innovation*, 43.

[369] Graham and Schuldner, *Corning and the Craft of Innovation*, 55-58.

[370] Scheiffele, "Typofoto und Jenaer Haushaltglas," 232-233.

[371] Christian Gries, "Johannes Molzahn (1892-1965) und der 'Kampf um die Kunst' im Deutschland der Weimarer Republik" (Ph. D. dissertation, Universität Augsburg, 1996), 1:77.

Kunst- und Kunstgewerbe in Breslau (now Wrocław or Wrozlaw, Poland),[372] and he moved to Berlin, where he lived in a state of immobility caused by depression.[373] Ilse Molzahn, a poet, novelist and writer of feature articles for newspapers, had been engaged to write essays and advertising copy for Jenaer Glas by Sibyl, who paid her directly, presumably with funds supplied by the firm to Moholy for his studio costs.[374] Sibyl also served as initial editor for what Ilse wrote in spite of her own busy schedule in the film industry, and sent the edited texts to Moholy in Amsterdam.[375] Interestingly, Ilse had her own direct connection with the Bauhaus, when she was invited by the school to present a reading of her own poems in 1919.[376]

Moholy suggested to Jenaer Glas that a new film be made to be used in home-making classes.[377] Sibyl worked on the Jenaer Glas film for her husband, then spending most of his time in Amsterdam. Still active in the Berlin-area film industry, she contacted Wolfgang Kaskeline (1892-1973), prominent director of industrial and advertising films for his family enterprise, the UFA-Kaskeline studio.[378] On October 9, 1934, she reported to László that on that day she had conferred for two and one-half hours with an UFA dramaturge named Podehl about the script, and had also conferred about the film with another person named Reichert.[379] On October 14 Sibyl wrote to László that she had spoken with Kaskeline's special effects specialist and that Kaskeline had promised that by the end of October he would send László complete sketches for special effects sequences

---

[372]Gries, "Johannes Molzahn," 1:244-249.

[373]Sibyl Moholy-Nagy to László Moholy-Nagy, October 4, 1934. Sibyl wrote of Molzahn that: ". . . Depression bereits alle Initiave kaputt gemacht hat." [Depression has taken away almost all of his initiative.]

[374]Sibyl Moholy-Nagy to László Moholy-Nagy, TLS, August 21, 1934, microfilm reel 951, frames 0134 and 0135, Moholy-Nagy files, Archives of American Art, Washington, D.C Moholy made a reference to an honorarium from Schott in a letter, thus indicating it was his responsibility to pay his collaborators, including writers, directly; see: László Moholy-Nagy to Sibyl Moholy-Nagy, November 30, 1933. See also: Gries, "Johannes Molzahn," 251 (where Lucia is mistakenly substituted for Sibyl).

[375]Sibyl Moholy-Nagy to László Moholy-Nagy, August 21, 1934; and Sibyl Moholy-Nagy to László Moholy-Nagy, November 8, 1934.

[376]Ilse Molzahn mentioned reading her poems at the Bauhaus in a short autobiographical essay in an appendix to her: *Dieses Herz Will Ich Verspielen; Gedichte* (Heidenheim, Germany: Verlag Werner Jerratsch, 1977), [59].

[377]Scheiffele, "Typofoto und Jenaer Haushaltglas," 231,

[378]Sibyl Moholy-Nagy to László Moholy-Nagy, TLS, October 4, 1934, microfilm reel 951, frames 0157 and 0158, Moholy-Nagy files, Archives of American Art, Washington, D.C.

[379]Sibyl Moholy-Nagy to László Moholy-Nagy, TLS, October 9, 1934, microfilm reel 951, frame 0151, Moholy-Nagy files, Archives of American Art, Washington, D.C..

involving a mirror.[380] However, before the film was sent to Schott in Jena early in November, she and Kepes altered the title frames to comply with László's decision that the title appear as a negative image, and completed the final editing.[381] In a letter to László, Sibyl pointed to a few minor flaws in the film but wrote that she was pleased with the final product: "Es ist aber ein hübscher Film geworden und wird Jena sicher gefallen."[382] [But it has resulted in an attractive film and will surely please {Schott at} Jena.] It is not known if copies of the film survive.

Moholy's frequent trips to Jena can be documented by letters he wrote to Sibyl.[383] His comprehensive advice for Jenaer Glas was summarized in an internal memorandum of January 28, 1937.[384] It should be emphasized that, although he offered suggestions for product design,[385] there is no evidence that his studio did provide any such designs.

One key graphic-design commission, this one for the London publisher of *The New Architecture and the Bauhaus* of 1935 by Gropius,[386] came during the period when Moholy was moving to London. The book was the first English-language book-length publication about the Bauhaus, and made the British public aware of the school's achievements. Moholy's own book, *The New Vision*, had already appeared in 1932, but only with an American imprint and thus would have been less readily available in Britain. The design of *The New Architecture and the Bauhaus* was completed in London but had been begun in Berlin, with the help of extensive correspondence, and thus the design process is well documented.[387] (DVD figure 284)

----

[380] Sibyl Moholy-Nagy to László Moholy-Nagy, TLS, October 14, 1934, microfilm reel 951, frames 0152-0154, Moholy-Nagy files, Archives of American Art, Washington, D.C..

[381] Sibyl Moholy-Nagy to László Moholy-Nagy, TLS, November 6, 1934 and TLS, November 8, 1934, microfilm reel 951, frames 0159-0160, and 0161-1062, respectively, Moholy-Nagy files, Archives of American Art, Washington, D.C.

[382] Sibyl Moholy-Nagy to László Moholy-Nagy, November 8, 1934.

[383] *E.g.,* a reference is made to a trip to Jena early in December, 1933, in: László Moholy-Nagy to Sibyl Moholy-Nagy, November 30, 1933.

[384] Excerpts from this memorandum appeared in: Scheiffele, "Typofoto und Jenaer Haushaltglas," 229-232.

[385] Scheiffele, "Typofoto und Jenaer Haushaltglas," 231-232.

[386] Walter Gropius, *The New Architecture and the Bauhaus*, translated from the German by P. Morton Shand, with an introduction by Frank Pick (London: Faber and Faber, limited, 1935).

[387] Senter, "Moholy-Nagy in England," 21-24, 161-162, 327-328 and illustrations 4 and 4a; David and Diserens, editors, *László Moholy-Nagy* (Valencia), 321; and David, editor, *László Moholy-Nagy* (Kassel), 289.

It was through the marketing magazine, *Shelf Appeal*, that Moholy became widely known for his ability as a graphic designer shortly after his move to England, when he designed the color cover for the November, 1935, issue.

Other British graphic-design commissions came from Jack Pritchard (1899-1992; originally known as John Craven Pritchard). Trained as an engineer and economist,[388] he became a key figure in introducing Modernism in design and architecture in Great Britain. From 1925 to 1936 he worked for Venesta, a British associate of the international plywood firm Luterma, which had factories in Finland, Lithuania and Estonia. Originally the two companies had become associated to find a suitable method for packing tea, and Pritchard was hired to try to broaden Venesta's activities. In that capacity he worked in sales and advertising and, occasionally, as a designer. His work at Venesta brought him into contact with leading Modernists, including Gropius, Breuer, Wells Coates, P. Morton Shand and Moholy.[389] Pritchard brought in Moholy to design a Venesta advertisement for the February, 1936, issue of *The Architectural Review*.[390] (DVD figure 285) But what was published in *The Architectural Review* was less an advertisement than a colored illustration, assigned a figure number by the editors, and with a caption that barely mentioned Venesta;[391] it appeared in an issue devoted to timber, including an informative article on plywood by Moholy's friend Shand. Moholy's contribution, an imaginative connection of plywood with its arboreal origins, provided leavening for an issue laden with extensive historical and technical data about wood.[392]

The announcement of the formation of the Isokon Furniture Company was made in January, 1936.[393] The firm was set up by Pritchard, his wife, Molly (née Cooke), and Coates, with Gropius as Controller of Design.[394] Isokon went on to make use of the talents of Moholy and especially Breuer, who designed a number of pieces of furniture for the firm. Breuer's first design for Isokon was his signature piece for both him and the

---

[388] Cheryl Buckley, *Isokon Exhibition, Hatton Gallery, University of Newcastle-upon-Tyne, April-May, 1980, Catalogue* (Newcastle-upon-Tyne: Hatton Gallery, University of Newcastle upon Tyne, 1980), 6. (This catalogue is hard to locate, but a copy is in the Pritchard Papers, Library of the University of East Anglia, Norwich.)

[389] Jack Pritchard, *View from a Long Chair: the Memoirs of Jack Ptritchard* (London: Routledge & Kegan Paul, 1984), 53-61 and 122-123

[390] Pritchard, *View from a Long Chair*, 122-123.

[391] *The Architectural Review: a Magazine of Architecture and Decoration*, volume LXXIX, number 471 (February, 1936), plate vi opposite page 80.

[392] Pritchard recalled that his colleagues had considered the advertisement a waste of money: Jack Pritchard to J.M. Richards, carbon copy of TLS, December 4, 1946, Pritchard Papers, Library of the University of East Anglia, Norwich.

[393] Buckley, *Isokon*, 15-16.

[394] Pritchard, *View from a Long Chair*, 111.

firm: the lounge chair of 1936 known as the long chair.[395] Moholy designed a brochure to help to launch it.[396] (DVD figure 286) His other work for the firm included stationery enlivened by a rendering of a bent-wood cantilever chair. Beyond this, Pritchard recalled that Moholy's contribution to Isokon lay in "general encouragement and advice," and the two men bonded. They later met in Chicago, as discussed in the next chapter, and it had been Pritchard who saw Moholy off at the docks when he sailed for America:

> I shall never forget seeing Moholy off for America. He travelled in . . . the *Manhattan*, and as we were seeing him off at Waterloo [*i.e.*, a railroad station in London] he suddenly found ten minutes before the train went [that] he had no keys for the special packages he had made which contained all the stuff he required for a most important conference in New York on arrival which was to start off the Bauhaus, and I promised to meet Moholy at Southampton before the ship sailed with the keys. This we did with twenty minutes to spare, and I will never forget being embraced by Moholy as a result![397]

Southampton is about sixty miles from London, and about two hours away by rail. Pritchard also saw Sibyl, Hattula and Claudia off at the station when they left for America.[398]

It was Herbert Read who mentioned Moholy and his talents as a designer to Marcus Brumwell (1901-1993), managing director of the Stuart Advertising Agency.[399] Moholy went on to receive a number of commissions through the Stuart Agency, including his work for Imperial Airways.[400] In addition to his work for Imperial Airways as an exhibition designer, noted below, Moholy was active as a graphic designer for them; a highlight was the exhibition catalogue for *The Empire's Airway* of 1935. (DVD figure 287) In several of his graphic designs for Imperial Airways, including this catalogue cover, he

---

[395]Pritchard, *View from a Long Chair*, 111-115; and Buckley, *Isokon*, 17-18. Moholy had a long chair in his apartments in Chicago; see: László Moholy-Nagy to Jack Pritchard, TLS, November 29, 1937, Institute of Design Papers, University of Illinois Library, Chicago.

[396]Buckley, *Isokon*, 20.

[397]Jack Prithard to J.M. Richards, December 4, 1946; a slightly embellished version of this tale appeared in: Pritchard, *View from a Long Chair*, 125.

[398]László Moholy-Nagy to Jack Pritchard, November 29, 1937.

[399]Senter, "Moholy-Nagy in England," 53; and *idem*, "Moholy-Nagy: the Transitional Years," 88.

[400]Michael Gifford, "Imperial Airways' Publicity," *The Penrose Annual; Review of the Graphic Arts*, volume XL (1938), 55-59 and illustrations on unnumbered pages following page 58, here 56.

Imperial Airways, in existence from 1924 to 1940, was a public company that sold shares and paid dividends to shareholders. It nevertheless operated with a government subsidy, and in 1940 it was absorbed into the newly formed government entity, British Overseas Airways Corporation. See: A.J. Quin-Harkin, "Imperial Airways, 1924-40," in: Peter J. Lyth, editor, *Air Transport* (Aldershot, England: Scolar Press, 1996), 24-45.

employed a speed-bird motif. This had originally been conceived by sculptor Barbara Hepworth in clay, then used in her cover design for an Imperial Airways booklet.[401]

It was perhaps Moholy's work on the Charing Cross exhibition for Imperial Airways, described below, that led to some commissions from the London Passenger Transport Board, commonly known as London Transport, which was responsible for transportation in London and its environs. For them Moholy designed at least two leaflets[402] and a small number of posters.[403] (DVD figure 288) London had a tradition of excellent transportation posters,[404] and Moholy's work was seen by more Londoners through his leaflets and posters for London Transport than through all of his other work there.

Tales of Domesticity among the Avant-Garde

THE SOCIAL LIFE THAT Moholy enjoyed during the period immediately following his return to Berlin in 1928 was dominated by his relationship with Ellen Frank. Very little is documented about this relationship, but since Ellen was the sister-in-law of Gropius through his wife, Ise (née Frank), and since, as noted above, she visited the Gropiuses in Dessau, she possibly met Moholy there. And although Lucia noticed an attraction between the two as early as May, 1928,[405] she and László continued to live together until about May, 1930,[406] and, as Julien Levy noted on a visit to Berlin, they spent some of their weekends together as late as summer, 1931.[407]

But it was not just László who found another companion as the marriage between him and Lucia gradually disintegrated. As noted in Chapter Three, there is no indication that either László or Lucia had much contact with Theodor Neubauer during the seven months when all three lived in Weimar. That changed when they all were living in Berlin as Lucia turned to Neubauer at about the time Moholy was turning to Ellen Frank. Although no

---

[401] Senter, "Moholy-Nagy in England," 179 and illustration 114; and Gifford, "Imperial Airways' Publicity," 56.

[402] Senter, "Moholy-Nagy in England," illustrations 126 and 127.

[403] Senter, "Moholy-Nagy in England," 186-188 and illustrations 125 and 125; Sibyl Moholy-Nagy, *Moholy-Nagy: Experiment in Totality*, 119-120; and Sheila Taylor, editor, *The Moving Metropolis; a History of London's Transport since 1800* (London: Laurence King, 2001), 211.

[404] Senter, "Moholy-Nagy in England," 186-187; and Taylor, editor, *The Moving Metropolis*, 103, 178-179, 184-185 *et passim*.

[405] In her note stemming from the beginning of May, 1929, cited in note 1.

[406] See note 2.

[407] Julien Levy, *Memoir of an Art Gallery* (New York: G.P. Putnam's Sons, 1977), 66; reprinted, with a new introduction by Ingrid Schaffner, by MFA Publications in Boston in 2003.

exact date can be documented, Lucia turned to Theodor well before the divorce of László and Lucia had become legally valid on March 3rd, 1934.

Neubauer's personal life was somewhat complex. When his first wife, Hedwig, died, their son and daughter were infants.[408] One can only speculate, but widower Neubauer's second, hasty marriage might have been for the sake of the children; his new wife, Elisabeth (née Bischoff; died 1961),[409] was probably a friend more than a lover (who, in any case, remained a source of support for her husband during the years of Nazi turbulence). After leaving Weimar, Neubauer had moved to Dusseldorf and become an *Abgeordnete*, or legislator, elected on the Communist ticket to the national parliament, the Reichstag, on December 7th, 1924. Meanwhile his second wife and children continued to live in their home in the district he represented in Dusseldorf, until 1931, when they moved to Berlin.[410] None of Neubauer's biographers mentions Lucia Moholy in any way, so how she and Elisabeth Neubauer might have interacted is not known.

Although it is impossible to set a date for the beginning of the liaison between Lucia and Theodor, it is known that by the end of 1929 Lucia had a rubber stamp that read "Lucia Moholy-Neubauer," and used it to stamp the backs of some of her photographs.[411] (The reader of these pages will be aware that Lucia is far from the only one of her contemporaries to change her or his name.)[412] While most details of their relationship remain unknown, surely a high point would have been Lucia's masterful photographs made about 1930 of her lover interviewing veteran Communist politician Clara Zetkin (née Eissner; 1857-1933). (DVD figure 289)

If we do not know precisely when the liaison between Lucia and Theodor began, we do know when they saw each other for the last time. This was August 3rd, 1933,[413] when, as

---

[408] Sonja Müller, *Theodor Neubauer,* Lebensbilder großer Pädagogen (Berlin: Volk und Wissen Volkseigener Verlag Berlin, 1969), 77. Sonja Müller is the daughter of Theodor and Hedwig. Her mother died May 13, 1923, in childbirth.

[409] Müller, *Theodor Neubauer*, 79-80. The wedding of Theodor and Elisabeth took place in September, 1923.

[410] Müller, *Theodor Neubauer*, 102.

[411] Rolf Sachsse and Sabine Hartmann, *Lucia Moholy, Bauhaus Fotografin* (Berlin: Bauhaus-Archiv, 1995), 23.

[412] Lucia herself had published an essay and a poem under a pseudonym, Ulrich Steffen, in an issue of the quarterly published by the Barkenhoff commune in Worpswede, Germany: *Neubau*, volume I, number 1 (June, 1919), 9-11; see: Oliver Botar, *Technical Detours: the Early Moholy-Nagy Reconsidered* (New York: Art Gallery of the Graduate Center of The City University of New York and The Salgo Trust for Education, 2006), 89 and 91.

[413] Elizabeth Bibesco, "German Concentration Camps; to the Editor of the Times," *The Times* (London), April 21, 1934, 15.

noted in Chapter Three, Neubauer was arrested in Lucia's apartment,[414] when she was living at Badensche Straße 6. He escaped and was re-captured while being transported via the Berlin subway system (in the manner of the 1971 film, *The French Connection*).[415] Elisabeth Neubauer was in a hospital at the time and her children were living with a nanny. One evening before Neubauer was arrested, when the nanny was visiting their mother and the children were alone, fourteen-year old Hartmut was questioned by brown-shirted Storm Troopers [*i.e.*, *S.A.* or *Sturmabteilung*] as to where his father might be hiding, and letters, books and photographs were seized. Neubauer remained in Germany until he was murdered by the Nazis on January 8th, 1945.[416] Lucia left Germany shortly after Neubauer's arrest,[417] and did not return to Germany during his lifetime.

THE ONLY COMMENT Ellen Frank made in writing about her relationship with Moholy was when she wrote: "I was deeply friend[ly] with him for 3 ½ years, we had wonderful trips together to France and Finland."[418] This deep friendship, then, evidently began to develop in May, 1928, and lasted until some time late in 1932. On November 14, 1932, László wrote a letter to Sibyl reporting on a quarrel he had had with Ellen, evidently involving his closeness to her, and he told Sibyl that they should not meet for a while until he had time to work things out by himself.[419] It would seem that by year's end László and Sibyl had bonded, and the close personal relationship between him and Ellen had come to an end. In any case Sibyl made a Christmas visit to her family in Loschwitz, near Dresden, and sent a telegram to László about her return to Berlin: "GUTE

---

[414]Lucia Moholy to Heinrich Jacoby, January 10, 1947, Bauhaus-Archiv, Berlin; portions published in: Sachsse and Hartmann, *Lucia Moholy, Bauhaus Fotografin*, 81-83, here 81.

   Lucia Moholy had known Jacoby since at least 1923, when she would have met him while accompanying her husband to a dinner party in Berlin where Jacoby was a guest; see: Hans Heinz Stuckenschmidt, "Musik am Bauhaus," in: Karin von Maur, *Vom Klang der Bilder: die Musik in der Kunst des 20. Jahrhunderts* (Munich: Prestel Verlag, 1985), 408-413, here 409.

   It is not clear why Neubauer was arrested; perhaps merely because he was a Communist, or perhaps he was suspected of having a role in the setting of the Reichstag fire that broke out on February 27, 1933. The Nazis and their collaborators were very arbitrary in whom they arrested.

[415]Willibald Gutsche, *Dr. Theodor Neubauer: ein Leben im Kampf um ein besseres Deutschland* (Erfurt: Wissenschaftlichen Kollektiv zur Erforschung der erfurter Stadtgeschichte, 1955), 44.

[416]Lucia Moholy to Heinrich Jacoby, January 10, 1947, 82.

[417]Lucia Moholy to Heinrich Jacoby, January 10, 1947, 81-82.

[418]Ellen Frank to David Travis, TLS, November 10, 1976, files of the Photography Department of the Art Institute of Chicago.

[419]László Moholy-Nagy to Sibyl Peach, MLS, November 14, 1932, Moholy-Nagy files, microfilm reel 951, frames 0037-0038, Archives of American Art, Washington, D.C.

NACHT SCHLAF GUT MORGEN BIN ICH BEI DIR = SIBYL."[420] [Good night sleep well tomorrow I will be with you, Sibyl.]

Ellen Frank went on to have a relationship with Sibyl's soon-to-be ex-husband, Carl Dreyfuß (1898-1969) of Frankfort am Main.[421] Dreyfuß was a close friend of Theodor W. Adorno, who described him as ". . . a philosopher by training, a major industrialist [owner and manager of a varnish factory] by profession and out of necessity, and a man of letters by inclination."[422] When Ellen met Carl he was still legally married to Sibyl (they were married September 30th, 1929, and their divorce was effective on November 6th, 1933).[423] Sibyl had left Carl when she moved to Berlin at some time around mid-1931, but she spent the Christmas holidays with him in Thuringia later that year.[424] Carl Dreyfuß was thereby

---

[420]Telegram sent through Deutsche Reichspost, December 29, 1932, microfilm reel 951, frame 0045, Moholy-Nagy files, Archives of American Art, Washington, D.C..

[421]According to an interview with Ellen Frank by Hattula Moholy-Nagy, discussed below.

Carl Dreyfuß was also known as Karl Ludwig Dreyfuß, Carl Dreyfuss and Carl Dreyfus, and under the pseudonym of Ludwig Carls; as co-authors he and Theodor W. Adorno were jointly known under the pseudonym of Castor Zwieback.

On Dreyfuß and Adorno as co-authors, see: Theodor W. Adorno, *Vermischte Schriften II: Aesthetica, Miscellanea* (Frankfurt am Main: Suhrkamp Verlag, 2003), [587]-597 and 818. Adorno had been known as Theodor Wiesengrund, but changed his last name to Adorno (his mother's maiden name) and made W. his middle initial.

[422]Theodor W. Adorno to Alban Berg, January 15, 1927, in: Lonitz, editor, *Correspondence, 1925-1935, Theodor W. Adorno and Alban Berg*, 92.

On the enduring friendship of Adorno and Dreyfuß, see: Stefan Müller-Doohm, *Adorno; a Biography*, translated by Rodney Livingstone (Cambridge, England: Polity Press, 2005), 99-100, 474-475 *et passim*; *idem*, *Adorno, eine Biographie* (Frankfort am Main: Suhrkamp Verlag, 2003), 149-150, 721 *et passim*.

[423]See the wedding document as altered to reflect their divorce and the divorce document itself, microfilm reel 946, frames 0873 and 0874, and 0870-0872, respectively, Moholy-Nagy papers, Archives of American Art, Washington, D.C.

[424]Sibyl Moholy-Nagy (as Sibyl Peach), "My Life in Germany - Two Years Before and Two Years After the Start of the Hitler Regime," microfilm copy of carbon copy of typed manuscript, pages 1-181 on microfilm reel 946, frames 0628-0814, here pages 25-27 on frames 655-657, Moholy-Nagy papers, Archives of American Art, Washington, D.C.

On the page preceding the title page is a note: "This manuscript was written for the contest sponsored by the psychological and historical departments of Harvard University in Spring 1940," *ibid.*, frames 628 and 629.

Some of the same characters appear in a somewhat autobiographical novel: Sibyl Moholy-Nagy (as S.D. Peech), *Children's Children* (New York: H. Bittner and Company, 1945), with a

(continued...)

involved with three actresses at the same time, because in addition to his relationships with Ellen and Sibyl he was for some years the lover of the actress Marianne Hoppe (1909-1999), whom he had met in 1930;[425] moreover, until 1926 he had been married to still another actress, Ellen Dreyfus-Herz,[426] and during the next year his "lady friend" was the dancer and silent-film actress Ilona Karolevna.[427] This set of relationships, of course, somewhat resembled László's, who was involved with Ellen and Sibyl at the same time, while legally married to Lucia. Moreover, with the exception of Lucia, all of these women were active on the stage and/or the screen (and even in Lucia's case, it could be said that she was extraordinarily good at photographing theatrical settings).

As noted in Appendix D, while Sibyl and Carl were married and living in Frankfurt some leading intellectuals joined in discussions in their living room. Among those present were Adorno and Benjamin.

Ellen's slender beauty, skillfully photographed by László, made her one of the most fashionable models in Berlin, as she posed frequently for him, often appearing on covers of *die neue linie* (DVD figures 272, 274 and 275) and in a sequence in one of his films (film clip 2) That did not lead to much success as an actress. During most of her long career, first as a dancer, then to some extent on German stages and as a night-club chanteuse, but mostly in films, she worked steadily, except for a fifteen-year period beginning in 1939,

---

[424](...continued)
dust jacket designed by Moholy. Both *Children's Children* and "My Life in Germany" include factual and as well as fanciful passages. The same is true of Sibyl's *Moholy-Nagy: Experiment in Totality*, but to a lesser degree. In many passages the texts of these writings contain inconsistencies with each other, and one of her goals was to present a well-crafted narrative.

Concerning the writing of *Children's Children*, see: Senter, "Moholy-Nagy in England," 49.

All three of these writings should be evaluated in terms of the history of autobiographical writings. These writings, as discussed in Appendix D, are quite commonly more valuable for the insights offered than for the seemingly factual material that is often elusively presented. In the case of Sibyl Moholy-Nagy, I have cited her writings as factual sources when the facts were corroborated by other sources or at least when her assertions seemed factually credible.

[425]Petra Kohse, *Marianne Hoppe: eine Biografie* (Berlin: Ullstein, 2001), 18, 76-79, 120-121 *et passim*.

Kohse makes no mention of Sibyl Peach (as Sibyl Pietzsch was known at the time) or Ellen Frank.

[426]Müller-Doohm, *Adorno; a Biography*, 99-100; *idem, Adorno, eine Biographie*, 149-150; and Kohse, *Marianne Hoppe*, 78.

[427]Theodor W. Adorno to Alban Berg, January 15, 1927, 92.

but did not achieve stardom.[428] Her later career consisted mainly of television roles and it was on television that she finally gained some recognition.[429] But in 1932 Sibyl reported to László that she had tried to get theater and film work for her but she was frustrated in that attempt because Ellen was perceived as *unbegabt* [untalented].[430] Moreover, it seems that Ellen did not work as a model, at least not very much, after Moholy left Germany; in any case, she modeled for Moholy at a time when few models reached celebrity status.

Moholy retained some photographs of Ellen Frank and brought them with him to Chicago. From there they were sent to Gropius in 1949 by Sibyl Moholy-Nagy, as she was weeding out her belongings in preparation for a move to San Francisco. She thought that Gropius would pass them along to his sister-in-law who ". . . might want to show them to her [*i.e.*, Ellen's] daughter."[431] (Ellen Frank was married to Georg Arm in 1939 and had a daughter, Evelyn, with him; Ellen and Georg were divorced in 1952).

Hattula Moholy-Nagy interviewed Ellen Frank in 1981 and 1982.[432] Frank recalled meeting László through Piscator; the earliest date she would have met Moholy through him was at or shortly before the opening of Sinclair's *The Singing Jailbirds*, which would be March 1st, 1928, as discussed above. Since she did not recall meeting him at the Bauhaus, this indicates that if, contrary to her memory, she had met him there, he could not have made much of an impression on her. Among the things she talked about with Hattula was her father's asking her to serve him as a typist. She also remembered how polite Moholy was and that he remained polite even when they were squabbling.

In 1981 Hattula Moholy-Nagy also interviewed György Kepes, who spoke of Ellen Frank and other topics. He remembered that Moholy's studio included his own bedroom, and that Moholy and Ellen did not actually share an apartment but rather that she had an

---

[428]Ellen Frank's movie roles are well documented in Internet web sites featuring movie databases. See also: Ursula von Wiese, *Vogel Phönix; Stationen meines Lebens* (Bern: Klio-Verlag, 1994), 127-128.

[429]*Ibid.*

[430]Sibyl Pietzsch to László Moholy-Nagy, TLS, August 19, 1932, microfilm reel 951, frame 0033, Moholy-Nagy files, Archives of American Art, Washington, D.C.

Not everyone who knew her thought that Ellen Frank was untalented; see: Ursula von Wiese, *Vogel Phönix*, 127-128.

[431]Sibyl Moholy-Nagy to Walter Gropius, TLS, May 28, 1949, Bauhaus-Archiv, Berlin.

[432]Notes made by Hattula Moholy-Nagy from her interviews with Ellen Frank in Munich,th April 29, 1981 and June 28th, 1982; copies are in my files.

apartment in a nearby building. Kepes recalled later serving as Hattula's baby sitter in the studio.[433]

Some of the meager documentation about Ellen Frank's life concerns Ascona where, as noted in Chapter Three, Oskar Schlemmer had described how that southern Swiss community had become, by the later 1920s, a center for intellectuals, actors, dancers, artists and just about anyone with an interest in the arts. Among the latter was Max Emden (1874-1940), an art collector[434] who had earned a doctorate in chemistry and mineralogy[435] but preferred to make a career in his family's department store in Hamburg, *M.J. Emden Söhne*. This business was consolidated into *Rudolph Karstadt A.G. [i.e., Aktien-Gesellschaft]* early in 1927.[436] Max Emden's direct participation was no longer needed, while he continued to enjoy revenue from Karstadt's, probably in the form of dividends on shares of stock. Thus at the age of 54 he was enabled to spend the rest of his life in leisure activities. He made his mark at Ascona by acquiring two nearby islands on Lake Maggiore known as the Brissago Islands.[437] On the larger of the two, known as San Pancrazio, he built a large mansion (Hans and Oskar Gerson with Alfred Breslauer and E. Vogt, 1928) and a marble outdoor swimming pool.[438] (DVD figure 290) The islands were located in the most southerly area of Switzerland, and were also at the country's lowest point above sea level. The previous owner had taken advantage of the mild climate to landscape the islands with exotic plants brought in from many parts of the world, and Emden expanded that effort.[439]

---

[433]Hattula Moholy-Nagy interviewing György Kepes, May 11th, 1981.

[434]Ulrich Luckhardt and Uwe M. Schneede, editors, *Private Schätze: über das Sammeln von Kunst in Hamburg bis 1933* (Hamburg: Christians Verlag, 2001), 71, 75, 221-222 and 261-262.

[435]Max Emden, "Über die Reduktionsprodukte der Phenylglyoxyldicarbonsäure" (Ph.D. dissertation, Üniversität Leipzig, 1898).

[436]Rudolf Lenz, *Karstadt; ein deutscher Warenhauskonzern, 1920-1950* (Stuttgart: Deutsche Verlags-Anstalt,1995), 99-100.

[437]Robert Landmann [Werner Ackermann], *Ascona — Monte Verità; auf der Suche nach dem Paradies*, von Ursula von Wiese überarbeitete und ergänzte Ausgabe, unter Mitarbeit von Doris Hasenfratz (Frauenfeld, Switzerland: Verlag Huber, 2000), 253-254; and Curt Riess, *Ascona: Geschichte des seltsamsten Dorfes der Welt*, 2. Auflage (Zurich: Europa Verlag A.G., 1964), 98 and 101-102.

[438]Wolfgang Voigt, *Hans und Oskar Gerson: Hanseatische Moderne*, mit Beiträgen von Hartmut Frank und Ulrich Höhns (Hamburg: Dölling Verlag, 2000), 67-68 and 113.

[439]Landmann, *Ascona — Monte Verità; auf der Suche nach dem Paradies*, 249 and 255-261; and Ursula von Wiese, *Vogel Phönix*, 128-129.

At about the time Emden had retired, his Chilean wife, Anita (later Gräfin [Countess] Einsiedel) left him,[440] and after that he had proposed marriage to another woman, someone he had known and admired for some time. She was fond of Ascona and its surroundings, and it was because of her that he had turned his attention to the Lake Maggiore Region. But she nevertheless rejected Emden's marriage proposal because she said that she would never marry him because he was a Jew, and this rejection left him in a state of severe depression.[441]

ASCONA HAD A TRADITION of semi-public nudity, but in earlier years it was associated with reform life styles or experimental modern dance efforts.[442] The nudity that prevailed on San Pancrazio had an erotic element because Emden's guest list included seven comely young women who frolicked naked in the marble pool as well as in his palace.[443] One of these was Ellen Frank, who appears in an archway from a ruined antique building with two other female guests in a photograph, made in 1929,[444] that was later included in an exhibition about Ascona.[445] (DVD figure 291). In the picture she is seen fully nude, from the back. During her interview with Hattula Moholy-Nagy she complained about publication of the photograph and its inclusion in an exhibition because she had not given her permission. She can be identified as the woman in the center, because the partially clothed woman on the right faces the camera and is obviously not Ellen, and the woman on the left was identified by Ursula von Wiese (1905-2002) as herself during an interview.[446] In another photograph (DVD figure

---

[440] Ursula von Wiese, *Vogel Phönix*, 128; Riess, *Ascona*, 98; and Luckhardt and Schneede, editors, *Private Schätze*, 221.

[441] Riess, *Ascona*, 98. I have not found the name of the woman Emden wanted to become his second wife.

[442] Landmann, *Ascona — Monte Verità; auf der Suche nach dem Paradies*, 97-115, 147 and 172; and Edmund Stadler, "Theater und Tanz in Ascona," in: Gabriella Borsano, editor, *Monte Verità, Berg der Wahrheit* [exhibition catalogue] (Milan: Electa Editrice, 1978), 128-132.

[443] Landmann, *Ascona — Monte Verità; auf der Suche nach dem Paradies*, 258; Riess, *Ascona*, 97 and 104-105; and Ursula von Wiese, *Vogel Phönix*, 127-129.

[444] The photograph was published in: Alfred Flechtheim, "Ascona, Lausanne, Winterthur," *Der Querschnitt*, volume IX, number 10 (October, 1929), 726-727 plus illustrations on unnumbered pages, here illustration facing page 726.

[445] Willy Rotzler, "Der Baron auf dem Monte Verità," in: Borsano, editor, *Monte Verità*, 103. The photograph later appeared in: Landmann, *Ascona — Monte Verità; auf der Suche nach dem Paradies*, 153; and in: Max Dohner, "Das 'Würstchen' Verdarb den Spass [The Little Clown Spoils The Fun]," *Limmattaler Tageblatt*, September 1, 2001, section 3, page [1].

[446] Dohner, "Das 'Würstchen' Verdarb den Spass," section 3, page [1].

Ursula von Wiese was later married to Werner Johannes Guggenheim (1895-1946).

292) of 1929 that was also included in an exhibition,[447] Ellen also appears nude with a group of women in the marble outdoor swimming pool; she is seen from behind, the second woman from the right,[448] and in still another photograph of 1929 she is one of three nude women in the pool (DVD figure 293 left). The photographs were made by Ado von Achenbach, a theatre director from Kassel, whose wife, Lilo, was one of the seven women who were regular guests of Emden.[449]

Ellen recalled that during her first summer at Ascona (1929),[450] while she was one of Emden's unclothed guests, he fell in love with her and bought her a Fiat open automobile. She is seen behind the Fiat's large steering wheel (a characteristic of Fiat automobiles at the time), on a Moholy-designed magazine cover for *die neue linie* for December, 1930. (DVD figure 274) Ellen, however, was not forthcoming with any further details of her relationship with Emden. Nevertheless, ironically, it was in Ellen's Fiat that she drove Moholy to Marseille in 1931, and also to Finland in the same year. In an interview she later described how she and László had fun together as they traveled in this open car.[451]

Evidently Emden was smitten by Ellen Frank during a period of emotional vulnerability following the rejection of his marriage proposal to another woman, referred to above. It is hard to get exact dates from the available accounts, but it was likely not long after his gift of the Fiat to Ellen Frank that Emden became enamored of a young woman he had admired in Hamburg. She moved to Ascona at age eighteen and bonded with Emden partly because he admired her physical beauty and partly because she had a

---

[447]Landmann, *Ascona — Monte Verità; auf der Suche nach dem Paradies, 160*

[448]Identified in Ursula von Wiese, *Vogel Phönix*, 126.

[449]Ursula von Wiese, *Vogel Phönix*, 127; and Dohner, "Das 'Würstchen' Verdarb den Spass," section 3, page [1].

[450]As for Moholy, he was in Ascona during part of the summer of 1930, at least from July 30 to August 15; see: Alexander Dorner to László Moholy-Nagy, TLS, August 1, 1930; and László Moholy-Nagy to Alexander Dorner, ALS, August 9, 1930. Both letters are in the Dorner-Archiv, Sprengel Museum in Hanover, and are reproduced in: Monika Flacke-Knoch, *Museumskonzeptionen in der Weimarer Republik; die Tätigkeit Alexander Dorners im Provinzialmuseum in Hannover* (Marburg: Jonas Verlag, 1985), 164-166.

The August 1, 1930, letter is reproduced, and both letters are transcribed, in: Christoph Brockhaus and Manfred Fath, editors, *Malewitsch-Mondrian, Konstruktion als Konzept, Alexander Dorner gewidmet; eine Ausstellung des Wilhelm Hack Museum, Ludwigshafen: Kunstverein Hannover, 27. März bis 1. Mai 1977*, 2. veränderte Auflage (Ludwigshafen: Wilhelm-Hack-Museum, 1977), 8-9 and 12-13. See also: László Moholy-Nagy to Alexander Dorner, ALS, July 30, 1930, Dorner-Archiv, Sprengel Museum in Hanover, transcribed in *ibid.*, 14.

[451]Notes made by Hattula Moholy-Nagy from her interviews with Ellen Frank in Munich, April 29th, 1981, and June 28th, 1982.

gift for humor, and was able to cheer up an often moody companion.[452] I could not ascertain her real name, only her nickname, Würstchen. (The name means little clown [a diminutive of *Hanswurst*], but it is also a synonym for a small sausage.)[453] In any case it remains unknown whether Ellen Frank's attraction to Moholy or Max Emden's attraction to Würstchen prevented a deeper relationship from developing between Max and Ellen.

The trip to Finland began June 26th, 1931.[454] Moholy had met Alvar Aalto in 1929, and had renewed his acquaintance in Berlin in 1930. He and Ellen spent some time with Aalto in Berlin in 1931, when he was visiting the *Deutsche Bauausstellung* there[455] (that event is discussed below). Aalto's biographer, Göran Schildt, provided more details about the trip itself and how it came about:

> In Berlin, Aalto depicted the fascination of the northern summer and the beauty of Finland in such glowing colours that Moholy and Ellen were possessed by the desire to see this miracle with their own eyes. Why not go to Finland during their approaching summer holidays and spend some more time with their cheerful Finnish friend?
>
> So it was that Laszlo and Ellen arrived in Ellen's Fiat in Turku on June 3rd, 1931 [*sic*; see note 454], where they were welcomed by Alvar and Aino [Alvar's wife, née Mandelin, 1894-1949]. They toured the interior together via Savonlinna in the east to Oulu in the northwest, where Moholy photographed Aalto's newly completed factory buildings for the Toppila Pulp Mill. In Oulu their ways parted. . . . Laszlo and Ellen left their car in Finland and set out for Oslo and Stockholm. . . .
>
> As souvenirs of his trip, Moholy brought back an experimental film, a quantity of photographs, and an unforgettable memory of the medieval church of Hattula.[456]

---

[452] Riess, *Ascona*, 102-103 and 106; Dohner, "Das 'Würstchen' Verdarb den Spass," section 3, page [1]; and Doris Hasenfratz, *Das Schicksal der Brissago-Inseln: vom Venustempel zum Eukalyptusbaum/Il Destino delle Isole di Brissago: dal Tempio di Venere all'Albero Eucalipto* (Ascona: Edizione Ferien-Journal Ascona, 1994), 36 and 38.

[453] Riess, *Ascona*, 103.

[454] See: László Moholy-Nagy to Raoul Hausmann, June 24, 1931, written in ink on a postcard with rubber-stamp impression listing the Fredericiastraße address, Künstler-Archive, Berlinische Galerie, Berlin. A transcript of the letter appeared in: Eva Züchner, editor, *Scharfrichter der bürgerlichen Seele, Raoul Hausmann in Berlin 1900-1933; unveröffentlichte Briefe, Texte, Dokumente aus den Künstler-Archiven der Berlinischen Galerie* (Ostfildern, Germany: Hatje, 1998), 369-370.

[455] Schildt, *Alvar Aalto*, 70-71.

[456] Schildt, *Alvar Aalto*, 74. Schildt does not make clear what the details of the itinerary were nor what modes of transportation were used in addition to Ellen's car.

(continued...)

Another city they visited was Narvik in northern Norway, and from there Moholy telegraphed Aalto that they had run out of money and asked him for a loan.[457]

Numerous photographs were made by Moholy on this trip. Some were made at the waterfront in Stockholm; (DVD figures 294 and 295 left) one of these shows an odd affinity to an earlier photogram. (DVD figure 295 right). A photograph of an elderly woman and a baby beside a Finnish lake (DVD figure 296) makes a nice contrast with a photograph of an Aalto-designed wood-pulp mill at Toppila. (DVD figure 297) Aino Aalto made a photograph of Moholy during the visit that shows him wearing a beret and a slicker and holding his Ernemann camera.[458] (DVD figure 55) Another photograph, probably also made by her, shows him and Ellen drinking coffee at an outdoor table on which what appears to be a movie camera is perched. (DVD figure 298)

Meanwhile, the man who gave the car to Ellen Frank, Max Emden, did not fare well during the Depression, at least partly because it had hit *Rudolph Karlstadt A.G.* very hard. Emden's son, Hans-Erich, a New York banker, tried to warn his father of the impending 1929 stock market crash, but his warnings went unheeded.[459] By 1931 shares of stock in *Rudolph Karlstadt A.G.* were worth only a small fraction of their previous value.[460] On June 9th of that year, Emden's extensive art collection (or at least part of it) was put up for auction in Berlin. Included were paintings by Feuerbach, Courbet, Degas, Monet, Munch and Gauguin, as well as ceramics, furniture and other items.[461] The days of the lavish pool-and-palace parties had evidently come to an end, although Emden did have the resources to retain his home on San Pancrazio and another nearby on the mainland until his death in 1940.[462]

---

[456](...continued)
Sibyl mentioned a film made in Sweden that Moholy was editing in Berlin in 1933: "I am cutting some old film which I made two years ago in Finnland [*sic*] . . ."; Sibyl Moholy-Nagy, "My Life in Germany," page 131, microfilm reel 946, frame 0763, Moholy-Nagy files, Archives of American Art, Washington, D.C.

[457]László Moholy-Nagy to Alvar Aalto, telegram, July 25, 1931, Alvar Aalto Archives, Helsinki and Jyväskylä, Finland.

[458]Schildt, *Alvar Aalto*, 220.

[459]Riess, *Ascona*, 193.

[460]Lenz, *Karstadt*, 332.

[461]*Die Sammlung Dr. Max Emden, Hamburg: Gemälde, deutscher und französischer Meister des 19. Jahrhunderts, Möbel. Teppiche, Bronzen, deutsches Silber, Fayencen*, Katalog Nr. XIII (Berlin: Hermann Ball, Paul Graupe, 1931); and Luckhardt and Schneede, editors, *Private Schätze*, 222 and 261-262.

[462]Riess, *Ascona*, 159.

Film-script editor, author and actress Sibyl Pietzsch (1903-1971)[463] entered Moholy's life at some point before the end of 1931 and from then on was a significant part of it as long as he lived. She wrote that: "*Madame Butterfly* was still playing in the Kroll Opera House when I took over the scenario office of a large motion-picture company in Berlin [*i.e.*, Tobis])."[464] As noted above, the last performance of *Butterfly* at the Kroll was July 2nd, 1931. She also wrote that she met her future husband "in the winter of 1931," by which she evidently meant that she had met him shortly before the end of the year, after she had been working at Tobis for about six months. This is borne out by her first known letter to Moholy, sent from Oberhof, Thuringia, and dated December 30, 1931.[465]

In any case it was their mutual interest in film that brought them together. Sibyl had been an acclaimed actress, on stage and screen.[466] As the head of the scenario office at Tobis,[467] she was working for a pioneer of the sound film at a time when written screenplays for sound films were still an innovation. In her appearances as an actress, and in her work as editor of film scenarios, she was known as Sibyl Peach. After leaving Tobis, she worked at other film-production companies in Berlin until she moved with her husband to London in June of 1935.[468]

---

[463] Sibyl Pietzsch was known professionally in the late 1920s and early 1930s as Sibyl Peach; and occasionally in the 1940s she was known as Sibyl Peech. Her name on her birth certificate was: Dorothea Pauline Maria Alice Sibylle Pietzsch.("Geburtsurkunde," microfilm reel 946, frame 0867, Moholy-Nagy papers, Archives of American Art, Washington, D.C.)

She was the daughter of Dresden architect Martin Pietzsch (1866-1961) and Fanny Henriette (née Clauß; 1866-1945). For more about her life, see: Appendix D.

[464] Sibyl Moholy-Nagy, *Moholy-Nagy, Experiment in Totality*, 57.

[465] Sibyl Moholy-Nagy to László Moholy-Nagy, MLS, December 30, 1931, Moholy-Nagy papers, microfilm reel 951, frames 0021 and 0022, Moholy-Nagy files, Archives of American Art, Washington, D.C.

[466] Gero Gandert, editor, *Der Film der Weimarer Republik, 1929; ein Handbuch der zeitgenössischen Kritik* (Berlin: Walter de Gruyter, 1993), [333]-335; clippings of newspaper reviews of stage and screen productions in which Sibyl Peach appeared, most preserved without dates, are on microfilm reel 948, frames 0510-0536; published and unpublished photographs documenting her roles on stage and screen are on microfilm reel 946, frames 1193 to 1267; and a listing of her stage roles is on microfilm reel 944, frame 3108, Moholy-Nagy papers, Archives of American Art, Washington, D.C.

[467] Sibyl Moholy-Nagy, "My Life in Germany," microfilm reel 946, pages 15-20 on frames 0646-0650, pages 34-36 on frames 0664-0666 *et passim*, Moholy-Nagy files, Archives of American Art, Washington, D.C.

[468] Sibyl Moholy-Nagy, "My Life in Germany," microfilm reel 946, pages 50-54 on frames 0680-0684 *et passim*, There are also numerous letters that she wrote to Moholy discussing her work in film, *e.g.*, Sibyl Moholy-Nagy to László Moholy-Nagy, TLS, November 8yh, 1934, microfilm reel 951, frames 0161 and 0162, Moholy-Nagy files, Archives of American Art, Washington, D.C.

A LTHOUGH THEY REMAINED on good terms with their former spouses, László and Sibyl had each experienced a failed marriage, and neither initially seemed to feel a need for formalizing the new relationship into which they had entered. It was Sibyl who began to change her mind. On October 17, 1934, she wrote from Berlin to László in Amsterdam about getting married, and acknowledged that he might find the idea bourgeois: "Ich weiss, dass es Dir sicher sehr spiessig vorkommt, dass ich jetzt plötzlich heiraten möchte. . . ." [I know that it will surely seem very bourgeois to you that I suddenly might want to get married. . . .] She pointed out some of the practical difficulties Hattula and they might face if they remained unmarried. Sibyl had already discussed some of these difficulties with her attorney. She also showed concern for the political uncertainties they faced, as well as what would happen to László's works of art if he should die.[469] Plans to have a wedding in Berlin had to be scrapped because of xenophobic regulations making marriages between Germans and foreigners almost impossible.[470] So Sibyl and László were married in London on January 25th, 1935.[471]

Sibyl and László had two daughters, Hattula Moholy-Nagy (born 1933), who became a Mesoamerican archaeologist, as well as the steward of her parents' legacy, and Claudia Moholy-Nagy (1936-1971), who taught theatre at Kendall College in Evanston, Illinois, and was director of the Victor Gruen Foundation for Environmental Studies at the time of her premature death.

In addition to his Berlin studio on Fredericiastraße, which he used as living quarters from time to time, as noted above, László and Lucia had occupied all or part of a garden house at Spichernstraße 20, at least by July, 1928.[472] There they had a darkroom and studio in addition to living quarters[473] and probably also storage space. Moholy continued to list the Spichernstraße address after he and Lucia no longer lived together, perhaps because of the darkroom and studio facilities. At some point in 1933 László

---

[469] Sibyl Moholy-Nagy to László Moholy-Nagy, TLS, October 17, 1934, microfilm reel 951, frames 0155 and 0156, Moholy-Nagy files, Archives of American Art, Washington, D.C.

[470] Sibyl Moholy-Nagy, "My Life in Germany," pages 132-133 on microfilm reel 946, frames 0764 and 0765, Moholy-Nagy files, Archives of American Art, Washington, D.C.

[471] A microfilm copy of the wedding document is in the Moholy-Nagy papers, microfilm reel 946, frame 0881, Archives of American Art, Washington, D.C. Witnesses were Philip Morton Shand and his fourth wife, Sybil Mary née Sissons. The London address for the wedding couple was given as the Cumberland Hotel at the Marble Arch in Hyde Park.

Philip Morton Shand and his first wife, Edith Marguerite née Harrington, were the grandparents of Camilla, Duchess of Cornwall.

[472] Lucia Moholy to Katherine Dreier, ALS, July 23, 1928, Katherine Dreier papers, box 24, folder 701, Beinecke Library, Yale University, New Haven, Connecticut.

[473] Max Gebhard described his beginning to work for Moholy in the autumn of 1928 at the dwelling of the Moholys on Spichernstraße, and mentions the studio and darkroom and also that they sometimes shared lunch with him there; see his "Erinnerungen," 181-182.

moved into an apartment on Lietzenseeufer 2 that had cellar storage;[474] Sibyl and Hattula moved into another apartment in the same building, this one with attic storage, around the end of March, 1934.[475]

Lietzenseeufer parallels the shoreline of a small lake (*Lietzensee*) in a leafy area of the Charlottenburg borough of Berlin, near where László and Lucia had lived in 1920. By the time of the move to the Lietzenseeufer apartment László had begun his work in Holland so he lived there only sporadically, but Sibyl and Hattula lived there until they moved to London. Also living at Lietzenseeufer 2 was a nursemaid for Hattula, who did not accompany her mother on trips to Amsterdam and London.

The move to London was facilitated when Moholy met with the British consul in Berlin by March 31st, 1935. This consul was sympathetic to him, at least in part because he knew something about Gropius.[476] Herbert Read served as a sponsor for Moholy's immigration to Britain.[477]

AFTER ARRIVING IN LONDON on Sunday, May 19th, or Monday, May 20th, 1935,[478] László lived in a small furnished apartment he had rented at number 16 Lawn Road Flats (Wells Coates, 1933-1934) while Hattula and Sibyl remained in Berlin arranging the move of their possessions. When the latter two arrived in England about June 25th,[479] Sibyl shared the small apartment in the Lawn Road Flats with her

---

[474] Moholy made reference to a cellar storage area that went with the apartment on Lieteznseeufer in: László Moholy-Nagy to Ise and Walter Groipius, TLS, December 23, 1934, Bauhaus-Archiv, Berlin; an English translation is in: Senter, "Moholy-Nagy in England," 323-324. Moholy's places of residences, beginning with his move to Germany, are listed in a forthcoming catalogue raisonné of Moholy' photograms.

[475] The information is from a letter from Sibyl Moholy-Nagy to her family in Loschwitz near Dresden, March 27, 1934; a copy of the letter is in the files of Hattula Moholy-Nagy, Ann Arbor, Michigan. The letter was sent from Meerscheidtstraße 13-15; her previous address had been: Wacholderweg 9. Both addresses are in the Charlottenburg borough of Berlin.

Concerning the attic, used to store paintings, see: László Moholy-Nagy to Sibyl Moholy-Nagy, TLS, October 7, 1934, in the files of Hattula Moholy-Nagy, Ann Arbor, Michigan.

[476] László Moholy-Nagy to Walter Gropius, TLS, March 31, 1935.

[477] Kostelanetz, editor, *Moholy-Nagy*, xvii.

[478] László Moholy-Nagy to Walter Gropius, TLS, May 13, 1935, Bauhaus-Archiv, Berlin; a transcription of the German text and English translation appeared in: Senter, "Moholy-Nagy in England," 328.

[479] Sibyl Moholy-Nagy to László Moholy-Nagy, TLS, June 18, 1935, microfilm reel 951, frames 0169 and 0170, Moholy-Nagy files, Archives of American Art, Washington, D.C.

husband, an apartment next to one occupied by Carola Giedion-Welcker[480] and one occupied by Ise and Walter Gropius.[481] Meanwhile Hattula stayed with architect Ernő Goldfinger and his wife, Ursula (née Blackwell), in London.[482] Sibyl and László later stayed at the manor house of film producer John Mathias in the ancient fishing town of Bosham, on the Sussex coast near Chichester.[483] Mathias was described by Sibyl as "a wealthy young Englishman who in the best amateur tradition had switched from polo to movies," and remembered his family with whom she and László had stayed as "eccentric"; it was while staying with the Mathias family that László began to shoot the film *Lobsters*, discussed below.[484] The Goldfingers brought Hattula to Bosham for at least one visit.[485]

Moholy had met Ernő Goldfinger (1902 - 1987) at least by 1933 at the *CIAM* Congress in Athens, but he probably first met him in 1930 in Paris at the Deutsche Werkbund exhibition there, discussed below. In 1934 he asked Moholy to create some photomurals for a hairdressing salon for Helena Rubinstein that he was designing, but although elegant models for the murals were made the salon project was not carried out.[486] (DVD figures 299A and 299B)

Temporary living arrangements for Moholy and his wife and daughter continued during three months of house hunting; among those who aided in the search was J.G. Crowther's German wife, Francisca.[487] In early August László rented a house for his family at 7 Farm Walk, dating from about 1907,[488] (DVD figure 300-302) which included a garden. (DVD figure 303) It is near the Golders Green station on the London Transport system, a grade-level station built just to the north of the Hampstead underground station. The Hampstead station served a favored neighborhood for artists

---

[480]Pritchard, *View from a Long Chair*, 111; and Sibyl Moholy-Nagy to Jack Pritchard, TLS, February 12, 1970, Pritchard Papers, Library of the University of East Anglia, Norwich.

[481]László Moholy-Nagy to "mr. hobson," carbon copy of TLS, April 10, 1935, Bauhaus-Archiv, Berlin.

[482]Senter, "Moholy-Nagy in England," 42.

[483]Sibyl Moholy-Nagy, *Moholy-Nagy, Experiment in Totality*, 126. Goldfinger had known John Mathias since their school days in Switzerland; see: Senter, "Moholy-Nagy in England," 64.

[484]Sibyl Moholy-Nagy, *Moholy-Nagy, Experiment in Totality*, 126.

[485]Senter, "Moholy-Nagy in England," 42.

[486]Senter, "Moholy-Nagy in England," 21.

[487]Senter, "Moholy-Nagy in Engand," 42.

[488]See: Sibyl Moholy-Nagy to László Moholy-Nagy, TLS, January 30, 1937, microfilm reel 951, frame 0199, Moholy-Nagy files, Archives of American Art, Washington, D.C. The letter contains a reference to a rental of twenty-six pounds and five shillings due on February 1, 1937, to Donald Overy of London.

and writers. When the Golders Green station was opened in 1907, its neighborhood had been only sparsely populated. Actually the unrealized Helena Rubenstein project of 1934 (DVD figure 299) was for a salon in the Golders Green neighborhood.[489]

At 7 Farm Walk, Moholy lived under the same roof as Hattula for the first time, and shortly after her birth, on March 25th, 1936, his second daughter, Claudia.[490] Moholy referred to himself as a *familienvater* in a letter to his friend, Paul Citroen, describing the joys of being able to spend a whole day with his family on the Easter holiday and, indeed, he seemed to have become a settled family man when he wrote of his newfound "*netten familienleben*" [pleasant family life].[491] A bit later he wrote to his friends the Giedions of living with five women under one roof: wife, two daughters, nanny and maid.[492]

IF SOME ASPECTS OF HIS NEW LIFE STYLE might be considered by some as bourgeois, the same could be said for the house on Farm Walk, a stark contrast to the modernist Lawn Road Flats. The latter had been designed for "young professional men and women with few possessions."[493] Planned jointly by Wells Coates, who had been trained as an engineer,[494] and by the two people who put together funding for the project, Jack Pritchard and his wife Molly, it is considered one of the most important structures in early English Modernism, with its lack of ornament, exposed reenforced-concrete surfaces and horizontal massing.[495] Among the building's admirers were Walter and Ise Gropius, who lived there for two-and-a-half years;[496] another resident was Marcel Breuer. The house Moholy chose on Farm Walk, however, is a simple gabled, semi-detached house; the architectural historian Sir John Summerson memorably remarked: "what a comic setting the neat little bourgeois house was for such a personality."[497]

---

[489]Senter, "Moholy-Nagy in England," 21.

[490]Claudia Moholy-Nagy died September 21st, 1971. I did have the pleasure of meeting her in Chicago not long before her tragic early death.

[491]László Moholy-Nagy to Paul Citroen, ALS, April 13th, 1936, Bauhus-Archiv, Berlin.

[492]László Moholy-Nagy to Sigfried Giedion and Carola Giedion-Welcker, May 22nd, 1936, ALS, Giedion Family archives, Zurich.

[493]Pritchard, *View from a Long Chair*, 79-80.

[494]Buckley, *Isokon*, 4-5.

[495]On the Lawn Road Flats, see: Pritchard, *View from a Long Chair*, 78-98; and Buckley, *Isokon*, 5-9 and 11-13.

[496]Pritchard, *View from a Long Chair*, 96.

[497]Senter, "Moholy-Nagy in England," 42, 274 and 369.

Of course the appearance of the house did not limit what went on inside, which was usually anything but bourgeois. There was room for Moholy to have his own studio, and many of his exploratory works of fine art, along with innovative graphic design, emerged from the house on Farm Walk. Moreover, Sibyl began her career as a writer there. The guest list for gatherings at the house included numerous names of people who could best be described as avant-garde. Among them were: artists Ben Nicholson, Barbara Hepworth, Hans Arp, and Max Ernst; art-historian Carola Giedion-Welcker; film-maker Vincent Korda; documentary film-maker John Grierson; architect-designers Wells Coates and Marcel Breuer along with Walter Gropius and Serge Chermayeff and their wives Ise and Barbara (née Barbara Maitland May; 1904–2000); designers György Kepes and Harry Blacker as well as Jan Tschichold; writer and editor J.M. (Sir James Maude) Richards; science writer J.G. Crowther and his wife, Francisca; and biologist and writer Julian Huxley.[498] Probably also present from time to time (although documentation is lacking) was editor and art historian Sir Nikolaus Pevsner, whom Moholy had met in Dresden in 1926 and with whom he corresponded later when he was living in Chicago and Pevsner was living in England.

Sibyl got the Farm Walk house ready to move into while László was spending part of August at La Sarraz in Switzerland,[499] having left London about August 7th.[500] Sibyl and Hattula moved into the house about August 10th, and Lucia Moholy was a temporary member of the household, with plans to move out on September 15th, 1935.[501]

During a five-day stay in Budapest in early spring, 1934, Moholy had visited his mother whom he had not seen recently.[502] A longer visit to Hungary took place in 1936. Moholy secured a leave of absence from his demanding job at Simpson, Piccadilly, described at the end of this chapter, and had planned a leisurely vacation to be spent mostly in Budapest and at Hungary's Lake Balaton,[503] one of the largest in Europe. Just before leaving London, however, he accepted an offer from a London picture agency to document the Olympic Games, held August 1st through 16th, 1936, in Berlin, with a sixteen-millimeter film plus whatever number of still photographs he wished to make. Moholy explained to his wife that: "They want me to catch the spectator psychology, the

---

[498]Senter, "Moholy-Nagy in England," 46-47 *et passim*.

[499]Antoine Baudin, *Hélène de Mandrot et la Maison des Artistes de la Sarraz* (Lausanne: Edition Payot, 1998), 319; Sibyl Moholy-Nagy to László Moholy-Nagy, TLS, August 15, 1935, microfilm reel 951, frames 0174 and 0175, Moholy-Nagy files, Archives of American Art, Washington, D.C.

[500]Sibyl Moholy-Nagy to László Moholy-Nagy, TLS, August 10, 1935, microfilm reel 951, frames 0172 and 0173, Moholy-Nagy files, Archives of American Art, Washington, D.C.

[501]*Ibid*.

[502]The information is from a letter from Sibyl Moholy-Nagy to her family in Loschwitz near Dresden, March 27, 1934.

[503]Sibyl Moholy-Nagy, *Moholy-Nagy, Experiment in Totality*, 131.

physiognomic contrast between an international crowd and the rabid German nationalists."[504]

Moholy sailed for Germany in the middle of July. However, he found the atmosphere in Berlin unbearably oppressive and shortly after the games had begun he left Germany.[505] The reader will feel the loss of Moholy's film especially strongly since his withdrawal from the scene meant there would be no leavening of the aura created by the skillful but uncritical Olympic coverage by famed film director and Nazi sympathizer Leni Riefenstahl (1902-2003).[506]

While in Berlin, Moholy also discovered that some of his works that had been stored in Berlin with a former housekeeper of Sibyl's had been destroyed because she had decided that they were examples of *Kulturbolschevismus*. Sibyl had found that on moving from Berlin to London she had not had room on the van for about thirty canvases and metal constructions. No second truck was available so she left them with her former housekeeper. The works were described as ". . . Moholy's earliest work, representing the transition from representational to abstract painting." [507] Sibyl later regretted her "personal ignorance" in trying to cope with this situation.[508]

The chronology for the 1936 visit to Hungary is impossible to reconstruct exactly from the available evidence. Sibyl wrote to her mother that she would be in Hungary on August 15th, and asked if she could leave Hattula and Claudia with her in Loschwitz while she was in Hungary.[509] Assuming the daughters were dropped off beforehand and Sibyl was in Hungary on August 15th, it is not clear where Moholy was after leaving the Olympic games early, but most likely he was in Budapest; Sibyl wrote only that he joined her at Lake Balaton.

In any case, Sibyl and László seemed to have a relaxing vacation after arriving at the Sporthotel at Tihany,[510] a resort town on a peninsula jutting into Lake Balaton. Sharing

---

[504]*Ibid.*

[505]Sibyl Moholy-Nagy, *Moholy-Nagy, Experiment in Totality*, 131-133.

[506]*Olympia*, two parts, both released in 1938.

[507]Sibyl Moholy-Nagy, *Moholy-Nagy, Experiment in Totality*, 132-133.

[508]Sibyl Moholy-Nagy to Lucia Moholy, TLS, November 15, 1947, Bauhaus-Archiv. Berlin.

[509]Sibyl Moholy-Nagy to Fanny Pietzsch, June 22, 1936; a copy of the letter is in the files of Hattula Moholy-Nagy, Ann Arbor.

[510]Sibyl Moholy-Nagy to Fanny Pietzsch, August 25, 1936; a copy of the letter is in the files of Hattula Moholy-Nagy, Ann Arbor.

their vacation was Sibyl's sister Eva from Loschwitz.[511] Sibyl, visiting Hungary for her first time, remembered floating at night on a flat-bottomed boat and drinking Badaconyi [*sic*; *i.e.*, Badacsony] wine in the courtyard of an old castle.[512] She also recalled that it was the last real vacation that her husband ever had. While they were in Hungary, visits were made to Moholy's mother Karolin (surname uncertain at the time, either Weisz or Nagy) and to his brother Jenő Nagy in Budapest.[513]

The vacation ended early in September as Moholy left for the 1936 CIRPAC meeting held September 8th through 12th at La Sarraz, Switzerland (see page 490).[514] Moholy wrote to Citroen from Tihany on August 29th that he had planned to be back in London on September 15th. He added that the vacationers were very happy in Tihany, the weather was fine and activities included swimming and excursions.[515] Moholy's mother made one visit to London, as recalled by her granddaughter, Hattula; this was a visit made in 1936, as documented by a photograph of Karolin made in Paris by Ergy Landau. (DVD figure 304) Perhaps Karolin met her son in Paris after he left La Sarraz and accompanied him to London. If not, then Karolin made a separate trip, perhaps meeting her son in Paris later in 1936, and then traveling on to London with him. In any case she is shown wearing a sweater, indicating that she was in Paris after summer had ended.

Moholy had an ability to maintain contact with women with whom he had been romantically involved, and Sibyl seemed to have little jealousy of social relationships based on past attachments of her husband. An example is the invitation to Ellen Frank in the Spring of 1937 to stay with László and Sibyl in August, when she had planned to do something in London, although, in the end, her stay at 7 Farm Walk did not take place.[516]

Vision in Motion: New Ideas for Sound and Movies

Two of Moholy's experimental films were basically an extension of his idea of creating sounds by scratching them into a phonograph record, as described in earlier

---

[511]Sibyl Moholy-Nagy to Fanny Pietzsch, August 25, 1936.

[512]Sibyl Moholy-Nagy, *Moholy-Nagy, Experiment in Totality*, 132.

[513]Sibyl Moholy-Nagy, *Moholy-Nagy, Experiment in Totality*, 133-134.

[514]Baudin, *Hélène de Mandrot*, 203.

[515]László Moholy-Nagy to Paul Citroen, MLS (*i.e.*, postcard), August 29, 1936, Bauhaus-Archiv, Berlin.

[516]László Moholy-Nagy to Walter and Ise Gropius, photocopy of TLS, May 28, 1937, and photocopy of TLS, June 18, 1937, Bauhaus-Archiv, Berlin.

chapters (see pages 170, 191-192 and 250-253) but now updated for sound film.[517] Both are now lost, and if they had titles there is no record of them. The first probably was never more than informal, untitled footage and seemingly dates from 1931 because it was shown to Sibyl when László had first met her. Sibyl wrote: that he ". . . worked on a sound film engraving linear shapes on film negative." She added:

> When he played it back on a sound projector he achieved a coincidence of tone and line that had never been demonstrated before. "I can play your profile," he would say to a friend, sketching the outline of the face in his notebook. "I wonder how your nose would sound."[518]

The other film seemed tame by comparison:

> That night [*i.e.*, at one of a series of "open house" Sunday-evening gatherings in Berlin] Moholy showed his latest film experiment—the ABC's scratched into a sound track. Played back it produced a strange tone sequence, a third dimension, so to speak, to the written and spoken alphabet.[519]

The date would have been in late in 1933, because that evening Moholy also showed movie sequences of his older daughter, Hattula, born on October 11th of that year.[520] It is not clear where the gathering took place, but it was likely in Sibyl's apartment at Meerscheidtstraße 13-15, in the Charlottenburg borough of Berlin.[521] The birth of Hattula, by the way, was celebrated by her father in a very characteristic way, as he recorded her in a movie begun when she was one day old. Her younger sister, Claudia, was also honored with a film.[522]

The first documented theatrical showing of the ". . . sound film engraving linear shapes on film negative" took place in London on December 10th of the same year, 1933, as one of "two experimental synthetic sound tracks by Professor L. Moholy-Nagy and

---

[517]Moholy had begun thinking about the optophonetic possibilites of sound film as early as 1928; see: László Moholy-Nagy, "elementare buchtechnik," footnote on page 62.

[518]Sibyl Moholy-Nagy, *Moholy-Nagy, Experiment in Totality*, 68.

[519]Sibyl Moholy-Nagy, *Moholy-Nagy, Experiment in Totality*, 96-97.

[520]These were evidently an early sequence from a movie of Hattula's earliest years, shot from 1933 to about 1936. The film, about twenty minutes in length, is a silent film usually known as *Hattula*. A print is in the Hattula Moholy-Nagy files, Ann Arbor, Michigan.

[521]Sibyl Moholy-Nagy, *Moholy-Nagy, Experiment in Totality*, 96-97; see also note 474.

[522]*Claudia*, 1936, 20 minutes, silent; Walter Gropius appears in one sequence shot in the house occupied by the Moholy-Nagys at 7 Farm Walk Lane in London. A print is in the Hattula Moholy-Nagy files, Ann Arbor, Michigan.

Oscar Fischinger."[523] This lost sound track was called by Moholy *Tönendes ABC*, or as *The Sound ABC* when he described it in *Vision in Motion*:

> I used all types of signs, symbols, even the letters of the alphabet, and my own finger prints. Each visual pattern on the sound track produced a sound which had the character of whistling and other noises. I had especially good results with profiles of persons.[524]

For the London showing, sponsored by the Film Society and seen at the Tivoli Palace Theatre, the film was billed as *A.B.C. in Sound.* The description in *The Film Society Programme* suggested a touch of humor:

> In this light-hearted experiment, Professor Moholy-Nagy indicates the difference in sound produced by arbitrary manipulation of the sound-track. Every change in the pattern of the track, whether typography, profile or other design, is immediately audible. The sound-track has been re-photographed so as to appear on the screen, simultaneously with the sound it is responsible for.[525]

Another early showing of *The Sound ABC* was on March 5th, 1934, at Masaryk University in Brno. (DVD figure 352)

It should be noted that not only did Moholy's experiments with using images directly on a film sound-track grow out of his earlier idea of scratching sounds into a wax disc to create a phonograph record, they also were part of the contemporary dialogue among avant-garde musicians. Moholy had entered that dialogue even before his Bauhaus years, as noted in Chapter Two. By 1923 his article in *Der Sturm*, "Neue Gestaltung in der Musik: Möglichkeiten des Grammophons," (July, 1923) had caught the attention of Hans Heinz Stuckenschmidt, as discussed in Chapter Three, while both were present in Weimar during the summer of 1923.

Moholy's role in the direct manipulation of sound in the sound track of motion pictures has recently been summarized by Thomas Y. Levin:

> . . . Moholy-Nagy immediately recognized in the new *optical* film sound processes being adopted in the late 1920s a means to effectively realize his long-standing groove-script vision. Here the technical difficulties posed by the

---

[523]"The Film Society," *The Times* (London), December 1, 1933, 12.

Oscar Fischinger (1900-1967) was a German experimental film-maker who later worked in the United States. There is no record of any contact between Fischinger and Moholy other than that sometimes their films were shown on the same program.

[524]László Moholy-Nagy, *Vision in Motion*, 277.

[525]The Film Society Programme, December 10, 1933, reprinted in: *The Film Society Programmes, 1925-1939* (New York: Arno Press, 1972), [272]-[275], here 274.

miniature scale of the groove-script inscriptions were eliminated by a graphic transcription of sound that was visible to the human eye.[526]

Levin's assertion is based, not only on the creation of *The Sound ABC*, still influential in spite of being lost, but also on two challenging articles in the Hungarian-language magazine *Korunk*.[527] They have been reprinted in various languages and were utilized by Moholy in subsequent lectures, but the initial appearance in Hungarian meant that Moholy could work directly with the language he knew best and left it to translators to make these articles available in other languages. In the first of these articles he insisted that: "The sound film ought to enrich our aural experience sphere by giving us entirely unknown sound values, just as the silent film has already begun to enrich our vision."[528] In the second article he crowed that:

> We are in a position today to be able to play written sounds, music written by hand, without involving an orchestra, by the use of the apparatus of the sound film. It is a great pleasure for me to be able to report on this acoustical phenomenon; inasmuch as I had already explained it in articles and lectures ten years ago. . . . I am very happy today to witness the successful realization of those of my suggestions previously labelled absurd. At the time, my starting point was that phonograph records could be made on the basis of an "etched alphabet."[529]

PRIOR TO HIS EXPERIMENTS with film sound-tracks, Moholy was present at a concert of *Gramaphonmusik* in Berlin which featured music created directly on the phonograph disc by Hindemith and Ernst Toch (1887-1964), an event he took note of in a lecture and related article.[530] The concert took place Wednesday evening, June 18th, 1930, at the *Hochschule für Musik* as part of a five-day festival, "Neue Musik

---

[526]Thomas Y. Levin, "'Tones from out of Nowhere': Rudolf Pfenninger and the Archaeology of Sound," *Grey Room 12* (Summer, 2003), 32-79, here 47-48.

[527]László Moholy-Nagy, "Az új Film Problémái," *Korunk*, number 10 (1930), 712-719; later republished in translation, *e.g.*, "Problems of the Modern Film," in: Passuth, *Moholy-Nagy*, 311-315; and László Moholy-Nagy, "Új Filmkísérletek," *Korunk*, number 3 (1933), 231-237; later republished in translation, *e.g.*, "New Film Experiments," in: Passuth, *Moholy-Nagy*, 319-323. *Korunk* was a Hungarian-language periodical published in Cluj, Romania (formerly Kolosovár, Hungary). These somewhat overlapping essays are likely based on Moholy's lectures introducing screenings of Moholy's films in Budapest.

[528]László Moholy-Nagy, "Problems of the Modern Film," 314.

At the end of his text the dates 1928-1930 appear, as if Moholy had been developing the ideas in the essay for some time prior to their publication in 1930. In fact, many of these ideas appear in German in a concise form in: László Moholy-Nagy, "Die Optik im Tonfilm," *Film und Volk*, volume II, number 6 (July, 1929), 9-10; reprinted as "Dok. 126," in: Gaßner, editor, *Wechsel Wirkungen*, 464-465.

[529]László Moholy-Nagy, "New Film Experiments," 322.

[530]László Moholy-Nagy, "New Film Experiments," 322.

Berlin."[531] By the time of the *Gramaphonmusik* concert, Moholy and Hindemith probably knew they would be working together on Hindemith's *Here and There*; it opened November 29th, 1930, at the Kroll Opera, as discussed above. It should also be noted that the young American composer John Cage (1912-1992), who later taught music for Moholy in Chicago, was among those present at the *Gramaphonmusik* concert in Berlin.[532]

Recently an author of a book on the interaction of music and technology summed up:

> . . . if we consider nearly any major development in later twentieth-century music we can see its germination and anticipation in the music and thinking of Hindemith, Toch, Moholy-Nagy, Stuckenschmidt, and others. The idea behind electronic synthesis—the creation of music independent of traditional instruments and performance—was prefigured by disc inscription.[533]

It should be emphasized that there is no record that Moholy had any formal musical training; even in secondary school he did not take advantage of the singing lessons offered to his school's choristers.[534] On the other hand, he did include two examples of printed music in *Buch neuer Künstler* which he co-edited in 1922, as discussed in Chapter Two, and for the series of Bauhaus Books he co-edited he had planned two books on music (although in the end neither one was published).[535]

Since Germany was to become one of the countries where John Cage achieved the most renown, it should be noted that besides attending the *Gramaphonmusik* concert, the only other recorded activity in Germany on his first European trip was a visit to the

---

[531] Alfred Einstein, "Neue Musik Berlin 1930, I," *Berliner Tageblatt*, June 19, 1930, [3]; *idem*, "Berlin's New Music Festival," *New York Times*, August 10, 1930, X 5; Josef Häusler, *Spiegel der Neuen Musik: Donaueschingen; Chronik, Tendenzen, Werkbesprechungen* (Kassel: Bärenreiter-Verlag, 1996), 112-113 and 430-431; Martin Elste, "Hindemiths Versuche 'grammophonplatten eigener Stücke' im Kontext einer Ideengeschichte der Mechanischen Musik im 20. Jahrhundert" in: *Hindemith-Jahrbuch/Annales Hindemith 1996/XXV* (Mainz: Schott, 1996), 195-221, here 195-197 and 211-221; and Mark Katz, *Capturing Sound; How Technology Has Changed Music* (Berkeley: University of California Press, 2004), 99-104.

[532] Lawrence Wechsler, "My Grandfather's Tale," *The Atlantic*, volume CCLXXVIII, number 6 (December, 1996), 86-90, 92, 94, 96, 98, 101-102 and 104-106, here 96; reprinted in *idem*, *Vermeer in Bosnia; a Reader* (New York: Pantheon Books, 2004), 205-233, here 218.

[533] Katz, *Capturing Sound*, 112.

[534] According to published records in Szeged; see DVD figure 9 on the DVD accompanying *Moholy-Nagy: Mentor to Modernism* for a sample page.

[535] One would have been written by George Antheil and the other would have been written by Heinrich Jacoby; see text figure 11, DVD figure 178 the DVD accompanying *Moholy-Nagy: Mentor to Modernism*.

Bauhaus in Dessau; this took place, however, only after Moholy had left the Bauhaus.[536] But it should be added that since he spent some time in Paris in the spring and summer of 1930, and during part of that time studied with the Modernist Hungarian architect Ernő Goldfinger,[537] it is likely that Cage saw the German Werkbund exhibition in Paris, shown there from May 14th through July 13th, 1930. As discussed below, he would have seen a lot of work by Moholy and other Bauhäusler there. His traveling companion at the time, Don Sample (also known as Don St. Paul), had brought back from Europe to Southern California, where he and Cage were living at the time, what one of their acquaintances referred to as "the Bauhaus catalogue," with commentary on furniture and design detail.[538] That was probably the bi-lingual guidebook to the Werkbund exhibition in Paris (see note 758).

Moholy tried to interest the motion-picture company Tobis in his experimental film *Ein Lichtspiel Schwarz Weiß Grau,* or *A Lightplay Black White Gray* (DVD figure 352), but nothing came of the effort except that Sibyl began to become interested in his work.[539] The film was evidently newly finished when he met Sibyl, because Moholy had written on October 26th, 1931, that he was still making sketches for it.[540]

A Lightplay Black White Gray (DVD figure 432) was passed by the censor, and was first shown publicly on Friday, March 4th, 1932, at the Kamera Cinema on *Unter den Linden* in Berlin, where it was billed as *Konstruktives Lichtspiel.*[541] What was completed was only one of six projected parts according to Moholy's published outline, as discussed below. The duration was probably something in the range of five to eight minutes.[542]

---

[536] Christopher Shultis, "Cage and Europe," in: David Nicholls, editor, *The Cambridge Companion to John Cage* (Cambridge, England: Cambridge University Press, 2002), 20-40, here 22-23.

[537] Shultis, "Cage and Europe," 21.

Goldfinger was discussed above in connection with Moholy's move to London in 1935.

[538] Stuart Timmons, *The Trouble with Harry Hay, Founder of the Modern Gay Movement* (Boston: Alyson Publications, 1990), 57-58.

[539] Sibyl Moholy-Nagy, *Moholy-Nagy; Experiment in Totality*, 57-62.

[540] László, Moholy-Nagy to Matthew Josephson, October 26, 1931.

[541] Jeanpaul Goergen, *m-n 100; Zum 100. Geburtstag von László Moholy-Nagy. 20. Juli 1995, Arsenal* [*i.e.,* Arsenal Cinema], *20.00 Uhr* (Berlin: Bauhaus-Archiv [und] Freunde der Deutschen Kinemathek, e.V., 1995), 2.

[542] Goergen, *op. cit.,* 2.

György Kepes recalled that he had made the opening sequence.[543] This consists of a transparent turning globe, around which is inscribed: "moholy=nagy zeigt ein lichtspiel." Shadows of the inscribed globe are thrown on a pale wall. This sequence recalls Kepes's work on the dust jacket for *The Outline of the Universe*, a 1931 book by J.G. Crowther and Moholy's first British commission, as discussed above. (DVD figure 269) When Crowther visited Moholy's Berlin studio in 1931 he observed that Kepes ". . . seemed to be doing all the work while Moholy acted as a supervisory manager," so one might conclude that since a motive similar to the opening sequence in *A Lightplay Black White Gray*, namely a globe with words circling it, was used on the dust jacket of *The Outline of the Universe* and two studies for it, both the opening sequence of the film and the dust jacket were made by Kepes.[544]

The showing of *A Lightplay Black White Gray* at Kamera Cinema is significant because it was obviously set up with the general public in mind (even if, on *Unter den Linden*, it would have been an upscale sector of the public), since featured on the program was German-American director William Wyler's 1930 Hollywood "Western" sound film, *Hell's Heroes* (billed in German as *Galgenvögel*), a critical and commercial success. Also on the program, as noted below, was Moholy's *Impressionen vom alten Marseiller Hafen* [*Impressions of the Old Port of Marseille*]; its duration was probably a bit over ten minutes.[545] And finally, after *Hell's Heroes*, there was a lecture by Moholy.[546] And, on top of all that, the theatre offered an exhibition of his work.[547]

THE REASON A COMMERCIAL CINEMA featured Moholy-Nagy so prominently might have had something to do with the familiarity he had developed with an upscale milieu of Berliners who by 1932 were familiar with his work principally through the Berlin showing of the traveling photography-and-film exhibition usually known as *FiFo* (discussed below), through his stage designs for the Kroll Opera and for Piscator, and through *die neue linie*.

---

[543] György Kepes interviewed by Lloyd C. Engelbrecht and Shirley McCollum in his home in Cambridge, Massachusetts, October 7th and 8th, 1978. Four tape cassettes and a copy in CD (compact-disc) format are in my collection.

[544] Senter, "Moholy-Nagy: the Transitional Years," 85; *idem*, "Moholy-Nagy in England," 151 and illustrations 1 a-c; and James Gerald Crowther, *Fifty Years with Science* (London: Barrie & Jenkins, 1970), 62. Senter reported that there were six studies for the cover ("Moholy-Nagy: the Transitional Years," note 5 on page 172).

Kepes told an interviewer only that he and Moholy had collaborated on the book jacket, but did not give details; see: György Kepes, interviewed by Robert Brown, March 7 and Aug. 30, 1972, and Jan. 11, 1973, pages 9.

[545] Goergen, *op. cit.*, 4; *Impressions of the Old Port of Marseille* is available from the Moholy-Nagy Foundation.

[546] Goergen, *op. cit.*, 2.

[547] Goergen, *op. cit.*, 2.

THE KAMERA SHOWING might have been the only time *A Lightplay Black White Gray* was offered to the general public and moreover the bill including it (but presumably without Moholy's lecture) played for just a week.[548] The other documented showings were in film-society, museum, or educational settings, and usually involved one or two screenings, but there were nevertheless so many such showings that the film must be considered a success. It was also Moholy's only film, except for *Impressions of the Old Harbor of Marseille* which shared the bill on March 4th, 1932, for which reviews were published the day after the opening.[549] One of these reviews appeared in *Vossische Zeitung*:

> Das Kameraprogramm bringt zwei neue Arbeiten von Professor Moholy-Nagy. Der Reportagefilm "Alter Hafen von Marseille" arbeitet scharf den Gegensatz zwischen dem weiten Hafen mit seinem geschäftigen Leben und den finsteren, engen schmutzigen Gäßchen des Hafenviertels heraus. Ein "Lichtspiel" in des Wortes ursprünglichem Sinn will der kurze zweite Bildstreifen sein. Er will nur Bewegungsbeziehungen geben und das Spiel von Licht und Schatten in einem Tanz von Gittern, Kugeln und Stäben festhalten. Gewiß ein eigenartiger Versuch, der sich allerdings in größerem Umfang kaum durchsetzen dürfte. Als Hauptfilm läuft in neuer Bearbeitung W. Wylers "Galgenvögel" (Hells Heroes).[550] [The program at the Kamera brings two new works from Professor Moholy-Nagy. The documentary film "Old Harbor of Marseille" brings out sharp contrast between the wide harbor with its busy activity and the dark, narrow, dirty alleys of the harbor neighborhood. The second short film is a "lightplay" in the original sense of that word. It presents only relative motion and the play of light and shadow caught in a dance of lattices, spheres, and rods. Surely a strange experiment that will, doubtless, scarcely be permitted to succeed in broader domains. The main feature is a new adaptation of W. Wyler's "Jailbirds" (Hell's Heroes).]

The two additional reviews published in Berlin on March 5, 1932, were more or less like the review in *Vossische Zeitung* in that *Impressions of the Old Harbor of Marseille*

---

[548]In a letter, Moholy stated that his films would run through Thursday [March 10th, 1932], László Moholy-Nagy to "Hausmanns" [*i.e.*, household of Raoul Hausmann], March 8, 1932, TLS with pencil corrections, Raoul Hausmann Archive, Berlinische Galerie, Berlin. A transcript and a reproduction of the letter appeared in: Züchner, editor, *Scharfrichter*, 418-419.

See also*: Reichsfilmblatt; Offizielles Organ des Verbandes Lichtspieltheater Berlin Brandenburg e. V.*, volume X, number 11 (March 12, 1932), [4], where it was reported that: "Die 'Kamera' brachte in ihrem vorigan Wochenprogramm zwei neue kleine Filme des ultramodernen Filmnammes Moholy-Nagy. . . ." [In its program for the previous week the "Kamera" brought two new short films by the ultramodern film-personality Moholy-Nagy . . .] The full *Reichsfilmblatt* review was reprinted in: Goergen, *op. cit.*, 3.

[549]Goergen, *op. cit.*, 2-3.

[550]"Abstrakter Film in der Kamera," *Vossische Zeitung: Berlinische Zeitung von Staats- und gelehrten Sachen*, Abend-Ausgabe, March 5, 1932, [6].

was better understood and treated more warmly than was *A Lightplay Black White Gray.* One was written by playwright and dramaturge Hermann Gressieker (1903-1983):

> Die Kamera zeigt vor der Reprise des Films "Galgenvögel" von Wyler, der für amerikanische Verhältnisse einmal sehr fortschrittlich war, zwei sehr verschiedene kleine Filmarbeiten von Moholy-Nagy. Die eine, "Alter Hafen in Marseille," ist eine klare und fesselnde Reportage. Sie unterscheidet sich von den meisten ihrer Art durch die Erlesenheit und Treffsicherheit der Aufnahmen. Vor allem wird hier nicht der oberflächlichen Reiselyrik gehuldigt, sondern gerade das, was nicht im Baedeker sieht, die Rückseite der Romantik, der tote und lebende Abhub der Gassen und Gossen wird hier sehr stark erfaßt. Der andere Kurzfilm, der sich "Ein Lichtspiel" betitelt, ist ein Experiment. Wie Professor Moholy-Nagy in einer kurzen Einführung erklärte, sollte hier hauptsächlich zweierlei versucht werden: eine Verkoppelung bewußt gestalteten Licht- und Schattenwirkungen mit bewußt gestalteten Bewegungswirkungen und zugleich die Uebertragen unseres Raumempfindens (der "Raumproblematik") in die Zweidimensionalität des Films. Doch dies "Zugleich" war wohl schon ein Zuviel. Das Glänzend photographierte Kreisen und Pendeln bizarrer Metallkonstruktionen ergab zwar alles: interessante Lichter und Schatten, interessante Bewegungskombinationen, interessante Raumphantasien. Aber es war so überfüllt mit Problematik, daß sich eine eindeutige Wirkung nicht einstellte. Wenn dies Experiment jedoch nicht "überzeugen," sondern anregen soll, dann hat es sein Zweck erfüllt.[551] [Before the Kamera shows its presentation of "Hell's Heroes" by Wyler, a film that at the time was very progressive for America, two very different short works on film from Moholy-Nagy are shown. One, "Old Harbor in Marseille," is clear and captivating reportage. It distinguishes itself from most films of its kind through choice and unerring camera work. Above all it does not indulge in superficial travelogue stuff, but on the contrary presents what is not seen in Baedeker, the reverse of the romantic, the living and dead trash in the alleys and gutters here becomes strongly evident. The other short film, titled "A Lightplay," is an experiment. As Professor Moholy-Nagy explains in a short introduction, two kinds of things are principally tested here: a joining of deliberately formed moving light-and-shadow effects and at the same time a merging of our sense of space (the "spatial uncertainties") into the two-dimensionality of film. Though the "simultaneity" was probably already excessive. The brilliance of the filmed oscillations of the metal construction to be sure produces everything: interesting lights and shadows, interesting spatial fantasies. But it was so overlaid with uncertainties that a clear effect did not emerge. If, however, this experiment was intended not to "convince," but to stimulate, then it achieved its purpose.]

The other review appearing on March 5 was written by Lotte H. Eisner for the *Film-Kurier.*[552]

---

[551]H[ermann] Gr[essieker], "Filme von Moholy-Nagy," *Berlin Börsen-Courier; Tagezeitung für alle Gebiete*, March 5, 1932, Abend-Ausgabe, 2.

[552][Lotte H. Eis]ner, "Zwei Moholy-Nagy-Filme, Kamera," *Film-Kurier, Tagezeitung* [Berlin], March 5, 1932, [2]. Reprinted in: Goergen, *op. cit.*, 3.

On March 19th; 1932, a joint review of *A Lightplay Black White Gray* and *Impressions of the Old Harbor of Marseille* appeared in newspaper in Frankfurt am Main; it was written by Siegfried Kracauer (1889-1966), who was to become the best-known writer about Weimar-era film:

> . . . Luckily, Moholy-Nagy seems to be aware of the threat posed by a preoccupation with purely formalist artistic activity. His other film takes up the topic of Marseille, and as such he wanders through the city, however not as a man about town, but instead chooses to illuminate the despair visible in the city. . . . If the images are not successful in achieving what they had set out for themselves, the reason for this is that less weight was placed on the clear visual expression of this despair than on the assessment of the painterly effects created by said images. The mosaic is run past one so quickly that next to nothing is retained. Long shots ought to have been used more often to interrupt the many close ups and a momentary slowing of the film's tempo would have been more effective.[553] (Translation by Robin Curtis)

Because *Impressions of the Old Harbor of Marseille* and *A Lightplay Black White Gray* played for a week in a commercial cinema along with a progressive yet successful major Hollywood feature and because three reviews were published the day after the opening, it should be emphasized that for one week Moholy was part of mainstream cinema.

Additional showings of *A Lightplay Black White Gray* quickly followed. It was shown by The Film Society of London on Sunday, November 20th, 1932, at the New Victoria Theatre (now the Apollo Victoria Theatre; E. Walmsley Lewis & William E. Trent, 1930).[554] This theatre has 2,860 seats, and was available to The Film Society because no other film showings were held in London on Sunday afternoons, and the American film critic Harry Alan Potamkin pointed out that London had the largest of the film societies because it hosted some two-thousand viewers.[555]

Soon after the London showing the film, billed as *Lichtspiel*, was presented on February 26th, 1933, by The Film Society of New York at 361 West 57th Street, where it was shown to the Society's members and their guests on a program that included a

---

[553] Siegfried Kracauer's review was called "Abstrakte Kunst," though it discusses both films. It originally appeared in the *Frankfurter Zeitung*, March 19, 1932; it was reprinted in: Siegfried Kracauer, *Kleine Schriften zum Film*, in: *idem*, *Werke*, Band 6, [Teil] 3, 1932-1961, edited by Inka Mülder-Bach (Frankfurt am Main: Suhrkamp Verlag, 2004), 37-38. The entire original German text appears in Appendix G, pages 741-742.

[554] Senter, "Moholy-Nagy in England," 7-8; *The Film Society Programme*, November 20, 1932, reprinted in: *The Film Society Programmes, 1925-1939*, [234]-236, here 235.

[555] Harry Alan Potamkin, "The Ritual of the Movies [part one]," *National Board of Review Magazine*, volume VIII (May, 1933), 3, 6 and 8; reprinted in: *idem*, *The Compound Cinema; the Film Writings of Harry Alan Potamkin*, selected, arranged and introduced by Lewis Jacobs (New York: Teachers College Press, 1977), 216-221, here 220.

feature film and a number of short films, among them *Ballet Mécanique* by Fernand Léger.[556]   Directors of The Film Society of New York included Potamkin and Julien Levy, who served as president.[557]   Another director was Iris Barry, who had co-founded The Film Society of London.[558]   Moholy had written to Julien Levy about the possibility of showing or selling *A Lightplay Black White Gray* and his Marseille film, and offered to send frames of the films in case Levy wanted something to be written about them.[559] Levy replied that he was interested in both films but his plans were still indefinite as to how to handle films, and mentioned the possibility of establishing the film society that eventually was to be the New York venue for *A Lightplay Black White Gray*.[560]

Two additional early showings took place in Germany in December, 1932: on December 4th it was presented at the Gloria-Palast in Frankfurt am Main by the *Filmliga* in co-operation with the journal, *Das neue Frankfurt*;[561] later in the month, billed as *Abstraktes Lichtspiel*, it was shown in Nuremberg at the *Neue Bilderbühne* in a special showing for the *Theatergemeinde der Volkshochschule*.[562]   As noted below, there were early showings in Budapest, but no exact dates can be cited.

ONE REASON for Moholy's flourishing creative life in Europe was his interaction with creative colleagues whose work he admired.   Usually this occurred during direct contacts and no paper trail would be left.   An exception is Moholy's request to Raoul Hausmann for his reaction to *A Lightplay Black White Gray* and *Impressions of the Old Marseille Harbor.*   He asked Hausmann's opinion of both films

---

[556]"Pictorial Backgrounds," *New York Times*, February 26, 1933, X 5. (It should be pointed out that George Antheil did not provide music for Léger's film.)

[557]Levy, *Memoir of an Art Gallery*, 153; and Ingrid Schaffner and Lisa Jacobs, editors, *Julien Levy: Portrait of an Art Gallery* (Cambridge: The MIT Press, 1998),188.

[558]Schaffner and Jacobs, editors, *Julien Levy: Portrait of an Art Gallery*; 37 and 39; and Russell Lynes, *Good Old Modern; an Intimate Portrait of the Museum of Modern Art* (New York: Atheneum, 1973), 108 and 110-111.

[559]László Moholy-Nagy to Julien Levy, TLS, September 25, 1932, Julien Levy archive, Newtown, Connecticut. The frames from A *Lightplay Black White Gray* and *Impressions of the Old Harbor of Marseille* were sent to Levy and are now in the Philadelphia Museum of art; see: Katherine Ware, "Between Dadaism and MoMA-ism at the Julien Levy Gallery," in: Katherine Ware and Peter Barberie, editors, *Dreaming in Black and White: Photography at the Julien Levy Gallery* (Philadelphia: Philadelphia Museum of Art, 2006), 13-121, here 58.

[560]Julien Levy to László Moholy-Nagy, TLS, October 10, 1932, Julien Levy archive, Newtown, Connecticut.

[561]Goergen, *op. cit.*, 2. See also: Levin, "'Tones from out of Nowhere'," note 35 on page 72.

[562]Goergen, *op. cit.*, 2.

in a letter pointing to their showing at the Kamera Cinema,[563] but Hausmann missed that showing and later viewed only *A Lightplay Black White Gray*, probably in Moholy's studio while he was out of Berlin. Basically, Hausmann advised his friend that what would improve the film would less complication and more clarity, and concluded: "Also, weniger wäre mehr gewesen" [thus, less would be more].[564] Moholy replied:

> . . . sie haben in vielem recht; wenn das "werk" dasteht, muss man [es] als kritisierbares ganzes nehmen, und als solches ist mein lichtspiel tatsächlich nur ein formaler einbruch in die filmindustrie. doch ist beglückend gewesen schon die unzulängliche und durch vieles gehandicapte arbeit.[565] [You are right to a great extent; as the "work" stands, one must consider it as open to criticism. And as such my lightplay is really only a formal break into the film industry. Though it is fortunate already to have an imperfect work made in spite of handicaps.]

On no later occasion did *A Lightplay Black White Gray* have a regular theatrical booking, and Moholy never got around to revising it, in part because, as he wrote to Hausmann explaining why he was unable to collaborate on a book with him, he was *wahnsinnig beschäftigt* [insanely busy].[566]

Except for the brief film used in *The Tales of Hoffmann*, and *A Lightplay Black White Gray*, Moholy had not completed any films when he first met Sibyl in 1931 even though he had been planning unrealized films for ten years. It proved to be the meeting of someone with practical knowledge about how films were currently being made in Germany that was the catalyst that turned friendship and mutual attraction into love and marriage.

Actually, the field work on *Impressionen vom alten Marseiller Hafen* was accomplished in the summer of 1931,[567] but, as noted, the film was first seen March 4th, 1932, at the Kamera Cinema in Berlin, which suggests that Sibyl Pietzsch helped get the film ready for its première showing. The more ambitious movie, *Berliner Stilleben*, was completed in the same year, 1932,[568] but no German screening before Moholy's

---

[563]László Moholy-Nagy to "Hausmanns" [*i.e.*, household of Raoul Hausmann], March 8, 1932.

[564]Raoul Hausmann to László Moholy-Nagy, TLS, May 3, 1932, Künstler-Archive, Berlinische Galerie, Berlin. Transcription of text in: Züchner, editor, *Scharfrichter*, 423-424.

[565]László Moholy-Nagy to Raoul Hausmann, May 8, 1932, written in ink on a postcard with rubber-stamp impression listing the Fredericiastraße address, Künstler-Archive, Berlinische Galerie, Berlin. A transcript of the letter appeared in: Züchner, editor, *Scharfrichter*, 424-425.

[566]*Ibid.*

[567]László, Moholy-Nagy to Matthew Josephson, October 26, 1931.

[568]Sibyl Moholy-Nagy, *Moholy-Nagy: Experiment in Totality*, 74-75; see also note 570.

emigration can be documented.[569] The account of the making of *Berliner Stilleben* by Sibyl Moholy-Nagy in her 1950 biography of her husband provided a clear date, since she stated that she met him late in 1931 and worked with him on the film before she left her job at Tobis at some point after the beginning of April, 1932.[570]

As Sibyl Moholy-Nagy has pointed out, the films about Berlin and Marseille provide a neat contrast. Both show aspects of modernity, such as the *pont transbordeur* [transporter bridge] in Marseille (Ferdinand Arnodin, 1905; no longer extant), connecting the north and south quays of the old harbor (*Vieux port*), (DVD figures 306 and 307) and in Berlin street-car tracks and the steel skeletons of buildings under construction. And both films also show slum quarters that contrast with images of modernity.[571]

D URING MOST OF the city's history, stretching back more than two millennia, the port of Marseille was located in a natural inlet, oblong in shape, stretching east and west. During the nineteenth century this facility proved to be inadequate owing to its small scale and lack of railroad access, so a new port was built to the north. Soon the neighborhood of the north quay of the old harbor developed into a slum after being abandoned by its bourgeois residents and many of its businesses. What fascinated Moholy was the liveliness of this slum community's street life which contrasted with the Berlin slum neighborhood where, as Sibyl put it, "Life is crushed by the city where in Marseille it is sheltered by it."[572]

Moholy's reportage of the fabled slum quarter in Marseille actually serves to preserve its memory, since its residents were evacuated and nearly all of its buildings dynamited during the Nazi occupation of the early 1940s.[573] But his work on his film there was almost defeated by its subject. He reported that:

---

[569]Goergen, *op. cit.*, 5; *Berliner Stilleben* is available from the Moholy-Nagy Foundation.

[570]Sibyl Moholy-Nagy, *Moholy-Nagy: Experiment in Totality*, 57-58 and 74-75; and *idem*, "My Life in Germany," pages 34-36 on microfilm reel 946, frames 0664, 0665 and 0666, Moholy-Nagy files, Archives of American Art, Washington, D.C.

[571]Sibyl Moholy-Nagy, "Six Films by Moholy-Nagy," a one-sheet flyer issued by the Solomon R. Guggenheim Museum in New York to accompany films showings on Sunday afternoons from February 22 through April 19, 1970. The same text was reproduced on two sheets of paper and distributed at the earlier showing at the Museum of Contemporary Art in Chicago. Copies of both are in my collection.

Another discussion of the contrast in the two films appears in Horak, *Making Images Move*, 122-130.

[572]Sibyl Moholy-Nagy, "Six Films by Moholy-Nagy."

[573]Sheila Crane, "Digging Up the Present in Marseille's Old Port: Toward an Archaeology of Reconstruction," *Journal of the Society of Architectural Historians,* volume LXIII, number 3 (September, 2004), [296]-319, here 299.

> I had a predetermined length (300 m.) of film stock, and decided that there was
> no way to capture a large city in so few metres. So I chose a small slice of the
> city, the *Vieux port*, one hitherto little known to the public due to its bad social
> circumstances, poverty and dangerous character. I tried to approach it with
> reportage that was not merely impressionistic; but finally I had to make do with a
> sketchy picture of the situation, since I was not even able to shoot from some
> higher point in order better to portray the totality of the processes before me. In
> this gloomy quarter, when after a long struggle I finally entered an apartment
> situated several stories up, I was received in such an unfriendly manner that I had
> to flee from the house; in fact, I was often physically threatened even on the
> street.[574]

Moholy nevertheless made a still photograph from inside an apartment (DVD figure 305)
as well as a film sequence that he incorporated into the movie. The still photograph was
shot through a decorative grill or railing, and looks west along the street known as La
Canebière.

Another writer reported that by the early twentieth century the neighborhood was
inhabited by ". . . small shopkeepers, artisans and fishing families, many of whom were
of Italian or Corsican origin," and added ". . . the Vieux-Port quarter was renowned,
particularly from the 1920s through the beginning of World War II, as a notorious den of
prostitution, criminality and [unauthorized] immigration."[575]

Sibyl summarized the street life of the neighborhood as seen in the film:

> The old port quarter is populated by an intensely extrovert group of
> people—women gesticulating, laughing, quarreling; children playing, dancing,
> running; men settling down on the sunny steps along the water, or sitting in tight
> groups in the small bistros. Even the very, very old—the rag picker, the ancient
> matriarch minding her grandchild, the beggar, the cripple—seem to be content to
> be part of this tightly knit community life. The filth in the narrow streets, the
> total lack of sanitary facilities, the poverty seem less repulsive where one is not
> alone. . . .[576]

In contrast, *Berliner Stilleben* documents with special force the grim apartment
buildings which stretch back from the streets beyond one light court after another. But
the isolated figures there and in the streets display no sense of community comparable to
what was filmed in Marseille.

---

[574] László Moholy-Nagy, "New Film Experiments," 321. The article was based on talks given at
several venues in Germany which had been accompanied by a screening of *Impressionen vom
alten Marseiller Hafen.*

[575] Crane, "Digging Up the Present in Marseille's Old Port," 298.

[576] Sibyl Moholy-Nagy, "Six Films by Moholy-Nagy."

T HE TRANSPORTER BRIDGE, which moved people and freight from one side of the
old harbor to the other, has been described as the "Eiffel Tower of Marseille,"
because a horizontal track was supported by ironwork towers reaching one-
hundred and fifty feet above the water level. (DVD figure 306) From an electric-
powered rail car that traversed the track a gondola was suspended over the water. (DVD
figure 307) Moholy, who made studies of the transporter bridge, some documentary in
nature (DVD figure 308), others bordering on the abstract (DVD figure 309), was one of
a number of Modernist photographers fascinated by it.[577] Concerning the bridge Moholy
wrote:

> Boats by the hundreds are rocking and there, above them all floats and radiates
> the famous Pont Transporteur. Inexhaustible, to and fro, from one shore to the
> other, it makes its way across and strangers admire and value it for its beauty.
> The suspended bridge is truly a wonder of technical precision and elegance. The
> fine-lined steel structure supporting on its long steel beams the "wandering"
> bridge is a remarkably attractive sight, and time and again it is a delight to see as
> the slightly rocking and swaying suspended vessel crowded with people once
> again begins its crossing above the water to the opposite side.[578]

The Berlin reviewers of the première of *Impressionen vom alten Marseiller Hafen*
left their (presumably entertainment-oriented) readers in no doubt about the grim scenes
that were part of the film. Griessekier's review, quoted above, made clear that the film
presented the flip side of what might appear in *Baedeker* guides, and another reviewer
stressed that in place of picturesque charm there were scenes such as children playing
amid mud and filth in narrow alleys.[579] Clearly the film was described for the film-going
public as representing current social reality. Nevertheless Moholy argued that claims by
producers, distributors and cinema owners that film-goers did not like film reportage
were hard to gauge because of difficulties presented by government censorship and the
refusal to grant tax concessions to educational films, as well as by timidity and self-
censorship within the film industry.[580]

The 1932 movie *Großstadt Zigeuner* [Big City Gypsies] was planned by Moholy as a
feature-length sound-film study of Berlin's "outsider" gypsy community. Sibyl
remembered that: "Gypsies had been the romantic element in his (Moholy's) Hungarian
childhood,"[581] but sadly, as Oliver Botar has pointed out, in Southern Hungary and
northern Serbia a fascination with Gypsies was permeated with anti-Gypsy prejudices

---

[577] Jan-Christopher Horak, "The Films of Moholy-Nagy," *Afterimage*, volume XIII, numbers 1-2
(1985), 20-23, here 22.

[578] Quoted from: "László Moholy-Nagy: Marseille," in: Passuth, *Moholy-Nagy*, 403. The original
German text is in the files of Hattula Moholy-Nagy.

[579] [Lotte H. Eis]ner, "Zwei Moholy-Nagy Filme," [2].

[580] László Moholy-Nagy, "New Film Experiments," 321.

[581] Sibyl Moholy-Nagy, *Moholy-Nagy, Experiment in Totality*, 78.

that were "as strong as anywhere . . .".[582]   Moholy had, of course, no way of predicting the future of Berlin's Gypsies, but as events unfolded, the Nazis murdered most of the Gypsies living in Germany and in much of German-occupied Europe as well. The surviving footage,[583] about eleven minutes in length,[584] thus preserves a vanished world.[585] Ellen Frank appears briefly in the film as she has her palm read. (film clip 2)

The chief source of information about the making of *Großstadt Zigeuner* is Sibyl Moholy-Nagy, who collaborated with her future husband in making it.[586] In fact, on a personal level, this was likely another experience that contributed to the bonding that brought them together and eventually to wedlock. It was Sibyl who had the practical knowledge of how films got made in Berlin, and László who supplied the creative ideas.

There was one brief press report on the making of the film. *Film-Kurier,* a Berlin film-industry daily, reported on April 19th, 1932, that:

> Professor Moholy-Nagy dreht augenblicklich gemeinsam mit Helmuth Brandis und Sibyl Peach einen Kulturfilm, der das Leben der Zigeuners in ihren Winterquartieren zeigt und voraussichtlich den Titel "Großstadtzigeuner" tragen wird.[587] [Professor Moholy-Nagy, joined currently by Helmuth Brandis and Sibyl Peach, is shooting a documentary film that shows the life of gypsies in their winter quarters and the title will probably be Big City Gypsies.]

---

[582]Oliver Botar, "Films by Moholy-Nagy" [review of films by Moholy distributed by The Moholy-Nagy Foundation], *Journal of the Society of Architectural Historians*, volume LXVI, number 3 (September, 2008), 460-462, here 462.

[583]Robin Curtis has discussed a version of the film dating from 1971 that was once available on a DVD disc, *Weltbühne Berlin: die zwanziger Jahre* [*sic*], issued by Chronos Classics but no longer available because of copyright violations. Although the frames listing Moholy as editor were retained, there was extensive re-editing by Irmgard zur Mühle. See: Robin Curtis, "The Stranger in a City Filled with Strangers: Moholy-Nagy's *Urban Gypsies,*" *Framework: the Journal of Cinema and Media*, volume XLIV, number 2 (Fall, 2003), [42]-56, here 44-47.

[584]*Großstadt Zigeuner* as issued on DVD by The Moholy-Nagy Foundation is about eleven minutes long.

The film is described in: Horak, *Making Images Move*, 124-130.

[585]Robin Curtis pointed out that it is impossible to ascertain from the film whether the people shown were Roma or Sinti; see her "Strangers in a City Filled with Strangers," note 1 on page 53.

[586]Sibyl Moholy-Nagy, *Moholy-Nagy, Experiment in Totality*, 78-84.

[587]"Moholy-Nagy filmt 'Großstadt-Zigeuner'; Autorenarbeit von Hellmuth [*sic*] Brandis," *Film-Kurier, Tagezeitung* [Berlin], April 19, 1932, [2].

Not much is known about Helmuth Brandis, except that the *Film-Kurier* account also mentions his work with Erich Waschneck, a successful director of feature films at the time.

The sound for the film was to be a narrator, along with a musical score. Evidently the sound track never was completed, but Sibyl wrote of her frustration in her attempts to create one:

> Der Film ist mein Tod: Jetzt hat sich ergeben, dass bei der neuen Aufnahme die Cembalo[n]begleitung wie zehn Schwanz getretene Katzen klingt. Es geht so keinesfalls und so werden wir morgen früh nochmals aufnehmen, allerdings eben nur gesprochenen Text ohne unterlegung der Musik, wie es ursprüunglich vorgesehen war.[588] [The film will be the death of me. It develops that the cembalon accompaniment sounds like ten cats whose tails are being stepped on. It is unacceptable and so we will make another recording early tomorrow, but only the spoken text without the accompaniment of music, as was foreseen from the beginning.]

The first public showing of *Big City Gypsies* was March 5th, 1934, at Masaryk University in Brno, as documented in DVD figure 352.

ALSO ANNOUNCED AS PART OF PROGRAM at The Film Society in London in December, 1933, that included Moholy's experimental sound tracks, was "an amateur film diary of the 1933 International Architectural Congress at Athens."[589] This, of course, as The Film Society members were to find out, was not actually an amateur film, but rather Moholy's *Architekturkongres Athen*, a twenty-nine minute documentary "made under amateur conditions." It was shown at The Film Society in London on December 10th, 1933, billed as *Architects' Congress* and sharing a program, as noted, with Moholy's *A.B.C. in Sound* along with short films by other film-makers. *Architekturkongres Athen* had been edited by Moholy on November 22nd and 23rd while he was staying at the Regent-Palace Hotel near Piccadilly Circus in London. Moholy endeavored to record, in a kind of "film diary, the intimacy and progress of an architectural congress held on board ship."[590] This was the fourth *CIAM* Congress which, as noted above, opened in Marseille, continued on board the Athens-bound *S-S Patria II*, and concluded in Athens; the dates were July 29th through August 14th, 1933. Sigfried Giedion photographed Moholy with his movie camera in Greece. (DVD figure 310)

With the works we have been discussing, Moholy emerged not just as a film-maker but also as a film theorist. And some of his ideas relate specifically to *Architects Congress*. One of his most important theoretical statements on film, "New Film Experiments," appeared in print in 1933; it was based on lectures given in several venues

---

[588] Sibyl Moholy-Nagy to László Moholy-Nagy, TLS, August 24, 1932, microfilm reel 951, frame 0036, Moholy-Nagy files, Archives of American Art, Washington, D.C.

[589] *The Times* (London), December 10, 1933, 12,

[590] *The Film Society Programmes*, December 10, 1933, [273]; *Architekturkongres Athen* is available from the Moholy-Nagy Foundation.

in Germany that had been accompanied by showings of some of his films[591] He saw the role of the amateur as crucial for the development of film, and proclaimed: "Amateurs of the film forward! Amateurs of the film, to work!"[592] This was a prescient rallying cry, and might seem to be a premonition of the most famous of all amateur films, the one made in 1963 by Abraham Zapruder, who filmed the assassination of John F. Kennedy using 8 millimeter color film.[593] In the twenty-first century it is taken for granted that everyone who wants to work with moving images and who has at least a modest income is able to do so, and with digital equipment far superior to what Moholy or Zapruder owned.

Moholy was careful to delineate for his London viewers of *Architects Congress* that the means used were truly what an amateur would be using at the time:

> The film was made under typically amateur conditions, with a hand camera devoid of tripod, with a very limited quantity of film stock, bought at different times and therefore of different qualities, and with no prepared scenario or pre-determined order of shots, but was taken when and where occasion offered. The final editing was directed toward displaying the actual work of the congress and the national and personal characteristics of the individual delegates. It is by such means, working within a limited compass, Professor Moholy-Nagy believes, that the amateur can make his contribution to the art of the film.[594]

Moholy's burst of film creativity continued in England, with a sixteen-minute documentary, *Lobsters* (1935-1936).[595] Terence Senter argued that Lobsters was strongly influenced by John Grierson's 1929 documentary film *Drifters*.[596] *Lobsters* is available in two editions: one is silent and one has narration by BBC radio newsman Alan Howland and a score by Modernist composer Arthur Benjamin (1893-1960).[597] The film also provides one of the rare examples of one of Moholy's films being offered to the general public. The Leicester Square Theatre in London ran it for an indefinite

---

[591] László Moholy-Nagy, "New Film Experiments," in: Passuth, *Moholy-Nagy*, 319.

[592] László Moholy-Nagy, "New Film Experiments," 320.

[593] Zapruder used a Bell & Howell Model 414PD Zoomatic Director Series camera that is now in the National Archives in Washington, D.C.

[594] *The Film Society Programmes*, December 10, 1933, [273].

[595] *Lobsters* is available in DVD format from the Moholy-Nagy Foundation. On *Lobster*s, see: Senter, "Moholy-Nagy in England," 64-76; and *idem*, "Moholy-Nagy's English Photography," *The BurlingtonMagazine,* volume CXXIII, number 944 (November, 1981), 659-671, here 669.

[596] Senter, "Moholy-Nagy in England," 67-68.

[597] A film copy of the version with sound is in the British Film Institute, London.

period beginning December 1ˢᵗ, 1936, and The Tatler, on Charing Cross Road in the same city, began a six day run on March 15ᵗʰ, 1937.[598]

While Moholy was away from London in August, 1935, it was Sibyl who met regularly with an impatient John Mathias, the recent seaside host for her and her husband, to discuss *Lobsters*, for which he was co-director,[599] and whether Moholy's planned return to London could be hastened.[600] At a luncheon meeting Mathias reported that he wanted to take advantage of the August 16ᵗʰ new moon to go to Littlehampton, which has a broad beach on the English Channel; there he planned to make time-lapse photographs of the tide at its monthly swiftest and highest, utilizing a vintage camera he had found.[601]

The New Architecture and the London Zoo was commissioned by the Museum of Modern Art in New York and was first seen there on February 10ᵗʰ, 1937,[602] in connection with an exhibition, *Modern Architecture in England*, which Ernestine (née Fantl) Carter, the Museum's Curator of Architecture and Industrial Design, had set up.[603] Moholy and Fantl had met the previous September, when both attended the CIRPAC meeting at La Sarraz in Switzerland (see page 490).[604]

This influential MOMA exhibition highlighted the changing attitudes toward Modernism in England that Moholy had witnessed during his visits to and residence in England during the years 1933 to 1937, a development summarized on a flap of the dust jacket for the exhibition's catalogue: "Although England has had, within recent times, the reputation of extreme conservatism in all the arts, the last few years have witnessed there an enthusiastic acceptance of modern architecture."[605] Moreover, in the same catalogue, architectural-historian and early promoter of International Style Modernism in the United States, Henry-Russell Hitchcock (1903-1987), wrote: "For quantity of sound

---

[598]Senter, "Moholy-Nagy in England," 74 and note 74 on page 281.

[599] In the film's credits, John Mathias and Moholy are each listed as a director. About the credits, see: Senter, "Moholy-Nagy in England," note 25 on page 279.

[600]Sibyl Moholy-Nagy to László Moholy-Nagy, TLS, August 16, 1935, microfilm reel 951, frames 0176-0177, Moholy-Nagy files, Archives of American Art, Washington, D.C.

[601]Sibyl Moholy-Nagy to László Moholy-Nagy, August 16, 1935.

[602]There were three showings per day throughout the run of the exhibition; see: Edward Alden Jewell, "Georgia O'Keefe Shows New Work . . . Zoo Movie at Museum," *The New York Times*, February 6, 1937, 7; see also: "Architecture in England of Today," in *ibid*., February 14, 1937, X 9.

[603]Senter, "Moholy-Nagy: the Transitional Years," note 52 on page 173.

[604]Baudin, *Hélène de Mandrot*, 204 and 313; and Senter, "Moholy-Nagy in England," 101-102.

[605]Ernestine N. Fantl, editor, *Modern Architecture in England* (New York: The Museum of Modern Art, 1937).

modern building and for quality as well, the English school is certainly ahead of the American," and added : ". . . the work of the English contemporary school in the last few years, still so evidently expanding and improving, sets a mark which we will not easily pass in America."[606]

The showings of *The New Architecture and the London Zoo* at the Museum constituted Moholy's film debut there. (DVD figure 311) Although the exhibition provided a progressive modern context for what was for many Americans their introduction to Moholy's work, it must be said that this film was not well received generally or critically and did little to build his reputation, even though it had financial support from the Department of Architecture at Harvard University, the Zoological Society of London, and the London architectural firm of Tecton (designers of the zoo structures shown in the film); moreover, it was aided by the efforts of Julian Huxley (1887-1975)[607] of the Zoological Society of London and Joseph Hudnut of Harvard.[608] Nevertheless Huxley himself, a sometime documentary film-maker,[609] seemed satisfied with the film: he arranged a special showing at the London Zoo on May 28th, 1937, for some of his guests who had come to London for the coronation of King George VI.[610] The reader with special interest in *The New Architecture and the London Zoo* is directed to the lively and well-researched account by Terence Senter.[611]

Moholy was also involved in film-making with two fellow Hungarians, Alexander Korda (1893-1956), head of London Films, and his brother, set designer Vincent Korda (1897-1979). While both were living in Hungary Moholy was almost certainly aware of Alexander's work, as discussed in Chapter One, and he had made Vincent's acquaintance in 1930.[612] For one film, *Rembrandt* (1936), sometimes considered

---

[606]Henry-Russell Hitchcock, "Modern Architecture in England," in: Fantl, editor, *Modern Architecture in England*, 25-41, here 39.

[607]Knighted as Sir Julian Huxley in 1958.

[608]Fantl, editor, *Modern Architecture in England*, [6].

[609]In 1934 Huxley, in collaboration with the naturalist R.M. Lockley, directed a natural-history documentary film for Alexander Korda, *The Private Life of the Gannets*. The cinematographers were Osmond Borradaile and John Grierson and it won an Academy Award (from the Academy of Motion Picture Arts and Sciences, Los Angeles).

[610]László Moholy-Nagy to Walter and Ise Gropius, photographic copy of MLS, May 28, 1937, Bauhaus-Archiv, Berlin.

[611]Senter, "Moholy-Nagy in England," 100-105; see also: Peder Anker, "The Bauhaus of Nature," *Modernism/modernity*, volume 12, number 2 (April 28, 2005), [229]-251, here 235-236.

The New Architecture and the London Zoo is available from the Moholy-Nagy Foundation.

[612]Senter, "Moholy-Nagy's English Photography," 663.

Vincent's finest achievement, he built a set in the firm's studios.[613] Moholy's role included using contacts in Holland to arrange for photographs of windmills and other features of old Holland that would be a useful resource for Vincent.[614]

FOR ANOTHER FILM on which Vincent worked as a set designer, *Things to Come* (1936), based on a novel by H.G. Wells, Moholy did a lot of work at the Worton Hall Studios, Isleworth, on sequences shot in futuristic sets he had designed.[615] (DVD figure 312) Moholy spent a lot of time working on the film; he had begun by December 1st, 1935, and he was still working on it on February 24th of the next year.[616] He was assisted by special effects specialist Wally Veevers (died 1983), then still a young trainee.[617] Nevertheless, Moholy's work was all but unutilized in the film as completed, leaving him bitterly disappointed.[618] However, about five minutes of this unutilized footage survives.[619] Moholy retained stills from this footage and they were used by him in various ways, most notably in the design of the front and back of the cover for the catalogue of the New Bauhaus in Chicago. (DVD figures 430 and 431)

---

[613] John Halas, "Korda, Vincent," in: Naylor, editor, *Contemporary Designers*, second edition, 308-309.

[614] László Moholy-Nagy to Paul Citroen, MLS, April 13, 1936, Bauhaus-Archiv, Berlin. Moholy gave an outline of what was needed and how much money the photographer might earn and suggested that Hajo Rose, formerly of Moholy's Berlin studio and at the time teaching at a school that Citroen had set up in Amsterdam, might be asked to make the photographs. On Rose in Amsterdam, see: Brüning and Droste, editors, *Das A und O des Bauhauses*, 326; and Hochensmith, "Hajo (Hans-Joachim) Rose," 244.

[615] The best overall source for *Things to Come* is: Christopher Frayling, *Things to Come* (London: British Film Institute, 1995); the best source for Moholy's involvement with the film is: Senter, "Moholy-Nagy in England," 108-121.

[616] László Moholy-Nagy to Paul Citroen, TLS with MLS note, December 1, 1935; and *idem* to Paul Citroen, MLS February 24, 1936, Bauhaus-Archiv, Berlin.

[617] Senter, "Moholy-Nagy in England," 114-115; *idem*, "Moholy-Nagy's English Photography," 664. In 1969 Wally Veevers shared an Academy Award (from the Academy of Motion Picture Arts and Sciences, Los Angeles) for special visual effects for the 1968 film *2001, a Space Odyssey*.

[618] Senter, "Moholy-Nagy in England," 111-118; *idem*, "Moholy-Nagy's English Photography," 664.

[619] "Senter, Moholy-Nagy's English Photography," 664; and Frayling, *Things to Come*, 72-73

The 1929 Film and Photography (FiFo) Exhibition
in Stuttgart and at Other Venues

THE EVENT THAT FIRMLY ESTABLISHED Moholy's international reputation as a master photographer was the massive international *Film und Foto* exhibition presented by the German Werkbund and first shown in Stuttgart in 1929.[620] It was often known as *FiFo* while it was still hanging, a designation later usually used by historians. It was international in two senses: in the range of venues where it was shown following the Stuttgart première, and in the scope of the photographs included. Moreover, the photographic section constituted one of the largest photographic exhibitions held anywhere up until that time, and its largest single component consisted of photographs by Moholy.

The impact of the Stuttgart exhibition went beyond increasing Moholy's own reputation as a photographer. The Stuttgart art-historian and critic, Hans Hildebrandt (1878-1957), called it a turning-point in the history of the photographic art, because it forcefully documented the clear emergence of photography from its original painterly concerns.[621]

After being exhibited in Stuttgart from May 18th through July 7th, 1929, a portion of the exhibition was seen elsewhere: in Zurich (August 28th through September 22nd)[622] where films were shown for one week;[623] in Berlin (photographs were shown October 19th through November 17th and films were shown October 19th through November

---

[620]Gustav Stotz, editor, *Internationale Ausstellung des deutschen Werkbunds Film und Foto, Stuttgart, 1929* (Stuttgart: Das deutsche Werkbund, 1929); reprint: New York: Arno Press, 1979); also reprinted in the same year from a more complete copy of the catalogue by the Deutsche Verlags-Anstalt GmBh of Stuttgart. The Stuttgart reprint includes additional material not part of the other reprint. Moreover the New York reprint includes only 791 numbered items, while the Stuttgart reprint inludes 977 numbered items; both reprints include some listed but unnumbered items.

[621]Hans Hildebrandt, "Die Fifo in Stuttgart," *Photographische Rundschau und Mitteilungen,* volume LXVI, number 10 (May, 1929), 211.

[622]Das Kunstgewerbemuseum der Stadt Zürich, *Wegleitungen des Kunstgewergemuseums der Stadt Zürich 88: Film und Foto, Wanderausstellung des Deutsches Werkbundes, 28. August bis 22. September 1929* (Zurich: Kunstgewerbemuseum, 1929); Ute Eskildsen and Jan-Christopher Horak, editors, *Film und Foto der zwanziger Jahre* (Stuttgart: Verlag Gerd Hatje, 1979), 192, 194; Gustav Stolz to Hannah Höch, June 26, 1929, Künstlerarchiv der Berlinischen Galerie, Berlin; published in: Eberhard Roters, Eva Züchner, Ralf Burmeister and Eckhard Fürlus, editors, *Hannah Höch: eine Lebenscollage*, Band II, 1921-1945, 2. Abteilung (Ostfildern-Ruit, Germany: Verlag Gerd Hatje, 1995), 350-351.

[623]"g" [*i.e.*, Sigfried Giedion], "Die Neue Optik," *Der Cicerone; Halbmonatschrift für Künstler, Kunstfreunde und Salmer*, volume XXI, number 18 ([September 15], 1929), 532.

21st);[624] and still later in the same year it was seen in Gdańsk (Danzig), Poland.[625] Early in 1930 it was seen in Vienna (February 20th through March 31st)[626] with added photographs by Austrian photographers[627] (none at all had been shown in Stuttgart). Although only twenty-four photographs by Moholy were shown in Vienna, far fewer than had been seen in Stuttgart (see below), his work still constituted the second-largest component of the exhibition there. There were showings later in 1930 in Zagreb (Agram), then in Yugoslavia, now in Croatia;[628] and in the German cities of Essen, Dusseldorf, Dessau and Breslau (now Wrocław or Wrozlaw, Poland).[629]

Moholy was living in Berlin when *FiFo* was shown there, and helped with the installation, evident in the simple explanatory panels of enlarged typewritten text, with white letters on a black background.[630] (DVD figure 313) These were similar to what he had used in a typographic exhibition earlier in 1929 at the *Kunstbibliothek* in Berlin, as discussed above.

Extensive selections from the exhibition were seen in Tokyo and Osaka in 1931 (evidently without any cinematic component), presented under the title: *German*

---

[624] *Film und Foto: internationale Wanderausstellung des deutschen Werkbundes, vom .19 Oktober bis 17. November, im Lichthof des ehemaligen Kunstgewerbemuseums, Frinz-Albrecht-Strasse 7* (Berlin: Das Museum, 1929); Advertisement, *Die Form; Zeitschrift für gestaldende Arbeit*, volume 4, number 21 (November 1, 1929), inside front cover; Leo Hirsch, "'Film und Foto,' Werkbund-Ausstellung im Kunstgewerbemuseum," *Berliner Tageblatt*, October 19, 1929, Abend-Ausgabe, [3]; B.E.W., "'Film und Foto'; Wanderausstellung der Werkbund," *Deutsche Allgemeine Zeitung*, October 26, 1929, Beiblatt, fourth unnumbered page; and Eskildsen and Horak, editors, *Film und Foto der zwanziger Jahre*, 192, 194 and 201.

[625] Eskildsen and Horak, editors, *Film und Foto der zwanziger Jahre*, 194.

[626] Eskildsen and Horak, editors, *Film und Foto der zwanziger Jahre*, 192, 194.

[627] Österreichischer Werkbund, *Internationale Ausstellung Film und Foto; Wanderausstellung des Deutsches Werkbundes, Österreichisches Museum. 20. Februar bis 31. März 1930* (Vienna: Michael Winkler, 1930); reprinted in: Stotz, editor, *Internationale Ausstellung des deutschen Werkbunds Film und Foto, Stuttgart, 1929* [Stuttgart: 1979]), following page [96].

[628] Eskildsen and Horak, editors, *Film und Foto der zwanziger Jahre*, 171, 192.

[629] Eskildsen and Horak, editors, *Film und Foto der zwanziger Jahre*, 192.

[630] Kühn, editor, *Neues Sehen in Berlin: Fotografie der Zwanziger Jahre*, 18-19 and 133.

International Traveling Photography Exhibition.[631] The showings in Japan were first suggested by Sōzō Okada (1903-1983; also known as Hikaru Yamauchi) who was studying theatre in Germany in 1929, and who, together with Tomoyoshi Murayama (1901-1977), had been active in Dadaist circles in Berlin from 1921 to 1923,[632] approached the Asahi newspaper company, publisher of two Japanese newspapers, the *Tokyo Asahi* and the *Osaka Asahi*;[633] Asahi was also publisher of *Asahi Camera* and *The Japan Photographic Annual*. The company was very pleased with the attendance.[634]

THE SHOWING IN TOKYO, on the top storey of the Tokyo Asahi Building, was very brief, from April 4th through 22nd, 1931; moreover, since over 1,100 photographs were to be shown, there was only enough space for half of them to be on display at one time, so the exhibition was changed midway through its duration in order to show the other half.[635] There was no catalogue, but a list of the photographers was published in a photographic magazine. Included were Moholy, Heartfield, Höch, Cunningham, El Lissitzky and others whose photographs had been shown in Stuttgart, along with photographs by Baron Albert von Schrenck-Notzing and the copy prints of historic photographs[636] described below.

---

[631] Akiko Okatsuka, "Consciousness and Expression of the Modern," in: Tokyo Metropolitan Museum of Photography, *The Founding and Development of Modern Photography in Japan (Nihon kindai shashin no seiritsu to tenkai)* [bi-lingual exhibition catalogue; Japanese text translated into English by The Word Works] (Tokyo: Tokyo Metropolitan Museum of Photography, 1995), 18-27, here 22; and Takeba Joe, "The Age of Modernism: from Visualization to Socialization," in: Anne Wilkes Tucker, Dana Friis-Hansen, Kaneko Ryūichi and Takeba Joe, editors, *The History of Japanese Photography* (New Haven: Yale University Press, 2003), [142]-183, here 146.

[632] Akiko Okatsuka, "Consciousness and Expression of the Modern," 22; Klaus Weber, editor, *Avantgarde im Dialog: Bauhaus, Dada und Expressionismus in Japan: eine Ausstellung in Zusammenarbeit mit dem National Museum of Modern Art, Kyoto und der Insho Domoto Memorial Foundation for Modern Art* [exhibition catalogue] (Berlin: Bauhaus-Archiv, 2000), 31; and Ichiro Haryu, "Avantgarde Kunst in Japan: Vergangenheit und Gegenwart" and Yoshio Shirakawa, "Eine Botschaft von MAVO," in: Jutta Hüsewig, Yoshio Shirkawa and Stephan von Wiese, editors, *Dada in Japan: japanische Avantgarde, 1920-1970* (Dusseldorf: Kunstmuseum Düsseldorf, 1983), 12-16, here 13, and 19-20, here 19, respectively. For illustrations see: *ibid.*, 38-41.

[633] Kohtaro Iizawa, "The Bauhaus and Shinko Shashin," in: Masafumi Fukagawa, editor, *bauhaus fotografie (tenrankai korokiumu: bauhausu no shashin)* (Kawasaki: Kawasaki City Museum, 1997), 134-139 [*i.e.*, 139-134 in Japanese pagination], here 138; see also: Gustav Stolz to Hannah Höch, December 21, 1931, Künstlerarchiv der Berlinischen Galerie, Berlin, in: Roters, Züchner, Burmeister and Fürlus, editors, *Hannah Höch: eine Lebenscollage*, Band II, 1921-1945, 2. Abteilung, 417.

[634] Gustav Stolz to Hannah Höch, December 21, 1931.

[635] *Asahi Camera*, (March, 1931), 316.

[636] *Ibid.*, 316-317.

The exhibition moved to Osaka in July, 1931, where it was seen in the Osaka Asahi Building.[637] (DVD figure 314) It is possible that the exhibition was seen in the newspaper's present twelve-storey building (Junichiro Ishikawa, 1930-1931), now a Modernist landmark but not quite completed in July and not formally dedicated until November 25th.[638] Perhaps the space for one of the multi-use building's many tenants was utilized for the exhibition before it was outfitted for its tenant. In any case both the exhibition and the new building suggest that *Osaka Asahi* was striving to seem up-to-date.

The large number of Moholy's photographs on view in the Japanese venues of *Fifo*, and the large number of viewers attracted, were key factors in the influence of Moholy in Japan, as mentioned below.

In Stuttgart, the exhibition was seen in the municipal exhibition halls (*Städtischen Ausstellungshallen*) dating from 1925 that had been designed by Stuttgart architect Bernard Pankok (1872-1943),[639] who was a member of one of the *Die Aufnahmekommission* [organizing committees] of *Film und Foto*.[640] The exhibition was set up to utilize one of the features of Pankok's building: everyone passed through Room One, the largest of the thirteen galleries used for the exhibition.[641] The gallery used for Room One had been designed as a dramatically high-walled and spacious "Grand Gallery," well-lit from a large skylight and two rows of clerestory windows. Room One of *Film und Foto* was planned and installed by Moholy.[642] (DVD figure 315) He was

---

[637] *Osaka Asahi shinbun*, July 1, 1931, 5.

[638] "Asahi Building One of the Most Modern Structures in Osaka," *The Japan Times & Mail*, November 27, 1931, [3].

[639] Baedeker, Karl, *Süddeutschland; Handbuch für Reisende* (Leipzig: Karl Baedeker, 1929), 193; Hans Volmer, editor, *Allgemeines Lexikon der bildenden Künstler von der Antike bis zur Gegenwart* (Leipzig: Verlag von E.A. Seemann, 1932), 26:197.

Illustrated in: Karl Steinorth, "Die Internationale Werkbundausstellung 'Film und Foto' und ihre Organisatoren," unpaginated, in: Stotz, editor, *Film und Foto* (Stuttgart: 1979).

[640] Steinorth, "Die Internationale Werkbundausstellung 'Film und Foto' und ihre Organisatoren," unpaginated; Stotz, editor, *Film und Foto* (New York: 1979), 10; *idem* (Stuttgart: 1979), *ibid*.

[641] See the ground plan in: Stotz, editor, *Film und Foto* (New York: 1979), [9]; *idem* (Stuttgart: 1979), *ibid*.

[642] Walter Riezler, "'Form,' Foto und Film," *Die Form; Zeitschrift für gestaldende Arbeit*, volume 4, number 14 (July 15, 1929), 365-369, here 365; Stotz, editor, *Film und Foto* (New York: 1979), 49; *idem* (Stuttgart: 1979), *ibid*.; and Lusk, *Montagen ins Blaue*, 156-159. There is only one known photograph of Room One of the exhibition; it was originally published in a Stuttgart newspaper and was later published in Lusk, *Montagen ins Blaue*, 158, in Eskildsen and Horak, editors, *Film und Foto der zwanziger Jahre*, 171, 191, and in Steinorth, "Die Internationale Werkbundausstellung 'Film und Foto' und ihre Organisatoren," unpaginated. A photograph of the

(continued...)

one of a panel of collaborators from Germany, the United States, Holland, the Soviet Union and Switzerland who helped to organize the exhibition,[643] and he had been asked to set up a comprehensive survey of the ways in which photography was used in modern industrial societies, as well as a survey of the commercial network of manufacturers and suppliers that supported the work of photographers and film-makers. As a contemporary account noted: "Before one reached the pictures grouped after their original countries and personalities, one went through a room created by Prof. L. Moholy-Nagy that represented the development since Daguerre and the spheres of scientific, reporting and advertising photography in large, distinct lines. . ."[644]

The only available photograph of Room One is a bit grainy. (DVD figure 315) However, one of the works on view, in a prominent spot, was Moholy's 1924 study for an advertisement for automobile tires of that provided a touch of color for a room dominated by black, white and gray images and also allows us to better imagine the actual appearance of the room when a reproduction of is viewed along with the vintage photograph. (DVD figure 316 left)

THE FILM SHOWINGS that were part of *Film und Foto*[645] took place in a separate building near the *Städtischen Ausstellungshallen*. Moholy had as yet only completed one film, which was running concurrently in Berlin as part of the production he had designed for *The Tales of Hoffmann*, discussed above, so even though he was not represented in the *FiFo* screenings in Stuttgart or in Berlin, visitors to *FiFo* in Berlin could see his *Mirakel* elsewhere in the city. As noted, Moholy did include the film industry in Room One of the Stuttgart exhibition. Because the films shown, chosen by Hans Richter (1888-1976),[646] included feature films, such as Carl Theodor Dreyer's *The Passion of Joan of Arc* (1928), and short films, such as René Clair's *Entr'acte* (1924), Man Ray's *Emak Bakia* (1926), and Marcel Duchamp's *Spirals* (1926; also known as *Anémic Cinéma*) along with Richter's own *Inflation* (1928), pushed the boundaries, Moholy was doubtlessly encouraged (if he needed encouragement) to experiment further in the films that he already had in planning stages.

---

[642](...continued)
gallery as set up for another purpose is in *ibid*.

[643]Concerning Moholy's role in the organization of *FiFo* in addition to setting up Room One, see: Oliver Botar, "László Moholy-Nagy's New Vision and the Aestheticization of Scientific Photography in Weimar Germany," *Science in Context*, volume XVII, number 4 (December, 2004), [525]-556, here 544-546.

[644]A. Kraszna-Krausz, "Exhibition in Stuttgart, June, 1929, and its Effects," *Close Up*, December 29, 1929; reprinted in: David Mellor, editor, *Germany: the New Photography, 1927-1933* (London: Arts Council of Great Britain, 1978), 35-36.

[645]"Programme der Filmvorführungen mit Produktionsdaten der Filme," in: Eskildsen and Horak, editors, *Film und Foto der zwanziger Jahre*, 198-201; and Stotz, editor, *Film und Foto* (Stuttgart: 1979), unpaginated.

[646]Stotz, editor, *Film und Foto* (New York: 1979), 10, 16-17; *idem* (Stuttgart: 1979), *ibid*.

THE LIST OF PHOTOGRAPHERS represented in Room One included some who did work for picture agencies, who accepted photographic commissions, or who used photographs in graphic design. Among these were Moholy himself and Lucia Moholy, and others such as Francis Bruguière (1879-1945), Erich Comeriner (discussed above in connection with Moholy's Berlin studio), and Moholy's old friend Erzsi Landau.[647] Some picture agencies were represented, such as the Berlin office of the picture service of the *New York Times*,[648] and there were technical photographs, such as microphotographs from the Techno-Photographisches Archiv, which had offices in Berlin and Stuttgart.[649] Manufacturers represented included I.G. Farben's Agfa, which showed an X-Ray photograph plus a "straight" photograph of a beach scene.[650] One of the most striking images in Room One, evident in a vintage photograph, was a full-body X-ray (source not determined).

The inclusion in *Film und Foto* of photographs supplied by commercial firms was in line with a key goal of the Werkbund: to forge close ties with industry. Moholy also designed the prospectus for the exhibition.[651] The large number of advertisements in the catalogue by commercial firms involved with photography and film demonstrates that, thanks in large part to Moholy's prospectus and his work in organizing Room One, the Werkbund did attract the attention of industry to the exhibition.

Also in Room One were copy prints of historic photographs made from vintage examples owned by the Berlin professor of photochemistry (at the *Technische Hochschule*, now *Technische Universität*) and collector Erich Stenger (1878-1957),[652]

---

[647]Stotz, editor, *Film und Foto* (New York: 1979), 49-50; *idem* (Stuttgart: 1979), *ibid*.

[648]Stotz, editor, *Film und Foto* (New York: 1979), 50; *idem* (Stuttgart: 1979), *ibid*. In addition to 23 illustrations of items from *Film und Foto* reproduced in the original catalogue, some also appeared in: Franz Roh und Jan Tschichold, editors, *Foto-Auge, 76 Fotos der Zeit=Oeil et Photo, 76 Photographies de Notre Temps=Photo-Eye, 76 Photoes [sic] of the Period* (Stuttgart: Akademischer Verlag Dr. Fritz Wedekind & Co., 1929; Tübingen: Verlag Ernst Wasmuth, unveränderter Nachdruck, 1973). A photograph from *The New York Times* picture service appeared as plate 2 in *ibid*.

[649]Stotz, editor, *Film und Foto* (New York: 1979), 50; *idem* (Stuttgart: 1979), *ibid*; and Roh and Tschichold, editors, *Photo-eye*, plate 51.

[650]Stotz, editor, *Film und Foto* (New York: 1979), 50; *idem* (Stuttgart: 1979), *ibid*; and Roh and Tschichold, *Photo-Eye*, plates 12 and 20.

[651]Lusk, *Montagen ins Blaue*, 156-157; and Eleanor M. Hight, *Moholy-Nagy: Photography and Film in Weimar Germany* (Wellesley, Massachusetts: Wellesley College Museum, 1985), 40.

[652]László Moholy-Nagy to Erich Stenger, July 17, 1929, manuscript, signed note on back of postcard, Bauhaus-Archiv, Berlin, quoted in Eskildsen and Horak, editors, *Film und Foto der zwanziger Jahre*, 68. As noted below, Stenger had recently provided photographs for other photographic exhibitions. On Stenger see: "Stenger, Erich," in: Robert Volz, editor, *Reichshandbuch der deutschen Gesellschaft; das Handbuch der Persönlichkeiten in Wort und Bild*

(continued...)

including some from the earliest years of photography.[653] An astronomical photograph from Mount Wilson Observatory was shown.[654] The importance of photography to police work was demonstrated by examples from the criminal division of the provincial police office in Stuttgart.[655] And the most curious pictures shown were "photographs from the sphere of Parapsychology" ("*Aufnahmen aus dem Gebiet der Parapsychologie*") supplied by Baroness Gabriele von Schrenck-Notzing from the files of her recently-deceased husband.[656] These were some of the much-publicized photographs of "ectoplasm" made by Baron Albert von Schrenck-Notzing (1862-1929),[657] a medical doctor who had been a fellow student of Sigmund Freud and who

---

[652](...continued)

. . . (Berlin: Deutscher Wirtschaftsverlag, Aktiengeselshaft, 1930), 2:1840-1841.

Stenger was the most prolific author on the history of photography of his generation. Among his publications was a book for which he had served as co-author that described his collection of early photography as probably the largest in the world; see: Wilhelm Drost and Erich Stenger, *Die Daguerreotypie in Berlin, 1839-1860: ein Beitrag zur Geschichte der photographischen Kunst* (Berlin; R. Bredow, 1920; reprinted in: Robert Sobieszek, editor, *The Daguerreotype in Germany: Three Accounts* (New York: Arno Press, 1979), 119.

[653]Beaumont Newhall, "Photo Eye of the 1920s: the Deutsche Werkbund Exhibition of 1929," *New Mexico Studies in the Fine Arts*, volume II (1977), 5-12, here 7 and 12; Eskildsen and Horak, editors, *Film und Foto der zwanziger Jahre*, 73-75; and Stotz, editor, *Film und Foto* (New York: 1979), 50; *idem* (Stuttgart: 1979), *ibid*.

Part of Stenger's collection is now in the Museum Ludwig, Cologne.

[654]Roh and Tschichold, *editors, Photo-Eye*, plate 53.

[655]Stotz, editor, *Film und Foto* (New York: 1979), 50; *idem* (Stuttgart: 1979), *ibid*; and Roh and Tschichold, *editors, Photo-Eye*, plate 73.

[656]Stotz, editor, *Film und Foto (New York)*, page I following page 94; *idem* (Stuttgart: 1979), page [I] following page 80 and unnumbered pages following page VI that followed page 80. One of the Schrenck-Notzing photographs shown at *Fifo* was reproduced in: László Moholy-Nagy, "Die wichtigsten Epochen aus der Geschichte der Fotografie," *Das Werk: Schweizer Monatsscrift für Architektur, freie Kunst, angewandte Kunst*, volume XVI, number 9 (September, 1929), 258-267, here 261.

Obituaries of Albert Schrenck-Notzing appeared in: *Berliner Tageblatt und Handels-Zeitung*, Abend-Ausgabe, February 13, 1929, [7]; and in *Vossische Zeitung: Berlinische Zeitung von Staats- und gelehrten Sachen*, Post Ausgabe, February 13, 1929, [5].

[657]Schrenck-Notzing, Baron Albert von, *Phenomena of Materialisation; a Contribution to the Investigation of Mediumistic Teleplastics*, translated by E.E. Fournier d'Albe (London: K. Paul, Trench, Trubner & Co., Ltd.; New York: E.P. Dutton & Co., 1920); and *idem*, *Materialisationsphaenome: ein Beitrag zur Erforschung der mediumistischen Teleplastie*, [second, extensively revised edition] (Munich: Verlag von Ernst Reinhardt, 1923 [1913]). Both editions are illustrated with numerous photographs made by Schrenck-Notzing and other photographers.

went on to become a well-known researcher in parapsychology.[658] Except for a cryptic comment in 1925 to his friend Hannah Höch about ectoplasm, described in Chapter Two, there is no evidence as to whether Moholy had a personal interest in parapsychology or was merely trying to be encyclopedic. Photographs of ectoplasm, including those of Schrenck-Notzing, finally became the subject of artistic discourse in 2003.[659]

Over the opening through which one entered the other rooms from Room One a question was posted in large capital letters: *WOHIN GEHT DIE FOTOGRAFISCHE ENTWICKLUNG?* [WHITHER GOES THE DEVELOPMENT OF PHOTOGRAPHY?] (DVD figure 315)

BECAUSE THE IMPACT of Room One in Stutgart was due in part to the configuration of the exhibition space available and its gateway position to the other galleries, it is not clear how the images shown in Room One were set up in the tour venues and what impact the images shown might have been in a different physical environment. In the case of the space available in Berlin, the light court of the Kunstgewerbemuseum (DVD figure 313), however, Oliver Botar has documented that the effect was comparable.[660] He was also able to document Leonardo's *Mona Lisa* as part of a group of art-historical reproductions, presumably also shown in Stuttgart and aimed at demonstrating the impact of photography on making art masterpieces more widely available.

Room One reflected the ideas on photography Moholy had first set forth in his book, discussed in Chapter Three, *Painting, Photograph, Film*, which had just been published in a new German edition (1927; earlier edition 1925). (The first foreign-language edition appeared in Russian in Moscow in 1929.)[661] In his book Moholy had condemned photography that tried to imitate painting trends, such as Romanticism or Impressionism,[662] and instead turned to a range of images free from that pre-occupation including, among others, press photographs, sports photographs, microphotographs,

---

[658]Eskildsen and Horak, editors, *Film und Foto der zwanziger Jahre*, 240-241; Karl Steinorth, *Photographen der 20er Jahre* (Munich: Prisma Verlag, 1987), 88-89; J. Gordon Melton, editor, *Encyclopedia of Occultism & Parapsychology*, fourth edition (Detroit: Gale Research, 1996), 2:1138-1139; and Rosemary Ellen Guiley, *The Encyclopedia of Ghosts and Spirits* (New York: Facts on File, 1992), 294-295.

[659]Karl Schoonover, "Ectoplasm, Evanescence, and Photography," *Art Journal*, volume LXII, number 3 (Fall, 2003), 30-41.

[660]Botar, "László Moholy-Nagy's New Vision and the Aestheticization of Scientific Photography in Weimar Germany," 549-551.

[661]The Russian cover and title page are illustrated in Passuth, *Moholy-Nagy*, figures 245-246.

[662]László Moholy-Nagy, *Painting, Photography, Film*, 48-49. See also: Andrea Nelson, "László Moholy-Nagy and *Painting Photography Film*: a Guide to Narrative Montage," *History of Photography*, volume XXX, number 3 (Autumn, 2006), [258]-266, here 261-263.

X-ray photographs, photograms, photograms and photographs used in graphic design, photocollages, photographs of reflections in convex mirrors, negative prints, superimpositions of images through double exposure, film stills, a photograph of lightning, striking details from natural settings including a herd of zebras, and extreme close-ups.[663] Most of the images in his book were not made by professional photographers, but what all the images had in common was that they were not derived from pictorial trends (except, of course, for two images that Moholy used as examples of photographs influenced by painting).[664]

Moholy later clearly summed up the importance of photography as used "in scientific records, in police work and in reporting."

> In these fields, photography has been employed without art ambitions, but with a knowledge of its working conditions, its science and technology, physical optics and chemistry. Here alone it proved to be the pioneer of an original development, of one peculiar to itself, it being irrelevant whether it was called "art" or not.[665]

Not surprisingly the introductory text to *Photo-Eye*, written by Franz Roh as a way of explaining the *Film und Foto* exhibition, reflected Moholy's point of view as, *e.g.*, when Roh condemned the prevalent practice of "a frank or disguised attempt to imitate the charm that belongs either to painting or graphic art" as "a deviation of the proper task of photography."[666] And the exhibition as a whole was carefully described at the time by

---

[663] László Moholy-Nagy, *Painting, Photography, Film*, *passim*.

[664] László Moholy-Nagy, *Painting, Photography, Film*, 48-49. One of the two was a photograph of 1911 by Alfred Stieglitz that Moholy dismissed as Impressionist; it showed a Paris bi-level street scene. This was, however, the same Alfred Stieglitz from whom he had requested assistance in moving to New York early in 1923, as described in Chapter Two. Stieglitz would have seen his photograph reproduced in: *idem*, *Malerei, Photographie, Film*, Bauhausbücher 8 (Munich: Albert Langen Verlag,1925), 40; and/or in: *idem*, *Malerei, Fotografie, Film*, Bauhausbücher 8, 2. veränderte Aufl. (Munich: Albert Langen Verlag), 1927), 47.

Stieglitz was evidently hurt by being identified as a photographer caught up by the dead hand of the past. In 1941 he refused to comment on a Moholy photograph because he said he had a "personal prejudice against him"; see: Mary Street Alexander and Andrea Gray Stillman, editors, *Ansel Adams: Letters and Images, 1916-1984* (Boston: New York Graphic Society, 1988), 123.

[665] Laszlo Moholy-Nagy, "Photography in the Study of Design," *The American Annual of Photography, Volume Fifty-nine, 1945* (Boston: American Photographic Publishing Co., 1944), 158-164, here 158.

[666] Franz Roh, "The Essence and Value of Photography," in Roh and Tschichold, editors, *Photo-Eye*, unpaginated.

one reviewer as an exhibition that had nothing to do with that kind of *pseudokünstlerische* [pseudo-artistic] photograph.[667]

It was not principally his work on Room One that was important in fostering Moholy's international reputation, but rather the work he showed in Room Five, which was devoted solely to him. No individual photographs were listed; instead the catalogue referred to 97 photographs, photograms and photocollages from a forthcoming book by the Munich publisher Albert Langen.[668] In the end only 60 photographs appeared in a 1930 book called *60 Fotos*, brought out by another publisher,[669] but it was still a prestigious publication, with text and captions in German, French and English, and it allows us to get a good idea of what was shown by Moholy in Stuttgart. Included in *60 Fotos*, the only monograph on Moholy as a photographer brought out during his lifetime, were worm's-eye and bird's-eye photographs (DVD figures 177 and 317), "straight" photographs emphasizing diagonals (DVD figure 176), negative prints (DVD figure 317 right), photocollages (DVD figure 318) and photograms.

Another publication, *Photo-Eye* of 1929, illustrated three photographs by Moholy, along with much more work of other photographers who showed in Stuttgart than was illustrated in the exhibition catalogue.[670] For this reason *Photo-Eye* thrust Moholy, more forcefully than did *60 Fotos*, into an international context of innovation, especially for those who had not seen the *Film und Foto* exhibition itself, since *60 Fotos* was made up entirely of Moholy's work.

In his essay in *Photo-Eye*[671] Roh referred to the three Moholy photographs included in the book. Concerning the reaction to *Paris Drain* (1925; *Photo-Eye* plate 38) (DVD figure 188), he wrote: " . . . I remember how some people, otherwise quick at grasping, would not make allowances for the taking of [a photograph of] the Paris sewerage canal, until those very same people finally arrived at understanding how expressive and almost symbolic such fragments of reality can become." He grouped negative prints by Moholy (*Boat under Tow*, 1927; *Photo-Eye* plate 69) and by himself (*Photo-Eye* plates 64-65) as a variety of the "reality-photo," employing the principle of inversion. (DVD figure 317

---

[667]Riezler, "'Form,' Foto und Film," 365-366.

[668]Stotz, editor, *Film und Foto* (New York: 1979), 69; *idem* (Stuttgart: 1979), *ibid*.

[669]László Moholy-Nagy, *60 [i.e. Sechzig] Fotos*, 1st volume of Fototek (books of modern photography), edited [and with an introduction] by Franz Roh (Berlin: Klinkhardt & Biermann Publishers, 1930).

[670]Roh and Tschichold, editors, *Photo-eye*. Cited fully in note 648.

[671]Roh, "The Essence and Value of Photography," unpaginated. In *Photo-Eye*, the tri-lingual book cited fully in note 648. The English text is a charming but somewhat quaint translation.

right) And he praised Moholy's photomontage, *Leda and the Swan*[672] (1925; *Photo-Eye* plate 55): "How flexible, transparent and delicate is the play of forms . . ." (DVD figure 318)

IT IS IMPOSSIBLE TO KNOW exactly how many works were shown at *Film und Foto* in Stuttgart, but the number exceeded one thousand. A careful reading of the catalogue indicates that there were 977 numbered entries plus some unnumbered ones, in addition to whatever was shown in Room One, for which no individual entries or numbers were listed. Even so, Moholy's 97 photographs in Room Five, plus whatever of his work was shown in Room One, means that about ten per cent of the exhibition was devoted to him, and that his work constituted the largest single component. John Heartfield (1891-1968) was the only individual other than Moholy to have a room devoted solely to him.[673] Born Helmut Herzfeld, he had been a leading Berlin Dadaist and went on to become a highly creative photocollage artist. Room Four, organized by Moholy's old friend El Lissitzky,[674] showed individual Soviet photographers and also documented the work of the Russian Aerodynamics Institute.

Some photographers were grouped by academic institutions, including the Bauhaus;[675] this was probably the first time that the Bauhaus was brought to the attention of a broad audience as a school noted for its work in the field of photography. Also represented was the photochemical department of the Berlin women's vocational school known as *Lette-Verein*, which showed an X-ray photograph.[676]

----

[672] The original photomontage is in the George Eastman House, Rochester; see also the photograph with Moholy's inscription on *recto* in: Lusk, *Montagen ins Blaue*, 134-135.

[673] A gallery photograph appears in: Eskildsen and Horak, editors, *Film und Foto der zwanziger Jahre*, 191; two gallery photographs appear in: Steinorth, *Photographen der 20er Jahre*, 51.

[674] Stotz, editor, *Film und Foto* (New York: 1979), 10, 73-74; *idem* , *Film und Foto* (Stuttgart: 1979), *ibid*.; Steinorth, *Photographen der 20er Jahre*, 66-67; and "Film und Foto Stuttgart: das Ausland und die Werkbundausstellung," *Die Form; Zeitschrift für gestaltende Arbeit*, volume 4, number 5 (March 1, 1929), 123.

[675] "Werkbundausstellung Stuttgart 1929 Film und Foto . . . die Ausstellung und die deutschen Fachschulen," *Die Form; Zeitschrift für gestaldende Arbeit*, volume 4, number 7 (April 1, 1929), 177; Stotz, editor, *Film und Foto (New York: 1979)*, 51-53; *idem* (Stuttgart: 1979), *ibid*.; Eskildsen and Horak, editors, *Film und Foto der zwanziger Jahre*, 77-79 and 81. Bauhaus photographers also showed as a group in Vienna; see: Österreichischer Werkbund, *Internationale Ausstellung Film und Foto*, 5.

[676] Stotz, editor, *Film und Foto* (New York: 1979), 50; *idem* (Stuttgart: 1979), *ibid*; Roh and Tschichold, *Photo-Eye*, plate 21. The X-ray photograph is illustrated in: László Moholy-Nagy, "Die wichtigsten Epochen aus der Geschichte der Fotografie," 262.

The director of the *Lette-Verein* was Lilly Hauff (born 1876). Concerning the *Lette-Verein*, see: Lilly Hauff, *Der Lette-Verein in der Geschichte der Frauenbewegung* [The Lette-Verein in the history of the women's movement] (Berlin: J. Jastrow, 1928); Doris Obschernitzki, *Der Frau*

(continued...)

Edward Weston (1886-1958) was listed as one of two collaborators from the United States, along with Edward Steichen, who helped to organize the exhibition.[677] Nevertheless Weston wrote that Richard Neutra (1892-1970) had asked him to choose the American photographs because he (Neutra) was "Representing in America an important exhibit of photography to be held in Germany this summer. . . ." Weston added that: ". . . he has given me complete charge of collecting the exhibit, choosing the ones whose work I consider worthy of showing. . . ."[678] All nine of the photographers chosen by Weston lived in New York or in or near the San Francisco Bay Area (it is not clear who chose Man Ray, who was then living in Paris.) New Yorkers included Berenice Abbot (who was later to make a brief appearance in Chicago at the Institute of Design), Paul Outerbridge, Charles Sheeler, Edward Steichen and Ralph Steiner; Californians included Imogen Cunningham, Roger Sturtevant, Brett Weston and Edward Weston himself. Eight years later Moholy, from his base in Chicago, began to alter the geography of photography in the United States, so to say. It is now generally agreed that *three* major circles of photographers developed in twentieth-century America, centered in New York, in San Francisco, and in Chicago, respectively, for, as critic Andy Grundberg noted in 1976:

> [There] was an experimental, as-yet-unnamed axis of photographic activity that set down in Chicago; its impresario was Laszlo Moholy-Nagy, its crucible the Bauhaus, its blossoming in the 1950s and early '60s with the emergence of a number of important younger photographers.[679]

The Zurich venue was reviewed by Moholy's friend, art-historian Sigfried Giedion, who reminded his readers of the success the Wurtemburg branch of the Werkbund had had two years earlier in their well-received Weißenhof-Siedlung architecture-and-design exhibition in Stuttgart, and proclaimed that *Film and Foto* was comparable in importance. He compared the opportunities opened up by the development of photography with the new possibilities opened up for architecture by industrialization,

---

[676](...continued)
ihre Arbeit!: Lette-Verein: zur Geschichte einer Berliner Institution 1866 bis 1986 [For Every woman her own career!: Lette-Verein: on the history of a Berlin institution from 1866 to 1986] (Berlin: Edition Hentrich, 1987); and Eskildsen and Horak, editors, *Film und Foto der zwanziger Jahre*, 87-88.

[677]Stotz, editor, *Film und Foto*, 10. See also: Steinorth, "Die Internationale Werkbundausstellung 'Film und Foto' und ihre Organisatoren," unpaginated.

The best source on the American role in the organization of *Film und Foto* is Beaumont Newhall in his 1977 essay, "Photo Eye of the 1920s: the Deutsche Werkbund Exhibition of 1929," cited fully in note 648.

[678]Edward Weston, *The Daybooks of Edward Weston*, edited by Nancy Newhall (Millerton, New York: Aperture, 1973), 2:102-103.

[679]Andy Grundberg, "Photography: Chicago, Moholy and After," *Art in America* (September/October, 1976), 34-39.

and compared architects who used the new materials of construction provided by modern industry, such as steel or reenforced concrete skeletons, merely as a support for derivative carved-stone façades, to photographers who used photography merely to imitate traditional art media. He therefore praised the inclusion in *FiFo* of photographs used for police work, botanical studies, news reporting, microcopying, X-rays, etc., as well as those produced by innovators such as Man Ray and Moholy, as being free of the taint of imitating other art media.[680] In short, Giedion endorsed Moholy's ideas about the direction photography should take.

The Stuttgart *Film und Foto* exhibition can be seen as the climax of a series of more modest exhibitions staged earlier.[681] The first comprehensive photographic exhibition in Germany since the pre-war years was called *Kino- und Photo- Ausstellung* and was also known as *Kipho*; it was held in the *Funkhaus Berlin* from September 25th to October 4th, 1925.[682] The exhibition was evidently set up with more ambition than skill; it was summed up by Ise Gropius, who commented: "Looked at the 'Kipho,' which was so badly and confusingly arranged that nothing created a real effect."[683] Perhaps the exhibition was a bit too comprehensive for its sponsors; it had been organized by a broad range of organizations and incorporated scientific, technical, sport and police photographs as well as artistic and amateur photographs, most or all of this following precedents seen in pre-war German exhibitions.[684] Not seen earlier was the incorporation of nineteenth-century artistic and applied photography, made possible by loans from the collection of Erich Stenger;[685] another innovation was the inclusion of films. Other important photographic exhibitions were seen in Frankfurt am Main, with an opening on

---

[680] Sigfried Giedion, "'Film und Foto; zur Wanderausstellung des deutschen Werkbundes im Zürcher Kunstgewerbemuseum," *Neue Zürcher Zeitung*, September 1, 1929, zweite Sonntagsausgabe, Blatt 9, 1.

[681] "Ausstellungsübesicht zur Fotografie und zum Film in Deutschland, 1920-1933 (Gruppenausstellungen),"in: Eskildsen and Horak, editors, *Film und Foto der zwanziger Jahre*, 190-192; and Oliver Botar, "Prolegomena to the Study of Biomorphic Modernism: Biocentrism, László Moholy-Nagy's 'New Vision' and Ernő Kállai's 'Bioromantik'" (Ph.D. dissertation, University of Toronto, 1998), 505-513.

[682] Eskildsen and Horak, editors, *Film und Foto der zwanziger Jahre*, 190; and Kühn, editor, *Neues Sehen in Berlin*, 136-137.

[683] Day-book entry by Ise Gropius for October 2, 1925.

[684] Botar, "Prolegomena," 507-508; and *idem*, "László Moholy-Nagy's New Vision and the Aestheticization of Scientific Photography in Weimar Germany," note 14 on page 540.

[685] Botar, "Prolegomena," 508.

August 14th, 1926;[686] in Basel in April and early May, 1927;[687] in Berlin with an opening on February 12th, 1928, at the *Itten-Schule*, the school there that had been organized by Johannes Itten;[688] and, as discussed near the end of Chapter Three, in Jena from March 25th to May 6th, 1928. Just before *FiFo* opened in Stuttgart, there was a large photographic exhibition, *Fotografie der Gegenwart* [Contemporary Photography] at the Folkwang Museum in Essen, seen from January 20th to February 17th, 1929;[689] a lecture by Moholy, "Fotografie und Film der Zukunft" [Photography and Film of the Future] was presented on the closing day.[690] *Fotografie der Gegenwart* toured to other cities after its closing in Essen, including Berlin, Dresden, Vienna and London.[691]

While there was precedent for most of what was accomplished in Stuttgart, the scale and the clear and appealing organization of the exhibition there, and the fact that it toured extensively, set it apart from these precedents. It also proved to be the last of the series.

After *FiFo*: Moholy's Photographs in Exhibitions and Publications, 1929-1937

As far as can be ascertained, Moholy did not print any of his black-and-white camera photographs. Initially Lucia did a lot of the printing and after they split up he sent all of the negatives to printing firms. Also he did not make photographic records of his works. Again, this was initially done by Lucia and then by commercial firms. As discussed in Chapter Three, Lucia photographed the photocollages.

---

[686]Botar, "Prolegomena," 509-512; and Ute Eskildesn, "Photography and the Neue Schlichkeit Movement," in: Mellor, editor, *Germany: the New Photography, 1927-1933*, 101-112, here 110.

[687]Botar, "Prolegomena," 512-513.

[688]Botar, "Prolegomena," 520-523; and *idem*, "László Moholy-Nagy's New Vision and the Aestheticization of Scientific Photography in Weimar Germany," 340-342.

[689]Botar, "Prolegomena," 527-528; and *idem*, "László Moholy-Nagy's New Vision and the Aestheticization of Scientific Photography in Weimar Germany," 543-544. An invitation is in the Hattula Moholy-Nagy files.

[690]Botar, "Prolegomena," 527; *idem*, "László Moholy-Nagy's New Vision and the Aestheticization of Scientific Photography in Weimar Germany," 543; and Ute Eskildsen, "Fotokunst statt Kunstphotographie: die Durchsetzung des fotografischen Mediums in Deutschland, 1920-1933," in: Eskildsen and Horak, editors, *Film und Foto der zwanziger Jahre*, [8]-25, here 11.

[691]Botar, "László Moholy-Nagy's New Vision and the Aestheticization of Scientific Photography in Weimar Germany," note 19 on page 543; and Kühn, editor, *Neues Sehen in Berlin*, 171-177.

The first in-depth discussion in the United States of Moholy's photography was a 1930 article by Harry Alan Potamkin, "Moholy-Nagy and his Theories of Photography."[692] Potamkin is discussed further below.

Two photographs by Moholy appeared in a German photographic annual for 1930: images of the face of a smiling man (DVD figure 277) and a cat, both made with his Ernemann Camera.[693] In an introductory essay, it was explained that "The publisher of this yearbook has examined 29,000 pictures; those seen here appeared to be the best." Moholy's work was referred to: "Moholy-Nagy the Inexorable; you are spared nothing—not one bump, not one gap in the teeth, not one wrinkle." Moholy's international reputation as a photographer was further enhanced when he participated in the *Premier Salon International du Nu Photographique* in Paris in 1933. This was a truly international exhibition with photographs from the United States, France, and at least eight other European countries. No catalogue was published, but some of the photographs, selected for technical and artistic quality, appeared in a book. Included was the negative image from Moholy's pair of images, *Nude Positive and Negative* of 1931.[694] (DVD figure 319 left) Among the other photographers shown were Man Ray, former Bauhaus student Andreas Feininger, and Moholy's old friend, Ergy Landau.[695]

Perhaps Moholy had helped to pave the way for the *Premier Salon International du Nu Photographique*; a French painter and critic, Jacques Mauny, stressed the importance of the 1929 *Film und Foto* exhibition, and added that in its wake "Paris has suddenly become deeply interested in photography."[696] Readers are reminded that *FiFo* toured but was not shown in France.

Forty-three of Moholy's photographs were shown October 12th through 25th, 1931, in the Delphic Studios, operated by Alma Reed (née Sullivan; 1889-1966) at 9 East Fifty-Seventh Street, New York.[697] The photographs for the exhibition had been obtained from

---

[692] Harry Alan Potamkin, "L. Moholy-Nagy and his Theories of Photography," *American Photography*, volume XXIV, number 5 (May, 1930), 254 and 256; reprinted in: *idem*, *The Compound Cinema*, 540-542.

[693] *Das Deutsche Lichtbild: Jahresschau 1930* (Berlin: Verlag Robert & Bruno Schultz, 1930), plates 23, 76 and 25th unnumbered page following plate 112.

[694] Daniel Masclet, *Daniel Masclet Présente La Beauté de la Femme: Album du Premier Salon International du Nu Photographique, Paris 1933* (Paris: Daniel Masclet, 1933), 51.

[695] Masclet, *Daniel Masclet Présente*, 9, 41, 93 and 94, respectively.

[696] Jacques Mauny, "New Galleries . . ." *The New York Times*, May 11, 1930, X 13.

[697] *Exhibition of Photographs by Moholy-Nagy at the Delphic Studios, 9 East 57 Street, New York City* (New York: Delphic Studios, 1931). The catalogue listed forty-three photographs by title, including three negative photographs, ten photograms and ten photoplastics, and there are quoted texts by Potamkin.

(continued...)

Moholy by a man with whom he had been in contact for some time and who helped Reed with setting up the exhibition,[698] Harry Alan Potamkin (1900-1933); he was the most accomplished and widely published American film critic of his time as well as a poet and a writer about photography.[699] Moholy was not the first photographer shown at the Delphic Studios; Potamkin thought of it as a leading place to exhibit photographs,[700] and in fact in 1930 Edward Weston had had his first exhibition in New York there.

A review of the Moholy exhibition in the Delphic Studios (which was shown alongside work by artist Grace H. Turnbull) appeared in *Art News*:

> The photographic record of Mr. Maholy-Nagy [*sic*], Hungarian artist, showing in America for the first time, is one of individuality and decorative charm. He plays his camera game now straight, now prankishly, taking his effects as they come from nature or else adding his own inventions and manipulations to produce results that are decidedly "modern" in feeling. A word in the catalog refers to this camera-artist as one to whom the "photo is the differentiation of light phenomena, for expressiveness as well as objectivity, for interpenetrations organized as commentary or narration, as well as for projections of absolute patterns." Perhaps this will serve to give some clue to the artist's intentions. But his work, taken by and large, really speaks for itself, and often achieves really beautiful and original results.[701]

Shown at the Delphic Studios were twenty-one photographs that Moholy wished to be priced at sixty dollars each, intended to be part of a group exhibition of European photographers planned by Potamkin,[702] plus twenty-two photographs Moholy had sent to him for publications he was working on.[703]

---

[697](...continued)

On the Delphic Studios, see: Antoinette May, *Passionate Pilgrim; the Extraordinary Life of Alma Reed* (New York: Paragon House, 1993), 227-231, 242 and [244]-245.

[698]László Moholy-Nagy to Julien Levy, TLS, November 7, 1931, Julien Levy archive, Newtown, Connecticut. Potamkin had mentioned Moholy in his writings at least as early as 1929; see: Harry Alan Potamkin, "The Work of Francis Bruguiere," *Transition; an International Quarterly for Creative Experiment*, number 18 (November, 1929), 81-82, here 82. (There are six plates of Bruguiere's photographs preceding page 81.)

[699]Potamkin, *The Compound Cinema, passim.*

[700]Harry Alan Potamkin to László Moholy-Nagy, July 20, 1931; a copy of the letter is in the Julien Levy archive, Newtown, Connecticut.

[701]"Grace H. Turnbull, L. Maholy-Nagy [*sic*], Delphic Studios," *Art News*, volume 30 (October 17, 1931), 8.

[702]Harry Alan Potamkin to László Moholy-Nagy, July 20, 1931.

[703]László Moholy-Nagy to Julien Levy, November 7, 1931.

Julien Levy (1906-1981), mentioned earlier in this chapter, had visited Moholy in Berlin in the summer of 1931 and bought some photographs from him,[704] and had planned to stage a single-artist exhibition for him in his gallery in New York.

The Delphic Studios exhibition in effect meant that Levy never staged a single-artist showing of Moholy's photographs, because he cancelled his plans to do so when he found out about the Delphic Studios exhibition.[705] Instead he included photographs by Moholy in two group exhibitions in 1932.[706] Moholy explained to Levy the circumstances of his sending his photographs to Potamkin[707] and tried, unsuccessfully, to mollify him by sending him enlargements of photographs he had made in the summer of 1931 (which surely included his Finnish photograph now in the Philadelphia Museum of Art).[708] (DVD figure 296)

Levy, who had recently inherited a generous stipend from his mother,[709] and also enjoyed specific financing for his gallery from his widower father,[710] provides quite a contrast with Potamkin, his colleague at the Film Society.[711] Whatever income Potamkin might had derived through Reed from sales of a few of Moholy's photographs would have been minimal. In spite of his accomplishments as a writer about film, Potamkin lived much of his life in poverty, and he died in 1933 at thirty-three years of age from a stomach condition that two of his friends blamed on his poverty-stricken living

---

[704]Levy, *Memoir of an Art Gallery*, 65-66.

[705]Julien Levy to László Moholy-Nagy. ALS, October 27, 1931, Julien Levy archive, Newtown, Connecticut.

[706]"Photography Exhibitions at the Julien Levy Gallery," in: Ware and Barberie, editors, *Dreaming in Black and White*, 320-322, here 320.

[707]László Moholy-Nagy to Julien Levy, November 7, 1931.

[708]László Moholy-Nagy to Julien Levy, November 7, 1931; and Ware and Barberie, editors, *Dreaming in Black and White*, 229.

[709]Ware, "Between Dadaism and MoMA-ism at the Julien Levy Gallery," 15; and Steven Watson, "Julien Levy: Exhibitionist and Harvard Modernist," in: Schaffner and Jacobs, editors, *Julien Levy: Portrait of an Art Gallery*, 80-95, here 83.

[710]Ingrid Schaffner, "Introduction: Portrait of an Art Dealer," in: Levy, *Memoir of an Art Gallery* (2003), xv-vvi.

[711]Levy, *Memoir of an Art Gallery*, 153.

conditions.[712] Although he was a Marxist[713] he wrote for a wide variety of publications, but most of them paid him little or nothing. Potamkin wrote a study of Moholy's photography that appeared in *American Photography*, cited above, a study that was meant as a part of a larger work in preparation, as well as an essay, "New Eyes, New Compositions, New Conscience," that included a discussion of his photography (the essay appeared in a book a copy of which was sent to Moholy but bibliographical information is lacking).[714] In stark contrast, Levy wrote nothing about Moholy except for a passage in his memoirs, much of which was devoted to his worries that he had paid too much for some photographs he bought from him.[715]

Alma Reed had a reputation for being unbusinesslike. Even her close friend and co-founder of the Delphic Studios, José Clemente Orozco (1883-1949),[716] an artist whose career had benefitted enormously from the help she and the gallery gave him, complained in 1931 that her commission from sales could be as high as fifty percent,[717] that she had no records of recent sales, and he did not know what was owed to him.[718] Moholy wrote to Julien Levy that he had written to Reed more than once and never received an answer.[719] In any case, business records of the Delphic Studios have not survived.[720] Delphic Studios had still retained some photographs of Moholy in 1939,

---

[712]Lewis Jacobs, "Introduction," in: Potamkin, *The Compound Cinema*, xxv-xliii, here xxvii. Jacobs wrote: "My last remembrance of Potamkin was the paleness of his face and his effort to smile as we awkwardly tried to make polite conversation. The next morning at age 33 he was dead."

See also: Kenneth Rexroth, "The Function of Poetry and the Place of the Poet in Society," in: *idem*, *World Outside the Window: the Selected Essays of Kenneth Rexroth*, edited by Bradford Morrow (New York: New Directions Pub. Corp., 1987), 1-2. Rexroth knew Potamkin personally and wrote that he died of ". . . an illness which was the direct result of semi-starvation."

[713]Jacobs, "Introduction," xxxiv-xxxv; and Levy, *Memoir of an Art Gallery*, 153-154.

[714]Harry Alan Potamkin to László Moholy-Nagy, July 20, 1931.

[715]Levy, *Memoir of an Art Gallery*, 66.

[716]May, *Passionate Pikgrim*, 227-229.

[717]Potamkin considered the usual gallery fee to be fifteen percent; see: Harry Alan Potamkin to László Moholy-Nagy, July 20, 1931.

[718]Alejandro Anreus, *Orozco in Gringoland; the Years in New York* (Albuquerque: University of New Mexico Press, 2001), 44 and note 71 on page 154.

[719]László Moholy-Nagy to Julien Levy, TLS, undated [early 1933], and TLS, March 14, 1933, and TLS, April 20, 1933, all in the Julien Levy archive, Newtown, Connecticut.

[720]Anreus, *Orozco in Gringoland*, 36, 41 and 43-44.

when most of them were purchased for five-hundred dollars for the Museum of Modern Art in New York by Beaumont Newhall.[721]

Levy did no better than Reed in selling Moholy's photographs (or, indeed, those of the other photographers shown in his gallery). After including Moholy's photographs in the two group showings in 1932, Levy reported that none were sold; how many, if any, were sold in his gallery later is not known. But, as noted in the following paragraph, many of them eventually entered museum collections.

To sum up, the long-term results for Moholy of the efforts of Julien Levy, Harry Alan Potamkin and Alma Reed were that Moholy had a one-artist showing of his photographs in the Delphic Studios in New York in 1931; also his work was included by Julien Levy in two group photography exhibitions in New York in 1932; thirty-seven of his photographs were acquired from the Delphic Studios by the Museum of Modern Art in New York in 1939; the Art Institute of Chicago acquired numerous examples of Moholy's work from Julien Levy, beginning in 1975;[722] and a modest number of good examples of his work entered the Philadelphia Museum of Art, as part of their acquisition of photographs from the Julien Levy estate in 2001 and 2004.[723] Moreover, Moholy's photographs were shown at the *International Exhibition of Photography* at the George Walter Vincent Smith Art Gallery, Springfield, Massachusetts, from February 4th to 16th, 1933. Included were twelve photographs lent by the Delphic Studios.[724]

It should be added that while Levy was visiting Moholy in Germany in 1931, he had spent a weekend with him and his wife,[725] and as a result he also acquired a number of

---

[721] Lynes, *Good Old Modern*, 160; and Beaumont Newhall, *Focus; Memoirs of a Life in Photography* (Boston: Little, Brown and Company, 1993), 57-58.

The number of photographs purchased for the Museum of Modern Art was thirty-seven and they were catalogued under accession numbers 473.39-510.39.

It can be assumed that after Potamkin's death in July, 1933, the photographs sent to him by Moholy for publication stayed in the Delphic Studios, which was why more were still available there in 1939 than just the twenty-one photographs Moholy had specifically sent for sale. Moholy wrote that Reed had sold some pictures for Potamkim, but did not specify how many, although those sold were evidently few in number; see: László Moholy-Nagy to Julien Levy, TLS, March 14, 1933, Julien Levy archive, Newtown, Connecticut.

[722] Ingrid Schaffner, "Alchemy of the Gallery," in: Schaffner and Jacobs, editors, *Julien Levy: Portrait of an Art Gallery*, 20-53, here 52-53; and David Travis, *Photographs from the Julien Levy Collection, Starting with Atget* (Chicago: The Art Institute of Chicago, 1976), 7, 22 *et passim*.

[723] Ware and Barberie, editors, *Dreaming in Black and White*, 7, 10-11, 58-60, 229, 237 and 254.

[724] An exhibition list is in the Julien Levy archive, Newtown, Connecticut.

[725] Levy, *Memoir of an Art Gallery*, 66.

photographs by Lucia Moholy, some of which are now in the Art Institute of Chicago and in the Philadelphia Museum of Art.[726]

Contributing to Moholy's international reputation as a photographer was his article, "How Photography Revolutionizes Vision," published in a British weekly late in1933.[727] The article was translated by P. Morton Shand, and was one result of their meeting at the *CIAM* in the summer of that year.

Sixteen of Moholy's photographs appeared in *Photography Year Book* for 1935, an ambitious publication of 464 pages.[728] There was no text, except for a brief introduction, but the photographs were thoughtfully arranged into a number of categories. One was trick photography, and items by Moholy included in this section were a photocollage, two sets of positive-and-negative prints, and two photograms.[729] Numerous pages were devoted to the camera in advertising, and included was an item designed by Moholy for *Der Konfektionär*.[730] (DVD figure 281) Moholy was also well represented in a similar volume of *Photography Year Book* that appeared in 1937.[731]

The only one-person showing of Moholy's photographs in England during his residence there took place April 4th through 30th, 1936, when forty-six of his photographs were shown at the Royal Photographic Society galleries at 35 Russell Square in London, an exhibition set up by Charles Sewter.[732] No catalogue or checklist can be located, but an anonymous review appeared in *The Times*:

> An adventurous use of the camera, but strictly on photographic lines, is shown in the exhibition of 46 works by Mr. L. Moholy-Nagy at the Royal Photographic Society, 35, Russell Square. Some "stills" of special effects for the film *Things to Come* are included, but, taken from their context, they do not convey very much, and the interest of the exhibition is in the pictures taken at odd angles or of unusual subject matter, such as "Scaling the Mast" and "Fish Bones," and the photomontages and "Photogrammes"—which may be described as a sort of

---

[726] Ware and Barberie, editors, *Dreaming in Black and White*, 59-61 and 240.

[727] László Moholy-Nagy, "How Photography Revolutionizes Vision," *The Listener*, November 8, 1933, 688-690. *The Listener* was published by the British Broadcasting Corporation (BBC).

[728] T. Korda, editor, *Photography Year Book* [volume I, 1935] (London: "Photography" and Cosmopolitan Press, Ltd., 1935), 132, 158, 173, 177, 180, 209, 210, 216, 253, 262, 264 and 289.

[729] Korda, editor, *Photography Year Book* [1935], 253, 262 and 263, respectively.

[730] Korda, editor, *Photography Year Book* [1935], 289.

[731] T. Korda, editor, *Photography Year Book; the International Annual of Camera Art, Vol. II, 1936-37* (London: "Photography" and Cosmopolitan Press, 1937), 128, 222, 224, 255, 288, 291, 319 and 323. *Photography*, edited by T. Korda, was described in *Photography Year Book* as "the world's leading professional and amateur photo monthly."

[732] Senter, "Moholy-Nagy in England," 125-126.

photographic surrealism. But the net result of the exhibition is to confirm the belief that the artistic possibilities of photography come before exposure.[733]

NOT LONG BEFORE LEAVING ENGLAND, at some point before March 26th, 1937, Moholy made a sequence of photographs at Hull, a major English port.[734] As noted below, he had been invited to lecture at the Hull School of Architecture by its founder, Leslie Martin (1908-1999), one of several friends he had met through the Modern Architecture Research Group (MARS), the British section of *CIAM*. The photographs came about because while in Hull Moholy, staying at the home of Leslie Martin (knighted in 1957 as Sir Leslie Martin) and his wife, the architect Sadie Speight, Moholy made a morning stroll with them through the docks, photographing as they proceeded along an area described by Terence Senter as a " . . . half-mile right angle of busy streets formed by Humber Dock Street . . . Minerva Terrace . . . and Nelson Street waterfront.[735] (DVD figures 320 and 321) Senter has reported on his interviews with Martin in 1972 and 1980:

> Sir Leslie recalls Moholy's spontaneous choice of subjects, and his darting and diving for unusual viewpoints with his manœverable, unobtrusive 35 mm Leica camera that had proved so convenient for candid work on his books.[736]

Senter went on to point out that the sequence of seventy photographs survive only in a series of contact prints once owned by Martin; each print bears a frame number, thus preserving the order of Moholy's creative procedure. Senter also pointed out that Moholy had "manœvered the pictorial elements in his view finder" and went on to analyze the carefully calculated results.[737]

There was a social element to the pictures as well, since many document unemployed men loitering around the docks.[738] Moreover, the sequence documents a lost world (as do Moholy's films *Impressions of the Old Harbor at Marseille* and *Big City Gypsies*, as discussed above) because the scenes Moholy photographed in Hull had become "derelict, altered or demolished" by 1981.[739]

---

[733]"Unusual Photography," *The Times* (London), April 7, 1936, 14.

[734]Senter, "Moholy-Nagy's English Photography," 665-668 and 670-671.

[735]Senter, "Moholy-Nagy's English Photography," 670.

[736]Senter, "Moholy-Nagy's English Photography," 670.

[737]Senter, "Moholy-Nagy's English Photography," 670.

[738]Senter,"Moholy-Nagy's English Photography," *e.g.*, photographs 43 and 48 on page 666 and photograph 69 on page 667.

[739]Senter, "Moholy-Nagy's English Photography," 670.

WHILE MOHOLY was still living in England, some of his photographs were shown at the Museum of Modern Art in New York as part of the exhibition of photographs and motion-picture stills, *Photography 1839-1937,* seen there from March 17th to April 18th, 1937; Moholy's work on view consisted of thirteen black-and white photographs (including five photograms, a still from *Thing to Come* and a photograph of set construction for the film), two Dufaycolor transparencies and a four-color photo-engraving of one of the transparencies.[740] Among the black-and-white photographs were a photograph of a nude shown in both positive and negative prints. (DVD figure 319) The exhibition was organized by Beaumont Newhall (1908-1993) with help from Moholy,[741] who met with Newhall in London during the autumn of 1936.[742]

It should be emphasized that the photographs published or exhibited during his lifetime do not represent the totality of Moholy's work in the medium. Among photographs never published or illustrated during his lifetime are eighteen covering the coronation parade for King George VI, May 18th, 1937 (a natural subject for someone who as a child had been convinced that he was a prince!).[743] (DVD figures 322 and 323)

Innovations in Exhibition Design

Room One at *FiFo* in Stuttgart proved to be typical of Moholy's heavy involvement in exhibition design, which began shortly after he left the Bauhaus and continued throughout the rest of his life. And this was the only design field in which he did on-site work in Germany, France, the Netherlands, Belgium, the United Kingdom and the United States.

The first of these designs was for an autumn, 1928, open-air exhibition Moholy and Gropius set up to promote a housing-estate project of Adolf Sommerfeld (1886-1964), one of the latter's principal patrons, dating back to 1921 when Bauhaus students began decorative work on his wooden house in Berlin (Walter Gropius and Adolf Meyer, 1921-1922, demolished). Sommerfeld, a real-estate developer, was collaborating with another housing enterprise under the overall banner *Bauen und Wohnen* [Building and Living], in

---

[740]Beaumont Newhall, editor, *Photography, 1839-1937* (New York: The Museum of Modern Art. 1937), 115, 119 and plates 69-70.

[741]Newhall, editor, *Photography, 1839-1937,* 5-7.

[742]Newhall, *Focus; Memoirs of a Life in Photography,* 47, 49; idem, "*Vision in Motion,* by L. Moholy-Nagy," *Photo Notes: Official Publication of the Photo League, Inc., New York* (March, 1948), 9-11 (portions reprinted in: Kostelanetz, Moholy-Nagy, 70-71); Lynes, *Good Old Modern,* 155-157; and Senter, "Moholy-Nagy in England," 126-127.

[743]Nine of the coronation photographs are illustrated in: David and Diserens, editors, *László Moholy-Nagy* (Valencia), [383]. The coronation photographs are nine pasted contact prints on each of two sheets; they were formerly in the collection of Helmuth Franke and are now in a private collection. Franke is discussed below.

an exhibition seen in September and October, 1928. It was located in the neighborhood
known as *Fischtalgrund* in the outlying Berlin *Bezirk* [borough] of Zehlendorf.
Evidently Gropius was in general charge of *Bauen und Wohnen*;[744] in any case Moholy
was in charge of the signage.

Fischtalgrund and other Zehlendorf neighborhoods offered ample building
opportunities in a wooded countryside. Here homes could be built to relieve a severe
Berlin housing shortage. Moreover, the new residents would be served by growing
rapid-transit facilities that could move them readily to other parts of the city.

There were three large-scale housing schemes in Zehlendorf at the time, one merely
proposed and two actually built, all best known by their acronyms. Sommerfeld's
company was known as AHAG-Sommerfeld; AHAG was an acronym for *Allgemeine
Häuserbau A.G.* [General Housing Construction Corporation]. The partner of AHAG in
the exhibition *Bauen und Wohnen* was GAGFAH, an acronym for *Gemeinnützige
Aktiengesellschaft für Angestellten-Heimattstätten* [Communal Corporation for Workers'
Homes]. In addition to its exhibition pavilion on the grounds of *Bauen und Wohnen*,
GAGFAH made its recently built housing estate, adjacent to an attractive stretch of
recently landscaped greenery known as *Fischtal Park*, part of the exhibition. For an
admission fee of one mark visitors could examine one-hundred-and-twenty dwelling
units in twenty-eight buildings, ranging from single-family houses to a twelve-unit
apartment building, all ready to be occupied at the close of the exhibition. Heinrich
Tessenow (1876-1950) was in overall charge, and the buildings erected were designed by
a total of sixteen architects, most of them more or less conservative, but one a leading
Modernist (Hans Poelzig).[745]

P ART OF THE AMBIENCE of the exhibition was the modernist housing estate built by
the third acronym-designated enterprise, GEHAG, or *Gemeinnützige Heimstätten-,
Spar- und Bau-Aktiengesellschaft* [Community Home Saving and Building
Corporation], with buildings designed by Bruno Taut, Otto Rudolf Salvisberg and Hugo
Häring, much of which had been built before the *Bauen und Wohnen* exhibition
opened.[746] Some of the GEHAG estate faced GAGFAH houses across the street known
as *Am Fischtal*. It was on an empty lot on the northeast corner of *Am Fischtal* and *Onkel*

---

[744]Annette Bossmann and Andreas Teltow, *Drei Architekten in Berlin* (Berlin: Märkische Museum,
1993), 49.

[745]Bossmann and Teltow, *Drei Architekten in Berlin* 44-54; and Annemarie Jaeggi, "Waldsiedlung
Zehlendorf 'Onkel Toms Hütte'," in: Norbert Huse, editor, *Siedlungen der zwanziger
Jahre—heute; Vier Berliner Großsiedlungen 1924-1984* (Berlin: Bauhaus-Archiv, 1984), [137]-
158, here 146.

[746]Jaeggi, "Waldsiedlung Zehlendorf 'Onkel Toms Hütte',"[137]-158.

The GEHAG estate was also known as *Onkel-Toms Siedlung*, which took its name not directly
from Harriet Beecher Stowe's well-known book, *Uncle Tom's Cabin*, but from Onkel Toms Hütte,
a venerable Zehlendorf establishment set up to provide refreshments and shelter to people making
excursions to the forests and picturesque small lakes in the area.

Tom Straße (known at the time as *Spandauer Straße*) that the exhibition buildings constructed for *Bauen und Wohnen* were located, slightly west of the GEHAG estate.

The immediate reason Sommerfeld participated in the exhibition was that he owned property adjacent to the GEHAG housing estate on which he had hoped to build five-hundred houses integrated with a large green area. AHAG-Sommerfeld had even taken over the basic costs for extending the subway (*U-Bahn*) system to the area, but in the end its planned houses were not built.[747]

Moholy had no reason to suspect that Sommerfeld's project would not be realized, and he threw himself into the task at hand with characteristic vigor and creative imagination. Meanwhile, Xanti Schawinsky (1904-1979), still a student at the Bauhaus, designed and set up the GAGFAH exhibition space in its pavilion, with help from other students in the school's printing-and-advertising workshop.[748]

The common portion of the exhibition grounds included a large wooden open-air restaurant with a grandstand-type roof. (DVD figures 324, 325 and 326) AHAG was spelled out in suspended lettering on the open side, indicating an entrance to its portion of the exhibition. The restaurant was enlivened with brightly-colored accents presented in pennants and hanging colored discs. From one side of the restaurant visitors progressed to the AHAG-Sommerfeld portion of the exhibition grounds, consisting of nine interconnecting demountable structures, resembling market stalls, painted green and enlivened with bright color accents. Visitors, who could approach the "stalls" from the courtyard or from a pathway separated by a some trees from *Onkel Tom Straße*, (DVD figure 324) could see each of them in partial or "teaser" views from openings facing the courtyard (DVD figures 327 and 328) or from windows facing the pathway (DVD figure 330), as well as from the inside, where they were connected by a long straight hallway. (DVD figure 331) Moholy explained to his friend Sigfried Giedion what the visitor would see in these "stalls":

> Moveable walls lettered with new slogans, rotating color filters, light projectors, signal demonstrations and reflectors: transparency, light and movement all in the service of the public. Everything was so arranged that it can be handled and understood by the simplest individual. Then also the exciting use of new materials: huge sheets of celluloid, lattice work, enlargements, small and large sheets of wire meshing, transparent displays, with lettering suspended in space, everywhere clear and brilliant colors.[749]

---

[747]Nerdinger, *Walter Gropius*, 108; and Jaeggi, "Waldsiedlung Zehlendorf 'Onkel Toms Hütte'," 147 and 149.

[748]Brüning and Droste, editors, *Das A und O des Bauhauses*, 244-245 and 314.

[749]Sigfried Giedion, *Walter Gropius, Work and Teamwork* (New York: Reinhold Publishing Corporation, 1954), 49. No color photographs or renderings are available; the colors are known only through verbal descriptions.

The most dramatic of the slogans presented was: *"Heraus aus dem Steinmeer—Wohnen im Grünen"* [Out of the stone sea—living in the green]. (DVD figure 330) That is, in some of the densely-populated neighborhoods of Berlin one saw only stone and other hard surfaces, with little or no greenery, but in the new neighborhoods on its southern outskirts one could live in and interact with a green landscape. (The urban "stone sea" was carefully documented in Moholy's 1932 film *Berliner Stilleben*.) Another slogan was *"So Baut Amerika,"* marking a room devoted to American building practices that, it was argued, could be utilized in Germany to lower the cost of new housing.[750] (DVD figure 331)

Both the open-air restaurant and the exhibition pavilions incorporated a play of light and shadow through the "lettering suspended in space" and the open-work construction of the support of the restaurant roof. Moholy described these in *von material zu architektur*[751] and in *The New Vision*. In the latter he wrote: "A 'section of space' is cut out of cosmic space by a network of strips, wires and glass, just as if space were a divisible, compact object. The new architecture is in complete interpenetration with outer space."[752]

Basically, Gropius and Moholy wanted exhibition visitors to enjoy a lively and festive occasion during which they would learn much about Modernist views on housing, including siting, design, interior spaces, and cost reductions through innovative construction methods and the use of new building materials. The results were extensively documented by Lucia Moholy.[753]

Adolf Behne praised the work of Moholy and Gropius: "Diese Sonderausstellung der 'AHAG,' von Walter Gropius und Moholy-Nagy künstlerisch besorgt, ist ausgezeichnet gelungen und kann als Beistpeil einer guten Ausstellung dienen." [This special exhibition of AHAG, artfully managed by Walter Gropius and Moholy-Nagy, is splendidly laid out and can serve as a good example.] Behne went on to praise the effect of the touches of humor in the exhibition.

---

[750] Hartmut Probst and Christian Schädlich, *Walter Gropius* (Berlin: Ernst & Sohn Verlag für Architektur und technische Wissenschaften, 1986-1988), 2:149.

[751] László Moholy-Nagy, *Von Material zu Architektur*, Bauhausbücher 14 (Munich: Albert Langen Verlag, 1929),220; *idem*, *Von Material zu Architektur*, Bauhausbücher 14. Faksimilie der 1929 erschienen Erstausgaben, neue Bauhausbücher (Mainz: Florian Kupferberg, 1969), 220.

[752] László Moholy-Nagy, *The New Vision* (2005), [190].

[753] *Ibid.*; Sachsse and Hartmann, *Lucia Moholy; Bauhaus Fotografin*, 144. More of her photographs of the *AHAG-Sommerfeld* exhibition can be seen in: Brüning and Droste, editors, *Das A und O des Bauhauses*, 242-245; Nerdinger, *Walter Gropius*, 108; *idem*, editor, *Walter Gropius Archive*, 2:91-92; Reginald R. Isaacs, *Gropius; an Illustrated Biography of the Creator of the Bauhaus* (Boston: Little, Brown, and Company, 1983), 151; Jeannine Fiedler and Peter Feierabend, editors, *Bauhaus* [English-language edition] (Cologne: Könemann, 1999), 498; and Probst and Schädlich, *Walter Gropius*, 2:148-149.

> Hier ist endlich einmal eine Austellung, die nicht Materialmassen irgendwie
> hinbaut und mit ihrer Gestaltlosigkeit und Undurchschaubarkeit selbst der
> wertvollste Material ungenießbar und unfruchtbar macht. Hier ist vielmehr ein
> Gedanke prägnant und logisch und auch mit Witz so durchgeführt, daß unser
> Auge das locker ausgebreitete Material mit Vergnügen aufnimmt.[754] [Here is at
> last an exhibition that does not build up masses of material in some way or other
> and with its lack of structure and opaqueness render even the most valuable
> material unpleasant and sterile. Rather here is a pithy and logical idea and it is
> also executed with so much humor that our eye takes in with pleasure the loosely
> arranged material.]

Moreover, in another review Behne clearly recognized that Moholy had created a new type of exhibition: an organized path was presented to the visitor, rather than presenting a scattered array of things in one large hall:

> In Ausstellung der AHAG (Adolf Sommerfeld) am Fischtalgrund in Zehlendorf,
> von Walter Gropius und Moholy-Nagy gebaut und eingerichtet, ist ein neuer Typ
> der Ausstellung. Hier ist nicht in einergenügend großen Halle irgendwelches
> Material irgendwie untergebracht und wird nicht der Besucher irgendwo vor der
> Materialmassen gestellt. Hier ist vielmehr die Ausstellung der organisiete Weg
> des aufmerksamen Besuchers, und dieser Weg an bestimmten Objecten in
> bestimmter eindeutiger Führung und Folge entlang ist identisch mit dem
> Gedankengang der Aussteller. Die Prinzipien einer modernen Buchregie sind
> hier zum ersten Male auf eine Ausstellung angewandt.[755] [The AHAG (Adolf
> Sommerfeld) exhibition at the Fischtalgrund in Zehlendorf, constructed and
> arranged by Walter Gropius and Moholy-Nagy, is a new kind of exhibition.
> Here material is not accumulated randomly requiring an appropriately large hall
> and thus here the visitor is not confronted in some way by masses of material.
> Rather here the exhibition is the organized path of the alert visitor, and this path
> along particular objects in a clear sequence and direction is identical with the
> intent of the exhibitors. For the first time, the principles of a modern book-
> design have been applied to an exhibition.]

The approach to exhibition design that Behne lauded was evident at the *Section Allemande* of the *Salon des Artistes Décorateurs* in Paris, presented from May 14th through July 13th, 1930, at the *Grand Palais des Champs-Elysées* in Paris.[756] Moholy,

---

[754]Adolf Behne, "Bauen und Wohnen: die Musterhäuser am Fischtalgrund—Siedlung und Ausstellung der GEHAG—die Aufgabe des Bauens," *Die Welt am Abend*, September 3, 1928, 2. Beilage, [1].

[755]Adolf Behne, "Ausstellung der AHAG am Fischtalgrund, Architekt: Walter Gropius, Ausstellungsleitung: L. Moholy-Nagy," *Das neue Berlin: Grosstadtprobleme*, volume I, number (January, 1929), 20. A review by Behne with nearly identical wording appeared in: *idem*, "AHAG-Ausstellung," *i 10; Internationale Revue,* volume 2, numbers 17-18 (December 20. 1928), 94-95.

[756]Section Allemande," in: Société des Artists Décorateurs, *Catalogue du 20e Salon du 15 Mai au 13 Juilliet, 1930* (Paris: Grand Palais des Champs-Elisées, Rue Jean-Goujon, 1930), [165]-205;

(continued...)

Gropius, Bayer and Breuer set up a planned sequence of spaces on two levels through which the visitor was guided among the exhibited items.[757] (DVD figures 332 and 333)

To supplement the catalogue of the showing in Paris, an illustrated bi-lingual guidebook was available, designed by Herbert Bayer, with drawings and diagrams by Stefan Sebök and Rudolf Luderer .[758] (DVD figures 333 and 337)

At the request of the German Werkbund, which had been entrusted by the German government to stage a showing at the Paris *Salon des Artistes Décorateurs*, Gropius organized the *Section Allemande*,[759] which marked the first display of German work in decorative arts and design in the French capital since the war's end. This seemed to herald as improvement of relations between two former adversaries in World War I and, indeed, while the exhibition was still on view, the French ended their occupation of the Rhineland, a conciliatory move overwhelmingly favored by Germans, across the political spectrum.[760] Gropius traveled with Moholy and Bayer to Paris to study the space available and to negotiate details with the officials of the *Salon*; they were there from December 14th to 19th, 1929.[761] During this trip and during subsequent visits to Paris by Gropius and his assistants,[762] and with the aid of measured drawings and photographs,[763] the utilization of the allotted space was carefully worked out. The resulting ease of circulation was favorably noted by one French critic.[764]

---

[756](...continued)
and "Deutscher Geist in Paris," *die neue linie*, volume I, number 11 (July, 1930), 12-13.

[757]Probst and Schädlich, *Walter Gropius*, 2:150 and 152.

[758]Deutscher Werkbund, *Section Allemande: Exposition de la Société des Artistes Décorateurs, Grand Palais, 14. mai-13. juillet* [a bi-lingual, illustrated guidebook] (Berlin: Verlag Hermann Reckendorf, 1930) ; and Brüning and Droste, editors, *Das A und O des Bauhauses*, 251.

[759]Joachim Driller, "Bauhäusler zwischen Berlin und Paris: zur Planung und Einrichtung der 'Section Allemande' in der Ausstellung der Sociéte des Artistes Décorateurs Français 1930," in: Isabelle Ewig, Thomas W. Gaehtgens and Matthias Noell, editors, *Das Bauhaus und Frankreich, Le Bauhaus et la France, 1919-1940* (Berlin: Akademie Verlag, 2002), [255]-258.

[760]"The Rhineland Evacuated: Departure of the Last French Troops," *Manchester Guardian Weekly*, July 4, 1930, 4.

[761] Driller, "Bauhäusler zwischen Berlin und Paris," 258-263.

[762]Driller, "Bauhäusler zwischen Berlin und Paris," 264-270.

[763]Isaacs, *Gropius; an Illustrated Biography*, 156.

[764]Léandre Vaillat, "Au Salon des Artistes décorateurs, II. La section allemande," *Le Temps*, May 27, 1930, 3; reprinted in: Ewig, Gaehtgens and Noell, editors, *Das Bauhaus und Frankreich*, 342-344, here 344.

Harry Kessler, who was mentioned above and who had close ties to France, commented on the *Section Allemande*: "It has caused a considerable sensation here. There is no doubt whatever that it is much more interesting than the French arts and crafts exhibition which is set alongside it."[765]

There was much comment on the *Section Allemande* in the French press, but comment on Moholy's work there, while positive in tone, was confined to brief general remarks.[766]

In the *Section Allemande* Sebök's idea for a cellar wine café, first seen in *The Tales of Hoffmann*, assumed another form as a social room for a high-rise apartment building,[767] part of *Salle 1*, designed by Gropius. (DVD figure 332)

MOHOLY WAS IN CHARGE of *Salle 2*, devoted to lighting, photography, theatre, ballet and the development of modern design in Germany. Mass-produced lamps were shown, some with real examples, others in photographs. (DVD figure 335) The latter included photographs of lamps designed in his metal workshop at the Bauhaus; one of the Bauhäusler included was Marianne Brandt.[768] Also featured was theatrical lighting, using, as one example, as noted above, a photograph by Lucia of his first-act Kroll Opera setting for *Tales of Hoffmann*. The development of new trends in photography was demonstrated with examples of recent German and Soviet photographs, and there were also images of post-war Germany automatically projected on the wall of a small half-open room.[769] (DVD figure 338) Another set of images and text was projected on a wall documenting the development of modern design in Germany in the twentieth century.[770]

Punctuating *Salle 2* were some of Bauhäusler Oskar Schlemmer's costumes. His impressions of the exhibition appeared in a letter:

---

[765]Kessler, *Berlin in Lights*, 389.

[766]Ewig, Gaehtgens and Noell, editors, *Das Bauhaus und Frankreich,* 317-346 *passim.*

[767]A page from the bi-lingual guidebook (cited in note 758) with a rendering credited to Sebök is reproduced in: Fleischmann, editor, *Bauhaus Drucksachen, Typografie, Reklame*, 283; another rendering was published in: Nerdinger, *Walter Gropius*, 143.

[768]László Moholy-Nagy to Marianne Brandt, March [need day], 1930, Bauhaus-Archiv, Berlin.

In the letter Moholy asked Marianne Brandt to rush photographs of her work at the Bauhaus so that he could have enlargements made for the exhibition.

[769]Marcel Breuer, "Die Werkbund Ausstellung in Paris 1930," *Centralblatt für Bauverwaltung*, volume 50, number 27 (July 9, 1930), 477-480, here 477.

[770]*Ibid.*

Three of my ballet figurines are on display there, and I was asked to supervise the installation. Gropius and Moholy had been put in charge . . . and had asked me to participate. Probably they just wanted to get whatever would make the greatest impression. It is remarkable to see what Gropius always manages to produce, a good example being this exhibition in Paris, the first since the war, which was, all in all, pretty impressive.

The association with old Bauhaus comrades revived some old conflicts. Schlemmer added: "There were a few rather unfortunate personality conflicts, especially in connection with Moholy."[771]

It was in the theatrical section of *Salle 2* that Moholy publicly introduced his *Light Prop for an Electrical Stage* (sometimes referred to as *Light Space Modulator*), thus emphasizing its theatrical possibilities.[772] (DVD figures 336 and 337) The origins of this device go back well before 1930; he always dated it as 1922-1930. He was careful to include a rendering of 1922, signed and dated in his hand (DVD figure 106), in his 1929 book, *von material zu architektur*;[773] this rendering, though actually made for the *Kinetic Constructive System*, discussed below, does contain the seeds of the *Light Prop*, as pointed out on page 179 in Chapter Two. One indication that the drawing was also related to the *Light Prop* is that it appeared in the sculpture section rather than the architecture section of *von material zu architektur*. Nevertheless it is not clear how much was accomplished toward constructing the *Light Prop* before 1930, and Moholy seems to have put the idea on hold during his Bauhaus years. Still, the *Light Prop* was in the back of his mind, and, as Winfried Nerdinger has suggested, a number of things that had come to his attention after 1922 seem to have had an impact on his developing thoughts about it.

One of these might be the complex, spiraling outdoor fountain that sculptor Rudolf Belling (1886-1972) designed for the Goldstein Villa that had been erected 1922-1924 (demolished 1957) in the *Westend Bezirk* [borough] of Berlin from designs of Arthur Korn. Belling's fountain dates from 1923; Nerdinger illustrated and discussed the fountain and related works, including Moholy's *Light Prop for an Electrical Stage*.[774] Certainly Moholy would have been aware of the Goldstein Villa, since it was extensively

---

[771] Oskar Schlemmer to Otto Meyer, June 29th, 1930, reprinted in: Oskar Schlemmer, *The Letters and Diaries of Oskar Schlemmer*, selected and edited by Tut Schlemmer, translated from the German by Krishna Winston (Middletown, Connecticut: Wesleyan University Press, 1972), 260-261.

[772] For a comprehensive account of the *Light Prop* and its context see: Hannah Weitemeier Steckel, *Light-Visionen: ein Experiment fon Moholy-Nagy* (Berlin: Bauhaus-Archiv, 1972).

[773] László Moholy-Nagy, *von material zu architektur*, 205. The rendering, a collage with pen and watercolor on paper, 61 by 48 centimeters, is now in the Bauhaus-Archiv, Berlin.

[774] Winfried Nerdinger, *Rudolf Belling und die Kunstströmungen in Berlin 1918-1923, mit eine Katalog der plastischen Werke* (Berlin: Deutscher Verlag für Kunstwissenschaft, 1981), 171-[190].

covered in *MA* in its issue for July 1ˢᵗ, 1924,[775] the issue directly preceding the journal's September 15, 1924, issue that included his renowned *Filmváz* (see Chapter Three, note 571). Although the fountain itself was not illustrated in *MA*, a waterless model had been exhibited in the Große Berliner Kunstausstellung in 1923,[776] and this was an exhibition in which Moholy himself had been represented.

ANOTHER TRANSITIONAL IDEA that led to the *Light Prop* was Moholy's *Kinetic Constructive System.*[777] The rendering of this project, carried out by Stefan Sebök,[778] (DVD figure 107) included carefully-drawn spiral forms, made with mechanical instruments, along with collage elements, including photographs of human figures, strategically placed arrows, and a small color photograph of the American flag.[779] Although Sebök's earlier collages were evidently a bit tame, to judge by the one available example, an invitation to an international festival of 1926,[780] by 1929 his work was good enough to be shown in an international photocollage exhibition in Berlin that included work by Moholy, Höch, Haußmann and other leading practitioners of that medium.[781] His rendering of the *Kinetic Constructive System* is further evidence of Sebök's mastery of photocollage.

The *Kinetic Constructive System* must have seemed like a dead end to Moholy and Sebök after their work on the *Tales of Hoffmann* because it did not encompass the idea of a play of shadows in a theatre (or other enclosed space), while the *Light Prop* could be used for a theatrical play of shadows. Certainly Moholy's explanation of the rendering of the *Kinetic Constructive System* in *von material zu architektur* is confusing and

---

[775]Arthur Korn, "Analitikus és Utopisztikus Architektura," *MA; Aktivista Folyóirat*, volume IX, numbers 6-7 (July 1, 1924), unpaginated (includes 11 illustrations). The translation is by Sándor Vajda.

[776]Willi Wolfradt, "Große Berliner Kunstaustellung," *Der Cicerone; Halbmonatschrift für Künstler, Kunstfreunde und Salmer*, volume XV, number 11, ([June 15], 1923), 522-523, here 523.

[777]For a recent exegesis of the *Kinetic Constructive System* see: Botar, *Technical Detours*, 173-177. The rendering of the *Kinetic Constructive System* probably entered the Theatre Collection of the University of Cologne Institute of Theatre-, Film- and Television Studies because it was borrowed for but not included in an exhibition; see: Niessen, editor, *Das Problemtheater*.

[778]The size is 76 by 54.5 centimeters. It is now in the Theatre Collection of the University of Cologne Institute of Theatre-, Film- and Television Studies.

[779]Reproduced in black-and-white in: László Moholy-Nagy, *von Material zu architektur*, 204; reproduced in color in: David, editor, *László Moholy-Nagy*, 145 and 344.

[780]Reproduced in Fleischmann, editor, *Bauhaus Drucksachen, Typografie, Reklame*, 244.

[781]*Fotomontage; Ausstellung im Lichthof des ehemaligen Kunstgewerbemuseums . . . 25. April bis 31. Mai 1931* (Berlin: Staatliche Museen, Staatliche Kunstbibliothik, 1931), "verzeichnis der aussteller" on unnumbered page.

unconvincing, both in the original German[782] and in the English translation appearing in all five English-language editions (known as *The New Vision*).[783]

However, as Oliver Botar has pointed out, in the 1922 manifesto that Moholy wrote with Alfréd Kemény, "The Dynamic-Constructive System of Forces," discussed in Chapter Two, there was one idea that the *Kinetic Constructive System* implemented and the *Light Prop* did not: this was the idea of the viewer of the work of art moving beyond being "merely receptive." Botar pointed to the relevant passage in the manifesto:

> [With the] Dynamic-Constructive Energy System, man, merely receptive in his observation of works of art produced until now, experiences a heightening of his own faculties, and becomes an active partner along with the unfolding energies.[784]

Botar went on to point to Moholy's love of amusement parks, and, with the help of Peter Yeadon, interpreted the *Kinetic Constructive System* as a rather demanding amusement-park interactive ride, using digital modeling to demonstrate the point.[785] Nevertheless the *Kinetic Constructive System* was never actually implemented.

What brought the *Light Prop* to fruition was the opportunity to show it in Paris, and to get a subvention from a large German electrical company, *Allgemeine Elektrizitäts Gesellschaft*, generally known as *AEG*, for the construction of the device.[786] What evidently interested *AEG* was that the firm was already selling lighting equipment for theatres, and Moholy's *Light Prop* would, in the short term, attract a lot of attention to what was being shown by *AEG* in Paris, and might possibly lead to some promising developments in the future as well. Moreover, the reader is reminded that, as noted above in discussing the character Olympia in *The Tales of Hoffmann*, automata in theatres has a long history, and the *Light Prop* can be seen as one more step in that development, in this case emphasizing the theatrical possibilities of lighting.

---

[782]László Moholy-Nagy, *Von Material zu Architektur*, 204-205.

[783]*E.g.*, László Moholy-Nagy, *The New Vision* (2005), 186-187.

[784]Alfréd Kemény and László Moholy-Nagy, "The Dynamic-Constructive System of Forces," quoted in Botar, *Technical Detours*, 171.

[785]Botar, *Technical Detours*, 170-177 and 204.

[786]László Moholy-Nagy, "Lichtrequisit einer elektrischen Bühne," *Die Form; Zeitschrift für gestaldende Arbeit*, volume V, numbers 11-12 (June, 1930), 297-298, here 297; reprinted in Gaßner, *Wechsel Wirkungen*, 252-257; English translation in: Passuth, *Moholy-Nagy*, 310-311, here 310.

The construction of the *Light Prop* was prepared by Sebök through a series of drawings[787] (DVD figure 339) and executed by the theatrical department of *AEG*.[788] It was displayed in the *Grand Palais* in a cubic box with a circular opening at the front and with over a hundred yellow, green, blue, red and white light bulbs installed inside. When the *Light Prop* was set in motion, bulbs flashed according to a pre-arranged plan, and the results could be viewed through the opening.[789] (DVD figure 337) It was noted that: "If the projection takes place in a darkened room, the rear wall of the box may be removed and the colors and shadows thrown behind the box upon a sheet of any size,"[790] but it is not clear if those viewing conditions were realized at the Paris Exhibition. What is known is that a photograph of Moholy's Act One set for the Kroll Opera production of *The Tales of Hoffmann* (DVD figure 228), still on view in Berlin on a repertory basis, was displayed next to the *Light Prop*, thus suggesting the kinship I am arguing for.

DURING HIS LIFETIME the *Light Prop* never achieved the acclaim Moholy had hoped for. It was shown in single-artist exhibitions in London and Chicago,[791] but it seemed to have attracted little attention at either venue. He lamented that: "Almost no one could grasp the technical wit or the future promise of the experiment."[792] More successful was a black-and-white film of 1931, *A Lightplay Black White Gray*, first shown in 1932 and discussed above. It lacked the color effects that were possible, but Moholy also enhanced its expressive possibilities by utilizing specifically cinematic devices such as juxtapositions, superimpositions and dissolves. Moreover, by eliminating color, Moholy was able to make clear that his cinematic vision had been enriched by his study of photograms, an idea hinted at in his unrealized plans for a film utilizing photograms, discussed in Chapter Two. On the other hand, Moholy also did

---

[787]Some of the drawings are reproduced in: David, editor, *László Moholy-Nagy*, 146-149. Some of the drawings are in the Theatre Collection of the University of Cologne Institute of Theatre-, Film- and Television Studies (see: David, editor, *László Moholy-Nagy*, 146-147 and 344) and some are in the Bauhaus-Archiv in Berlin.

The drawings in Cologne probably are there because they were borrowed for an exhibition; see: Niessen, editor, *Das Problemtheater*, 30-31.

[788]László Moholy-Nagy, "Lichtrequisit," 297; and László Moholy-Nagy, *The New Vision from Material to Architecture*, translated by Daphne M. Hoffmann (New York: Brewer, Warren & Putnam Inc., 1932), 137.

[789]László Moholy-Nagy, *Vision in Motion*, 238; idem, *The New Vision* (1932), 136.

[790]László Moholy-Nagy, "Abridged Translation: Lighting Requisite for an Electric Stage," *Die Form; Zeitschrift für gestaldende Arbeit*, volume V, numbers 11-12 (June, 1930), 299.

[791]Senter, "Moholy-Nagy in England," 251-252; and "If Art Is Moving, Then This Is It," *Chicago Daily Times*, January 9, 1940, page number not available. This article did not appear in the edition of the *Chicago Daily Times* available on microfilm in the Illinois State Historical Library, Springfield. A xerox copy of a clipping is in the Photography Department, Art Institute of Chicago.

[792]László Moholy-Nagy, *The New Vision* (2005), 227.

some paintings which seemed to suggest the expressive possibilities of the *Light Prop* when used with colored lights.[793] (DVD figure 519 and back cover of volume Two) *A Lightplay Black White Gray* was made possible by grants from *AEG* and from the camera-film company *AGFA*,[794] but evidently only enough aid was available to complete one of a planned six parts. Moholy's description makes it seem likely that at least one other part was completed, namely part VI, which would have documented the construction of the Light Prop, something that could only have been done at the time.[795] If that part of the film was actually shot, evidently no footage survives.

We have seen that the origins of the *Light Prop* were not sculptural, but in the 1932 and 1938 editions of *The New Vision*, the Light Prop was illustrated in the section on sculpture, where it was referred to both as sculpture and as a "stage lighting device"; meanwhile the *Kinetic Constructive System* continued to be illustrated in the space-and-architecture section.[796] This circumstance might prompt a reader to recall the kinship between the *Light Prop* and Moholy's *Nickel Construction* of 1921, also illustrated in the sculpture section. Moreover, placing the *Light Prop* in the sculptural section of the book gives it a pioneering place in the history of sculpture with moving parts. In his 1944 essay "Abstract of an Artist," added to *The New Vision* in 1946, Moholy discussed it under the heading "Sculptures and Mobiles" and provided a good extended description of the work and discussed some of what he had learned from making it.[797]

After Moholy died, the *Light Prop* did finally achieve fame. As the *AEG* connection faded from memory, it was easy to associate it with Dada, and, since it is a machine that does not seem to have a function, at least not in the usual machine sense, it is easy to associate it with Moholy's own Dada drawings of 1920, such as *The Machine of Emotional Discharge*. Not only were careful copies of the *Light Prop* made, but artists paid homage to it. The Swiss neo-Dadaist Jean Tinguely (1925-1991) provided an example with his massive *Chaos I* of 1974, installed in an indoor shopping mall in Columbus, Indiana. Moholy had used a slotted orb of billiard-ball size that ran back and forth on a small curved track as parts of the device shifted; (DVD figures 336 and 362) Tinguely devised a similar feature employing a bowling-ball size orb.

---

[793] *E.g.*, "Color variation of part IV [*sic.*, actually part VI]," in: László Moholy-Nagy, *Vision in Motion*, second printing (Chicago: Paul Theobald, 1947), 172 (not included in the first printing).

[794] László Moholy-Nagy, "Probleme des neuen Film," *Die Form*, volume 7, number 5 (ay 15, 1932), 247-255, here editor's note 1 on page 250.

[795] László Moholy-Nagy, *Vision in Motion*, 288-289. An earlier version of this scenario appeared in *Korunk* in 1931 as "Fényjáték-fil"; an English translation appeared in: Passuth, *Moholy-Nagy*, 316-317.

[796] László Moholy-Nagy, *The New Vision* (1932), 136-137 and 164-165; and *The New Vision* (1938), [140]-141 and 186-187.

[797] László Moholy-Nagy, *The New Vision* (2005), 224 and 227.

Asort of afterglow of the Werkbund Ausstellung in Paris was planned, shortly after that exhibition closed, by Alexander Dorner (1893-1957), director of the *Niedersächsisches Landesmuseum* (at the time known as the *Provinzialmuseum*) in Hanover. He had been one of the fiercest supporters of the beleaguered Bauhaus and wrote an impassioned letter in an attempt to avert its closing in Weimar.[798] Dorner had pondered the idea of having a room in his museum that would present the latest ideas in Western visual culture. After visiting the Paris exhibition he was determined to bring his idea to fruition, and used that exhibition as his model, although for a facility to be designed by Moholy on a much smaller scale and to be called the *Raum der Gegenwart* [Room of Our Own Time].[799] A precedent within the *Landesmuseum* was El Lissitzky's *Abstract Cabinet*, or *Kabinett der Abstrakten*, designed and constructed from 1926 to 1928 as another of his "Demonstration Rooms"[800] discussed in Chapter Three, this one designed to highlight the pioneering collection of abstract art Dorner had assembled at the *Landesmuseum* in Hanover; a changing display in that room sometimes included two paintings by Moholy that, although seen in photographs of the *Abstract Cabinet*, cannot now be located.[801] (DVD figure 369)

In the end the *Room of Our Own Time* was not completed, because, even though Dorner had hoped to persuade Werkbund Ausstellung exhibitors to donate parts of their

---

[798]*Pressestimmen für das Staatliche Bauhaus Weimar; Auszüge, Nachtrag, Kundegebungen, 1924,* mit einem Nachwort zur Reprintausgabe von Peter Hahn (Munich: Kraus Reprint, 1980), 130-131.

[799]Samuel Cauman, *The Living Museum; Experiences of an Art Historian and Museum Director, Alexander Dorner*, with an introduction by Walter Gropius (New York: New York University Press, 1958), 109.

[800]A "Demonstration Room" had been set up in Dresden in 1926 and visited by Dorner, who promptly engaged El Lissitzky to design a similar room for the *Landesmuseum* in Hanover; see: Maria Gough, "Constructivism Disoriented: El Lissitzky's Dresden and Hannover *Demonstrationsräume*," in: Nancy Perloff and Brian Reed, editors, *Situating El Lissitzky: Vitebsk, Berlin, Moscow* (Los Angeles: Getty Research Institute, 2003), [76]-125, here [76], 78 and 98.

[801]One painting appears in two photographs of the *Abstract Cabinet* reproduced in: Cauman, *The Living Museum*, 98-99. On the verso of one of these photographs Dorner identified it only as "eine Arbeit von Moholy"; see: Flacke-Knoch, *Museumskonzeptionen in der Weimarer Republik*, 144-145. The painting evidently vanished after seizure by the Nazis in 1937 (see pages 506-508).

The other painting appears in a photograph of the Abstract Cabinet published in Dietrich Helms, "El Lissitzky," in: Eberhard Roters and Hannah Weitemeier Steckel, editors, *Avantgarde Osteuropa 1910-1930* (Berlin: Deutsche Gesellschaft für bildende Kunst [Kunstverein Berlin]), 1967), 26-33, here [31]. That painting also evidently vanished after seizure by the Nazis.

On the *Abstract Cabinet*, see also: Alexander Dorner, "Zur Abstrakten Malerei; Erklärung zum Raum der Abstrakten in der Hannoverschen Gemäldegalerie," *Die Form: Zeitschrift für Gestaltende Arbeit*, volume III, number 4 ([March?], 1928), 110-114; and Gough, "Constructivism Disoriented," [76] and 98-107.

display and ship them directly from Paris to Hanover,[802] construction was delayed due to a shortage of funds after the Landesmuseum had made a major purchase of a medieval altarpiece.[803] The effort to construct the *Room of Our Own Time* was also hindered by political opposition.[804] Nevertheless Moholy and Dorner worked very hard on the project, as attested to by the forty-six letters they exchanged from July 15th to November 26th, 1930,[805] and the four blueprints and a pencil-and-ink drawing made with the assistance of Sebök and Rudolf Luderer.[806] (text figure 13, DVD figure 340) The model they took was *Salle 2* of the *Section Allemande* in Paris, and included the planned installation in Hanover of the *Light Prop for an Electrical Stage*.[807] Although never completed, the *Room of Our Own Time* was opened in an unfinished state, but no photographs have been found.

---

[802]Cauman, *The Living Museum*, 109. See also: László Moholy-Nagy to Alexander Dorner, July 15th, 1930, Dorner-Archiv, Sprengel Museum, Hanover; portions transcribed in: Flacke-Knoch, *Museumskonzeptionen in der Weimarer Republik*, 83-84. The entire letter was transcribed in: Brockhaus and Fath, editors, *Malewitsch-Mondrian,* 7 and 12-13.

In his July 15th, 1930, letter to Dorner, Moholy lists items that could be used in Hanover along with the person or firm from whom requests were to be made. Curiously, in the case of the *Light Prop* Moholy advised Dorner to apply to a Herr Saalbach of the *AEG*, thus implying that he did not own it. As will be seen below, Moholy showed the *Light Prop* in a gallery in London in an exhibition that opened in 1936, and offered to sell it for 300 guineas. In any event, it was in his possession when he died.

[803]Cauman, *The Living Museum*, 51, 53-55 and 110-111. See also: Alexander Dorner to László Moholy-Nagy, TLS, November 5th, 1930, Dorner-Archiv, Sprengel Museum in Hanover; a transcription is in: Brockhaus and Fath, editors, *Malewitsch-Mondrian,* 14.

[804]Alexander Dorner, *The Way Beyond "Art"—The Work of Herbert Bayer* (New York: Wittenborn, Schultz., Inc., 1947), 18; *idem*, *The Way Beyond "Art"* (New York: New York University Press, 1958), 17. See also: Alexander Dorner to László Moholy-Nagy, November 5, 1930.

[805]These letters, and other documents relating to the project, are in the Dorner-Archiv, Sprengel Museum, Hanover. A selection was published in: Flacke-Knoch, *Museumskonzeptionen in der Weimarer Republik*, 160-166; another selection was published in: Brockhaus and Fath, editors, *Malewitsch-Mondrian,* 7-14.

[806]Reproduced in: Veit Loers, "Moholy-Nagys 'Raum der Gegenwart' und die Utopie von Dynamisch-Konstruktiven Lichtraum," in: Catherine David, editor, *László Moholy-Nagy* [exhibition catalogue] ([Stuttgart]: Gerd Hatje, 1991), 36-51, here 38-39.

Stefan Sebök and by Rudolf Luderer had earlier worked with Moholy on the *Section Allemande* of the Deutscher Werkbund exhibition in Paris..

[807]Cauman, *The Living Museum*, 102-103 and 109-111; Flacke-Knoch, *Museumskonzeptionen in der Weimarer Republik*, 78-80; and Sabine Lange, "Der 'Raum der Gegenwart' von Laszlo Moholy-Nagy," in: Anette Kruszynski, Dirk Luckow and Freya Mülhaupt, editors, *Museum der Gegenwart, Kunst in öffentlichen Sammlungen bis 1937: 1937, Europa vor dem 2. Weltkrieg* (Dusseldorf: Kunstsammlung Nordrhein-Westfalen, 1987), 58-69, here 60 and 63.

Actually, the *Light Prop* would have been the only original work in a space devoted to photographs, viewed on a continuous horizontal roll and on a cluster of panels swiveling from a corner of the room, along with still and moving projected images (DVD figure 341), dynamic elements suggested by El Lissitzky's "Demonstration Rooms" in Dresden (1926) and Hanover (1928). Samuel Cauman, Dorner's biographer, wrote that the room ". . . was intended to present the latest developments in Western visual culture," and added:

> According to its plan, photography and film were to be accorded, for the first time, their proper place in modern art and in museum programs, together with the entire visual design enterprise of modern industrial civilization—technical structures, airplanes, motor cars, factories, machines.

> When a button was pushed a projector was to show, on a screen in the center of the room, the newest stage designs. . . . On another wall two other buttons were to release short films on two magnifying glass screens set in the wall. . . . Projection equipment and actuating buttons were installed, but proved technically unsatisfactory, and the room was opened before it was possible to show films. Even though robbed of this portion of its impact, the room constituted an unforgettable presentation.[808]

Another exhibition Moholy and Gropius worked on together was the *Deutsche Bauausstellung* [German Building Exhibition], held in the Berlin exhibition grounds (*Messegelände*) (Martin Wagner and Hans Poelzig, 1928-1929) at the *Funkturm* [radio tower] (Heinrich Strauer, 1924-1926), from May 9th through August 2nd, 1931.[809] Incidentally, Moholy was fascinated with the radio tower, and made a number of

---

[808]Cauman, *The Living Museum*, 109. Cauman worked closely on *The Living Museum* with Dorner, who died as the book was going to press.

[809]Ausstellungs-, Messe- und Fremdverkehrs-Amt der Stadt Berlin, *Deutsche Bauausstellung, Berlin, 1931: Amtlicher Katalog und Führer* (Berlin: Bauwelt Verlag/Ullsteinhaus, 1931), front cover.

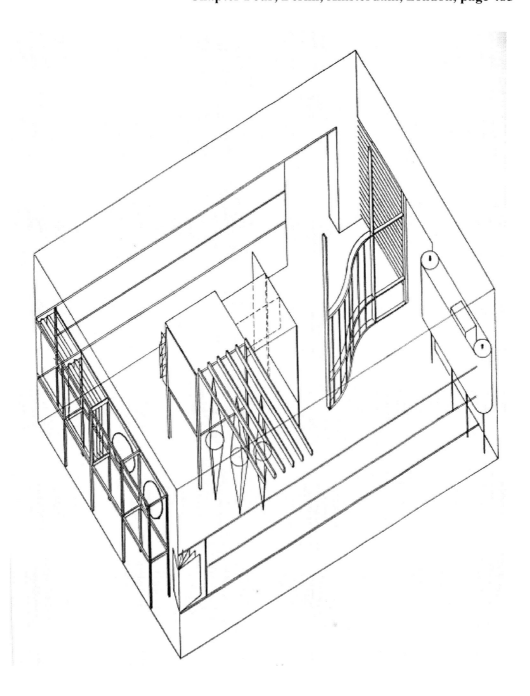

Raum der Gegenwart [Room of Our Own Time], 1931
rendering by Stefan Sebök and Rudolf Luderer

text figure 13, DVD figure 340

photographs of it, such as these of 1928 contrasting the open-work steel of the structure with the almost abstract appearance of the tables and chairs at the base of the tower when seen in a bird's-eye view. (DVD figure 342)

At the German Building Exposition Moholy was credited with setting up [*Einrichtung*] a section Gropius was in charge of, *Grundriß*, which in this context can be translated as planning of dwelling space.[810] He played a similar role for *"Siedlungsform" — Hausform und Baublockgestaltung*, conceived by Bruno Taut to illustrate his ideas on housing developments.[811]

Also at the German Building Exhibition Moholy collaborated with Herbert Bayer in designing exhibition space for the *Deutscher Baugewerksbund*, or German construction unions; the devices they employed included swiveling panels like those in the *Room of Our Own Time* to display pictures and texts, and also photographs on a continuous roll, this time vertically oriented in contrast to the horizontal roll in Hanover.[812] (DVD figure 343 right) In their work for the *Deutscher Baugewerksbund* Moholy and Bayer were assisted by Hin Bredendieck.[813] (DVD figure 343)

Although Moholy was not directly involved, still one more embodiment of Gropius's social room for dwellers in a tall apartment building,[814] ultimately derived from Sebök's *Weinstube* in *The Tales of Hoffmann*, was set up as part of a major section of the German Building Exhibition known as *Die Wohnung unserer Zeit* [The Modern Dwelling].[815] This section was organized by Ludwig Mies van der Rohe (1886-1969), who had been appointed Director of the Bauhaus in Dessau in August of the previous year, and he relied heavily (but not exclusively) on present and former faculty and students of the school. Mies provided not only a demonstration for the general public of what the Bauhaus was currently accomplishing, but also a kind of reunion of Bauhäusler, which surely delighted Moholy. With its houses by Ludwig Hildesheimer, Mies and Breuer, exhibition spaces by Lilli Reich, and its interiors by Gropius, Kandinsky, and Josef Albers assisted by Anni Albers and Xanti Schawinsky, *Die Wohnung unserer Zeit*

---

[810]*Deutsche Bauausstellung, Berlin, 1931: Amtlicher Katalog*, 128 and 129.

[811]*Deutsche Bauausstellung, Berlin, 1931: Amtlicher Katalog*, 129-131.

[812]Herbert Bayer, Walter Gropius and Ise Gropius, eds., *Bauhaus 1919-1928* (New York: The Museum of Modern Art, 1938), 208; *Deutsche Bauausstellung, Berlin, 1931: Amtlicher Katalog*, 26; Probst and Schädlich, *Walter Gropius*, 2:155-157; Brüning and Droste, editors, *Das A und O des Bauhauses*, 260-263; and Fiedler and Feierabend, editors, *Bauhaus*, 500-501.

[813]Virginia Bredendieck to Walter Gropius, TLS, June 24, 1937, Bauhaus-Archiv, Berlin.

[814]Nerdinger, editor, *Walter Gropius Archive*, 2:150-153; *Deutsche Bauausstellung, Berlin, 1931: Amtlicher Katalog*, 163; and Reginald R. Isaacs, *Walter Gropius, der Mensch und sein Werk* [translated and revised from the American edition by Georg G. Meerwein] (Berlin: Gebr. Mann Verlag, 1983-1984), 2:545.

[815]*Deutsche Bauausstellung, Berlin, 1931: Amtlicher Katalog*, 160-177.

encompassed a Bauhaus celebration within a mammoth, mostly humdrum exhibition, one more dance on the edge of the volcano that was about to erupt.

The American architect Philip Johnson (1906-2005) provided some pithy comments on the exhibition:

> The Berlin Building Exposition of 1931 was the largest of its kind ever to be held. With Teutonic thoroughness every material, every method, every theory that had to do with building was shown in the Exposition. The result of this thoroughness, plus an extraordinary lack of funds for proper presentation, made the Exposition, with brilliant exceptions, boring.[816]

Johnson, of course, excepted the contribution of Mies (his future collaborator), which he resoundingly praised,[817] and went on to praise the work of Moholy and Bayer as well:

> . . . these men, drawing undoubtedly partially from Russian Constructivism, employ settings that are, or seem to be, actual constructional units. Much use is made of moving arrows, startling primary colours and shiny materials such as chrome steel, tubing and glass.[818]

Early in 1935 László and Sibyl went to Utrecht to plan and install the exhibition of rayon, or artificial silk (*kunstzijde*), of the Arnhem firm *Algemene Kunstzijde Unie* for the spring fair held from March 13th to 22nd at the *Jaarbeurs* [Trade Exhibition Center]. Although Pallas Studio had helped him obtain the commission, he designed and installed the exhibition covering 900 square meters on his own.[819]

According to Sibyl, "The Utrecht workmen would listen to Moholy's instructions, take a look at the blueprints, and walk away." The only exception was a man with an Indonesian family background, identified by her only as "Teng." She described their joint efforts:

> From thousands of samples Moholy had chosen some seven hundred fabrics. A fourth of those Teng and I cut with pinking scissors into free forms. With library paste we glued them on matting board mounted on a curved plywood wall that extended across the whole exhibition hall.[820]

---

[816] Philip Johnson, "The Berlin Building Exposition of 1931," in: *Oppositions 2* (January, 1974), 86-91, here 87 (see also page 81 where the source is listed as "*T-Square*, 1932").

[817] Johnson, "The Berlin Building Exposition of 1931," 87-88.

[818] Johnson, "The Berlin Building Exposition of 1931," 91.

[819] László Moholy-Nagy to Walter Gropius, March 31, 1935; amd Senter, "Moholy-Nagy in England, 194-196 and illustrations 133a-e.

[820] Sibyl Moholy-Nagy, *Moholy-Nagy; Experiment in Totality*, 111.

Moholy described the exhibition preparation for Gropius: "There was a tremendous lot of work involved because I had to finish everything—without any substantial help—in twelve days."[821]

There were cut-out panels in the curved plywood wall that kept the space open and flowing, and a variety of devices were used to display the fabrics in addition to pasting them on that wall.[822] (DVD figures 344, 345, 346 and 347) Moholy's work was highly praised,[823] and, as one result, the same client asked him to design a more modest installation of six square meters, shown in Brussels at the *Exposition Universelle et Internationale* held from April through November, 1935.[824] (DVD figure 348)

MOHOLY WAS POISED TO CONTINUE his work as an exhibition designer in England, where his major exhibition client was Imperial Airways. He and Australian Modernist architect and interior designer Raymond McGrath (1903-1977) collaborated on the design of an exhibition that was provisionally known as *The Future Is in the Air*.[825] It opened as *The Empire's Airway* in the Science Museum in the South Kensington neighborhood of London, where it was seen from December 6th, 1935, to February 2nd, 1936.[826] The exhibition was very complex and presented demanding challenges for Moholy and McGrath. Included were working and static models of aircraft and a push-button activated sound recording of aircraft engines.[827] Also on view were photographs, including some that were made by Moholy with a Leica camera and later enlarged.[828] Moholy designed the catalogue,[829] as noted above. (DVD figure 287) The attendance was 147,000,[830] and with that encouragement Imperial Airways, aided by

---

[821] László Moholy-Nagy to Walter Gropius, March 31, 1935.

[822] For illustrations, see: Senter, "Moholy-Nagy in England," illustrations 133 a-e.

[823] Senter, "Moholy-Nagy in England," 195; Sibyl Moholy-Nagy, *Moholy-Nagy; Experiment in Totality*, 112-113.

[824] László Moholy-Nagy to Walter Gropius, March 31, 1935; John Gloag, "The Brussels Exhibition," *The Architectural Review*, volume LXXVIII, number 464 (July, 1935), [xl] and 1-8, here 4; and Senter, "Moholy-Nagy in England," 194, 196 and illustrations 134 a-d.

[825] Senter, "Moholy-Nagy in England," 197-198.

[826] Senter, "Moholy-Nagy: the Transitional Years," note 34 on page 173; *idem*, "Moholy-Nagy in England," 199.

[827] Senter, "Moholy-Nagy in England," 197-198 and illustrations 136a-c.

[828] Senter, "Moholy-Nagy in England," illustration 136e.

[829] Senter, "Moholy-Nagy in England," 179-181, 198 and illustrations 115a-b.

[830] Senter, "Moholy-Nagy in England," 198.

Moholy, went on to stage followup exhibitions in other venues.[831] One of these was seen in London Transport's Charing Cross Underground station, from June 18th until July 7th, 1936.[832] At the very end of his stay in London, Moholy was still doing exhibition work for Imperial Airways, forcing him to delay his trip to Chicago for an interview with his future employer there. He had already been paid part of his honorarium, and he found the task to be very interesting: an advertising display for Imperial Airways installed in two rail cars fitting them out for a tour.[833] The exterior of the cars was in the same sky-blue hue Moholy had already used for the catalogue cover of *The Empire's Airway*; on this blue surface was applied in red lettering: "The aeroplane in the sky carries us above mediocre things." A key element in the interior display was curving plywood panels. The cars toured to railroad stations throughout England, Scotland and Wales.[834]

Moholy took time out from his work for Imperial Airways for a quick trip to Paris to visit the *Exposition Internationale des Arts et Techniques dans la vie Moderne* [International Exposition Dedicated to Art and Technology in Modern Life], held May 25th through November 25th, 1937. He planned to leave London on Tuesday, June 22nd, for Paris, and return to London on Thursday, June 24th.[835] While in Paris he was able to see his old friend, Sigfried Giedion, and had his only documented meeting with Pablo Picasso when he photographed the two of them at the *Exposition*.[836] (DVD figure 349) Moholy would have seen the Spanish Pavilion, still under construction, designed by his friend from the C.I.AM., José Luis Sert, with the assistance of Luis Lacasa, for the embattled Republican, anti-Fascist, Loyalist Spanish Government.[837] The Pavilion's most famous feature, Picasso's *Guernica*, had been installed in mid-June in the still-not-completed Pavilion, and thus not yet open to the public during Moholy's visit;[838] surely either Picasso or Sert arranged for Moholy to visit the Pavilion anyway. *Guernica* commemorated the bombing by Nazi German and Italian Fascist warplanes of innocent

---

[831] Senter, "Moholy-Nagy in England," 199-203 and illustrations 135, 137a-d, and 138a-d.

[832] Senter, "Moholy-Nagy in England," 199 and illustrations 137 a-d.

[833] László Moholy-Nagy to Walter and Ise Gropius, photocopy of TLS, June 13th, 1937, Bauhaus-Archiv, Berlin.

[834] Senter, "Moholy-Nagy in England," 199-203, 317 and illustrations 138 a-d.

[835] László Moholy-Nagy to Walter and Ise Gropius, photocopy of TLS, June 18th, 1937, Bauhaus-Archiv, Berlin.

[836] "Moholy-Nagy, Picture Hunter, Looks at the Paris Exposition," *Architectural Record,* volume LXXXII, number 4 (October, 1937), 92-93.

[837] Josefina Alix, "From War to Magic: the Spanish Pavilion, Paris 1937," in: William H. Robinson, Jordi Falgàs and Carmen Belen Lord, editors, *Barcelona and Modernity: Picasso, Gaudí, Miró, Dalí* (Cleveland: Cleveland Museum of Art in Association with Yale University Press, 2006), 450-457.

[838] Magdalena Dabrowski, "Picasso: Guernica and His Reaction to the Civil War," in: *ibid.*, 461-467, here 462.

civilians in a defenseless Spanish village on April 26th, 1937, in support of an ultimately successful Fascist coup led by Francisco Franco. *Guernica* was later shown in a number of American cities, including a 1940 showing in the San Francisco Museum of Art where Moholy lectured about the mural in the gallery in which it was shown there, as discussed in Chapter Five. (DVD figure 465)

Moholy and Mme. Hélène de Mandrot, Patroness of Art and Architecture

In addition to Ascona, another destination for Moholy in Switzerland was La Sarraz, near Lausanne, where Mme. Hélène de Mandrot (née Revilliod; 1867-1948), wealthy designer of furniture and interiors, artist and art patron, was a generous host to annual summer gatherings at Château La Sarraz. The Château of which she was *la châtelaine* was a real castle, its oldest parts dating back to the eleventh century. Nearly all of those assembled there were men, except for de Mandrot herself, with only a few other exceptions, such as art-historian Carola Giedion-Welcker, who sometimes attended with her husband, Sigfried Giedion.[839] Moholy was at La Sarraz during a portion of the summer or early autumn in 1930, 1931, 1932, 1933, 1935 and 1936.[840]

Moholy's absence in 1934 was the occasion for a letter of greeting to de Mandrot and his artist colleagues of previous years who were in La Sarraz that year, a letter that summed up what the annual gatherings meant to him: "endroit merveilleux de repos, de rassemblement et parfois de travail intensif" [a place of wonderful rest and at times intensive work by those assembled].[841]

Some photographs document Moholy relaxing and having a good time at La Sarraz in 1932.[842] A playful mood enlivens his contributions to the creatively humorous annual entries by her summer guests in de Mandrot's guest book.[843] (DVD figure 350) This change of pace was especially important for Moholy because he was normally very busy. Nevertheless, the relaxation did not get in the way of "intensive work" at La Sarraz, as he usually made some paintings and photographs,[844] and as he played a key role in the collective work accomplished in regular gatherings.

---

[839]Baudin, *Hélène de Mandrot*, 314.

[840]Baudin, *Hélène de Mandrot*, 319 *et passim*.

[841]László Moholy-Nagy to Hélène de Mandrot, August 12, 1934, Archives de la Maison des Artistes-Hélène de Mandrot, Lausanne.

[842]Baudin, *Hélène de Mandrot*, 113, 114, 137 and 143.

[843]Baudin, *Hélène de Mandrot*, 110 and figures 15 and 20.

[844]Some of these are illustrated in: Baudin, *Hélène de Mandrot*, 103, 105, and figures 24, 28 and 35, and in: Sibyl Moholy-Nagy, *Moholy-Nagy, Experiment in Totality*, figure 31.

Those present at La Sarraz included artists and architects as well as theater and film producers and directors. The gatherings of artists constituted what was known as *La Maison des Artistes*, and in their meetings in 1930 they discussed the future of La Sarraz, including a role for modern art in the *Musée romand* which was housed in the Château and had been set up by Helen's husband, Henry de Mandrot (1861-1920), as a regional museum; also discussed were strategies for getting modern art into other museums.[845]

GROPIUS WAS PRESENT at *La Maison des Artistes* in 1935, as was Moholy, and they were part of an advisory committee. Their key role in the discussions that year was alluded to by de Mandrot when she regretted their absence from the advisory committee in 1936: "Je regret beaucoup l'absence de Moholy qui, avec Gropius, représentes, je crois, les tendences le plus extrème de notre comité."[846] [I very much regret the absence of Moholy who, along with Gropius, represents the most extreme tendencies of our committee.] That Moholy made such an impact was a neat feat for him because of his limited command of French. Also present at *La Maison des Artistes* in 1935 was former Bauhaus student Xanti Schawinsky,[847] whose comments on Moholy's use of German was discussed in Chapter Three. He described the linguistic difficulties Moholy faced at La Sarraz:

> . . . French was spoken at the table. So when Moholy wanted to say something he had to translate his Hungarian thought into German, which still would have been easiest for him, but then he had to re-think it into English (being a [newly settled] Londoner at this time, this primarily preoccupied him) and finally to express himself in French The result: utter despair, since meanwhile a completely new thought got conveyed.[848]

Actually, Gropius and Moholy were present at La Sarraz in 1936 but only in September for their work in CIRPAC (*Comité International pour la réalization des problèmes architecturaux contemporains*), the steering committee of *CIAM* (*Congrès internationaux d'architecture moderne*).[849] The idea of organizing the *CIAM* had come from Hélène de Mandrot,[850] and it was organized at La Sarraz in 1928 by an invited group of architects from various European countries.[851] The aim of *CIAM* was to open

---

[845]Baudin, *Hélène de Mandrot*, 285-288.

[846]Baudin, *Hélène de Mandrot*, 300.

[847]Baudin, *Hélène de Mandrot*, 323.

[848]Xanti Schawinsky to Sibyl Moholy-Nagy, August 25, 1948.

[849]Baudin, *Hélène de Mandrot*, 201-204, 315 and 319.

[850]Baudin, *Hélène de Mandrot*, [189]-190 and 272-275.

[851]Baudin, *Hélène de Mandrot*, 299, 308 and 312; and Sigfried Giedion, "Introduction," in: José Louis Sert, *Can Our Cities Survive?; an ABC of Urban Problems, their Analysis, their Solutions, based on the Proposals Formulated by the C.I.A.M., International Congresses for Modern*

(continued...)

up discussions about architecture and city planning to a wide international public in the hope that the *CIAM* members could rationalize architecture through the use of machines and new building materials and adapt it to the prevailing socio-economic order through careful planning of cities.[852]

It was de Mandrot who provided the initial impulse for the organization of the *CIAM* by contacting key figures such as Giedion and Le Corbusier and urging them to form the organization.[853] Although Moholy was not invited to the organizational meeting he soon became active in the group's steering committee, CIRPAC, and also made the film, *Architekturkongres Athen*, described above, that documented the fourth congress of the *CIAM*, held in 1933 in Athens and on a cruise ship that traveled from Marseille to Athens and back.

For Moholy, La Sarraz provided an opportunity for close association with leading artists who were not Constructivists, including Hans Arp and Max Ernst.[854] But the most important role of *La Maison des Artistes* in his career was his exhibition in Brno and Bratislava in 1935, discussed below, followed by extensive coverage of his work in a special edition of the Brno journal *telehor*, edited by František Kalivoda (1913-1971), also discussed below. Kalivoda participated in *La Maison des Artistes* in 1934, 1935 and 1936, and he was assisted with the publication of the special edition of *telehor* by Sigfried Giedion and Hélène de Mandrot.[855]

By contrast, Moholy's other time in Switzerland was spent in Ascona, where there was no organized activity such as there was at La Sarraz, so there was more relaxation.

---

[851](...continued)
Architecture . . . (Cambridge: The Harvard University Press, 1944), ix-xi, here ix.

[852]On the aims of the members of the *CIAM* see: Mitchell Schwarzer, "CIAM, City at the End of History," in: R.E. Somol, editor, *Autonomy and Ideology: Positioning an Avant-Garde in America* (New York: The Monacelli Press, Inc., 1997), [232]-261.

A succinct history of the *CIAM* is in Sert, *Can Our Cities Survive?*, ix-xi (see note 853) and 242-249. A lengthier history, cited above, is Eric Mumford's *The CIAM Discourse on Urbanism*; Mumford devoted pages 73 to 92 to the 1933 *CIAM* meeting. See also Woud, *Het Nieuwe Bouwen*, and Steinmann, editor, *CIAM*. All three of these books are cited fully in note 245.

[853]Sigfried Giedion, "Introduction," in: Sert, *Can Our Cities Survive?*, ix-xi, here ix.

[854]Baudin, *Hélène de Mandrot*, 131-134, 308 and 312.

[855]Baudin, *Hélène de Mandrot*, 316-317, 319 and plate 28.

For the special quadrilingual (Czech, French, German and English) issue of *telehor*, Giedion wrote the foreword, and Hélène de Mandrot made the translations into French.

As noted above, he spent much time in Ascona with people he had met earlier, including Ellen Frank.[856]

The Persistence of Painting

THE FIRST SHOWING of Moholy's works in fine arts after he left the Bauhaus is notable because it included him in a select group of leading European artists. This was in the Kunsthaus in Zurich where an exhibition, *Abstrakte und Surrealistische Malerei und Plastik*, was seen October 6th through November 3rd, 1929. One-hundred-and-fifty works were shown, among them three paintings by Moholy. Included were his *Axl II* of 1927, an oil on canvas, offered for 1500 Swiss francs; the same price was asked for *B 100* of 1928, another oil on canvas; and 1000 Swiss francs was asked for *G IV* of 1926, a painting on Galalith (a thermoplastic discussed in Chapter Three).[857] *Axl II* later entered the collection of the Solomon R. Guggenheim Museum in New York.[858] The Zurich exhibition, primarily organized by Giedion, was later seen at other venues, including the *Graphisches Kabinett* in Munich.[859]

After the German monarchy collapsed at the end of World War I, some Royal-Imperial residences were used for gallery space. One of these, the Berlin Palace of the Crown Prince (*Das Kronprinzen-Palais*; 1633, remodeled in 1733 by Philipp Gerlach and in 1863 by Johann Heinrich Strack; no longer extant), located on *Unter den Linden,* next to the State Opera House or *Staatsoper*, became a venue for contemporary art, as a new branch, or *neue Abteilung*, of the National Gallery. In this role the Palace was used to house recent purchases of contemporary art, as well as contemporary works on loan,[860]

---

[856]Xanti Schawinsky to Sibyl Moholy-Nagy, August 25, 1948.

[857]Kunsthaus Zürich, *Ausstellung Abstrakte und Surrealistische Malerei und Plastik, 6. Oktober bis 3, November 1929, Katalog mit Abbildungen* (Zurich: Kunsthaus Zürich, 1929), 15; *idem, Ausstellung Abstrakte und Surrealistische Malerei und Plastik, 6. Oktober bis 3, November 1929, kleine Ausgabe* (Zurich: Kunsthaus Zürich, 1929), 13.

[858]Angelica Zander Rudenstine, *The Solomon R. Guggenheim Museum Collection, Paintings, 1880-1945* (New York: The Solomon R. Guggenheim Museum, 1976), 2:550-551. *A XLII*, intended by Moholy to be a letter followed by a Roman numeral, was listed as *Axl II*, evidently because part of the title as inscribed by Moholy on the verso was obscured by the stretcher.

[859]Franz Roh, "Malerei des Abstrakten und der Surrealisten," *Der Cicerone; Halbmonatschrift für Künstler, Kunstfreunde und Sammler*, volume XXII, number 5, ([March 1], 1930), 141-142, here 141.

[860]Annegret Janda, "The Fight for Modern Art; the Berlin Nationalgalerei after 1933," in: Stephanie Barron, editor, *"Degenerate Art," the Fate of the Avant-Garde in Nazi Germany* (Los Angeles: Los Angeles County Museum of Art, 1991), [104]-119, here [104]-107; and Elizabeth M. Grady, "The Politicization of Public Opinion on Modern Art at the National Gallery in Berlin, 1918-1933" (Ph.D. dissertation, Northwestern University, 2002), 25-42 *et passim*.

a program that in many ways was a pre-cursor of the Museum of Modern Art in New York, as well as other similar institutions.

In the late spring of 1930 Moholy had a painting in an exhibition that was shown in the Palace of the Crown Prince set up to showcase some recent acquisitions. The painting, shown in a gallery photograph published in 1930,[861] cannot be identified, but it is similar to *Q 1*, of 1923, now in the collection of the Museum of Modern Art in New York, and was probably painted in the same year.

The director of the National Gallery since 1909, Ludwig Justi (1876-1957),[862] who had set up the program in the Palace of the Crown Prince in 1919, was suspended from his position on July 1, 1933.[863] The way he carried out the re-utilization of the Palace of the Crown Prince as a branch of the National Gallery had made him somewhat of an embattled figure. Many people in the right-wing part of the political spectrum vehemently opposed Justi's policies, but he was also criticized by some on the left, including Modernist artists and critics, who were generally sympathetic but occasionally had some specific criticisms, such as that Justi did not show much Constructivist art.[864] Thus the acquisition of a work by Moholy was probably part of an effort to placate disgruntled Modernists who were basically supportive of Justi's policies. Max Osborn, who had favorably reviewed Moholy's work, as discussed in Chapter Two, was a member of Justi's acquisition commission,[865] so it is possible that he (Osborn) had a role in adding a work by Moholy to the collection. Justi's commitment to the Bauhaus had been shown when he added his name to the signatories of a letter to the Thuringian

---

[861] Ernst Kállai, "Kronprinzenpalais," *Die Weltbühne*, volume 26 (July 15, 1930), 100-102; reprinted in: Annagret Janda and Jörn Grabowski, editors, *Kunst in Deutschland 1905-1937: die Verlorene Sammlung der Nationalgalerie im ehemaligne Kronprinzen-Palais* (Berlin: Gebr. Mann, 1992), 16-19; Moholy's painting is seen in the gallery photograph on reprint page 18; and in Janda, "The Fight for Modern Art," [104].

See also: Annegret Janda, editor, *Das Schicksal einer Sammlung; Aufbau und Zerstörung der neuen Abteilung der Nationalgalerie im ehemaligen Kronprinzen-Palais Unter den Linden, 1918-1945* (Berlin: Staatliche Museen zu Berlin/DDR, Nationalgalerie, 1988), where a painting by Moholy is visible in the photograph on the front cover.

[862] On Justi, see; "Justi, Erich," in: Volz, editor, *Reichshandbuch der deutschen Gesellschaft*, 1:865.

[863] Grady, "The Politicization of Public Opinion on Modern Art," 79; and Janda, "The Fight for Modern Art," 107.

[864] Grady, "The Politicization of Public Opinion on Modern Art," 125-129 and 152-156; and Adolf Behne, "Berliner Bericht: das Kronprinzenpalais," *Das neue Frankfurt; Monatsschrift für die Probleme moderner Gestaltung*, volume IV, numbers 4-5 (April-May, 1930); reprinted in: Hirdina, editor, *Neues Bauen, neues Gestaltung*, 306.

[865] Grady, "The Politicization of Public Opinion on Modern Art," 128-129.

Legislature protesting the closing of the Bauhaus in Weimar;[866] moreover, he showed several other Bauhaus painters in addition to Moholy, including Oskar Schlemmer.

Ernst Kállai wrote a review of the 1930 exhibition showcasing new acquisitions for the collection housed in the Palace of the Crown Prince. His review showed evidence of his newly developed negative attitudes toward Moholy, in sharp contrast to his earlier efforts to support his work beginning when he was still not a widely known artist.[867] After praising some paintings in the exhibition, Kállai wrote that, in contrast, in the case of works by Juan Gris, Oskar Schlemmer and Moholy-Nagy, what was purchased was not their best work (*Juan Gris, Oskar Schlemmer und Moholy-Nagy dagegen sind nicht in besser Form gekauft worden*). He added that:

> Moholy-Nagys raffinierte ästhetische Aufmachung is ja zumeist nur Blendwerk fürs Auge, ohne wesentliche Gehalt.[868] [Moholy-Nagy's clever, effete theatrics lack significant merit and provide, at most, eyewash.]

Thus Kállai provided little aid for Justi in his attempts to placate some of his Modernist critics!

Moholy showed his work in one-artist exhibitions in the Hans Goltz Galerie in Munich in 1929 and 1930, his first showings there since 1926. Concerning the 1929 showing, that opened in March, Franz Roh wrote that the abstract paintings on new materials, including Galalith and Trolitan, were characterized by purity of form, and that the transparent forms in his paintings employed entirely new color harmonies; he also noted that the abstract paintings contrasted with non-abstract works of photography and photomontage.[869] The invitation to the 1930 exhibition, which opened on March 17th, also announced lectures by Moholy on March 14th and 17th, on painting and photography, and on the film of the future, respectively. On the verso of the invitation was an essay by Roh highlighted by these words: "Moholy wurde für Deutschland, was Mondrian für Paris und Lyssitzky für Rußland sind, Führer der rein konstruktivistischen Malerei" [Moholy is becoming for Germany what Mondrian is for Paris and Lissitzky is for Russia, a leader in pure constructivist painting].[870]

---

[866] *Pressestimmen für das Staatliche Bauhaus Weimar*, 117-119.

[867] As recently as 1925 Kállai had viewed Moholy's work in a very positive way; see Ernst Kállai, *Neue Malerei in Ungarn* (Leipzig: Klinghardt & Biermann, 1925), 88, 110-115 and illustrations 68-71. (The jacket and title page were designed by Moholy.) Kállai's entire text was reprinted in his: *Ernst Kállai: Schriften in deutscher Sprache, 1920-1925* (Budapest: Argumentum Kiadó, 1999), 83-159.

[868] Kállai, "Kronprinzenpalais," *Die Weltbühne*, 102.

[869] Franz Roh, "Münchner Ausstellungen," *Der Cicerone; Halbmonatschrift für Künstler, Kunstfreunde und Sammler*, volume XXI, number 7, ([April 1], 1929), 203.

[870] The Jan and Edith Tschichold papers, Getty Research Institute, Los Angeles.

His interest in new materials on which to paint originated during Moholy's Bauhaus years. In the 1925 and 1927 editions of *Painting, Photography, Film* he had discussed some of these new materials:

> Valuable artificial materials are being produced today for the electro-technical industry: turbonite, trolite, neolith, galilith, etc., etc. These materials, like aluminum, cellon [essentially a nylon plastic, also known as celon and Zellon], celluloid, are much more suitable for pictures which have to be accurately executed than are canvas and wood-panel. I do not doubt that these or similar materials will soon become the ones most often used for easel paintings and that it will be possible to achieve quite new and surprising effects with them. Experiments with painting on highly polished black panels (trolite), on coloured transparent and translucent plates (galalith, matt and translucent cellon), produce strange optical effects: it looks as though the colour were **floating** almost without material effect in a space in front of the plane to which it is in fact applied [emphasis in original].[871]

After his Munich exhibition of 1930, Moholy did not have another single-artist exhibition until 1934; as he wrote to František Kalivoda in June of that year:

> you are surprised that i am again arranging a growing number of exhibitions of both my earlier and more recent work. it is true that for a number of years i had ceased to exhibit, or even to paint. i felt that it was senseless to employ means that i could only regard as out of date and insufficient for the new requirements of art at a time when new technical means were still waiting to be explored.[872]

Moholy went on to lament that some of his ideas, such as large-scale outdoor light shows on natural and artificial mists, were not possible because of the way the capitalist economy was functioning. With Moholy's whole career in mind, it would seem that most of all he was trying to convince himself that by the mid-1930s the time for painting had passed. As interested as he might have been in light shows on artificial mist, and taking into account the effort he put into photography, film, stage, exhibition and typographic design, his passion for painting nonetheless persisted. As will be seen in Chapter Five (page 553), in Chicago Moholy confessed to Gropius that he still thought of himself primarily as a painter. Moreover, two scholars who have concentrated on Moholy's photography came to the same conclusion. Eleanor Hight wrote: "Even

---

[871]László Moholy-Nagy, *Malerei, Photographie, Film*, (1925), 19; *idem*, *Malerei, Fotografie, Film*, Bauhausbücher 8, 2. veränderte Aufl. (1927), 23; (also available in a facsimile editions of 1986 and 2000 published in Berlin by Gebr. Mann Verlag of Berlin): *idem*, *Painting, Photography, Film*, 25.

On Moholy's use of plastics in his painting, see: Angelica Zander Rudenstine, *The Guggenheim Museum Collection, Paintings, 1880-1945*, 2:541-545.

[872]The letter was reprinted in: *telehor; the international review new vision*, numbers 1-2 (February 28, 1936), 30-32, here 30. The same ideas in a slightly different text appeared in an English journal: "Light Architecture," *Industrial Arts*, volume I, number 1 (Spring, 1936), 15-17; reprinted in: Kostelanetz, editor, *Moholy-Nagy*, 155-159.

though his writings on painting were few, we can sense an underlying desire on his part to be seen first and foremost as a serious painter."[873] Andreas Haus wrote: "It was as a painter that he had raised photography to the status of an art, but exclusively in the sense that he had reconstructed it as a new painting technique."[874]

It was in Paris and in several Dutch cities that Moholy began to present the first one-artist showings of his work since his 1930 showing in Munich.

In Paris he exhibited June 1st through June 15th, 1934, at a gallery operated by *Abstraction-Création*, located at 44, avenue de Wagram.[875] (DVD figure 351) *Abstraction-Création,* in existence from 1931 to 1936, was a group of painters and sculptors (and "friends").[876] From 1932 through 1936 the group published a series of lively, illustrated annuals, *Abstraction-Création: Art non-figuratif*, and for about a year, during 1934 and 1935, they showed work of artist members.

Moholy was a member of *Abstraction-Création*, and his work appeared in each of the group's annuals. In the first two, issued in 1932[877] and 1933,[878] only his earlier work was illustrated; in 1934, a work was illustrated dating from the previous year;[879] in 1935, two works dating from 1930 were illustrated;[880] and in the last annual, in 1936, two works dating from that year were illustrated.[881] Thus there was no clear pattern, but evidently for the issues of 1932 and 1933 he did not show recent work because he produced relatively few works of fine arts in those years. Nevertheless during a period of about four years, during which he did not exhibit his work in fine arts and when his work as a painter and sculptor was suspended or at least reduced, his membership in *Abstraction-*

---

[873]Eleanor M. Hight, *Picturing Modernism; Moholy-Nagy and Photography in Weimar Germany* (Cambridge: The M.I.T. Press, 1995), 212.

[874]Andreas Haus, *Moholy-Nagy: Photographs and Photograms*, translation from the German by Frederic Samson (New York: Pantheon Books, 1980), 7.

[875]An invitation is in The Jan and Edith Tschichold papers, Getty Research Center, Los Angeles; another copy, mailed as a postcard with a message to Roth Figyelné (see Chapter One) dated May 17, 1934, is in the Hattula Moholy-Nagy archives.

[876]On *Abstraction-Création* see: Norbert Novis and Hagen Röhrig, editors, *Abstraction Création 1931-1936* (Munster, Germany: Westfälisches Landesmuseum für Kunst und Kunstgeschichte, 1978). This is a bi-lingual publication in German and French.

[877]*Abstraction-Création: Art non-figuratif*, volume I (1932), 24. A reprint of the five annuals was published in New York in 1968 by the Arno Press.

[878]*Abstraction-Création: Art non-figuratif*, volume II (1933)*, 30.

[879]*Abstraction-Création: Art non-figuratif*, volume III (1934), 31.

[880]*Abstraction-Création: Art non-figuratif*, volume IV (1935), 21.

[881]*Abstraction-Création: Art non-figuratif*, volume V (1936), 19.

Création, and the illustration of his work in the group's annual, maintained his presence in the art scene. Actually, an examination of listings of dated paintings in exhibition catalogues makes it seem likely that the only calendar year in which he did no painting at all would be 1931, the year he met Sibyl, and she recalled that he told her then that he did not paint anymore.[882]

One highlight of the texts that accompanied the illustrations in the *Abstraction-Création* annuals was Moholy's assertion that: "Je ne peint pas des nus parce que je peux mieux les photographier." [I do not paint nudes anymore because I can do that better with photography]   This was in answer to a question posed by the editors, "Pourquoi ne peignez-vous pas des nus?" [Why do you not paint nudes?]—a strange question from the editors of a publication that illustrated only abstract art![883]

The Paris show marked a change in Moholy's attitude toward his work in fine arts. Near the end of August he wrote to Jan Tschichold: "ich bin jetzt ganz leidenschaftlich hungrig meine bilder überall zu zeigen"[884] [I am now passionately hungry to show my pictures everywhere].

Another one-artist exhibition followed soon after the Paris showing. This was in Utrecht, and was seen from September 22nd through October 15th, 1934, in the Kunstzaal W. Wagenaar at 25 Niewe Gracht.[885] Moholy worried that his paintings were not being understood and that the Utrecht public perceived them as repetitive. But he emphasized to Sibyl that he wanted to take every opportunity to exhibit them anyway so that people would realize that he was a painter and not just a photographer.[886]

THE UTRECHT EXHIBITION was to be presented soon after in Amsterdam by the committee for changing exhibitions of modern applied art in the Stedelijk Museum. The members of the committee belonged to the Amsterdam chapter of a group known as V.A.N.K., an acronym for *Vereeniging voor ambachts- en Nijverheidskunst* [Dutch Association for Crafts and Industrial Arts], described by Moholy as "*kameraden*" [comrades].[887] Moholy's work, as listed on the Amsterdam

---

[882] Sibyl Moholy-Nagy, *Moholy-Nagy, Experiment in Totality*, 69-71.

[883] *Abstraction-Création: Art non-figuratif*, volume II (1933), 1 and 30.

[884] László Moholy-Nagy to Jan Tschichold. TLS, August 29, 1934, The Jan and Edith Tschichold papers in the Getty Research Institute in Los Angeles.

[885] An announcement of the Utrecht exhibition is in The Jan and Edith Tschichold papers in the Getty Research Institute in Los Angeles.

[886] László Moholy-Nagy to Sibyl Moholy-Nagy, October 9, 1934, MLS, microfilm reel 951, frames 0147-0150, Moholy-Nagy files, Archives of American Art, Washington, D.C.

[887] László Moholy-Nagy to Paul Citroen, TLS, December 12, 1934, Bauhaus-Archiv, Berlin.

(continued...)

invitation, consisted of paintings, photograms, photomontages and designs for stage settings, seen in the Stedelijk Museum from November 24th to December 9th, 1934. He also presented a lecture, "Vom Tafelbild zur Lichtarchitektur" [from framed picture to light architecture], in the Museum on November 27th.[888] A third Dutch showing of the exhibition took place at Studio 32 in Rotterdam, from December 13th, 1934, through January 12th, 1935. Moholy asked his friend Paul Citroen if had heard how his work had been judged by his colleagues in Amsterdam, and also asked him to view the exhibition in Rotterdam and write to him as to whether the order in which the paintings were hung was pleasing.[889]

Sibyl Moholy-Nagy described the pains Moholy took to select works to be shown in 1934: "He made a trip to Berlin where all his work was still stored, and for days and nights lined up his paintings, collages, and water colors along walls of our apartment to make a selection."[890]

In 1935 Moholy showed in Brno and Bratislava in a one-artist exhibition set up by František Kalivoda. Moholy was no stranger to Brno, having lectured there in 1924 at the invitation of the Brno branch of Devětsil.[891] An article based on his talk had appeared in a 1924/1925 issue of its journal, *Pásmo: Revue Internationale Moderne*,[892] and later *Pásmo* reprinted selections from his writings in translation.[893] Moreover, in 1934 Brno was the venue for an early showing of his films, including one première. (DVD figure 352)

---

[887](...continued)
The poster for the exhibition is reproduced in: Sibyl Moholy-Nagy, *Laszlo Moholy-Nagy, Experiment in Totality*, 120. An invitation to the exhibition, and to a lecture by Moholy, is in The Jan and Edith Tschichold papers, Getty Research Institute, Los Angeles.

[888]Portions of the lecture appear in English in: Sibyl Moholy-Nagy, *Laszlo Moholy-Nagy, Experiment in Totality*, 108-110. The lecture was written with help from Sibyl; see: Sibyl Moholy-Nagy to László Moholy-Nagy, November 8, 1934.

An invitation to the exhibition, and to a lecture by Moholy, is in The Jan and Edith Tschichold papers, Getty Research Institute, Los Angeles.

[889]László Moholy-Nagy to Paul Citroen, December 12, 1934, TLS, Bauhaus-Archiv, Berlin.

[890]Sibyl Moholy-Nagy, *Laszlo Moholy-Nagy, Experiment in Totality*, 107.

[891]Rostislav Svácha, editor, *Devětsil; Czech Avant-Garde Art, Architecture and Design of the 1920s and 1930s* (Oxford: Museum of Modern Art Oxford, 1990), 110.

[892]László Moholy-Nagy, "Richtlinien für eine synthetische Zeitschrift" [Guidelines for a Synthetic Newspaper], *Pásmo; Revue Internationale Moderne*, volume I, numbers 7-8 (1924/1925), 5; reprinted in facsimile in: Eskildsen and Horak, editors, *Film und Foto der zwanziger Jahre*, [156].

[893]Iva Mojžišová, "Moholy-Nagy in Brünn und Preßburg," in: Gaßner, editor, *Wechsel Wirkungen*, 282-283.

T HE BRNO SHOWING of Moholy's one-artist exhibition opened at the *Künstlerhaus* on Saturday, June 1st, 1935; four of his films were shown on Friday, June 7th: *Impressions of the Old Harbor at Marseille, ABC in Sound, A Lightplay Black White Gray* and *Big City Gypsies*.[894] The list of media on the announcement seemed to be about the same as were illustrated the next year in *telehor*: oil and tempera paintings on canvas, trolit,[895] silberit and aluminum;[896] enamel-on-steel paintings; sculpture; camera photographs, photograms, and photocollages; and Lucia Moholy's photographs of his stage settings. (DVD figure 352; see also DVD figures 355, 356, 357 and 358)

telehor was a short-lived magazine; indeed only one issue appeared, but this consisted of 136 pages and had numerous color and black-and-white illustrations. The text included a foreword by Giedion and Moholy's letter to Kalivoda, mentioned above, along with reprints of four of his essays as well as his film script, "Once a Chicken Always a Chicken," in Czech, French, English and German. In fact, *telehor* constituted the most thorough publication of Moholy's work during his lifetime.[897] As noted above, the publication of *telehor* as well as the exhibition that had toured Czechoslovakia the previous year, grew out of contacts at La Sarraz.

The other city showing Moholy's one-artist exhibition was Bratislava (also known as Preßburg), where it was seen, preceding the Brno showing, from May 2nd to 11th, 1935.[898] (DVD figure 354) Shortly before the exhibition opened, the four films soon to be screened in Brno, were seen in Bratislava. Moholy had earlier had a presence in Bratislava (once a part of Hungary), when he presented a cycle of five lectures there on March 5th, 7th, 9th, 11th and 12th, 1931.[899]

---

[894] An announcement of the exhibition and the accompanying film showings is in The Jan and Edith Tschichold files, Getty Research Institute, Los Angeles; it is reproduced in: Vladimir Šlapeta, "Das Bauhaus und die Avantgarde in der Tschechowakei um 1933," in: Peter Hahn, editor, *Bauhaus Berlin* (Berlin: Weingarten, 1985), 241-252, here 244.

[895] Also known as Trolitan, a phenol-formaldehyde resin introduced in 1926; it is similar to Bakelite in appearance.

[896] Silberit, also known as silverit, was a new form of highly-polished aluminum, very reflective in character.

[897] *telehor* is cited fully in note 872.

[898] Ranier Wick, "Prüfstand Bauhaus-Pädagogik; die Kunstgewerbeschule in Bratislava," in: Susanne Anna, editor, *Das Bauhaus im Osten; Slowakische und Tschechische Avantgarde 1928-1939* (Ostfildern-Ruit, Germany: Verlag Gerd Hatje, 1997), 14-31, here 15. An announcement of the Bratislava exhibition is in the Jan Tschichold Collection, Museum of Modern Art, New York.

[899] Wick, "Prüfstand Bauhaus-Pädagogik; die Kunstgewerbeschule in Bratislava," 15; Iva Mojžišová, "Die persönlichen Beziehungen zwischen den Angehörigen des Bauhauses und der Kunstgewerbeschule in Bratislava im Lichte neuendeckter Dokumente," *Wissenschaftliche Zeitschrift der Hochschule für Architektur und Bauwesen Weimar*, volume XXXIII, numbers 4, 5 and 6 (1987), 335-338, here 336; and *idem*, "Moholy-Nagy in Brünn und Preßburg," 282-283.

The works shown in Czechoslovakia would have been returned to Moholy in London, since he had already moved there by the time the exhibition opened in Brno. Although no catalogue or checklist was issued at the time, a checklist of the Brno showing was eventually published, so that clearly this exhibition of one-hundred and fifty works[900] (DVD 355, 356, 357 and 358) was the largest exhibition of his works shown during his lifetime. (DVD figures 359, 360, 361 and 362) While the Cincinnati exhibition of 1946, discussed in Chapter Five, was more comprehensive in that it encompassed works from throughout his career, including his American years, that exhibition was smaller, comprising only sixty-six works; moreover it did not include as many types of media as did the Brno exhibition. (See Chapter Five.)

A work possibly similar to two of the works shown in Brno was *sil 1*, 1933, oil on silberit, now in the Scottish National Gallery of Modern Art in Edinburgh. (DVD figure 363 and front cover of Volume Two). Shown at Brno were *sil 2* and *sil 3*, both also 1933.[901] J.G. Crowther had commissioned a painting from Moholy when he visited him in London in connection with the dust jacket for his 1931 book, *The Outline of the Universe*; it was delivered by Moholy during his London visit begun November 13th, 1933 and bore the title *sil 1*.[902]

An excellent example of Moholy's European paintings of his post-Bauhaus period and of his continuing exploration of new supports for his paintings, *sil 3* was created on highly-polished aluminum[903] as a support for a playful image, abstract but resembling kites flying above the clouds. Three kite-like forms seem to be tethered by strings, represented by scratches in the surface. The off-white cloud forms at the bottom are indication of a more open attitude about the use of curves and in that respect anticipate his paintings made in Chicago.

A highlight of Moholy's last year in London was his exhibition that opened December 31st, 1936, at the London Gallery, 20 Cork Street.[904] Only forty-three works were displayed,[905] and the London Gallery show encompassed fewer types of media than shown in Brno (*e.g.*, photograms were shown but not camera photographs or photocollages), but it did include some recent works created after the Czech showings. Nevertheless, the generously illustrated thirty-seven page catalogue accompanying the London Gallery

---

[900]František Kalivoda, editor, *Výstava László Moholy-Nagy, Katalog* (Brno: Dům Umění Města, 1965), 10-12.

[901]*Ibid.*, 10.

[902]Senter, "Moholy-Nagy: the Transitional Years," 86.

[903]As in note 895.

[904]On the London Gallery see: Senter, "Moholy-Nagy in England," 245-255.

[905]London Gallery Ltd., *L. Moholy-Nagy, [with text] by Sigfried Giedion . . . First Exhibition in England of L. Moholy-Nagy, Dec. 31st, 1936 — Jan. 27th, 1937 [at] London Gallery Ltd., 28 Cork Street* (London: London Gallery, Limited, 1936), 5-7.

exhibition was the largest one issued for his single-artist showings during his lifetime. (DVD figures 364, 365 and 366)

Moholy wrote a detailed description of one of the works on display in London, *Transparent Rho 51* of 1936 (DVD figure 365; also visible hanging on the wall in the same figure) and described its importance and its possibilities for interaction with the viewer:

> The abstract has now seized upon colour as the medium of more objective expression. But it has not yet been possible to create the highest intensity of colour, as expressed in nature (through reflection or absorption of light by certain bodies). It is thus once more a question of the same ancient problem, but no longer upon a naturalistic plane.
>
> I made an experiment on these lines in the transparent picture, one which accompanies this article (*Rhodoid 52* [*sic*; actually *Rhodoid 51*]). The picture is painted on the front and back of a transparent material. Adjacent to the coloured surface there is a perforation. This admits unfiltered light, so that in addition to the pigmentary effect of the painted spaces we have a direct material effect derived from the light striking through upon the background. Thus a kind of spatial kinetics also begins to play its part. When the picture is secured at a certain distance from its background, we have effects of light and shade which appears to move as the spectator walks past the picture.[906]

THE LONDON GALLERY EXHIBITION was the first in England to bring wide attention to Moholy's work in the fine arts there, since his earlier contributions to group exhibitions in the fine arts there had attracted little attention to that aspect of his career.[907] Athough this exhibition was by far the most widely reviewed of any of his single-artist exhibitions during his lifetime, nearly all of the reviews were unfavorable. The advertisement in *The Times* (London) had billed Moholy as "late Professor at 'Bauhaus,' leader of Constructivism,"[908] and that seemed to have set the tone for the reviewers. The anonymous reviewer in *The Times* found that ". . . it is difficult to resist the impression that they [the works on view] represent an attempt to assert the individuality of the artist, as painter, in circumstances in which it is no longer relevant,"

---

[906]László Moholy-Nagy, "Paths to the Unleashed Colour Camera" in: *The Penrose Annual; a Review of the Graphic Arts, volume XXXIX* (London: Lund Humphries & Co., Ltd., 1937), 25-28, here 27-28. (An error in labeling caused the picture illustrated in *The Penrose Annual* to be mis-identified as *Transparent Rho 52* in the picture caption and on page 28 of the text.)

The text of the essay, but with differing illustrations that did not include the work cited by name in his *Penrose Annual* text, was published in Chicago in: *Printing Art Quarterly*, volume LXVII, number 3 (Winter, 1938), 28-32.

The essay was originally published as "A Feslzabadult Szin-fényképezé Felé," *Korunk*, 1936, number 12, 1014-1016.

[907]Senter, "Moholy-Nagy: the Transitional Years," 89; *idem*, "Moholy-Nagy in England," 243-245.

[908]Advertisement in *The Times* (London), December 31, 1936, page 8, bottom of column 4.

and went on to assert that "All of the implications of the paintings, or 'Constructions' as most of them are called, are of a communal art which is fundamentally architectural. . . ."[909] This and other reviews were summed up in *Art and Industry*,[910] which noted that *The Yorkshire Post* critic had said that some of the paintings "reveal him as an architect rather than a painter," and went on to assert that "*The Daily Telegraph's* critic [T.W. Earp] said some strange things" and quoted him at some length:

> Whatever its significance with regard to (his) other activities, constructivism, so far as painting is concerned, proves from this exhibition to be simply a new name for a very old thing. . . . The architect's tracings or engineers' diagrams, which the pictures faintly resemble, are not very interesting apart from their purpose toward constructing something else. But constructivism that constructs nothing, and is of little visual attraction in itself, might better be called zeroism.

Giedion's statement (part of an excerpt from his *telehor* essay reprinted in the London catalogue) that: "Moholy-Nagy's painting is the vital thread linking all his manifold activities,"[911] did not seem to have had much effect on the reviewers.[912] Nor did the assertion by Gropius in his noon-time talk at the opening that: "He has succeeded in projecting all his various interests into his painting and thus captured a new Pictorial unity peculiar to himself."[913] An exception to the negative reviews was written by Modernist architect Dora Cosens, who wrote for *The Architects' Journal*. She quoted the assertion by Gropius and much of the rest of his talk as well, and found that Moholy's work ". . . in its preoccupation with spatial relationships and recession of planes, probably approximates more nearly than that of any other painter to the aesthetics of architecture." She went on to give a very sympathetic description of his works on view (two of which were illustrated):

> His paintings and constructions . . . show the openness of a mind that is experimenting all the time with the textures and reflecting qualities of new and improbable materials, and the effect of light on and through their surfaces—sprayed paint on polished aluminium, tempera on light-absorbing canvas, coloured and incised designs on sheets of rhodoid which, set concave or

---

[909] "Mr. Moholy-Nagy," *The Times* (London), January 2, 1937, 8.

[910] "L. Moholy-Nagy, Experimentalist," *Art and Industry*, volume XXII, number 129 (March, 1937), 110-115, here 112. The article also included numerous photographs of Moholy's graphic and exhibition designs.

[911] Sigfried Giedion, "The Work of L. Moholy-Nagy," in: London Gallery Ltd., *L. Moholy-Nagy*, 9-13, here 13.

[912] Additional summaries of reviews, most of them unfavorable, are in Senter, "Moholy-Nagy in England," 253-254.

[913] Walter Gropius, quoted in: "L. Moholy-Nagy, Experimentalist," 112; on Gropius's talk, see: Senter, "Moholy-Nagy: the Transitional Years," 85; and *idem*, "Moholy-Nagy in England," 248-249.

convex to reflect or transmit the light, make the cast shadows and the light part of the design.[914]

It is possible that Moholy's paintings were generally viewed more favorably in Basel where, while the London exhibition was still on view, twenty-two of his paintings were shown in the context of a Constructivist exhibition that included work by Mondrian, van Doesburg, Malevich and Sophie Taeuber-Arp, among others. The Basel exhibition, which opened January 16th, 1937, included, among other works by Moholy, two paintings on transparent celluloid, three paintings on transparent rhodoid, two paintings on galilith and one painting on aluminum; two of his paintings, including *Komposition Q VIII*, 1923, were illustrated in the catalogue.[915]

Terence Senter has compiled a useful list of the paintings, sculpture and drawings created by Moholy during the years 1935, 1936 and 1937.[916] The total number of these works is forty-three, and all, or nearly all, would have been made by him in London. Thus Senter's list provides a useful context for Moholy's accomplishments in graphic and exhibition design, photography and film during his London years.

In 1936 Moholy was included in two American exhibitions, each of which, by chance, opened on March 3rd of that year. One of these was at the Museum of Modern Art in New York, when *Cubism and Abstract Art* was seen there from March 3rd through April 12th, 1936.[917] Moholy was represented by a painting, two lithographs, a photogram and three examples of his graphic design for the Bauhaus.[918] Illustrated in the catalogue were the photogram and the examples of graphic design.[919]

Charleston, South Carolina, was the other March 3rd venue for Moholy; five of his paintings were included in the first exhibition of the Solomon R. Guggenheim Collection of Non-Objective Paintings, held at the Gibbes Museum of Art (then known as Gibbes

---

[914]Dora Cosens, "Exhibitions, Moholy-Nagy," *The Architects' Journal* (January 7, 1937), 2, 5, 6 and 7, here 6.

[915]*Konstruktivisten: Van Doesburg, Domela, Eggeling, Gabo, Lissitzky, Moholy-Nagy, Mondrian, Pevsner, Taeuber, Vantongerloo, Vordemberge, u. a., vom 16. Januar bis 14. Februar 1937* (Basel: Kunsthalle Basel, 1937), 18, 19 and two unnumbered pages following page 20. The catalogue was reprinted in 1974 by the Silver Fox Press of Reddington, Connecticut.

[916]Senter, "Moholy-Nagy in England," 318-321.

[917]Edward Alden Jewell, "Shock Troops in Review; Museum of Modern Art Opens a Pageant of the Cubists and Abstractionists," *New York Times*, March 8, 1936, X 9; and Lynes, *Good Old Modern*, 137-141.

[918]Alfred H. Barr, *Cubism and Abstract Art*, first paperbound edition (New York: The Museum of Modern Art, 1974), 217, 225 and 230.

[919]*Ibid.*, [159] and [171].

Memorial Art Gallery) from March 3ʳᵈ through April 12ᵗʰ, 1936.[920] (Guggenheim maintained a winter home in Charleston.)

Moholy had met Solomon R. Guggenheim (1861-1949) in Berlin in June, 1930,[921] and made a photographic portrait of him there (DVD figure 367);[922] he had known Guggenheim's close friend and the initiator and curator of the Solomon R. Guggenheim Collection, Hilla Rebay (1890-1967),[923] since 1923.[924] A Moholy photograph of 1932 shows Guggenheim with Rebay's friend Rudolf Bauer (1889-1953); this was made in

---

[920]Hilla Rebay, editor, *Solomon R. Guggenheim Collection of Non-objective Paintings, on Exhibition from March 1, 1936 through April 12, 1936; Presented by the Carolina Art Association at the Gibbes Memorial Art Gallery, Charleston, South Carolina* (New York, The Bradford Press, inc., 1936), 82-86. On the organization of this exhibition see: Joan M. Lukach, *Hilla Rebay: in Search of the Spirit in Art*, with postscript by Thomas M. Messer (New York: George Braziller, 1983), 37-38.

Two of the works shown in Charleston are currently owned by the Solomon R. Guggenheim Museum; see: Rudenstine, *The Guggenheim Museum Collection, Paintings, 1880-1945*, 2:548-549 and 552.

[921]Lukach, *Hilla Rebay*, 75.

[922]László Moholy-Nagy to Hilla Rebay, September 9, 1930, Hilla von Rebay Foundation, The Solomon R. Guggenheim Museum, New York; portions published in English translation in: Lukach, *Hilla Rebay*, 75-76.

The photographic portrait of Guggenheim Moholy referred to is probably the one illustrated in: Haus, *Moholy-Nagy: Photographs and Photograms*, page 69 and plate 62. The inscription on the verso, *Kupferkönig*, or copper king, refers to Guggenheim's activities as a major developer and owner of copper mines, and thus connects him with Moholy's activities as a teacher in the metal workshop at the Bauhaus.

[923]For two contrasting views on the relationship of Hilla Rebay amd Solomon Guggenheim, see: Lukach, *Hilla Rebay*, 307-308 *et passim*; and Rolph Scarlett and Harriet Tannin, *The Baroness, the Mogul, and the Forgotten History of the First Guggenheim Museum* (New York: Midmarch Arts Press, 2003), [100]-103.

[924]Hilla Rebay, art collector and curator, was also a prolific and accomplished artist who had shown at Der Sturm in Berlin and whose work had been illustrated in its magazine. She had earlier been known as Hildegarde Anna Augusta Elisabeth Rebay, Freifrau [Baroness] von Ehrenwiesen. She never married, and during most of her life she was known as Hilla Rebay, or, occasionally, as Hilla von Rebay. On Rebay see: Lukach, *Hilla Rebay*; Jo-Anne Birnie Danzker, Brigitte Salmen and editors, *Art of Tomorrow: Hilla Rebay and Solomon R. Guggenheim* (New York: Guggenheim Museum, 2005); and Karole Vail, editor, *The Museum of Non-Objective Painting: Hilla Rebay and the Origins of the Solomon R. Guggenheim Museum* (New York: Guggenheim Museum, 2009).

Rebay and Moholy had corresponded since 1923; see: Robert L. Herbert, Eleanor S. Apter and Elise K. Kenney, editors, *The Société Anonyme Bequest at Yale University: a Catalogue Raisonné* (New Haven: Yale University Press, 1984), 464.

Bauer's *das Geistreich* [the realm of the spirit], his residence and gallery in Berlin (four pictures are visible on a wall).[925] (DVD figure 368)

In 1929, even before he met Guggenheim, one of Moholy's paintings, *T1*, 1926, had been bought for his collection.[926] Rebay collected Moholy's paintings as well, and two of Moholy's paintings in the Charleston exhibition belonged to her.[927] There was another showing of Moholy's work in the context of The Solomon R. Guggenheim Collection while he was still living in Europe; this took place in Philadelphia, February 8th to 28th, 1937.[928]

WHEN HILLA REBAY WAS IN PARIS in 1930 in connection with a display of her work at the Bernheim-Jeune gallery, Moholy was there working on the German Werkbund exhibition at the *Grand Palais des Champs-Elysées*, seen from May 14th through July 13th, as discussed above. Moholy helped her to hang her pictures at Bernheim-Jeune, and then returned several times bringing friends to the exhibition.[929] In turn she visited the Werkbund exhibition with its carefully planned sequence of spaces on two levels through which the visitor was guided among the exhibited items, perhaps providing a germ of an idea for the Solomon R. Guggenheim Museum in New York, eventually erected, as described in Chapter Five, from Frank Lloyd Wright's design, but only after Guggenheim and Rebay considered other architects.

Moholy served as mentor to Rebay and helped her to expand the range of artists she and Guggenheim were collecting. It was Moholy who suggested Piet Mondrian and Fernand Léger for the Guggenheim collection and who introduced her to both artists in 1930.[930] As will be seen in Chapter Five, Moholy's friendship with Rebay continued in the United States, and sales of his work to the Guggenheim Collection continued there.[931]

---

[925]The photograph was formerly owned by Helmut Franke; on the back an inscription in Mohnoly's hand reads, in part: "Rudolph [*sic*] Bauer & S.R. Guggenheim 1932." Franke is discussed below.

[926]Lukach, *Hilla Rebay*, 63-64; and Rudenstine, *The Guggenheim Museum Collection, Paintings, 1880-1945*, 2:548-549.

[927]Rebay, editor, *Solomon R. Guggenheim Collection of Non-objective Paintings, on Exhibition from March 1, 1936 through April 12, 1936*, 37-38.

[928]Hilla Rebay, editor, *Second Enlarged Catalogue of the Solomon R. Guggenheim Collection of Non-objective Paintings, on Exhibition from February 8, 1937 Through February 28, 1937, Presented by the Philadelphia Art Alliance, Philadelphia, Pennsylvania* (New York, The Bradford Press, inc., 1937), 42-43; see also: Lukach, *Hilla Rebay*, 96-98.

[929]Lukach, *Hilla Rebay*, 64.

[930]Lukach, *Hilla Rebay*, 64-68.

[931]Rudenstine, *The Guggenheim Museum Collection, Paintings, 1880-1945*, 2:546-548, 558-559 and 562-563.

During a brief visit to Paris in late September, 1936, Moholy sought the company of Rebay. She had been in and out of Paris during summer and early fall,[932] and Moholy, after being unsuccessful in telephoning her during his visit, wrote her a letter expressing his enthusiasm for a large Cézanne exhibition he had just visited at the *Musée de l'Orangerie* that had opened there on June 20th; included were one-hundred-and-thirteen oil paintings and more than eighty drawings and watercolors.[933] About Cézanne he wrote:

> Cézanne, by the way, was a great experience for me. Very positive in many respects. I thought it was nice that even so capital a painter as Cézanne had to learn to paint. Look at the trousers and the jacket in the portrait of his father. But I think the last abstracting paintings are really "grand." I would really have liked to have seen this exhibition with you in order to know exactly what appeals to you.[934]

To his friend Franz Roh he wrote in a similar vein, stressing how much he had learned at the exhibition.[935] And it was shortly after this exhibition that he wrote of the French painter's importance to experiments in color photography: "It is my conviction that Cézanne's artistic development will for a long time to come remain the practical foundation of color photography . . ."[936]

The last time Rebay saw Moholy's work on exhibition in Europe was a very special occasion, the now infamous "degenerate" art exhibition, billed as *Entartete Kunst* when it opened July 19th, 1937, in the arcade rooms of the *Residenz* in Munich, before moving on to other venues. Rebay saw it in Munich and wrote about it to her artist friend Rudolf Bauer. In her letter she noted that the exhibition was extremely crowded with visitors, and that she had seen works by Schwitters, Grosz, Klee, Kandinsky and Moholy there.[937]

---

[932]Lukach, *Hilla Rebay*, 94-96.

[933]Douglas Lord, "Shorter Notices: Paul Cézanne," *The Burlington Magazine for Connoisseurs,* volume LXIX, number 400 (July, 1936), 32-33 and 35; and Paris, Musée de l'Orangerie, *Cézanne. Avant-propos de J[acques]-E[mille] Blanche, Préf. de Paul Jamot*, deuxième édition corrigée (Paris: Musée de l'Orangerie, 1936).

[934]László Moholy-Nagy to Hilla Rebay; the letter is in the Hilla Rebay Foundation archives and is quoted in English translation in: Lukach, *Hilla Rebay*, 77. It is undated, but would have been written near the end of September because of the date on a letter he wrote to Franz Roh about his visit to the Cézanne exhibition: László Moholy-Nagy to Franz Roh, September 27, 1936, ALS, Franz Roh files, Getty Research Center, Los Angeles.

[935]László Moholy-Nagy to Franz Roh, September 27, 1936.

[936]László Moholy-Nagy, "Paths to the Unleashed Colour Camera," 26-27.

[937]Hilla Rebay to Rudolf Bauer, August 17, 1937, Hilla Rebay Foundation archives, New York. An English translation was published in: Lukach, *Hilla Rebay*, 120.

The treatment of modern art and artists by the Nazis was barbarous and outrageous, and Moholy had a premonition of this during his work with the Kroll Opera, discussed above. For him (and many others) the Nazi disdain for Modernist art meant that there was no way they could continue to work in Germany. All modern art was denounced by the Nazis as "*entartete*," which translates as degenerate: in practice they denounced the paintings of Van Gogh and Cézanne as well as all later works that showed any sign of modern tendencies. They attempted to seize all such works of art in public collections in Germany, a huge undertaking.[938]

Selections from these seized works were shown in the *Entartete Kunst* exhibition. Rebay, in her letter to Bauer, cited above, was not specific as to what works of Moholy she had seen. After the war, and the end of the Nazi era, detailed information about art seized by the Nazis and where it had been exhibited became available. Reconstructed lists of the works that had been shown in Munich in the summer of 1937 included just one work by Moholy, described as a watercolor in one list[939] and as *Konstruktion*, seized from the Folkwang Museum in Essen, in another.[940]

A 1949 listing of artists whose works were seized and the number seized indicated that twelve works by Moholy had fallen victim to the Nazis.[941] In 1962, Moholy's old friend Franz Roh published the results of a survey of the directors of the public museums and galleries in Germany that he had conducted in order to assemble a list of seized works. Although not all museums were able to provide information for his survey, he did identify nine of the works by Moholy that had been seized. These came from three museums: from the Landesmuseum, Hanover, one painting and three works under the category of drawings and prints; from the Städtische Kunsthalle, Mannheim, two works under the category of drawings, watercolors and prints; and from the Folkwang Museum, Essen, three works under the category of drawings and watercolors.[942] In other words, of twelve works described as seized in an account dating from 1949, only nine could be identified in 1962. One of the three works not listed in 1962 might have come from the Folkwang Museum, which in 1929 published a handbook that provided a checklist of their holdings. Four works by Moholy were listed under the category of drawings and

---

[938] Jonathan Petropoulos, *Art as Politics in the Third Reich* (Chapel Hill: The University of North Carolina Press, 1996), 51-57; and Franz Roh, *"Entartete" Kunst; Kunstbarbarei im Dritten Reich* ["Degenerate" art: art barbarism in the Third Reich] (Hanover: Fackelträger-Verlag Schmidt-Küster GMbH, 1962), 51-53 and [122]-[248].

[939] Paul Ortwin Rave, *Kunst Diktatur im dritten Reich* (Hamburg: Gebr. Mann, 1949), 80.

[940] Barron, editor, "Degenerate Art," 79 and 302.

[941] Rave, *Kunst Diktatur im dritten Reich*, 88.

[942] Roh, *"Entartete" Kunst*, 167, 194, 198 and 222.

watercolors;[943] these would have been hard to hide from the seizing officials because of the checklist, so it seems likely that four works were seized from the Folkwang Museum, even though only three of them could be identified in 1962.

At least one of the works seized from Hanover can now be tentatively identified. This is *Konstruktion*, which resembles closely the work known as *KVII*, dating from 1923, now in Bielefeld. (DVD figure 124) The Hanover version can be seen in photographs of El Lissitzky's *Abstract Cabinet* in the Landesmuseum in Hanover. (DVD figure 369)

The seized works were handled in a variety of ways, including sales abroad through dealers or in auctions,[944] a massive secret burning,[945] and storage in warehouses until the end of the war.[946] The most likely avenue through which Moholy would have known that any of his works had been seized or exhibited as "degenerate" would have been through his contact with Rebay while they were both living in the United States. Ironically, on the same page in an American architectural journal dated October, 1937, there appeared a brief report on the showing of "degenerate" art in Munich (no specific artists were mentioned) and a story about the opening of Moholy's New Bauhaus in Chicago.[947]

Moholy and Japan

Moholy never went to Japan, but he had an enormous influence there. Ironically, his work on *Madama Butterfly* early in 1931, described above, directly preceded the residence in Japan of his brother, Ákos Nagy, which began in July of 1931 when he

---

[943] Agnes Waldstein, editor, *Museum Folkwang, Band I, Moderne Kunst: Malerei, Plastik, Grafik* (Essen: Museum Folkwang, 1929), items 606-609 on page 53.

Each of the items was listed as *Konstruktion*. These were *Konstruktion: A*, "Deckfarben u. Klebearbeit" (47 by 35.9 centimeters); *Konstruktion: Schiff*, "Deckfarben" (48.6 by 36 centimeters); *Konstruktion*, "Deckfarben u. Klebearbeit" (34.6 by 24.9 centimeters); and *Konstruktion: 19*, "Deckfarben u. Klebearbeit" (48.6 by 36.5 centimeters). It was indicated that each was signed (i.e.: "Bezeichnung: Moholy-Nagy"). Each item was also designated as "Folkwang," which meant that it had been purchased during or before 1922; see: Waldstein, editor, *op. cit.,* [3].

[944] Roh, *"Entartete" Kunst*, 56-57; Petropoulos, *Art as Politics*, 76-83; and Alice Goldfarb Marquis, *Alfred H. Barr, Jr., Missionary for the Modern* (Chicago: Contemporary Books, 1989), 177-179.

[945] Petropoulos, *Art as Politics*, 82; and Marquis, *Alfred H. Barr, Jr.*, 177.

[946] Petropoulos, *Art as Politics*, 76-77 and 82.

[947] See: *Architectural Record*, volume LXXXII, number 6 (October, 1937), 91.

began his service as a correspondent for the Russian news agency TASS in Tokyo.[948] The Japanese version of the *FiFo* exhibition, which included a large number of photographs by his brother László, was possibly still showing in Osaka when he arrived in Japan with his family, but there is no record that he saw it. Nevertheless this exhibition, that opened in Tokyo and Osaka while *Madama Butterfly* was still playing in Berlin, did stimulate interest in Moholy's work.

While one more European incarnation of Puccini's popular opera would be little noted in Japan, the year 1931 also saw the publication in that country of Moholy's last Bauhaus Book, *von material zu architektur*,[949] (DVD figures 370m 371, 372, 373, 374, 375 and 376) but it seemingly created about as much interest as still one more production of *Madama Butterly* in far-off Berlin. One can only speculate as to the reason; perhaps the publisher was not good at book distribution, or perhaps the economic Depression intervened and some copies were printed but none were distributed through commercial channels. The only known copy of the Japanese version was in Moholy's collection when he died, and is now in a private collection.

Not surprisingly there was no mention of the first Japanese edition of *von material zu architektur* in the proceedings of a 1997 symposium on Bauhaus photography, published in connection with an exhibition at the Kawasaki City Museum.[950] Nevertheless the 1997 Kawasaki symposium provides ample information about the influence of Moholy in Japan. For example, his *Painting, Photography, Film* had been known in Japan since 1930 because it was issued serially in a Japanese photography magazine, in a translation by Zen Ogida, in 1930 and 1931.[951]

Moholy in London and Attempts at Assembling a Modernist Movement

Although Moholy lived in London for a mere two years, it was especially appropriate for him to work there. The Industrial Revolution underlay his career, and London and nearby areas in western England were where it had originated during the late eighteenth century. Moreover, key elements of that revolution, including the increasing availability and use of metals, the mechanization of the textile industry, technical innovations in paper-making and printing, and the rapid growth of freight and passenger transportation all are reflected in his career in one way or another.

---

[948]See appendix B.

[949]*László Moholy-Nagy, Zairyō kara kenchiku e* [From Material to Architecture] (Tokyo: Kōyōsha, 1931).

[950]Published in Japanese and English as part of a catalogue: Fukagawa, editor, *bauhaus fotografie*, cited fully in note 633.

[951]Kohtaro Iizawa, "The Bauhaus and Shinko Shashin," in: Fukagawa, editor, *bauhaus fotografie*, 134 and 137.

London was also the center of the English Arts and Crafts Movement that rose in opposition to the Industrial Revolution. In fact, major centers of activity within that movement were centers of industry and commerce and, as will be seen in Chapter Five, Chicago constitutes a good example. The Arts and Crafts Movement provided a powerful thrust toward design reform that continued after the movement had waned. One Arts and Crafts figure, Edward Johnston (1872-1944), developed into a Modernist graphic designer whose 1916 sans-serif type face for London Transport[952] was used by Moholy in his own work for the London transportation system, discussed above. Moreover, Moholy was briefly associated with Eric Gill in his work for Simpson's of Piccadilly, discussed below; Gill was another Arts and Crafts figure who had become a Modernist graphic designer (see page 525 and DVD figure 397 right).

Of course London had become one of the world's major metropolises, and more than eight million people lived in greater London when Moholy worked there from 1935 to 1937. Moreover London, unlike Berlin, continued as an imperial capital, and the British Empire was on a much larger scale than the empire for which Berlin had once served as capital. Thus London was even more bustling than indicated by the size of its resident population, and of course much busier than Berlin. All of this made London an ideal location for a design practice.

Perhaps more important than all this for Moholy was Britain's long tradition of political and religious liberty, including tolerance for Jews, in the face of his growing uneasiness with the repression in Nazi Germany. Those at risk in Germany included Gypsies and political dissidents (among them Lucia Moholy's lover, Theodor Neubauer), but also and most prominently Jews. Although Moholy was not openly identified as a Jew in Germany, some of his friends, including Herbert Read, were aware of his Jewish background that had obliged him to leave Germany.[953]

Although Moholy's residence in Britain was relatively brief, he did make a modest contribution to the cause of intellectual liberty there. He was associated with a group known as For Intellectual Liberty; its members were mostly literary figures, along with some scientists and artist Henry Moore. The group's president was novelist Aldous Huxley, brother of Moholy's friend Julian. As noted above in connection with his writing about films, Moholy was an opponent of censorship, and his cover for the group's *Bulletin* of November, 1936, used chains as symbols of censorship.[954] (DVD figure 377)

---

[952]Taylor, editor, *The Moving Metropolis*, 179 and 184-185; and Justin Howes, *Johnston's Underground Type* (Harrow Weald, England: Capital Transport Publishers, 2000).

[953]Senter, "Moholy-Nagy in England," 24 and 53. The statement about Read's concern for Moholy's safety as a Jew in Germany is from an interview Senter had with Marcus Brumwell on June 1, 1972; see: *ibid.*, 53, 276 and 371.

[954]Senter, "Moholy-Nagy in England," 190 and illustration 130.

The British capital was, during the time of Moholy's residence there, one of only four cities in the world, along with Berlin, Paris and New York, that had a comparable range and scale of museum resources. Despite our lack of any specific documentation, one can suppose Moholy immersed himself in some of London's museums with the same enthusiasm he displayed when he described his three-and-a-half hour visit to the Art Institute of Chicago shortly after his arrival in the Illinois metropolis (see Chapter Five).

One reason that Moholy did not feel contented in England was that there was no way to teach, other than to give lectures, including a few academic guest lectures, *e.g.*, at Oxford University in spring, 1937,[955] at Hull School of Architecture (at the invitation of Leslie Martin) early in 1937,[956] and at Cambridge University in the spring of 1937.[957]

THE LECTURE AT CAMBRIDGE cannot be dated exactly, but Moholy was invited in February[958] and the lecture took place after Gropius had moved to Massachusetts (near the end of March, 1937). The context for the lecture is important because Cambridge had become a battleground for Modernism. Moholy was invited to lecture by the influential biologist Conrad Hal Waddington (1905-1975), who taught at Christ's College. It was Waddington who turned to Gropius for a design for a student dormitory at Christ's College that was to fit in with traditional and venerable surroundings but should be contemporary and modern. As a result Gropius and his partner at the time, Maxwell Fry (1899-1987), working with two traditional architects, were commissioned to make preliminary designs.[959] Moholy was invited at a time when there was still hope that the dormitory would be erected from the design by Gropius and his collaborators, but by the time he lectured the commission had already been cancelled. (The building was finally erected in 1948 in a traditional manner).[960] Gropius had not been successful in establishing a bastion of Modernism in the most traditional part of England, and Moholy lectured at a time that must have seemed anticlimactic for his host. Not much is documented about the content of his lecture, but nevertheless Moholy's comments on his visit to Cambridge are amusing:

> in cambridge war ich durch waddington gast bei einem feast in christcollege
> [*sic*]. Ich erinnerte mich an deinen bericht von dem feast, bei dem du seinerzeit

---

[955]László Moholy-Nagy to Walter and Ise Gropius, May 28, 1937.

[956]Senter, "Moholy-Nagy's English Photography," 670; *idem*, "Moholy-Nagy in England," 242; and László Moholy-Nagy to Walter and Ise Gropius, TLS, May 28, 1937, Bauhaus-Archiv, Berlin.

[957]Information from a letter from Sibyl Moholy-Nagy to her family in Loschwitz near Dresden, February 20, 1937; a copy of the letter is in the files of Hattula Moholy-Nagy, Ann Arbor, Michigan.

[958]*Ibid.*

[959]J.M. (James Maude) Richards, *Memoirs of an Unjust Fella* (London: Weidenfeld and Nicolson, 1980), 135.

[960]Winfried Nerdinger, *Walter Gropius*, 190-191.

warst und habe mich auf alkoholkonsum und mittelalterliche sitte vorbereitet. Es
war sehr interesant, besonders master [of Christ's College, Charles Galton]
darwin [1887-1962], der enkel des affenerfinders [*sic*; evidently a simplistic
colloquial description of evolution].[961] [In Cambridge I was invited by
Waddington as guest at a feast in Christ's College. I remembered your account
of the feast you had there earlier and I was prepared for a lot of drinking and
medieval customs. It was very interesting, especially Master {of Christ's
College Charles Galton} Darwin (1887-1962), the grandson of the evolutionist.]

   In addition to lack of teaching opportunities, another element of Moholy's
unhappiness in England surely was that no opportunities to work in the theatre came his
way. The most promising avenue in England for both activities was at Dartington Hall in
Devonshire, where, in 1925, Dorothy and Leonard Elmhirst had begun to set up a variety
of enterprises, among them craft production, a school, a dance program and a theatre.[962]
Gropius worked with the Elmhirsts for several years,[963] but none of their seemingly
promising initiatives enabled Gropius to forge any Bauhaus-like institution under their
auspices. This in spite of the fact that he once referred to Dartington Hall as "a kind of
an English Bauhaus,"[964] and had provided the Elmhirsts with a chance to explore
Bauhaus ideas by giving them a copy of Moholy's *The New Vision*.[965] Although the
restored medieval buildings at Dartington Hall were supplemented by some of the
earliest examples of modern architecture in England,[966] the only accomplishment
Gropius could point to at Dartington Hall was the conversion of an antique barn into a
theatre.[967] He attempted to involve Moholy in this theatre project, and at his request

---

[961]László Moholy-Nagy to Walter and Ise Gropius, May 28, 1937.

[962]Dennis Hardy, *Utopian England; Community Experiments*, *1900-1945* (London: E & FW Spon,
2000), 144-162.

[963]Isaacs, *Gropius; an Illustrated Biography*, 192-194.

[964]Isaacs, *Gropius; an Illustrated Biography*, 193.

[965]Walter Gropius to Leonard Elmhirst, May 9, 1933, Dartington Hall Trust Archive, Totnes,
Devonshire.

[966]Michael Young, *The Elmhirsts of Dartington; the Creation of an Utopian Community* (London:
Routledge & Kegan Paul, 1982), 170, 265-266, plate 24 facing page 278, and pages 300-301;
Gerald Heard, "The Dartington Experiment," *The Architectural Review: a Magazine of
Architecture & Decoration,* volume LXXV, number 449 (April, 1934), 119-122 and plates ii and
iii following page 120; Fantl, editor, *Modern Architecture*, plates 37, 38 and 40 following page 41;
and Alan Powers, *Modern: the Modern Movement in England*, photography by Morley von
Sternberg (London: Merrell, 2005), 164-167.

[967]Young, *The Elmhirsts*, 229; and Anthony Emery, *Dartington Hall* (Oxford: The Clarendon
Press, 1970), 10 and 222-224.

Moholy produced a proposal for stage effects.[968] Gropius wrote to Moholy in February, 1935, that:

> At my visit to Dartington Hall I handed your theatre plan personally to Mrs. Elmhirst and asked her to have it translated by [Kurt] Jooss. I told her about you and she would very much like to see you some time at Dartington Hall. I will fix that as soon as you are here.[969]

The translator of this theatre plan, Kurt Jooss (1901-1979), had been a pioneer of modern dance in Germany and beginning in 1934 had been based at Dartington Hall.[970] A key part of Moholy's plan, along with Jooss's translation, follows:

> wir müssen wieder zu einer kultur der farben züruck, die wir im grunde schon einmal besessen haben. die moderne malerei versucht diese farbkultur der menschheit züruckzugeben und zu ihrer ausbreitung und ihrem verständnis kann keine bessere und durchdringendere aktion erdacht werden, als die bewusst vom optischen ausgehende bühnenbildgestaltung. dazu gehört die leichte handhabung der künstlichen (elektrischen) lichtquellung, die eine gesteigerte, weil leuchtendere und transparentere farbwirkung, als sie die pigmentmalerei je erzielen kann, ermöglichen. [We must return to a colour culture which at one time we have actually possessed. The modern painter seeks to give back this colour culture to humanity, but to reach a wider public no better way can be found than through the theatre. Besides, this easy handling of artificial (electric) light gives much greater effect than the pigment painter can ever hope to achieve because of their translucent and transparent colour effects.]

Moholy evidently did make at least one trip to Dartington Hall,[971] but nothing came of his theatre plan.

The most cohesive group of English Modernists was known as Unit One.[972] It brought together eleven painters, sculptors and architects under the leadership of Herbert Read (1893-1968),[973] curator, theorist, critic, historian and editor. In 1935 Read described the group in these words:

---

[968]Moholy's typed nine-page proposal, in German, with two drawings in the text, and three typed pages of excerpts in English, are in the Dartington Hall Trust Archive, Totnes, Devonshire.

[969]Walter Gropius to László Moholy-Nagy, February 2, 1935, Bauhaus-Archiv, Berlin; English translation in: Senter, "Moholy-Nagy in England," 324-325.

[970]Isa Partsch-Bergsohn and Harold Bergsohn, *The Makers of Modern Dance in Germany, Rudolf Laban, Mary Wigman, Kurt Jooss* (Hightstown, New Jersey: Princeton Book Company, Publishers, 2003), 70-75; and Young, *The Elmhirsts*, 225-229.

[971]Senter, "Moholy-Nagy in England," 50, 275, 368 and 371.

[972]Herbert Read, "Unit One," *The Architectural Review: a Magazine of Architecture & Decoration*, volume LXXIV, number 444 (October, 1935), 125-128.

[973]Read was knighted in 1953 as Sir Herbert Read.

. . . the aims of the Unit are strategical: to form a point in the forward thrust of modernism in architecture, painting and sculpture, and to harden this point in the fires of criticism and controversy.[974]

But in spite of Read's eloquent rhetoric, the group proved to be short-lived.[975]

Read had helped Moholy emigrate to England,[976] and the two had corresponded at least since 1933.[977] Their friendship continued as Read visited the Institute of Design in Chicago in 1946, as described in Chapter Five. Two other members of Unit One, painter Ben Nicholson (1894-1982) and sculptor Barbara Hepworth (1903-1975), were already known to Moholy through Paris-based *Abstraction-Création*.[978] After his arrival in England Moholy had some significant contact with two other members of the group, architect Welles Coates and sculptor Henry Moore.

In the early 1970s, through interviews and correspondence, Terence Senter has reconstructed discussions Moholy initiated with Nicholson, Naum Gabo, Roland Penrose, Jack Pritchard and others, aimed at setting up an English Bauhaus.[979] But, in short, no such efforts were actively pursued. The same could be said for the efforts of Gropius, who discussed the possibility of an English Bauhaus with Henry Moore, Frank Pick and others.[980] Pick was Chairman of the Council for Art and Industry, set up by the Board of Trade, an arm of the British government.[981]

---

[974]Herbert Read, editor, *Unit 1; the Modern Movement in English Architecture, Painting and Sculpture* (London: Cassell and Company Ltd., 1934), 12.

[975]Richards, *Memoirs,* 132.

[976]Senter, "Moholy-Nagy in England," 30.

[977]Senter, "Moholy-Nagy in England," 13, 24-25 and 322-323.

[978]Senter, "Moholy-Nagy in England," 10-11; and Sibyl Moholy-Nagy to László Moholy-Nagy, August 22, 1934. Nicholson and Hepworth were married to each other from about 1933 to 1951.

[979]Senter, "Moholy-Nagy: the Transitional Years," 87-88; *idem*, "Moholy-Nagy in England," 52, 276, and 370-371; and Terence Senter to Jack Pritchard, ALS, September 10, 1971, Pritchard Papers, Library of the University of East Anglia, Norwich.

[980]Senter, "Moholy-Nagy in England," 40-41.

[981]*Ibid.,* 40.

Books for Britain

NOT LONG BEFORE leaving Germany, Moholy wrote to Gropius about reviving the Bauhaus publishing program, even suggesting proposed manuscripts.[982] He actually identified a possible (unnamed) publisher; the letter was dated March 31st, 1935, and, given the timing, it was a German publisher he had in mind, in spite of the political as well as financial difficulties that publisher would have faced. A more modest scheme for a book on exhibition design was submitted on November 8th, 1935, by Gropius to the Architectural Press on behalf of himself and Moholy.[983] But nothing came of any plan to revive the Bauhaus Books until both Moholy and Gropius were living in the United States. Nevertheless, Moholy was active in publication in London through his work on one lengthy magazine article and three books.

Almost book length is an article Moholy designed for the July, 1936, issue of *The Architectural Review*; called "Leisure at the Seaside," it was an aptly-timed comprehensive survey of England's popular seaside resorts.[984] Included is a foreword and essays by four authors. Making good use of a large page-size (nearly fourteen inches in height), Moholy employed a variety of devices, including a blank page with six round cutouts of various sizes inserted between pages [10] and 11. When viewed through the holes, some of the small photographs on page 10 make the page seem like a photocollage; at the same time, the holes remind one of the "peepholes" in his exhibition designs that provide hints of what the visitor will experience as he or she proceeds. All of the photographs are black and white, but swaths of color are added to highlight some key photographs as well as to enhance key lines in the type, such as authors' names. Color is also used to highlight some elements of line-drawn illustrations, and in other ways as well. (DVD figures 378, 379, 380 and 381)

J.M. Richards, assistant editor of *The Architectural Review*, engaged Moholy to do the photographs and the layout for "Leisure at the Seaside."[985] As Richards and Moholy

---

[982] László Moholy-Nagy to Walter Gropius, March 28, 1935.

[983] Senter, "Moholy-Nagy in England," 204-206.

[984] Osbert Lancaster, H.B. Brenan, Harry Roberts and Peter Maitland [pseudonym of Serge Chermayeff], "Leisure at the Seaside," *The Architectural Review: a Magazine of Architecture & Decoration*, volume LXXX, number 476 (July, 1936), front cover; plate i (tipped in) facing page 1, with caption on page 1; pages 7-[28]; plate ii facing page 18, with caption on page 18; and plate iii facing page 42, with caption on overleaf. On page 7: "The lay-out of these pages on the Seaside has been designed, and the photographs accompanying them have been taken by L. Moholy-Nagy" [*sic*; some vintage photographs were included].

On Chermayeff's pseudonym, see: Alan Powers, *Serge Chermayeff, Designer, Architect, Teacher* (London: RIBA Publications, 2001), 80. Also, Serge Charmayeff was sometimes known in England as Sergius Ivan Chermayeff.

[985] Richards, *Memoirs*, 134-135.

traveled together to the sites covered,[986] Richards had found that: "His sparkling round spectacles and amiable grin gave him an air of bonhomie that quickly made him friends."[987]

The resort that receives the most coverage is the justly admired and much published De La Warr Pavilion in Bexhill, designed by Eric Mendelsohn and Serge Chermayeff, and was Britain's first all-welded steel building.[988] It had opened December 12th, 1935.[989] Restored by John McAlsan & Partners in 2005, it serves as a national center for contemporary art.[990] Herbrand Sackville, the 9th Earl De La Warr (1900-1976), chiefly responsible for the erection of the Pavilion as a publicly-funded enterprise, was Bexhill's first socialist mayor. An anonymous photographer made a photograph of Moholy at work in Bexhill, consulting a light meter and standing next to a large view camera mounted on a tripod (Tate Gallery, London).[991] (DVD figure 382) Chermayeff's article in *The Architectural Review*, "The Architect," summarizes some of the problems of poor planning and lack of planning at seaside resorts and used the carefully planned Bexhill Pavilion as an example of what can be achieved by good planning.[992] (Since he had been jointly responsible for the design at Bexhill, he wrote under a pseudonym, evidently in order to avoid seeming to be immodest and any appearance of conflict of interest.) Chermayeff worked very closely with Moholy on the photographs taken at Bexhill, because they were jointly commissioned by him and *The Architectural Review*.[993] Serge Chermayeff (1900-1996) was later to become Moholy's successor at the Institute of Design in Chicago.

Much of Moholy's fame in Britain stems from three documentary books illustrated with his black-and-white photographs brought out by a London publisher, John Miles.

---

[986] Senter, "Moholy-Nagy in England," 97; and *idem*, "Moholy-Nagy's English Photography," 670.

[987] Richards, *Memoirs*, 134.

[988] Bill Addis, "Concrete and Steel in Twentieth Century Construction: from Experimentation to Mainstream Usage," in: Michael Stratton, editor, *Structure and Style: Conserving Twentieth Century Buildings* (London: E & FN SPON, 1997), [103]-142, here 115.

[989] Alastair Fairley, *De La Warr Pavilion: the Modernist Masterpiece*, foreword by Richard Rogers (London: Merrell Publishers Limited, 2006).

[990] *Ibid.*, 135-147.

[991] Arts Council of Great Britain, *L. Moholy-Nagy* (Arts Council of Great Britain, 1980), [4] and 63.

[992] "Peter Maitland" [*i.e.*, Serge Chermayeff], "The Architect," in: "Leisure at the Seaside," [18-19] and 22-[28].

[993] Senter, "Moholy-Nagy in England," 99, 285 and 367.

John Betjeman, author of one of the books, had recommended Moholy,[994] who had already met his wife, Penelope, in Berlin, as noted below.

Terence Senter has ascertained the vantage point used by Moholy at various sites to make some of the photographs for John Miles. He also commented on changes in some of the sites which had already occurred by 1975.[995]

The first of these three John Miles books, *The Street Markets of London*,[996] appeared in the autumn of of 1936 and was the only one of the three to appear while Moholy was still resident in England.[997] It was written by Mary Benedetta[998] and had a two-page foreword by Moholy. The text was completed before the photographs, although it was still being written as late as the end of January, 1936.[999] In some cases the photographs were attempts to "underline" portions of the text and in others Moholy developed his own ideas while visiting the shabby yet picturesque markets. (DVD figures 383 and 384)

A list of illustrations appears at the front of *The Street Markets of London*, and the pictures are presented without captions, interspersed into the text. In a reprint of 1972 the role of author and photographer are reversed on the title-page and in the format: the list of illustrations is converted to captions appearing at the bottom of the photographs, and the photographs precede Benedetta's text but not Moholy's foreword. The order of the photographs is changed slightly, and the photographs suffer a slight lack of clarity.[1000] At least some of the negatives were taken by Moholy to the United States; his widow gave them to Helmut Franke in 1949,[1001] so they were not available for use in making new plates.

---

[994] Senter, "Moholy-Nagy in England," 78, 282 and 369; and *idem*, "Moholy-Nagy's English Photography," 670.

[995] Senter, "Moholy-Nagy in England," 93-96.

[996] *The Street Markets of London* by Mary Benedetta; photography by L. Moholy-Nagy (London: John Miles, Ltd., 1936). A foreword by Moholy is on pages vii and viii.

[997] Senter, "Moholy-Nagy in England," 79-80.

[998] Later known as Mary Benedetta Bois; see: Senter, "Moholy-Nagy in England," 367.

[999] Senter, "Moholy-Nagy in England," 80.

[1000] *The Street Markets of London*; photographs by L. Moholy-Nagy, text by Mary Benedetta (New York: Benjamin Blom Inc., Publishers, 1972).

[1001] The negatives of the photographs of the markets formerly owned by Helmut Franke, 6 by 9 centimeters in size, were evidently made with the Ernemann camera Moholy had begun using in Germany. They are now in another private collection. Included are 15 negatives, all 9 by 6 centimeters in size, taken in connection with Moholy's illustrations for *The Street Markets of London*. About half portray the Caledonian Market and about half the Petticoat Lane Market. Some were used in the book—others were close enough to the images in the book that they could be identified.

Sibyl Moholy-Nagy gave a lot of ephemera relating to her late husband, including photographs (mostly negatives and contact prints, newspaper clippings, etc.) to Helmut Franke, a printer in a photography studio and an admirer of Moholy's work. Franke returned the favor by preserving this invaluable collection of documentary material.

Curiously, in his foreword to *The Street Markets of London* Moholy stated his preference "to work with a large camera in order to obtain the minutely graded black-white-grey values of the contact print," but went on to report that "after several attempts with a large camera I always returned to the Leica." However, the only negatives that can now be located are 6 by 9 centimeters in size and were made from cut film,[1002] while the Leica uses roll film and makes negatives 35 millimeters in size. In his foreword Moholy found it easy to re-affirm his contention that "the days of the merely 'beautiful' photograph are numbered," as he clearly was caught up in documenting markets that he recognized were "the shopping-centre, in fact, for a large part of the working-class."

The second book for publisher John Miles that Moholy illustrated with photographs was *Eton Portrait,*[1003] by Bernard Fergusson (1911-1980), an Eton alumnus;[1004] it appeared in November, 1937.[1005] The photographs were evidently begun by late spring, 1936,[1006] and probably finished at or near the end of the year,[1007] while the text was evidently begun in 1936 and finished during the following year.[1008]

Dating back to the fifteenth century, Eton College, a residential secondary school for boys, is a "public" school in the British sense, which means it is available to members of the public who are eligible for admission, and who can afford the tuition, room and board (rather expensive in the case of Eton, even though it is officially a not-for-profit charity) or qualify for scholarships. It was then, and still in many respects remains, a bastion of the upper classes, and (to mix metaphors) a stepping-stone to the upper echelons of society, government and business.

In spite of the picturesque Thames-side setting, twenty miles west of central London, nearly all of Moholy's pictures center on the students. Although Hungary, along with most other countries, lacks a near equivalent to Eton, Moholy's experience in a boys'

[1002]As in note 1001.

[1003]Bernard Fergusson, *Eton Portrait*, with a chapter on college by Philip Brownrigg [and] photographs by L. Moholy-Nagy (London: John Miles, Ltd., 1937).

[1004]The author later became Sir Bernard Edward Fergusson, Baron Ballantrae.

[1005]Senter, "Moholy-Nagy in England," 79.

[1006]Three of the photographs can be dated from their content as June 4, 1936.

[1007]Senter, "Moholy-Nagy in England," 79. It should be noted that two of the photographs show students in winter overcoats against a background of leafless trees.

[1008]Senter, "Moholy-Nagy in England," 80.

gimnázium in Szeged, with its rigorous academic standards and all-male environment, helped him to identify with the students at Eton. Moreover, one student at work at a machine in a workshop, surely reminded him of the Bauhaus, in spite of dress more formal than would have been worn at the Bauhaus. (DVD figure 385)

W HEN ASKED TO PREPARE A NEW EDITION of *Eton Portrait*, Fergusson used a new title and provided a new introduction;[1009] moreover, he omitted the entire text of the earlier edition. More a new publication than a new edition, *Portrait of Eton* of 1949 not only included all of Moholy's photographs from the 1937 edition, but the author also added some informative anecdotes about Moholy's work on the book. Since Moholy had left London in early summer and the book did not appear until November, 1937, it seems likely that he had not been involved with all the details of preparing the photographs for publication. The negatives were returned to Sibyl in July, after her husband had sailed for New York.[1010] In any case, nearly all of the photographs in the 1937 *Eton Portrait* are cropped on the right and left edges; with the evident benefit of the original plates, the publisher of *Portrait of Eton* did away with the cropping, or at least made it less severe. In the cases of most of the photographs the cropping made little difference, but in some cases the uncropped images are more attractive and intelligible.

The choice of a photographer was clearly made by the publisher, and there is no reason to believe Fergusson had even heard of Moholy when they began to work together. Fergusson recognized that "his heart was in the Constructivist School," and observed that "He took me to an exhibition of his work in that field, and I thought there must be something wrong with me."[1011] Nevertheless he recognized that photography was another matter, and Fergusson was fascinated by Moholy's methods and the resulting pictures.

In spite of Fergusson's evident lack of appreciation of Constructivism, and in spite of Moholy's recently expressed reluctance to make "beautiful" photographs, one photograph nevertheless ended up being "beautiful" in a Constructivist sense: *Books in Chapel* showed books neatly stacked in piles on pew-top tables that provided enough rectilinear emphasis so that the photograph seems to be a shot of a massive Constructivist sculptural installation. (DVD figure 386)

Fergusson recalled that ". . . I went down there half-a-dozen times with Moholy-Nagy to tell him what to photograph," and "In all, Moholy took over four hundred pictures, and the business of selection was difficult." His fondness for Moholy's pictures is revealed in his lament that "I regret the destruction of all the negatives which were not used for

---

[1009]Bernard Fergusson, *Portrait of Eton*, photographs by L. Moholy-Nagy (London: Frederick Muller Ltd., 1949).

[1010]Sibyl Moholy-Nagy to László Moholy-Nagy, TLS, July 9, 1937, microfilm reel 951, frames 0227 and 0228, Moholy-Nagy files, Archives of American Art, Washington, D.C.

[1011]Fergusson, *Portrait of Eton* (1949), 10. This would have been Moholy's exhibition at the London Gallery, which opened on the last day of 1936, a time-frame confirmed by the circumstance that some of the Eton photographs were clearly made in winter.

the book." He explained that: "I had hoped to make up an album for the school, as an authentic record of Eton in the 'thirties; but Moholy feared a cheapening of his market and forbade it. He destroyed the negatives himself."[1012]

On first looking at Moholy's Eton photographs one might guess that his subject was a school for undertakers, but formal dress, including silk top hats, was a trade mark of Eton.[1013] (DVD figure 387) This provided another reason for the ever fastidiously dressed Moholy to identify with Eton students. The most revealing of Fergusson's anecdotes involves one of Moholy's efforts at documenting Eton attire that came about ". . . when I asked Moholy to photograph Tom Brown's barrow as it distributed the pressed suits for the following week." (DVD figure 388)

> With his superb tactical eye he plunged into Mr. Hope-Jones's house, dashed upstairs to a first-floor window and began work. I stood nervously between the window and the door of the room. Mr. Hope-Jones's dame [*i.e.*, matron],[1014] summoned by a suspicious boy's-maid, swept in, ignored me, tugged Moholy by the tails of his mackintosh, and asked what he was doing and how dare he. He paid no attention to her tugs, but continued to kneel on the ottoman and take photographs. Only when he had finished did he turn to face her . . . He began an explanation in broken English." Are you a German or what?" she said; and then I had to overcome my own shyness and intervene. He and I were escorted from the house by the bootboy, he triumphant, I red as beetroot; but we had our photographs.[1015]

Further insight was provided by Fergusson when he wrote:

> Hardly any of the photographs were posed; I think only three. He excelled in seizing the moment, and it was a lively experience to see him at work. He used a Leica for all except one or two of the interiors, and if he caught the eye of somebody whom he was about to photograph he pouted and walked away, saying "he is schpoilt [*i.e.*, spoiled]."[1016]

[1012]Fergusson, *Portrait of Eton* (1949), 9-10.

[1013]*E.g.*, Fergusson, *Portrait of Eton* (1949), 27; and *idem, Eton Portrait* (1937), facing page 22.

[1014]Fergusson, *Portrait of Eton* (1949), 79.

[1015]Fergusson, *Portrait of Eton* (1949), 9-10; the resulting photograph is on page [65]. In *idem*, Fergusson, *Portrait of Eton* (1937) it is on an unnumbered page following page 136..

[1016]Fergusson, *Portrait of Eton* (1949), 10.

The third book that Moholy illustrated for Miles was *An Oxford University Chest*,[1017] which appeared in December, 1938.[1018] The text was by John Betjeman (1906-1984), a poet and a writer on architecture who had studied at Magdalen College at Oxford. Knighted in 1969 as Sir John, he was Poet Laureate and one of the great popularizers of British architecture, especially the then-maligned, particularly by the Modernists, Victorian!

AT FIRST GLANCE a reader might feel that a good title for the book would be "Oxford Town and Gown," (DVD figure 394), since the neighborhood of Christminster (which includes the remains of a market town already old when the University was founded), along with the Morris Motor Works, and workers' neighborhoods such as the notorious Jericho are discussed and illustrated. However, the University is clearly the book's focal point. When it was re-issued with a new title in 1990 the publisher took advantage of the late author's reputation, which had grown over the years with his continuing achievements, and called the book *John Betjeman's Oxford*.[1019] The original photographic plates were evidently not used, so *John Betjeman's Oxford*, along with an earlier reprint of 1979,[1020] lack the clarity of those in the original edition.

For this book, Moholy's photographs were not the only illustrations, as there were also numerous drawings by Osbert Lancaster (1908-1986), along with illustrations based on vintage drawings and prints as well as uncredited photographs documenting "Motopolis, scenes in the Morris works and Oxford's outer suburbs."

Moholy's approach at Oxford differed from his work at Eton. Although there were some spontaneous photographs of students and faculty members who resembled his caught-off-guard subjects at Eton, because of the contagious enthusiasm of John Betjeman and his wife Penelope, much attention was given to the architecture of what is surely the world's most picturesque university.

John Betjeman's wife, Lady Penelope (1910-1986), whose pen name was Penelope Chetwode, had already been known as Lady Penelope Betjeman before her husband was knighted because of her father's position. She had, as noted above, become Moholy's friend in Berlin during her three-month visit in 1933 and 1934 to the German

---

[1017] John Betjeman, *An Oxford University Chest*, illustrated in line and half-tone by L. Moholy-Nagy, Osbert Lancaster, the Rev. Edward Bradley and others (London: John Miles, Ltd., 1938).

[1018] Senter, "Moholy-Nagy in England," 79.

[1019] John Betjeman, *John Betjeman's Oxford*, illustrated in line and half-tone by L. Moholy-Nagy, Osbert Lancaster, the Rev. Edward Bradley . . . and others (Oxford: Oxford University Press, 1990).

[1020] John Betjeman, *An Oxford University Chest* (Oxford: Oxford University Press, 1979).

metropolis,[1021] where he made four portrait photographs of her.[1022] (DVD figures 389 and 390) Possibly Shand played a role in bringing them together. He had met Moholy during the previous summer,[1023] and was fluent in German; he was also an admirer of Moholy's photographs.[1024] (DVD figures 391, 392 and 393) She also could have met him through Gerda Busoni (née Sjöstrand), the widow of composer Ferruccio Busoni who, as noted in Chapter Three, participated in the 1923 summer festival at the Bauhaus.[1025] In any case Penelope stayed with Gerda Busoni in Berlin.[1026]

It was to be Penelope who guided Moholy, whom she called "Mowli-Wogie,"[1027] while they scampered across rooftops to get just the right angle for his Oxford photographs:

> Moholy was tremendous fun to be with and full of enthusiasm for the things that interested him, especially architecture: and he was fascinated by Oxford and we both greatly enjoyed our scramble over the roofs.[1028]

[1021] Penelope left England for Germany on October 15, 1933; she returned to London on January 15, 1934, as documented in: Candida Lycett Green, editor, *John Betjeman Letters*, edited and introduced by Candida Lycett Green (London: Methuen, 1994), 1: 127-128 and 130.

[1022] Senter, "Moholy-Nagy in England," 266 and 367. One of these portraits is illustrated in: Senter, "Moholy-Nagy's English Photography," [662] and 670; and in: Imogen Lycett Green, *Grandmother's Footsteps; a Journey in Search of Penelope Betjeman* (London: Macmillan, 1994), facing page 146.

[1023] Moholy and Shand had met at the 1933 CIAM. Congress held on a cruise between Marseille and Athens, as discussed above; see: Mumford, *The CIAM Discourse on Urbanism*, 77 and note 65 on page 293. See also: László Moholy-Nagy to Walter Gropius, MLS, December 16, 1935, Bauhaus-Archiv, Berlin. A typescript of the body of the letter and most of the marginal notes is also in the Bauhaus-Archiv. An English translation by Karen Duckworth appeared in: Senter, "Moholy-Nagy in England," 329-332, here 330.

[1024] Philip Morton Shand, "New Eyes for Old," *The Architectural Review: a Magazine of Architecture & Decoration*, volume LXXV, number 446 (January, 1934), 11-12, plate ii facing page 12 and plate iv facing page 20 (with caption on verso of plate iv: "At Close Range: Convolutions in Concrete").

[1025] Busoni's stay in Weimar during the 1923 summer festival is documented in carbon copies (and microfilm copies) in the Thüringisches Hauptstaatsarchiv, Weimar.

[1026] Senter, "Moholy-Nagy in England," 9, 266 and 367.

[1027] John Betjeman, quoted in: Bevis Hillier, *John Betjeman; New Fame, New Love* (London, John Murray, 2002), 118.

[1028] Senter, "Moholy-Nagy in England," 87, 283 and 367.

Interviewed in 1974, she judged Moholy's Oxford photographs "among the best ever taken of Oxford."[1029]

While there are by no means enough photographs in the book to document every important building on the campus, Moholy did include the breath-taking interior of the Museum of Natural History (1855-1859), for which the architects, Dean & Woodward, had some input from John Ruskin.[1030] (DVD figure 396)

Moholy made a preliminary visit to Oxford early in June, but left after four days because of unfavorable weather.[1031] The Oxford photographs were made in a couple of days, one of which can be dated from the circumstance that Penelope's father, Philip Lord Chetwode (1869-1950), was awarded an academic honor at Oxford on Wednesday, June 24th, 1936, and the academic procession in which he took part was documented by Moholy with two photographs.[1032] (DVD figure 395) The short time-frame in which Moholy worked had more to do with his busy schedule than the demands of his publisher, since, according to Terence Senter, it is unlikely that Betjemen's text had even been begun before the photography had been completed.[1033] In spite of that short time-frame, Betjeman later recalled that his collaborator "had a Leica" and made "hundreds of little prints . . . and from these he selected those which were to be enlarged."[1034]

Betjeman added:

> That was where his genius lay. He knew just which to choose, showing the beauty of crumbling stone, the crispness of carved eighteenth-century urns, and members of the public who were quite unconscious that they were being photographed . . .[1035]

[1029] *Ibid.*

[1030] Betjeman, *An Oxford University Chest*, 175-176.

[1031] The information is from a letter from Sibyl Moholy-Nagy to her mother, Fanny Pietzsch, copy of TLS, June 7, 1936 A copy of the letter is in the files of Hattula Moholy-Nagy, Ann Arbor, Michigan.

[1032] Senter, "Moholy-Nagy in England," 79; Betjeman, *An Oxford University Chest,* illustrations facing pages [5] and 15; and John Betjeman, quoted in: Hillier, *John Betjeman; New Fame, New Love*, 118.

[1033] Senter, "Moholy-Nagy in England," 80-81.

[1034] John Betjeman, quoted in: Hillier, *John Betjeman; New Fame, New Love*, 118-119. Betjeman's statement can be backed up by the circumstance that at least one roll of 35 millimeter film with images of Oxford was brought to the United States by Moholy; it was given by his widow to Helmut Franke and is now in another private collection.

[1035] John Betjeman, quoted in: Hillier, *John Betjeman; New Fame, New Love*, 119.

Merchandising to Men: a New Kind of Store

F OR THE FINAL EXAMPLE of Moholy's diverse intents and activities in the years between the Bauhaus and the New Bauhaus, I turn to his work for Alexander ("Alec") Simpson (1902-1937), who, in 1932, had become head of the family business, S. Simpson Limited.[1036] Moholy worked tirelessly as he helped to make his client's new men's clothing store, Simpson, Piccadilly, into a stunning success that lured upscale customers into an active but elegant lifestyle.[1037]

Moholy's work for Alex Simpson would be a good example of his devotion to a client, because he developed a close relationship with him;[1038] as with Moholy's work with fashion magazines in Berlin and Amsterdam, his work for Simpson provides one more example of his passion for being well dressed making him sympathetic to his client's goals. And Moholy once again demonstrated his ability to stimulate the creativity of his assistants, some of whom, in this endeavor, worked with a great deal of independence.[1039]

Moholy benefitted greatly from his work for Simpson because of the economic stability it made possible due to a generous annual salary as payment for his part-time services[1040] for display design and supervision and also for the design of direct-mail brochures.[1041] Moholy was assisted by György Kepes and Harry Blacker, who had offices in the new store, where they, in turn, were assisted by a small staff.[1042] In the Simpson workshop on Whitfield Place Moholy was assisted by craftsmen who worked in

---

[1036]The best sources of information about Moholy's work for Simpson are: Senter, "Moholy-Nagy in England," 128-150, 206-207, 291-293 and illustrations 139 a-n; David Wainwright, *The British Tradition; Simpson—a World of Style* (London: Quiller Press, 1996), 13-14, 17-18 and [25]-35; and Michael Havinden, Richard Hollis, Ann Simpson and Alice Strang, editors, *Advertising and the Artist: Ashley Havinden* (Edinburgh: National Galleries of Scotland, 2003), 13, 19, 46 and 67-68.

[1037]Bronwen Edwards, "A Man's World? Masculinity and Metropolitan Modernity at Simpson Piccadilly," in: David Gilbert, David Matless and Brian Short, editors, *Geographies of British Modernity: Space and Society in the Twentieth Century* (Oxford, England: Blackwell Publishing, 2003), [151]-167.

[1038]Senter, "Moholy-Nagy in England," 134-136 and 148.

[1039]Senter, "Moholy-Nagy in England," 143-148.

[1040]Havinden, Hollis, Simpson and Strang, editors, *Advertising and the Artist*, 19; and Senter, "Moholy-Nagy in England," 135-136.

[1041]Senter, "Moholy-Nagy in England," 135-136; and Wainwright, *The British Tradition,* [25]-35.

[1042]Senter, "Moholy-Nagy in England," 143.

wood and sheet glass; in addition, the Strand Electric Company nearby produced needed items from designs by Moholy, Kepes and Blacker.[1043]

Moholy helped to make the new six-storey-and-basement building for Simpson[1044] ready for its opening at the end of April, 1936. The architect was Joseph Emberton (1889-1956), one of Britain's earliest Modernist architects, who utilized innovative steel-frame and brick-panel structural methods[1045] and designed not only the exterior but also the carefully worked-out lighting of the interior, as well as the counters, showcases, etc., to ensure a harmonious ambience.[1046] It was announced that: "A supply of filtered fresh air at a uniform temperature automatically controlled, is maintained throughout the entire Store,"[1047] an amenity that could not be taken for granted in the retail establishments of the time.

The new building was flanked by older buildings on either side, but had façades on Piccadilly and on Jermyn Street seventy-one feet in width.[1048] The steel frame permitted an unobstructed view through the store from one street to the other.

The Piccadilly façade was simple, with horizontal bands of windows on each floor, much like Eric Mendelsohn's earlier department stores in Germany, but this time emblazoned with colored lighting. Emberton installed red, blue and green neon lighting strips, set above and beside the windows, thus dramatizing the daily fading of the twilight.[1049] The top band of windows was recessed and topped by a canopy, providing a counterpoint to the recessed windows of the ground floor. (DVD figure 397)

Since Simpson, Piccadilly, was a subsidiary of S. Simpson Limited, known for its innovative attire that was high in quality but inexpensively mass produced in its London factory on Stoke Newington Road, the mission of the Piccadilly store was, in part, to serve as a showplace for retailers who visited London. Among the innovations were

---

[1043]Senter, "Moholy-Nagy in England," 144,

[1044]The store survived until 1999, and the building is now a bookstore, Waterstone's, Piccadilly.

[1045]Addis, "Concrete and Steel in Twentieth Century Construction," 115.

[1046]Senter, "Moholy-Nagy in England," 132; Wainwright, *The British Tradition,* 7-13 and 33; "Three London Shops, Two [*sic*; *i.e.*, Simpson, Piccadilly]," *The Architectural Review: a Magazine of Architecture & Decoration*, volume LXXIX, number 475 (June, 1936), 270-271; and Rosemary Ind, *Emberton* (London: Scolar Press, 1983), 30-33 and plates 72-78.

[1047]Advertisement for Carrier-Ross, *The Architectural Review: a Magazine of Architecture & Decoration*, volume LXXIX, number 475 (June, 1936), lxi.

[1048]Wainwright, *The British Tradition,* 7.

[1049]Wainwright, *The British Tradition,* 15; advertisement for Claude General Neon Lights Ltd, *The Architectural Review: a Magazine of Architecture & Decoration*, volume LXXIX, number 475 (June, 1936), liii; and Ind, *Emberton*, 31.

DAKS self-supporting trousers, patented by Alec Simpson in 1932; these were held in place by rubber pads sewn into the waistband, thus allowing a more elegant appearance for men engaged in activities such as golf or cricket. Still another innovation was shirts with buttons down the full length of the front, (DVD figure 398) making them more like a jacket and less like a tunic than the shirts that had been common in Britain. Nevertheless, for men who eschewed ready-to-wear clothing, a well-staffed custom ("bespoke" in British usage) tailoring shop was included on an upper floor of Simpson's. In addition to men's clothing, the store sold sporting equipment and there was also a gift shop, a pet shop and a floral shop, all of which helped to establish a leisure-time atmosphere.

In the new store, Moholy, who had been hired as Design Consultant,[1050] was assisted by Kepes, who was hired by Simpson as Chief Designer,[1051] and by Harry Blacker, hired as Art Director.[1052] The three provided changing designs within the dramatic, non-reflecting concave show windows (DVD figures 398 and 399) and they were also responsible for the changing display of merchandise within the store.[1053]

ALEC SIMPSON WAS COMMITTED to a strikingly modern store, and drew on the talents of a wide range of versatile creative people. It was Emberton who designed the Simpson logo, in collaboration with Ashley Havinden (1903-1973), employing a type face closely related to Gill Sans.[1054] Simpson was spelled out in black and white, with the initial sans-serif capital "S" and the lower-case descending "p" in black, with the white letters outlined against the gray background. But the black "p" also served as a capital "P" for a lower line followed by the rest of "Piccadilly" in small black capital letters. (figure 400) This logo appeared in Simpson's advertisements much like a calling card, as a label in its clothing, was used in window display (DVD figure 398) and also was adapted by a Modernist sculptor and graphic designer, Eric Gill (1882-1940), for colored neon exterior signage.[1055] (DVD figure 397 right)

[1050] Senter, "Moholy-Nagy in England," 135-136; and Wainwright, *The British Tradition,* 13-14.

[1051] Senter, "Moholy-Nagy in England," 136; and György Kepes interviewed by Lloyd C. Engelbrecht and Shirley McCollum in Cambridge, Massachusetts, October 7 and 8, 1978.

[1052] Senter, "Moholy-Nagy in England," 136-137.

[1053] Senter, "Moholy-Nagy in England," 143-145.

[1054] Wainwright, *The British Tradition,* 9.

[1055] Ind, *Emberton,* caption to plate 72; see also: Wainwright, *The British Tradition,* 13. Eric Gill is now best known as the designer of the Gill Sans type face,

It was Havinden, whose professional name was simply Ashley, who brought Moholy and Simpson together.[1056] Ashley was a Modernist art director for W.S. Crawford, a London-based international advertising agency, and Alec Simpson was one of their clients; in 1932 Ashley had designed the DAKS trade name in the form of four bold capital letters widely spaced. For Simpson, Piccadilly, he became more involved with detail than, as an art director, he was accustomed to;[1057] his contributions included designing a cursive script (Ashley Script) as well as twenty designs for rugs to enliven the selling floors,[1058] designs for direct-mail brochures,[1059] and extensive consultations with Emberton and Moholy. Moholy made clear his high opinion of Ashley in a letter sent from Chicago.[1060]

ALVAR AALTO DESIGNED curved plywood-and-leather chairs as well as plywood tables as furnishings for the store.[1061] Moholy tried to enlist the help of sculptor Henry Moore (a friend of his as well as Ashley's), but Moore was uninterested in the idea of creating relief panels for the Piccadilly elevation.[1062] Moore had already created a relief panel, *West Wind*, for another London building, 55 Broadway (Adams, Holden & Pearson, 1929), headquarters of London's underground transportation system,[1063] but evidently that was carried out by Moore because of his close friendship with one of the architects.[1064]

Moholy, of course, regularly used ideas from his works of fine art in his commercial work, and his work for Simpson, Piccadilly, was no exception. For example, his work in painting on rhodoid was reflected in his experimentation with white lettering on transparent rhodoid price tickets.[1065] But sometimes a process that originated with his commercial work was later used in creating works of fine art. For Simpson he bent

---

[1056]Senter, "Moholy-Nagy in England," 45-46 and 132-136; idem, "Moholy-Nagy's English Photography," 659 ; and *idem*, "Moholy-Nagy: the Transitional Years," 89.

[1057]Senter, "Moholy-Nagy in England," 131.

[1058]Havinden, Hollis, Simpson and Strang, editors, *Advertising and the Artist*, 67-68.

[1059]Wainwright, *The British Tradition*, 35.

[1060]László Moholy-Nagy to E. Ashley Havindon, November 23, 1937, xerox copy in my files.

[1061]Ind, *Emberton*, 32.

[1062]Senter, "Moholy-Nagy in England," 138 and 229.

[1063]Taylor, editor, *The Moving Metropolis*, 202-203.

[1064]Senter, "Moholy-Nagy in England," 229.

[1065]Senter, "Moholy-Nagy in England," 148.

transparent rhodoid into curved numerals[1066] and he displayed shirts and jackets on heat-formed body shapes of transparent plastic;[1067] in Chicago, beginning in 1940, he created pieces of sculpture by bending heated Plexiglas.

The fifth floor of Simpson, Piccadilly, had been set aside as an exhibition area, and Moholy installed a small biplane for the opening,[1068] evidently by benefitting from a contact from the exhibition he had recently worked on for Imperial Airways, described above. In July, the aircraft was replaced by boats, described in an advertisement as: ". . . speedboats, outboards, sailing dinghies, collapsible boats and all manner of small crafts."[1069]

In order to draw attention to his new store Alec Simpson spent much money on advertising.[1070] The opening was widely covered in the daily press, as well as in professional journals in merchandising and architecture.[1071]

His lucrative relationship with Simpson's would not have been something he could have relied on had Moholy remained in England. Alec Simpson died of cancer on May 15th, 1937.[1072] Moreover, his new store had already run into serious financial difficulties because, although it proved to be good at attracting people inside, too few of them became customers. Moholy's employment by the store was ended,[1073] wages were cut, women's clothing was added, but the store remained in operation only because it managed to attract new investors.[1074] As things developed, Moholy never had to try to fit into the post-Alec-Simpson era at the store, because his first contact with his future employer in Chicago was a telegram he received on May 23rd, as described in Chapter Five.

[1066] Senter, "Moholy-Nagy in England," 148.

[1067] Wainwright, *The British Tradition,* 14 and [25]-26.

[1068] Senter, "Moholy-Nagy in England," 143 and illustration 139b; and Wainwright, *The British Tradition,* 17-18 and 32.

[1069] Wainwright, *The British Tradition,* 35.

[1070] Havinden, Hollis, Simpson and Strang, editors, *Advertising and the Artist,* 46 and [48]-49; and Wainwright, *The British Tradition,* 34-36.

[1071] Wainwright, *The British Tradition,* 32-34; Senter, "Moholy-Nagy in England," 140-142; and Edwards, "A Man's World?" [151] and 161-163.

[1072] László Moholy-Nagy to Walter and Ise Gropius, May 28, 1937.

[1073] *Ibid.*

[1074] Wainwright, *The British Tradition,* 36-37.

Chapter Four, Berlin, Amsterdam, London, page 530

By the time he was contacted by his future employer in Chicago, Moholy had given up on England, in large part because Gropius had left late in March of 1937 to take up a position at Harvard University. At the end of May he wrote in despair to the Gropiuses:

> . . . ich seit deinem wegzug fühle, dass man hier in geistiger hinsicht nichts oder
> nur minimales erreichen kann und dass jeder stimulus und jeder enregung fehlen.
> und dir wirst ja wie sehr ich an dem gedanken hänge, wieder an einr schule zu
> arbeiten. ich bin dir also sehr dankbar für diese brücke, zu der du die ersten
> pfeiler so rasch aufgerichtet hast.[1075] [. . . since your departure I am aware that
> nothing intellectual, or only little, can be achieved and that each attempt or
> suggestion will fail. And you know well how much I depend on your ideas. I
> am very grateful to you for this bridge, the first pillar of which you so rapidly
> erected.]

[1075]László Moholy-Nagy to Walter and Ise Gropius, May 28, 1937.

Chapter Five: The Chicago Years, 1937-1946

"I never saw a busier place than Chicago was at the time of our arrival. . . . There was much gaiety going on at Chicago, as well as business."
—Harriet Martineau, 1837

"Of the great cities of the World, Chicago is the youngest. It has grown the fastest."
—László Moholy-Nagy, 1940

"It would be roughly true to say that Moholy-Nagy is to William Morris what Einstein is to Sir Isaac Newton."
—Eric Newton, 1939

"Without question Moholy-Nagy was one of the most original and talented men ever to work in Chicago."
—Frank Holland, 1947

Summary of Chapter Five

THE CAREER MOHOLY HAD FORGED WAS CAPPED BY HIS ACHIEVEMENTS in the Illinois lakeside metropolis where, despite some serious setbacks, he was successful as an educator, designer, writer and lecturer, while his national reputation grew as he traveled widely throughout the United States, lecturing, teaching and participating in symposia. With his experiences in World War I still haunting him, Moholy developed widely-praised educational programs for wounded World War II veterans and their care-givers. The planning of Chicago's future was another of his active concerns, an indication of the roots he put down in the city in which he lived longer than any other. He continued to make black-and-white and color photographs, paintings, drawings and sculpture, but sales of them were sparse and he showed mainly in group exhibitions in Chicago; New York City; Oakland, California; Charleston, South Carolina; and elsewhere. He had one-artist showings in four Florida locations in 1938, in Chicago in 1939 and 1940, and in Cincinnati in 1946, plus a one-artist exhibition of his photographs in San Francisco in 1940. Curving forms dominated most of his Chicago paintings and drawings, and his innovative Plexiglas sculptures were bent into complex curves.

Home life for Moholy was centered on his wife, Sibyl, and their two young daughters, while the New Bauhaus that he had set up and later its successor schools, the School of Design in Chicago and the Institute of Design (I.D.), were so absorbing for both parents that each school must have seemed like another member of the family. (DVD figure 401) Attempts to get a visa for Lucia Moholy, then living in London, so that she could teach photography at the School of Design in Chicago, were unsuccessful.

Contacts by mail kept Moholy in touch, at least sporadically, with relatives and friends overseas. Moholy's social life was dominated by his teacher-colleagues, their students, and the patrons who were school supporters, but he also enjoyed the company of his European friends who visited or settled in the United States, as well as the ethnic Hungarians he met in Chicago. He became an American citizen and a bit of a political activist. In the summer of 1946 Moholy and faculty-colleague Arthur Siegel presented a very successful symposium featuring visiting photographers; the symposium was set up to highlight the emergence of a photography curriculum within the I.D. Meanwhile a fountain of letters flowed from Moholy's pen. His death from leukemia was marked by a funeral at the I.D. addressed by Walter Gropius, and a separate memorial event arranged by the Hungarian community in Chicago, followed by a large memorial exhibition at the Art Institute of Chicago.

Chicago, a City in Search of a Bauhaus?

THE ASSOCIATION OF ARTS AND INDUSTRIES was founded in 1922 and was to become, as events unfolded, the group that invited Moholy to Chicago, and thus became the connecting link between the original Bauhaus and a Chicago school which was set up to pursue some of the same aims. Manufacturer William Nelson Pelouze (1865-1943) of the Pelouze Scale Company and artist and designer Norma K. Stahle (1891-1950) were the Association's founders.[1]

The basic goal of the Association of Arts and Industries was to improve the quality of design of manufactured goods in the Chicago region. Although the Association engaged in a variety of activities in pursuit of this goal, from its earliest years it devoted the major portion of its resources to design education. Initially this took the form of providing money to the Art Institute of Chicago for a "School of Industrial Art."[2] The Art Institute had never been only an art museum; from its earliest days it had operated a large school.[3] After several years of negotiations, an agreement was signed between the Association of Arts and Industries and the Art Institute of Chicago on August 31st, 1928, calling for an industrial art school at the Art Institute, subsidized by a fund of $260,000, to be provided by the Association of Arts and Industries.[4] "The School of Industrial Art" as set up

---

[1] Lloyd C. Engelbrecht, "The Association of Arts and Industries: Background and Origins of the Bauhaus Movement in Chicago" (Ph.D. dissertation, University of Chicago, 1973), 41-43; please note that three pages have been mis-numbered in the bibliography of my dissertation: page 355 should be page 354, page 356 should be page 355, and page 354 should be page 356.

[2] Lloyd C. Engelbrecht. "Modernism and Design in Chicago," in: Sue Ann Prince, editor, *The Old Guard and the Avant-garde: Modernism in Chicago, 1910-1940* (Chicago: University of Chicago Press, 1990), 119-138 and 252-256, here 124-129.

[3] Charlotte Moser, "'In the Highest Efficiency': Art Training at the School of the Art Institute of Chicago," in: Prince, editor, *The Old Guard and the Avant-garde*, 193-208 and 261-263.

[4] Engelbrecht, "The Association of Arts and Industries," 43-59 and 68-77.

under this agreement was never a separate school, but more like a curriculum within the Art Institute's existing art school.

On December 31ˢᵗ, 1929, the Association of Arts and Industries completed the turning over of the agreed-upon sum to the Art Institute. The largest part, $150,000, had been raised from the General Education Board, a Rockefeller family philanthropic trust. The balance came from a variety of individuals and firms, including $50,000 from mail-order merchant and philanthropist Julius Rosenwald (1862-1932).[5]

Since the School of the Art Institute had been offering work in industrial design and related subjects for some time, there is no clear starting date for the "School of Industrial Art" at the Art Institute.

In order to understand why the Association of Arts and Industries was formed, certain aspects of Chicago's history must be borne in mind. None of the world's large cities has been more profoundly shaped by the Industrial Revolution than has Chicago. Modern industrialization, born in England in the eighteenth century, spread to the European continent, and then moved westward through the young American republic. Chicago, while still a small village, became the western outpost of the Industrial Revolution.

WHILE THERE IS MUCH ABOUT THE FAVORABLE LOCATION of Chicago, on the southwestern shore of Lake Michigan (DVD figure 402), that helps to explain its rapid growth from a village of 150 people in 1832 into one of the world's major industrial centers, with a 1940 population of about 3,400,000, a more complete explanation is possible only by factoring in the contributions of a type of person who was attracted to Chicago—someone adept at inventing new ways to utilize the possibilities opened up by industrialization. Thus Chicago's role in the Industrial Revolution was not merely to transplant what had been achieved elsewhere, but rather to create new ways to utilize those new possibilities.

An excellent example of the kind of enterprise that was to shape the future city can be found as early as 1832: the balloon frame, devised in that year by George Washington Snow (1797-1870), was first used as a structural system for building a warehouse, located, coincidentally, just a few feet to the north of the present building of the Art Institute of Chicago.[6] Moholy's friend Sigfried Giedion, who has been discussed in

---

[5]*Ibid.*, 74-77.

[6]Paul E. Sprague pinpointed the location of the first balloon-frame structure in his "The Origin of Balloon Framing," *Journal of the Society of Architectural Historians*, volume XL, number 4 (December, 1981), 311-319; see also: *idem*, "Chicago Balloon Frame: the Evolution During the 19th Century of George W. Snow's System for Erecting Light Frame Buildings from Dimension Lumber and Machine-made Nails," in: H. Ward Jandl, editor, *The Technology of Historic American Buildings: Studies of the Materials, Craft Processes, and the Mechanization of Building Construction* (Washington, D.C.: The Foundation for Preservation Technology, 1983), 35-61.

previous chapters, was a Swiss art historian and also a trained engineer[7] who was fascinated with Chicago's history. He pointed out that it was the balloon frame, making use of newly available machine-cut nails, and other products of industrialization, that transformed wood construction into an industry, as industrialization began to penetrate housing.[8] (DVD figure 403)

Giedion's research in Chicago was aided by Robert Bruce Tague (1912-1985), a young Chicago architect who had begun part-time evening studies in photography at the School of Design in Chicago in February, 1939.[9] He recalled that in the spring of that year, when there was little work in the office of George Fred Keck, for whom he was then working, he (Tague) spent "quite a bit of time" assisting Giedion in various ways in his Chicago research, going around the city with him.[10] He made one hard-to-accomplish photograph for which he was credited in *Space, Time and Architecture*.[11]

Giedion also pointed to some of the innovators, men such as Swift, Armour and Wilson, who brought the young city of Chicago to a unique position among early centers of meat packing.[12] Some of the key factors in the mechanization of meat packing had appeared elsewhere, but only in Chicago did meat packing attain a scale that transformed a huge section of the country to the west of Chicago, stretching from Texas to the

---

[7]"Totentafel: Sigfried Giedion Gestorben," *Werk; die Schweizerische Monatsschrift für Bildeten und Angewandte Kunst*, volume LV, number 5 (May, 1968), 337-338. See also "Sigfried Giedion: a Biographical Sketch," in the translation of his *Bauen in Frankreich*: Sigfried Giedion, *Building in France, Building in Iron, Building in Ferro-Concrete*, translated by Sokratis Georgiadis (Santa Monica, California: The Getty Center for the History of Art and the Humanities, 1995), 226-227, here 226.

[8]Sigfried Giedion, *Space, Time and Architecture: the Growth of a New Tradition; the Charles Eliot Norton Lectures for 1938-1939* (Cambridge: Harvard University Press, 1941), 269-271. (This book was later revised and enlarged and has gone through many editions.)

[9]"Student list - semester - February-June, 1939," Robert J. Wolff files, microfilm reel 69-73, frame 0471, Archives of American Art, Washington, D.C.

[10]Betty J. Blum, "Interview with Robert Bruce Tague," Chicago Architects Oral History Project, Department of Architecture, The Art Institute of Chicago, revised edition, 2005, 18-20.

[11]Blum, "Interview with Robert Bruce Tague," 19-20; and Giedion, *Space, Time and Architecture,* xiv and figure 179 on page 306.

[12]Sigfried Giedion, *Mechanization Takes Command: a Contribution to Anonymous History* (New York: W.W. Norton, & Company, Inc., 1948), 211-228.

Giedion's lecture, "The Anonymous History of the Nineteenth Century and the Spirit of Invention," based on the early stages of his research for *Mechanization Takes Command*, was given at the School of Design in Chicago, April 17th, 1942; an announcement is in the Institute of Design Papers, University of Illinois Library, Chicago.

Canadian border, into what Giedion called "a gigantic reservoir of cattle."[13] Chicago meat-packing innovations included intensive use of railroad transportation, refrigeration, and the packaging of cooked beef in metal cans.[14]

A NOTHER CHICAGO INNOVATOR was Cyrus Hall McCormick (1809-1884), an inventor who turned his talents to farm machinery and later established the firm which, more than any other, prospered by the opening up of increasing agricultural acreage in the nineteenth century. Giedion maintained that McCormick knew the secret of making things work and also of exploiting them. He arrived in Chicago in 1847 and by 1851 was ready to show his Chicago-made reaper in the Great Exhibition in London, where its unrivaled superiority was acknowledged.[15] Another McCormick innovation was simply the scale of his manufacturing enterprise, made possible by his skill in marketing.

It was also in Chicago that manufacturers utilized the potential opened up by large-scale production of uniforms during the Civil War to develop an industry devoted to men's ready-to-wear clothing.[16] And it was two Chicago companies, Sears, Roebuck, along with Montgomery Ward, that expanded the practice of mail-order merchandising to unprecedented levels through efficient marketing of mass-produced items made available, as a result of industrialization, in virtually limitless quantities.[17]

I T WAS IMPORTANT for Moholy's success in Chicago that the kind of businessman who made innovative use of opportunities opened up by industrialization did not exist only in Chicago's earlier years. A more recent example would be Walter P. Paepcke (1896-1960), who was to become very closely involved with Moholy's efforts in Chicago. As a young man Paepcke had become president of a family business, Chicago

---

[13]Giedion, *Mechanization*, 219; see also: William Cronon, *Nature's Metropolis: Chicago and the Great West* (New York: W.W. Norton & Company, 1991), [207]-259.

[14]Howard Copeland Hill, "The Development of Chicago as a Center of the Meat Packing Industry," *The Mississippi Valley Historical Review*, volume X, number 3 (December, 1923), 253-273, here 256-273.

[15]Giedion, *Mechanization*, 153.

[16]Harold M. Mayer and Richard G. Wade, *Chicago, Growth of a Metropolis*, (Chicago: University of Chicago Press, 1969), 230; and Bessie Louise Pierce, *A History of Chicago* (New York: Alfred A. Knopf, 1937, 1940), 2:109-110 and 3:171-174.

[17]Mayer and Wade, *Chicago, Growth of a Metropolis*, 230-[231] and 351; Cronon, *Nature's Metropolis*, 333-340; Perry Duis, *Chicago; Creating New Traditions* (Chicago: Chicago Historical Society, 1976), 106-111; Boris Emmet and John Jeuck, *Catalogues and Counters: a History of Sears, Roebuck and Company* (Chicago: University of Chicago Press, 1950); Gordon L. Weil, *Sears, Roebuck, U. S. A.: the Great American Catalog Store and How it Grew* (New York: Stein and Day, 1977); Frank B. Latham, *1872-1972, a Century of Serving Consumers: the Story of Montgomery Ward* (Chicago: Montgomery Ward & Co., 1972); and Daniel J. Boorstin, "A. Montgomery Ward's Mail-Order Business," *Chicago History*, new series, volume II, number 3 (Spring-Summer, 1973), 142-152.

Mill and Lumber Company. In 1926, however, he organized the Container Corporation of America around his belief that paper and fiber cartons would replace wooden boxes and crates for most uses. The success of this new venture vindicated his faith in the growth of paper packaging.[18] The firm's functional and well-designed containers showed that Paepcke quickly realized the importance of good design for his firm.[19] In 1937 the Container Corporation began its series of highly-regarded advertisements.[20] An early example, dating from July, 1937, was created by the French graphic designer A.M. Cassandre (1901-1968); the simple wording clearly states Paepcke's faith in paper and fiber packaging: "Folding cartons, corrugated and solid fibre shipping cases for every industry." (DVD figures 404 and 405) DVD figure 405 depicts a black-and-white full-page advertisement in *Fortune*, one of eight similar Cassandre advertisements for the Container Corporation published in that magazine in the last eight months of 1937.[21] Significantly, Paepcke went on to become Moholy's strongest backer during his years as head of the School of Design in Chicago and the Institute of Design.

While large-scale industrialization brought many benefits, for the workers, who were essential to these innovative enterprises, it often meant repetitive hand motions and labor-intensive operation of machinery and equipment during lengthy, fatiguing workdays in large, impersonal workplaces. Thus the work experience of those employed in Chicago enterprises is another key part of the story: the new opportunities opened up by industrialization meant harsh working conditions for the majority of workers. While the extent of the day-by-day tedium and hardships experienced by workers cannot be

---

[18]Teal Triggs, "Fusion of Art and Industry: the Bauhaus Ideal and Container Corporation of America" (M.A. thesis, University of Texas, Austin, 1983), 21-32.

[19]Engelbrecht, "The Association of Arts and Industries," 217-20, 297, 317-21 and 325; and Victor Margolin, *The Struggle for Utopia: Rodchenko, Lissitzky, Moholy-Nagy, 1917-1946* (Chicago: University of Chicago Press, 1997), 236-238.

[20]Daniel Catton Rich, editor, *Modern Art in Advertising: Designs for the Container Corporation of America* (Chicago: Paul Theobald, 1946).

[21]*Fortune*, volume XV, number 5 (May, 1938), 189; *ibid.*, volume XV, number 6 (June, 1937), 175; *ibid.* volume XVI, number 1 (July, 1937), 145; *ibid.*, number 2 (August, 1937), 141; *ibid.*, number 3 (September, 1937), 177; *ibid.*, number 4 (October,

1937), 177; *ibid.*, number 5 (November, 1937), 201; and *ibid.*, number 6 (December, 1937), 217.

Seven of these advertisements were reproduced in: Rich, editor, *Modern Art in Advertising*, items 20, 21, 22, 23, 24, 25 and 26; Cassandre's work for the Container Corporation extended until 1946 (Rich, editor, *Modern Art in Advertising*, items 28-32).

On Cassandre in America, see: "Projects for Four Posters: a Portfolio for Four Posters by A.M. Cassandre," *Fortune*, volume XV, number 3 (March, 1937), front cover and 120-[124]. See also a portfolio of five drawings by Cassandre for American posters reproduced in: *Printing Art Quarterly*, volume LXVII, number 3 (Winter, 1938), 23-27; four of these drawings were shown in the *Exhibition of Advertising Art, 1938*, sponsored by the Art Directors Club of Chicago; see *ibid.*, 22, 23, 24, 25 and 26.

gauged solely by the occasional outbreak of violence, Chicago is known for three major incidents resulting in the violent repression and death of workers. Significantly, the industries involved were farm machinery, railroads and steel. These incidents were the Haymarket Square bombing of 1886, which grew out of a dispute at the McCormick Harvester Works; the strike at the Pullman Palace Car Company in 1894; and the "Memorial Day Massacre" of 1937, during a strike at Republic Steel.[22]

The "Memorial Day Massacre" of 1937 took place during a strike at Republic Steel not long before Moholy's arrival in Chicago. Ten striking steel workers were killed by police on Sunday, May 30th;[23] this incident showed that labor unrest in the city, followed by harsh repression, continued into the modern era. Moreover, Moholy surely was aware of the incident, because, in a fascinating circumstance, an article about labor unrest in *Fortune* magazine, including pictures and several paragraphs about the "Memorial Day Massacre,"[24] appeared in the same issue of the magazine in which also appeared Moholy's only camera photograph made and published while he lived in Chicago. Moholy's photograph is discussed below.

WIDESPREAD CONCERN over the quality of the work experience helps to explain how Chicago became a center of the Arts and Crafts Movement, which, in turn, was to have an influence on Chicago's future design environment. A hallmark of the English Arts and Crafts Movement was its opposition to inhumane working conditions. John Ruskin (1819-1900) had resoundingly denounced work which would "unhumanize" workers by demanding that they "make their fingers measure degrees like cogwheels, and their arms strike curves like compasses. . . ."[25] William Morris (1834-1906) had called for an end to labor which was "mere wearing away of body and

---

[22]Sidney Lens, *The Labor Wars, from the Molly Maguires to the Sitdowns* (Garden City, New York: Doubleday & Company, Inc., 1973); *idem, The Labor Wars, from the Molly Maguires to the Sitdowns* (Garden City, New York: Anchor Books, 1974). See also: Paul Avrich, *The Haymarket Tragedy* (Princeton, New Jersey: Princeton University Press, 1984); James R. Green, *Death in the Haymarket: a Story of Chicago, the First Labor Movement and the Bombing That Divided Gilded Age America* (New York: Pantheon Books, 2006); Nick Salvatore, *Eugene V. Debs, Citizen and Socialist* (Urbana: University of Illinois Press, 1982); and John Tebbel, *The Marshall Fields: a Study in Wealth* (New York: E.P. Dutton & Co., Inc., 1947), 52-58.

[23]Daniel Leab, "The Memorial Day Massacre," *Midcontinent American Studies Journal*, volume VIII, number 1 (Fall, 1967), 3-17; and Lens, *The Labor Wars* (1973), figure 37. There is also a newsreel, *Memorial Day Massacre*, filmed live on May 30th, 1937, by Paramount Pictures, with a duration of nineteen minutes.

[24]"The Industrial War," *Fortune*, volume XVI, number 5 (November, 1937), 104-110, 156, 158, 160, 162, 164, 166, 168, 171-172, 174, 176 and 179-180, here [106-107] and 171-172.

[25]John Ruskin, "The Nature of Gothic," Chapter VI, *The Stones of Venice*, Volume II, "The Sea Stories," in: *The Complete Works of John Ruskin*, volume X (London: George Allen, 1904), 192. This portion of *The Stones of Venice* was first published in 1853.

mind."[26] Hence, one indirect but crucial result of industrialization in Chicago was a strong local Arts and Crafts Movement. In fact, one of the most active centers of arts-and-crafts activity outside England was Chicago, where the Chicago Arts and Crafts Society, begun in 1897, and the Industrial Art League, organized in 1899, were the most important groups.

The constitution of the Chicago Arts and Crafts Society, published in 1898, directly reflects Ruskin's and Morris's attitudes toward labor, as well as an awareness of actual working conditions in Chicago's factories, since one of its stated aims was:

> To consider the present state of the factories and the workman therein, and to devise lines of development which shall retain the machine in so far as it relieves the workman from drudgery, and tends to perfect his product; but which shall insist that the machine no longer be allowed to dominate the workman and reduce his production to a mechanical distortion.[27]

The Arts and Crafts Movement was beset with inner contradictions. Thus while some aspects of the movement, such as the emphasis on hand work, might seem unrelated, or even antithetic, to industrialization, in fact the chief centers of arts-and-crafts activity were also centers of industry. Many individual figures had ties both to assembly-line mass production and its products as well as to the Arts and Crafts Movement. One good example is Julius Rosenwald, a major executive and share-owner in Sears, Roebuck. Thus, as noted above, he was a generous supporter of efforts to improve the education of designers for mass-production industries, while he was also a close friend of Jane Addams (1860-1935) and a member of the board of trustees at Hull House.[28] Addams, pacifist, social reformer and co-founder of the Hull-House settlement in an impoverished working-class neighborhood in Chicago,[29] was an early member of

---

[26]William Morris, "The Lesser Arts, Delivered before the Trades' Guild of Learning, December 4, 1877," in: *The Collected Works of William Morris, Volume XXII, Hopes and Fears for Art: Lectures on Art and Industry* (London: Longmans Green and Company, 1914), 3-17, here 5.

[27]The constitution of the Chicago Arts and Crafts Society was published in: Chicago Architectural Club, *Catalogue of the Eleventh Annual Exhibition by the Chicago Architectural Club at the Art Institute of Chicago, March 23 to April 10, 1898* (Chicago: Chicago Architectural Club, 1898), 118.

[28]M. R. Werner, *Julius Rosenwald, the Life of a Practical Humanitarian* (New York: Harper & Brothers Publishers, 1939), 90-94; and Eleanor J. Stebner, *The Women of Hull House: a Study in Spirituality and Friendship* (Albany: State University of New York Press, 1997), 149.

[29]Victoria Bissell Brown, "Addams, Jane," in: Rima Lunin Schultz and Adele Hast, editors, *Women Building Chicago, 1790-1990: a Biographical Dictionary* (Bloomington: Indiana University Press, 2001), 14-22.

the Chicago Arts and Crafts Society, which held some of its key meetings at Hull House.[30]

The Arts and Crafts Movement, in Chicago and internationally, had pretty much run its course by 1910, but a lot of what developed later in terms of design and related fields derived from it. Moholy himself was made aware that the concerns of the Arts and Crafts Movement were not forgotten in Chicago. He was present at a 1939 lecture by Frank Lloyd Wright (1867-1959), one of the best Chicago examples of a creative person who was strongly influenced by the Arts and Crafts movement but who also was frustrated by its inner contradictions. Wright, speaking at Hull House, vividly remembered a bitter battle nearly forty years earlier, within the Chicago Arts and Crafts Society, over his criticism of the group's emphasis on handicraft. Specifically mentioned was a disagreement with the ideas of Oscar Lovell Triggs (1865-1930), but the precise nature of that disagreement is impossible to reconstruct now.[31]

Two years after hearing Wright's talk, Moholy wrote that: "In 1903, Frank Lloyd Wright launched in Hull House, Chicago, an offensive against Ruskin and Morris. He proclaimed the machine the legitimate tool in the hands of the creative artist." Moholy added: "This was a brave challenge to the governing ideas of that time," but went on to point to ways in which mass-production factories had, nevertheless, not used machines as well as they should have, and also had mis-used workers. He agreed with Wright's proclamation that "the machine must be studied and understood in order to be used rightly," and declared that "the Bauhaus followed this principle."[32]

THE ASSOCIATION OF ARTS AND INDUSTRIES that, as noted above, dates from 1922, was clearly aware of Chicago's arts-and-crafts heritage, and, since one of the Association's principal aims was the training of designers, it is worth noting that, although the educational ideas of the leaders of the Arts-and-Crafts Movement in Chicago seldom got beyond the discussion stage, the carefully worked-out ideas of the Industrial Art League's Oscar Lovell Triggs, who called for industrial education concerned with real objects and processes, but integrated with a broader range of studies,

---

[30] Engelbrecht, "The Association of Arts and Industries," 4-5; and Wilbert R. Hasbrouck, *The Chicago Architectural Club: Prelude to the Modern* (New York: The Monacelli Press, 2005), 222-223.

[31] See: "Dinner Talk at Hull House, November Eighth, 1939," in: *Frank Lloyd Wright Collected Writings, Volume 4, 1939-1949*, edited by Bruce Brooks Pfeiffer (New York: Rizzoli, 1994), 19-26, here 20. Ludwig Mies van der Rohe was also present; see: "An Interview with Katharine Kuh," conducted by Avis Berman, edited by William McNaught, *Archives of American Art Journal*, volume XXVII, number 3 (1987), 2-36, here 23-24; Katherine Kuh, *My Love Affair with Modern Art: Behind the Scenes with a Legendary Curator*, edited & completed by Avis Berman (New York: Arcade Publishing, 2006), 78-80; and Engelbrecht, "Association of Arts and Industries," 5-6, 8-11 and 15-21.

[32] Laszlo Moholy-Nagy, "Education in Various Media for the Designer," in: National Society for the Study of Education, *The Fortieth Yearbook; Art in American Life and Education* (Bloomington, Illinois: Public School Publishing Company, 1941), 652-665.

had not been forgotten.[33] The spade-work of Triggs and other arts-and-crafts figures makes it easier to understand why the education of designers was a central concern of the Association of Arts and Industries. If Moholy and Triggs had ever met, Moholy would no doubt have considered the older man a bit old-fashioned; nevertheless in many ways the kind of school operated by Moholy in Chicago put into practice on a continuing basis concepts Triggs had argued for more than three decades earlier. (text figure 15, DVD figure 406)

text figure 15, DVD figure 406

"R.S." [Robert C. Spencer ?], emblem of the Industrial Art League, 1902

CLEARLY, BY 1922 the influence of the Arts and Crafts Movement's fascination with handmade goods was giving way to a concern for the products of modern industry. Hence, the Association of Arts and Industries had as its goal the improvement of manufactured goods in the Chicago region. Its members included manufacturers, bankers, department-store executives, publishers, art patrons, artists, architects and designers. In support of its aims the Association presented exhibitions, lectures, symposia and design competitions, but it is remembered today chiefly for its two main educational efforts. These were, first, as referred to above, the provision of funds to the School of the Art Institute of Chicago to enable it, through its "School of Industrial Art," to strengthen and increase its efforts to educate students who would then work for industry; later, after the results of these efforts fell short of the Association's

---

[33] Oscar Lovell Triggs, "A School of Industrial Art," *The Craftsman*, volume III, number 2 (January, 1903), 216 and 221-223; and *idem, The Changing Order; a Study of Democracy* (Chicago: Oscar L. Triggs Publishing Company, 1905), 250, 258-260.

On Triggs, see: Engelbrecht, "The Association of Arts and Industries," 6, 13-21; and Eileen Boris, "'Dreams of Brotherhood and Beauty:' the Social Ideas of the Arts and Crafts Movement," in: Wendy Kaplan, editor, *The Art that is Life: The Arts & Crafts Movement in America, 1875-1920* (Boston: Museum of Fine Arts, 1987), 212-215.

As is evident in his talk, discussed above, Wright, for one, had not forgotten Triggs.

expectations, the decision to start its own school, and the resulting invitation to Moholy, as a major figure in European Modernism, to serve as its founding director.

SEARS, ROEBUCK can be taken as an example of the kind of Chicago firm that viewed the educational efforts of the Association of Arts and Industries as crucial. A.J. Snow, director of the firm's design department, lamented that it was hampered by the ". . . failure of a true industrial arts school to emerge in Chicago," and was "constantly on the alert to find talent with sufficient design promise to merit employment."[34] Thus the firm turned to out-of-town consulting designers such as New York-based Raymond Loewy (1893-1986), designer of Sears, Roebuck's much-admired "Coldspot" electric refrigerators. The 1934 model (DVD figure 407) proved to be Loewy's first major success as a designer, and Sears introduced new Loewy-designed models annually in the following years. By 1936 Loewy had opened a branch office in Chicago.[35] As events were to develop, in the August, 1938, issue of the *Magazine of Art*, acclaim for Loewy's "Coldspot" refrigerator redesign of 1938 was balanced by a reference to the reading lamp of 1928 (DVD figure 142) designed by Moholy's Bauhaus students Marianne Brandt and Hin Bredendieck; these products were cited as part of an attempt to define the emerging profession of industrial design.[36] Of course by 1938 Bredendieck had become Moholy's faculty colleague at the New Bauhaus and the irony, as seen below, was that Moholy's initial educational endeavor in Chicago was floundering just as high-profile recognition in the August, 1938, issue of *Magazine of Art* appeared.

In addition to its educational efforts, the Association of Arts and Industries became a battleground, during the early 1930s, for fights over changes in taste. In these struggles it was Frank Lloyd Wright who was relied on to articulate the Modernist position, as lecturer and symposium participant, at a time when he was no longer living in the

---

[34] A.J. Snow, quoted in: Sheldon Cheney and Martha Candler Cheney, *Art and the Machine: an Account of Industrial Design in 20ᵗʰ-Century America* (New York: Whittlesey House, 1936), 269.

[35] Emmet and Jeuck, *Catalogues and Counters*, 391-392; Cheney and Cheney, *Art and the Machine*, 90 and 252; and Sears, Roebuck and Company, *Spring and Summer, 1935, Catalog No. 170* (Chicago: Sears, Roebuck and Co., 1935), 576-577.

[36] Eugene Schoen, "Industrial Design: a New Profession," *Magazine of Art*, volume XXXI, number 8 (August, 1938), 472-479, here 476-477.

Chicago area.[37] Thus Wright helped create an understanding of the Modernist approach underlying that invitation to Moholy from the Association of Arts and Industries.

Wright's influence on the first generation of European Modernists has been well chronicled,[38] and his early recognition in Europe is in ironic contrast to the slow pace of the recognition given to his work in the United States. (Indeed, widespread appreciation of Wright's work by Americans did not begin until after 1940.) Thus in 1924 Alfonso Iannelli (1888-1965), a faculty member of the School of the Art Institute, was deeply impressed, during visits to Germany and Holland to observe design schools there, by the acclaim Wright was receiving in Europe. In fact, Wright was regarded as a crucial influence on the formal vocabulary and creative outlook of European Modernists. Iannelli had been one of Wright's collaborators on the 1914 Midway Gardens commission in Chicago, but only after his talks with European architects and designers did he fully understand Wright's significance. This point is clearly evident from a speech given by Iannelli at the Art Institute on November 25th, 1924, shortly after his return. In that speech he declared:

> The modern movement in architecture had its beginnings
> in America. [Henry H.] Richardson, [Louis H.] Sullivan
> and Frank Lloyd Wright have been its greatest exponents,
> but the work of these men is more generally recognized in
> Europe than in their own country, and the modern
> architecture in Germany and Holland is far more advanced
> than in America.[39]

Shortly after his arrival in Chicago to organize the New Bauhaus for the Association of Arts and Industries, Moholy tried to get Wright to join his faculty.[40] It is almost

---

[37]Wright's contributions at events set up by the Association are described in: Engelbrecht, "Association of Arts and Industries," 109-119; and in: *idem*, "Modernism and Design in Chicago," 124-128. See also: Norma K. Stahle to Frank Lloyd Wright, TLS, February 2nd, 1931 (with a handwritten, unsigned reply by Frank Lloyd Wright on bottom and reverse of letter); Norma K. Stahle to Frank Lloyd Wright, TLS, February 9th and 18th, March 23rd, April 17th, June 2nd and 9th, and July 2nd, 1931, and April 21st and 29th, May 6th and 17th, and June 1st, 1932; Frank Lloyd Wright to Norma K. Stahle, unsigned carbon copies of letters dated April 27th and May 18th, 1932; and Alfonso Iannelli to Frank Lloyd Wright, ALS, February 5th, 1931; all of these are in the Frank Lloyd Wright Archives, Frank Lloyd Wright Foundation, Scottsdale, Arizona.

[38]See, *e.g.*, Reyner Banham, *Theory and Design in the First Machine Age*, second edition (New York: Praeger Publishers, 1967), 144-147, 156-157, 271-272 and 292; and Lloyd C. Engelbrecht, "Bauhäusler: a Case Study of Two-Way Traffic Across the Atlantic," in: *Yearbook of German-American Studies,* volume XXII (1987), 149-172, here 150 and 153-159.

[39]"Art Institute of Chicago News Letter," mimeographed, November 29, 1924.

[40]László Moholy-Nagy to Walter Gropius, TLS, October 8th, 1937, Bauhaus-Archiv, Berlin. See also: William A. Kittredge to Frank Lloyd Wright, TLS, October 11th, 1937; Frank Lloyd Wright to William A. Kittredge, TLS with AL passage added, October 12th, 1937; and Frank Lloyd Wright

(continued...)

needless to add that nothing came of the invitation; teaching in someone else's school was not a high priority for Wright! As it happened, Moholy soon became aware of the pioneer Chicago Modernist architect George Fred Keck (1895-1980),[41] who did join his faculty, and added a strain of native American Modernism.

N O DISCUSSION OF MODERNISM in the fine arts in Chicago is complete without some mention of Rudolph Weisenborn,[42] whose best pictures vivify a vigorous variation on Cubism.[43] He was born October 31st, 1881, in Chicago, and died there March 15th, 1974. His exhibition of Modernist paintings and drawings in commercial galleries and in the Art Institute of Chicago, and his work as a teacher at Hull House and other Chicago institutions and as a private teacher, had much to do with changes in taste in Chicago. In fact this pioneer Chicago Modernist showed works on more occasions at the Art Institute than did any other artist (on one occasion, as noted below, in a group exhibition with Moholy), but nevertheless worked tirelessly to organize other venues for local artists to show their work.[44] Moholy and Weisenborn participated in a group exhibition at the Renaissance Society of the University of Chicago,[45] and both artists also showed at the Katharine Kuh Gallery, but on separate occasions.[46] Weisenborn helped to turn veteran *Chicago Tribune* art critic Eleanor Jewett (1892-1968) from a staunch opponent of Modernism in the fine arts into someone who was sympathetic to Modernism, as noted below. And both Weisenborn and Moholy

---

[40](...continued)
to William A. Kittredge, carbon copy of TLS, October 19th, 1937; all of these are in the Frank Lloyd Wright Archives, Frank Lloyd Wright Foundation, Scottsdale, Arizona. (William A. Kittredge [1891-1945] was a member of the board of the Association of Arts and Industries.)

[41]On Keck, see: Robert Boyce, *Keck and Keck* (New York: Princeton Architectural Press, 1993); and Narciso Menocal, *Keck & Keck, Architects* (Madison: Elvehjem Museum of Art, University of Wisconsin, 1980).

[42]On Weisenborn, see the forthcoming monograph by Lloyd C. Engelbrecht to be published in Cincinnati by the Flying Trapeze Press at a date to be announced.

[43]*E.g., Portrait of Herman Spertus*, 1940 (DVD figure 408); see also: Engelbrecht, "Association of Arts and Industries," 204-205 and figures 37 and 38.

[44]Paul Kruty, "Declarations of Independents: Chicago's Alternative Art Groups of the 1920s," in: Sue Ann Prince, editor, *The Old Guard and the Avant-garde*, 77-93 and 242-248, *passim*.

[45]The Renaissance Society of the University of Chicago, *Drawings by Contemporary Artists, May 20 - June 10, 1944* (Chicago: The Renaissance Society of the University of Chicago, 1944).

[46]On Weisenborn at the Katharine Kuh Gallery, see: John and Molly Thwaites, "Rudolph Weisenborn at the K. Kuh Gallery, Chicago," *Magazine of Art*, volume XXX, number 6 (June, 1937), 389-390; Fritzi Weisenborn, "Plastic Painting 'Speaks'," *Chicago Times, Sunday Times Magazine*, April 6,1941, 11-M; and Clarence J. Bulliet, "The Divine Rage of Rudolph," *The Chicago Daily News*, April 12, 1941, Art, Antiques & Interiors Section, 15.

were friends of British documentary film-maker John Grierson,[47] who had spent some time in Chicago prior to Moholy's arrival there; moreover, Weisenborn had been the first to publish comment on Grierson's work.[48] John E. Walley, who taught at the I.D. and who, as discussed below, was one of Moholy's most enthusiastic welcomers to Chicago, considered Weisenborn his most important teacher.[49] Chicago art critic Molly Thwaites co-wrote (with her husband John) favorable reviews of Weisenborn's work;[50] she was to become crucial to the daily operation of the School of Design in Chicago and the I.D. with the title of registrar, beginning in the Fall semester of 1940.[51] She might even have played an indirect role in the coming of Robert J. Wolff to the School of Design, since she had co-written favorable reviews of his work in 1937.[52] As registrar Molly Thwaites helped to run the School of Design office, and as part of her contribution was to type

---

[47]Terence A. Senter, "Moholy-Nagy in England: May 1935-July 1937" (Master of Philosophy thesis, University of Nottingham, 1975), 61-62; and Jack C. Ellis, *John Grierson: Life, Contributions, Influence* (Carbondale: Southern Illinois University Press, 2000), 23-24.

[48]This was on Grierson's work as a newspaperman and art writer, before he had turned to film-making; see: Jack C. Ellis, *John Grierson: a Guide to References and Resources* (Boston: G.K, Hall & Co., 1986), 87.

[49]John E. Walley, interviewed by Lloyd C. Engelbrecht, Chicago, January, 1973; Engelbrecht, "Association of Arts and Industries," 206 and figure 39; and John E. and Jano Walley to Rudolph and Fritzi Weisenborn, TLS, November 11th, 1965, microfilm reel 856, frames 0044 and 0045, Rudolph Weisenborn Papers, Archives of American Art, Washington, D.C.

[50]John and Molly Thwaites, "Rudolph Weisenborn at the K. Kuh Gallery, Chicago"; and *idem*, "Seeing the Shows in Chicago," *Magazine of Art*, volume XXX, number 9 (September, 1937), 576-578.

[51]Moholy repeatedly relied on Molly Thwaites for a variety of tasks and to assure operation of the school when he was out of town. She is mentioned in numerous letters concerning the operation of the School of Design in Chicago and the I.D.; *e.g.*, Sibyl Moholy-Nagy to László Moholy-Nagy, TLS, June 16th , 1942, microfilm reel 951, frames 0414-0415, and László Moholy-Nagy to Sibyl Moholy-Nagy, ALS, June 16th, 1942, microfilm reel 951, frames 0410-1413, both in the Moholy-Nagy Papers, Archives of American Art, Washington, D.C.

Molly Thwaites left her job as registrar in June, 1945, but returned in November. See: "The President's Report [*i.e.*, the report by Moholy to the I.D. board]," June 5th, 1945, mimeographed, Institute of Design Papers, University of Illinois Library, Chicago; and Sibyl Moholy-Nagy to Robert J. Wolff, TLS, November 25th, 1945, microfilm reel N69-72, frames 0407-0408, Robert Jay Wolff files, Archives of American Art, Washington, D.C.: "Did you hear that next Monday Molly Thwaites is coming back to her old job at the Institute?"

[52]John and Molly Thwaites, "Robert Jay Wolff, the Quest Gallery, Chicago," *Magazine of Art*, volume XXX, number 6 (June, 1937), 388; and *idem*, "Seeing the Shows in Chicago," *ibid.*, volume XXX, number 9 (September, 1937), 576-577.

numerous letters for Moholy,[53] she no doubt used her literary skills to improve Moholy's English as she typed.

It happened that the largest-ever Weisenborn exhibition took place shortly after Moholy's arrival in Chicago. It was seen from February 1st to March 1st, 1938, in a former automobile showroom on the ground floor of the art-deco masterpiece known as the 333 North Michigan Avenue Building (Holabird & Root, 1928).[54] In the catalogue John and Molly Thwaites were listed as sponsors and Moholy was on the list of those "The Sponsors Wish to Thank." The most generous patron was John Grierson, of "London, England," listed as the lender of eight canvases.[55] One can only speculate, but perhaps, on the recommendation of Grierson, who surely was aware of Moholy's extraordinary skills at exhibition design (discussed in Chapter Four), he might have installed Weisenborn's works in a challenging space for showing art. In any case, a description of the exhibition describes juxtapositions that make it seem like a Moholy installation:

> On one side the huge windows brought the Tribune Tower and Wrigley Building across the Chicago River and into the room between the canvases. On the other, the glass thrust out the painting into the "crazy slamming roar of the street." *Chicago* [a painting by Weisenborn] faced Chicago; and the Loop skyscrapers [were] reflected in the windows on either side.[56]

One can further speculate that this exhibition provided the opportunity for Moholy to meet Molly Thwaites.

A 1996 catalogue for an exhibition on art in Chicago after 1945 did not even mention Weisenborn.[57] A bit earlier, a European writer assured his readers that Weisenborn ". . .

---

[53] One of the earliest letters Thwaites typed is: László Moholy-Nagy to Robert Delson, TLS, October 4th, 1940, Robert Delson Papers, University of Illinois Library, Chicago.

[54] Mitchell Siporin, "The Weisenborn Retrospective," *The Chicago Artist* [published by the Artists Union of Chicago], volume I, number 6 (February, 1938), 2.

[55] *Retrospective Exhibitition of the Paintings and Drawings of Rudolph Weisenborn, February First to March First [1938]*, a folder with six unnumbered pages. A copy is in the Library of the Art Institute of Chicago, pamphlet box P-05500.

[56] John Thwaites, from a revised manuscript for an unpublished monograph on Weisenborn, probably written in 1947, microfilm reel 856, frame 0269, Rudolph Weisenborn Papers, Archives of American Art, Washington, D.C.

[57] Lynn Warren, editor, *Art in Chicago, 1945-1995* (Chicago: Museum of Contemporary Art, 1996). It should be emphasized that Weisenborn had exhibited new work in Chicago into the mid-1950s; moreover, Weisenborn was not even mentioned on pages 36-58, which primarily contained background information on earlier developments.

has now faded into total obscurity."[58] At the present time, when Modernist artists whose work has received little notice in recent decades, including Hilla Rebay, Katherine Dreier, Rudolf Bauer and Rolph Scarlett (a favorite painter of Rebay's), are being re-evaluated, Weisenborn might be ripe for re-evaluation as well.[59] One of his finest works is his *Portrait of Herman Spertus* of 1940. (DVD figure 408)

The Association of Arts and Industries and the New Bauhaus

NORMA K. STAHLE,[60] a designer who was executive director of the Association of Arts and Industries during its entire existence, managed most of the group's affairs, and was the most influential voice within it. But she never wrote anything that clearly set forth her ideas about design or design education, so what is known about her ideas is what can be gleaned from newspaper accounts of her activities, and from the few pieces of her correspondence which survive. Moreover, nothing is known about her education, despite the probing and meticulous research of Connie Heaton Goddard into Stahle's early life.[61] What is known, however, is that something in her background enabled her to develop a sophisticated understanding of the issues involved in modern design.

The statement by Stahle, in a letter to Moholy in 1937, that "we have always subscribed to the plan of the Bauhaus,"[62] is somewhat of an exaggeration. But this indication of an underlying sympathy with the Modernist position, at least in design, is borne out by other letters, in which she indicated admiration for Wright and his ideas,[63]

---

[58] Ian Aitken, *Film and Reform: John Grierson and the Documentary Film Movement* (London: Routledge, 1990), 62.

[59] A beginning of a possible re-evaluation of Weisenborn can be seen in: Elizabeth Kennedy, editor, *Chicago Modern, 1893-1945: Pursuit of the New* (Chicago: Terra Museum of Art, distributed by the University of Chicago Press, 2004), [16], 18, 155, 160, 168 and 171.

[60] On Stahle, see: Connie Heaton Goddard, "Stahle, Norma K.," in: Schultz and Hast, editors, *Women Building Chicago,* 831-833.

[61] Goddard, "Stahle, Norma K.," 831.

[62] Quoted from a letter, now lost, Norma K. Stahle to Professor Moholy-Nagy, dated May 29th, 1937; the entire letter is quoted in: Sibyl Moholy-Nagy, *Moholy-Nagy, Experiment in Totality*, second edition (Cambridge: The M.I.T. Press, 1969), 139-140; an earlier statement, describing the invitation to Moholy as a "real opportunity to establish [a] project along bauhaus lines," appeared in a telegram, now lost, Norma K. Stahle to László Moholy-Nagy, sent about May 21st, 1937, and quoted in: László Moholy-Nagy to Walter Gropius, TLS, May 28th, 1937, photographic copy in the Bauhaus-Archiv, Berlin.

[63] Norma K. Stahle to Frank Lloyd Wright, TLS, February 2nd, 1931, February 9, 1931, February

(continued...)

and by her interest in the activities of two pioneer West-Coast Austrian-American Modernist architects, Rudolph Schindler and Richard Neutra.[64] By the time the New Bauhaus was announced to the press, Stahle was clearly articulating the Bauhaus orientation of the new school.[65] Thus it seems unlikely that differences over concepts of Modernism led to the later falling out between Stahle and Moholy.

The Association's eventual dissatisfaction over the New Bauhaus, discussed below, was prefigured by the Association's dissatisfaction with the Art Institute over its operation of its "School of Industrial Art."[66] Because of this dissatisfaction with the school at the Art Institute, Stahle had decided by 1935 that the time had come to cut the Association's ties with it. The Association's board agreed, and on June 1st, 1935, it invoked a clause in the joint agreement with the Art Institute, permitting it to take back some of the money provided for the Institute's School.[67] Early the following year, plans for its own school were announced by the Association. It was to be located in the Marshall Field house, built for the founder of a Chicago dynasty of department-store, wholesale-store and newspaper tycoons, which had recently been donated for that purpose by Marshall Field III (1893-1956).[68] During the summer of 1936 the dissolution

---

[63](...continued)
18th, 1931, March 23rd, 1931, April 17th, 1931, June 2nd, 1931, June 9th, 1931, July 2nd, 1931, April 21st, 1932, April 29th, 1932, May 6th, 1932, May 17th, 1932 and June 1st, 1932, Frank Lloyd Wright Archives, Frank Lloyd Wright Foundation, Scottsdale, Arizona.

[64]Norma K. Stahle to Frank Lloyd Wright, TLS, June 9th, 1931, Frank Lloyd Wright Archives, Frank Lloyd Wright Foundation, Scottsdale, Arizona. The letter reads, in part: "I was very much interested in your letter to Rudolph Schindler and in the Schindler-Neutra circular. Sometime I have some interesting side-lights to give you in this connection."

[65]Norma K. Stahle, quoted in: "American School of Design to Open Here This Fall," *The Chicago Daily News*, August 23, 1937, 11; and in: "Chicago Fosters Progressive Art, New Bauhaus, American School of Design, Opens Tomorrow," *The New York Times*, October 17, 1937, 8 N.

[66]On the Association's dissatisfaction with the operation of the School of Industrial Art, see: Engelbrecht, "Association of Arts and Industries," 86-107, 338 *et passim*.

[67]Engelbrecht, "Association of Arts and Industries," 213-215.

[68]Al Chase, "Marshall Field Gives Family Residence to Industrial Art School," *Chicago Tribune*, January 5, 1936, part 5, page 10. However, Field himself was otherwise not active with the Association of Arts and Industries. In later years he contributed modest sums to the School of Design, *e.g.*, $100.00, in 1943; see: Gesine Heller, "Secretary to Mr. Field," to Walter P. Paepcke, December 22nd, 1943, and Walter P. Paepcke to Marshall Field, December 27th, 1943; both letters are in the Institute of Design Papers, University of Illinois Library, Chicago.

Additional support for the School of Design and the I.D. came from the Marshall Field Department Store and from its executives, and through tuition payments for the store's employees who studied part-time. As of the spring semester of 1944, there were twenty "designers and artists" from Marshall Field enrolled in evening classes; see: László Moholy-Nagy to Robert Delson, TLS, March 16th, 1944, Robert Delson Papers, University of Illinois Library, Chicago; and

(continued...)

of the joint agreement was announced, and later that year the Art Institute returned $131,500 to the Association.[69] This sum of money, plus the Field house, constituted the principal resources used to start the school which was to become known as the New Bauhaus.

Clearly, by 1937 Stahle had decided that she wanted the new school to be run along Bauhaus lines. Walter Gropius, the founder and first director of the German Bauhaus, had arrived in the United States in March of 1937 to accept a position as professor of architecture at Harvard University. Stahle wrote to him on May 14th, asking him if he would be interested in coming to the Association's planned new school. Gropius promptly replied that he intended to remain at Harvard for an indefinite period, but he recommended Moholy for the position of director in Chicago. Gropius described Moholy as "my nearest collaborator in the Bauhaus" and added that Moholy "is endowed with that rare creative power which stimulates the students."[70]

On May 23rd, 1937, Moholy received a telegram from Stahle:

> Starting industrial design school in Fall backed by industrialists. Modest beginning but real opportunity to establish project along lines Bauhaus. Looking for head, Gropius recommends you highly. Would you consider it? At what figure? Cable.

Moholy promptly cabled back:

> For plan highly interested. Please send more details. Not knowing American life standard, difficult to specify figure. My last contract here was fifteen hundred pounds a year.[71]

---

[68](...continued)
Walter P. Paepcke to John Cuneo, carbon copy of TLS, April 4th, 1944, Institute of Design Papers, University of Illinois Library, Chicago.

[69]Engelbrecht, "Association of Arts and Industries," 215.

[70]Walter Gropius to Norma K. Stahle, TLS, May 18th, 1937, Bauhaus-Archiv, Berlin; reproduced in: Peter Hahn, "Vom Bauhaus zum New Bauhaus," in: Peter Hahn and Lloyd C. Engelbrecht, editors, *50 Jahre New Bauhaus; Bauhausnachfolge in Chicago* (Berlin: Argon Verlag, 1987), [12].

[71]The telegrams, now lost, are quoted in: László Moholy-Nagy to Walter and Ise Gropius, photographic copy of TLS, May 28th, 1937, Bauhaus-Archiv, Berlin.

An account differing somewhat from mine appeared in: Sibyl Moholy-Nagy, *Moholy-Nagy; Experiment in Totality* (as in note 62, above), 139-140 (the first edition was published in 1950). In a letter to Richard Kostelanetz, Sibyl Moholy-Nagy wrote: "When I wrote the biography in 1948 (my first objective book) I frequently made up imaginative references if I couldn't 'document' a piece. Unfortunately, I have been brainwashed by the establishment to a point where my academic honor no longer permits me to do this—and other tight-rope acts of the imagination." Sibyl

(continued...)

Moholy also wrote to Walter and Ise Gropius, on May 28th, that: "Das Telegramm . . . schlug natürlich wie der Blitz ein" [of course the telegram struck like lightning].[72] After Stahle received Moholy's reply, she spent two days with Walter Gropius, questioning him about Moholy.[73] Then she contacted the European referees whose names had been supplied by Gropius: Julian Huxley, *International Textiles*, and Simpson, Piccadilly.[74] It is not clear whether replies were received from the latter two, but Huxley assured Moholy that he had given him "a magnificent testimonial."[75] Shortly afterward, Moholy was invited to Chicago for an interview. He sailed for New York on the steamship "Manhattan," arrived there on July 8th, 1937,[76] and stayed at The Barclay, 111 East 48th Street.[77] Meeting him at his steamship was art historian James Johnson Sweeney (1890-1986).[78] Moholy talked with Norma Stahle by telephone, and it was arranged that he would have lunch in New York with Elkan Harrison Powell, who had recently succeeded Pelouze as president of the Association of Arts and Industries; then Moholy was to visit Walter and Ise Gropius in their summer place on Cape Cod before traveling on to Chicago.[79] Meanwhile Sibyl left with Hattula and Claudia for a farewell visit to Sibyl's

---

[71](...continued)
Moholy-Nagy to Richard Kostelanetz, October 5th, 1969, carbon copy of typed letter, microfilm reel 945, frame 0285, Moholy-Nagy Papers, Archives of American Art, Washington, D.C. See also Chapter Four, note 410, and Appendix D, pages 721-722.

Actually, since *Moholy-Nagy, Experiment in Totality* is, to some extent, autobiographical, it will be discussed in that context in Appendix D, pages 721-722, where it is observed that it is not unusual to find that details in autobiographic writings and ascertainable fact are at odds.

[72]László Moholy-Nagy to Walter and Ise Gropius, May 28th, 1937.

[73]Walter Gropius to László Moholy-Nagy, photographic copy of carbon copy of a typed letter, June 10th, 1937, Bauhaus-Archiv, Berlin.

[74]László Moholy-Nagy to Walter and Ise Gropius, photographic copy of TLS, May 28th, 1937, and Walter Gropius to László Moholy-Nagy, photographic copy of carbon copy of a typed letter, June 1st, 1937; both are in the Bauhaus-Archiv, Berlin.

[75]László Moholy-Nagy to Walter and Ise Gropius, photocopy of TLS, June 13th, 1937, Bauhaus-Archiv, Berlin. See also: Ise Gropius to Julian Huxley, photocopy of carbon copy of TLS, June 7th, 1937, Bauhaus-Archiv, Berlin.

[76]Immigrant Identification Card, United States Department of Labor, 11-187802, reel 951, frames 0468-0469, Moholy-Nagy files, Archives of American Art, Washington, D.C.

[77]László Moholy-Nagy to Sibyl Moholy-Nagy, ALS, July 9th, 1937, reel 951, frames 0215-0226, Archives of American Art, Washington, D.C.

[78]Sibyl Moholy-Nagy, *Moholy-Nagy; Experiment in Totality*, 142; and László Moholy-Nagy to Sibyl Moholy-Nagy, July 9th, 1937.

[79]Engelbrecht, "Association of Arts and Industries," 216-217; and László Moholy-Nagy to Sibyl Moholy-Nagy, July 9th, 1937.

family in Dresden on July 11th and returned to London on July 18th;[80] Sibyl was not to see any of her family again until 1950.

In Chicago an appointment was offered and accepted, and a public announcement was made on August 22nd that Moholy would be director of "the New Bauhaus, an American School of Design."[81] Announcements soon followed in American magazines concerned with art, architecture and design.[82]

THUS THE STAGE was set for the beginning of Moholy's educational undertaking in Chicago at the New Bauhaus, which operated in 1937 and 1938; this was followed by an independent school begun by Moholy in 1939, the School of Design in Chicago; and this, in turn, was re-organized in 1944 and renamed the Institute of Design.[83] The I.D. later became a unit of the Illinois Institute of Technology, a liaison that continues.

Before discussing each of the schools in turn, it is worth noting what they shared. Most important was a creative ferment that had a liberating effect on the students, and that was a key ingredient in the success Moholy achieved in realizing his basic aim of nurturing the creative potential of each student. Since there was an effort to avoid any attempt to bring the work of the students to a pre-conceived result, there is no easily recognizable common or "I.D." look in the work of the students.

There was also an informal, freewheeling atmosphere, including many opportunities for casual contacts between faculty and students.[84] And, since many of the faculty had also been students in one of these schools, it was sometimes not easy to tell the difference between students and faculty. Many students found this milieu to be exciting and stimulating, and open to wide-ranging experimentation.

At the same time, it should be noted that, just as there was some discontent among students at the German Bauhaus, some Chicago students were dissatisfied. Some simply left and little documentation of their discontent is available. On the other hand, some

---

[80] Sibyl Moholy-Nagy to László Moholy-Nagy, TLS, July 9th, 1937, microfilm reel 951, frames 0227-0228, and *idem*, TLS, July 18th, 1937, microfilm reel 951, frames 0232-0233, Archives of American Art, Washington, D.C.

[81] "American School of Design to Open Here This Fall," *The Chicago Daily News*, August 23, 1937, 11; and *Chicago Tribune*, August 22, 1937, part 1, page 19.

[82] Many are cited in: Engelbrecht, "Association of Arts and Industries," 229-231.

[83] On the re-organization of the School of Design in Chicago into the Institute of Design, see: Alain Findeli, "Design Education and Industry: the Laborious Beginnings of the Institute of Design in Chicago in 1944," *Journal of Design History*, volume IV, number 2 (1991), 97-113.

[84] Examples of the sharing of apartments and off-campus studio space by faculty and students are described in: Beatrice Akiko Takeuchi, "School of Design in Chicago: Refugees East and West," unpublished manuscript, 1998, 33-37 and 41-43, Archives of American Art, Washington, D.C.

persevered and completed their studies and re-evaluated their discontent in a broader context.[85]

MANY OF THE STUDENTS at the New Bauhaus and its successor schools had already had considerable education or experience in art or related fields. Richard Koppe (1916-1973), one of the original students at the New Bauhaus and later a faculty member of the I.D., has written that: "Some students entered the New Bauhaus in the spirit of graduate students," and added: "In my particular case, for example, I had already felt the effects of contemporary European thought, influence, and education in four years at the St. Paul School of Art in Minnesota. . . ."[86] Margaret de Patta (née Strong; 1903-1964), who had already studied extensively in New York and California, and had already acquired a considerable reputation as a jewelry designer,[87] initially enrolled in the School of Design in Chicago in the summer session of 1939;[88] it is possible that her enrollment was stimulated by Moholy's talks in San Francisco in April of that year.[89] She was also enrolled in the spring semester of 1940.[90] Moholy once wrote that ". . . the best jewelry in the country is made by a former student of ours,

---

[85]*E.g.,* Richard Koppe, "The New Bauhaus, Chicago," in: Eckhard Neumann, editor, *Bauhaus and Bauhaus People; Personal Opinions and Recollections of Former Bauhaus Members and their Contemporaries,* revised edition (New York: Van Nostrand Reinhold, 1993), 258-266, here 263-264.

[86]Koppe, "The New Bauhaus, Chicago," 261.

[87]On de Patta, see: Jeannine Fiedler, "Kurzbiografien," in: Peter Hahn and Lloyd C. Engelbrecht, editors, *50 Jahre New Bauhaus: Bauhausnachfolge in Chicago,* 261; Toni Greenbaum, *Messengers of Modernism; American Studio Jewelry 1940-1960* (Montreal: Montreal Museum of Decorative Arts and Flammarion, 1996), 62-69; Robert Cardinale and Hazel Bray, "Margaret de Patta: Structure, Concepts and Design Sources," *Metalsmith,* 3 (Spring, 1983), 11-15; and Yoshiko Uchida, *The Jewelry of Margaret de Patta: a Retrospective Exhibition* (Oakland, California: Oakland Museum, 1976).

[88]Telephone interview with Martha Bielawski of Richmond, California, December 19, 2006. Martha Bielawski was the second wife of the late Eugene Bielawski, who, before marrying her, had been Margaret de Patta's second husband.

An example of de Patta's student work at the School of Design in Chicago appears in: David Travis and Elizabeth Siegel, editors, *Taken by Design: Photographs from the Institute of Design, 1937-1971* (Chicago: The Art Institute of Chicago in association with the University of Chicago Press, 2002), [34-35] and 253. In *Moholy-Nagy: Mentor of Modernism* I have corrected errors in the text of my article in *Taken by Design*: "Educating the Eye: Photography and the Founding Generation at the Institute of Design, 1937-46," [16]-33 and 229-231, here 30.

[89]László Moholy-Nagy, "The Bauhaus Education" and "The New Vision," *Proceedings of the Pacific Arts Association Fourteenth Annual Convention, San Francisco, California, April 1, 2, 3, 4, 1939,* edited by Alfred Neumeyer, 59-68 and 75-82, respectively.

[90]Georg W. Költzsch and Margarita Tupitsyn, editors, *Bauhaus: Dessau, Chicago, New York [exhibition catalogue] Museum Folkwang* (Essen: Museum Folkwang, 2000), 257.

Mrs. Margaret de Patta. . . ."[91] A photograph of one of her rings was included in *Vision in Motion*.[92]

Paepcke was sometimes troubled by what he considered "chaotic procedures" on Moholy's part. His confidant in these matters was Gropius, who, in a letter of February 28th, 1945, tried to explain Paepcke's point of view to Moholy, with suggestions to meet some of Paepcke's objections.[93] Gropius had recently explained in a letter to Paepcke that since the school was ". . . mainly a laboratory of design, some undefined conditions and procedures must be accepted."[94] Paepcke, as a skilled administrator of a large industrial enterprise, knew the value of carefully delegated responsibilities within an organization. He feared that if Moholy were to become overextended, and had a breakdown from overwork, then the organization might not be strong enough to keep the school going in his absence.[95] Procedures were put into place within the Institute of Design to take some of the burden of administration and attention to details off of Moholy. This mattered little to his actual pace of activities, since he carried on a busy schedule of speaking, writing, designing, and creating works of art. And, following Moholy's death on November 24th, 1946, the Institute of Design survived as a force in design education primarily because Moholy had left as his legacy the creative milieu of a laboratory of design, although the administrative procedures sought by Paepcke were no doubt a factor in its survival.

The intercession by Gropius, on behalf of Moholy, with Paepcke, recalls the relationship that Gropius and Moholy had had at the Bauhaus, as described in Chapter Three. It will be recalled that there the "level-headed" Gropius often tried to explain the aims and methods of his "freewheeling" associate.

It had never been Moholy's aim to train specialists in graphic design, photography, or any discipline that circumscribed. He insisted on a many-sided approach that educated the whole student.[96] He once wrote to Nikolaus Pevsner that education in his school

---

[91] László Moholy-Nagy to Marion Becker, TLS, September 14th, 1943, Archives and Rare Books Department, University of Cincinnati Libraries.

[92] László Moholy-Nagy, *Vision in Motion* (Chicago: Paul Theobald & Co., 1947), figure 112 on page [94].

[93] Walter Gropius to László Moholy-Nagy, carbon copy of TLS, February 28th, 1945, Bauhaus-Archiv, Berlin.

[94] Walter Gropius to Walter P. Paepcke, photocopy of carbon copy of TLS, February 16th, 1945, Bauhaus-Archiv, Berlin.

[95] Walter Gropius to László Moholy-Nagy, February 28th, 1945.

[96] For an overview of Moholy's educational aims and methods in Chicago, see: Alain Findeli, "The Methodical and Philosophical Foundations of Moholy-Nagy's Design Pedagogy in Chicago (1937-1946)," *Design Issues: History, Theory, Criticism*, volume VII, number 2 (Fall, 1990), 4-19;

(continued...)

". . . is more general in scope than a limited vocational training," and hence ". . . is valid for anyone in any profession whether he be a lawyer, doctor, designer or architect."[97] Thus the curriculum included academic subjects, with Moholy himself presenting informal seminars on avant-garde literature.[98] There was also a steady stream of guest lecturers[99] and exhibitions. One result of this kind of educational experience was that an individual student would produce work in a variety of media.

Moholy had not wanted to include work in the fine arts in the school's curriculum, even though he continued with his own fine-arts efforts while serving as director. In fact, in a revealing letter to Gropius in the spring of 1938, he wrote: "Ich selbst fühle mich in erster Linie als Maler. . . ." [I see myself primarily as a painter].[100] Moholy regarded successful work in the fine arts as creative activity on the highest level of a cultural epoch, and was convinced that this kind of expression could not be taught. But, as discussed in Chapter Three, Moholy also believed that all students could learn to use the elements of art. Moreover, the open-ended character of avant-garde twentieth-century art permeated the I.D. and was often evident in student work. Nevertheless, as discussed below, sometimes the de-emphasis on the fine arts was unsettling for the students.

IT IS ALSO EVIDENT that a great deal of what would normally have been thrown away in most schools was saved by the students and faculty of the I.D. and its precursors in Chicago. Thus, there has been preserved a rich array of items, including actual examples as well as photographs of student class-work; course outlines and notes the faculty used in their classes; press releases; invitations to lectures, exhibitions and

---

[96](...continued)
reprinted in: Victor Margolin and Richard Buchanan, editors, *The Idea of Design* (Cambridge: The MIT Press, 1995), 29-43.

See also Margolin's own summary of Moholy's educational efforts in Chicago that appeared in his *The Struggle for Utopia*, Chapter Six, [214]-250.

Findeli's book-length account of Moholy as pedagogue in Chicago appeared as: *Le Bauhaus de Chicago: L'Œuvre Pédagogique de László Moholy-Nagy*, préface de Frank Popper (Sillery, Quebec: Les Éditions du Septentrion, 1995). Carefully researched, thoroughly documented and profusely illustrated, it remains the only comprehensive account of the New Bauhaus, the School of Design in Chicago, and the early years of the Institute of Design.

[97] László Moholy-Nagy to Nikolaus Pevsner, TLS, March 18th, 1943, Bauhaus-Archiv, Berlin.

[98] The late Pat Parker Filipowski recalled in an interview with Lloyd C. Engelbrecht, in Lexington, Massachusetts, August, 1978, her experiences in Moholy's Wednesday morning literature seminars. See also: Takeuchi, "School of Design in Chicago," 15-16. Moholy summarized these seminars in a chapter, "Literature," in his *Vision in Motion*, 292-357.

[99] An extended but partial list of guest lecturers is in: László Moholy-Nagy, *Vision in Motion*, 70.

[100] László Moholy-Nagy to Walter Gropius, TLS, June 8th, 1938, Bauhaus-Archiv, Berlin; portions quoted in: Hahn, "Vom Bauhaus zum New Bauhaus," 14-15.

special events; posters; academic catalogues and brochures; and correspondence. Hence, there is much material of this kind in public and private collections, including the Chicago Historical Society, the Library of the University of Illinois in Chicago, the Archives of the Illinois Institute of Technology, the Archives of American Art in Washington, D.C., the Archives and Rare Books Library of the University of Cincinnati Libraries, and the Bauhaus-Archiv in Berlin. The sheer volume of what has been preserved makes it obvious that both faculty and students thought of their work at the I.D., and at its precursors, as a very special experience.

On his arrival in Chicago Moholy lived at the Knickerbocker Hotel (Rissman & Hirschfield, 1927) on East Walton Street, not far from Lake Michigan. (DVD figure 409) After the August 22nd, 1937, announcement of his appointment to direct the New Bauhaus, he sent for his family to join him from London, while he remained in Chicago to work on preparations for opening the new school. When his family arrived in Chicago they all made a temporary home at the Knickerbocker before moving to an apartment, as noted below.

The school's home, the Marshall Field house, is no longer extant, but it stood at 1905 South Prairie Avenue, near the shore of Lake Michigan (the site of the house is no longer close to the shore because of extensive landfill in the lake bed). (DVD figure 401) It was designed in a relatively restrained "Second Empire" or neo-grec style by Richard Morris Hunt (1827-1895). When completed in 1875 it was the first house in Chicago to be provided with electricity.[101] (DVD figures 410, 411 and 412)

Henry K. Holsman (1866-1963), an architect who was a member of the Association's board,[102] was in charge of remodeling the Field house for use as the New Bauhaus, but Moholy assisted in this after he was appointed director.[103] The extent to which the remodeling reflected Moholy's ideas can only be guessed at. Stahle no doubt wanted the remodeling to go in a Modernist direction and, giving the timing, and the fact that the remodeling was quite extensive, input by Moholy must have been limited. Holsman himself tended to be conservative in expression; although he was later to be associated with Ludwig Mies van der Rohe in the famed 860-880 Lake Shore Drive apartment buildings, completed in 1951,[104] this was primarily due to his knowledge of technical innovations in apartment-house construction.

---

[101] Tebbel, *The Marshall Fields: a Study in Wealth*, 48-49; and Susan Benjamin and Stuart Cohen, *Great Houses of Chicago, 1871-1921* (New York: Acanthus Press, 2008), 20-21 and 44-49.

[102] On Holsman, see: Engelbrecht, "Association of Arts and Industries," 220-224 and figures 47-50.

[103] László Moholy-Nagy, "Why Bauhaus Education?", *Shelter; a Correlating Medium for Housing Progress*, volume III, number 1 (March, 1938), [6]-21, here [12], 13, [14] and [16]; and László Moholy-Nagy to Walter Gropius, ALS, March 11th, 1938, Bauhaus-Archiv, Berlin.

[104] William H. Jordy, *American Buildings and Their Architects: the Impact of European Modernism in the Mid-Twentieth Century* (Garden City, New York: Anchor Books, 1976), 233.

As a result of the remodeling, the limestone-trimmed, red-brick exterior of the Field house was enhanced with a new pink travertine-marble frame around the entrance, with cast-aluminum letters spelling out the name of the school. (DVD figure 413) A conservatory that formed part of the south side of the house (DVD figure 410) was demolished, and in place of its curving glass façade a box-like cement-block office wing was built, severely modern in appearance, inside and out. (DVD figures 414, 415, 416, 417, 418, 419 and 422) But the remodeled interior of the existing house was scarcely less modern. Included was a strikingly modern office for Moholy, in the original portion of the structure, just to the east of the added office wing. (DVD figures 411, 419, 420 and 421)

The entrance and stair hall of the Field house was photographed in 1884, and one can see details such as the double-flued fireplace above which one can see the dining room (later Moholy's office). (DVD figure 423) The removal of the fireplace, along with the removal or plastering over of other details, resulted in a severe, modern appearance of the interior (DVD 424) The transformation of the interior was most dramatically seen in the circular walnut staircase, where the carved balustrade on the older part of the stairway was plastered over. Although the building was demolished in 1955, the sweeping forms of the resulting spiral may still be experienced in a marvelous photograph made by Henry Holmes Smith in 1937, making a stark contrast with the original staircase as viewed in the photograph of 1884. (DVD figure 425) In a photograph dating from November 9th, 1937, Moholy and Gropius look down from the stairwell railing with a triumphant expression on their faces. (DVD 426)

The lighting fixtures in the galleries, consisting of cylindrical opaque glass with a concentric-circle mesh at the bottom (DVD figure 429), were designed by Moholy himself,[105] and he probably also designed the globular hanging fixtures, used in the workshop room (DVD figures 427 and 428) and elsewhere (DVD figures 421 and 424). As far as is known, these two examples would be the only lighting fixtures Moholy himself designed.

The spacious workshop room utilized the entire north part of the second storey. (DVD figures 412, 427 and 428). The exhibition area was comprised of adjoining west and east galleries, the latter serving as a lecture area as well. (DVD figure 429) As seen in DVD figure 411, the two principal lower-storey rooms of the original house were used. These were very accessible for visitors, who could enter the west gallery on their left just after arriving through the main entrance, clearly identified on the exterior as the New Bauhaus. (DVD figures 413, 414 and 415)

If the remodeled Field house presented an appearance of the world of today, the covers of the school's catalogue suggested the world of tomorrow, by making use of stills from unused footage of special effects Moholy had designed for Alexander Korda's film, *Things to Come,* discussed in Chapter Four. (DVD figures 416 and 417)

---

[105]László Moholy-Nagy, "Why Bauhaus Education?", [16].

On an inside page of the catalogue was the emblem Moholy devised for the New Bauhaus, based on a 1922 design by his former Bauhaus colleague, Oskar Schlemmer. (text figure 16, DVD figure 418) In what was probably an unprecedented tribute, the entire twelve pages of the catalogue (including the covers) were reprinted in a Chicago graphic-design quarterly (see note 119).

emblem for the New Bauhaus, 1937

text figure 16, DVD figure 432

After the catalogue was sent to the printers, Moholy left to visit Walter and Ise Gropius at their summer residence on Cape Cod. On the way Moholy paused for an interview with *The New York Times*, during which he outlined his plans for the New Bauhaus.[106] A little later, in a Sunday edition, *The New York Times* featured a lengthy article on its art pages which described the European background and educational aims of the New Bauhaus.[107] In addition, on the editorial page on the same day it was pointed out that while nothing could compensate for the evil done by the Nazis in persecuting minorities, the United States had benefitted incidentally by being able to "import genius." Specifically named as examples were: Albert Einstein, Thomas Mann, Walter Gropius, and Moholy.[108]

---

[106]*The New York Times*, September 2, 1937, 23. The *Times* had earlier reported on the plans for opening the school: "Bauhaus Will Open in Chicago in Fall; Old Marshall Field Residence to House School of Design," *ibid.*, August 22, 1937, section 2, page 6.

[107]Edward Alden Jewell, "Chicago's New Bauhaus," *The New York Times*, September 12, 1937, X 7. A German translation, "Das Neue Bauhaus in Chicago," appeared in a German-exile anti-Nazi Paris publication, *Das Neue Tage-Buch*, volume 5, number 10 (October, 1937), 954-955.

[108]"America Imports Genius," *The New York Times*, September 12, 1937, section 4, page 8; reprinted in facsimile in: Lloyd C. Engelbrecht, "Moholy-Nagy und Chermayeff in Chicago," in: Hahn and Engelbrecht, editors, *50 Jahre New Bauhaus*, 51-68, here 54.

This coverage, in America's most prestigious newspaper, proved to be a harbinger of things to come. Just as had earlier happened in Europe, Moholy's infectious enthusiasm inspired editors in publications of many kinds: newspapers in large and small cities, art, photography, architecture and business magazines, avant-garde and academic quarterlies, and trade and technical publications. Sometimes the result was an article he himself wrote, and at other times articles were written about him, his school, and his work.

ON HIS WAY BACK TO CHICAGO from Cape Cod, Moholy visited the Museum of Modern Art in New York, and signed the guest book on September 8th. Lower on the same page were signatures by Herbert Bayer and Marcel Breuer (September 13th) and Ludwig Mies van der Rohe (September 23rd).[109] Thus signing the guest book at MOMA seemed to be the New York equivalent of signing the guest book at Der Sturm gallery in Berlin (see Chapter Two).

One of the things Gropius and Moholy talked about at Cape Cod was another attempt at starting a publishing project aimed at producing a series of books comparable to the one they had co-edited at the Bauhaus. As noted in Chapter Four, a European attempt in 1935 for a similar project came to nothing. But now Moholy succeeded in engaging William Warder Norton (1891-1945), president of W.W. Norton & Company, a prestigious New York publisher, in the project. Moholy had met with him in Wilton, Connecticut.[110] Details of the visit are not documented, but Wilton is a town on the northeastern outer edge of a commuter-rail network, just over one hour away from Manhattan by rail. On returning to Chicago, Moholy wrote letters to William W. Norton dated September 16th and September 22nd,[111] and received a reply from him dated

---

[109]This page from "Museum of Modern Art Guest Book, 1929-1943," is reproduced in: Cammie McAtee, "Alien #5044325: Mies's First Trip to America," in: Phyllis Lambert, editor, *Mies in America* (Montreal: Canadian Centre for Architecture, 2001), [132]. The "Guest Book" is housed in the Archives of the Museum of Modern Art.

[110]László Moholy-Nagy to WalterGropius, photographic copy of MLS, August 12th, 1937; and William Warder Norton to László Moholy-Nagy, photocopy of carbon copy of TLS, September 30th, 1937. Both of these items are in the Bauhaus-Archiv, Berlin.

[111]The letters are not available to me, but are referred to in the letter cited in the previous note.

```
List of Possible books:

Dr. S. Giedion              "Recreation & Leisure"
Dr. S. Giedion              "Chaos and Construction"
J. J. Sweeney               "New Painting"
D. A. Dorner                "Gropius-Monography"
L. Moholy-Nagy               (Reprint) "New Vision"
L. Moholy-Nagy              "Painting Photo Film" (Light new medium of
                                                  expression)
L. Moholy-Nagy and Gropius  "Exhibition Architecture"
J. Albers                   "Lectures for Basic Design"
J. Tychichold               "The New Typography"
P. Nelson                   "Social Services"      (hospitals etc.)
LeCorbusier                 "America"
R.J. Neutra                 "Hollywood"
P. Morton Shand             "Cinemas"
O. Schlemmer and       )
Xanty and Dr. Curjel)       "Theater"
Br. Kiesler and Calder      "Tomorrow"
Lönberg-Holm and Kocher     "Integrated House"
N. Gabo and Pevsner         "New Assembly"
H. Bayer                    "Advertising"
A. Barr                     "The New Museum"
Prof. Bernal                "Utopia of Today"
O. Berger                   "Textiles"
H. Morris                   "Village-Colleges"
Prof. H. Reed               "Surrealism"
Dr. C. Welcker              "Constructivism"
J. Richards                 "London New"
F. Lager                    "Cubism"
H. Arp                      "Poetry"
```

table three: photocopy of typed original of list of possible books list of books proposed for The New Bauhaus Books; photocopy of typed original is in the Bauhaus-Archiv, Berlin

September 30th. Norton pointed out that his firm had not made any money on the art and architectural books it had published thus far. He pointed to a book he had shown to Moholy in Wilton, *The International Style*.[112] He wrote that 1,500 copies had been printed and only 702 had been sold, not enough to show a profit. (Norton had no way of knowing at the time that the book would eventually be considered a classic that proved to be a long-term money-maker for his firm.) Therefore he sought some kind of

---

[112] Henry-Russell Hitchcock and Philip Johnson, *The International Style: Architecture since 1922* (New York: W. W. Norton & Company, Inc., 1932).

subsidy if he were to publish a series of books, such as a loan to be repaid when production, advertising and overhead costs had been recovered.[113]

---

corrected list of books proposed for The New Bauhaus Books, 1937

Dr. S. Giedion, "Recreation and Leisure"; *idem*, "Chaos and Construction"; J. J. Sweeney, "New Painting"; Dr. A. Dorner, "Gropius Monograph"; L. Moholy-Nagy, (Reprint) "New Vision"; *idem*, "Painting Photo Film" (Light new medium of expression) [translation of existing book]; L. Moholy-Nagy and Gropius, "Exhibition Architecture"; J. Albers, "Lectures for Basic Design"; J. Tschichold, "The New Typography" [translation of existing book]; P. Nelson, "Social Services" (hospitals, etc.); Le Corbusier, "America"; R.J. Neutra, "Hollywood"; P. Morton Shand, "Cinemas"; O. Schlemmer, Xanti Schawinsky and Dr. H. Curjel, "Theater"; Dr. F. Kiesler and A. Calder, "Tomorrow"; K. Lønberg-Holm and A. Kocher, "Integrated House"; N. Gabo and A. Pevsner, "New Assembly"; H. Bayer, "Advertising"; A. Barr, "The New Museum"; Prof. J. Bernal, "Utopia of Today"; O. Berger, "Textiles"; H. Morris, "Village Colleges"; Prof. H. Read, "Surrealism"; Dr. C. Welcker, "Constructivism"; J. Richards, "London New"; F. Léger, "Cubism"; H. Arp, "Poetry"

---

table four: corrected list of possible books list of books proposed for The New Bauhaus Books

---

Moholy proposed a series of twenty-eight books, mostly new books but also a reprint (*The New Vision*) and a few translations of existing books.[114] (tables three and four) Evidently some kind of subsidy from the Association of Arts and Industries was promised. In any case, *The New Vision* was brought out in a new edition by W.W. Norton; facing the title page was a series description: "The New Bauhaus Books, editors Walter Gropius, L. Moholy-Nagy, No. 1." As noted below, the book included numerous examples of work by New Bauhaus students. But since the New Bauhaus did not proceed beyond its first year, the continuation of the series became a moot point.

---

[113]William Warder Norton to László Moholy-Nagy, September 30th, 1937.

[114]A photocopy of one typed sheet, undated but probably made in the latter part of September, 1937, is in the Gropius files at the Bauhaus-Archiv in Berlin. A shorter, preliminary list is in a letter to Gropius: László Moholy-Nagy to WalterGropius, photographic copy of MLS, August 13th, 1937, Bauhaus-Archiv, Berlin.

One of the hoped-for authors, Alfred Barr, who had been invited to participate by Moholy in a letter of September 15th, 1937, had already declined, in a letter of September 30th, to be part of the project.[115] Gropius and Moholy, however, did not give up. They later began a series of I.D. Books with Chicago publisher Paul Theobald, but, as noted below, only two titles were issued, one written by Gropius and the other written by Moholy.

After returning to Chicago from Cape Cod, Moholy's appearances included a speech before the Illinois Society of Architects on September 28th, 1937. His talk included an outline of the Bauhaus approach but the bulk of it was devoted to architecture and space perception.[116] It was probably similar to an article published a short time later.[117] He was also scheduled for a radio interview on the subject of "everybody is talented" on October 2nd, at 8:15 in the evening, on labor-union oriented station WCFL, operated by the Chicago Federation of Labor.[118]

From the New Bauhaus to the Institute of Design and from Prairie Avenue to Ontario Street to State Street: Moholy as Educator in Chicago

In a diagram inscribed in a circle, the first year of the New Bauhaus was represented in the outer ring, labeled "Preliminary Courses."[119] (table five) This constituted the heart of the program for the first, and as it turned out, the only, year of the New Bauhaus. Basically what was taught, then, was an altered and updated form of the *Vorkurs*, or foundation course, of the German Bauhaus.[120]

---

[115]László Moholy-Nagy to Alfred Barr, photocopy of typed copy of TLS, September 15th, 1937, Bauhaus-Archiv, Berlin; and Alfred Barr to László Moholy-Nagy photocopy of typed copy of TLS, Bauhaus-Archiv, Berlin.

[116]Arthur Woltersdorf, "From Fair to Fabrication: Illinois Society of Architects Learns of Paris and the New Bauhaus," *Illinois Society of Architects Monthly Bulletin*, volume XXII, numbers 4-5 (October-November, 1937), [1]-2.

[117]László Moholy-Nagy, "The New Bauhaus and Space Relationship," *American Architect and Architecture*, volume XLI, number 2664 (December, 1937), [22]-28.

[118]László Moholy-Nagy to Walter Gropius, photographic copy of MLS, September 20th, 1937, Bauhaus-Archiv, Berlin.

[119]*The New Bauhaus: American School of Design* [Catalogue for 1937-1938], 4; a copy is in the Institute of Design Papers, Library of the University of Illinois in Chicago. All twelve pages of the catalogue were reprinted in: *Printing Art Quarterly*, volume LXVII, number 2 (Autumn, 1937), following page 24.

[120]On the foundation course as taught in Chicago, see: Lloyd C. Engelbrecht, "Grundkurs," in: Hahn and Engelbrecht, editors, *50 Jahre New Bauhaus*, 121-135.

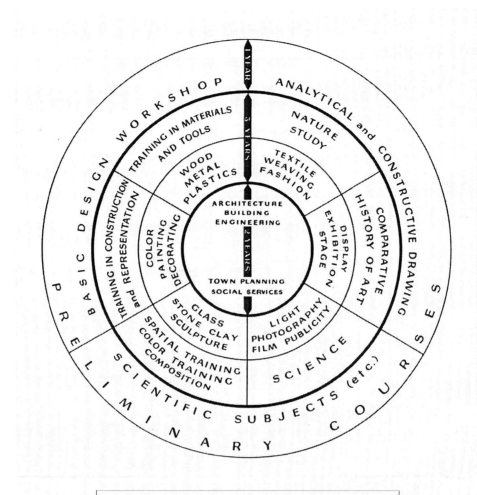

table five: curricular outline of the program of studies at the New Bauhaus, 1927

Sparking the educational program of the New Bauhaus were lectures by Moholy based on his book, *The New Vision*. Workshop instruction in the foundation course was given by Moholy's former Bauhaus student Hin Bredendieck,[121] assisted by Andi Schiltz.[122] A photography and light workshop was offered by György Kepes and

[121]Bredendieck described his foundation course instruction in Chicago in: Hin Bredendieck, "The Legacy of the Bauhaus," *Art Journal*, volume XXII, number 1 (Fall, 1962), 15-21. Bredendieck was assisted in preparing this article by Henry Holmes Smith, then serving as art director of the *Art Journal*.

[122]Schiltz had studied at the University of Cincinnati (Lloyd C. Engelbrecht interview with Andi Schiltz, New Preston, Connecticut, July, 1975). See also: *University of Cincinnati Record, Annual Catalogue, 1929-1930*, series I, volume XXVI, number 3, part 1 (July, 1930), 472. Schiltz also studied at the Art Academy of Cincinnati, where he earned a degree in 1929; see: "Minutes of Board of Directors' Meeting of Institute of Design, January 9, 1945," mimeographed; a copy is in

(continued...)

Henry Holmes Smith (1909-1986). AlexanderArchipenko taught sculpture, while David Dushkin (about 1898-1986)[123] taught music. In addition, Bredendieck taught projective geometry and lettering, and Kepes taught a drawing and color workshop. Academic subjects at the New Bauhaus were taught by three professors from the University of Chicago: philosopher Charles Morris (1901-1979), biologist Ralph W. Gerard (1900-1974) and physicist Carl Eckart (1902-1973); in addition, Howard Vincent O'Brien (1888-1947), columnist for *The Chicago Daily News*, gave a series of six lectures on "the meaning of culture."[124]

Exercises originated by Bredendieck at the New Bauhaus included making hand sculptures, which could be held in the hand and perceived by the sense of touch (DVD figure 433), and "wood cuts," or exercises in cutting into wooden blocks with hand and power saws and drills. (DVD figures 434, 453, 454 and 456) Part of the reason for these exercises was a practical one: the students were provided with free materials in the form of pieces of expensive hardwood removed from the woodwork during the remodeling of the Field house.[125] The hardwood included a number of varieties which had been brought from around the world. Bredendieck also continued foundation course exercises from his own student experience at the German Bauhaus, including paper cutting and folding (DVD figure 435), and tactile charts; one tactile chart by Alexander Corrazzo, now lost, was photographed by Corrazzo. (DVD figure 436)

Kepes, who had been assisting Moholy with design projects in Europe, was brought to Chicago but he did not arrive until several weeks after the opening of classes.[126] In the absence of Kepes, Henry Holmes Smith (1909-1986),[127] a photographer who had been attracted to Moholy's ideas through the 1932 edition of *The New Vision*, was asked to

---

[122](...continued)
the Institute of Design Papers, University of Illinois Library, Chicago.

[123]On Dushkin, see: Dorothy Smith Dushkin Papers, Sophia Smith Collection, Smith College, Northampton, Massachusetts.

[124]László Moholy-Nagy to Walter Gropius, photocopy of TLS, October 20th, 1937, Bauhaus-Archiv, Berlin; and *The New Bauhaus: American School of Design* [Catalogue for] *Night Class and Spring Semester, 1938*, unpaginated folder; a copy is in the Institute of Design Papers, Library of the University of Illinois in Chicago.

[125]Marie Zoe Greene-Mercier, interviewed by Lloyd C. Engelbrecht, Chicago, February, 1976.

[126]The reason for the late arrival of Kepes was that he remained in Europe while trying, unsuccessfully, to enter Spain so that he could join the international volunteers fighting alongside the Loyalist Republican, anti-Fascist forces in Spain. Lloyd C. Engelbrecht interviewing György Kepes, Cambridge, Massachusetts, October 7th and 8th, 1978; and György Kepes interviewed by Robert Brown, March 7th and August 30th, 1972, and January 11th, 1973, pages 10-12 in a typescript in the Archives of American Art, Washington, D.C.

[127]On Smith, see: Howard Bossen, *Henry Holmes Smith, Man of Light* (Ann Arbor, Michigan: UMI Research Press, 1983).

begin the photography classes.[128] Smith, then at the outset of his career, has stated that the experience of working with Moholy and Kepes and the students at the New Bauhaus has influenced his entire development as an artist.[129] Smith returned the favor in advance since it was his generous loan of his own photographic equipment and supplies, and some technical photography manuals, that enabled the school to set up a darkroom.[130]

In their classes, Kepes and Smith sought to involve the students in a broad exploration of the technical and aesthetic possibilities available to the photographer. A thorough grounding was provided in the early history of photography, the nature and properties of light, and the opportunities opened to the photographer by the direct manipulation of light. Class exercises included studies of leaves, cloth, and cellophane and other translucent materials; superimposed images; multiple exposures; negative prints; studies of the action of prisms and distorting mirrors; studies of overlapping rays of light or "additive light records"; solarization; and "light volume studies," in which varying distances from a light source are measured by variations in size.[131]

Alexander Archipenko[132] had been an essential part of the creative artistic ferment in Paris during the years immediately preceding World War I. Following the War, as described in Chapter Two, he worked and taught briefly in Berlin where he had met Moholy, before emigrating to the United States in 1923. To Archipenko can be credited

---

[128]The first class sessions were described by Smith in "Into Light: the New Bauhaus and Nathan Lerner," an essay of 1973 based on a lecture given that year at Indiana State University, Terre Haute, marking the opening of an exhibition by Nathan Lerner; published in: *Henry Holmes Smith: Collected Writings 1935-1985* (Tucson: Center for Creative Photography, University of Arizona, 1986), 106-108.

[129]Engelbrecht, "Association of Arts and Industries," 280-281.

[130]Engelbrecht, "Association of Arts and Industries," 276.

[131]Engelbrecht, "Association of Arts and Industries," 279-284 and figures 108-114; and *idem*, "Educating the Eye," 22 and 24-27.

[132]On Archipenko, see: Donald H. Karshon, *Archipenko: Sculpture, Drawings and Prints, 1908-1964* (Danville, Kentucky: Centre College, 1985); Katherine Janszky Michaelsen, *Archipenko; a Study of the Early Works, 1908-1920* (New York: Garland Publishing, 1977); *idem, Alexander Archipenko, a Centennial Tribute* (Washington, D.C.: National Gallery of Art, 1986); and Alexander Archipenko, *Archipenko: Fifty Creative Years, 1908-1958*, "by Alexander Archipenko and fifty art historians" (New York: Tekhne, 1960).

In 1922 Moholy and Kassák had included work by Archipenko in their *Buch neuer Künstler,* discussed in Chapter Two.

Chicago critics praised Archipenko's work. John and Molly Thwaites hailed him as an innovator and ". . . one of the masters of modern art"; see their: "Archipenko's Recent Work at the Kuh Gallery, Chicago," *Magazine of Art*, volume XXXI, number 2 (February, 1938), 103-105. Clarence J. Bulliet considered him "perhaps the most inventive genius in sculpture the ages have known;" see: *The Chicago Daily News*, May 14, 1938, 25.

a number of innovations in sculpture, including the representation of solid forms through the shaping of voids, and creating an illusion of convex forms through the use of concave forms, both of which can be observed in the work of his students in Chicago. Archipenko was also a pioneer in the use of color with three-dimensional forms; he had planned to give his students exercises involving color, but Moholy talked him out of it.[133]

The musical instruction provided by Dushkin included playing instruments, and analytic listening. In addition there were musical crafts, or studies of the tonal characteristics of common materials such as wood and metal, and the adaptation of them to musical uses by fashioning them into forms that provided definite pitch and also resonance.[134]

It was Charles Morris (1901-1979), a philosopher and semiotician,[135] who lined up colleagues from the University of Chicago to teach at the New Bauhaus.[136] A letter written by Morris in 1968 recalls his fondness and respect for Moholy: "I think of Moholy-Nagy as one of the most vital and significant persons I have been privileged to have as a friend."[137] This provides a measure of Moholy's ability to relate to the university scholarly community. Morris once gave a copy of John Dewey's *Art As Experience* (1934) to Moholy; Dewey wrote in a letter to Morris that: "I was amazed by the congruence of his ideas with ours."[138]

Moholy had tried to get art and literary critic James Johnson Sweeney, then serving as curator at the Museum of Modern Art, as lecturer for "History of Art and other subjects," but Sweeney initially accepted and then rejected the appointment, although too late to allow his name to be removed from the printed catalogue.[139] Moholy had hoped to bring in Sigfried Giedion from Zurich to replace Sweeney, beginning with the second

---

[133]Engelbrecht, "Association of Arts and Industries," 285.

[134]Engelbrecht, "Association of Arts and Industries," 285-286.

[135]On Morris, see: Richard A. Fiordo, *Charles Morris and the Criticism of Discourse* (Bloomington: Indiana University, 1977).

[136]Morris had met Moholy through Rudolf Carnap; see: Charles Morris to Lloyd C. Engelbrecht, TLS, June 3rd, 1968, Institute of Design Papers, University of Illinois Library, Chicago.

[137]*Ibid.*

[138]*Ibid.*

[139]Walter Gropius to László Moholy-Nagy, photocopy of carbon copy of TLS, September 26th, 1937; and László Moholy-Nagy to Walter Gropius, MLS, Septembr 28th, 1937; both letters are in the Bauhaus-Archiv, Berlin.

semester of the New Bauhaus,[140] but although Giedion was a frequent guest lecturer for Moholy, he never joined his faculty.

As noted above, Moholy also tried to invite Frank Lloyd Wright to join the faculty. Moholy was assisted in contacting Wright by an Association board member, William A. Kittredge, director of design and typography at R.R. Donnelley & Sons Company, a large printing and publishing firm. Moholy described Kittredge as "a great admirer and personal friend of him" [*ein grosser bewunderer und persönlicher freund von ihm*]."[141] But the end result was only a student visit to Wright's home in Spring Green.[142]

The opening of classes at the New Bauhaus on October 18th, 1937, was widely covered in newspapers and magazines,[143] the latter including two national news-weeklies, *Time* and *News-Week*.[144]

Gropius gave an official dedication speech after a banquet in his honor at a downtown hotel on the evening of November 9th. The title of his talk was "Education toward Creative Design."[145] (DVD figure 437) Preceding the evening event was a three o'clock tea at the New Bauhaus.[146]

The Field house occupied by the New Bauhaus had been a centerpiece of a "Gold Coast" neighborhood of impressive residences, a neighborhood now best known for the most architecturally distinguished of them, Henry H. Richardson's Glessner house (1886-1887), still extant on the southwest corner of East Eighteenth Street and South

---

[140] László Moholy-Nagy to Walter Gropius, photocopy of MLS, October 20th, 1937; László Moholy-Nagy to Walter Gropius, photocopy of MLS, October 23rd, 1937; László Moholy-Nagy to Walter Gropius, photocopy of TLS, October 29th, 1937; and Sigfried Giedion to Walter Gropius, photocopy of TLS, October 25th, 1937. All four letters are in the Bauhaus-Archiv, Berlin.

[141] László Moholy-Nagy to Walter Gropius, TLS, October 8th, 1937.

[142] László Moholy-Nagy to Frank Lloyd Wright, August 12th, 1941, Frank Lloyd Wright Archives, Frank Lloyd Wright Foundation, Scottsdale, Arizona

[143] *E.g.*, Eleanor Jewett, "School for Design Will Open Oct. 18," *Chicago Tribune*, October 10, 1937, part 8, page 5; and "Chicago Fosters Progressive Art, New Bauhaus, American School of Design, Opens Tomorrow," *The New York Times*, October 17, 1937, 8 N. See also: Engelbrecht, "Association of Arts and Industries," 229-231.

[144] "New in Old," *Time: the Weekly Newsmagazine*, October 25, 1937, 41; and "Hungarian Professor Directs New School in Chicago," *News-Week*, September 20, 1937, 36. (*News-Week* was later known as *Newsweek*.)

[145] The invitation to the banquet and lecture, held in the Red Lacquer Room of the Palmer House, is shown in: Hahn and Engelbrecht, editors, *50 Jahre New Bauhaus*, 96.

[146] Judith Cass, "Tea to Mark Dedication of New Bauhaus," *Chicago Tribune*, November 2, 1937, 13.

Prairie Avenue.[147] (DVD figure 438) The "Gold Coast" was conveniently located near a lakefront commuter-railroad station at Sixteenth Street from which residents could travel in a few minutes to offices, places of business and theatres in downtown Chicago, although it was common to walk downtown, which took about thirty minutes. (The commuter- railroad station had been moved south to Eighteenth Street by the time the New Bauhaus opened.)

By 1937 the ambience of this south-side "Gold Coast" neighborhood was disintegrating, but Addie V. Gregory (née Hibbard; born 1859), widow of wholesale-hardware merchant Robert B. Gregory, still maintained her home at 1638 South Prairie Avenue.[148] As the unofficial historian of that neighborhood she welcomed her new neighbors as she poured the tea for the three o'clock reception on November 9th,[149] later noting their presence in her role as historian.[150] (DVD figures 439 and 440) Among those greeting guests at the reception was Norma K. Stahle; among the guests was architect George Fred Keck, who was later to teach at the School of Design in Chicago. (DVD figure 441). The guests were also greeted by a speech by Moholy, who went over his text on the school grounds beforehand. (DVD figure 442)

The Field family retained a tenuous hold in the neighborhood through Gus Klemm, retired driver for the family, who had his residence on the upper level of the two-storey carriage house to the rear of the mansion. He remained as a sort of caretaker through the New Bauhaus year and also during the years when the mansion served as classrooms for an aeronautical university and until it and the carriage house were demolished in 1955.[151]

The fading of the old "Gold Coast" neighborhood was accompanied by the development of some elegant streets on the Near North Side lined with mansions, town houses and apartment buildings.[152] From autumn, 1937, until late in 1940, this was the

---

[147]Benjamin and Cohen, *Great Houses of Chicago, 1871-1921*, 136-147.

[148]*Chicago Social Register, 1937*, volume LI, number 4 (November, 1936), 59; and Addie Hibbard Gregory, *A Great-Grandmother Remembers* (Chicago: A. Kroch, Publisher, 1940), 103, 224 and 231.

By the time the New Bauhaus opened the neighborhood was no longer near the lakefront because the shoreline by then lay a considerable distance to the east due to extensive landfill.

[149]Cass, "Tea to Mark Dedication of New Bauhaus," 13.

[150]Gregory, *A Great-Grandmother Remembers*, 120.

[151]Joseph Egelhof, "House Built to Last 1,000 Years Won't," *Chicago Tribune*, February 28, 1955, [1] and 6. In conversations with me, former New Bauhaus student Nathan Lerner remembered being aware of Klemm's presence, especially when he attended Archipenko's sculpture class on the ground level of the carriage house.

[152]Gregory, *A Great-Grandmother Remembers*, 117, 133-134 and 224-226; and Arthur Meeker, *Chicago, with Love: a Polite and Personal History* (New York: Alfred A. Knopf, 1955), 61-62

(continued...)

neighborhood where Moholy and his family occupied a spacious apartment on the second floor of the seven-storey McConnell Apartments at 1210 North Astor Street, at the northwest corner of Astor and East Division Street (Holabird & Roche, 1897).[153] (DVD figures 443, 444, 445, 456 and 457) Moholy described the apartment for his English friend Ashley Havinden: "After a very long search we found an apartment in a very, very old [*sic*] Chicago apartment house, which we remodeled completely and which now makes a very fine dwelling."[154] Floors were covered with tatami mats. One room was converted by Moholy into his studio.[155] (DVD figures 445 and 446) From the curved corner window nook of the McConnell one can look eastward along Division Street and get a view of nearby Lake Michigan. As Moholy noted: "It overlooks the lake and this really means everything in this town."[156]

Richard Koppe recalled that: "Students were often invited to Moholy's apartment on Astor Street, which was painted entirely in white. Here he had a foyer gallery for his Constructivist paintings and light modulators."[157]

D URING THE SPRING SEMESTER of 1938 there was a series of twelve evening lectures presented at the New Bauhaus from February 14th through May 26th, offered free to day students and for a fee of ten dollars to night students and the general public. Included were two lectures by Franz Alexander on psychoanalysis; two by J.J. Sweeney on "Invention and Form"; and one by Moholy on photography and cinema, plus another on painting. Also H. Ede of the Tate Gallery in London lectured on English painting; J.G. Crowther lectured on "American Scientists with Emphasis on the Work of Edison"; Clarence J. Bulliet lectured on a "Human Approach to Art Criticism"; and two University of Chicago professors, Louis Leon Thurstone and Rudolf Carnap, spoke on "Measurement of Intelligence" and "The Task of Science," respectively.[158]

---

[152](...continued)
and 119-122.

[153] On the McConnell, see: Robert Bruegmann, *Architects and the City: Holabird and Roche of Chicago, 1880-1918* (Chicago: University of Chicago Press, 1997), 171-173 and 452; and *idem, Holabird & Roche, Holabird & Root: an Illustrated Catalog of Works, Volume I, 1880-1911* (New York: Garland Publishing, Inc., 1991), 168-169.

[154] László Moholy-Nagy to Ashley Havinden, TLS, November 29, 1937. The letter was sold at auction in Bern by Kornfeld und Klipstein in June, 1976, and its present location is unknown; xerox copies are in my files and in the files of Hattula Moholy-Nagy, Ann Arbor, Michigan.

[155] This was the northernmost bedroom, conveniently furnished with a sink; see: Hattula Moholy-Nagy, "Chicago Memories," Appendix E, page 727.

[156] László Moholy-Nagy to Ashley Havinden, November 29th, 1937.

[157] Richard Koppe, "The New Bauhaus, Chicago," 262.

[158] *The New Bauhaus: American School of Design* [Catalogue for] *Night Class and Spring Semester, 1938*, unpaginated folder.

Psychiatrist Franz Alexander (1891-1964) had likely been one of Moholy's acquaintances in Budapest. In any case his lectures at the New Bauhaus demonstrated Moholy's continued interest in psychoanalysis and his conviction that it was important in a context of the arts. Alexander, as noted below, went on to support Moholy's efforts to help wounded war veterans and their care-givers.

In his speech Clarence J. Bulliet (1883-1952), of *The Chicago Daily News*, demonstrated that he was especially sympathetic to what Moholy was doing. He pointed out that creative work of modern artists had often been reduced to formulas which were then applied by people with little creativity or imagination, but that in contrast ". . . the Bauhaus has as a fundamental idea in its operation, the seeking and finding of new ideas and the blazing of new trails."[159]

Another of these guest lecturers at the New Bauhaus was J.G. (James Gerald) Crowther, who had been one of Moholy's friends in England and who, as noted in Chapter Four, is credited with the creation of the field of science journalism. He described his experience in Chicago in terms of his current lecture tour:

> I spoke for an hour and a half on American scientists; the audience was
> the most appreciative and understanding that I had in America. I stayed
> with the Moholy-Nagys, who were striving hard to consolidate the
> school and their position.[160]

The impressive series of lectures was a form of community outreach and provided an occasion for many Chicagoans to visit the New Bauhaus. Among the visitors were three sight-impaired men. An appealing photograph by Henry Holmes Smith shows Moholy making notes while György and Juliet Kepes guide the visitors in perceiving tactile charts and hand sculptures. (DVD figure 448)

The first field trip for the students was offered by George Fred Keck, a future faculty member at the School of Design in Chicago: on October 25th, 1937, Moholy hired a bus for a visit to the recently completed Bertram Cahn house in Lake Forest, Illinois, designed by Keck; the tour was preceded by a discussion of Keck's drawings for the house.[161] Keck's wealthy client had asked for "a house for the day after tomorrow" and Keck had responded with an attractive Modernist masterpiece.[162]

---

[159] A copy of Bulliet's speech, headed "The New Bauhaus, April 7, 1938," is in the Clarence J. Bulliet Papers, the Archives of American Art, Washington, D.C.

[160] James Gerald Crowther, *Fifty Years with Science* (London: Barrie & Jenkins, 1970), 195. Actually, all of the out-of-town speakers stayed at the Moholy-Nagy apartment; see: Sibyl Moholy-Nagy to Ise Gropius, TLS, February 7th, 1938, Bauhaus-Archiv, Berlin.

[161] László Moholy-Nagy to George Fred Keck, TLS, October 25th, 1937, Keck Papers, State Historical Society of Wisconsin, Madison.

[162] On the Bertram Cahn house: see: Boyce, *Keck and Keck*, 60-63.

Moholy was also busy giving lectures "off-campus," as noted above. Among the earliest of these was an appearance at the Lakeside Press Galleries in Chicago where a December 6th, 1937, lecture on the New Typography movement supplemented an exhibition called "Printing for Commerce";[163] a March 1st, 1938, lecture at the Minneapolis Institute of Arts on "Painting with Light";[164] and a May, 1938, lecture at the Pratt Institute in Brooklyn, where the subject was the educational program at the New Bauhaus.[165] Still another lecture was given on July 27th, 1938, as part of a series of lectures on miscellaneous topics in Woodstock, New York, in the setting of a former Arts-and-Crafts colony known as Byrdcliffe.[166] Moholy spoke on "Bauhaus Education," ironically speaking of the New Bauhaus in the present tense because he was unaware that it would shortly cease to exist.[167]

AN ACCOUNT OF A MORE INFORMAL MEETING held not long after Moholy's arrival in Chicago has been provided by John E. Walley (1910-1974), one of Moholy's most enthusiastic supporters in the Windy City who was later to join his faculty. Moholy was invited to speak to a group of politically radical but artistically conservative artists, organized into a union affiliated with the Congress of Industrial Organizations (the Congress is now part of the AFL-CIO). The union's invitation was given to Moholy only after a heated discussion within the group. Writing in 1965, Walley recalled:

> I can still see Moholy's arrival at the union headquarters with a large
> movie projector, two slide projectors, films and large scale photo
> blow-ups. The shock, the impact of the new ideas turned into a
> marathon debate lasting well after midnight. Moholy was never at a
> disadvantage in a heated discussion, even when completely
> outnumbered. The group finally shifted to a nearby bar and continued
> until closing time.[168]

---

[163] *Paper and Printing Digest*, volume 4, number 1 (January 1938), 3-5.

[164] "Members' Lecture," *The Bulletin of the Minneapolis of Arts*, February 26, 1938, [41]-42.

[165] Ruth Green Harris, "The New Bauhaus: a Program for Art Education," *The New York Times*, May 29, 1938, section 10, page 7.

[166] On Byrdcliffe, see: Nancy E. Green, editor, *Byrdcliffe: an American Arts and Crafts Colony* (Ithaca, New York: Herbert F. Johnson Museum of Art, Cornell University, 2004).

[167] László Moholy-Nagy, "Bauhaus Education," in: *Byrdcliffe Afternoons; a Series of Lectures Given at Byrdcliffe, Woodstock, New York, July 1938* (Woodstock, New York: The Overlook Press, 1939), 101-111. See also: László Moholy-Nagy to Katherine Dreier, MLS, July 19th, 1938, Katherine Dreier Papers, box 41, folder 1204, Beinecke Rare Book and Manuscript Library, Yale University.

[168] John E. Walley, "The Influence of the New Bauhaus in Chicago," in *Selected Papers, John E. Walley, 1910-1974*, edited by Donald Dimmitt and Elinore Pawula (Chicago: Department of Art, University of Illinois at Chicago Circle, 1975), 75.

Two major touring exhibitions were brought to the New Bauhaus by Moholy. Late in 1937 there was a show of abstract art, which included work by Alexander Calder, Naum Gabo, Ben Nicholson, Barbara Hepworth, Jean Hélion, Henry Moore, Piet Mondrian, John Piper and Moholy himself. (DVD figure 429) Also included was work by sculptor Eileen Holding, who organized the exhibition.[169] On display was the work of some of the best-known artists of the twentieth century who were then little known, if known at all, in Chicago at the time.

The second touring exhibition, *A Brief Survey of Photography from 1839-1937*, seen at the New Bauhaus from April 25th through May 7th, 1938,[170] was a selection of photographs that, as discussed in Chapter Four, had been shown at the Museum of Modern Art in New York during the previous year; it was part of an exhibition, *Photography, 1839-1937*, organized by Beaumont Newhall (with help from Moholy, as noted in Chapter Four). *A Brief Survey of Photography from 1839-1937* also included work by Moholy,[171] who on April 27th interpreted the Chicago showing by means of a public lecture called "Development of Photography."[172] His emphasis on the importance of the history of photography to its practice was later to be reinforced by Arthur Siegel, a New Bauhaus student who, as noted below, went on to teach photography at the I.D. Newhall had secured Moholy's place in the history of photography through the exhibition's catalogue,[173] one of the earliest attempts at a comprehensive history of

---

[169]Forthcoming . . . Debate," *Magazine of Art*, volume XXXI, number 2 (February, 1938), 66; Clarence J. Bulliet, "Around the Galleries . . . Abstractions at Bauhaus," *The Chicago Daily News*, November 27, 1937, 24; *idem*, "Around the Galleries . . . Abstracts at the New Bauhaus," *ibid.*, December 4, 1937, 11; and László Moholy-Nagy, "Why Bauhaus Education?" [16].

Holding probably met Moholy when they both participated at a symposium in London; see: László Moholy-Nagy, Naum Gabo, Eileen Holding and Herbert Read, "Modern Art and Architecture: Reports on the Principal Speeches at the Informal General Meeting on Wednesday, 9 December, 1936," with an introduction by Serge Chermayeff, *Journal of the Royal Institute of British Architects*, third series, volume XLIV, number 5 (January 9, 1937), [206] and 209-219.

[170]Clarence J. Bulliet, "Around the Galleries . . . Photo Show at Bauhaus," *The Chicago Daily News*, April 23, 1938, 33; concerning the traveling exhibition, see: John Raeburn, *A Staggering Revolution: a Cultural History of Thirties Photography* (Urbana: University of Illinois Press, 2006), 91-92; and Museum of Modern Art Archives, New York, Department of Circulating Exhibitions, C/E 111.1 65 (1).

[171]"Photography by the New Bauhaus School," *Townsfolk; Society, Sports, Travel and the Fine Arts*, volume XX, number 5 (June, 1938), 18; and Museum of Modern Art Archives, New York, Department of Circulating Exhibitions, C/E 11.1/91(9) and C/E II.1/42(3).

[172]Clarence J. Bulliet, "Around the Galleries . . . Photo Show at Bauhaus," *The Chicago Daily News*, 33.

[173]Beaumont Newhall, editor, *Photography, 1839-1937* (New York: The Museum of Modern Art. 1937), 94, 115, 119 and plates 69 and 70.

photography. Revised in 1938 as *Photography: a Short Critical History*,[174] it led to Newhall's classic *The History of Photography from 1939 to the Present Day*.[175]

Also, Newhall wrote the only article about Moholy to be published in a literary quarterly during his lifetime: this was his "The Photography of Moholy-Nagy," published in *The Kenyon Review* in 1941.[176] Included in Newhall's essay was the best description I have read of Moholy's exploitation of camera angles:

> Moholy-Nagy was by no means the first to break the "rule" that the
> back of the camera must be kept plumb, but he was perhaps the first to
> revel in the results so obtained. By tipping the camera precariously
> down, new forms are created by the establishment of a new vision. The
> converging verticals play against the unfamiliar birdseye view of
> common objects to create exciting patterns and forms. We cannot call
> such pictures "wrong." We have simply seldom seen that way before.
> We never looked down, down, down, until we had built tall buildings,
> or until flying had become common. We had never seen what
> existed—converging verticals and plane profiles.[177]

Newhall ended his essay by warning his literate readers of Moholy's oft-repeated prediction: "'The illiterate of the future,' he says, 'will be ignorant of the use of camera and pen alike.'"

Moholy was shown a draft of the essay and wrote to Newhall: "You have done more than justice to my humble efforts and you have seen this work under so new an angle that I myself have learned a lot from your writing."[178] After seeing the article as published he wrote to Newhall:

> Congratulations on your article in the Kenyon Review. I was very
> agreeably surprised to see that you had written a completely new
> article! I liked the old one very much too but I think that this article
> was even more comprehensive as it mentions also my other activities

---

[174] Beaumont Newhall, *Photography: a Short Critical History*, second edition, revised and emended (New York: Museum of Modern Art, 1938); coverage of Moholy is on pages 68, 206, 220 and plates 69 and 70.

[175] Beaumont Newhall, *The History of Photography from 1839 to the Present Day* (New York: Museum of Modern Art, 1949). This book was later revised and enlarged and has gone through many editions.

[176] Beaumont Newhall, "The Photography of Moholy-Nagy," *The Kenyon Review,* volume III, number 4 (Summer, 1941), [344]-351 and four un-numbered plates preceding page 345.

[177] *Ibid.*, 347.

[178] László Moholy-Nagy to Beaumont Newhall, carbon copy of TLS, February 24th, 1939, microfilm reel 951, frame 0331, Moholy-Nagy files, Archives of American Art, Washington, D.C.

and I feel that for many years nobody has so clearly seen my directions
toward light as you do in this article.[179]

There was a follow-up in the widely-read magazine *Minicam Photography* when
Newhall's *Kenyon Review* text was presented "with new illustrations and revisions,"[180]
integrated with skill, presumably by the magazine's associate editor, former New
Bauhaus faculty member Henry Holmes Smith.

Another sort of follow-up to Newhall's article was provided by John Crowe Ransom
(1888-1974), an influential literary figure and the editor of *The Kenyon Review,* who had
recently written:

> The photograph is a mechanical imitation perhaps but not a
> psychological one. It was obtained by the adjustment of the camera and
> the pressing of the button, actions so characterless that they indicate no
> attitude necessarily, no love; but the painting reveals the arduous pains
> of the artist.[181]

After reading Newhall's article and thinking about the photographs illustrated, Ransom
had clearly changed his mind about photography and wrote: "The functional use
disappears; they become at once remarkable, in shape, in light effect, and even in texture;
they are pure particularity now, not function."[182]

Moholy has been described by many of those who knew him as naively optimistic.
Nothing better illustrates his optimism than his plans to construct a new workshop
building on the grounds of the Field house. Since only three of the autumn enrollees had
failed to return for the spring term, and there were twenty-three new day students and
eighteen in the evening classes, there was a shortage of space.[183] Moholy fought "wie ein

---

[179]László Moholy-Nagy to Beaumont Newhall, carbon copy of TLS, June 23rd, 1941, microfilm
reel 951, frame 0359, Moholy-Nagy files, Archives of American Art, Washington, D.C.

[180]Beaumont Newhall, "Photography of Tomorrow: Moholy-Nagy Creates New Vision," *Minicam
Photography*, volume V, number 5 (January, 1942), 50-58. Newhall's entire text was included
without any change; the added text consisted of picture captions and a sidebar containing the text
of Moholy's "The 8 Categories of Photographic Vision," an early version of his "eight varieties of
photographic vision," included in *Vision in Motion*, 207-208.

[181]John Crowe Ransom, *The World's Body* (Baton Rouge: Louisiana State University Press, 1968),
209. Ransom's book had originally appeared in 1938.

[182]John Crowe Ransom, "Moholy-Nagy's New Arts," *The Kenyon Review,* volume III, number 4
(Summer, 1941), [372]-374, here 374.

[183]Sibyl Moholy-Nagy to Ise Gropius, February 7th, 1938.

A documented listing of New Bauhaus students by name is in: Engelbrecht, "Association of
Arts and Industries," 340-343. I made one error on page 340, by listing Mary Zoe Greene-Mercier

(continued...)

löwe" [like a lion] for the new building because he wanted it ready for the autumn term.[184] The proposed building would have enclosed 250,000 cubic feet and would have had five floors plus a basement; Moholy had been told by the board of the Association of Arts and Industries that sixty to seventy-five thousand dollars would be available.[185] In a letter to Gropius written in March, 1938, Moholy explained that he had made drawings (now lost) for the proposed building quickly "because I am anxious to get along with the construction" so that it could begin before September, even though he was not sure who would make the necessary working drawings; he wrote that he thought they would be made by "Messrs Holsman and Holsman," and added, "I worked very nicely together with them at the remodeling of the old house."[186] Gropius answered Moholy's letter rather promptly with some specific suggestions, such as what kind of Venetian blinds could be used, and offering a construction estimate of one-hundred and twenty-five thousand dollars.[187] But as Moholy and Gropius were to find out only a few months later, the Association of Arts and Industries had entered a period of financial instability that put an end to any thought of expanding the physical facilities of its fledgling school.

In an exchange of letters between Moholy and Gropius about setting up an architectural curriculum at the New Bauhaus, Gropius was a bit more cautious. Moholy had evidently asked Gropius for advice about having such a curriculum at the New Bauhaus. Gropius, still new in the United States, consulted with Joseph Hudnut, dean of Harvard's Graduate School of Design, of which the Architecture Department, then headed by Gropius, was a part. As a result, Gropius was able to advise Moholy about the practical problems presented by American educational and certification practices for architecture. Gropius was also concerned about the impact of the possible appointment of Mies as head of the Architecture Department at the Armour Institute of Technology in Chicago, and pointed out that if Mies did become head of the architectural program at the Armour Institute (later combined with the Lewis Institute to form the Illinois Institute of Technology), an appointment they knew was under consideration, it would be even harder for Moholy to overcome the practical difficulties of setting up his own program.[188]

---

[183](...continued)
twice, once as "Mrs. Leslie Greene" and once as "Mary Zoe Greene." I made one omission: Henry Holmes Smith should be listed as a spring-semester student, according to his "My Year with Moholy-Nagy: a Brief Memoir," October 26, 1976, typescript, Center for Creative Photography, Tucson, 7.

[184]Sibyl Moholy-Nagy to Ise Gropius, TLS, April 8th, 1938, Bauhaus-Archiv, Berlin.

[185]Sibyl Moholy-Nagy to Ise Gropius, TLS, August 16th, 1938, Bauhaus-Archiv, Berlin.

[186]László Moholy-Nagy to Walter Gropius, ALS, March 11th, 1938. As described above, Henry K. Holsman assisted Moholy in remodeling the Field house for the New Bauhaus; he was principal architect of Holsman & Holsman.

[187]Walter Gropius to László Moholy-Nagy, TLS, March 15th, 1938, Bauhaus-Archiv, Berlin.

[188]Walter Gropius to László Moholy-Nagy, carbon copy of TLS, January 24th, 1938, Bauhaus-

(continued...)

By March 9th, Gropius had been informed that Mies would accept the position at the Armour Institute, and wrote a letter to Moholy informing him of this.[189]

W HEN MOHOLY LEARNED THAT MIES was going to accept the position at the Armour Institute he tried to arrange a meeting with him, so that they could in some way co-ordinate their programs. But when Moholy mentioned the possibility of co-operating with Mies in a joint program to Stahle and the Association board, they were strongly against the idea.[190] This was probably because architectural education was not one of the Association's priorities, and also because the Armour Institute conducted its architectural classes, at the time, in classrooms in the Art Institute of Chicago. Since the Association had gone to great lengths to free its educational program from the Art Institute, it was not likely that they would have wanted any sort of affiliation that involved the Art Institute in any way. But in the face of this, Moholy's naive optimism again asserted itself; in a letter to Gropius Moholy described the aversion of the Association board to any approach to Mies, and went on to detail his own plans for adding architecture to his curriculum, including the appointment of Chicago architect George Fred Keck to the faculty planned for the next year.[191]

No relationship ever developed in Chicago between Moholy and Mies, although Moholy and his wife did attend the ceremonial dinner marking the installation of Mies at the Armour Institute, given by the Chicago Chapter of the American Institute of Architects on October 18th, 1938, in the Red Lacquer Room of the Palmer House; both Mies and Frank Lloyd Wright spoke. Sibyl Moholy-Nagy wrote about the event a few days later in a letter to Gropius.[192] Part of what she wrote was:

> Was Mies machte, war urälteste Blut und Boden Ideologie, "beseelter Stein"' "funktioneller Axthieb," "ewig Melodie der Formen"—der ganze alte Zimmt [*sic*]![193] Ich war erleichtert, dass wenigstens die

---

[188](...continued)
Archiv, Berlin.

[189]Walter Gropius to László Moholy-Nagy, TLS, March 9th, 1938, Bauhaus-Archiv, Berlin.

[190]László Moholy-Nagy to Walter Gropius, ALS, June 8th, 1938.

[191]*Ibid.*

[192]Sibyl Moholy-Nagy to Walter Gropius, two-page supplement to a letter of October 25th, 1938, TLS, Bauhaus-Archiv, Berlin. Most of the original German text of the letter was published in: Peter Hahn, "Vom Bauhaus zum New Bauhaus," 17.

[193]The best published account of Mies' speech appeared in: Peter Blake, *The Master Builders: Le Corbusier, Mies van der Rohe, Frank Lloyd Wright* (New York: W.W. Norton & Company, Inc., 1976), 229-232.

The fullest account is a five-page press release, possibly never published, dated October 18, 1938, issued by Alexander Schreiber on behalf of the Armour Institute, headed: "L. MIES

(continued...)

> Hälfte der Zuhörer kein deutsch verstand und da er anscheinend noch
> nicht ein Wort englisch kann. . . . [What Mies produced was the most
> ancient blood and soil ideology, "inspired stone," "functional axe strokes,"
> "eternal melodies of form"—all the old rubbish. It was easier to bear
> since at least half of the audience understood no German and since he
> appeared not yet to have learned any English . . .]

There were two interpreters, Arthur Woltersdorf and John Barney Rodgers; the
former was not very effective, so Rodgers took over. Evidently Sibyl Moholy-Nagy
thought that those in the audience who did not know German were not getting much
out of Woltersdorf's translation.

About Wright, Sibyl Moholy-Nagy added:

> F.L. Wright, heftig verärgert, durch eine zu kurze Einführung, machte
> einen pathetischen und sehr inhaltlosen speech auf Mies und verliess
> dann in der Mitte des Dinners den Saal, was recht peinlich war. Wir
> trafen ihn dann zufällig in der Bar und er lud uns unter dem Eindruck,
> dass das Bauhaus tot sei, gnädigst nach Taliassen [*sic*] ein. Es gibt
> natürlich keinen Zweifel an seinem Genie—aber seine persönliche
> Gegenwart ist widerlich und peinlich durch diese masslose
> Aufgeblasenheit. [F.L. Wright, greatly angered by a too short
> introduction, made a pathetic and very empty speech about Mies and
> then left the hall in the midst of dinner, in a way that was really
> embarrassing. We then encountered him by chance in the bar and,
> under the impression that the Bauhaus was dead, he most graciously
> invited us to Taliassen (*sic*). Of course there is no doubt about his own
> genius—but his personal presence is repulsive and embarrassing
> because of this enormous arrogance.]

As will be seen below, in the passages about the Guggenheim Museum, Wright made
his own unflattering comments about Moholy.

Henry T. Heald, the President of the Armour Institute of Technology, also wrote an
account of the evening, in which he described the difficulties Woltersdorf had in
interpreting Mies' speech as well as Wright's abrupt departure, and reported that after
the meeting "I found him [Wright] at the bar, where he'd been waiting out the rest of the
program."[194]

---

[193](...continued)
VAN DER ROHE ADDRESS AT TESTIMONIAL DINNER—PALMER HOUSE
10/18/38—CHICAGO." The translation varies from the excerpts that are quoted by Blake. A
copy of the press release is in the Elmer Ray Pearson papers, Chicago Historical Society.

[194]Henry T. Heald, "Mies van der Rohe at I.I.T.," *Four Great Makers of Modern Architecture:
Gropius, Le Corbusier, Mies van der Rohe, Wright; the Verbatim Record of a Symposium Held at
the School of Architecture, Columbia University, March-May, 1961* (New York: Da Capo Press,
1970), 106.

The only other documented contact between Mies and Moholy in Chicago was at the speech by Wright referred to above as described by Katharine Kuh (née Woolf; 1904-1994), who noted Mies' rudeness to Moholy on that occasion.[195]

D URING THE SUMMER of 1938 the increasingly precarious financial position of the Association was becoming more and more evident, while on campus a good bit of tension and animosity had developed, along with the creative ferment. Things came to a head during the summer and early autumn. Elkan Harrison Powell (1888-1966), a Sears, Roebuck & Company executive who was also president of the Sears-owned *Encyclopædia Britannica*, had recently become president of the Association of Arts and Industries. As Powell explained the financial situation in a letter to Gropius:

> At about the time the school opened, in October 1937, we entered a
> very bad general business depression. We were forced to sell securities
> to operate the school at 50% to 60% of their former value, and have
> been unable to secure additional funds from new sources or from
> sources that have subscribed liberally to the Association in the past.[196]

When it became apparent that funds were not available to continue the school into the second year, letters were sent out to the faculty informing them the school likely would not reopen in the fall, as detailed below. But Moholy himself was able to remain in Chicago because he signed a contract, probably in October, with Spiegel, Inc., a Chicago merchandising firm, as discussed below. Under this contract he received a salary of $10,000 for one year of service as an art advisor.[197]

Norma Stahle, who served as assistant director of the New Bauhaus while continuing as executive director of the Association, became dissatisfied with Moholy's direction of the school, although initially she and Moholy had gotten along very well together.[198]

---

[195]"An Interview with Katharine Kuh," conducted by Avis Berman, 23-24; and Kuh, *My Love Affair with Modern Art*, 78-79.

[196]E. H. Powell to Walter Gropius, ALS, August 30th, 1937, Bauhaus-Archiv, Berlin; quoted in: Sibyl Moholy-Nagy, *Moholy-Nagy; Experiment in Totality*, 162. Powell's letter was in answer to a letter to him from Gropius, photographic copy of carbon copy of TLS, August 19th, 1938, Bauhaus-Archiv, Berlin.

Powell and Gropius had met in New York for dinner on May 26th, 1938; an exchange of telegrams dated May 25th, 1938, documents the meeting. Photographic copies of Powell's telegram to Gropius, and of Gropius' telegram to Powell, are in the Bauhaus-Archiv, Berlin.

[197]Sibyl Moholy-Nagy, *Mohly-Nagy; Experiment in Totality*, 161, 163.

[198]László Moholy-Nagy to Sibyl Moholy-Nagy, MLS, August 1st, 1937, microfilm reel 951, frames 0243-0244, Moholy-Nagy papers, Archives of American Art, Washington, D.C. Moholy wrote of being Stahle's guest at a play, *You Can't Take It with You*, a comedy written by Moss Hart and George S. Kaufman. He wrote that: "Sie—glaube ich—später richtig eine freundin für uns sein wird mit ihrer bereitschaft die dinge ähnlich zu sehen wie wir. Sie hat auch eine eigene

(continued...)

Although Powell continued to support Moholy, his support was not enough, since most of the executive committee of the board of directors of the Association, some of the students, and even for a time, a few faculty members, sided with Stahle. Moreover, by November, 1938, Powell had been replaced as president of the Association by Glenn Hayes, who was also director of the Chicago Wholesale Market Council.[199] It is difficult to reconstruct all of the reasons for the dissatisfaction with Moholy, but it is evident that to some people Moholy seemed rigid in his ideas.[200] Moreover, some of the students were upset over the de-emphasis on painting in the school; they had thought of the Bauhaus in Germany in terms of the painting of Kandinsky, Klee and Moholy himself.[201]

In addition to the executive committee, the board of the Association of Arts and Industries included other members, some of whom were industrialists. They had not been active on the board, and their belated support for Moholy did little to change things. In particular Sewell Avery, president of both United States Gypsum and Montgomery Ward, and, not surprisingly, Paepcke, supported Moholy.[202]

In the end it was simply the financial failure of the Association that led to the closing of the New Bauhaus, leaving many conflicts unresolved. Stahle and the majority of the board were, in effect, saying to Moholy that they no longer had the financial resources necessary to operate the school, but that even if they did, they would not want Moholy to direct it.

Nevertheless there was a final burst of glory in the form of the student exhibition. This opened July 5th, 1938, and continued on into September.[203] (DVD figures 449, 450, 451 and 452) A large part of the credit for the success of the exhibition is due to Bulliet, who was not only a perceptive critic but a gifted writer as well. His brilliant and

---

[198](...continued)
Kultur, ich würde sagen sehr liberalreiche." [She, I believe, will later be truly a friend for us with her readiness to see things similarly to us. She is a cultured person, and I would say, very liberal.]

[199]Glenn Hayes to Walter Gropius, photographic copy of ALS, November 5th, 1938, Bauhaus-Archiv, Berlin. The letter is written on New Bauhaus stationery and signed by Glenn Hayes as President.

[200]Hin Bredendieck disagreed with Moholy's ideas about organization of the workshops, and about his own role, and Stahle seemed to agree with Bredendieck. Moholy described the situation in a letter, László Moholy-Nagy to Walter Gropius, ALS, June 6th, 1937, Bauhaus-Archiv, Berlin.

[201]Discussed at length by Moholy in: László Moholy-Nagy to Walter Gropius, photographic copy of ALS, June 6th, 1937, Bauhaus-Archiv, Berlin; the point of view of some of the students is discussed in: Koppe, "The New Bauhaus, Chicago," 239-242.

[202]Sibyl Moholy-Nagy to Ise and Walter Gropius, photographic copy of TLS, January 5th, 1939, Bauhaus-Archiv, Berlin.

[203]"Exhibition: Work from the Preliminary Course, 1937-1938, The New Bauhaus, American School of Design," mimeographed. A copy is in the Institute of Design Papers, Library of the University of Illinois in Chicago.

intriguing review for *The Chicago Daily News*[204] was promptly quoted by art magazines published in New York[205] and London.[206] The exhibition also received a favorable review in the well-known weekly news-magazine, *Time*.[207] (Actually, there had been an exhibition of student work at the end of the autumn semester also, but it received less attention.)[208]

Forceful attention was brought to the school by a national commercial printers' journal, *More Business*, in its November, 1938 issue, devoted entirely to the New Bauhaus. Included was a cover in color designed by Kepes and two articles by Moholy,[209] accompanied by illustrations featuring student work and a color photograph by Moholy, respectively.[210] (DVD figure 453)

Further recognition came with the inclusion of student and faculty work from the New Bauhaus in the large exhibition, *Bauhaus 1919-1928*, at the Museum of Modern Art in New York,[211] referred to in Chapter Three. The exhibition opened December 6th, 1938, and included work by New Bauhaus students Nathan Lerner and Richard Koppe.[212]

---

[204] "Around the Galleries," *The Chicago Daily News*, July 9, 1938, 13. Bulliet's review was re-published, in English, in Hahn and Engelbrecht, editors, *50 Jahre New Bauhaus*, 109-110.

[205] "The Bauhaus Touch," *Art Digest*, volume XII, number 19 (August 1, 1938), 27.

[206] B. Holme, "Chicago," *The London Studio: an Illustrated Magazine of Fine and Applied Art*, volume XVI, number 116 (November, 1938), 268-269.

[207] "Bauhaus: First Year," *Time: the Weekly Newsmagazine*, July 11, 1938, 21.

[208] Sibyl Moholy-Nagy to Ise Gropius, February 7th, 1938; and László Moholy-Nagy to Walter Gropius, TLS, Bauhaus-Archiv, Berlin.

[209] László Moholy-Nagy, "New Approach to Fundamentals of Design," and "Color Photography," *More Business: the Voice of Letterpress Printing and Photo-engraving*, volume III, number 11 (November, 1938), 4-8 and 13, respectively.

The front cover of *More Business*, Moholy's illustrated article on color photography, and two pages of student work are reproduced in: Hahn and Engelbrecht, editors, *50 Jahre New Bauhaus*, 244-247.

[210] The photograph on page 13 of *More Business* (December, 1938) is *Moebius Rings*, a Dufay color photograph of 1935.

[211] "Nazi-Banned Art Is Exhibited Here; Museum of Modern Art Honors Bauhaus, Famous School, by Showing Examples of Work; 700 Items Are Included; Institution Had Wide Influence on Modern Design Until It Displeased Hitler Regime," *The New York Times*, December 4, 1938, 40.

[212] Herbert Bayer, Walter Gropius and Ise Gropius, editors, *Bauhaus 1919-1928* (New York: The Museum of Modern Art, 1938), 216. Moholy had taken the initiative by writing to Alfred Barr, the Director of the Museum of Modern Art, "I wanted to ask your collaboration in incorporating our new Bauhaus in a nice way in this exhibition . . .", László Moholy-Nagy to Alfred Barr, photocopy

(continued...)

(DVD figures 434, 454, 455 and 456) Lerner's contribution, *Light Volume* (DVD figure 455), was made with the light box that he invented as student at the New Bauhaus.[213]

Of course *Bauhaus 1919-1928* helped to build Moholy's reputation as well, and it was for its catalogue that he wrote his summary of his work in the Metal Workshop at the Bauhaus, "From Wine Jugs to Lighting Fixtures."[214] He also wrote about his foundation course at the Bauhaus.[215] At least three of his paintings and drawings were shown,[216] in addition to six of his photographs,[217] examples of his work in graphic and exhibition design,[218] and his *Light Prop for an Electrical Stage*,[219] shown in motion.[220]

At about the same time as *Bauhaus 1919-1928* was showing at the Museum of Modern Art, a new edition of Moholy's *The New Vision* appeared, published by W.W. Norton & Company of New York, as mentioned above, and it was stunning. This edition contained still more New Bauhaus student work.[221] More than 1,000 copies had

---

[212](...continued)
of carbon copy of TLS, September 15th, 1937, Bauhaus-Archiv, Berlin.

[213] Concerning the light box, see: Engelbrecht, "Educating the Eye: Photography and the Founding Generation at the Institute of Design, 1937-46," 25 and 27.

[214] László Moholy-Nagy, "From Wine Jugs to Lighting Fixtures," in: Herbert Bayer, Walter Gropius and Ise Gropius, editors, *Bauhaus 1919-1928*, 134-[139].

[215] *Ibid.*, [88]-89 and 122-125.

[216] *Ibid.*, 191 and 197.

[217] *Ibid.*, 152-153 and [155].

[218] *Ibid.*, 78-79, 146-147, 149, 206, 208 and 210.

[219] *Ibid.*, 210.

[220] The exhibition was installed by Herbert Bayer and Beaumont Newhall (see: Beaumont Newhall to Lloyd C. Engelbrecht TLS, January 20th, 1979, original in my files and a copy in the Bauhaus-Archiv, Berlin). After the exhibition closed, but while the *Light Prop* was still at the Museum of Modern Art, Moholy asked Newhall to have a photograph taken of it while it was in motion; see: László Moholy-Nagy to Beaumont Newhall, February 24th, 1939.

[221] László Moholy-Nagy, *The New Vision: Fundamentals of Design, Painting, Sculpture, Architecture,* translated by Daphne M. Hoffmann, revised and enlarged edition, The New Bauhaus Books, no. 1, editors Walter Gropius, L. Moholy-Nagy (New York: W.W. Norton & Company, Inc, 1938), figures 11-15, 16a, 16b, 43-50, 77, 78, 105a, 105b, 138, 163, 164, 177, 178 and 179. This edition was also published in London in 1939 by Faber & Faber.

been sold by Christmas of 1938,[222] and before the holiday, booksellers had already been told that the edition had been completely sold out.[223]

All of these successes must be seen in the context of the financial crisis the Association of Arts and Industries was experiencing, but this crisis did not extinguish Moholy's optimism. He would not give up his cherished plans without a struggle and sought to raise funds to continue operating the New Bauhaus. He thought he had the approval of the Association's board for these efforts, and that the board would cover his travel expenses; hence he spent the period of July 18th to August 11th, 1938, in attempts at fund raising,[224] traveling through Michigan, Ohio, Pennsylvania, Delaware, New York and New Jersey. No money was raised, but gifts of materials were secured and valuable contacts for the future were made.[225] But the full extent of the Association's financial troubles was probably not made clear to Moholy until after he returned to Chicago from his trip.

WHILE HE WAS ON THE EAST COAST, Moholy gave a lecture at Byrdcliffe on July 27th (as described above) and renewed his acquaintance with Katherine Dreier when he and Sibyl visited her and her art collection at her home, "The Haven," in West Redding, Connecticut.[226] In her living room they saw two works of Marcel Duchamp, *The Large Glass* (first shown at an exhibition at the Brooklyn Museum in 1926 in which Moholy was also represented) as well as *Tu m'*, installed above the living-room bookcase in 1931 in the space for which it had been created. *The Large Glass* had been severely damaged in 1927 and reconstructed by Duchamp in Dreier's home, a reconstruction completed in the summer of 1936. (DVD figure 457) Moholy thus was among the small group of people who saw the reconstructed work before it went on public display in 1943.

In her thank-you note for Dreier's hospitality, Sibyl wrote: "Moholy recalled all the works of art he saw, mainly of course the Duchamps, which left him deeply

---

[222] Sibyl Moholy-Nagy to Ise and Walter Gropius, photocopy of ALS, December 24th, 1938, Bauhaus-Archiv, Berlin.

[223] Katherine Dreier to László Moholy-Nagy, carbon copy of TLS, January 10th, 1939, Katherine Dreier Papers, box 24, folder 700, Beinecke Rare Book and Manuscript Library, Yale University, New Haven, Connecticut.

[224] See the court documents cited in note 241.

[225] Sibyl Moholy-Nagy, *Moholy-Nagy: Experiment in Totality*, 157-159; and Sibyl Moholy-Nagy to Ise Gropius, August 16th, 1938.

[226] László Moholy-Nagy to Katherine Dreier, MLS, July 19th, 1938, Katherine Dreier Papers, box 24, folder 700, Beinecke Rare Book and Manuscript Library, Yale University, New Haven, Connecticut; and Sibyl Moholy-Nagy to Ise Gropius, August 16th, 1938.

impressed."[227] Moholy also admired some of Dreier's own works, and because of his comments to her about them he was asked to write an introduction to the set of reproductions of her lithographs to be issued in an edition of eighty copies.[228] Reproductions of the lithographs had been made in Paris under the supervision of Duchamp.[229] Moholy promptly accepted the invitation to write the introduction.[230]

The summer itinerary of the Moholys included first visits to two houses now considered masterpieces; at the time one was nearly finished and one was recently finished. These are the Gropius house at Lincoln, Massachusetts (Gropius and Breuer, 1937-1938),[231] and "Fallingwater," the Kaufmann house at Bear Run, Pennsylvania (Frank Lloyd Wright, completed 1936).[232]

Moholy had developed plans for the second year of the New Bauhaus, and a catalogue was issued. The starting date was to be September 26th. Xanti Schawinsky, who had studied with Moholy at the Bauhaus, was to join the faculty; another faculty member was to be Herbert Bayer, who had studied and taught at the Bauhaus.[233] Also announced as a faculty member in the catalogue was Jean Hélion (1904-1987), a French painter who had instead returned to Europe, joined the French army, was captured and held as a German prisoner of war, and then escaped.[234] He gave a lecture on his war experiences for the School of Design in Chicago early in 1943, followed by another lecture, "Simplicity and Complexity in Art."[235] Two of the possible appointments are

---

[227] Sibyl Moholy-Nagy to Katherine Dreier, MLS, August 30th, 1938, Katherine Dreier Papers, box 24, folder 702, Beinecke Rare Book and Manuscript Library, Yale University.

[228] Katherine Dreier, *1 to 40 Variations*, Introduction by L. Moholy-Nagy (Springfield, Massachusetts: The Pond-Ekberg Company, 1939). See also: Katherine Dreier to László Moholy-Nagy, January 10th, 1939.

[229] Katherine Dreier to László Moholy-Nagy, January 10th, 1939.

[230] László Moholy-Nagy to Katherine Dreier, MLS, January 10th [*sic*], 1939, Katherine Dreier Papers, box 24, folder 700, Beinecke Rare Book and Manuscript Library, Yale University, New Haven, Connecticut.

[231] Walter and Ise Gropius and their daughter Ati moved into their new house on September 21st, 1938; see: Peter Gittleman, "The Gropius House: Conception, Construction, and Commentary" (M.A. Thesis, Boston University, 1996), 44-45.

[232] Sibyl Moholy-Nagy to Ise Gropius, August 16th, 1938.

[233] *The New Bauhaus: American School of Design* [Catalogue for 1938-1939], 8.

[234] Jean Hélion, *They Shall Not Have Me (Ils Ne M'auront Pas): the Capture, Forced Labor, and Escape of a French Prisoner of War* (New York: The Golden Eagle Press, and Books, Inc., distributed by E.P. Dutton & Company, Inc., 1943).

[235] László Moholy-Nagy to F.P. Keppel, carbon copy of typed letter, January 7th, 1943, Institute of

(continued...)

intriguing, even though the second year of the New Bauhaus did not take place: Jean (Hans) Arp (1887-1966) and Piet Mondrian.[236]

OMINOUS LETTERS were sent to the faculty members of the New Bauhaus beginning with one dated August 16th, 1938. The first of these letters, sent by Edna Vergonet, secretary of the New Bauhaus, advised that "It is probable that the Bauhaus will not open this fall," and that ". . . if you are offered any other position you had better take it." She added that: "An official notice will be sent from the Association later."[237] On September 12th, 1938, a letter was sent to the faculty members signed by Norma K. Stahle and advising them of the probability that the school would not open in the fall, and that they should plan accordingly, although the letter still held out the hope that the school would reopen "at some future time."[238] Finally, September 26th passed and the school indeed did not reopen.

Moholy tried meeting with the executive committee of the Association's board to work out a fund-raising plan, but no agreement was reached.[239] On October 14th, 1938, Moholy, who had, after all, once planned to be a lawyer, brought a law suit against the Association of Arts and Industries, which had given him a five-year contract.[240] He had sued for $2,750 in back wages and re-imbursement of expenses;[241] his attorney was J.

---

[235](...continued)
Design Papers, University of Illinois Library, Chicago; and László Moholy-Nagy to Myron Kozman, TLS, December 14th, 1942; copies are in my files and in the files of Hattula Moholy-Nagy.

[236] Sibyl Moholy-Nagy, *Moholy-Nagy; Experiment in Totality*, 154. According to a letter Mondrian wrote in 1939, Sweeney negotiated with him and Arp: ". . . Pictures, sculptures decoration are of no use in new life and are an obstacle to realize it now in the present. Because I am sure that you feel most of this above as I do feel it, I do not understand that you have spoken to Mr. Sweeney, as he told me, not only about me, but also about Arp to have at the [New] Bauhaus. Arp is a great artist, but nothing for our future environment." Mondrian's letter was published in: Richard Kostelanetz, editor, *Moholy-Nagy*, Documentary Monographs in Modern Art (New York: Praeger Publishers, 1970), 176-177; and in: Piet Mondrian, *The New Art—the New Life; the Collected Writings*, edited by Harry Holtzman and Martin S. James, translated by the editors (Boston: G.K. Hall & Co,, 1986), 310-311.

[237] A xerox copy of one of these letters, Edna Vergonet to Henry Holmes Smith, TLS, September 12th, 1938, is in the Institute of Design Papers, University of Illinois Library, Chicago.

[238] A xerox copy of one of these letters, Norma K. Stahle to Henry Holmes Smith, TLS, August 16th, 1938, is in the Institute of Design Papers, University of Illinois Library, Chicago.

[239] Sibyl Moholy Nagy, *Moholy-Nagy: Experiment in Totality*, 160-162.

[240] *Chicago Tribune,* October 16, 1938, 18.

[241] *Ibid.*; "Bauhaus Blowout," *Time: the Weekly Newsmagazine*, October 24, 1938, 38; and *Moholy-Nagy (plaintiff) vs. Association of Arts and Industries (defendant)*, File No. 38c14366, Docket #

(continued...)

Robert Cohler of Kelly & Cohler. Eventually the suit was settled out of court;[242] there was some consideration of awarding Moholy a mortgage on the Field house,[243] but in the end only chairs and equipment still in the Field house (as described below) proved to be the only benefit Moholy received from the suit. As one measure of the bitterness of the proceedings, Norma Stahle stated in a deposition that the only reason Gropius had recommended Moholy to the Association was because Moholy had had a love affair with his sister-in-law.[244] Of course Moholy and Ellen Frank, the sister of Ise Gropius, did have a love affair, as described in Chapter Four. But Moholy found this statement to be "mean and low,"[245] and he knew that Gropius's support was based on an assessment of his professional abilities and the similarities of their aims. Stahle's bitterness was not anticipated by Moholy, upon whom she had made a very positive first impression, as described above.

Perhaps behind Stahle's bitterness was a situation similar to what might have helped to make her unhappy with the Association's arrangement with the Art Institute: her concern with the lack of hands-on co-management in that case had its echo in the New Bauhaus. In spite of Moholy's very positive first impression of Stahle, and even though he had written of her that: "In fifteen years of quiet and persistent work she broke the ground and prepared the understanding for the idea of Bauhaus education in this country,"[246] he somehow never seemed to have realized the true nature and extent of her efforts. In fact she had presented guest speakers, organized symposia and exhibitions, and recruited to the Association's cause leading figures in the arts and design.[247] (Her contacts with Frank Lloyd Wright, mentioned above, provide an example of this.) Moholy does not seem to have involved Stahle in his own efforts to bring in guest speakers and to set up exhibitions.

---

[241](...continued)
92, Fee Book 394/539, Pg. 588, Register 129, Judge Harry M. Fisher, Circuit Court of Cook County.

[242] As recorded on an undated one-page stipulation signed by the attorneys for both sides, probably late in November; the stipulation is part of the file cited in the previous note.

[243] Sibyl Moholy-Nagy to Ise and Walter Gropius, photocopy of TLS, December 24th, 1938, Bauhaus-Archiv, Berlin. The letter, in German, mentioned only the possibility of a mortgage, and I have not found any documentation of a mortgage or possible mortgage other than this letter. Nevertheless, in her book, possibly with the intent of making a cleaner narrative, Sibyl stated that her husband *had* been awarded a mortgage (*Moholy-Nagy; Experiment in Totality*, 162-163).

[244] László Moholy-Nagy to Walter Gropius, photocopy of ALS, November 15th, 1938, Bauhaus-Archiv, Berlin.

[245] *Ibid*.

[246] László Moholy-Nagy, "Why Bauhaus Education?", 10.

[247] Engelbrecht, "The Association of Arts and Industries," 60-67, 77-85 and 109-124 *passim*.

But there was another legal issue between Moholy and the Association, in addition to Moholy's salary. Gropius and Moholy actually took legal action to block the Association's possible future use of the name "Bauhaus."[248] In spite of its financial difficulties, the Association of Arts and Industries sought to re-open the school late in 1938 with Archipenko as director and Bredendieck as a member of the faculty.[249] Sibyl Moholy-Nagy was especially taken aback because Archipenko had been at her apartment the day before the announcement and had seemed very friendly.[250] On the other hand, Glenn Hayes, who, as noted, had succeeded Powell as president of the Association of Arts and Industries, made efforts, directly and through Bredendieck, to get Kepes to continue teaching at the school but these efforts came to nothing, despite both bribes and threats, because of the continuing loyalty Kepes felt toward Moholy.[251] Ironically these attempts to retain three teachers from the New Bauhaus were a kind of *de facto* tribute by Hayes to the quality of the educational enterprise Moholy had set up. But efforts to retain part of Moholy's faculty were beside the point because the Association simply lacked the resources to continue. It never did re-open the New Bauhaus, and instead went out of existence not long after the school's closing, probably at some time in 1939. But in the end it is worth noting that Moholy bore no long-term grudge against Bredendieck or Archipenko, and both were later invited by him to teach at the I.D.[252]

Early in 1939, Moholy and some sympathetic teachers organized a new school, initially known as the School of Design, a name later lengthened to School of Design in Chicago. The teachers, all of whom initially taught without salary,[253] included Moholy, Kepes, Schiltz and Dushkin from the faculty of the first year of the New Bauhaus, Keck from the planned additions to the faculty for its canceled second year, and Robert J. Wolff (1905-1977), a sculptor and painter. The continuing service of physicist Eckart, biologist Gerard and philosopher Morris from the New Bauhaus faculty received

---

[248] Glenn Hayes to Walter Gropius, ALS, November 5th, 1938; Walter Gropius to J. Robert Cohler, photocopies of carbon copies of typed letters, November 17th, November 19th and November 29th, 1938; two-page typed draft of a letter, Walter Gropius to Association of Arts and Industries, November, 1938; J. Walter Cohler to Walter Gropius, photocopy of ALS, November 12th and November 29th, 1938; all of these are in the Bauhaus-Archiv, Berlin.

[249] Sibyl Moholy-Nagy to Walter Gropius, October 19th, 1938, ALS, Bauhaus-Archiv, Berlin; and György Kepes interviewed by Robert Brown, March 7th and August 30th, 1972, and January 11th, 1973, page 16.

[250] *Ibid.*

[251] György Kepes interviewed by Robert Brown, March 7th and August 30th, 1972, and January 11th, 1973, pages 16-17 and 19.

[252] On the re-appointment of Archipenko, see: "Minutes of Board of Directors' Meeting of Institute of Design, January 15, 1946," mimeographed, item 11; a copy is in the Institute of Design Papers, University of Illinois Library, Chicago.

[253] Sibyl Moholy-Nagy to Ise and Walter Gropius, TLS, March 6th, 1939, Bauhaus-Archiv, Berlin.

favorable notice in the influential journal *Parnassus*, published by the College Art Association.[254]

Moholy and his colleagues co-signed an announcement dated January 17th, 1939, which went out to prospective students.[255] The announcement offered to open classes "at the end of February" if sufficient enrollment could be obtained. A more confident follow-up announcement set registration for February 23rd, with classes to begin the next day.[256] The opening was promptly reported in *Time*, notable because it is a general news-magazine that covers only a limited number of art-related stories:

> Mid snow and ice in Chicago last week, Ladislaus Moholy-Nagy, famed Hungarian designer and onetime head of Chicago's ill-nurtured New Bauhaus, marched on, opened his own School of Design with three new instructors and seven New Bauhauslers, 30 [*sic*] faithful students.[257]

QUARTERS WERE FOUND FOR THE SCHOOL in a former commissary, with a ceiling height of seventeen feet, on the second storey of a loft building at 247 East Ontario Street on the Near North Side (Benjamin Marshall & Charles Eli Fox,1917).[258] (DVD figures 458, 459, 460 and 461) In an informal agreement with the Association of Arts and Industries, New Bauhaus faculty members who were still owed salary were allowed to take chairs and equipment from the former Field house as compensation.[259] Enrollment consisted of eighteen day students and twenty-nine night students, many of them from the student body of the New Bauhaus.[260] Moholy was especially pleased with the student exhibition held in July, after the School of Design had been in operation for one only semester; he wrote to Gropius that: "We have had a great number of visitors and it seems to me that our reputation is revived in this country.

---

[254]John Alford, "Practical Courses in College Art Departments: a Survey," *Parnassus*, volume XII, number 7 (November, 1940), 11-[15], here 13-[15].

[255]A copy of the announcement is in the Institute of Design Papers, University of Illinois Library, Chicago.

[256]A copy of the anouncement is in the Institute of Design Papers, University of Illinois Library, Chicago.

[257]"Excelsior," *Time: the Weekly Newsmagazine*, March 6, 1939, 25.

[258]Takeuchi, "School of Design in Chicago," 7-8, 10-12, 15-18, 20-21, and 30-32.

The commissary had originally been used for Horn & Hardart cafeterias, and most recently for the disbanded Raklios chain of Chicago restaurants. The massive commissary ovens were converted into photography studios.

[259]György Kepes interviewed by Robert Brown, March 7th and August 30th, 1972, and January 11th, 1973, pages 18-19; and Sibyl Moholy Nagy, *Moholy-Nagy: Experiment in Totality*, 163.

[260]"Student list - semester - February-June, 1939," Robert J. Wolff files, microfilm reel 69-73, frame 0471, Archives of American Art, Washington, D.C.

This was exactly the goal I set for myself when these gangsters [*i.e.*, the Association of Arts and Industries] almost ruined us."[261]

   Two of the visitors to the July, 1939, exhibition of the School of Design were Al and DeVera Bernsohn, who wrote an illustrated article on the school's photographic achievements for the San Francisco magazine *Camera Craft*. Their article began with these words:

> We met Moholy-Nagy. And the barriers, that formerly indicated to us the limitations of photography, tumbled—to be supplanted by new, flexible boundaries, farther apart. Photography broadened, widened, deepened.[262]

They added:

> Probably the most striking phase of the new approach taught at the School of Design is the unusual, but perfectly logical, conception of light. Nathan Lerner, a brilliant scholar in the school, explained his interpretation of light to us: "Usually light was not considered as plastic means, only as an auxiliary medium to indicate material existence. Now a new period starts wherein light will be used as a genuine means of expression because of its own qualities, own characteristics."[263]

Of Moholy and the photogram, the Bernsohns wrote: ". . . we find Moholy-Nagy the foremost exponent of photograms in the world. . . . He achieves effects of almost metaphysical power with his photograms."[264] These observations led to a note on the creation of photograms in the School of Design as part of the discussion of photograms in their small but comprehensive manual for photographers, wherein the Bernsohns described photograms as "a branch of photography as yet almost completely unexplored and uncharted."[265]

   Another visitor to the July, 1939, student exhibition at the School of Design was *Chicago Tribune* critic Eleanor Jewett, who, as noted below, still had a considerable reputation as an opponent of modern art and, indeed, before the year was out would write an unfavorable review of a showing at the Katharine Kuh Gallery of the work of

---

[261] László Moholy-Nagy to Walter Gropius, photocopy of TLS, July 15th, 1939. Bauhaus-Archiv, Berlin.

[262] Al and DeVera Bernsohn, "Moholy-Nagy, Iconoclast," *Camera Craft*, August, 1939, 357-364, here 357.

[263] *Ibid.*, 360.

[264] *Ibid*, 362.

[265] Al and DeVera Bernsohn, *Developing, Printing and Enlarging*, Little Technical Library (Chicago: Ziff-Davis Publishing Company, 1939), 84.

Moholy's one-time Bauhaus colleague Paul Klee.[266] But Jewett nevertheless had earlier hailed the opening of the New Bauhaus,[267] and went on to write this about the student exhibition:

> The School of Design, 247-257 East Ontario street, under the direction of L. Moholy-Nagy, is doing much that is interesting. Did you by chance happen to see, in their student exhibition held recently, the new type of chair made entirely from plywood slabs? It weighed no more than six pounds and was a delightful achievement.
>
> The summer session is now on in the school, but if you should go in to visit do not miss the work of the class in sculpture [taught by Robert J. Wolff]; here something most remarkable is being achieved, especially through the investigation of new space problems.[268]

THE NEW SCHOOL WAS LAUNCHED with very limited financial resources. Of the former board members of the Association of Arts and Industries, only Walter Paepcke stepped forward to support the new school. After his wife, Elizabeth, known as "Pussy" (née Nitze; 1902-1994), enrolled in the evening class in photography during the initial semester,[269] the Paepckes decided to make available to the school an abandoned farm house and two acres of land in northern La Salle County, Illinois, just south of the small village of Somonauk and about seventy miles southwest of Chicago.[270] (DVD figures 462A and 462B) This became the location for a series of summer sessions beginning in 1939, for the most part managed by Sibyl Moholy-Nagy, as described in numerous letters she exchanged with her husband.

Walter Paepcke began to give the school even more active support in 1940. He had been a board member only during the final year of the Association of Arts and Industries, but he evidently was not very active in that capacity, and hence was aloof from the tension between Moholy and Stahle. But Paepcke proved to have the fund-raising ability that the Association had demonstrated in the 1920s. The funds raised through his efforts,

---

[266] Avis Berman, "The Katharine Kuh Gallery: an Informal Portrait," in: Prince, editor, *The Old Guard and the Avant-garde*, 155-169 and 258-259, here 160.

[267] Eleanor Jewett, "School for Design Will Open Oct. 18."

[268] Eleanor Jewett, "Artist Tells Background of New Painting" [*i.e.*, column heading not related to the School of Design], *Chicago Tribune*, August 13, 1939, part 8, page 4.

[269] "Student list - semester - February-June, 1939," Robert Jay Wolff files, microfilm reel 69-73, frame 0471, Archives of American Art, Washington, D.C.

[270] The village of Somonauk is located in southern De Kalb County, but the farm used by the school was located just over the border in La Salle County. The property was known as the "Rumney Farm," and is described in a document for a four-year renewal of the lease (for the nominal sum of one dollar per year) dated February 23rd, 1945, signed by Elizabeth and Walter Paepcke, and signed and dated March 8th, 1945 by Moholy, microfilm reel 951, frame 0449, Moholy-Nagy Papers, Archives of American Art, Washington, D.C.

along with his personal gifts of money and those of his family, and the grants from his firm, the Container Corporation, were essential to the continuity, growth and enhancement of the School of Design in Chicago and, later, the I.D. Paepcke put quite a bit of effort into this, as evidenced by thick files of letters now in the Institute of Design Papers, University of Illinois Library, Chicago. Generally he solicited donations from men who headed major Chicago business concerns, but, late in 1945, reporting on what was surely his most intensive campaign, he reported having sent out ". . . about 1200 letters to all types of individuals who might be prospective donors to the school."[271]

As a means of engaging them in financial support and other means of assisting the School of Design, Paepcke put a considerable amount of effort into convincing business leaders that it could serve their needs in various ways, such as offering training for their employees in night classes. One early example of his efforts to engage business leaders is the meeting he set up on June 6th, 1940, to discuss "how the School of Design can best meet the industrial and business needs of Chicago." This meeting took place at the Racquet Club, an upscale establishment at 1365 North Dearborn Street (Andrew Rebori, 1923). Among those who attended were meat-packer Oscar Mayer, then serving as president of the Chicago Association of Commerce; clothing manufacturer Ray Manning of Hart Schaffner & Marx; A.J. Snow of Sears, Roebuck; Carl V. Haecker, head of display at Montgomery Ward; Frank B. Cornell, an executive of dry-goods distributor Butler Brothers; and furniture manufacturer William Bachrach of The Dearborn Company.[272] Those who attended the June 6th meeting were then invited to a preview on June 11th of the year-end exhibition at the School of Design.[273]

An indication of community support for the School of Design came from John H, Millar, publisher of *Millar's Chicago Letter*. In summer, 1940, he devoted an entire eight-page issue to the school. Included were illustrations, a two-page article by Moholy, "Relating the Parts to the Whole," and a description of a recent commission from the

---

[271] Walter P. Paepcke to Walter Gropius, carbon copy of TLS, December 17[th]tt, 1945, Institute of Design Papers, University of Illinois Library, Chicago.

[272] Oscar Mayer to Walter P. Paepcke, TLS, June 3rd, 1940; Ray Manning to Walter P. Paepcke, TLS, May 31st, 1940; Frank B. Cornell to Walter P. Paepcke, TLS, May 31st, 1940; William Bachrach to Walter P. Paepcke, TLS, May 31st, 1940; and "Acceptances, School of Design luncheon, Racquet Club, June 6" (mimeographed); all of these are in the Institute of Design Papers, University of Illinois Library, Chicago.

   As noted below, Bachrach later served as chair of the Committee on Education of the Chicago Association of Commerce, and his name appeared on School of Design letterhead as a member of its Sponsors Committee.

[273] László Moholy-Nagy to Oscar Mayer, carbon copy of TLS, June 6th, 1940; and László Moholy-Nagy to Frank B. Cornell, carbon copy of TLS, June 6th, 1940; both of these are in the Institute of Design Papers, University of Illinois Library, Chicago.

Kaufmann Department Store of Pittsburgh for an exhibition apartment, complete with student-made furnishings.[274]

By mid-1942 Paepcke had not found his early efforts to support the School of Design sufficiently encouraging,[275] and he had decided that the school would be best served if it could be incorporated into an existing educational institution. One early choice was the Illinois Institute of Technology,[276] but the first efforts to bring the School of Design into that institution bore no fruit, a bit ironic in view of the fact that after Moholy died the Institute of Design did merge with I.I.T. In the short term, Moholy seems to have inspired Paepcke to continue his support with a letter of August 5th, 1942:

> I have said it so often, and I know that with words such things cannot be expressed adequately enough, that without you we could not have gotten so far. Your unemphasized, none the less radiating confidence in us helped us to withstand our difficulties.
>
> When you became active in soliciting funds for the School it electrified not alone Sibyl and myself but all the people around us. This concrete assurance of your confidence in the School is as much to us as the financial help which we have received through you, and I hope that the development of the School will give you the justification of your devotion.[277]

Moholy's assertions in his letter were not exaggerated. In spite of Paepcke's recurring doubts, it is clear that without his own financial support and his fund-raising efforts, Moholy could not have continued his educational efforts in Chicago for very long. But equally important was Paepcke's moral support of Moholy and his ability to interpret Moholy's educational program to the business and industrial community of Chicago. Much of this was in person and cannot be documented, but a three-page memorandum, dated December 20th, 1944, provides an example of how effective Paepcke was. At that time I.D. board member Leverett S. Lyon was serving as Chief Executive Officer of the Chicago Association of Commerce. Some tough questions

---

[274]"The School of Design in Chicago," *Millar's Chicago Letter*, volume II, number 23 (August 5, 1940).

[275]Sibyl Moholy-Nagy to László Moholy-Nagy, TLS, June 8th , 1942, microfilm reel 951, frames 0404 and 0405, Moholy-Nagy Papers, Archives of American Art, Washington, D.C.

[276]*Ibid.*

Further consideration was given to a merger with I.I.T. in the autumn of 1945, but no action was taken because Moholy had become seriously ill with leukemia. See: "Minutes of Board of Directors' Meeting of Institute of Design, October 2nd, 1945," item 8, and *ibid.*, November 6th, 1945, item 6, mimeographed. See also Walter P. Paepcke, carbon copy of TLS, December 21st, 1945. All three items are in the Institute of Design Papers, University of Illinois Library, Chicago.

[277]László Moholy-Nagy to Walter P. Paepcke, TLS, August 5th, 1942, Institute of Design Papers, University of Illinois Library, Chicago.

about the I.D. and its fund-raising efforts had been presented to Lyon by the manager of the Association's subscription-investigating department, Jesse A. Jacobs. For example, one question was whether the I.D. was "a one-man school" centered around Moholy and thus unable to carry on the work outlined in its bulletins. These questions were turned over to Paepcke, whose memorandum, addressed to Jacobs, gave thoughtful and effective answers to each of the questions, and concluded:

> . . . I may say that while the Institute is being given support by a substantial number of commercial and industrial concerns, it also is receiving the support of scores of individuals who believe, as I do, that the Institute provides a cultural stimulus to this area and who feel that all of us do more to support human beings when they are down and out and not enough to teach and equip the talented members of the younger generation to become useful and vital participants in the life of the city through an education which combines science, craftsmanship and art.[278]

In addition to the money Paepcke donated and raised, the most important financial support came from two New York-based philanthropic foundations: $10,000 from the Carnegie Corporation in 1940,[279] and $7,500 in 1941,[280] plus $7,500 from the Rockefeller Foundation in 1942.[281] The latter grant for the School of Design in Chicago was ". . . to enable it to incorporate into its curriculum work with silent and sound motion pictures." Interestingly, it was added: "The School will offer fundamental training for students as well as amateurs who want to learn cinematic technique,"[282] thus demonstrating Moholy's continuing interest in the role amateur film-makers can play, as seen in Chapter Four.

The prestige of the School of Design was enhanced by the "Sponsors Committee," announced in the handsome sixteen-page catalogue issued for the 1939-1940 school year.[283] Initially the committee included: John Dewey, Walter Gropius, Joseph Hudnut and Alfred H. Barr. Another member was William Bachrach, the furniture manufacturer

---

[278] Typed memorandum, "Mr. Jacobs" to "Mr. Lyon," December 12th, 1944, and Walter P. Paepcke to Jesse A. Jacobs, TLS, December 20th, 1944; both are in the Institute of Design Papers, University of Illinois Library, Chicago.

[279] "School of Design Is Given $10,000 'for Pioneering'; Bauhaus Art College Gets Carnegie Grant to Extend Work," *The Chicago Daily News*, February 7th, 1940, 17.

[280] László Moholy-Nagy to Walter Gropius, copy of TLS, August 13th, 1941, Bauhaus-Archiv, Berlin.

[281] "Educational," *The Architectural Forum*, volume LXXVII, number 2 (August, 1942), 106. On the Rockefeller foundation and Moholy's schools in Chicago, see: Margolin, *The Struggle for Utopia*, 239-241.

[282] *Ibid*.

[283] *School of Design, 247 East Ontario Street, Chicago, Illinois*, [Catalogue for 1939-1940], inside of front cover.

who chaired the Committee on Education of the Chicago Association of Commerce. Later the name of biologist Julian Huxley was added.[284] While the committee, whose members' names appeared on its letterhead, may have added to the prestige of the School of Design, it never met as a group, and most of the members were not active in support of the school. However, Moholy did have a more active relationship with Dewey and Barr. He had two meetings with Dewey in New York late in 1938.[285] During one of these visits Dewey presented Moholy with a copy of his recently-published *Experience and Education*.[286] And Moholy developed friendly relations with Barr and co-operated on a notable project, even though, curiously, he had forgotten Barr's visit to the German Bauhaus[287] (discussed in Chapter Three). The Sponsors Committee served until March, 1944, when the school's name was changed to the Institute of Design and a functioning board of directors was set up by Paepcke and Moholy.

T HE PRINCIPAL ACTIVITY by Chicagoans related to the Museum of Modern Art in New York while its Director, Alfred Barr, served on the Sponsors Committee of the School of Design in Chicago was a traveling exhibition, *Light As a Means of Expression*. It was seen at the Museum of Modern Art from September 16th to November

---

[284]Huxley, who had become friends with Moholy while both were living in England, as described in Chapter Four, wrote about the School of Design in Chicago in a letter, Julian Huxley to James M. Landis, February 12th, 1942; Huxley wrote that he ". . . was much impressed with the extraordinary ingenuity displayed and with the valuable results obtained when there is a synthesis of artist, scientist, and the craftsman and expert in materials." Huxley sent a copy to Moholy with a covering note; the copy and the note are in the Institute of Design Papers, University of Illinois Library, Chicago.

[285]Sibyl Moholy-Nagy to Ise and Walter Gropius, January 5th, 1939, photocopy of carbon copy in Bauhaus-Archiv, Berlin.

[286]John Dewey, *Experience and Education*, Kappa Delta Pi Lecture Series (New York: The Macmillan Company, 1938).

Dewey wrote of this encounter with Moholy in a letter to Charles Morris, then Professor of Philosophy at the University of Chicago and part-time faculty member at the New Bauhaus and the School of Design in Chicago. The encounter was later described in a letter, Charles Morris to Lloyd C. Engelbrecht, TLS, June 3rd, 1968, Institute of Design Papers, University of Illinois Library, Chicago.

See also: Findeli, "Moholy-Nagy's Design Pedagogy," 14-15. Findeli dated the letter from Dewey to Morris as December 2nd, 1938, and reported that a copy of the letter was owned by the late Elmer Ray Pearson.

Dewey had been closely involved with educational innovation in Chicago around the turn of the last century, and in particular had been a supporter of the manual training movement, which aimed to "send the whole boy to school." This was no doubt part of the reason for his interest in Moholy's school. See Engelbrecht, "Association of Arts and Industries," 24-25.

[287]László Moholy-Nagy to Walter Gropius, photographic copy of MLS, September 21st, 1937, Bauhaus-Archiv in Berlin. Moholy wrote of Barr: ". . . er hat mich in Europa nie besucht. . . ." [. . . he never visited me in Europe . . .]

2nd, 1942. Preceding that showing had been a tour of eight boys preparatory schools in New England and Illinois begun November 15th, 1941. There was also a tour of three universities (including North Texas State Teachers College in Denton) in 1943 and a final showing in 1947 at the Everhard Museum in Scranton, Pennsylvania.[288] The exhibition, organized by Moholy, Kepes and Lerner, consisted of fifteen panels of photographs and photograms and a penlight drawing created by faculty and students of the School of Design, along with two photograms by Man Ray.[289]

Although a total of only forty-seven students had registered during the spring, 1939, semester, this number greatly increased in succeeding semesters. By the autumn, 1942, semester there were twenty day students and 188 night students, for a total enrollment of 208. Many of the night students were employees of business and industrial firms which encouraged selected employees to attend the school. These firms then paid all or part of their tuition fees. Factors which limited the size of the student body were, first, the lingering economic depression, and then the War.

Additions to the faculty in the autumn of 1939 included George Barford, Eugene Bielawski (1911-2002), Leonhard Nederkorn and Marli Ehrman (1904-1982; née Marie Helene Heimann).[290] Ehrman, who had studied at the Bauhaus in Germany, organized a textile and weaving workshop.[291] Her studies at the Bauhaus included the foundation course under Moholy; the two of them, plus Bredendieck, were the only members of the faculty with direct links to the Bauhaus except for Werner Drewes (1899-1985), a former Bauhaus student who taught briefly at the I.D. in 1945.[292]

A SOCIAL HIGHLIGHT of the first full year of the School of Design was reminiscent of the social life of the German Bauhaus. This was student participation on January 12th, 1940, in Chicago's third annual Architects Ball, a fund-raising event for architectural education. It was held in the spacious Trianon Ballroom (no longer

---

[288] Michelle Harvey to Elizabeth Siegel, TLS, August 10th, 1998, files of the Photography Department of the Art Institute of Chicago; and László Moholy-Nagy, *Vision in Motion*, [196]-197.

[289] Museum of Modern Art Archives, New York, Department of Circulating Exhibitions, C/E 111.1 65 (1).

[290] *School of Design, 247 East Ontario Street, Chicago, Illinois*, [Catalogue for 1939-1940], 10.

[291] On Ehrman, see: Sigrid Wortmann Weltge, *Women's Work; Textile Art from the Bauhaus* (San Francisco: Chronicle Books, 1993), 10, 172, 176-179, 202 *et passim*. It should be noted that in the United States Ehrmann sometimes dropped the second letter "n" in her name.

[292] László Moholy-Nagy, *Vision in Motion*, [6] and [148]; Caril Dreyfuss, editor, *Werner Drewes Woodcuts* (Washington, D.C.: Published for the National Collection of Fine Arts, by the Smithsonian Institution Press; for sale by the Supt. of Documents, U.S. Government Printing Office, 1969), 11; and Peter Hahn, "About Werner Drewes, Zu Werner Drewes," in: Ingrid Rose, *Werner Drewes; a Catalogue Raisonné of his Prints, Das Graphische Werk*, edited by Ralph Jentsch (Munich: Verlag Kunstgalerie Esslingen, 1984), 19-24, here 23-24.

extant), that was located at the corner of East 62nd Street and South Cottage Grove Avenue. School of Design student participation included making decorations for the ball, known as "Call Out the Gods," and guests were costumed as their favorite mythological figures. *Life* magazine covered the event.[293] Its story included a photograph of "A wire-and-plywood Venus . . . constructed by pupils at the Moholy-Nagy school of design." That Venus was made by Robert Preusser and two other students; there was also a photograph of Preusser and three other students carrying another Venus, "Venus on the Half Shell," this one featuring a live model.[294] (DVD figures 463 and 464)

The use of tools at the School of Design can be illustrated by an account written by a student in Eugene Bielawski's foundation course. Beatrice Takeuchi wrote:

> Gene put us through an intense primer on the use of the power tools—table saw, band saw, jigsaw, jointer and planer, drill press, belt sander, disk sander, grinder, buffer, wood and metal lathes, and later, the pipe bender, corrugating machine, and assorted welding equipment. Although women students were outnumbered by men, we were not excluded from shop work nor did we seek exemption. The big table saw was a terror, but as we each received instruction from Gene in passing the wood material with our hand safely inches away from the shrieking blade, the knowledge of the machine and training in its use finally demystified the monster. The tools did not have the safety features they have now. One of the endearing sounds heard throughout the school at any time was that of the table saw cutting through plywood, which seemed to be the loudest.[295]

This provides a sharp contrast with the attitudes at the German Bauhaus. Because one of Moholy's star pupils in the tool-intensive Metal Workshop there was a woman (Marianne Brandt), it should not be overlooked that Gropius was usually opposed to admitting women into the tool-intensive workshops such as metal and carpentry.[296]

---

[293]"Life Goes to the Architects Ball: 2,000 Chicagoans Cavort as their 'Favorite Myths'," *Life*, February 5, 1940, 80-82 (picture credits on page 83).

[294]*Ibid.*, 80 and 81, respectively; and Robert Preusser to Lloyd C. Engelbrecht, TLS, undated, from an envelope postmarked January 10, 1978 (in my files).

[295]Takeuchi, "School of Design in Chicago," 11.

[296]Anja Baumhoff, *The Gendered World of the Bauhaus: the Politics of Power at the Weimar Republic's Premier Art Institute, 1919-1932* (Berlin: Peter Lang, 2001), 59-61.

Additions to the faculty during the later years of the School of Design[297] included Nathan Lerner (1913-1997),[298] Charles Niedringhaus, Frank Barr (1906-1955), Calvin Albert (1918-2007), Frank Levstik,[299] Hubert Leckie (1913-1993), Frank Sokolik, James Prestini (1908-1993),[300] Myron Kozman (1916-2002), Johannes Molzahn,[301] Robert Delson (1909-1955),[302] Sarah Taylor Leavitt, Yuichi Idaka (born 1914),[303] Robert Bruce Tague[304] and others. Prior to teaching, Tague had been an evening student at the school, in the spring and fall semesters of 1939.[305] Else Regensteiner (1906-2003) was assistant

---

[297]Although it is not quite complete, the best listing of Moholy's faculty colleagues in Chicago is to be found in: Findeli, *Le Bauhaus de Chicago*, Annexe 1 following page 417.

[298]On Lerner, see: Nicholas Pavkovic, "Nathan Lerner and the New Bauhaus," *Pulp Magazine* (Winter, 1989), front cover, [3-4] and 43-59; Lloyd C. Engelbrecht, "Lerner, Nathan Bernard," in: Kenneth T. Jackson, editor, *The Scribner Encyclopedia of American Lives* (New York: Charles Scribner's Sons, 2002), 338-340; and Astrid Böger and Robert Manley, editors, *Modernist Eye: The Art and Design of Nathan Lerner* (Raleigh: Gallery of Art & Design, North Carolina State University, 2000).

[299]*School of Design in Chicago*, [Catalogue for Spring and Fall, 1941], 12.

[300]*School of Design in Chicago*, [Catalogue for Spring and Fall, 1941], 12. On Prestini, see: Lloyd C. Engelbrecht, "Prestini, James," in: Colin Naylor, editor, *Contemporary Designers*, second edition (Chicago: St. James Press, 1990), 466-467.

[301]László Moholy-Nagy to Johannes Molzahn, TLS, December 31st, 1942; Johannes Molzahn to László Moholy-Nagy, carbon copy of typed letter, January 5th, 1943; László Moholy-Nagy to Johannes Molzahn, TLS, January 12th, 1942 [*sic*; should read 1943]; László Moholy-Nagy to Johannes Molzahn, TLS, February 2nd, 1943; Sibyl Moholy-Nagy to Walter Gropius, photographic copy of carbon copy of typed letter, February 8th, 1943; László Moholy-Nagy to Johannes Molzahn, TLS, August 24th, 1943; all of these are in the Bauhaus-Archiv, Berlin. On Molzahn, see: Herbert Schade, *Johannes Molzahn; Einführung in das Werk und die Kunsttheorie des Malers* (Munich: Schnell & Steiner, 1972).

[302]László Moholy-Nagy to Robert Delson, TLS, April 25th, 1944, May 3rd, 1944 and February 19th, 1945; all three letters are in the Robert Delson Papers, University of Illinois Library, Chicago.

[303]Idaka was a photographer who was born in Seattle in 1914, lived in Japan from 1915 to 1928, and was graduated in 1937 from the University of Chicago with a B.S. degree in chemistry. On Idaka, see: "Institute of Design, Meeting of the Board of Directors, November 14, 1944," mimeographed, Institute of Design Papers, University of Illinois Library, Chicago.

[304]Költzsch and Tupitsyn, editors, *Bauhaus: Dessau, Chicago, New York*, 257; and *School of Design in Chicago*, [Catalogue for Spring and Fall, 1941], 12.

[305]From lists of students at the School of Design on a microfilm reel 69-72, frames 0471 and 0472, Robert J. Wolff files, Archives of American Art, Washington, D.C. On Tague, see: Blum, "Interview with Robert Bruce Tague."

to Ehrman beginning in 1939, and joined the faculty in 1942.[306] Children's classes were headed by Gordon Webber (1912-1986), Juliet Kepes, Robert D. Erickson (1917-1991) and others.

ONE VERY SPECIAL ATTEMPT to bring a new faculty member into the School of Design did not meet with success: Lucia Moholy was invited to join the faculty in 1940 but was blocked by her inability to get a visa from the United States Consulate in London and to book passage while resident in England. Since Britain and Germany were belligerents there was no possibility she could visit her German lover, Theodor Neubauer, or aid him in any way, and thus she had no personal reason to remain in Europe.

The effort to bring Lucia to Chicago began with a letter of July 15th, 1940, confirming an agreement on a three-year contract to begin September 15th, 1940, with a monthly salary of two-hundred dollars.[307] At the time Britain was at war but the United States was not. The documents submitted to the American Consul General in London seemed to be adequate to support a visa and the requisite passage on a commercial carrier from wartime Britain to neutral United States. There was a letter of record from Moholy to the Consul General of September 12th, 1940, affirming the offer of a contract, and a letter from Lucia to the Consul General of November 27th, 1940, applying for a visa. There are numerous other papers in the Lucia Moholy files in the Bauhaus-Archiv in Berlin that document the efforts to bring Lucia to Chicago, among them copies of two telegrams from Johannes Itten confirming that Lucia Moholy had taught in his school for two years.[308] Documents submitted by her brother, Franz Spencer, included a copy of his United States income-tax form covering the year 1939 showing a good income as a screen-writer as well as from some investments.[309] But what followed for Lucia was an extended tale of missed opportunities, the difficulty of getting commercial transportation out of wartime England and nitpicking by American consular authorities as to her professional qualifications in spite of the offer to her of a contract to teach at the School of Design. Meanwhile Lucia had to move from her London apartment in Mecklenburgh

---

[306]Weltge, *Women's Work*, 179, 180, 182, 183 and 204.

[307]László Moholy-Nagy to Lucia Moholy, TLS, July 15th, 1940, Bauhaus-Archiv, Berlin.

[308]The telegrams from Johannes Itten are dated October 23rd and November 21st, 1940. In the former Itten wrote that "I confirm Luzia [*sic*] Moholy was teacher and lecturer of photography in my school for two years 1930 to 1931," and in the latter he wrote "I confirm that Miss Lucia Moholy was leading the photo class of the Itten School at Berlin as a head teacher and this to the satisfaction of all."

[309]The Lucia Moholy files in the Bauhaus-Archiv, Berlin, include an embossed and notarized four-page income-tax form, plus one page with supporting information; a signed and notarized "Affidavit of Support," listing a house Spencer owned and some income from investments, addressed to "Cunard White Star Ltd."; and a signed and notarized letter to the American Consul in London from a bank officer in Beverly Hills listing the amount Spencer had on deposit and offering the opinion that he is "financially responsible for any commitment he may undertake."

Square after a bomb fell near it (she moved to a remote location on the outer reaches of the London underground railway system).

Moholy was careful to include music in his curriculum in Chicago. David Dushkin was listed in the School of Design's academic year 1939-1940 catalogue as teaching a course in music and building musical instruments.[310] In the following academic year it was announced that: "Music Appreciation will be given by David Dushkin with the assistance of Miss Patricia Berkson."[311] Dushkin and Berkson were initially listed to teach music appreciation in the fall of 1941,[312] but were not listed in later announcements for the 1941-1942 academic year.[313] In their place John Cage taught "sound experiments" on Wednesday evenings during that academic year.[314] In the fall quarter, Cage reported that: "Gordon [Webber] is taking my class at the Bauhaus (I have 4 other students all of them free)."[315] He had met Webber the previous year at Mills College, as recounted below. Since the faculty was still not being paid, Cage was evidently to receive no salary unless he had paying students.

C AGE WAS INTERESTED IN TEACHING at the School of Design in Chicago partly because he was looking for a base for his idea of establishing a Center for Experimental Music. Moholy supported the idea, but had no money to fund it and Cage would have had to do the fund-raising, which he was unable to do.[316] Cage earned some income from working as composer-accompanist for dance teacher Kay Manning at the University of Chicago, and as an accompanist at Hull House, while he tried, without success, to get Northwestern University in Evanston to fund "experimental work in Radio music."[317]

---

[310] *School of Design, 247 East Ontario Street, Chicago, Illinois*, [Catalogue for 1939-1940], 10.

[311] *School of Design in Chicago, Day and Evening Classes, 1940-41*, folder with no pagination.

[312] *School of Design in Chicago*, [Catalogue for Spring and Fall, 1941], 12.

[313] *School of Design in Chicago, Day and Evening Classes . . . 1941-42*, folder with no pagination.

[314] *School of Design in Chicago, Evening Session [1941-1942]*, 4 and [19].

Cage's classes were described in: Robert J. Wolff, *Essays on Art and Learning* (New York: Grossman Publishers, 1971), 12-13.

[315] John Cage to Doris Dennison, MLS, October 26th, 1941, John Cage Archive, Northwestern University, Evanston, Illinois, C5A.20.

[316] Richard Kostelanetz, *Conversing with Cage*, second edition (New York: Routledge, 2003), 10-11.

[317] John Cage to Doris Dennison, October 26th, 1941.

After Cage left, music at the school was dropped, except for occasional lectures by pianist Margit Varró and composer Ernst Krenek.[318] Krenek, whom Moholy had known about at least as early as the summer of 1923, appeared Saturday, February 19th, 1944, to introduce a recital of contemporary music; on that occasion Felix Witzinger played piano music by Bartók, Chavez, Gershwin, Honegger, Milhaud and Stravinsky.[319]

Although his interest in getting a faculty member to teach art history continued after his unsuccessful effort to engage either Sweeney or Giedion,[320] Moholy never was able to realize this goal. As noted above, he did bring in Giedion from time to time for lectures. The first of these lectures was in late spring, 1939, and drew two-hundred and fifty people.[321] A series of lectures enriched a summer session in Chicago when Giedion lectured daily from July 27th to August 5th, 1944, on "town planning problems."[322] One student remembered that he ". . . conducted a week-long seminar for students on planning, a subject new to us, on a scale that stretched the notion of design from a fountain pen to the penultimate." One assignment consisted of papers read in class based on readings in planning and its history.[323]

Additions to the part-time faculty who taught academic subjects included sociologist William Lloyd Warner (1898-1970), economist Maynard C. Krueger (1906-1991), and semanticist Samuel I. Hayakawa (1906-1992; Hayakawa was later to become a United States Senator from California).

Although I would like to emphasize that while the I.D. would not have survived and flourished without Moholy, he was a complex person, and one particular aspect of his personality sometimes led to difficulty with his faculty. In many ways, including in his educational philosophy, Moholy seemed anti-authoritarian; moreover, he had very generously re-hired both Archipenko and Bredendieck after they had tried to undercut him in his dealings with the Association of Arts and Industries. But there was, nevertheless, a streak of authoritarianism in Moholy; this was most evident in his relationships with Kepes and then with Molzahn, who had been brought in to serve as a

---

[318]László Moholy-Nagy, *Vision in Motion*, 70.

[319]Findeli, *Le Bauhaus de Chicago*, 66.

[320]"Report of Progress of the School of Design in Chicago under the Grant of the Carnegie Corporation of New York of $10,000. Dated February 1st, 1940." A carbon copy is in Institute of Design Papers, University of Illinois Library, Chicago. On page 4 appears these words: "We would like to have an art historian. . . ."

[321]László Moholy-Nagy to Walter Gropius, July 15th, 1939.

[322]László Moholy-Nagy to Robert J. Wolff, MLS, May 31st, 1944, reel 69, frames 0361 and 0362, Robert Jay Wolff files, Archives of American Art, Washington, D.C.; and "Institute of Design, President's Report, June 22, 1944," mimeographed, Institute of Design Papers, University of Illinois Library, Chicago.

[323]Takeuchi, "School of Design in Chicago," 19-20.

replacement for Kepes. This tendency was recognized by Sibyl Moholy-Nagy, who once confided in a letter to Gropius about ". . . occasional bursts of authoritarianism to which Moholy is prone."[324]

When a serious disagreement developed between Moholy and Kepes in the late autumn of 1942, Sibyl Moholy-Nagy observed that settling the matter was difficult because: ". . . Kepes could not find the right tone because too much of the past had stood between him and Moholy. . . ."[325] Briefly, Kepes and Moholy each wrote long, typed, stiff and formal but angry letters. Kepes' letter, dated October 23rd, was to Keck, with a copy to Moholy;[326] Moholy's letter was dated November 19th, 1942, and was to Kepes.[327] On November 3rd, 1942, Keck sought to mediate. In a brief note to Moholy on that date, with a copy to Kepes, he wrote:

> I received a letter from Jerry Kepes dated 23rd of October, of which you received a carbon copy.
>
> In the letter Jerry wants to do certain things, and I suggest that the three of us, you Jerry and I have a meeting at my office. This meeting to take place tomorrow at five o'clock (Thursday) at my office at the above address.[328]

On the surface most of the disagreement, hard to understand in retrospect, seemed to be about a course in camouflage; there was also an argument by Kepes that a constitution and a board of trustees would benefit the school; as noted, the School of Design in Chicago had only an advisory board called the Sponsors Committee.

A part of the difference was no doubt personal. Kepes had been associated with Moholy for a long time and, since he was eleven years younger, Moholy had been something of a father figure, or at least an older-brother figure to Kepes. Keck, on the other hand, was the same age as Moholy. Moreover, the design work accomplished by Kepes in Berlin and in London had been credited solely to Moholy, without acknowledging his contribution; this no doubt contributed to Kepes's conflicted feelings about Moholy. In the end Keck's efforts at mediation came to nothing. Perhaps no one could have mediated the dispute, or perhaps Sibyl Moholy-Nagy was right when she

---

[324] Sibyl Moholy-Nagy to Walter Gropius, photographic copy of TLS, February 8th, 1943, Bauhaus-Archiv, Berlin.

[325] Sibyl Moholy-Nagy to Walter Gropius, February 8th, 1943.

[326] György Kepes to George Fred Keck, carbon copy of typed letter, October 23rd, 1942, Keck Papers, State Historical Society of Wisconsin, Madison.

[327] László Moholy-Nagy to György Kepes, carbon copy of typed letter, November 19th, 1942, Keck Papers, State Historical Society of Wisconsin, Madison.

[328] George Fred Keck to László Moholy-Nagy, carbon copy of typed letter, November 3rd, 1942, Keck Papers, State Historical Society of Wisconsin, Madison.

wrote that: ". . . Keck is too much of a petit bourgeois, loathe to take sides. . . ."[329]
Kepes resigned from the School, effective as soon as he could be replaced; his original
plan was to do free-lance work in collaboration with his wife, Juliet (née Appleby; 1919-
1999),[330] a New Bauhaus and School of Design student and, as noted above, teacher of
children's classes.

Kepes soon decided to accept an offer to teach in the art department at North Texas
State Teachers College (now University of North Texas) in Denton, and began teaching
there in 1943. (DVD figures 465 and 466)   Moholy himself had given a lecture at the
Texas State College for Women (now Texas Woman's University), also in Denton, early
in 1942,[331] had visited there in April of 1942,[332] and had gone on to teach there from June
3rd to June 20th.[333]   Moholy was invited to the school by Mary Marshall, director of the art
department from 1930 to 1948, who is credited with modernizing the department and
creating a progressive atmosphere.[334]   She had visited Sibyl and László in Chicago.[335]

In Denton, both Moholy and Kepes developed a close working relationship with
Carlotta Corpron (1901-1987), a Modernist photographer who taught at the Texas State

---

[329]Sibyl Moholy-Nagy to Walter Gropius, February 8th , 1943.

[330]László Moholy-Nagy to Loretto and Johannes Molzahn, TLS, December 31st, 1942, Bauhaus-
Archiv, Berlin.

[331]The lecture was remembered by Dorothy Antoinette LaSelle, a faculty member of the Texas
State College for Women, as in the winter of 1942; see: Keri Kesler, editor, *Dorothy Antoinette
LaSelle: an Oral History, interviewed by Dawn Letson, October 25, 1994, December 7, 1994, and
January 26, 1995* (Denton, Texas: The Woman's Collection, Texas Soman's University, 2000),
29-30.

[332]László Moholy-Nagy to Johannes Molzahn, TLS, May 29th, 1942, Bauhaus-Archiv, Berlin.

[333]*College Bulletin—Catalogue, Texas State College for Women, Denton, Texas, Number 285,
February 15, 1942, Summer Session—1941*, 22.

[334]Erin L. Waugh, "'Designing with Light'": Carlotta Corpron and the New Bauhaus" (M.A. thesis,
University of North Texas, 1992), 15-16.

[335]Sibyl Moholy-Nagy to László Moholy-Nagy, TLS with manuscript addition at bottom of second
page, June 10th, 1942, microfilm reel 951, frames 0406-0407, Moholy-Nagy Papers, Archives of
American Art, Washington, D.C.

College for Women.[336] A photograph of 1944 by Corpron, *Pattern of Light on a Glass Brick*, was included in Moholy's *Vision in Motion*.[337]

At the urging of faculty member Dorothy Antoinette LaSelle (1901-2002), Marshall invited Moholy to present his June workshop at the Texas State College for Women. Founded in 1901 as the Girls Industrial College, and known from 1905 to 1934 as the College of Industrial Arts, the school's Art Department resembled the Bauhaus and the School of Design in Chicago in that it was organized into workshops. This facilitated Moholy's work in Denton, and thus the student newspaper reported:

> Laboratory work in the workshop conducted by Mr. Moholy, assisted by members of the TSCW art faculty, is being done each afternoon. Miss Mary Marshall, director of the department, has charge of paper construction; Miss Thetis Lemmon, metal and plastics; Miss Carlotta Corpron, photography; Miss Dorothy A. LaSelle, and Miss Elizabeth Mitchell, wood and plastics, tactile charts and textile studies; and Miss Mattie Lee Lacy, clay.
>
> Unique and already of far-reaching influence on design in America is Mr. Moholy's belief that talent is potential in everyone and that the function of education is "to uncover it, activate it, and develop it."[338]

Corpron's students made photograms, and also made light modulators using paper and then photographed them. Corpron remembered:

> At the end of the three-week workshop we were able to put up an exhibit of about fifty photograms and light modulators. Moholy-Nagy remarked that he had never known such empathy between teacher and students.[339]

---

[336]On Corpron, see: Waugh, "'Designing with Light'"; Martha A. Sandweiss, *Carlotta Corpron, Designer with Light*, foreword by Gyorgy Kepes (Austin: Published for the Amon Carter Museum, Fort Worth, by the University of Texas Press, 1980); Margaret K. Mitchell, *Recollections: Ten Women of Photography* . . . (New York: The Viking Press, 1979), 48-65 and 200; and Christian John Gerstheimer, editor, *Texas Bauhaus: the Photographs of Carlotta Corpron, Ida Lansky and Barbara Maples* (El Paso: El Paso Museum of Art, 2006).

[337]László Moholy-Nagy, *Vision in Motion*, 186. Moholy discussed the inclusion of this photograph in a lost letter, László Moholy-Nagy to Carlotta Corpron, August 26[h], 1946; excerpts are quoted on a single-page typed document "Opinions I value," by Carlotta Corpron, The Woman's Collection, Texas Woman's University, Denton.

[338]"Moholy-Nagy Lectures on Workshop Program," *The Lass-o: Student Weekly Publication of the Texas State College for Women*, June 12, 1942, 2.

[339]Carlotta Corpron, quoted in: Mitchell, *Recollections: Ten Women of Photography*, 49.

The showing of photographs, on Friday, June 19th, was described as a "big exhibit," and it was reported that preparing for it left students almost "too busy to talk."[340]

Moholy also gave a series of lectures.[341] Pleased with his work in Denton, László reported to Sibyl that his lectures were well attended and that the student group, numbering fifty, was good. He added:

> I have the good luck that the regular teachers—because they wanted to work with me—remained here and took over different groups: wood, plastic, metal, clay, photo, paper cut. In this way I can switch from one group to the other and give demonstration or advice and can leave the students with the teachers. Everything is well organized . . . the whole atmosphere is good. . . .[342]

There was a follow-up to the sessions in Denton: later in the summer of 1942 LaSelle observed the School of Design classes in Somonauk for two weeks and the next summer she enrolled for the summer term there.[343]

Kepes later taught at Brooklyn College and at the Massachusetts Institute of Technology. He maintained an intellectual connection with the School of Design in Chicago through *Language of Vision*, his book describing his teaching there, published in 1944;[344] this book has continued to serve as a basic text in many art and design schools, and has done more to spread Bauhaus teaching methods than any other single publication, except perhaps for the various editions of Moholy's *The New Vision*. Among the many illustrations Kepes included a photograph by Corpron,[345] along with many photographs of the work of students and faculty at the School of Design. For his part, Moholy included Kepes in the text and illustrations in his *Vision in Motion*. Moreover, as related below, in the summer of 1946 Moholy suggested Kepes as a possible successor to head the Institute of Design. Had Moholy lived longer it seems likely that his friendship with Kepes would have been renewed. Sibyl Moholy-Nagy was delighted by the appearance of *Language of Vision*, and made a point of sending a copy

---

[340]"Art Workshop Stresses Originality, Creatorship," *The Lass-o: Student Weekly Publication of the Texas State College for Women*, June 19, 1942, 2.

[341]"Moholy-Nagy Lectures on Workshop Program," 2.

[342]László Moholy-Nagy to Sibyl Moholy-Nagy, June 16th, 1942.

[343]Kesler, editor, *Dorothy Antoinette LaSelle: an Oral History*, 31-32.

[344]György Kepes, *Language of Vision* (Chicago: Paul Theobald, 1944). The first in-depth study of *Language of Vision* is: Michael Golec, "A Natural History of a Disembodied Eye: the Structure of Gyorgy Kepes's *Language of Vision*," *Design Issues*, volume XVIII, number 2 (Spring, 2002), 1-16.

[345]Kepes, *Language of Vision*, [61].

to Lucia Moholy in London.[346] Moholy also cited *Language of Vision* in his *Vision in Motion* as one of the "most important" books on the Bauhaus.[347]

Molzahn was appointed against the advice of Gropius. Since Moholy was busy, he asked his wife to respond to Gropius' concerns. Molzahn was three years older than Moholy, and Sibyl confided to Gropius (in a letter also quoted from above) that:

> I personally feel, and that has to remain between me and you, that the fact that Molzahn is a very matured person and a definitely shaped personality will provide a better balanced school government, since it will check occasional bursts of authoritarianism to which Moholy is prone.[348]

The hopes of Sibyl Moholy-Nagy were soon dashed. Molzahn was offered an appointment, and he accepted it on short notice. He arrived in Chicago on February 5th, 1943, and was a house guest of the Moholys on his arrival.[349] But by the end of the summer he had decided to leave the School of Design in Chicago. He did agree to teach an additional year to allow Moholy time to find a replacement.[350] But in a letter of resignation dated July 28th , 1944, he wrote that he wished to leave at the end of the summer term:

> You will remember that several times during this past year I have postponed my resignation. With the passing of the year however, I have come to a deeper realization that there is no possibility of a beneficial cooperative effort between us. The centering of our interests lie in opposite directions and seemingly cannot be reconciled. In addition, the methods you employ in handling school matters run counter to the belief[s] I hold.[351]

Moholy replied that in spite of ". . . apparent differences in educational and administrative practices, . . ." he was sorry to see Mohzahn leave, and assured him that: "Even though there have been differences of opinion concerning many points connected

---

[346] Sibyl Moholy-Nagy to Lucia Moholy, TLS, May 8th, 1946, Bauhaus-Archiv, Berlin.

[347] László Moholy-Nagy, *Vision in Motion*, 64.

[348] Sibyl Moholy-Nagy to Walter Gropius, February 8th, 1943.

[349] Johannes Molzahn to László Moholy-Nagy, carbon copy of typed letter, January 27th, 1943; László Moholy-Nagy to Johannes Molzahn, TLS, February 2nd, 1943; both are in the Bauhaus-Archiv, Berlin.

[350] László Moholy-Nagy to Johannes Molzahn, TLS, April 24th, 1943, Bauhaus-Archiv, Berlin.

Concerning Molzahn's classes, see: Takeuchi, "School of Design in Chicago," 38-40 and 48.

[351] Johannes Molzahn to László Moholy-Nagy, carbon copy of TLS, July 28th, 1944, Bauhaus-Archiv, Berlin.

with the running of the Institute I am convinced of your sincerity and goodwill."[352] One might conclude that Sibyl Moholy-Nagy's hunch about the role Molzahn might have played was insightful, but in the end Molzahn did not succeed in having much influence on Moholy. In any case, a highlight of his tenure at the School of Design in Chicago was an exhibition there of his work as part of a group exhibition of faculty and students that opened October 30th, 1943.[353]

SEPARATE SUMMER SESSIONS had been held in 1939 in both Chicago and Somonauk. But instead of these sessions, in the summer of 1940 the School of Design in Chicago presented a special visiting session at Mills College in Oakland, California, at the invitation of the head of its Art Department, Alfred Neumeyer (1901-1973).[354] It ran from June 23rd until August 3rd. Although Mills College is a women's college, the summer sessions are co-educational. The School of Design faculty who participated in the 1940 Mills summer session included Moholy, Kepes, Wolff, Prestini, Niedringhaus, Webber and Ehrman.[355] (Summer sessions were resumed at both Chicago and Somonauk in 1941.)

At Mills College Moholy himself gave an advanced seminar that met Fridays from 9:00-noon and from 2:00-4:00,[356] as well as a public lecture on the campus, "The Aims of Bauhaus Education," on June 28th. Three of his films were shown on Friday evening, July 12th: *Impressions of the Old Harbor at Marseille*, 1932, *Großstadt Zigeuner*, 1932, and *A Lightplay Black White Gray*, 1932.[357]

Moholy and Neumeyer carried on an extensive correspondence, and met in Chicago in January, 1940, during Neumeyer's visit there. The correspondence discussed

---

[352]László Moholy-Nagy to Johannes Molzahn, TLS, July 28th, 1944, Bauhaus-Archiv, Berlin.

[353]An announcement was printed by Frank Barr: see microfilm reel 69-73, frame 0405, Robert J. Wolff files, Archives of American Art, Washington, D.C.; see also: Christian Gries, "Johannes Molzahn (1892-1965) und der 'Kampf um die Kunst' im Deutschland der Weimarer Republik" (Ph. D. dissertation, Universität Augsburg, 1996), 1:290, 2:[9] and list of paintings shown in Chicago on unnumbered pages.

[354]On Neumeyer, see: Alfred Neumeyer, *Lichter und Schatten: eine Jugend in Deutschland* (Munich: Prestel-Verlag, 1967).

Neumeyer was a teacher of my wife, June, who also served as his graduate assistant. I met him in her company in the summer of 1961, and again met with him in December, 1967.

[355]"Mills College, California, June, 1940, Schedule for Art Courses in the Summer Session," mimeographed, microfilm reel N69-72, frame 0645, Robert J. Wolff files, Archives of American Art, Washington, D.C.

[356]*Ibid.*

[357]"Three Pictures Will Be Shown at Mills," *Oakland Tribune*, July 12, 1940, B-18.

equipment, exhibitions, and other details.[358] One letter sent by Moholy to Neumeyer contains a touching detail:

> . . . we agree that salaries will be paid in proportion to the amounts which the teachers receive (or should receive regularly) during the year. (The sense of this sentence is that we have basic salaries for our teachers but in the last year, for example, we did not pay a penny on salaries because we gave our services without any compensation to our school.)[359]

Of course Moholy and his faculty were paid at Mills College; the details were worked out by Moholy and Neumeyer.[360]

IN ADDITION TO the classes, Moholy organized an exhibition of faculty and student work for the Mills College Gallery; this was later circulated by the Western Association of Art Museum Directors to Portland, Oregon, and other locations.[361] Included were 17 works by Moholy (among them four paintings on rhodoid mounted on wooden frames); 14 works by Wolff (mostly drawings and watercolors); 23 photograms by Kepes; a woven wall hanging by Ehrman; 17 turned wooden bowls and trays by Prestini; and student work including pieces of sculpture, hand sculptures, tactile charts, paper cutting and folding exercises, weaving, posters and photograms.[362]

Neumeyer had prepared the way for the summer session by booking the traveling version of the Museum of Modern Art's *Bauhaus 1919-1928* into the Mills College Art Gallery; the traveling version was called *The Bauhaus: How It Worked*.[363] It was shown from April 3rd through May 5th, 1940, and was highlighted by an April 21st lecture by Neumeyer, "Contribution of the Bauhaus to Art and Education."

---

[358]This correspondence is in the Institute of Design Papers, University of Illinois Library, Chicago.

[359]László Moholy-Nagy to Alfred Neumeyer, October 12th , 1939, TLS, Institute of Design Papers, University of Illinois Library, Chicago. See also: Sibyl Moholy-Nagy to Ise and Walter Gropius, March 6th, 1939.

[360]Alfred Neumeyer to László Moholy-Nagy, carbon copies of typed letters, October 26th and November 16th, 1939; László Moholy-Nagy to Alfred Neumeyer, TLS, November 17th, 1939; all of these are in the Institute of Design Papers, University of Illinois Library, Chicago.

[361]"Faculty and Students in College Display," *Oakland Tribune*, June 30, 1940, B-7. The traveling exhibition was described in: "Exhibition of Work from the School of Design in Chicago, January 7 through January 31," *Portland Art Museum Bulletin*, volume II, number 5 (January, 1941), 2-3.

[362]A six-page mimeographed list of works shown, including instructions for mounting Moholy's four rhodoid pictures and a scheme for displaying the student work, is in the Institute of Design Papers, University of Illinois Library, Chicago.

[363]"Bauhaus Exhibit at Mills College," *Oakland Tribune*, April 14, 1940, page B-7; Alfred Neumeyer to László Moholy-Nagy, copy of TLS, November 11h, 1939, Institute of Design Papers, University of Illinois Library, Chicago.

The genesis for the invitation to Mills College was probably Moholy's two lectures in April, 1939, at an annual meeting of the Pacific Arts Association in San Francisco.[364] The meeting perhaps took on added importance since it was held during the Golden Gate International Exposition, which had opened on Treasure Island in San Francisco Bay on February 18th, 1939.

Not long after Moholy's two lectures in San Francisco, Mills College sent Dean Rusk (1909-1994), Associate Professor of Government at Mills College and Dean of the Faculty,[365] to visit the School of Design in Chicago to extend the invitation.[366] Later, the President of Mills College, Aurelia Henry Reinhardt, paid a visit to Moholy's school.[367] She wrote that: "I have spent two fruitful hours at the School of Design. Moholy-Nagy is business-like, efficient in plans, and clear in his exposition of equipment needs and expectation of achievement."[368]

The 1940 Summer Session was deemed a success, and actually made money for Mills College. An invitation to return the following summer was extended by Neumeyer, but Moholy decided not to accept it.

It is always hard to gauge the long-term effect of an educational endeavor. Designer David Rowland (born 1924) recently described the importance to him of his student experiences in the summer of 1940 at Mills College. Rowland related that as a young man in Stockton, California, he had told his father, a museum director, that he wanted to become a designer. His father sent him to the Mills summer session, where he attended Moholy's advanced seminar. Rowland assured me that the contact with Moholy, intense although brief, was crucial in his development as a designer.[369]

---

[364]The items of relevant correspondence are: Aurelia Henry Reinhardt to Alfred Neumeyer and Rosalind Cassidy, TLS, with manuscript additions, November 6th, 1939; László Moholy-Nagy to Alfred Neumeyer, TLS, July 3rd, 1939, and TLS, July 14th, 1939; all three letters are in the Institute of Design Papers, University of Illinois Library, Chicago. Concerning Moholy's lectures, see note 89.

[365]Dean Rusk later served as United States Secretary of State.

[366]László Moholy-Nagy to Alfred Neumeyer, TLS, July 14th, 1939, and TLS, August 4th, 1939; Alfred Neumeyer to László Moholy-Nagy, carbon copy of TLS, July 20th, 1939; all are in the Institute of Design Papers, University of Illinois Library, Chicago.

[367]Alfred Neumeyer to László Moholy-Nagy, carbon copy of TLS, November 7th, 1939; László Moholy-Nagy to Alfred Neumeyer, TLS, November 15th, 1939; both are in the Institute of Design Papers, University of Illinois Library, Chicago.

[368]Aurelia Henry Reinhardt to Alfred Neumeyer and Rosalind Cassidy, TLS, with manuscript additions, November 6th, 1939, Institute of Design Papers, University of Illinois Library, Chicago.

[369]This was related in an interview in New York, Lloyd C. Engelbrecht interviewing David Rowland, October 15th, 1994, supplemented by subsequent telephone calls. Rowland is best known for his "40/4" chair of 1963; it won the *Gran Premio* at the *Triennale di Milano* in 1964,

(continued...)

THE GOLDEN GATE INTERNATIONAL EXPOSITION of 1939, presented on Treasure Island in San Francisco Bay, had been held over for a second year, and a major accomplishment of its second year was *A Pageant of Photography*, curated by Ansel Adams and shown in the Palace of Fine Arts.[370] The presentation was in two parts: the eponymous "A Pageant of Photography," displaying the entire history of photography on an epic scale, including a photogram by Moholy, along with a series of changing exhibitions including some devoted to individual photographers. Accompanying the exhibition was a handsome publication, including an essay by Moholy and a reproduction of his photogram.[371] Moholy was also one of the photographers chosen for an exhibition devoted entirely to his own photography, and this conveniently took place July 1st through 15th, while he was in the Bay Area. An anonymous reviewer for the *San Francisco Examiner* called his photographs "abstractions";[372] a press release from Mills College called them "photographs and photograms (photographs without camera)."[373]

It is known that his photographs shown at the Exposition were seen by an influential group of visitors, because a trip to the Palace of Fine Arts was on the agenda of a three-day national meeting of the American Federation of Arts; the trip was planned for the evening of July 11th.[374] The American Federation of Arts, founded in 1909, was devoted to increasing public understanding of art and making original works of art more available through touring exhibitions. Its members include many leading American museum professionals.

---

[369](...continued)
and is included in the collections of the Museum of Modern Art and other leading museums.

[370]Ansel Adams, with Mary Street Alinder, *An Autobiography*, a New York Graphic Society Book (Boston: Little, Brown and Company, 1985), 196 and 204; and Mary Street Alinder, *Ansel Adams: a Biography* (New York: Henry Holt and Company, 1996), 158-160.

A lively description of *A Pageant of Photography* and its context at the Exposition is in: Raeburn, *A Staggering Revolution,* 285-292.

[371]Golden Gate International Exposition, San Francisco, *A Pageant of Photography*, introduction by Ansel Adams (San Francisco: Crocker-Union, 1940), unpaginated.

[372]"Fair Features New Exhibits, Clipper Sailing, Pageant of Photography, Paris Pre-War Pictures Among New Island Attractions," *San Francisco Examiner*, July 10, 1940, 12.

[373]From an undated eight-page mimeographed Mills College press release issued in the summer of 1940, Institute of Design Papers, University of Illinois Library, Chicago.

[374]"Three Day Art Meeting Opens Here Today; Hundreds Gather for Discussions by Painters, Teachers; Fine Arts Palace Visit Planned," *San Francisco Examiner*, July 11, 1940, 16. See also: Jane Watson, "Federation's First Far-Western Convention," *Magazine of Art*, volume XXXIII, number 7 (July, 1940), 429-431; *idem*, "Federation Conference Passes Resolution Which Stresses Importance of Government Art Projects," *ibid.*, volume XXXIII, number 8 (August, 1940), 478-479; and "A Page of News and Comment for Art Lovers . . . [American] Federation of Arts," *Architect and Engineer*, volume CXLII, number 1 (July, 1940), 4 and 12.

Also on the Federation's agenda in San Francisco was a discussion of "problems of art education, from grade schools through universities and art schools," chaired by Stephen Pepper of the University of California;[375] among the other participants was "L. Moholy-Nagy of the Chicago modern School of Design and the Mills College summer faculty,"[376] who was further identified as "L. Moholy-Nagy of the famous Bauhaus group."[377] On July 13th the Federation's members visited the summer session classes that Moholy directed at Mills College.[378]

The American Federation of Arts held its opening-day sessions on July 11th in the San Francisco Museum of Art (precursor of the San Francisco Museum of Modern Art)[379] that occupied the top storey of the Veterans Memorial Building (Arthur Brown, 1932; Museum opened 1935). A dramatic photograph by San Francisco photographer Romeo Rolette captured Moholy's lecture in front of Pablo Picasso's *Guernica* of 1937, mentioned in Chapter Four, for the benefit of the members of the Federation. Picasso's mural was shown in the Museum's skylight-enhanced central court as part of a traveling exhibition, *Picasso: Forty Years of His Art*.[380] In addition to Moholy, Wolff is identifiable in Rolette's photograph, seen at the upper right. (DVD figure 467)

Also noteworthy was Moholy's appearance, along with Ansel Adams, before the Associated Camera Clubs of Alameda County, which was hosting the annual Western Amateur Camera Conclave at the Hotel Leamington in Oakland on July 25th. A featured speaker was Edward Weston, whose lecture was called "Toward a Constructive Understanding of Good Photography."[381] It was presumably before or after that meeting that Moholy met with Newhall and Weston at the latter's home in Carmel.[382]

---

[375] In the interest of full disclosure, I recall Pepper as one of my professors in aesthetics when I studied for a degree at the University of California in Berkeley (B.A., 1950).

[376] "Three Day Art Meeting Opens Here Today," 16.

[377] "Art Federation Meet Opens Here Today," *San Francisco Chronicle*, July 11, 1940, 11.

[378] "300 Attend Meet Here to Discuss Art Instruction," *San Francisco Chronicle*, July 12, 13.

[379] This was the pre-cursor to the San Francisco Museum of Modern Art, now located on Third Street.

[380] Alfred H. Barr, editor, *Picasso; Forty Years of His Art*, [organized by the] *Museum of Modern Art in Collaboration with the Art Institute of Chicago* (New York: Museum of Modern Art, 1939); Alfred Frankenstein, "The Critic Finishes 'Forty Years of Art'," *San Francisco Chronicle*, *This World* [section], July 14, 1940, 24; and "A Page of News and Comment for Art Lovers," 4.

[381] "Amateur Photographers Will Hold Camera Conclave Here on July 25," *Oakland Tribune*, June 30, 1940, 4-A.

[382] Beaumont Newhall, "*Vision in Motion*, by L. Moholy-Nagy," *Photo Notes: Official Publication of the Photo League, Inc., New York* (March, 1948), 9-11, here 10; portions reprinted in: Kostelanetz, *Moholy-Nagy*, 70-71. On Beaumont and Nancy Newhall in California in the summer

(continued...)

ONE FACTOR THAT GAVE PROMINENCE to the School of Design's presence at Mills College was the organization of the Summer Session for 1940 as a grand event, featuring presentations by prominent members of the Mills faculty and distinguished visitors in the arts and in other fields.[383] Some of these presenters were well known, and others achieved fame later. In the latter category were University of Chicago sociologist William Lloyd Warner and musician John Cage; both, as noted above, were to join the School of Design faculty as part-time adjuncts the following year.

Direct interaction at Mills between Cage and the Chicagoans took place when Webber designed a setting for a percussion concert presented there by Cage on July 18th.[384] Webber, in turn, enrolled in Cage's class at the School of Design in the fall of the following year, 1941, as noted above.

Lighter moments punctuated the activities of the summer session at Mills College, including a celebration of Moholy's forty-fifth birthday on July 20th, 1940, on the shoes of Lake Aliso on the Mills campus. (DVD figures 468 and 469)

BACK IN CHICAGO, the awarding of scholarships on the basis of applications submitted from throughout the United States helped to broaden the student body and provided wide publicity for the school. The results of one competition were announced in October, 1940, with full scholarships awarded to Alfonso Carrara of Chicago, Milton Halberstadt of Cambridge, Massachusetts, and Homer Page of Oakland, California. Two partial scholarships were also awarded.[385]

One of Moholy's out-of-town lectures took place in September, 1941, at Brooklyn's elite Abraham Lincoln High School, a school that surely reminded him of his own student years in a prestigious *gimnázium* in Szeged, Hungary. Since its opening in 1929, Abraham Lincoln High School has spawned numerous notable alumni, including playwright Arthur Miller, already mentioned in Chapter Four for his studies with Erwin Piscator, as well as Nobel Prize winners in Chemistry and Medicine. Moholy lectured to the school's art students, who evidently benefitted from a faculty who had prepared them

---

[382](...continued)
of 1940, see: Alinder, *Ansel Adams: a Biography*, 161-164.

[383]*Mills College Week*, volume 23, number 27 (April 25, 1940), unpaginated; "Mills College Announces Its 15th Residential Summer Session for Men and Women Offering Both Graduate and Undergraduate Credit, Program for 1940" [leaflet], Charles Niedringhaus file, Bauhaus-Archiv, Berlin.

[384]David W. Bernstein, "The Roots of American Experimentalism at Mills College, 1933-41," *Mills Quarterly*, volume XCII, number 4 (Spring, 2004), 10–[14], here 12 and [14]. The program is reproduced on page 13.

[385]"School of Design Awards," *Magazine of Art*, volume XXXIII, number 10 (October, 1940,) 592.

for the lecture because a newspaper reporter noted that: "It was clear that the students already knew a good deal about him . . ."[386]

The School of Design in Chicago was organized into workshops. The light workshop included instruction in photography offered, over time, by Moholy, Kepes, Levstik, and others. The photographic studio was also utilized for "Experiments in the Motion Picture," headed by Moholy. The most ambitious film production at the School of Design was a 1944 color film, *Design Workshops*, discussed below, which was based on the activities in the workshops of the school.

Moholy regularly visited the various workshops and the foundation-course studio, and a brief sequence from *Exhibition of Student Work*, a color film of 1942 (a copy is owned by the Moholy-Nagy Foundation) shows him looking at student work in progress. (film clip 3). On one occasion Moholy himself conducted an exercise on paper, as described by Beatrice Takeuchi:

> One morning early in the semester, Moholy came to us in his white lab coat bringing with him sheets of typing paper and newsprint and talked to us about the nature of materials. He rolled up one sheet and noted the strength of the column of paper in contrast to the flimsiness of the flat sheet. He then accordion-folded another sheet and noted the rigidity of the transformed sheet. We were in the dark as to the ultimate goal of the exercise, and he did not give any. He only encouraged us to become children again, to experience the material as a child might, to play with it. Our task was to transform flat sheets into as many different forms as possible in the next two hours. Then he left the room. That led many of us, of course, to fold and cut, as in paper dolls and snowflakes, or to fold as in fans, wholly unsatisfying, a dead end. After a dismal critique, Moholy asked us to try again. This time, however, a few students broke through by folding and cutting to form sheets that stretched. Then the floodgates opened, followed by a huge array of rigid structural paper folds, expandable, contractible, strong, weight-bearing, heavy paper three-dimensional pieces that were sculptural, photogenic. These began to appear from what had started as a child-like task that was open-ended, with no practical application. Later some structural pieces made of corrugated cardboard were used as spacers for our own bookshelves. These principles, however, are universally used today in packaging design, as well as thin-wall reinforced concrete structures.[387]

The Product Design Workshop achieved especially fine results in its experiments in designing chairs and other pieces of furniture. Many of the best of these were made of bent plywood, used either alone or in combination with other materials. These were

---

[386]"Designs for a Future World—Moholy-Nagy Speaks on Art," *New York Herald Tribune,* September 14, 1941, section VI, page 5. No exact date is given for the lecture; it was described only as taking place "last week."

[387]Takeuchi, "School of Design in Chicago," 12-13.

shown in a year-end school exhibition in June, 1940,[388] and one piece, a tea table designed by student Kenneth Evertsen,[389] went into production the next year. (DVD figure 470) It was manufactured and distributed by Artek-Pascoe, Inc., of New York, a firm in which Aino and Alvar Aalto had a role.[390] Moholy reported receiving a first payment on royalties of $150, and explained that fifteen percent of all royalties are being paid to the students.[391]

When metal became scarce during the War, bedspring manufacturers looked for designs utilizing substitute materials. Moholy's students fashioned springs from wood, and a patent was obtained for a wooden bedspring in 1942. The Frank J. Seng Company, a manufacturer of furniture hardware, actually did put it into production[392] and began paying royalties to the School by the end of 1942.[393] But the wooden springs were noisy, and interest in wooden bedsprings ended when the War ended.

Moholy once wrote about the School of Design's policies on sales of furniture and textiles:

> We have often been asked to sell our furniture. We had to decline these requests because for the time being we are interested in selling our models to producers for royalties [rather] than to individual customers, since we cannot set up commercial workshops with employed workmen. The only exception is the weaving workshop where we already employ a weaver on a yardage basis of production.[394]

---

[388] Fritzi Weisenborn, "Design Students Hold Annual Show," *Chicago Sunday Times*, June 23, 1940, 10-M.

[389] László Moholy-Nagy, *Vision in Motion*, [59].

[390] Mary Wells Ridley, "Finnish Influence in Modern Furniture," *New York World-Telegram*, April 11, 1941, 10; see also: Lloyd C. Engelbrecht, "Aalto, Alvar," in: Colin Naylor, editor, *Contemporary Designers*, second edition (Chicago: St. James Press, 1990), [xvi] and [1]-2, here 2.

[391] László Moholy-Nagy to Mr. Lester, carbon copy of typed letter, September 27th, 1941, Institute of Design Papers, University of Illinois Library, Chicago.

[392] "Wooden Springs Ease Tension on Furniture Men," *The Chicago Daily News*, July 9, 1942 (from a clippings file in the archives of *The Chicago Sun-Times*; story not included in all daily editions); László Moholy-Nagy, "Modern Designs from Chicago," *Modern Plastics*, volume XX, number 4 (December, 1942), 62-64, 150 and 152; *idem*, *Vision in Motion*, [79]-80; and Sibyl Moholy-Nagy, *Moholy-Nagy: Experiment in Totality*, [174]-175, 186.

[393] László Moholy-Nagy to Myron Kozman, December 14th, 1942.

[394] László Moholy-Nagy to Mr. Lester, The Treasurer, Carnegie Corporation of New York, carbon copy of TLS, September 27th, 1941, Institute of Design Papers, University of Illinois Library, Chicago.

Moholy went on to report receipt of $590 for execution of hand-woven fabrics for different patrons.[395]

In 1942 a summary of student designs which had gone into production or had the potential to do so appeared in a magazine devoted to industrial innovation. Illustrations included the wooden bedspring of 1942, studies for screw-driver handles derived from foundation-course hand sculptures that provided an improved grip, jewelry utilizing new materials, and textiles woven from Dow Chemical Company's Saran plastic.[396]

P RECEDING THE OPENING of the spring, 1942, semester at the School of Design was a large exhibition in the school's quarters that garnered some recognition. A lengthy newspaper review took note of the wooden bedsprings, and also ". . . furniture that is not only striking, but beautiful in a dignified way and by personal test, sometimes very comfortable." The photography was described as "of high caliber, and examples were cited by Moholy and Kepes, along with a photograph of "two nuns on a long bridge, by Nathan Lerner."[397] (DVD figure 471)

Moholy's plans for a full architectural program, as a fifth and sixth year, could not be realized with the modest means of the School of Design. But the School did offer a workshop in architecture and interior design. The teachers included Keck, Tague and Moholy.

Keck was an innovative architect, an early enthusiast for passive solar heating, and always on the search for new methods and materials that could cut building costs while maintaining or improving quality. For the spring semester of 1944, which was Keck's final semester at the school, he and Moholy offered an evening research course on pre-fabricated housing.[398] The following February, Konrad Wachsmann was brought in for a lecture on prefabrication.[399]

The various workshops were not operated as isolated entities; often they collaborated. The Weaving and Textile Workshop, for example, supplied textile coverings for the chairs produced in the Product Design Workshop. Sometimes the

---

[395]*Ibid.*

[396]"New Slant on New Product Planning," *Modern Industry; for All Management Men Concerned with Making and Marketing Better Products at Lower Cost*, volume 5, number 6 (June 15, 1942), 46-47.

[397]"A.B.D." [*i.e.*, Alice Bradley Davey, who also wrote under the pen names of Alice B. Sheldon and James Tiptree Jr.], "School of Design on Threshold of Fourth Year; Classes Embody Principles Born at Weimar," *The Chicago Sun*, January 3, 1942, 16.

[398]A printed announcement for the course is in the Institute of Design Papers, Library of the University of Illinois in Chicago.

[399]László Moholy-Nagy to Marion Becker, February 27th, 1945, Contemporary Arts Center files, Archives and Rare Books Department, University of Cincinnati Libraries

workshops collaborated on commissions. One of these was given to the School in 1942 by Lanz Fifth Avenue, a women's apparel store in Chicago, which commissioned the complete interior design of its salesroom.[400] This was carried out by a group of students working under Moholy and Tague. (DVD figures 472 and 473) As noted above, in 1940 the Kaufmann Department Store of Pittsburgh had commissioned an apartment interior for an exhibition. The store was owned by Edgar J. Kaufmann, (1885-1955), Wright's client for "Fallingwater." For the department-store project the students made the complete furnishings, including fabrics, furniture and lighting fixtures. Moholy reported receipt of "1150.00 in fees and materials."[401]

The most direct involvement of Moholy and the School of Design in the American war effort was in the field of camouflage. On December 19th, 1941, shortly after the attack on Pearl Harbor of December 7th, 1941, and the resulting entry of the United States into World War II, Edward J. Kelly (1876-1950), Mayor of Chicago, appointed Moholy to an official city committee charged with investigating the possibility of camouflaging landmarks and key targets in Chicago.[402]

Kepes initiated a course in camouflage shortly after the United States entered the war.[403] Two students who took this course, Robert Preusser and Jesse Reichek, soon after went to work with the United States Army Research Department.[404] Later Kepes himself attended a course in camouflage at the United States Army Corps of Engineers School at Fort Belvoir, Virginia. The United States Office of Civilian Defense then

---

[400]László Moholy-Nagy, *Vision in Motion*, 87.

[401]László Moholy-Nagy to Mr. Lester, The Treasurer, Carnegie Corporation of New York, carbon copy of TLS, September 27th, 1941 Institute of Design Papers, University of Illinois Library, Chicago; and *Millar's, Chicago Letter*, volume 2, number 23, August 5, 1940, [8]. See also: "Report of Progress of the School of Design in Chicago under the Grant of the Carnegie Corporation of New York of $10,000. Dated February 1st, 1940." A carbon copy is in Institute of Design Papers, University of Illinois Library, Chicago.

[402]Sibyl Moholy-Nagy, *Moholy-Nagy: Experiment in Totality*, 183-184; and Laszlo Moholy-Nagy to Immigration & Naturalization Service, May 29th, 1942, carbon copy of TLS, microfilm reel 949, frame 0706, Moholy-Nagy Papers, Archives of American Art, Washington, D.C.

[403]Meyer Zolotaroff, "Study 'Science of Illusion'," *Chicago Herald-American*, January 12th, 1942, 13; reproduced in: Lloyd C. Engelbrecht, "Moholy à Chicago," in: Chantal Béret, editor, *Laszlo Moholy-Nagy* (Paris: Centre de Création Industrielle, Centre Georges Pompidou, 1976), 144-160, here 156-157; and "Outline of the Camouflage Course at the School of Design in Chicago 1941-1942," four pages, mimeographed, Institute of Design Papers, University of Illinois Library, Chicago.

[404]John L. Scott, "in collaboration with L. Moholy-Nagy and Gyorgy Kepes," "A Bird's-Eye View of Camouflage," *Civilian Defense*, volume I, number 3 (July-August, 1942), 10-14 and 37, here 10.

certified the School of Design in Chicago for training in camouflage,[405] and a "certified" course opened on September 16th, 1942,[406] and ran until January 13th, 1943. The enrollment was seventy students (out of a total School of Design enrollment of two-hundred-and- eight students).[407] The weekly classes were taught by Kepes and Keck from the School of Design and by visiting experts.[408] From April 12th to May 2nd, 1942, some of the exercises made in the class were exhibited as part of a "War Art" exhibition organized by the Renaissance Society of the University of Chicago.[409] While the course aimed at what was practical and useful, the results nevertheless proved to be visually fascinating. A 1942 film on camouflage at the School of Design remains unpublished, but some footage of camouflage is included on the 1944 film *Design Workshops*, available on DVD from the Moholy-Nagy Foundation.

M OHOLY HAD BECOME DISSATISFIED with the amateurish and ineffective techniques he had observed being applied to the rehabilitation of wounded personnel returning from World War II. Since he himself had suffered a battle wound while serving as an artillery officer during World War I, as discussed in Chapter One, he was able to speak directly out of his own experience. He gained support for his views from Franz Alexander, Director of the Institute for Psychoanalysis in Chicago[410] (and, as noted above, a guest lecturer for Moholy). Soon Moholy also enlisted the aid of Conrad Sommer, Deputy Director of the Mental Hygiene Service of the Illinois State Department of Public Welfare. Sommer wrote:

> The Institute of Design's method of group therapy can be likened to psychoanalysis in that it reaches down into the unconscious. It often causes discomfort and anxiety for a time, since it bids the student to loosen his moorings from his inhibiting past.

. . . .

---

[405]László Moholy-Nagy to Walter A. Jessup, carbon copy of TLS, October 19th, 1942, Institute of Design Papers, University of Illinois Library, Chicago.

[406]"Summary of the Introductory Lecture for the Camouflage Course by George [*sic*] Kepes, Head of the Camouflage Dept., School of Design in Chicago," mimeographed, Institute of Design Papers, University of Illinois Library, Chicago.

[407]László Moholy-Nagy to Walter P. Paepcke, TLS, October 1st, 1942, Institute of Design Papers, University of Illinois Library, Chicago.

[408]The visiting experts are listed in an undated flyer [September, 1942], "School of Design in Chicago . . . The Course in Principles of Camouflage, approved by the OCD, Washington, D.C. . . ."; a copy is in the Institute of Design Papers, University of Illinois Library, Chicago.

[409]Richard Kostelanetz, "An Essential Role: 1937-1962," in: Joseph Scanlon, editor, *A History of the Renaissance Society, the First Seventy-Five Years* (Chicago: The Renaissance Society of the University of Chicago, 1993), 35-57, here 35 and 43-44; see also: "Documentation," in *ibid.*, 133-194, here 143.

[410]On the Institute for Psychoanalysis, see: Franz Alexander, *The Western Mind in Transition: an Eyewitness Story* (New York: Random House, 1960), 107-122.

> The Institute's technique should be considered as an adjunct
> of psychotherapy . . .[411]

Alexander and Sommer arranged for Moholy to speak at the annual meeting of the American Psychiatric Association in May, 1943, in Detroit.[412] His speech was called "New Approach to Occupational Therapy." In a key passage Moholy urged that those educating the wounded veteran should aim at a therapy that avoided the mistakes made in treating World War I veterans:

> His best qualities must be brought out so that he may not only try to
> restore the standard of his previous state, but attempt to rise *beyond it* to
> a higher efficiency and a higher productive level [emphasis in
> original].[413]

In a Chicago speech, at the forty-eighth annual conference of the Illinois Welfare Association at the La Salle Hotel, on November 10th, 1943, Moholy recalled the effect his World War I experiences had on the development of his ideas on the rehabilitation of wounded veterans:

> Occupational therapy should discover the patients's dormant
> potentialities— dormant because of modern specialization, though they
> were not left dormant in primitive society. Prehistoric man was hunter,
> tailor, lawyer and various other things in one. Hence he was a rounded
> man. We can observe the type today in the peasant. My father was a
> landowner, and I did not appreciate the peasant till, as an army officer, I
> shared foxholes with him in the first World War. Then I discovered
> that the Hungarian peasant, a paleolithic man if you like, was
> wonderful.
>
> Prehistoric man was creative. Modern society reserves creativeness to
> the genius, and the rest walk in the shadows of the genius. That is all
> nonsense. Though our vocational education develops one's talent, each
> of us has a variety of potential talents, differing only in degree.

---

[411] From Sommer's statement of support for Moholy's effort at rehabilitation of wounded veterans, as quoted in: László Moholy-Nagy, *Vision in Motion*, 72.

[412] László Moholy-Nagy to Walter P. Paepcke, ALS, May 17th, 1943, with an appended nine-page manuscript by Moholy reproduced from a typed text, "New Approach to Occupational Therapy," Institute of Design Papers, University of Illinois Library, Chicago; and Sibyl Moholy-Nagy, *Moholy-Nagy; Experiment in Totality*, 184-185.

[413] Laszlo Moholy-Nagy, "New Approach to Occupational Therapy" (unpublished paper, 1943), [1]-[9], here 2, Institute of Design Papers, University of Illinois Library, Chicago.

He went on to insist that the patient "should be trained in the use of all of his faculties."[414] He put this even more succinctly in the title of an article he called "Better than Before."[415]

SINCE THE GOAL was not solely to train wounded veterans, but to teach students, nurses and social workers who would be involved with occupational therapy during and after the War, courses were also set up at the School of Design to teach the principles of occupational therapy to practitioners. A brochure of 1943 outlined two courses offered as "Courses in Rehabilitation Conducted by L. Moholy-Nagy and Eugene Bielawski, Sponsored by [Conrad Sommer] the Deputy Director of the Mental Hygiene Service of the Illinois State Department of Public Welfare."[416] The first course included workshop exercises and lectures on modern art, photography, architecture and literature, and was offered on Monday evenings from October 4th, 1943, to January 24th, 1944. The second course, offered on Friday evenings from October 8th, 1943, through January 29th, 1944, featured presentations by guests, including Sommer, who had expertise in areas relevant to rehabilitation, followed by discussion. Among the other guests were Russell W. Ballard, Director of Hull House and industrial efficiency innovator Lillian Gilbreth (1878-1972; née Moller) of the Newark Engineering College.

A beginning on the course had been made the previous summer (*i.e.*, 1943). Moholy reported that the students in the night classes included:

> . . . members of the Psychiatric Institute of the University of Illinois,
> who attend our reorientation classes on rehabilitation. They are a very
> alive group of doctors, nurses, recreational and occupational therapists,
> and the course is progressing very well.[417]

Still another way in which the School of Design was involved with the War and its tensions was its openness to enrollment of Japanese-American students. Those people living in Pacific Coast states who were natives of Japan, and native Americans of Japanese parentage or ancestry, regardless of citizenship, were interned in an action a few people (including Ansel Adams) criticized at the time[418] and many more criticized in

---

[414]"Offers Plan to Restore Wounded Men," *The Chicago Daily News*, November 10, 1943, 15.

[415]Laszlo Moholy-Nagy, "Better Than Before," *Technology Review* (published by the Massachusetts Institute of Technology), volume XLVI, number 1 (November 1943), 45-48.

[416]"School of Design in Chicago, Courses in Rehabilitation Conducted by L. Moholy-Nagy and Eugene Bielawski, Sponsored by [Conrad Sommer] the Deputy Director of the Mental Hygiene Service of the Illinois State Department of Public Welfare," five-page mimeographed brochure, [1943], Institute of Design Papers, University of Illinois Library, Chicago.

[417]László Moholy-Nagy to Myron Kozman, TLS, July 1st, 1943; copies are in my files and those of Hattula Moholy-Nagy.

[418]Ansel Adams, *Born Free and Equal: Photographs of the Loyal Japanese-Americans at Manzanar Relocation Center, Inyo County, California* (New York: U.S. Camera, 1944); and

(continued...)

retrospect.[419] Educational facilities at the camps were meager, but some internees were allowed to re-settle in states to the east, including Illinois, and some of these enrolled at the School of Design. One Japanese-American student, Beatrice Akiko Takeuchi (born 1921), who enrolled in the School of Design in the autumn of 1942, later recalled: "Moholy was very fair and democratic, without prejudices regarding sex and nationality."[420] Her statement must be understood in the context of the hatred and bitterness that characterized the attitude of many Americans during World War II towards anyone with any kind of Japanese background.

O N FRIDAY, June 5th, at the end of the spring semester of 1942, the School of Design held a graduation ceremony[421] for its first group of five students to complete the requirements for the degree of Bachelor in Design: Juliet Kepes, Grace Seelig, Myron A. Kozman, Nathan Lerner and Charles Niedringhaus.[422] An extensive show of student-designed furniture, complemented by a display of Moholy's paintings, was set up to mark the event. (DVD figure 474)

The event on June 5th, 1942, also marked the first showing of films made by the School of Design. This consisted of three reels of color film documenting the work of the school, made possible by a grant of $7,500 from the Rockefeller Foundation.[423] This footage was the beginning of a project that resulted in a film about the work of the I.D. called *Design Workshops*; the earliest documented showing was in New York on February 2nd, 1944;[424] the earliest documented showing in Chicago was at the I.D. on

---

[418](...continued)
Nancy Newhall, "Review: Adams, Ansel, *Born Free and Equal, Photographs of the Loyal Japanese-Americans at Manzanar Relocation Center, Inyo County, California,*" *Photo Notes: Photo League Bulletin* (June, 1946), 3-5.

[419]Wendy L. Ng, *Japanese American Internment During World War II: a History and Reference Guide* (Westport, Connecticut: Greenwood Press, 2002).

[420]Beatrice Akiko Takeuchi, "Fragebogen" [questionnaire], August 1980, Bauhaus-Archiv, Berlin.

[421]László Moholy-Nagy to Walter A. Jessup, carbon copy of typed letter, October 13th, 1942, Institute of Design Papers, University of Illinois Library, Chicago ("Last June we had our first graduating class. . . .").

[422]László Moholy-Nagy to Robert J. Wolff, MLS, June 7th, 1942, microfilm reel 69-73, frames, 0324-0326, Robert Jay Wolff files, Archives of American Art, Washington, D.C.; reprinted in Kostelanetz, editor, *Moholy-Nagy,* 177-179.

[423]László Moholy-Nagy to Robert J. Wolff, June 7th, 1942. See also: Walter P. Paepcke to David H. Stevens and John Marshall, carbon copy of TLS, April 17th, 1942; Walter P. Paepcke to E. Penn Brooks, carbon copy of TLS, December 29th, 1943; both in the Institute of Design Papers, University of Illinois Library, Chicago.

[424]László Moholy-Nagy to Sibyl Moholy-Nagy, MLS, February 2nd, 1944, microfilm reel 951,

(continued...)

February 9th, 1944.[425] Another early showing was at the Museum of Modern Art in New York in March, 1944.[426] Later *Design Workshops* was widely shown in Chicago, Cincinnati and elsewhere and all reports indicate that it was well received. A sound track was planned by Moholy but he never completed it.[427] In 2008 the film was released by the Moholy-Nagy Foundation on a DVD with a new sound track featuring narration written and spoken by Hattula Moholy-Nagy.

Besides *Design Workshops*, one additional color film was made at the school: *Do Not Disturb* of 1945 (as noted in Chapter Three), on the subject of jealousy, now available on DVD from the Moholy-Nagy Foundation. Moholy's collage *Jealousy* (first version, 1926, DVD figure 193) was actually re-created by his students in the course of the film and also illustrated in the published film script.[428] A film class offered for day and evening students beginning with the 1942-1943 school year was taught by Moholy, assisted by Robert Lewis and Edward Renker. *Do Not Disturb* was the culmination of student work on film at the I.D., since students were involved in every aspect of the film, from the writing of the script to acting to cinematography and editing.[429]

A highlight of 1943 was an evening guest lecture by José Luis Sert (1902-1983; also known as Josep Lluis Sert), "Urbanism versus Suburbanism: Problems of Planning Our Cities," presented March 22nd, 1943, and discussed below. The postcard announcement

---

[424](...continued)
frames 0455 and 0456, Archives of American Art, Washington, D.C. The showing was in the afternoon at an unspecified place; among those present were Sigfried Giedion, Robert J. Wolff and his wife, Elizabeth, and Gropius's former English partner Maxwell Fry and his wife, the architect Jane Beverly Drew.

[425]Walter P. Paepcke to E.J. Condon, carbon copy of TLS, February 10th, 1944, Institute of Design Papers, University of Illinois Library, Chicago.

[426]Walter P. Paepcke to William H. Yates (president of United Wall Paper Factories, Inc.), carbon copy of TLS, March 30th, 1944, Institute of Design Papers, University of Illinois Library, Chicago. Paepcke wrote: "This film was done pursuant to a grant from the Rockefeller Foundation and was shown in New York a few weeks ago at the Museum of Modern Art to some sixty or more industrialist[s], artists and educators at the invitation of the Rockefeller Foundation." See also: "Institute of Design, President's Report, June 22nd, 1944," mimeographed, Institute of Design Papers, University of Illinois Library, Chicago.

[427]Writing of the accommodation of visitors to the annual exhibition at the I.D., Moholy wrote: "If necessary, the exhibition can be supplemented, for larger groups, with the showing of the colored motion picture of the work of the school. One day I hope we shall be able to add sound to this film." This was part of: "Institute of Design, President's Report, June 22, 1944," mimeographed, Institute of Design Papers, University of Illinois Library, Chicago.

[428]László Moholy-Nagy, *Vision in Motion*, 290-291.

[429]The most complete discussion of *Do Not Disturb*, illustrated with frames, is in: Elizabeth Siegel, "Vision in Motion: Film and Photography at the Institute of
Design," in: Travis and Siegel, editors, *Taken by Design*, [214]-223 and 234-236, here 217-219.

for this event provides a good example of hundreds of simple and effective announcements printed by Frank Barr (DVD figure 475) for special events at the School of Design and the Institute of Design.

Barr's operation was described by James Prestini:

> Frank Barr was a self-taught graphic designer who operated in the
> Bauhaus tradition. He designed and produced the work with no
> division of labor between design and making it. He was a doer and not
> a talker. He utilized a simple letter press and used the typographer's
> font in a simple store front on Clark Street. He was so poor that he
> could not afford plates. This forced him to maximize the use of
> standard elements and some which he made from linoleum blocks.[430]

Early in 1944, Paepcke had become convinced that in order to broaden the base of support for Moholy's school it would be wise to set up a board of directors.[431] He proceeded to set up a board of nine members, plus Moholy serving ex officio, and considered the board he was organizing to be "rather distinguished."[432] The first members to serve on the board were Paepcke plus some Chicago business and industrial leaders. Paepcke rejected a suggestion by George Fred Keck that labor union leaders be invited to serve.[433] At its meeting of March 30th, 1944, the board ratified a change of name to the Institute of Design. New stationery for the I.D. was designed by Moholy in June.[434] (DVD figure 476)

During the fall semester of 1944, new faculty included Ralph Rapson (born 1914), an architect and furniture designer who succeeded Keck as head of the architecture

---

[430] James Prestini to Elmer Ray Pearson, TLS, July 25th, 1980, Elmer Ray Pearson files, Chicago Historical Society.

Numerous examples of Barr's work are in archives and museums, such as the Chicago Historical Society, the Bauhaus-Archiv in Berlin and the Institute of Design Papers, University of Illinois Library, Chicago. Historians usually need to do a bit of digging to verify the exact dates, since years were rarely if ever given by Barr.

[431] Findeli, "Design Education and Industry," 103-104.

[432] Walter P. Paepcke to Walter Gropius, telegram, February 7th, 1944, Institute of Design Papers, University of Illinois Library, Chicago.

[433] George Fred Keck to Walter P. Paepcke, carbon copy of typed letter, January 24th, 1944; George Fred Keck to László Moholy-Nagy, carbon copy of typed letter, January 31st, 1944; Walter P. Paepcke to George Fred Keck, ALS, February 7th, 1944; all in Keck Papers, State Historical Society of Wisconsin, Madison.

[434] The earliest use of the new stationery found is: László Moholy-Nagy to Walter P. Paepcke, TLS, June 23rd, 1944, Institute of Design Papers, University of Illinois Library, Chicago.

classes.[435] Rapson had graduated from the University of Michigan and also studied with Eliel Saarinen (1873-1950) at the Cranbrook Academy of Art in Bloomfield Hills, Michigan. In Chicago he worked in the office of Keck and also collaborated with Moholy on design commissions.

As noted above, some of the guest lecturers were brought in for several series of programs. On May 8th, 9th and 10th, 1945, James Johnson Sweeney, at the time serving as Director of Painting and Sculpture at the Museum of Modern Art in New York, lectured on *The Four Quartets* by T.S. Eliot (1888-1965), as part of a series on contemporary literature.[436] The I.D. also presented a tea in Sweeney's honor at the Arts Club on May 9th.[437]

LESLIE LLEWELLYN LEWIS gave a series of lectures on James Joyce on Tuesday evenings, March 6th, 13th and 20th, and April 3rd, 10th, and 17th, 1945,[438] including two lectures each on *Ulysses*[439] and *Finnegan's Wake.* The latter had been published in book form only six years before (although excerpts had earlier appeared in periodicals).[440] For his lectures, Lewis prepared charts presenting the structures of *Ulysses* and *Finnegan's Wake*; these were republished in *Vision in Motion*.[441] Lewis had a varied background in education, working for non-profit organizations, businesses, and as a writer, editor and editorial consultant for publishers of business books.[442] He

---

[435] On Rapson, see: Jane King Hession, *Ralph Rapson: Sixty Years of Modern Design* (Afton, Minnesota: Afton Historical Society Press, 1999).

[436] "The Institute of Design," *Educational Events in Chicago*, February, 1945, 3; "The Institute of Design," *ibid.*, March, 1945, 4.

[437] "Institute of Design, Meeting of the Board of Directors, May 1, 1945," mimeographed, Institute of Design Papers, University of Illinois Library, Chicago.

[438] Letter signed by László Moholy-Nagy to "Dear Friends," undated but evidently written in February, 1945, mimeographed—signed on the mimeograph stencil, Library, Illinois Institute of Technology, Chicago; and Annabelle Scroon, "Midwest Book Briefs; Spring Season Gets under Way with Parties and Such [and] Other News of the Literary Scene," *Chicago Sun Book Week*, March 4, 1945, 10.

[439] The first publication of any part of *Ulysses* was in *The Little Review*, at the time published in Chicago, from 1918 to 1920; as noted in Chapter Three, it first appeared in book form in 1922.

[440] James Joyce, *Finnegan's Wake* (New York: Viking Press, 1939).

[441] László Moholy-Nagy, *Vision in Motion*, 347. The charts were used to illustrate a lengthy discussion by Moholy of Joyce that appeared in *Vision in Motion* on pages 341 through 351, including Moholy's observation that "In spite of animosity and misunderstandings, Joyce's influence grows constantly."

[442] No published biographical materials on Lewis have been found. The only source available is a three-page letter, Leslie Lewis to Walter P. Paepcke, ALS, [about June 1st, 1946], Institute of

(continued...)

returned to the I.D. the next year to serve on the staff, first to help enlarge the Board of Directors and organize a fund-raising program,[443] and then as business manager.[444]

A NOTHER EXAMPLE of the ability of the I.D. to involve the public with special events can be seen in the visit to Chicago by Fernand Léger (1881-1955), the French artist described by Moholy as the most important twentieth-century painter after Picasso. (DVD figures 92 and 513) Moholy and Kassák had included a painting by Léger in their *Buch neuer Künstler* in 1922. Although Moholy explained that Léger "did not speak any English" and had to rely on a translator,[445] he gave two lectures for students as well as speaking informally with them for several weeks, and he also gave a public lecture at the Arts Club accompanied by a film showing.[446] In addition to that lecture, Moholy encouraged the interest of the general public through an exhibition of Léger's work at the I.D. from October 14th to November 8th, 1944.[447]

The Léger exhibition was also shown in Cincinnati, at the Cincinnati Art Museum, under the auspices of the Cincinnati Modern Art Society.[448] For Cincinnati the opening

---

[442](...continued)
Design Papers, University of Illinois Library, Chicago. One sentence suggests the possible genesis of Lewis' fascination with avant-garde literature: "During the early 20's, while studying in Paris, I was a part-time teacher and, later, assistant principal of the Lycée des Ormes and the École d'Auteuil."

[443]"Institute of Design, Meeting of the Board of Directors, June 10, 1946," mimeographed, Institute of Design Papers, University of Illinois Library, Chicago.

[444]"Institute of Design, Meeting of the Board of Directors, September 10, 1946," mimeographed, and "Institute of Design, Meeting of the Board of Directors, October 14, 1946," mimeographed; both are in the Institute of Design Papers, University of Illinois Library, Chicago.

[445]László Moholy-Nagy to Marion Becker, TLS, June 17th, 1944, Archives and Rare Books Department, University of Cincinnati Libraries.

[446]Walter Paepcke to Don Fairchild, carbon copy of TLS, October 17th, 1944, Institute of Design Papers, University of Illinois Library, Chicago. No record has been found as to which films were shown accompanying Léger's lecture, but his *Ballet Mécanique* was shown in connection with the Cincinnati showing of the exhibition, and surely also was shown in Chicago.

[447]Sigfried Giedion, *Exhibition of Paintings by Fernand Léger in the Institute of Design, October 14th to November 8th, 1944* (Chicago: Institute of Design, 1944). See also: *idem*, "Léger in America," *Magazine of Art: a National Magazine Relating the Arts to Contemporary Life*, volume XXXVIII, number 8 (December, 1945), 295-299.

[448]László Moholy-Nagy to Marion Becker, TLS, June 17th, 1944; László Moholy-Nagy to Marion Becker, TLS, July 12th, 1944; László Moholy-Nagy to Marion Becker, TLS, July 21st, 1944; László Moholy-Nagy to Marion Becker, TLS, July 27th, 1944; László Moholy-Nagy to Marion Becker, TLS, August 2nd, 1944; László Moholy-Nagy to Marion Becker, TLS, August 11, 1944; László Moholy-Nagy to Marion Becker, TLS, September 26th , 1944; László Moholy-Nagy to Marion Becker, TLS, October 5th, 1944; László Moholy-Nagy to Marion Becker, TLS, October

(continued...)

was enlivened by a miniature film festival: shown were Léger's *Ballet Mécanique* (1924), Moholy's *A Lightplay Black White Gray*, *L'Entr'acte* (1924) by Francis Picabia and Réné Clair, and *Le Chien d'Andalou* (1929) by Salvador Dali and Luis Buñuel.[449] Moholy requested that the showing of his own film be accompanied (presumably by means of a recording!) by Duke Ellington's "Mood Indigo."[450] Moholy designed an eight-page brochure (featuring an illustrated essay by Sigfried Giedion) for Chicago as well as the similar one used in Cincinnati.[451] He related this account of the two exhibitions to his board, showing his ability to manage all this on his limited budget:

> I would like to report briefly on the Leger exhibition which was shown in the Institute from October 14th to November 8th. We took in approximately $307.50 for the lecture and catalogs [*sic*; *i.e.*, brochures]. When the final receipts are collected, namely $100.00 from Cincinnati for the catalogs and ten percent commission on the four pictures sold, we will not only offset our expenses but make a moderate profit.[452]

Moholy tried to hire Léger as a faculty member of the I.D. to begin in the summer of 1945, but with the end of the War Léger preferred to return to France.

The best-attended and most significant public event presented by the I.D. during Moholy's presidency was the February 23rd, 1945, lecture by Walter Gropius, "Rebuilding Our Communities After the War." This was at a luncheon meeting in the Palmer House, a leading Chicago hotel. Originally planned for the hotel's Red Lacquer Room, with a capacity of 550 occupants, the turnout was so great that it had to be

---

[448](...continued)
11th, 1944; László Moholy-Nagy to Marion Becker, TLS, October 25th, 1944; László Moholy-Nagy to Marion Becker, TLS, November 2nd, 1944; and László Moholy-Nagy to Marion Becker, TLS, November 4t, 1944; all of these are in the Contemporary Arts Center files, Archives and Rare Books Department, University of Cincinnati Libraries.

[449]These films were listed in the invitation to the opening, with a showing at 8:00 p.m. on November 11th, 1944, in the Cincinnati Art Museum's Alms Auditorium; a copy of the invitation is in the Contemporary Arts Center files, Archives and Rare Books Department, University of Cincinnati Libraries.

[450]László Moholy-Nagy to Marion Becker, TLS, November 4th, 1944, Contemporary Arts Center files, Archives and Rare Books Department, University of Cincinnati Libraries. "Mood Indigo" was written about 1930 by Duke Ellington (1899-1974), an innovative but nevertheless famous and widely popular composer and band leader; by 1946 "Mood Indigo" had been recorded numerous times.

[451]Sigfried Giedion, *Exhibition of Paintings by Fernand Léger Shown by the Cincinnati Modern Art Society at the Cincinnati Art Museum, Eden Park, November 11th to December 17th* [1944].

[452]"President's Report," part of "Institute of Design, Meeting of the Board of Directors, November 14, 1944," mimeographed, Institute of Design Papers, University of Illinois Library, Chicago.

transferred to the hotel's ballroom, which seats 1,200.[453] It was co-sponsored by the I.D., the Chicago Plan Commission and the Chicago Association of Commerce. It was also part of an attempt by Paepcke to convince the I.D.'s board, as well as business leaders and public officials, of the relevance and quality of the I.D.[454] And it marked the beginning of what was intended to be a series of I.D. books: *Rebuilding Our Communities,* by Gropius, based on his lecture.[455] (In the end Moholy's posthumous *Vision in Motion* proved to be the only other book in the series.)

The lecture, which was preceded by a press conference,[456] received wide coverage in Chicago's newspapers.[457] The most extensive coverage was in the *Chicago Sun,* which began with a narrative account of Gropius' lecture,[458] mentioned the talk in an unsigned editorial early in the week following the lecture,[459] and followed that with a two-part summary, written by Gropius himself.[460] But it was the *Chicago Herald-American,* among all of Chicago's newspapers, that was most strongly impacted by the lecture. Its coverage included an article signed by William Tell,[461] the newspaper's leading reporter at the time.[462] The lecture impressed Tell partly because of the kind of stories he had developed for the newspaper, and perhaps it also helped set in motion, as described

---

[453]"City Leaders Go to 'School'," *Chicago Times,* February 24, 1945, 13.

[454]Findeli, "Design Education and Industry," 104.

[455]Walter Gropius, *Rebuilding our Communities*, ID book, Institute of Design (Chicago: Paul Theobald, 1945). "The first of a series of monographs written by eminent authorities in their field, under the editorship of L. Moholy-Nagy, expounding the basic philosophy and creative approach of the Institute of Design, Chicago."

[456]"Press Conference" [publicity release], undated [about February 20, 1945], mimeographed, Institute of Design Papers, University of Illinois Library, Chicago.

[457]*E.g.,* "City Leaders Go to 'School'," *Chicago Times,* February 24, 1945, 13; "Gap is Wide in Housing, Planning," *The Chicago Daily News,* February 23, 1945, 8; and "Urges Post-War Homes Built in Cultural Units," *Chicago Tribune,* February 24, 1945, 5.

[458]"Harvard Expert Forecasts Greatest Building Boom," *Chicago Sun,* February 24, 1945, 7.

[459]"Chicago's Need for a Master Plan," *Chicago Sun,* February 26, 1945, 8.

[460]Walter Gropius, "Prospective Boom a Chance to Plan Neighborhoods as Wellsprings of Democracy," and "Erection of Area Centers Practical First Step for Planned Chicago Housing," *Chicago Sun,* March 2, 1945, 12, and March 3, 1945, 4, respectively.

[461]William Tell, "Housing Expert Tells City Leaders How to Wipe Out Slums," *Chicago Herald-American,* February 23, 1945, 2.

[462]Little could be learned about Tell. He had evidently left the *Chicago Herald-American* before the winners of the City Plan Contest (described below) were announced. Born in 1892, his name had earlier been Roderick Arkell; see: *Who Was Who among North American Authors, 1921-1939* (Detroit: Gale Research Company, 1976), 1:53. During part of 1945, letters to the editor in the *Chicago Herald-American* were routinely headed: "Dear William Tell."

below, the newspaper's $25,000 City Plan Contest. It was Tell who took the lead in announcing and reporting the contest.

Gropius was deeply impressed by the favorable reception for his lecture, and by the size of his audience as well as by the presence within it of a number of well-known and influential Chicagoans.[463] In a letter to Paepcke, Gropius wrote thanking him ". . . for the confidence you have shown me by having taken the risk of inviting an audience to hear me which was certainly unique in its weight and importance."[464]

THE SPRING, 1945, semester, begun February 5th, marked the end of an era. It was the last semester in the building at 247 East Ontario Street. It was the last semester held during the War years, which was one reason why the total enrollment of 212 students was not substantially different from that of recent semesters. Only 29 of the students were able to study full time. Of the seventeen members of the faculty, four were engaged full time, two taught half time, and the rest taught only one course.[465] The full-time faculty included, in addition to Moholy: Andi Schiltz, returning after an absence of several years; and two new faculty members: Emerson Woelffer (1914-2003), a painter, and Crombie Taylor (1914-1999), an architect.[466] Taylor served as assistant director and secretary and, along with Ralph Rapson, who had a half-time appointment, taught courses in architecture. Moholy taught advertising arts, visual fundamentals and motion pictures, and shared a course in painting and drawing with Woelffer. Marianne Willisch (about 1900-1984) joined the part-time faculty to teach interior design; she was the only direct link to the I.D. from the prestigious Viennese designers' association known as *Wiener Werkstätte* [Viennese Wokshops]. At the insistence of Paepcke, the administrative and clerical staff had recently been expanded and now numbered five full-time persons.[467] Paepcke's purpose was to free Moholy from handling administrative details and publicity.

---

[463] A preliminary "list of those who have accepted places at the speaker's table" was included in "Press Conference" [publicity release], undated [about February 20, 1945], mimeographed, Institute of Design Papers, University of Illinois Library, Chicago. An updated typed list was dated February 23rd, 1945 (a photographic copy is in the Bauhaus-Archiv, Berlin). Both lists included leaders of business and industry, newspaper editors, a few political office holders, leaders of higher education, and a few influential architects, including Mies van der Rohe. If Mies did in fact attend, it would have marked a rare participation in an event sponsored or co-sponsored by the I.D.

[464] Walter Gropius to William P. Paepcke, TLS, February 28th, 1945, Institute of Design Papers, University of Illinois Library, Chicago.

[465] "Institute of Design, Salary Budget for 1945 as of February 1, 1945," mimeographed; and seven-page mimeographed brochure for the evening classes and the Saturday morning children's classes. Both are in the Institute of Design Papers, University of Illinois Library, Chicago.

[466] László Moholy-Nagy to Crombie Taylor, carbon copy of TLS, November 15th, 1944, Institute of Design Papers, University of Illinois Library, Chicago.

[467] "Institute of Design, Salary Budget for 1945 as of February 1, 1945," mimeographed.

A harbinger of the future at the end of the Spring, 1945, semester was the awarding of the first graduate degree by the I.D.;[468] this went to Robert D. Erickson (1917-1991), who remained at the school to teach the children's Saturday class. The title of his thesis was: "A Child Sees."

BECAUSE ITS BUILDING HAD BEEN SOLD and its lease was not renewed, the I.D. was required to move. New quarters were found at 1009 North State Street[469] and the move took place in September, 1945. These new quarters, in the upper storey of a two-storey multi-use building, with façades on North State Street, North Rush Street and East Oak Street (no longer extant), were more attractive, but were also a bit smaller. (DVD figures 477, 481 and 484) This proved to be a problem since, with the end of the War, enrollment began to rise. Hence the I.D. remained on State Street only for the 1945-1946 academic year (including the summer of 1946).

It was during the autumn of 1945 that an unaccustomed exhaustion began to afflict Moholy. After a complete collapse in November, it was discovered that he had leukemia. After a three-week stay in a hospital he was released on December 2nd. His wife was informed that ". . . only his excellent heart and lungs saved his life when he was down to 40 % of his normal blood contents [*sic*; *i.e.*, blood count]."[470] He was sent home to rest while therapy continued by means of X-ray treatments. By January it seemed that he had completely recovered, and during the ensuing semester many persons assumed that his illness was behind him.

A record enrollment of 461 students greeted Moholy and his faculty during the fall semester of 1945. The long struggle to maintain enrollment levels during wartime conditions was now over. The increase was all the more impressive since most of it took place among full-time day students. This required a larger teaching staff, and Moholy asked several former faculty members to return during the year, including Nathan Lerner and Alexander Archipenko.

The greatest part of the post-War increase in enrollment was due to returning veterans, who were aided in returning to school by federal scholarships for military veterans as part of what was popularly known as "The G.I. Bill of Rights," officially known as the "Servicemen's Readjustment Act of 1944."[471]

---

[468] The idea of offering a graduate degree was presented to his board in the spring of 1944: "Institute of Design President's Report, June 22, 1944," mimeographed, Institute of Design Papers, University of Illinois Library, Chicago.

[469] "Minutes of Board of Directors' Meeting of Institute of Design, June 5, 1945," mimeographed, Institute of Design Papers, University of Illinois Library, Chicago.

[470] Sibyl Moholy-Nagy to Ise Gropius, photocopy of carbon copy of TLS, December 2nd, 1945, Bauhaus-Archiv, Berlin.

[471] On the "G.I. Bill," see: David R.B. Ross, *Preparing for Ulysses: Politics and Veterans During World War II* (New York: Columbia University Press, 1969).

Six-Week Summer Symposium of 1946:
"New Vision in Photography"

A renewed emphasis on the study of photography had now become possible at the I.D. But this was not due simply to increased enrollment. There was an upsurge of interest in photography nationally, in part owing to Moholy's enthusiasm for the medium and his ability to communicate that enthusiasm to the general public, as is evident from numerous articles about photography in a variety of American publications, as noted below. Moreover, Moholy's prestige as a photographer and the opportunities to study photography at the I.D. were becoming increasingly better known; e.g., in the summer of 1945, Alfred M. Frankfurter, influential editor of New York-based *Art News*, noted that: "As one of the great living pioneers of photography, Moholy-Nagy gives special attention to this most modern means of visual presentation."[472]

At the opening of the Spring, 1946, semester, former student Arthur Siegel was brought back as head of a newly instituted Department of Photography.[473] (DVD figure 478) Moholy continued making photograms in Chicago, sometimes in collaboration with faculty colleagues, including Siegel. (DVD figure 479)

Soon a four-year curriculum in photography was begun, leading to a baccalaureate degree. To launch the program, Moholy and Siegel presented a six-week summer symposium called "New Vision in Photography." This took place from July 8th to August 16th, 1946, and consisted of a program of lectures, seminars, exhibitions, film showings and other activities.[474] (DVD figure 480) It grew out of the decision to emphasize photography with a separate curriculum, and Moholy and Siegel clearly wanted to launch and publicize the new curriculum by staging a photographic event that would be comparable in significance to the Stuttgart *Film und Foto* exhibition of 1929.

While Moholy would not have had the means to set up a latter-day version of the 1929 Stuttgart exhibition, even if he had wanted to, he chose to do something different but, in his own mind, equally significant: he succeeded in bringing to his school Berenice Abbott (1898-1991), Rus Arnold, Erwin Blumenfeld (1897-1969), Gordon Coster (1906-1988), Stephen Deutch (1908-1997),[475] Beaumont Newhall, Edwin Rosskam (1903-

---

[472] Alfred M. Frankfurter, "Form and Function: a U.S. Bauhaus," *Art News*, volume XLIV, number 10 (August, 1945), 23.

[473] "Minutes of Board of Directors' Meeting of Institute of Design, January 15th, 1946," mimeographed, item 11; a copy is in the Institute of Design Papers, University of Illinois Library, Chicago.

[474] "New Vision in Photography, Six Weeks' Session from July 8-August 16, 1946, Institute of Design," mailer-brochure; a copy is in the Institute of Design Papers, University of Illinois Library, Chicago.

[475] On Deutch, see: Kenneth C. Burkhart and Larry A. Voskochil, editors, *Steven Deutch,*

(continued...)

1985), Frank Scherschel (about 1907-1981), Paul Strand (1890-1976), Roy Stryker (1893-1975) and Weegee (professional name of Arthur Fellig; 1899-1968). Some of the participants taught for only one day, others for two days or a week; on some days several of the visiting faculty were on hand at the same time. They joined Moholy, Siegel and Levstik, then a newly appointed faculty member. Levstik's contribution included making documentary photographs of the event. Also present was another newly-appointed faculty member, Harry Callahan (1912-1999),[476] who was soon to become crucial to the photography program. (DVD figure 481)

As late as March 6th Moholy had a smaller seminar in mind, limited (in addition to Siegel and himself) to Beaumont and Nancy Newhall, Man Ray, Stryker and Edward Weston.[477] It happened that of these only Beaumont Newhall and Stryker actually participated in the seminar. Weston was formally invited[478] but declined, evidently because of ill health.[479] It is not known why Man Ray did not come. He had visited Moholy in Chicago in October, 1940.[480] On April 27th, 1945, he had been photographed with Moholy at the Art Institute where he (Man Ray) was showing in an exhibition.[481]

---

[475](...continued)
Photographer: from Paris to Chicago, 1932-1989, with foreword by Studs Terkel and essay by Abigail Foerstner (Chicago: TriQuarterly Books/Another Chicago Press, 1989).

[476]Crombie Taylor, typed summary of a telephone conference with Moholy, June 14th, 1946; Crombie Taylor to Harry Callahan, xerox copy of TLS, July 9, 1946; both documents are in the Elmer Ray Pearson papers, Chicago Historical Society. Callahan was appointed for the ten-week summer term, and continued teaching in the fall.

On Callahan, see: John Pultz, "Harry Callahan and American Photography, 1938-1990" (Ph.D. dissertation, New York University, 1993); Sarah Greenough, *Harry Callahan* (Washington: National Gallery of Art; distributed by the Bullfinch Press, Boston, 1996); and Keith F. Davis, "'To Open an Individual Way': Photography at the Institute of Design," in: Travis and Siegel, editors, *Taken by Design*, [68]-91 and 231-234, here [69], 71-76, 83-85 *et passim*.

[477]László Moholy-Nagy to Beaumont Newhall, March, 1946; photographic copies of this letter are in the files of the Photography Department of the Art Institute of Chicago and in the Bauhaus-Archiv in Berlin.

[478]Beaumont Newhall to László Moholy-Nagy, March 5th, 1946, and László Moholy-Nagy to Beaumont Newhall, March 6th, 1946; xerox copies of these letters are in the files of the Photography Department of the Art Institute of Chicago and in the Bauhaus-Archiv in Berlin.

[479]Beaumont Newhall to László Moholy-Nagy, March 14th, 1946; xerox copies of this letter are in the files of the Photography Department of the Art Institute of Chicago and in the Bauhaus-Archiv in Berlin.

[480]Neil Baldwin, *Man Ray: American Artist* (New York: Clarkson N. Potter, Publishers, 1988), 234.

[481]Rich, editor, *Modern Art in Advertising*, item 76; Egbert Jacobson, editor, *Modern Art in Advertising; an Exhibition of Designs for Container Corporation of America* (Chicago: Art

(continued...)

(DVD figures 482 and 483) During his 1945 visit to Chicago he had lectured at the I.D;[482] moreover, he later lent one of his films for showing there.[483]

Moholy had given Siegel "charge of all the arrangements for the summer seminar."[484] Siegel was doubtless primarily responsible for the list of scheduled participants that appeared in the July issue of *Popular Photography*, where some of the common experiences of these participants were described; these experiences included working for *Life* magazine and for two United States government agencies, the Farm Security Administration and the Office of War Information.[485] Siegel recalled that his choices were based on: "one, I wanted to find out what was going on in photography, in a way; and two, I knew a lot of these people and I wanted to bring them together to get some publicity for the program."[486]

Although he often seemed to be in good health, ominous signs of Moholy's declining condition were becoming increasingly apparent. During the summer Siegel had to support Moholy not only with management of the symposium but also physically, during recurrences of his leukemia, by following him around with a chair into which he would collapse.[487]

I discussed the summer seminar with Beaumont Newhall in November of 1978 in Albuquerque. He kindly agreed to send me xerox copies of his own files on the event. What I learned from them is that Moholy had wanted to publish the proceedings of the

---

[481](...continued)
Institute of Chicago, 1945); Eleanor Jewett, "Two Exhibitions of Commercial Art Have Merit," *Chicago Tribune*, April 26, 1945, 20; and Rosamund Frost, "This Business Ties Art into a Neat Package," *Art News*, volume XLIV, number 7 (May 15, 1945), 13.

[482]Baldwin, *Man Ray*, 252; and John Chancellor, "Institute of Design: the Rocky Road from the Bauhaus," *Chicago*, volume II, number 5 (July, 1955), 28-35, here 34. Chancellor was married to the former Barbara Upshaw, who had been a student at the I.D., had attended the summer seminar, and was the former wife of Siegel. See also: László Moholy-Nagy, *Vision in Motion*, 70.

[483]László Moholy-Nagy to Man Ray, TLS, October 11th, 1945, Man Ray papers, Getty Research Center, Los Angeles.

[484]László Moholy-Nagy to Beaumont Newhall, May 15th, 1946; xerox copies of this letter are in the files of the Photography Department of the Art Institute of Chicago and in the Bauhaus-Archiv in Berlin.

[485]"Institute of Design Offers Summer Seminar," *Popular Photography*, volume XIX, number 1 (July, 1946), 162.

[486]Arthur Siegel, interviewed by James McQuaid, assisted by Elaine King, October 29th to November 6th, 1977, transcribed by Carol Fladd, edited and corrected by James McQuaid; a copy of the transcription is in the Ryerson Library, Art Institute of Chicago.

[487]John Grimes, "Arthur Siegel: a Short Critical Biography," *Exposure*, volume XVII, number 2 (Summer, 1979), 27.

Institute, and that he wanted Newhall to help him. Poignantly, the correspondence about the project included a two-page handwritten letter from Moholy to Newhall, dated November 16th, 1946, little more than a week before Moholy's death from leukemia on November 24th.[488] Moholy had met in New York with some of the participants, namely Newhall, Strand, Abbott, Stryker, Weegee and Blumenfeld, to urge them to work with him on a book about the seminar;[489] Newhall himself agreed to do this, but, unknowingly, he did so in a letter dated the very day of Moholy's death.[490] Of course the publication never appeared, and there do not seem be sufficient archival materials to give the complete account Moholy had wanted (although when I talked with Newhall in 1978 he still had hopes that someone could do so).

Moholy was supremely pleased with the way the summer seminar had worked out, and hoped to make it the forerunner of an annual event. As he wrote to Newhall, "This is the first time in the history of photography that such a Seminar was carried out and I am sure that it will have repercussions especially if we are able to continue it yearly with similarly enthusiastic and devoted participants."[491]

AS DIFFERENT AS the two events, separated by a span of fifteen years, were, striking parallels with the 1929 Stuttgart exhibition and the 1946 Chicago symposium were nevertheless evident. Moholy, Blumenfeld and Abbott had shown in Stuttgart (as had Edward Weston and Man Ray, both considered for the Chicago seminar). Weegee was the foremost crime photographer in the United States, echoing those police photographs shown in Stuttgart. Moreover, Moholy's initial lecture, scheduled for the morning of July 8th, probably echoed Stuttgart themes, as it was to include an account of "The invention of photography, its degeneration at the turn of the century, and its rejuvenation through the amateur, police photography, scientific, reportage and technology."[492] (DVD figure 484) And although the Chicago event had

---

[488] Xerox copies of this letter are in the files of the Photography Department of the Art Institute of Chicago and in the Bauhaus-Archiv in Berlin.

[489] László Moholy-Nagy to Beaumont Newhall, November 5th, 1946, and Beaumont Newhall to László Moholy-Nagy, November 9, 1946; xerox copies of this letter are in the files of the Photography Department of the Art Institute of Chicago and in the Bauhaus-Archiv in Berlin.

[490] Beaumont Newhall to László Moholy-Nagy, November 24th, 1946; xerox copies of this letter are in the files of the Photography Department of the Art Institute of Chicago and in the Bauhaus-Archiv in Berlin.

[491] László Moholy-Nagy to Beaumont Newhall, August 29th, 1946; photographic copies of this letter are in the files of the Photography Department of the Art Institute of Chicago and in the Bauhaus-Archiv in Berlin.

[492] Arthur Siegel, "Photography Summer Seminar Program," mimeographed, Arthur Siegel Collection, Box 17, Folder 5, Art Institute of Chicago Libraries.

been announced as "New Vision in Photography," much emphasis was placed on film showings.[493]

The most complete account of the summer seminar is in a well-researched recent article by Mark Pohlad.[494] Since the proceedings were not published as Moholy had wished, there are only fragmentary sources for determining what went on, chiefly Siegel's preliminary schedule[495] and his notes on Strand's lectures,[496] Siegel's responses to interview questions in 1977, Newhall's fragmentary account in his autobiography,[497] and an account by two students published in *Popular Photography*.[498] In spite of some participants' ties to *Life* magazine, that publication covered only the field trip held by Weegee.[499] Weegee had probably been Moholy's choice for the seminar because Siegel did not share his (Moholy's) interest in police photography.[500]

There is no way of knowing exactly how many students were attracted to the seminar. Siegel recalled that there were thirty or forty students, that they "came from all over," and that they were of "all ages." The only names that can be recovered are those

---

[493] Arthur Siegel, "Photography Summer Seminar Program," mimeographed, Arthur Siegel Collection, Box 17, Folder 5, Art Institute of Chicago Libraries; and Mark B. Pohlad, "A Photographic Summit in the Windy City: the Institute of Design's 1946 'New Vision in Photography' Seminar," *History of Photography*, volume XXIV, number 2 (Summer, 2000), 148-154, here 150.

[494] Pohlad, "A Photographic Summit," cited fully in the previous note. See also: Davis, "'To Open an Individual Way': Photography at the Institute of Design," 70-72.

[495] Arthur Siegel, "Photography Summer Seminar Program," mimeographed, Arthur Siegel Collection, Box 17, Folder 5, Art Institute of Chicago Libraries.

[496] Arthur Siegel, handwritten notebook with "Paul Strand" on first line of first sheet, Arthur Siegel Collection, Box 17, Folder 1, Art Institute of Chicago Libraries.

[497] Beaumont Newhall, *Focus: Memoirs of a Life in Photography* (Boston: Little, Brown and Company, 1993), 170-172.

[498] Max Thorpe and Jane Bell Edwards, "From a Student's Notebook [*sic*; two students were credited with originating the notes]," *Popular Photography*, volume XXI, number 6 (December, 1947), 53-56, 174 and 176. "These notes [by] Thorpe and Edwards] have been combined, illustrated and digested. . . ." (Max Thorpe was identified as such on page 176, but his last name was given as "Tharpe" on page 53.) A note on page 176 lists Thorpe and the others whose photographs illustrated the article, but no illustration was identified with an individual photographer.

[499] "Speaking of Pictures: Weegee Shows How to Photograph a Corpse," *Life*, August 12th, 1946, 8-10 (photographs and text) and 19 (names of photographers).

[500] Arthur Siegel, interviewed by James McQuaid, assisted by Elaine King, October 29th to November 6th, 1977.

few mentioned in the *Popular Photography* and *Life* articles, plus a few who can be recognized in photographs.

When asked to comment on the social side of the seminar, Siegel recalled:

> So, Paul [Strand] would give these lectures and then there would always be questions, you know, interchange between the people at the seminar, you know, it really was a seminar. . . . I mean, there was an exchange; it was not giving a lecture and then leaving. Lots of us would eat together, and we would go out [to restaurants] . . . and sit and talk for a long time.[501]

Siegel's description of the seminar nature of "New Vision in Photography" is born out by a photograph showing Weegee and Newhall attending a joint lecture by Blumenfeld and Coster; holding a camera and seated next to Weegee is Harry Callahan.[502] (DVD figure 481)

Max Thorpe and Jane Bell Edwards (1908-2002), two professional photographers who had come to the I.D. just for the summer seminar, provided an assessment of Moholy that is important for two reasons: they witnessed the power of Moholy as a teacher near the close of his life, and they did so in a context of a rich assembly of master photographers. They wrote:

> When Moholy-Nagy stepped upon the stage you were immediately aware of a man who was a talented and creative artist. His ability to let you know that he liked humanity, was interested in you as an individual, and that he had something to tell you, all without his uttering a sound is something that one rarely encounters.[503]

Final Months of Moholy as Educator in Chicago: the Institute of Design on North Dearborn Street

Early in June, the I.D. bought the former building of the Chicago Historical Society at 632 North Dearborn Street,[504] a handsome neo-Romanesque stone-masonry building,

---

[501] Arthur Siegel, interviewed by James McQuaid, assisted by Elaine King, October 29th to November 6th, 1977.

[502] The photograph was published in: Thorpe and Edwards, "From a Student's Notebook," [55]; Callahan had been newly appointed to the faculty of the I.D., as noted above.

[503] Thorpe and Edwards, "From a Student's Notebook," 174.

[504] The price was $127,500.00. See: "Board of Directors, Institute of Design, April 30, 1946," mimeographed, Institute of Design Papers, University of Illinois Library, Chicago. Remodeling costs were about $45,000.00. See: "Board of Directors, Institute of Design, August 25, 1946,"

(continued...)

designed by Henry Ives Cobb (1859-1931) and completed in 1892. (DVD figures 485, 486, 487, 488 and 489A) It was still being remodeled when the Fall, 1946, semester opened there on September 23rd. (DVD figures 489B and 489C) It was used by the I.D. until 1956, and is currently shared by two thriving night clubs, Excalibur and Vision.

At the time of the move to North Dearborn Street, Moholy had been suffering from leukemia for over a year. As noted above, sometimes it drained all of his energy, but at other times it seemed to be in complete remission. It was perhaps because of his illness that he wrote a letter to Paepcke on July 31st, 1946, concerning a successor at the I.D., ". . . in case I should one day be unable to continue as its president," even though at the moment his leukemia was evidently in remission and he described his present condition as "excellent."

The successors suggested were his former Bauhaus colleague Marcel Breuer; José Luis Sert, author of *Can Our Cities Survive?*; former School of Design in Chicago faculty members Ralph Rapson and György Kepes; architect Knud Loenberg-Holm (1905-1972), director of the Sweet Catalogue Service; and architect and designer Charles Eames (1907-1978).[505] The last named was cited by Moholy for his emergence ". . . as a brilliant furniture designer." Although Eames had never formally studied with Moholy, he often conferred with him on trips to Chicago around 1940.[506] The acquaintance was renewed when Moholy met Charles Eames and his wife and design partner, Ray, in Washington, D.C., in May of 1944, and talked with them about their work making molded plywood splints for wounded servicemen and women.[507] Interestingly, although Moholy had known Serge Chermayeff since the days when they both lived in England, and in the end Chermayeff was Moholy's successor, he was not on Moholy's list.

Also not on Moholy's list was Gropius; however, at a faculty meeting on November 24th, 1946, ". . . it was the consensus that the Board invite Walter Gropius to become

---

[504](...continued)
mimeographed, Institute of Design Papers, University of Illinois Library, Chicago.

[505] László Moholy-Nagy to Walter P. Paepcke, TLS, July 31st, 1946, Institute of Design Papers, University of Illinois Library, Chicago.

[506] R. Craig Miller, "Interior Design and Furniture," *Design in America, the Cranbrook Vision 1925-1950* (New York: Harry N. Abrams, Inc., Publishers, 1983), page 109 and note 83 on page 306.

Miller's note is based on a transcript of an interview, "Jill Mitchell Speaks with Barbara Price," April, 1982, in the Cranbrook Art Museum, Design in America Archives, Bloomfield Hills, Michigan. On page 11, Mitchell, a design student of Eames at Cranbrook, is quoted as saying: "Eames would go back and forth on weekends to confer with Moholy-Nagy who had just gone to Chicago." Mitchell added: "They were good friends. He [Eames] was very interested and wanted to know what Moholy was doing." Eames taught design at Cranbrook from September, 1939, to June, 1941.

[507] László Moholy-Nagy to Sibyl Moholy-Nagy, ALS, May 23rd, 1944, reel 951, frames 0443-0448, Moholy-Nagy files, Archives of American Art, Washington, D.C.

President and Director of the Institute of Design." They added that: "No one is closer to the spirit and philosophy of Moholy-Nagy than is Doctor Gropius."[508] But there was no other evidence that the appointment of Gropius was seriously considered by either the Board or by Gropius himself.

As events unfolded, after Moholy died on November 24th, 1946, it was Nathan Lerner who served as Educational Director pending appointment of a permanent Director. Lerner served along with Business Manager Leslie Llewellyn Lewis and Secretary Crombie Taylor.[509] The search for a successor quickly narrowed to Serge Chermayeff;[510] his appointment was announced on December 16th, 1946, and he was to begin his duties as President of the I.D. on or before January 15th, 1947.[511] However, negotiations on details of Chermayeff's appointment continued, and it was not finally ratified by the I.D. Board of Directors until March 11th, 1947.[512] Chermayeff remained at the I.D. until 1951, and in the present context it should be pointed out that the milieu of creative ferment that had been stimulated by Moholy's leadership continued under Chermayeff.[513]

His death on November 24th meant that Moholy did not survive to see the end of the fall, 1946, semester. But he was aware that there was still another increase in enrollment, and he arranged for an expanded faculty. He appointed former faculty member Hin Bredendieck and former students Richard Koppe and Richard Filipowski to the faculty. And he was able to appoint his wife, Sibyl, to the faculty to teach

---

[508]"To the Chairman and Board of Directors," Institute of Design, November 24th, 1946 (mimeograph, signed), Institute of Design Papers, University of Illinois Library, Chicago. The statement is signed by: Crombie Taylor, Nathan Lerner, Alexander Archipenko, Arthur S. Siegel, H. Bredendieck, John E. Walley, George Barford, Calvin Albert, Emerson Woelffer, Myron Kozman, Frank T. Sokolik, Harry M. Callahan, Frank Levstik, Robert Bruce Tague, Hugo Weber, Molly S.C. Thwaites and Richard Filipowski.

[509]Walter Gropius to Nathan Lerner, TLS, November 29th, 1946, Nathan Lerner files, Chicago Historical Society; Walter Gropius to Walter P. Paepcke, TLS, December 3rd, 1946, and undated memorandum, "To All Students," about December 1st, 1946, mimeographed, both in the Institute of Design Papers, University of Illinois Library, Chicago. See also: Walter Gropius to Sibyl Moholy-Nagy, carbon copy of TLS, December 3, 1946, Bauhaus-Archiv, Berlin.

[510]On Chermayeff, see: Lloyd C. Engelbrecht, "Chermayeff, Serge," in: Colin Naylor, editor, *Contemporary Designers*, second edition (Chicago: St. James Press, 1990), 105-106.

[511]A mimeographed announcement over the name of "Walter P. Paepcke, Chairman of the Board of the Institute of Design," was dated December 16th, 1946.

[512]"Minutes of the Board of Directors' Meeting of Institute of Design, March 11th, 1947," mimeographed; a copy is in the Institute of Design Papers, University of Illinois Library, Chicago.

[513]Engelbrecht, "Moholy-Nagy und Chermayeff in Chicago," 51 and 64-67.

humanities. Moreover, the fall semester was when he added John E. Walley,[514] and the Swiss artist Hugo Weber (1918-1971) to the faculty.

Moholy's health had waned during the summer months, and it was only with difficulty that he could take part in the summer seminar on photography. In spite of periods when his usual vigor returned, his health continued to deteriorate. Late in November he was forced to return to the hospital, and he died of leukemia in Michael Reese Hospital.

Moving accounts of Moholy's death were written by Gropius and by Sibyl Moholy-Nagy. Gropius, in a letter to Lucia Moholy, then living in London, wrote:

> He has had a sad death but after all I think that for his active mind it was good that he didn't die slowly, which is what he was terribly afraid of. He knew that his days were numbered; he has explained that to me and also to others but he really died at the peak of his activities. A week before his death he came to a congress on Industrial Design in New York and he has played a leading role there, fighting brilliantly and heavily against reactionaries. Everybody told me how well he looked and extremely lively he was on that occasion. Then he came back to Chicago pretty tired but he refused to take the advice of his doctor not to carry things and to take it easy. He came back on Tuesday and on Wednesday he was with his students. As nobody was there when he arrived he lifted a heavy projector and felt heavy pains right after that. The reason was that his spleen had burst which happens in leukemia cases because of too many white corpuscles. This developed peritonitis. The hospitals were so over-crowded that they had to bring him into the general ward of Michael Reese Hospital and he was under great strain there because of other people dying around him. He had many pains on account of the inflammation. On Sunday morning he was then suddenly quiet and very characteristic of his optimistic nature, he told Sybil that he now hoped to pull through as he was always lucky but two hours later he was dead.[515]

In her book, *Moholy-Nagy; Experiment in Totality*, Sibyl Moholy-Nagy gave a longer account of her husband's last days. It included a similar account of the hospital conditions:

---

[514]On Walley, see: "John E. Walley Biography," in: *Selected Papers, John E. Walley*, 9-16; George J. Mavigliano and Richard A. Lawson, *The Federal Art Project in Illinois, 1935-1943* (Carbondale: Southern Illinois University Press, 1990), 55-60 *et passim*; José Patiño Girona, "Happy Days are Here Again for 'Lost' Mural; Restoration Reviving Lane's WPA Painting," *Chicago Tribune*, March 28, 1997, section 1, pages [1] and 12; and Heather Becker, *Art for the People: the Rediscovery and Preservation of Progressive- and WPA-Era Murals in the Chicago Public Schools, 1904-1943* (San Francisco: Chronicle Books, 2002), 38-39, 84, 86, 103, 151 and 220.

[515]Walter Gropius to Lucia Moholy, photographic copy of ALS, December 12th, 1946, Bauhaus-Archiv, Berlin.

> There was no single room available in the large private hospital to which he was
> taken, and there was no night nurse. The oxygen tent did not function and the
> blood transfusion clotted. A stream of relatives, doctors and orderlies brushed
> by his bed in an emergency ward, while wide-open doors gave on a noisy
> corridor. It was like dying in Union Station. But Moholy was no longer aware
> of his surroundings. Breathing had become such a torture that it occupied all his
> attention. And there was an excruciating thirst after the heavy loss of blood. An
> old man brought a tray of food at regular intervals, and he took it away,
> untouched, with equal regularity. Another old man wrapped the body of the
> patient in the next bed in paper strips and carted it away. An oxygen pump
> supplying the victim of an apoplectic stroke in another bed hammered on day
> and night. Over everything lay the stench of a menagerie.[516]

One cannot help but wonder, on reading these accounts, whether, to the extent that Moholy
was aware of his surroundings, he might have felt that he was back in the military hospitals of
World War I!

The meeting in New York that Moholy had attended was a symposium, "Industrial Design, a
New Profession," organized by Edgar J. Kaufmann, junior (1910-1989), Director of the
Department of Design at the Museum of Modern Art, for the Society of Industrial Designers.[517]
The symposium took place November 11th to 14th, 1946. Kaufmann published an extended
account of Moholy's participation, which included these passages:

> Moholy was asked to attend as an educator and designer, and he led the
> discussion on the day devoted to Education. A group of people had been invited
> whose points of view were quite diverse, and controversial matters were
> earnestly debated. Moholy's statements found robust opposition, but
> his clear, measured comprehension gave them unique authority.
>
> Some of us knew how sick Moholy was, and were concerned not only that he
> had taken the trip, but that he should spend hours in such hard-hitting debate.
> His face, always intense, showed the tautness that comes with unrelenting
> sickness, his gestures were as deliberate as those of a swimmer. These signs of
> bodily weariness made the acute perception of his thought the more poignant. It
> was not possible to hear him patiently and resolutely stating the basic ideas
> that underlie his life's work without feeling that Moholy was uttering his
> testament as a teacher. His determined gentleness and patience, even when
> sharply provoked, supported this impression.

Kaufmann went on to describe Moholy's ideas in some detail, including ". . . design education as
a process wherein the student was given the chance to increase his own awareness," and closed
his account with this observation:

---

[516]Sibyl Moholy-Nagy, *Moholy-Nagy; Experiment in Totality*, 245.

[517]Moholy's participation in the symposium was summarized in: Margolin, *The Struggle for Utopia*, 245-
247. For the complete minutes, see: *Minutes of the Conference on Industrial Design: A New Profession*
[November 11th to 14th, 1946] (New York: Museum of Modern Art 1946), mimeographed.

. . . his every word, his careful attention were bent on strengthening the belief of all present in the high value of design as he understood it. He spent himself in this effort, with a grace and completeness that showed his living devotion to an ideal. It was a moving sight to see a man who knew his days were numbered, give so unstintingly of his time and his energies to bring more truth and courage to his fellow men.[518]

Moholy as Designer in Chicago

One of Moholy's principal goals in Chicago was that he, his faculty, and his students would work closely with industry. And to a large extent this goal was accomplished. As one means to stimulate this, Moholy discussed his own design commissions with his students, one of whom, Beatrice Takeuchi, recalled:

> He frequently brought his own projects currently on the board, like the
> B & O double-decker train car designs, Parker Pen designs, and he
> would often discuss with us some of the problems of American
> industrial design[er]s, his impatience with their timidity.[519]

Moholy's first design contract in Chicago was important as a financial bridge for him and his school after the break-up of the New Bauhaus; this was with Spiegel, Inc., a merchandising firm that sold mostly through mail orders. Sibyl Moholy-Nagy wrote that Moholy's contract, at an annual salary of $10,000, was secured within a month after the closing of the New Bauhaus,[520] and he completed his work in August, 1939,[521] so evidently he began at Spiegel at the beginning of September, 1938.

Spiegel was changing its sales strategy to concentrate on reaching customers who enjoyed a higher income than most of Spiegel's traditional customers. This meant,

---

[518]Edgar J. Kaufmann, junior, "Moholy," *Arts and Architecture*, volume LXIV, number 3 (March, 1947), 25.

[519]Takeuchi, "School of Design in Chicago," 17.

[520]Sibyl Moholy-Nagy, *Moholy-Nagy: Experiment in Totality*, 161.

To put Moholy's salary into context: Spiegel's sales during October, 1937, for example, totaled $7,492,835, which constituted an increase of more than twenty percent over October, 1936. Also, that sales increase made October, 1937, the fifty-seventh consecutive month during which an increase had occurred. See: "Sales by Ward, Spiegel, Inc., Gain over '36," *The Chicago Daily News*, November 8, 1937, 25.

Although sales slowed in 1938, net sales for that year nevertheless totaled $49,733,000 and the net profit was $1,964,000; see: Orange A. Smalley and Frederick D. Sturdivant, *The Credit Merchants: a History of Spiegel, Inc.* (Carbondale: Southern Illinois University Press, 1973), [249].

[521]László Moholy-Nagy to Walter Gropius, July 15th, 1939.

among other things, that higher-quality merchandise would be offered and the firm's mail-order catalogues be upgraded in appearance and organization,[522] surely factors in the hiring of Moholy. However, his efforts were not viewed by the firm as productive. Although Sibyl recalled that for Spiegel her husband "arbeitet wie ein Kuli" [worked like a coolie],[523] his contract was not renewed. The two principal sources on Moholy's work for Spiegel are a brief unpublished essay by Robert J. Wolff, evidently written in 1976, and comments on Wolff's essay by M.J. ("Modie") Spiegel, the de facto chief operating of the firm, who had hired Moholy on Wolff's strong recommendation.[524]

Wolff's memory of Moholy's work for Spiegel was that the firm's ". . . first need for Moholy was as an educator and only incidently as a designer." He went on to recall that:

> As time passed and Moholy settled into his new work both he and the
> Spiegel management seemed quite pleased with the arrangement.
> While the job apparently involved him in some actual industrial design,
> mostly I believe of an experimental nature, it seems that Moholy's
> principal value to the company was in injecting its employees with a
> new awareness and interest in the structure and appearance of the mass
> produced products they sold.

Wolff added that: "I don't think Modie and Fred Spiegel ever took him as seriously as they might have."

"Modie" Spiegel's letter, commenting on Wolff's essay, began with his assurance that he had ". . . a vivid recollection of Moholy Nagy's employment and termination. With the passage of time my memory gets dim, but not in this case." Spiegel recalled that, after he had ". . . employed him for one day a week,"

> He was supposed to be innovative and creative, which he was, but
> thoroughly impractical for the times. I tried to get our various
> executives to take him seriously and did meet with him and them
> occasionally to see if there was anything that was usable.
>
> . . . After about a year or two, I terminated Moholy, against which he
> protested on the theory that in Hungary one couldn't dismiss a person
> so lightly but would have to go through channels. Naturally, I told him
> we weren't in Hungary and I could do what I wanted, and I thought I
> had gone pretty far to try to help support the Bauhaus without getting
> anything usable in return.

---

[522]Smalley and Sturdivant, *The Credit Merchants*, 224-226 and 232-234.

[523]Sibyl Moholy-Nagy to Ise and Walter Gropius, photocopy of ALS. December 24th, 1938, Bauhaus-Archiv, Berlin.

[524]The work of Moholy for Spiegel is described in an unpublished four-page manuscript, "Moholy and Spiegel, Inc. 1938-1939" [undated; about 1976] by Robert J. Wolff, and in a letter, M.J. Spiegel to Robert J. Wolff, TLS, May 18th, 1976; a xerox copy of Wolff's essay, and a xerox copy of the letter are in the Bauhaus-Archiv, Berlin.

> At that point, Moholy offered me one of his pictures, which I scoffed at.
> I think they are worth a lot of money today, which just proves how
> prescient I am not.

More productive was a 1940 commission from Foley & Company of Chicago, for which Moholy designed a clear-plastic (cellulose acetate) device to dispense "VITA-BILDS" vitamin tablets (concentrate of many vitamins), one at a time.[525] (DVD figures 490 and 491) Two-level sleeping cars designed in 1943 by Moholy, with the assistance of Ralph Rapson, for the Baltimore & Ohio (B & O) Railroad were not directly executed, but these were to become prototypes of post-War sleeping-car designs.[526]

Also in association with Rapson, Moholy made some exhibition designs for United States Gypsum, beginning in 1944. One example was a massive concave canopy for the firm's exhibits for the 1945 National Association of Home Builders Convention; (DVD figure 492) this and other canopies supported a series of panels utilizing bold outline forms to dramatize the firm's products. Special care was taken to incorporate creative lighting effects.[527] The invitation to work for U.S. Gypsum probably came directly or indirectly through George Fred Keck, who in 1941 had put together the "Trans-Duo House" system for the firm, making use of their building products, such as acoustic-tile ceilings; Keck was aided by his brother, William, as well as by Tague and Rapson.[528]

T HE AMERICAN FIRM for which Moholy worked most intensively on design was the Parker Pen Company of Janesville, Wisconsin, and his success there provides a striking contrast with the evident lack of success he had with his contract for Spiegel's. The work for Parker Pen began in 1945. Gropius had known the president of the Company, Kenneth S. Parker, since 1928,[529] but it is not clear whether this was a factor in the engaging of Moholy to work for Parker Pen. Moholy's work for the Company was both general and specific. He advised on every aspect of the company's work, during conferences with individual employees on work problems, along with general advice on packaging, display, posters, stationery and showrooms. He also made

---

[525]László Moholy-Nagy, *Vision in Motion*, 58.

[526]László Moholy-Nagy, *Vision in Motion*, 55; and Sibyl Moholy-Nagy, *Moholy-Nagy; Experiment in Totality*, 209.

[527]Sibyl Moholy-Nagy, *Moholy-Nagy; Experiment in Totality*, 209-210; and "The Art of Display," *Interiors*, volume CV, number 11 (April, 1946), 89-[113], 144 and 146, here 93-95.

[528]United States Gypsum Company advertisement, *Architectural Forum*, volume LXXV, number 4 (October, 1941), [54-57].

[529]László Moholy-Nagy to Walter Gropius, ALS, July 6th, 1945; and Walter Gropius to László Moholy-Nagy, carbon copy of TLS, July 12th, 1945, both in the Bauhaus-Archiv, Berlin

four patented designs for Parker,[530] with the assistance of Charles Wiley,[531] Beatrice Takeuchi[532] and Nolan Rhodes;[533] it is probable that most of these never actually went into production, but rather that they influenced what was produced by the company. (DVD figure 493) Takeuchi remembers an ink bottle, designed by her and Moholy's other assistants, as the only item that went into production.[534] There was also a striking design for sales-counter display of boxed bottles of ink,[535] but it is not known whether it actually went into production.

Moholy also created interiors for the Parker Pen Company's Chicago office, and ". . . completed the job just a few months before his death in November 1946." These interiors included the sales manager's office, a dealer's lounge, repair work stations and a retail service room.[536] (DVD figure 494) A description of one interior gave details of color and texture, evoking student tactile-chart exercises at the Bauhaus and at the I.D.:

> In the retail service room, walls are hushed pink and yellow; the ceiling blue. The natural white pine furniture is upholstered with coral, and other accents are blue and yellow. In the same room, natural leather, striated plywood, Flexglass, corrugated glass, plaster covered corrugated metal, and twist finish carpeting add a variety of textural effects.[537]

It should be added that Moholy did not have any connection with the "Parker 51" pen; this was designed by Kenneth S. Parker and Marlin S. Baker[538] and patented by

---

[530] Sibyl Moholy-Nagy, *Moholy-Nagy; Experiment in Totality*, 211-212, 226; U. S. Patent Office, Des. 146,806, May 20, 1947; Des. 150,311, July 20, 1948; Des. 150,312; July 20, 1948; and Des. 150,313, July 20, 1948. Des. 150,311 is illustrated in: Hahn and Engelbrecht, editors, *50 Jahre New Bauhaus*, 198.

[531] Sibyl Moholy-Nagy to Ise Gropius, December 2nd, 1945, photographic copy of TLS, Bauhaus-Archiv, Berlin.

[532] Takeuchi, "Fragebogen"; and Howard M. Herriot to Beatrice Takeuchi, TLS, August 14th, 1973, xerox copy in the Bauhaus-Archiv, Berlin.

[533] Sibyl Moholy-Nagy, *Moholy-Nagy; Experiment in Totality*, 211.

[534] Telephone interview, Lloyd C. Engelbrecht and Beatrice Takeuchi, July, 1996. An example of the ink bottle is owned by Cathy Erickson of Chicago.

[535] "L. Moholy-Nagy and the Institute of Design in Chicago," *Everyday Art Quarterly; a Guide to Well Designed Products* (Winter, 1946/Spring, 1947), 1.

[536] "Moholy Takes Pen in Hand," *Interiors*, volume CVII, number 10 (May, 1948), [88]-91.

[537] *Ibid.*, [89].

[538] Howard M. Herriot to Beatrice Takeuchi, August 14th, 1973.

them on August 8th, 1939.[539] Moholy has sometimes been credited with the design of the "Parker 51" pen, no doubt because he illustrated it in *Vision in Motion.*

Moholy described his work for the Parker Pen Company in an essay he wrote for an in-house publication, *Parker Pen Shoptalker*:

> The designer has to know about the industrial processes and the basic mechanical principles involved in a certain problem and has to try to add to the specialist's findings his experience in different fields from which sometimes useful analogies can be derived. This relationship is now well established with the firm and I am very happy about it. . . .[540]

Parker himself wrote a note about Moholy in another in-house publication, *Parkergrams*, shortly after Moholy's death:

> No matter how many designers we engage from now on, we shall not have the luck to find another like him. He was not only gifted as a designer, but one of the truest friends this company ever had. His interest in our success and welfare was such you would have thought he was the sole owner of the business.[541]

Years later Parker recalled his fondness for Moholy: "It would be hard to tell you how much Moholy has been missed at Parker Pen during the past seventeen years. Talking and working with him was not only valuable, but fun; and not only for me but for many others."[542]

SHORTLY AFTER HIS ARRIVAL IN THE WINDY CITY an editorial in a Chicago graphic-design magazine hailed Moholy as ". . . an eminent designer and artist whose work stands as an unmistakable prediction of the direction much of the future's advertising art will take . . ."[543] After this warm welcome to the design community Moholy maintained contacts with fellow designers. One of the ways he did this was by exhibiting with them: he showed in the *Exhibition of Advertising Art, 1938*, sponsored by the Art Directors Club of Chicago.[544] In that exhibition he showed two photographs of his *Light Prop* and a color photograph of 1935, *Dufay Color photography (Light*

---

[539]U. S. Patent Office, Des. 116,097, August 8th, 1939.

[540]*Parker Pen Shoptalker*, June, 1946; reprinted in: Kostelanetz, editor, *Moholy-Nagy*, 92.

[541]Kenneth Parker, "Obituary Note," *Parkergrams*, December, 1946; reprinted in: Kostelanetz, editor, *Moholy-Nagy,* 93.

[542]Kenneth Parker to Sibyl Moholy-Nagy, July 5th, 1963, TLS, microfilm reel 944, frames 0704 and 0705, Moholy-Nagy files, Archives of American Art, Washington, D.C.

[543]"What Will Be the Advertising Art of 1948," *Printing Art Quarterly*, volume LXVII, number 3 (Winter, 1938), 21-22, here 22.

[544]*Printing Art Quarterly*, volume LXVII, number 3 (Winter, 1938), 22, 28, 30 and 31.

filtering), that had appeared in *The Penrose Annual* during the previous year but probably had not been exhibited previously.[545] (DVD figure 495)

Moholy also showed in an exhibition organized by the American Designers' Institute that opened January 24th, 1942, at the Art Center at 820 North Michigan Avenue, Chicago, of "photographs and samples of outstanding designs executed and produced by its members in the past two years." A total of twenty designers participated, including Alfonso Iannelli.[546] Later the Institute elected Moholy to become a member of their Board of Directors, and placed him on their educational committee.[547]

Moholy, nevertheless, was not enthusiastic about some prevalent aspects of American design. On March 18th, 1943, in a long letter to Nikolaus Pevsner, Moholy lamented:

> The "streamlining" ideas are prevailing everywhere and it is certain that without the constructive tendencies of modern art in Europe, the streamlining produced here will be entirely the opposite of what we want. This is rather embarrassing and one cannot use any other term for it but "modernistic."[548]

On July 8th, 1944, at the close of its meeting in Chicago, about forty members of the American Designers' Institute visited the I.D. to view an exhibition of student work and a showing of the school's film, *Design Workshops*.[549]

---

[545] See Chapter Four, note 928; and László Moholy-Nagy, *Vision in Motion*, 170-[171].

[546] A flyer announcing the exhibition is in the Institute of Design Papers, University of Illinois Library, Chicago.

[547] "Institute of Design President's Report, June 22, 1944," mimeographed, Institute of Design Papers, University of Illinois Library, Chicago.

[548] László Moholy-Nagy to Nikolaus Pevsner, March 18th, 1943, TLS, Bauhaus-Archiv, Berlin. In a later essay, Moholy complained that though "Industrial streamlining was introduced originally for a more economical organizing of objects moving with great speed," it nevertheless "radiated into every type of *goods* [emphasis in original], mobile or static." See László Moholy-Nagy, "Design Potentialities," in: Paul Zucker, editor, *New Architecture and City Planning* (New York: Philosophical Library, 1944), 675-687, here 681.

My own attempt to summarize early modern design in Chicago appeared in 1990: Engelbrecht. "Modernism and Design in Chicago," 119-138 and 252-256.

[549] "Institute of Design President's Report, June 22, 1944," mimeographed; Loyal S. Baker to Walter P. Paepcke, TLS, July 25th, 1944; both are in the Institute of Design Papers, University of Illinois Library, Chicago.

Moholy and Architecture and Planning

Although Moholy worked closely with several architects, played an active role in the *C.I.A.M.* (*Congrès Internationaux d'Architecture Moderne*), and was active in kindred fields by designing a number of interiors, as well as by working extensively as an exhibition and stage designer yet, as far as can be determined, he identified himself as an architect in the United States on only three occasions. The first dates from 1938, when he submitted his name as an entrant for "A Competition to Select an Architect for a Proposed Art Center for Wheaton College," in Norton, Massachusetts, announced in *Architectural Forum* in February, 1938.[550] His participation is known only from a list of those who entered the competition, now in the Museum of Modern Art.[551] No drawing, or additional evidence of any kind, documents Moholy's work for this competition. It seems probable that he withdrew after he learned that Walter Gropius had been named an invited participant.[552] (Gropius, who submitted a design in collaboration with Marcel Breuer, did not win the competition.)

In the case of another competition Moholy was more active. This was for a "Festival Theatre and Fine Arts Building at the College of William and Mary in Williamsburg, Virginia, Sponsored by the American National Theatre and Academy." This competition was announced in *Architectural Record* in November, 1938; designs were due by January 31st, 1939. The theatre was to contain 1,500 seats.[553]

A formal drawing for the competition entry, titled "A Theater & Art Building," was designed, according to the label on the drawing (now in the Chicago Historical Society), by "George Fred Keck and L. Moholy-Nagy architects [and] Robert Bruce Tague collaborator."[554] (DVD figures 496, 497, 498 and 499) The drawings as submitted, on three sheets, contained no names (a requirement of the competition), but after the awards were announced it was revealed that the submission was credited only to "George Fred Keck and William Keck, Architects, and Robert Bruce Tague, Associate Architect," and

---

[550] *Architectural Forum*, volume LXVIII, number 2 (February, 1938), 68-71.

[551] James D. Kornwolf, editor, *Modernism in America, 1937-1941: a Catalog and Exhibition of Four Architectural Competitions [held by] Wheaton College, Goucher, College of William and Mary [and the] Smithsonian Institution* (Williamsburg, Virginia: Joseph and Margaret Muscarelle Museum of Art, College of William and Mary, 1985), 241 and 243.

[552] "Important Architectural Competition," *Magazine of Art*, volume XXXI, number 4 (April, 1938), 237-238.

[553] "Program for an Architectural Competition for a Festival Theatre and Fine Arts Building at the College of William and Mary, Williamsburg, Va., Sponsored by the American National Theatre and Academy," *Architectural Record*, volume LXXXIV, number 5 (November, 1938), 33-36.

[554] This presentation drawing, along with designers' names and descriptive text, is in the Architectural Collection of the Chicago Historical Society, a gift of Elmer Ray Pearson. It is rendered in red-and-black ink and black wash.

it did not win an award.[555] No changes were made in the theatre section as it appeared on the drawing that included Moholy's name. The building, of "reinforced concrete and steel, stone and local brick," included facilities for teaching painting, sculpture, architecture, drama and music, with space for a gallery, library and administrative offices. In addition to the formal drawing with Moholy's name on it, a note and rough sketches of a plan and elevation, in Moholy's hand, are on one side of a sheet; on the other side is this note:

> Dear Keck,
>
> Herewith 2 sketches of the project; perhaps an idea. You have to excuse the primitive representation; but the place—Nashville—and weather are so nice that I made them without great care, lying on the lawn.
>
> Best Greetings,
> Yours,
>
> Moholy=Nagy
> Easter sunday [April 17th, 1938][556]

These Nashville sketches, although made "without great care," do illustrate an elevation and plan that are close to the formal drawing that included Moholy's name.

In the brief at the upper left on the competition entry is a program description for the theatre portion of the multi-use building. (table six and DVD figure 492) A key part of the program description reads as follows:

> The projector booth in the large theater is hung so that it can be used for the reduced seating capacity as well. The small theater stage can be opened into the big stage. At the same time the projector booth allows for a projection of light displays, color organ, and motion picture, and simultaneous projections in any direction. In this case the theater walls may act as projection screens. Swivel chairs may be used.
>
> The . . . arena type, or space theater; orchestra pit and parts of the seating can be covered, and the stage stepped to different levels accommodating audience. The patent projector of the Vienna Hofberg Theater would allow projected stage designs without distortion and without darkening the front stage. Bridges with

---

[555]Kornwolf, editor, *Modernism in America*, 139-140, 145 and 173-175.

[556]The sketches were shown to me by George Fred Keck about 1967, when we talked in Chicago. The sketches and note, on one sheet of paper, are in the Keck Papers, State Historical Society of Wisconsin, Madison. A xerox copy is in my possession;

another xerox copy is in the Institute of Design Papers, University of Illinois Library, Chicago.

elevator principle lowered from the gridiron, Trotoir Boulants (moving platforms and bends) mounted on the revolving stage would allow unlimited scenic richness.

Construction: reinforced concrete and steel, stone and local brick.
The building is planned near the lake with possibility for terraces on the south side, with boat houses and lockers underneath. It provides for recreational and open air classes in covered and un-covered terraces.
Teaching departments are separated from public communications. Therefore public communication to the theater and gallery is a separate unit, visually and con-structively an independent entity located under the gallery.
The library is placed centrally for all departments and can function as a semi-public room, without interference with classrooms.
Administration rooms are also centrally placed.
Architecture, painting and sculpture studios are on the top floor with north light, high, that they may not be shaded by trees. They are near the library, lecture rooms and gallery on the second floor. In the lecture rooms a folding partition allows flexibility. Theater and Music divisions have south light, controlled by outside aluminum blinds and balconies. Theater workshop and stage design have north light, and are near the stage and rehearsal room. Actors reach the stage from their dressing rooms and musicians the orchestra pit through the under stage, and the stage designer the workshop by a little stairway, directly.
The projector booth in the large theater is hung so that it can be used for the reduced seating capacity as well. The small theater stage can be opened into the big stage.
At the same time the projector booth allows a projection of light displays, color organ, and motion picture, and simultaneous projections in any direct-ion. In this case the theater walls may act as projection screens. Swivel chairs may be used.
The the arena type, or space theater; orchestra pit and parts of the seating can be covered, and the stage stepped to different levels accomodating audience.
The patent projector of the Vienna Hofburg Theater would allow projected stage designs without distortion and without darkening the front stage. Bridges with elevator principle lowered from the gridiron, Trottoir Roulants (moving platforms and bends) mounted on the revolving stage would allow unlimited scenic richness.
The acoustics of the large theater will be regulated with isocoustic screens.
The main kitchen in the large theater has access to lobby, gallery and terraces.
Storage and packing room is on the ground floor with an elevator for gallery, model-ing and casting studios.
Ample stairways and fire-escapes are pro-vided, together with well located toilet facilities for all. The building is access-ible by cars and trucks, and has covered unloading platforms. Parking space is located conveniently on unwooded level space.

Table six: detail of DVD figure 492

Clearly Moholy envisioned theatre facilities in which productions similar to those he planned and carried out in Europe could take place. (tables six, seven eight and nine, DVD figures 492, 493, 494 and 495)

As noted above, the competition drawings as submitted did not list Moholy among those credited, so evidently he withdrew from this project as well, perhaps because Gropius and Breuer were invited to be participants.

The probable explanation for Moholy's making his preliminary sketch in Nashville is that he must have been visiting Leslie Cheek (1908-1992) at his family mansion and garden there, Cheekwood (Bryant Fleming, 1929-1932), now the Cheekwood Botanical Garden and Museum of Art.[557] Cheek, who taught at William and Mary,[558] was probably spending the holiday with his family and thus provided the opportunity for Moholy to visit him on Easter of 1938. Both were somewhat embattled Modernists. Cheek had played a key role in setting up the William and Mary competition,[559] but witnessed the failure to fund and build the winning design by Eero Saarinen, Ralph Rapson and Frederic James.[560] No doubt Cheek and Moholy discussed the competition, not as yet formally announced, and Cheek might have had with him in Nashville the site plan for the competition, or a copy of it.[561] The "lawn" mentioned in Moholy's note on the back of his sketches would have been part of the extensive grounds of the Cheek family mansion. (DVD figures 500 and 501)

---

[557] Cheek's family had made a fortune in the coffee business and had originated the Maxwell House Coffee brand.

[558] On Cheek see: Kornwolf, editor, *Modernism in America*, 247; see also: Leslie Cheek, Jr., "Art at William & Mary," *Magazine of Art*, volume XXXI, number 3 (March, 1938), 150-155.

I am indebted to James D. Kornwolf for sharing his insights on Cheek with me, and for providing the clue, namely Cheek's continuing ties in Nashville, that helps to explain why Moholy made his drawing in Nashville; telephone interview, August 30th, 1996.

[559] Kornwolf, editor, *Modernism in America*, 130.

[560] Kornwolf, editor, *Modernism in America*, 133-137 and 146-151

[561] Kornwolf, editor, *Modernism in America*, 132.

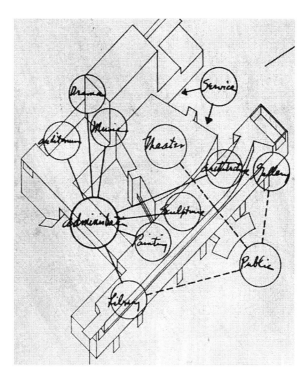

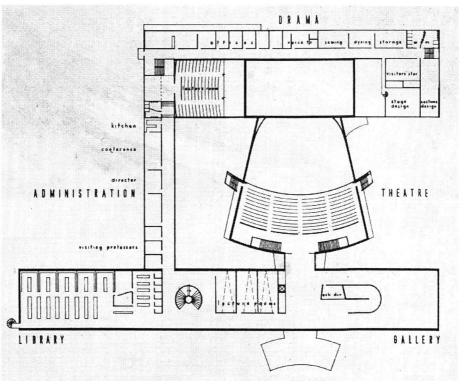

table seven: details of DVD figures 496 and 497

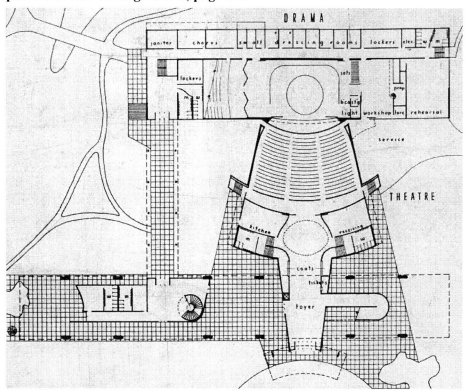

table eight: details of DVD figures 496 and 499

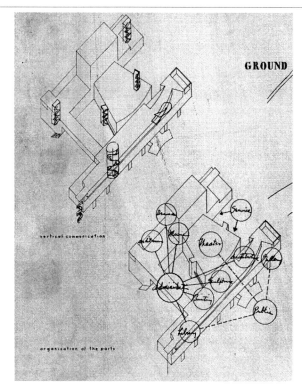

table nine: details of DVD figures 496 and 499

The third time Moholy offered his services as an architect was when he was approached in May, 1943, by Hilla Rebay, curator of the Solomon R. Guggenheim Foundation, for advice on who might be asked to design a building for the Foundation's art collection,[562] which already included a number of his paintings.[563] Moholy replied by including his name on a list of potential architects, along with Le Corbusier, Gropius, Neutra, Breuer, Keck, Aalto and Lescaze.[564]

I T SHOULD BE BORNE IN MIND that in 1939 Moholy had been involved with two architectural competitions for art buildings on college campuses, as discussed above. Moreover, as related in Chapter Four, Rebay had visited the German Werkbund exhibition in Paris in 1930 on which Moholy had collaborated in setting up a carefully planned sequence of spaces on two levels through which the visitor was guided among the exhibited items (although this space was in an existing building, it might have helped to plant a germ of an idea in Rebay's head about the kind of museum she wanted). It should not be overlooked that while they were both in Paris in 1930 Moholy had helped Rebay hang her paintings in a gallery show there, as related in Chapter Four. But perhaps more important, as Beatrice Takeuchi recalled from her student days, "Architecture, Moholy explained, was the mother art in which all other work was contained."[565]

Nevertheless, after Frank Lloyd Wright, who had not been on Moholy's list, received the commission, Moholy wrote a short note to Rebay: "Congratulation to [*sic*] your choice of Wright. He is certainly a grand architect."[566] However, Moholy went on to criticize one of Wright's early schemes for the Guggenheim Museum; this was evidently during a visit Moholy made to New York in late May, 1944,[567] at a time when Rebay

---

[562]Lukach, Joan M., *Hilla Rebay: in Search of the Spirit in Art*, with postscript by Thomas M. Messer (New York: George Braziller, 1983), 182; Hilla Rebay to László Moholy-Nagy, May 12th, 1943, Hilla von Rebay Foundation, Solomon R. Guggenheim Museum of Art, New York.

[563]These are listed in: Angelica Zander Rudenstein, *The Guggenheim Museum Collection: Paintings, 1880-1945* (New York: The Solomon R. Guggenheim Foundation, 1976), 2:546-549, 552, and 562-563. (Additional paintings by Moholy were added to the collection later.)

[564]Lukach, *Hilla Rebay*, 234; László Moholy-Nagy to Hilla Rebay, May 24th, 1943, Hilla von Rebay Foundation, Solomon R. Guggenheim Museum of Art, New York. Moholy added a handwritten note to his typed list of architects: "I love to do myself arch. tasks. I worked with a young architect, Robert Bruce Tague, very satisfactorily during the last year on such tasks."

[565]Takeuchi, "School of Design in Chicago," 21.

[566]László Moholy-Nagy to Hilla Rebay, ALS, July 26th, 1943, Hilla von Rebay Foundation, Solomon R. Guggenheim Museum of Art, New York.

[567]László Moholy-Nagy to Sibyl Moholy-Nagy, ALS, May 23rd, 1944, written "On/the/train/to NYC," microfilm reel 951, frames 0443-9448, Archives of American Art, Washington, D.C.

herself was having second thoughts.[568] Rebay's second thoughts were prompted by Wright's first set of sketches after site selection had been completed in March of 1944.[569] In his letter to her dated July 5th, 1944, Wright reacted sharply to Moholy's criticism, relayed to him by Rebay:[570] "Moholy-Nagy has the nerve to suggest what a museum should be like? I never did respect him for his brains."[571] In a letter to Rebay the following day Wright added: "What does [Rudolf] Bauer [a painter represented in the Guggenheim Collection who had known Rebay and Solomon R. Guggenheim in Berlin] know about an appropriate museum site? What does that show-off pretender, the Hungarian [*i.e.*, Moholy-Nagy], know about a building either? Ask anyone."[572]

It is unlikely that Moholy knew about Wright's comments. In any case, in 1945 he wrote to him asking for photographs of his "Fallingwater" to include in *Vision in Motion*, and added a tepid comment about pictures he had seen of a model of the Guggenheim.[573]

One more example of Moholy's many-sidedness is the strong interest he took in city planning, already seen through his interest in the *C.I.A.M.* As one result of Moholy's service as a juror for the "Better Chicago Contest,"[574] sponsored by the *Chicago Herald-*

---

[568] Brendan Gill, *Many Masks; a Life of Frank Lloyd Wright* (New York: G.P. Putnam's Sons, 1987), 438.

[569] Published in: Bruce Brooks Pfeiffer, editor, *Frank Lloyd Wright: the Guggenheim Correspondence* (Carbondale: Southern Illinois University Press, 1986), 31-36.

[570] I have not been able to establish how Rebay conveyed Moholy's criticism to Wright.

[571] Frank Lloyd Wright to Hilla Rebay, July 5th, 1944, published in Pfeiffer, editor, *Frank Lloyd Wright: the Guggenheim Correspondence*, 47.

[572] Frank Lloyd Wright to Hilla Rebay, July 6th, 1944, published in Pfeiffer, editor, *Frank Lloyd Wright: the Guggenheim Correspondence*, 47-48,

[573] László Moholy-Nagy to Frank Lloyd Wright, TLS, October 9th,1945; Wright agreed in a friendly note of October 18th; original of the former and carbon copy of the latter are in the Frank Lloyd Wright Archives, Frank Lloyd Wright Foundation, Scottsdale, Arizona.

[574] The initial list of judges was given in: *Illinois Society of Architects Monthly Bulletin*, in: "For a 'Better Chicago Plan'" in its issue of June/July, 1945 (page 8). These were listed as: ". . . Daniel Burnham, Jr., president of the Chicago Regional Planning Association; Arthur Cutts Willard, president, University of Illinois; Prof. Ovid Wallace Eshbach, dean of engineering, Northwestern University; Dr. Jesse E. Hobson, director, Illinois Institute of Technology; Most Rev. Bernard J. Sheil, D.D., Auxiliary Bishop, Catholic Archdiocese of Chicago; Walter Blucher, Municipal Finance Officers Association; Walter F. Dodd, Attorney; L. Moholy-Nagy, president, Institute of Design; John W. Root of the American Institute of Architects; Harold S. Buttenheim, editor, 'the American City'; and James C. Downs, Jr., chairman, Mayors Committee on Race Relations. Jerrold Loebl, chairman of the National Public Housing Conference of Chicago will act as professional advisor to the contest." They were also announced in the *Chicago Herald-American*, complete with short biographies of each juror (April 9, 1945, front page and page 8) and pictures of each juror (page 13). Evidently Professor F.M. Lescher of the University of

(continued...)

American, the City Planning Group was formed. Basically Moholy worked very hard reviewing the submissions for the "Better Chicago Contest"[575] (discussed in more detail below), and had been very favorably impressed by the quality of the entries, but he was so disturbed by the way significant ideas had been treated by what he considered to be reactionary jurors that he asked that his name be removed from the list of jurors.[576]

The City Planning Group was Moholy's instrument for doing something about the projects submitted to the contest. In March, 1946, Moholy had a luncheon with two young architects, Charles Wiley, who had worked with him for Parker Pen, and former School of Design student Harry Weese (1915-1998);[577] together they launched the City Planning Group,[578] which included young architects and planners.

THE CITY PLANNING GROUP was not to survive long, and Moholy's association with Weese was short-lived because of his early death. But it is worth noting that it was Weese who wrote a short account of the fledgling organization.[579] And a highlight of Weese's career was a major planning project: in 1966 he was named designer for the Washington, D.C., Metro subway rail system (operation began in 1976). The stations Weese designed for the Metro are noted for their spacious interiors and coffered vaulted ceilings, articulated by dramatic lighting, and also for functional and attractive signage and complete absence of advertisements.[580] (DVD figure 502)

---

[574](...continued)
Illinois alternated with Arthur Cutts Willard: see William Tell, "9 City Plans Vie for Top Prize," *Chicago Herald-American*, September 5, 1945, picture caption on page 4, and William Cartan, "Tell Better Chicago $25,000 Winners," *ibid.*, December 16, 1945, [1] and 5.

[575]László Moholy-Nagy to Robert J. Wolff, September 5th, 1945, TLS, Robert Jay Wolff files, microfilm reel N69-72, frame 0368, Archives of American Art, Washington, D.C.

[576]According to an account by noted Chicago architect Harry Weese, included in: Sibyl Moholy-Nagy, *Moholy-Nagy; Experiment in Totality*, 227.

[577]On Weese see: Kitty Baldwin Weese, *Harry Weese Houses*, with an introduction by Allan Temko (Chicago: Chicago Review Press, 1987); and Katsuhiko Ichinowatari, editor, *Harry Weese: Humanism and Tradition* (Tokyo: Process Architecture, 1979).

Weese was listed as a former student at the School of Design in a letter, Mollie Thwaites to Myron Kozman, TLS, July 3rd, 1943; xerox copies are in my files and in the files of Hattula Moholy-Nagy.

[578]Sibyl Moholy-Nagy, *Moholy-Nagy; Experiment in Totality*, 226-227.

[579]Published in: Sibyl Moholy-Nagy, *Moholy-Nagy; Experiment in Totality*, 227.

[580]Nory Miller, "Washington's Metro: It Works and It Looks Good," *Ekistics: the Problems and Science of Human Settlements,* volume XLIII, number 256 (March, 1977), 171-173.

Several years before Weese received the Washington subway commission, the continuing allure planning held for him was evident in a letter he wrote to Sibyl Moholy-Nagy about his delight at working on an earlier planning job:

> We are engaged in the planning of the 45 acres of the Chicago Dock and Canal Company whose first legal counsel was Abraham Lincoln and whose property formed the mouth of the Chicago River, lying now roughly between the Tribune Tower and Navy Pier. It is a marvelous assignment rooted in some interesting lore and tied to waterfront concepts.[581]

The *Chicago Herald-American* (no longer published) was part of the Hearst chain of newspapers headed by William Randolph Hearst. It seems surprising that in 1945 it was the *Herald-American* that began a major effort at influencing city planning, since it was a conservative newspaper and, with few exceptions, the articles that filled its pages were rather brief. Nevertheless, it was the *Herald-American* that held the "Better Chicago Contest," a project begun with high hopes, and one that represented a major effort for the newspaper. It also marked a culmination of William Tell's efforts for it. He had been brought in at the beginning of the year: ". . . to tell what he saw and what he found wrong with our town; to pull no punches, political or otherwise; to impress upon all of us the civic cleanup job we must do to keep Chicago from the kind of stagnation which threatens to rot the structure of so many American cities." And his editors found that: "Tell did his job well."[582]

Tell continued to do his job well as he announced the contest on April 9th, 1945,[583] and carefully explained, in an extensive series of informative and amply-illustrated articles, why planning was so important to Chicago and the Chicago region.[584] Nevertheless, by the time the contest winners were announced,[585] Tell had evidently left

---

[581] Harry Weese to Sibyl Moholy-Nagy, TLS, September 22nd, 1961, microfilm reel 944, frame 0660, Moholy-Nagy files; Archives of American Art, Washington, D.C.

[582] "Time for Planning Is Now," *Chicago Herald-American*, April 9, 1945, 8.

[583] The announcement featured a front-page, by-lined article, William Tell, "$25,000 City Plan Contest," *Chicago Herald-American*, April 9, 1945, [1] and 8, supplemented by separate articles, also split between the front page and page 8, "Purpose, Prizes and Rules of Contest," and "Members of Jury to Pick Winners." Three pages of pictures relating to the contest appeared on pages 11, 12 and 13.

[584] *E.g.*, William Tell, "Chicago—How It Grew," *Chicago Herald-American*, April 10, 1945, p. [1], 4 and 12; *idem*, "Chicago—Its Earlier Days," *ibid.*, [1] and 4; *idem*, "Chicago—Too Many Cooks!", *ibid.*, April 12, 1945, [1] and 9; *idem*, "William Tell Tells How Freehanded Generosity with Railroads Carved up Chicago's Streets," *ibid.*, April 15, 1945, 19; *idem*, "City System Pure Chaos," *ibid.*, April 16, 1945, 7; and *idem*, "Need New Laws in City Planning," *ibid.*, July 6, 1945, 7.

[585] Cartan, "Tell Better Chicago $25,000 Winners," [1] and 5. In spite of the resignation reported

(continued...)

the newspaper, perhaps for some of the same reasons Moholy had resigned as a contest judge. Tell's last article about the contest may provide the clue. He reported that of the eighteen entrants vying for the top prize of $10,000, nine remained for consideration, and nine others were eliminated, although "Several of these were tabled to be considered later as candidates for the secondary prizes totaling $15,000."[586]

Tell went on to describe the deliberations:

> The big problem for the jury, it appears, is to reconcile the different kinds of thought on city planning represented among the 11 members. Somewhere between the highly visionary school of city planning and the so-called realistic school may be the indicator that will point to the verdict and—the winning plan.[587]

In any case, Tell's educational efforts surely had an impact on Chicago's citizens, and, moreover, while Moholy was disappointed in the results as a whole, there were some "Better Chicago Contest" minor prizes awarded to members of the I.D. community. A $1,000 prize for an Administrative and Cultural Center was won by Ralph Rapson (jointly with Kazumi Adachi, Florence Schust and Herbert Stevens); Rapson was teaching architecture at the I.D. at the time. Another prize of $500 was won by three I.D. students, David Aaron, Stanley Kazdailis and Beatrice Takeuchi, in collaboration with Crombie Taylor, Assistant Director of the I.D.[588]

Moholy as Fine Artist, Photographer and Writer in Chicago

Although Moholy remained very active in Chicago in creating paintings, black-and-white and color photographs, drawings, prints, and sculpture, these works have not, until the 1990s, been discussed as a group.[589]

---

[585](...continued)
by Weese, Moholy was still listed as a juror. However, Moholy was evidently not present at the awards dinner; see: William Cartan, "Award Better City Planners $25,000," *Chicago Herald-American*, January 30, 1946, 3.

[586]Tell, "9 City Plans Vie for Top Prize," 4.

[587]Tell, "9 City Plans Vie for Top Prize," 4.

[588]Crombie Taylor to Walter P. Paepcke, December 20th, 1945, Institute of Design Papers, University of Illinois Library, Chicago; Cartan, "Tell Better Chicago $25,000 Winners," [1] and 5; *idem*, "Offer 100-City Chicago Plan," *Chicago Herald-American*, December 23, 1945, 9.

[589]The first comprehensive attempt to present the full range of Moholy's work in Chicago was made in the 1991-1992 exhibition, *Moholy-Nagy: a New Vision for Chicago*. The dates of the exhibition are given incorrectly in the catalogue on page [2]. It was actually shown in the Illinois

(continued...)

INCLUDED IN Moholy's art output during his Chicago years were innovative paintings made on Plexiglas and suspended over white-painted boards by means of brackets. Examples include *Mills I*[590] and *Mills 2* (DVD figure 503),[591] both painted at Mills College in the summer of 1940.[592] Although Plexiglas, a trade name for a poly-methyl-methacrylate plastic sheet, was first synthesized in 1910 in Germany, it was in the United States, in 1936, that it was first produced commercially in sheet form.[593]

Because Plexiglas had only been available commercially beginning in 1936, there had been no experience with Plexiglas over time, and in fact Moholy's work involving Plexiglas, and particularly his sculpture, has become unstable over the years.

The instability of Plexiglas is unfortunate, because the most innovative of Moholy's work in the fine arts in Chicago was his molded Plexiglas sculptures. These were molded into complex "warped surface" curves, a type of shape which had been rare up until then in the work of other sculptors. An example is *Ribbon Sculpture* of 1943. (DVD figure 505) Once owned by Moholy's faculty colleague, James Prestini, it was offered for sale in 2000.[594] Because Prestini took pains to store the work under ideal conditions it remains in good condition.[595]

Sometimes Moholy combined Plexiglas with steel rods, thus anticipating the molded plastic furniture, mounted on steel rods, which emerged as innovative post-War furniture shortly after Moholy had died; an example is *Twisted Planes*, Plexiglas and steel rods, 1946. (DVD figure 504)

---

[589](...continued)
State Museum in Springfield from October 20th, 1990, to January 6th, 1991, and at the State of Illinois Art Gallery in Chicago from January 14th to March 8th, 1991. See: Terry Suhre, editor, *Moholy-Nagy: a New Vision for Chicago* (Chicago: University of Illinois Press and the Illinois State Museum, 1990).

[590]Angelica Zander Rudenstine, *The Guggenheim Museum Collection, Paintings, 1880-1945* (New York: The Solomon R. Guggenheim Museum, 1976), 2:558-559.

[591]Sibyl Moholy-Nagy, *Moholy-Nagy; Experiment in Totality*, figure 58 facing page 180.

[592]Neumeyer was informed by Moholy that "two empty plexiglas sheets packed in plywood" were being sent to Mills College so that Moholy could "paint on them during the summer session." [László Moholy-Nagy to Alfred Neumeyer], June 7th, 1940, carbon copy of typed memorandum, "List of Pictures Sent to Mills College," Institute of Design Papers, University of Illinois Library, Chicago.

[593]Rudenstine, *The Guggenheim Museum Collection*, 2:545.

[594]Advertisement for Robert Henry Adams Fine Art of Chicago, *Art News*, volume IC, number 4 (April, 2000), 96.

[595]Hattula Moholy-Nagy explained in an E-mail message to me of October 13th, 2008: "Prestini kept it in a pillowcase on the top shelf of a closet in his apartment, which accounts for the unusually good preservation."

Moholy bent the Plexiglas for these sculptures with his own hands, using the cooking oven in his apartment as a heat source.[596] At times he was assisted by his daughters and by students.[597] After Moholy's death, Sibyl Moholy-Nagy wondered if her husband's work with plastics could have led to his leukemia. She consulted two doctors, both of whom advised her that there was no connection.[598]

The photographic output of Moholy in Chicago was to receive more attention in the 1990s when Hattula Moholy-Nagy began to publish her findings. Her first article on the subject appeared in 1993[599] and another followed four years later.[600] More recently she has teamed up with Jeannine Fiedler to curate an exhibition documented by a catalogue that concerns Moholy's color photographs in general, most of which were created in Chicago.[601]

Because there is only a single example of a camera photograph made by Moholy in Chicago and published while he lived there, some people have concluded that he had discontinued using a camera to make photographs. In fact, he continued using a camera but there was more emphasis on color slides.[602] The single example of a camera photograph made and published while Moholy lived in Chicago appeared in 1937 in *Fortune*, an upscale business magazine operated by the publishers of *Time* and *Life*. *Fortune* published a montage of two of his color photographs depicting a festive scene of

---

[596] Sibyl Moholy-Nagy, *Moholy-Nagy; Experiment in Totality*, 191; and László Moholy-Nagy to Robert J. Wolff, June 7th, 1942.

[597] "I remember . . . visits to the household, probably when baby-sitting the girls [Hattula and Claudia], when sometimes we would all help Moholy take out a Plexiglas sculpture from the oven, an exciting moment of truth for any cake or roast, but a serious moment of truth for Moholy, who excitedly instructed us when and how to bend it." Quoted from: Takeuchi, "School of Design in Chicago," 29.

[598] Sibyl Moholy-Nagy to Ise Gropius, September 29th, 1948, photographic copy of TLS, Bauhaus-Archiv, Berlin. Sibyl Moholy-Nagy wrote: "I talked to Laci's doctor about the cancer danger in working with plastics. He assured me that there was nothing in it and so did my surgeon cousin recently. But I would not be so sure."

[599] Hattula Moholy-Nagy, "A Reminiscence of My Father as Photographer," in: Adam J. Boxer, editor, *The New Bauhaus, School of Design in Chicago: Photographs, 1937-1944 . . . .* (New York: Banning + Associates, 1993), 16-17.

[600] Hattula Moholy-Nagy, "Moholy-Nagy: the Late Photography" and "Moholy-Nagy: die späte Photographie," in: Gottfried Jäger and Gudrun Wessing, editors, *über moholy-nagy* (Bielefeld: Kerber Verlag, 1997), 149-152 and 153-156, respectively.

[601] Jeannine Fiedler and Hattula Moholy-Nagy, editors, *Laszlo Moholy-Nagy: Color in Transparency; Photographic Experiments in Color, 1934-1946/Fotografische Experimente in Farbe, 1934-1946* [exhibition catalogue, Bauhaus-Archiv, Berlin, June 21 to September 4, 2006] (Göttingen: Steidl Publishers, 2006).

[602] Hattula Moholy-Nagy, "Moholy-Nagy: the Late Photography," 149-150.

a variety of commercial paper products that party planners could use.[603] (DVD figure 507) This appeared as leavening for the text, charts, and black-and-white portraits of paper-company executives in a lengthy article devoted to fifteen American paper companies.[604]

THE CHICAGO PHOTOGRAPHS include creative photographs, such as the single collage that exists from his Chicago years, *Zeus Has Troubles Too*, of 1943,[605] the studies of traffic lights taken at night, and light drawings made in the dark with a pinpoint flashlight. An example of automobile headlights taken at night is a curious photograph, evidently photographed while cars, traveling at night, approached traffic lights is *Three Shots of Traffic Lights*, 1939-1946 (DVD figure 506); Jeannine Fiedler and Hattula Moholy-Nagy have published a fascinating rumination on this photograph:

> For the Greek philosopher Plato, to research the secrets of light was to penetrate the secrets of the gods. The title of this composition, "3 shots of traffic lights," does little to clarify the method used, and indeed is confusing. Is this a superimposition of three shots using a slide sandwich technique? Do the flashbulb-like twitches stem from several spotlights or from one? Is the azure background a result of overexposure, or was Moholy shooting in twilight here? The light articulations, painted in the sky as if by the hand of a god, do not reveal the mystery of their genesis.[606]

No firm date can be established for *Three Shots of Traffic Lights*, but it has an affinity with one of Moholy's Plexiglas woks, *Ribbon Sculpture*, of 1943. (DVD figure 505)

One example of a light drawing made in the dark with a pinpoint flashlight was a carefully-articulated portrait of a man, known only as *a drawing made by a pinpoint flashlight*, 1941 or earlier.[607] (DVD figure 508) It was likely made on printing-out paper and was shown with a group of photograms that were made on that kind of light-sensitive paper. This portrait became one of Moholy's most widely exhibited photographs, since it was part of the traveling exhibition first seen in 1941, *Light As a Means of Expression*, discussed above.

There are documentary photographs from his automobile trip from Chicago to Mills College and back in 1940, as well as photographs made on the Mills campus. (DVD

---

[603] László Moholy-Nagy, "The Tinsel and the Glamour," *Fortune*, volume XVI, number 5 (November, 1937), 138-139.

[604] "Fifteen Paper Companies," *ibid.*, 132-137, 189-190, 192, 194, 196 and 199.

[605] László Moholy-Nagy, *Vision in Motion*, 215.

[606] Jeannine Fiedler and Hattula Moholy-Nagy, editors, *Laszlo Moholy-Nagy: Color in Transparency*, 138.

[607] László Moholy-Nagy, *Vision in Motion*, [196]-197.

figure 469) One of the people he photographed on the way to or from Oakland was a colorfully-dressed elderly Native American man, possibly Navajo, seen in New Mexico or Arizona. (DVD figure 509)

F AMILY PICTURES were prominent among the photographs Moholy made in the United States, including many in color, that were probably not intended to be exhibited or published, but since they were made with the same skill and insight that informs his other photographs they are now of interest outside his family circle. One of the most charming shows an impish Hattula, not quite six years old, possibly aware of something her father is unaware of; it was filmed in Somonauk in the summer of 1939. (DVD figure 510) A slightly later photograph shows Sibyl with her daughters lying in a grassy part of Lincoln Park in 1945, evidently dressed for brisk autumn weather. (DVD figure 511) Hattula remembers the scene as near the family's Lakeview Avenue apartment.[608]

A rare photographic self-portrait was made in color by Moholy in 1944. (DVD figure 512) He is seen elegantly dressed and in what Hattula has described as "the classical pose of the visionary."[609] At abut the same time he made three studio portraits of his friend Fernand Léger, then visiting the I.D., as noted above, in connection with an exhibition and some lectures; one of these portraits is seen in DVD figure 513.

It should be added that one Chicago photograph has been mis-attributed to Moholy. Actually made by an unknown photographer, it originally appeared in the *Chicago Tribune*.[610] Moholy gave the *Tribune* as the source when he published it in *Vision in Motion*,[611] but many writers have nevertheless taken it to be his own work.

Moholy's impact on photography in America is due in part to the articles that he wrote for three widely distributed American photography publications. These appeared in *Popular Photography* in 1939,[612] *Modern Photography* in 1940,[613] and *The American*

---

[608]Jeannine Fiedler and Hattula Moholy-Nagy, editors, *Laszlo Moholy-Nagy: Color in Transparency*, 190.

[609]Jeannine Fiedler and Hattula Moholy-Nagy, editors, *Laszlo Moholy-Nagy: Color in Transparency*, 138-139.

[610]Hattula Moholy-Nagy, "Moholy-Nagy: the Late Photography," 149-150.

[611] László Moholy-Nagy, *Vision in Motion*, 9 and 36.

[612] László Moholy-Nagy, "Making Photographs without a Camera," *Popular Photography,* volume V, number 6 (December, 1939), 30-31and 167-169; the first page of the article is illustrated in: Engelbrecht, "Educating the Eye," 31.

[613] László Moholy-Nagy "as told to Floyd B. Quigg," "Make a Light Modulator," *Modern Photography*, volume II, number 7 (March, 1940), 38-42.

Annual of Photography for both 1943[614] and 1945.[615] At the same time his photographic ideas were discussed in general publications, including an article in the *Chicago Tribune* in 1940 in which two of his photograms were illustrated,[616] and in 1938 and 1939 two illustrated articles appeared in a publication aimed at design professionals.[617]

In 1943 Moholy's article, "Surrealism and the Photographer," appeared in *The Complete Photographer*, edited by Willard Detering Morgan (1900-1967).[618] Morgan published articles by many leading photographers, including Moholy's old Dessau neighbor, Andreas Feininger, and Nancy and Beaumont Newhall.

Moholy surely qualifies as a Chicagoan because he spent more than nine years living and working in the Windy City and, since he always found time in his busy schedule to remain active as painter, sculptor and photographer, it can be said that no Chicago artist of his or an earlier generation is so well known locally, nationally, or internationally. Certainly that is true if one uses as a measure the amount of Moholy's work in permanent collections of major European, Japanese and American museums.

At the end of April, 1938, Moholy was represented in a group show at the Arts Club, one of the principal venues in Chicago for showing Modernist art.[619] Apart from being seen at the New Bauhaus, the group show at the Arts Club was the first time his work in fine arts was seen locally after his move to Chicago. Clarence J. Bulliet commented:

> L. Moholy-Nagy is exhibiting with the Arts Club for the first time
> one of his "abstracts," which he calls "Construction RH 6," built on a

---

[614] *Idem*, "Space-Time and the Photographer," *The American Annual of Photography, Volume Fifty-Seven, 1943* (Boston: American Photographic Publishing Co., 1942), 7-14.

[615] *Idem*, "Photography in the Study of Design," *The American Annual of Photography, Volume Fifty-Nine, 1945* (Boston: American Photographic Publishing Co., 1944), 158-164.

[616] Andrew B. Hecht, "Photography without a Camera," *Chicago Tribune*, April 7, 1940, F 11.

[617] László Moholy-Nagy, "A New Instrument of Vision," *Printing Art Quarterly*, volume LXVII, number 2 (Autumn, 1937), 21-23; and *idem*, "Paths to the Unleashed Colour Camera," *ibid.*, volume LXVII, number 3 (Winter, 1938), 28-32. The latter had already appeared in *The Penrose Annual*, as discussed in Chapter Four.

[618] László Moholy-Nagy, "Surrealism and the Photographer," *The Complete Photographer: a Complete Guide to Amateur and Professional Photography* (New York: National Educational Alliance, Inc, 1943), 9:3337-3342.

[619] On the Arts Club, see: Engelbrecht, "Association of Arts and Industries," 153-154, 162-163 and 190-192; Richard R. Brettell and Sue Ann Prince, "From the Armory Show to the Century of Progress: the Art Institute Assimilates Modernism," in Prince, editor, *The Old Guard and the Avant-Garde*, 209-225 and 263-266, here 216-219; and The Arts Club of Chicago, *Drawings 1916/1966: Catalogue of an Exhibition on the Occasion of the Fiftieth Anniversary of the Arts Club of Chicago, February 26/March 11, 1966* (Chicago: The Arts Club of Chicago, 1966).

bulging transparency to enhance its spatial qualities. It is the one
"problem piece" in the show—a new challenge to the understanding
of the lay visitor. Moholy-Nagy is director of the New Bauhaus.[620]

Another early display of Moholy's work in Chicago was at the Renaissance Society
of the University of Chicago, where a single-artist exhibition was held from April 7th
through May 7th, 1939.[621] A four-page brochure was issued,[622] and there was a review in
the student newspaper.[623] The Renaissance Society, which did not show Modernist art
exclusively, nevertheless had a distinguished record of ground-breaking Modernist
exhibitions dating back to 1917, and was evidently the first gallery in Chicago to show
work by Arp, Hélion, Léger and Mondrian.[624]

T HE FIRST AMERICAN single-artist showing of Moholy's works was a spring, 1938,
touring exhibition including paintings, photograms and sculpture shown in four
Florida cities: Jacksonville, Gainesville, Tallahassee and Pensacola. The tour was
set up by Robert Delson (1909-1955), a future faculty member of the I.D., who was
teaching at the time at the Federally funded WPA (Works Progress Administration) Art
Center in Jacksonville. At each venue Delson lectured on "Constructivist Art and the
Bauhaus" and showed Moholy's film, *A Lightplay Black White Gray*. The lecture and
film were presented on June 8th at the Jacksonville Federal Galleries.[625] (DVD figure
517)

The event at the Florida Union at the University of Florida in Gainesville attracted at
least 3,000 people. D.R. (Billy) Mathews, director of the Union, reported:

---

[620] Clarence J. Bulliet, "Around the Galleries, Arts Club Annual," *The Chicago Daily News*, April
30, 1938, 13.

[621] Kostelanetz, "An Essential Role," 40-42.

[622] "*Laszlo Moholy-Nagy, Paintings* (folder), 1939," xerox copy in my files. Listed, without exact
dates of the exhibition, in "Documentation." in: Scanlon, editor, *A History of the Renaissance
Society*, 142 and 185.

[623] Herbert Grossberg, "Moholy-Nagy Presents Two Roomsful of Abstract Art," *The Maroon*, April
13, 1939, page number not known; reproduced on microfilm reel 2401,frame 0938, Archives of
American Art, Washington, D.C. Portions were quoted in: Kostelanetz, "An Essential Role," 40.

[624] James Johnson Sweeney, editor, *A Selection of Works by Twentieth-Century Artists: Catalogue
of the Summer Exhibition, June 20 to August 20, 1934* (Chicago: The Renaissance Society of the
University of Chicago, 1934), unpaginated. Sweeney had organized the exhibition to highlight the
appearance of his book, *Plastic Redirections in Twentieth Century Painting* (Chicago: published
for the Renaissance Society of the University of Chicago by the University of Chicago Press,
1934). See also: Clarence J. Bullliet, "Around the Galleries," *The Chicago Daily News*,
September 22, 1934, 6 and *ibid.*, September 29, 1936, 6.

[625] Documented by an invitation dated June 8th and a clipping from an unidentified Jacksonville
newspaper dated June 10, 1938, Robert Delson Papers, University of Illinois Library, Chicago.

> It provoked the most attention of any exhibition that we have presented here in the union.

> Quite frankly most of the comments were not at first very favorable as far as appreciating the beauty of the exhibition. After your discussion [*i.e.*, lecture by Robert Delson], however, and after some deliberation I feel confident in saying that the exhibition did make the majority of students finally come to have a genuine appreciation for it.[626]

The director of the University's School of Architecture and Allied Arts added that: "I am glad to tell you that the exhibition of Moholy-Nagy and particularly your lecture on the subject was of much interest and value to our students. . . ."[627]

The showing at the Florida State College for Women (now Florida State University) in Tallahassee was described by Beatrice B. Williams, head of the Art Department:

> It caused a lot of excitement here which is a very good thing.

> It was nice to have you [*i.e.*, Robert Delson] lecture to us. As Miss Wilburn said, "You gave a clear, straight-forward talk expressing yourself so simply everyone should have been able to understand you.[628]

Later she added:

> All the members of the Art Faculty thought his [*i.e.*, Delson's] lecture excellent and felt he had interested not only the art majors but those who had had very little or no art training.[629]

The Katharine Kuh Gallery in Chicago gave Moholy a one-artist exhibition that was seen from January 4th through February 3rd, 1940.[630] Kuh operated her gallery in a balcony room facing the elegant, art-deco "Diana Court," the lobby of the Michigan Square Building (Holabird & Root, architects, 1929, no longer extant)[631] from the

---

[626]D.R. (Billy) Mathews to Robert Delson, carbon copy of TLS, April 13th, 1938, Robert Delson Papers, University of Illinois Library, Chicago.

[627]Rudolph Weaver to Robert Delson, carbon copy of TLS, May 2nd, 1938, Robert Delson Papers, University of Illinois Library, Chicago.

[628]Beatrice B. Williams to Robert Delson, carbon copy of TLS, April 27th, 1938, Robert Delson Papers, University of Illinois Library, Chicago.

[629]Beatrice B. Williams to Mrs. Walter Pliny Fuller, carbon copy of TLS, May 15th, 1939, Robert Delson Papers, University of Illinois Library, Chicago.

[630]Rudenstine, *The Guggenheim Museum Collection*, 2:555.

[631]Interior views of Diana Court are in: Stuart E. Cohen, *Chicago Architects* (Chicago: The

(continued...)

autumn of 1935 through the spring of 1941.[632] Kuh, who had studied with Alfred Barr at Vassar College,[633] displayed, in addition to Moholy, other European Modernists such as Picasso, Braque, Chagall, Kandinsky and Klee, along with a select group of American Modernists, including Charles Sebree (1914-1985)[634] and Rudolph Weisenborn, as well as Carlos Mérida (1891-1984), a native of Guatemala then active in Mexico.

A highlight of the Moholy exhibition at the Katharine Kuh Gallery was the *Light Prop* or *Light-Display Machine*. (DVD figures 336 and 337) Harold Allen, who was to go on to study at the School of Design in Chicago, attended the opening and recalled that sculptures were shown "with lights, and when they moved, it would make reflections all over the walls."[635] The *Chicago Daily Times* reported that, when asked of the *Light Prop*, "Does it move," Moholy, while "twirling it," replied "Yes." A picture caption for a photograph of the *Light Prop* as displayed in the gallery noted that "it moves when an electric switch is touched." But this report, without a byline, did not appear in all editions of the *Daily Times* ,[636] and the formal review by Fritzi Weisenborn (Alfreda "Fritzi" née Gordon, 1900-1968), Rudolph Weisenborn's wife and the regular art reviewer for the newspaper, did not mention the *Light Prop* specifically, referring only to "constructions."[637] One might have expected a more detailed response, since she was married to Chicago's pioneer Modernist painter.

Clarence J. Bulliet has been referred to above in connection with his speech at the New Bauhaus and his newspaper review of New Bauhaus student work; he had introduced the novel approach (at least novel for Chicago journalism) of reviewing Modernist art sympathetically. Nevertheless, like Fritzi Weisenborn, he did not mention the *Light Prop* directly, referring only to a "metal 'construction,' with no conceivable

---

[631](...continued)
Swallow Press, Inc., 1976), figures 53-54. Photographs of the gallery are in: Berman, "The Katharine Kuh Gallery: an Informal Portrait"; one photograph of December, 1937, on page163, and one photograph of November, 1940, on page 157. The December, 1937 photograph, made by Edmund Teske, is also reproduced in: Kuh, *My Love Affair with Modern Art*, 3.

[632]Berman,"The Katharine Kuh Gallery," 155-169; Kuh, *My Love Affair with Modern Art*, and 2-7 and 9-15.

[633]Avis Berman, "Preface," in: Kuh, *My Love Affair with Modern Art*, xvi-xvii.

[634]On Sebree, see: Kennedy, *Chicago Modern,* 49 and 149.

[635]Harold Allen, interviewed by David Travis, Liz Siegel and others, August 12th, 1998; sound tape and a transcript are in the Photography Department, Art Institute of Chicago.

[636]"If Art Is Moving, Then This Is It," *Chicago Daily Times*, January 9, 1940, page number not available. This article did not appear in the edition of the *Chicago Daily Times* available on microfilm in the Illinois State Historical Library, Springfield. A xerox copy of a clipping is in the Photography Department, Art Institute of Chicago.

[637]Fritzi Weisenborn, "What Our Galleries Are Showing: Katherine [*sic*] Kuh Gallery," *Chicago Sunday Times*, January 7, 1940, 10-M.

'usefulness'."[638] Bulliet's formal review was preceded by a preliminary report that also failed to mention *Light-Display Machine*.[639] So much for a work that in later years would become one of Moholy's most admired!

Only those versed in the history of art criticism in Chicago could fully appreciate the terse notice in the *Chicago Tribune* by Eleanor Jewett.[640] She wrote that "Those who enjoy abstract [missing word] and mathematics will revel in the exhibit of 'Transparencies, Mobiles, Photograms, Constructions' by Moholy-Nagy . . ." and went on to say that:

> The work is very different and attractive in a curiously odd way.
> Moholy-Nagy is director of the school of design and has an
> international reputation in modern art.

Jewett had spent years writing scathing reviews attacking Modernist art while at the same time supporting conservative artists.[641] Moholy's showing at the Katharine Kuh Gallery came just at a time when Jewett was beginning to soften her stand against Modernist art, and the fact that she found anything at all "attractive" means that Moholy was playing a demonstrable role in changing taste in art among Chicagoans.

Among the paintings shown at the Katharine Kuh Gallery was *Ch Beata I*, of 1939 (Solomon R. Guggenheim Museum).[642] (DVD figure 518) It is a large, nearly square painting, 118.9 by 119.8 centimeters, utilizing red, yellow, black, white and gray hues. Moholy is obviously as interested in transparency as ever, now achieving some of his effects of transparency by means of curving overlapping forms, some parts of some of which are created by masses of tiny, discrete and carefully varied brush strokes. Perforations in the most prominent of the forms suggest the *Light-Display Machine*.

---

[638]Clarence J. Bulliet, "Around the Galleries: Moholy's Fuddie-Duddies," *The Chicago Daily News*, January 20, 1940, 14.

[639]Clarence J. Bulliet, "Around the Galleries . . . Moholy-Nagy Show," *The Chicago Daily News*, January 6, 1940, 25.

[640]Eleanor Jewett, [art column headed] "Famed Exhibit of Italian Art to Close Tonight," *Chicago Tribune*, January 10, 1940, 2.

[641]On Jewett's long-time vehement attacks on modern art, see: Sue Ann Prince, "'Of the Which and the Why of the Daub and Smear': Chicago Critics take on Modernism," and Berman, "The Katharine Kuh Gallery," both in: Prince, editor, *The Old Guard and the Avant-garde*. See especially pages 103-117, 159-160, 163-164 and 166. See also: Kuh, *My Love Affair with Modern Art*, 5-7.

Curiously, neither Prince nor Berman discusses Jewett's later criticism written after she had become sympathetic to Modernist art.

[642]Rudenstine, *The Guggenheim Museum Collection*, 2:554-555.

The Art Institute had a series of exhibitions in its Room of Chicago Art in the 1940s; these included one on abstract painting and sculpture by Chicago artists that opened December 31st, 1942. The artists included Moholy and three others from the School of Design in Chicago: Emerson Woelffer, Alexander Corrazzo and Gyorgy Kepes, along with Rudolph Weisenborn.[643]

AFTER MOHOLY MOVED to Chicago, group exhibitions held outside that city frequently included his work. An early example is an exhibition organized by Hilla Rebay that opened on March 7th, 1938, in Charleston, South Carolina; it was another in a series begun by the two exhibitions of the Guggenheim Collection, discussed in Chapter Four, that had been staged in the United States and that showed his work while Moholy was still living in Europe. Included in the 1938 exhibition were five oil-on-Trollit paintings by Moholy (one of them owned by Rebay herself) and a work created with watercolor and chinese ink (also owned by Rebay); all were illustrated in the catalogue.[644]

In 1941 Moholy joined The American Abstract Artists and took part in the group's Fifth Annual Exhibition at the Riverside Gallery in New York,[645] and again in 1942 at the American Fine Arts Building in New York.[646] Moholy also showed in the group's Eighth Annual Exhibition in 1944 at the Mortimer Brandt Gallery in New York, along with the work of "the late Piet Mondrian."[647] American Abstract Artists was a group of mostly American artists who became embattled because of hostility from critics and indifference from art institutions.

───────────────

[643]"Chicago's Own," *Art Digest*, volume XVII, number 8 (January 15, 1943), 18; Dorothy Odenheimer, "Abstract Art—A challenge for 1943," *Chicago Sun*, January 3, 1943, 24; Clarence J. Bulliet, "Around the Galleries . . . Eight Abstractionists," *The Chicago Daily News*, January 2, 1943, 18; and *idem*, "Around the Galleries . . . Abstractions of War," *ibid.*, January 9, 1943, 6. See also: László Moholy-Nagy to Myron Kozman, TLS, January 21st, 1943; copies are in my files and in those of Hattula Moholy-Nagy.

[644]Hilla Rebay, editor, *Third Enlarged Catalogue of the Solomon R. Guggenheim Collection of Non-Objective Paintings, March 7th until April 17th, 1938, Gibbes Memorial Art Gallery, Charleston, South Carolina, Loan Exhibition from the Solomon R. Guggenheim Foundation, New York* (New York: Solomon R. Guggenheim Foundation, 1938), 50-51 and 104.

Two of Moholy's paintings shown, *T 1* of 1926 and *Tp 2* of 1930, are now in the collection of the Solomon R. Guggenheim Museum in New York: see Rudenstine, *The Guggenheim Museum Collection*, 2:548-549 and 552-553.

[645]George L.K. Morris, "The American Abstract Artists; a Chonicle, 1936-56," in: *The World of Abstract Art*, edited by The American Abstract Artists (New York: George Wittenborn, Inc., 1957), 140.

[646]Edward Alden Jewell, "Abstract Artists Hold Sixth Show," *The New York Times*, March 10, 1942, 24.

[647]Edward Alden Jewell, "Abstract Artists Hold 8th Annual," *The New York Times*, March 29, 1944, 25.

On June 20th, 1942, Moholy suffered serious injuries when a Braniff Airlines shuttle bus on which he was riding was hit by a "streetcar" [*i.e.*, trolley car] and he was pressed between the steel structure of the seats; as a result he was unable to paint or make sculpture during the summer months. He wrote to Rebay that ". . . through this accident I will not be able to paint the new pictures which I wanted to exhibit and sell in the Guggenheim Museum." He went on to ask her for a statement needed by his lawyer for his attempt to settle the case out of court.[648]

In the summer of 1945 a loan exhibition was presented by the Museum of Non-Objective Painting in its galleries at 24 East 54th Street, New York. Included were "thematic essays in spatial thought" by Moholy. One of Moholy's works on view, a painting called *Space Modulator*, was illustrated in the coverage of the exhibition in *Art News*.[649]

Paintings made by Moholy in Chicago include one made in 1942 on red Formica that is a color variation of a frame from his 1932 film *A Lightplay Black White Gray* that utilized his *Light Prop*. The red Formica not only serves as a ground, it also provides the red for the multicolored composition. The painting can serve as a reminder that one of the possibilities Moholy thought of for his *Light Prop* was as a modulator for projections of colored light. (DVD figure 519 and back cover of Volume Two)

ON PURELY VISUAL GROUNDS it would be hard to relate one of Moholy's works of 1945 to the leukemia from which he began suffering in that year. But the title, *Leuk 4*, is a giveaway. This is a square painting, oil and watercolor on canvas, 124.7 by 124.7 centimeters. A prominent transparent bright yellow arc, dominating the right side of the canvas, provides a cheerful note, perhaps expressing Moholy's hope that he might soon overcome the affliction. The black-and-white background suggests a textile pattern. There is no ready explanation for the play of four rectangles, two of them transparent, in the center of a large white circle that intersects with the yellow arc. Dotted lines extend from the edges of two of the rectangles. (DVD figure 520)

The most extensive showing of Moholy's work in the United States during his lifetime[650] was organized by Marion Becker (née Rombauer; 1903-1976), director of the

---

[648] László Moholy-Nagy to Hilla Rebay, September 21st, 1942, ALS, Hilla von Rebay Foundation, Solomon R. Guggenheim Museum of Art, New York.

Given the timing, it was evident that the Braniff flight was a link in his return to Chicago from his teaching job in Denton, Texas, most likely as a flight from Dallas to Chicago.

[649] "The Passing Shows," *Art News*, volume XLIV, number 9 (July, 1945), 6-7 and 26-28, here 26.

[650] Sibyl Moholy-Nagy summarized the exhibition and sale of Moholy's works during his residence in the United States in her *Moholy-Nagy; Experiment in Totality*, 205 and 207-208. (She erroneously referred to the Cincinnati Modern Art Society as the Contemporary Arts Society.) See also: Lukach, *Hilla Rebay*, 234-237.

Cincinnati Modern Art Society[651] (original name of the Contemporary Arts Center)[652] and staged in the Cincinnati Art Museum; it opened February 12th, 1946, and remained on view through early April.[653] It should be noted that in later years the Contemporary Arts Center acquired its own space, first in the Formica Building and Arcade (Harry Weese, 1971), and then in a building specifically designed for it, the The Lois & Richard Rosenthal Center for Contemporary Art (Zaha Hadid, 2003), on the northwest corner of Walnut and East 6th streets. It should also be noted that Cincinnati, before ceding that distinction to Chicago, had been the western outpost of the Industrial Revolution, and, as one result, its venerable industrial-worker neighborhood (five blocks to the north of the Zaha Hadid building and much of it still intact), still known by its colorful title of Over the Rhine, was at one time the most densely-populated space on earth.[654]

In retrospect it seems especially appropriate that the Contemporary Arts Center (under its earlier name) should have been the venue for a Moholy exhibition because he was a strong opponent of censorship and the Center has been best known ever since 1990 for its heroic battle against censorship. In that year it brought to Cincinnati a traveling photography exhibition organized by the Institute of Contemporary Art of the University of Pennsylvania, *Robert Mapplethorpe: the Perfect Moment*.[655] In a landmark legal case

---

[651] Marion Becker was a skilled, efficient and visionary curator, but she was better known as a writer on cooking; see: Anne Mendelson, *Stand Facing the Stove: the Story of the Women Who Gave America* The Joy of Cooking (New York: Henry Holt and Company, 1996). Mendelson devotes only a few pages to Becker's work as a curator: 189-190, 192, 204, 215, 304 and 407; anyone wishing for more extensive information on Becker's curatorial work should consult the Contemporary Arts Center files, Archives and Rare Books Department, University of Cincinnati Libraries.

[652] On the Cincinnati Modern Art Society, see: Ruth K. Meyer, *The Modern Art Society: the Center's Early Years, 1939-1954; an Exhibition in Celebration of the Fortieth Anniversary of the Contemporary Arts Center, Cincinnati, Ohio, October 13-November 25, 1979* (Cincinnati: Contemporary Arts Center, 1979); and "Cincinnati's New Collectors: To the Modern Art Society Which Encouraged Their Purchases of Modern Art, Local Collectors Lend [*sic*!]," *Art News*, volume XLIV (15-30 November, 1945), 14-15. The Society's forthcoming Moholy exhibition is mentioned in the text.

[653] The invitation to the exhibition, designed by Fred Lewy; and "Cincinnati Modern Art Society Secretary" [*i.e.*, Jane Brueggeman] to László Moholy-Nagy, carbon copy of TLS, April 9th, 1946; both are in the Contemporary Arts Center files, Archives and Rare Books Department, University of Cincinnati Libraries.

[654] Daniel Hurley, *Cincinnati: the Queen City* (Cincinnati: The Cincinnati Historical Society, 1982), 76-77; and Alan I. Marcus, *Plague of Strangers: Social Groups and the Origins of City Services in Cincinnati, 1829-1870* (Columbus: Ohio State University Press, 1991), 66-67, 86 and 141-143.

[655] Janet Kardon, editor, *Robert Mapplethorpe: the Perfect Moment* (Philadelphia: Institute of Contemporary Art, University of Pennsylvania, 1989), [4].

the Contemporary Arts Center successfully defended itself against charges that by bringing the exhibition to Cincinnati it had violated obscenity statutes.[656]

Moholy's exhibition staged by the Modern Art Society was not devoted solely to works made in Chicago, but was, rather, a unique retrospective of his entire career as a fine artist; hence work made as early as 1916 was included. A total of sixty-six works was shown, so that, although it was probably the second largest exhibition of his works held during his lifetime, it was the most extensive in terms of the range of dates of the work shown. Moholy himself designed the exhibition,[657] which required some temporary alterations in the Museum's first-floor Schmidlapp Gallery. His final drawing, sent to Cincinnati on January 28th,[658] was based on answers to his questions about the physical space and sketches and photographs sent to him from Cincinnati.[659] (DVD figures 521 and 522). Marion Becker wrote to Moholy that she was working ". . . with the gallery layout which looks perfectly beautiful in your drawing and which we will do our very best to carry out."[660] Among the conditions Moholy asked for was that the windows be covered, because, he wrote, "To hang pictures between the windows usually is not advisable because looking against light and dark does not allow good view;"[661] the windows were accordingly covered by panels, as shown in gallery photographs by Cincinnati photographer F.V. Raymond. (DVD figures 523 and 524) No color photographs are known to exist, but the walls were pale blue, the floor tiles a pale gray and the ceiling white.[662]

---

[656]Arthur Danto, "Playing with the Edge: the Photographic Achievements of Robert Mapplethorpe," in: Mark Holborn and Dimitri Levas, editors, *Mapplethorpe*, second, revised edition (Kempen, Germany: teNeues Publishing Company, 2007), 311-329, here 321-323.

[657]A thick sheaf of correspondence and sketches relating to the space and how it was to be used is in the Contemporary Arts Center files, Archives and Rare Books Department, University of Cincinnati Libraries.

[658]László Moholy-Nagy to Marion Becker, TLS, January 28th, 1946, Contemporary Arts Center files, Archives and Rare Books Department, University of Cincinnati Libraries.

[659]Moholy's large drawing of his design for the exhibition was published in: Engelbrecht, "László Moholy-Nagy in Chicago," 52; the drawing itself, a letter describing it (László Moholy-Nagy to Marion Becker, TLS, January 28th, 1946), and two photographs by F.V. Raymond of the exhibition as installed, are in the Contemporary Arts Center files, Archives and Rare Books Department, University of Cincinnati Libraries.

[660]László Moholy-Nagy to Marion Becker, TLS, January 31th, 1946, Contemporary Arts Center files, Archives and Rare Books Department, University of Cincinnati Libraries.

[661]László Moholy-Nagy to Marion Becker, TLS, January 5th, 1946, Contemporary Arts Center files, Archives and Rare Books Department, University of Cincinnati Libraries.

[662]Marion Becker to László Moholy-Nagy, TLS, January 7th, 1946, Contemporary Arts Center files, Archives and Rare Books Department, University of Cincinnati Libraries.

MOHOLY ALSO DESIGNED THE BROCHURE for the Cincinnati retrospective.[663] It was similar to the one he had designed for the 1944-1945 Léger exhibition, discussed above, that was presented by the I.D. and also by the Cincinnati Modern Art Society. Moholy had hoped to show his retrospective exhibition at the I.D. and also circulate it elsewhere,[664] but in the end only a scaled-down version containing twelve works (among them the Plexiglas pieces, *Spirals* and *Leda and the Swan*) was shown at the Department of Art at the University of Kentucky in Lexington.[665] Because of these hopes there was no reference to the Cincinnati Modern Art Society in the brochure itself. In any case, the brochure was illustrated but had no specific list of the works shown; moreover, with one or two exceptions, the works illustrated in the brochure were not in the exhibition. Only a two-page typed checklist with prices (DVD figure 528) contained that information,[666] and it is not clear in every case what was shown from the brief titles used in the checklist; moreover twenty-one works in frames[667] were listed only as "Sketches (1916-1945)."

The invitation was designed by Fred Lewy (formerly Fritz Lewy; 1893-1950), a Cincinnati designer and teacher of design who worked closely with the Cincinnati Modern Art Society. Lewy installed the exhibition,[668] and would have designed the

---

[663] *Moholy: Paintings, Sculptures, Photograms and Photographs by L. Moholy-Nagy, Institute of Design, Chicago.* [Text by] L. Moholy-Nagy, Siegfried [*sic; i.e.,* Sigfried] Giedion and Fr. Kalivoda. [Chicago: published for the Cincinnati Modern Art Society by the Institute of Design, 1946]. The brochure was printed in Chicago by Toby Rubovits Inc., Printers Binders Designers, as documented in "Shipping Advice" to Marion Becker, February 5th, 1946, Contemporary Arts Center files, Archives and Rare Books Department, University of Cincinnati Libraries. Some copies were retained in Chicago, and 350 were sent to the Cincinnati Modern Art Society.

[664] László Moholy-Nagy to Marion Becker, TLS, November 10th, 1945, Contemporary Arts Center files, Archives and Rare Books Department, University of Cincinnati Libraries.

[665] "Cincinnati Modern Art Society Secretary" [*i.e.,* Jane Brueggeman] to László Moholy-Nagy, carbon copy of TLS, April 9th, 1946; Edward Warder Rannells to Marie Blatherwick, TLS, April 4th, 1946; Jane Brueggeman [secretary for the Cincinnati Modern Art Society] to John Conway, carbon copy of TLS, April 5th, 1946; "Secretary" [*i.e.,* Jane Brueggeman] to Edward Warder Rannells, April 5th, 1946; all four letters are in the Contemporary Arts Center files, Archives and Rare Books Department, University of Cincinnati Libraries.

[666] The price list is in the Contemporary Arts Center files, Archives and Rare Books Department, University of Cincinnati Libraries. All of the works are individually listed, except for the 24 sketches and drawings, only three of which are itemized.

[667] Venice Barton ("Secretary to Mr. Moholy-Nagy") to Marion Becker, TLS, January 29th, 1946, Contemporary Arts Center files, Archives and Rare Books Department, University of Cincinnati Libraries.

[668] Marion Becker to László Moholy-Nagy, carbon copy of TLS, March 8th, 1946, Contemporary Arts Center files, Archives and Rare Books Department, University of Cincinnati Libraries.

brochure had Moholy not done so.[669] Lewy and Moholy had lived and worked in Weimar at the same time; although Lewy had been a designer, with the title of *Künstlerischer Beirat* [artistic advisor] at the *Deutsches Nationaltheater* in Weimar,[670] used by the Bauhaus for special events, there is no indication in any of the correspondence about the Cincinnati exhibition that they had known each other in Weimar.

The invitation to hold a retrospective in Cincinnati came about because of Moholy's work as an educator. In fact, at the beginning of 1944 Moholy had suggested showing School of Design student work in Cincinnati,[671] and Marion Becker referred in April, 1945, to ". . . our plan for showing your own work and that of your students." She added: "I think of the show as: 'Moholy-Nagy: Artist - Experimenter - Educator'." [672] As late as November 6th Becker had hoped Moholy would include "some evidence in the show of the teaching method you have developed as shown in your students' work."[673] He replied: "Of course I would like to emphasize mainly painting and photography, but I gladly agree to something which shows my approach to teaching."[674] As things developed, however, there was nothing directly didactic in the exhibition itself, possibly because Moholy's illness left him little time or energy to put together an educational component. Moreover, because of his illness, it had not been known in advance whether he would even attend the opening.[675] But in the end he did travel to Cincinnati and on Tuesday, February 12th, he presented some of his ideas on art pedagogy in an evening

---

[669] "I just talked with Fred Lewy and he is interested to know how we would handle your catalogue [*i.e.*, brochure]—will you do the typography and layout or will he?," Marion Becker to László Moholy-Nagy, carbon copy of TLS, November 6th, 1945, Contemporary Arts Center files, Archives and Rare Books Department, University of Cincinnati Libraries.

[670] An eight-page autograph autobiography of Lewy is in the Library of the Cincinnati Art Museum; files documenting his activities in Weimar are in the *Deutsches Nationaltheater* archives in the *Thüringisches Haupstaatsarchiv*, Weimar.

[671] László Moholy-Nagy to Marion Becker, TLS, January 26th, 1944, Contemporary Arts Center files, Archives and Rare Books Department, University of Cincinnati Libraries.

[672] Marion Becker to László Moholy-Nagy, carbon copy of TLS, April 4th, 1945, Contemporary Arts Center files, Archives and Rare Books Department, University of Cincinnati Libraries.

[673] Marion Becker to László Moholy-Nagy, carbon copy of TLS, November 6th, 1945, Contemporary Arts Center files, Archives and Rare Books Department, University of Cincinnati Libraries.

[674] László Moholy-Nagy to Marion Becker, November 10th, 1945.

[675] Mollie Thwaites to Marion Becker, TLS, December 11th, 1945, Contemporary Arts Center files, Archives and Rare Books Department, University of Cincinnati Libraries.

lecture at the Cincinnati Art Museum, "Design School,"[676] followed by the film *Design Workshops*.

In a bit of irony, one of Raymond's gallery photographs shows plaster casts of Greek sculpture just outside the entrance to the Moholy exhibition. (DVD figure 527) The irony was that Becker had wanted Moholy to display the work of his students to show an alternative to the traditional educational methods of the Cincinnati Art Academy, at the time housed in the Cincinnati Art Museum; the plaster casts, once ubiquitous in art schools, were placed where they were so that students could make sketches of the casts, a key element in traditional art instruction.

László and Sibyl traveled to Cincinnati via railroad. They stayed with Marion Becker and her husband, the Modernist architect John William Becker (1902-1974) of the firm of Garriott & Becker, in the house he had designed for his family in Newtown, near Cincinnati, in 1940 (since demolished).[677]

The Cincinnati exhibition was a mixed success. Nothing was sold from the exhibition,[678] even though, in his attempt to "sell really much," Moholy maintained that he had "set the prices rather low."[679] He was convinced, however, that the exhibition did aid sales in the period immediately following, and he reported on May 3rd that: ". . . in the last few days I sold six pictures and sculptures."[680]

CINCINNATI, on the north shore of the Ohio River, is the hub of a lively three-state (Ohio, Kentucky, Indiana) industrial, commercial and financial community as well as a center for arts and entertainment, where, historically, liberal and innovative tendencies had thrived along with conservative ones.[681] The latter tendencies

---

[676] László Moholy-Nagy to Marion Becker, TLS, January 31st, 1946, Contemporary Arts Center files, Archives and Rare Books Department, University of Cincinnati Libraries; and "Architect Is Scheduled to Address Art Society, *Cincinnati Enquirer*, [need date and page number].

[677] Marion Becker to László Moholy-Nagy, carbon copy of TLS, January 31st, 1946, Contemporary Arts Center files, Archives and Rare Books Department, University of Cincinnati Libraries.

[678] Marion Becker to László Moholy-Nagy, carbon copy of TLS, May 7th, 1946, Contemporary Arts Center files, Archives and Rare Books Department, University of Cincinnati Libraries.

[679] László Moholy-Nagy to Marion Becker, TLS, January 28th, 1946, Contemporary Arts Center files, Archives and Rare Books Department, University of Cincinnati Libraries.

[680] László Moholy-Nagy to Marion Becker, TLS, May 3rd, 1946, Contemporary Arts Center files, Archives and Rare Books Department, University of Cincinnati Libraries.

[681] This innovative/conservative dichotomy can be seen in the area's housing stock, as Walter E. Langsam and Alice Weston demonstrated in their *Great Houses of the Queen City: Two Hundred Years of Historic and Contemporary Architecture and Interiors in Cincinnati and Northern Kentucky*, photographs by Alice Weston, text by Walter E. Langsam, foreword by Michael Graves, third printing "with minor revisions and corrections" (Cincinnati: The Cincinnati Museum Center

(continued...)

could be seen in the complete lack of coverage of the Moholy exhibition by two of Cincinnati's daily newspapers and by the somewhat diffident tone of the comment by Mary L. Alexander in the *Cincinnati Enquirer*. Her review was in three parts. The first appeared on February 12th, evidently based on a preview; Moholy's background and educational ideas were discussed, as well as the ". . . 'Space Modulators.' They are all abstractions and very strange. . . ."[682] On February 17th she conceded that Moholy's work ". . . clears our mind of all the old traditional ideas and substitutes a refreshing new vision of light as a new medium of expression."[683] But the last word, on February 24th, was that Moholy's ". . . fine technique and lively imagination rarely lift his work above pedestrian performance, barring a few notable instances."[684]

Time magazine seemed more positive in its assessment, if only because its coverage was part of an article describing Moholy's career and the success of the I.D.:

> . . . Moholy directs and spark-plugs Chicago's Institute of Design, a U.S. version of the now defunct Bauhaus, which was closed by Nazi pressure in 1932 [*sic*; *i.e.*, 1933]. Recently installed in spacious new quarters, the Institute now has some 300 students and, for the first time in its eight-year history, a waiting list. And, to prove that it makes as much sense as nonsense, it has secured a long list of Chicago businessmen as backers, including top executives of United Air Lines, Container Corp. of America, Marshall Field & Co., Sears, Roebuck & Co. For the backers, the brave new Bauhaus is supposed to pay off in the form of broadly trained designers equipped to create new products for future markets.[685]

Nevertheless, given the timing, *Time* had taken note of the exhibition solely on the basis of an advance copy of the brochure.[686]

---

[681](...continued)
at Union Terminal, 2002).

[682]Mary L. Alexander, "Color Trick Played in Nagy Paintings; Show Opens Today," *Cincinnati Enquirer*, February 12, 1946, 9.

[683]*Idem*, "'Construction No. 19' by Moholy Nagy," *Cincinnati Enquirer*, February 17, 1946, 34.

[684]*Idem*, "Week in Art Circles," *Cincinnati Enquirer*, February 24, section 4, page 7.

[685]"Message in a Bottle," *Time*, February 18, 1946, 63.

[686]The point is confirmed by a piece of correspondence: Althea Lever to Marion Hendrie, TLS, March 11t, 1946, Contemporary Arts Center files, Archives and Rare Books Department, University of Cincinnati Libraries.

An intriguing passage in *Time* describing "a meaningless 'machine of emotional discharge,' which he designed for laughs," and going on to assert that: "A drawing of this 'machine' was included in a show of Moholy's paintings and sculptures which opened in the Cincinnati Art Museum this week," was one way of pretending that an un-named reviewer had actually been in

(continued...)

Six of Moholy's innovative Plexiglas sculptures, dating from 1939 to 1946, were shown in Cincinnati, according to the checklist. One of these, *Leda and the Swan*, 1946 (*Institut Valencià d'Art Modern*), about two feet in height (DVD figures 529 and 530), was suspended over the entrance, with a ball bearing so that it could turn easily, as per Moholy's instructions.[687] Another Plexiglas sculpture, *Rays*, 1945, barely discernable in a detail of one of the gallery photographs (DVD figure 525), was also skillfully photographed by Raymond on its mount, a tall black box containing a spotlight that shined through its glass top to illuminate *Rays*; the photograph has a magical quality because it was made with the spotlight in the black box on and with the gallery lights off. (DVD figure 526)

There is no record of any contemporary written comment at all, by anyone, about the Plexiglas sculptures shown in Cincinnati, with the exception of one letter. This was written by Raymond Barnhart, a young faculty member of the Art Department at the University of Kentucky in Lexington. In a generally admiring letter of March 16th, 1946, he wrote: "To avoid being classed as a uniformly and non-critical admirer, permit me to say that I felt that some of the plastic sculpture seemed to be made of an overly-thick material in relation to the size of the volumes involved, resulting in crowded spaces."[688]

---

[686](...continued)
Cincinnati. *Time* even claimed its reviewer had observed that: "Visitors smiled dutifully, but found the machine no more amusing and no less confusing than the rest of the show."

Nevertheless, even though *The Machine of Emotional Discharge* was illustrated on the outside back cover of the exhibition brochure (DVD figure 85), there is no evidence that Moholy still had the original drawing itself; hence an attempt on the part of *Time* to amuse its readers was no boon to historians.

But while it is unlikely that any actual drawing of a machine of emotional discharge was on view in Cincinnati, there was a painting, oil on canvas, identified in the checklist (DVD figure 528) as: "The great 4 (machine of emotional discharge II), 1920." (the date of 1920 may be a year off). This painting, as discussed in Chapter Two, is currently known as *The Great Wheel (Large Emotion Meter)*. (DVD figure 81, also visible in DVD figure 523) Moreover, the fact that *The Machine of Emotional Discharge*, illustrated on the outside back cover of the exhibition brochure, was, as discussed in Chapter Two, first published simply as *Rajz* [drawing], may indicate that Moholy made the drawing before the idea of calling it *The Machine of Emotional Discharge* came to him. So possibly the title for the drawing illustrated on the brochure cover, and the subtitle of *The great 4*, came to him as he was preparing the Cincinnati exhibition and recalling a time when he was young and when an aura of Dadaism permeated the avant garde. The drawing and the painting do not have a lot in common, but they both do include assemblages of modern industrial elements with no evident industrial purpose.

[687]László Moholy-Nagy to Marion Becker, TLS, January 31st, 1946; and Marion Becker to László Moholy-Nagy, carbon copy of TLS, April 9t, 1946. Both letters are in the Contemporary Arts Center files, Archives and Rare Books Department, University of Cincinnati Libraries.

[688]Raymond Barnhart to László Moholy-Nagy, TLS, March 16th, 1946, Contemporary Arts Center

(continued...)

Marion Becker was pleased with the reaction to the exhibition:

> . . . it has met with more response than any other modern show we have
> had. People study it, enjoy it, react to it with fervor, and the gallery
> almost always has visitors, which is not usual in the Cincinnati [missing
> word?] Museum.[689]

Moholy's own response to the exhibition is touching, since we now know that he had
less than a year to live: "The exhibition gave me quite a thrill because it allowed me to
think about my own development and it was only a pity that I could not go back again
and be alone with the pictures."[690] *Nickel Construction* of 1921 (DVD figure 60) was
among the works shown (visible in DVD figures 524 and 525); as discussed in Chapter
Two, Moholy would have remembered it as the first of his works to become widely
known.

A similar experience awaited Moholy in New York. Hilla Rebay, director of the
Museum of Non-Objective Painting (precursor of the Solomon R. Guggenheim
Museum), recalled, in her essay in the catalogue for a memorial exhibition in New York,
that:

> . . . a week before his death, Moholy unexpectedly arrived at our
> Museum from Chicago, where, to his surprise, that very day had been
> hung a new exhibition on the mezzanine floor. There he found one hall
> dedicated entirely to his work. He was overjoyed, claiming never to
> have seen his paintings presented so beautifully. One week later he was
> gone.[691]

---

[688](...continued)
files, Archives and Rare Books Department, University of Cincinnati Libraries.

[689]Marion Becker to László Moholy-Nagy, carbon copy of TLS. March 30th, 1946, László Moholy-
Nagy to Marion Becker, TLS, February 15th, 1946, Contemporary Arts Center files, Archives and
Rare Books Department, University of Cincinnati Libraries.

[690]László Moholy-Nagy to Marion Becker, TLS, February 15th, 1946, Contemporary Arts Center
files, Archives and Rare Books Department, University of Cincinnati Libraries.

Becker replied: "I need hardly tell you how thrilled I am that you were pleased with the
installation of the exhibition here. It does give me pleasure to see your things against it every time
I pass through the gallery . . ."; Marion Becker to László Moholy-Nagy, carbon copy of TLS,
February 26th, 1946, Contemporary Arts Center files, Archives and Rare Books Department,
University of Cincinnati Libraries.

[691]Hilla Rebay, "Moholy-Nagy the Painter and Friend," in: *In Memoriam László Moholy-Nagy, 15
May-10 July 1947* (New York: Museum of Non-Objective Painting, 1947), 21-23; the galleries
Moholy had visited in November, 1946, are illustrated on pages 22 and 23.

Concerning the New York exhibition that opened May 15th, 1947, see: Thomas B. Hess,
"Moholy=Nagy: Memorial to a Many-Sided Non-Objectivist," *Art News*, volume XLVI, number 4
(June, 1947), [1; *i.e.*, front cover], 5, 22-23, 49 and 51.

In Chicago itself, the first comprehensive exhibition of Moholy's works to be seen there was the memorial showing at the Art Institute, September 17th through October 26th, 1947. One room of the exhibition was devoted to a chronological presentation of eighty prints and drawings, dating from 1918 to 1946, selected and arranged by Carl Schniewind; the other room was devoted to twenty paintings and Plexiglas sculptures made in Chicago, installed by Katharine Kuh and Fred Sweet.[692] Accompanying the exhibition was a handsome illustrated catalogue.[693] In a lecture at the opening Moholy's old friend, Alexander Dorner, gave a summary of his entire career, going beyond his work in fine arts. Not surprisingly, considering his joint efforts with Moholy in Hanover to set up the *Room of Our Own Time,* described in Chapter Four, Dorner proclaimed Moholy "one of the great transformers" of exhibition design.[694]

Writing in the *Chicago Sun*, Frank Holland lamented:

> It is a pity that such a splendid presentation comes after the artist's death which occurred last November, as it is obvious in a glance at the works on view that he was a greater artist than most of us even suspected.

Holland added:

> It comes as something of a surprise to find that, in spite of local indifference and all of his energy and time consuming activities, he was through it all first and fundamentally a creative producing artist of important stature. Without question Moholy-Nagy was one of the most original and talented men ever to work in Chicago.[695]

Moholy's first extended writing effort in Chicago grew out of his work as a fine artist. This was his essay, "Abstract of an Artist," published as part of the third and fourth editions of *The New Vision*, which appeared in 1946 and 1947, respectively; the essay itself is dated "Chicago, 1944." This essay grew out of the text of a February, 1943, lecture, part of which can be heard in DVD sound clip 2. In the essay, he traces his development as an artist from his earliest interests in art through a period of twenty-five years during which ". . . I have been fascinated by phenomena not listed anywhere." The effect on Moholy of writing this essay is that he turned the invitation to exhibit in

---

[692]Katharine Kuh and Carl O. Schniewind, editors, *L. Moholy=Nagy: The Art Institute of Chicago, September 18 to October 26, 1947, an exhibition sponsored by the Society for Contemporary American Art* (Chicago: The Art Institute of Chicago, 1947); Frank Holland, "Laszlo Moholy-Nagy Memorial Exhibit Is Thrilling Show," *Chicago Sun*, September 21, 1947, 28.

[693]Kuh and Schniewind, editors, *L. Moholy=Nagy.*

[694]Alexander Dorner, "In Memoriam Moholy-Nagy (1895-1946)," 9 pages, mimeographed, Bauhaus-Archiv, Berlin. The quoted phrase is on page 8.

[695]Holland, "Laszlo Moholy-Nagy Memorial Exhibit Is Thrilling Show," 28.

Cincinnati, received in April of the following year,[696] into an opportunity to put together a retrospective exhibition; as noted above, the earliest work shown in Cincinnati dates from 1916. Moholy also took pains to make sure that the third edition of *The New Vision*, with the autobiographical essay included, was offered for sale during his exhibition in Cincinnati,[697] and asked that the book be shown "at the entrance to the exhibition."[698] Ten copies of the book were sent to the Cincinnati Modern Art Society by the publisher, George Wittenborn; of these seven were sold, for $2.00 each.[699] Moholy's only other extended writing effort in Chicago, in addition to "Abstract of an Artist," was his *Vision in Motion*; with the aid of editing by Sibyl Moholy-Nagy it appeared posthumously in 1947. At one time Moholy had hoped that it would be available as early as February, 1946,[700] a hope that proved to be unrealistic.

Moholy did continue in Chicago, as he had done in Europe, to write relatively brief articles for periodicals of all kinds, including the American photography magazines discussed above. The first of his American articles was his report on his visit to the Paris exhibition of 1937, noted in Chapter Four.

Continued Contacts with European Relatives and Friends

Contacts with Moholy's relatives after his move to Chicago were very limited. He had some contact with his mother while the United States was still neutral, and sent her money through a Swiss channel. Gropus helped in some way that is not explained in the sole letter documenting his aid, but one letter from Moholy's mother was received through him.[701] She died of natural causes on April 4th, 1945, in Budapest.

As noted in Appendix B, his brother Ákos was murdered on September 7th, 1938, by Soviet prison officials. Nevertheless, an autobiographical account written not long before his murder (discussed in Appendix B) makes it clear that Ákos did know his brother had moved to Chicago. There are no known documents that would show how he knew that. And Moholy himself died without any knowledge of his brother's earlier death. Moholy was in contact by mail with his brother Jenő even after the War had

---

[696]László Moholy-Nagy to Marion Becker, TLS, April 10th, 1945, Contemporary Arts Center files, Archives and Rare Books Department, University of Cincinnati Libraries.

[697]László Moholy-Nagy to Marion Becker, November 10th, 1945.

[698]László Moholy-Nagy to Marion Becker, February 15th, 1946.

[699]"Secretary" of the Cincinnati Modern Art Society to George Wittenborn, carbon copy of typed letter, April 22nd, 1946, Contemporary Arts Center files, Archives and Rare Books Department, University of Cincinnati Libraries.

[700]László Moholy-Nagy to Marion Becker, TLS, November 10th, 1945.

[701]László Moholy-Nagy to Walter Gropius, photographic copy of TLS, March 25th, 1941, Bauhaus-Archiv, Berlin. The letter from his mother cannot now be located.

begun in Europe,[702] but for most of the War years there was no mail service from the United States to Hungary.[703] In a letter to Jenő of December 10th, 1945, Moholy referred to the restored mail service.[704] A letter written to Jenő by Sibyl conveyed her husband's invitation to his son, Levente (also known as Venti), to study at the School of Design in Chicago with his tuition costs to be covered by a scholarship,[705] but Levente traveled to Chicago only in later years.

There were continued contacts with European friends during Moholy's Chicago years. These took various forms, and some are part of the previous narrative in this Chapter. In addition to his close association with Walter Gropius, Hilla Rebay, and Sigfried Giedion,[706] other contacts involved visits by Europeans to Chicago, attempts to help his friends immigrate to the United States, sending funds and CARE packages, and correspondence. As noted in Chapter Three, Gret Palucca received CARE packages from him after World War II. Still another recipient of these packages was Paul Citroen.[707]

GEORGE GROSZ AND MOHOLY had not known each other well in Europe, but they did have some contact there through Erwin Piscator. In 1937, when Grosz was teaching at the Art Students League in New York, he wrote a brief letter to Moholy recommending one of his students, "Anthony Smith," now better known as Tony Smith (1912-1980), as a good candidate for admission to the New Bauhaus.[708] Smith

---

[702]*E.g.*, Jenő Nagy to László Moholy-Nagy, MLS, April 10th, 1940, microfilm reel 949, frame 0709, Moholy-Nagy files, Archives of American Art, Washington, D.C.

[703]Levente Nagy, "Memories of Moholy-Nagy, in: Belena S. Chapp, editor, *László Moholy-Nagy: From Budapest to Berlin 1914-1923* (Newark: University Gallery, University of Delaware, 1995), 91-94, here [93].

[704]László Moholy-Nagy to Jenő Nagy, December 10th, 1945, Levente and Edith Nagy files, Budapest; the letter appears, in English translation, in: Passuth, *Moholy-Nagy,* 408.

[705]Sibyl Moholy-Nagy to Jenő Nagy, carbon copy of TLS, July 26th, 1940, microfilm reel 949, frames 0710-0711, Moholy-Nagy files, Archives of American Art, Washington, D.C.

[706]For most of his time in the United States Giedion was not accompanied by his wife, Carola Giedion-Welcker, but she was with him in an extended visit in the spring of 1939; see: László Moholy-Nagy to Walter Gropius, photocopy of TLS, July 15th, 1939, Bauhaus-Archiv, Berlin. In the letter Carola Giedion-Welcker is referred to as "CW."

[707]László Moholy-Nagy to Paul Citroen, October 30th, 1946, TLS, Bauhaus-Archiv, Berlin.

[708]George Grosz to László Moholy-Nagy, October 10th, 1937; the letter, along with a draft, is in container 730, George Grosz Papers, Houghton Library, Harvard University. A transcript of the letter (which was written in German) is in: George Grosz, *Briefe, 1913-1959*, herausgegeben von Herbert Knust (Reinbeck bei Hamburg: Rowolt Verlag GmBH, 1979), 263.

was admitted,[709] but studied in Chicago for only one year. Perhaps Grosz had unknowingly misled him as to the possibilities for studying architecture at the New Bauhaus. In any case, Smith was unhappy that no curriculum in architecture was offered during the initial year. When he learned that George Fred Keck would teach architecture during the planned second year, he decided he did not want to study with him and left Chicago to become an apprentice with Frank Lloyd Wright's Taliesin Fellowship.[710] In the context of his study at the New Bauhaus it is worth noting that Smith is now best known as a sculptor and also became an accomplished architect and painter.

AN ATTEMPT TO HELP ERZSI LANDAU immigrate to the United States was under way in the autumn of 1941, when Moholy wrote to Sibyl (who had remained in Chicago) from New York on September 4th: "For Landau Ergi we have to find some one or two persons who would give her affidavits. I shall speak about it to you later." No other information on Landau's attempt to enter the United States is available, and, since the letter was written during an extended visit to New York, one must assume that while there he talked with one of her friends: a good guess would be that it was Mondrian. While no contacts between Mondrian and Landau have been documented beyond the fact that both knew Moholy and that for more than a decade they both lived in Paris at the same time, Moholy's note about Landau was in a postscript to a long letter in which he ended by describing an extended visit to Mondrian's New York studio, thus indicating a connection in his mind.[711]

For his part, Mondrian had moved in October, 1940, to New York, where his first studio was at 352 East 52nd Street, at the corner of First Avenue. His 1939 letter from London expressing his disappointment at not being invited to teach at the New Bauhaus has already been discussed in this Chapter. Among the points he made was:

> I see by your letters that you are thinking I could do good work at the Bauhaus in the future. But why did you not think of me firstly? I am, among the different artists, perhaps the most free from "art" and the most near to "reality" and its aesthetic construction; the most near to architecture and industry.[712]

Moholy's account of his visit to Mondrian's studio is fascinating:

> . . . today I left an evening for Mondrian who has no telephone. He looks very frail but he does not care. Showed me old pictures, cartons

---

[709]Engelbrecht, "Association of Arts and Industries," 340-343.

[710]John Keenan, "Architecture," and Joan Pachner, "Chronology," both in: Robert Storr, editor, *Tony Smith: Architect, Painter, Sculptor* (New York: The Museum of Modern Art, 1998), 36-47, here 37, and 184-186, here 184, respectively.

[711]László Moholy-Nagy to Sibyl Moholy-Nagy, MLS, September 4th, 1941, microfilm reel 951, frames 0568-0573, Moholy-Nagy Papers, Archives of American Art.

[712]As in note 221.

[*sic*], + - [*sic*] drawings which are all derived from nature, sea scenes or churches, houses in Paris etc.

Moholy was also present at Mondrian's funeral in New York on February 3rd, 1944.[713] The principal speaker was Alfred Barr.[714]

There was also continued contact with Marianne Brandt, the Bauhaus student discussed in previous chapters. Her first such contact that can be documented was with Sibyl after Moholy had died,[715] but surely this followed exchanges of letters between Brandt and Moholy after he had moved to Chicago.

THE MOST EXTENSIVE EXCHANGE OF LETTERS with any of his European friends was with Raoul Hausmann at various addresses in Czechoslovakia and France. Moholy's letters to Hausmann are preserved in an archive in Berlin, but Hausmann's letters to Moholy cannot be located. The correspondence began in 1938, continued until late in 1940 and resumed early in 1945. The first letter is about the New Bauhaus Books published by W.W. Norton, and Moholy was not able to encourage Hausmann that Norton would choose to publish his book on optophonetics, or attempts to make sound and light waves correspond through his patented device called the optophon.[716] After Hausmann's 1939 move from Czechoslovakia to France Moholy sent him ten dollars in financial aid.[717] Four letters concerned advice about possible sales of Hausmann's works to Alfred Barr at the Museum of Modern Art (sales that did not take place).[718] On December 21st, 1940, Moholy offered to put Hausmann's name on a list for a Rescue Committee that was attempting to bring artists and writers out of occupied and unoccupied France.[719] On July 14th, 1945, Moholy inquired under what conditions Hausmann might join the I.D. faculty, and if he had enough command of English to lecture to students and could give time and enthusiasm to teaching, and on September 28th offered him a post at the I.D. as guest lecturer for four months.[720] Hausmann never

---

[713] László Moholy-Nagy to Sibyl Moholy-Nagy, February 2nd, 1944.

[714] Alice Goldfarb Marquis, *Alfred H. Barr, Jr., Missionary for the Modern* (Chicago: Contemporary Books, 1989), 213-214.

[715] Sibyl Moholy-Nagy to Ise Gropius, photographic copy of TLS, October 27th, 1947, Bauhaus-Archiv, Berlin.

[716] László Moholy-Nagy to Raoul Hausmann, TLS, March 17th, 1938, Raoul Hausmann Archive, Berlinische Galerie, Berlin.

[717] As in note 716, October 30th, 1939.

[718] As in note 716, December 27th, 1939, and January 5th, February 27th and December 21t, 1940.

[719] As in note 716, December 21st, 1940.

[720] As in note 716, July 14th and September 14th, 1945.

did set foot in the United States, but Moholy received some materials from him for use in *Vision in Motion*.[721]

Moholy also maintained institutional continuity with his friends through his continued participation in the *CIAM* (*Congrès Internationaux d'Architecture Moderne*). As discussed in Chapter Four, he had been an active member of the group while living in Europe. On May 13th, 1939, a *CIAM* meeting was held at the New York Architectural League with Giedion, George Fred Keck, Moholy and others. Giedion opened the meeting and asked for comments "regarding the advisability of forming an American group of architects which might become a unit of CIAM." (Giedion seems to have taken or been granted the power to organize new *CIAM* groups in the absence of other *CIAM* officers.) On the previous day, Giedion had participated in a symposium on contemporary architecture at the New York University Institute of Fine Arts that included his lecture, "American Architecture Viewed from Europe"; Moholy was in the audience.[722]

Moholy was also present at the organizing meeting for a New York chapter of the *CIAM*, held on May 20th, 1944, at the New School for Social Research in New York; also present were his friends from his European years, Gropius, Giedion, Chermayeff and Breuer.[723] Moholy served on the Board of Directors of the New York *CIAM* Chapter for Relief and Postwar Planning that emerged from that meeting, and was also present at its June 15th, 1945, meeting in a New York restaurant, Le Canard Bleu.[724] Moholy had invited José Luis Sert, who was also present at the two New York meetings that he had attended, to return to the School of Design in Chicago to lecture on March 22nd, 1943, about his 1942 book, *Can Our Cities Survive?*; this book had emerged from the 1933 meeting of the *CIAM* that both he and Moholy had taken part in, as discussed in Chapter Four.[725] (DVD figure 475)

---

[721] As in note 716, April 4th, 1946, postscript; and László Moholy-Nagy, *Vision in Motion*, 212.

[722] Eric Mumford, *The CIAM Discourse on Urbanism, 1928-1960* (Cambridge: The MIT Press, 2000), 126-127.

[723] Mumford, *The CIAM Discourse on Urbanism*, 145-147.

[724] Mumford, *The CIAM Discourse on Urbanism*, 147 and 149.

[725] José Louis Sert, *Can Our Cities Survive?; an ABC of Urban Problems, their Analysis, their Solutions, Based on the Proposals Formulated by the C.I.A.M., International Congresses for Modern Architecture . . .* (Cambridge: The Harvard University Press, 1942).

The *CIAM* had made only a short official statement at the time of its fourth meeting in 1933, a meeting discussed in Chapter Four. Sert's book is not an official *CIAM* document; see: Auke van der Woud, *Het Nieuwe Bouwen Internationaal/International [and] CIAM Volkshuisvesting. Stedebouw/Housing, Town Planning* [text in Dutch and English] (Delft: Delft University Press, 1983), 72, 74 and 163-167.

Other *CIAM* colleagues, two Warsaw architects and planners, lectured in May, 1946, at the I.D. These were Simon Syrkus and his wife Helena Syrkus (1900-1982); she had been an architect in the office of Le Corbusier. He was a survivor of the Nazi concentration camp at Auschwitz and she survived years of slave labor imposed by the Nazis.[726] The two gave lectures on the re-building of Warsaw, evidently making a good impression on Moholy, who considered them "magnificent city builders."[727] Chicago, of course, was a logical venue for these lectures, as a city with such a large population of Polish background that it is sometimes called the second largest Polish city in the world.

Myron Kozman, then serving in the United States Army and stationed in England, wrote to Moholy at the end of May of 1944 that he was surprised to find that Kurt Schwitters was in England, having traveled there from Norway with an artist whom Kozman had met.[728] In one of his letters to Kozman shortly after the war's end, Moholy asked him to get information about Schwitters: "Find out how Kurt Schwitters is—whether he can work, and the condition of his health."[729] With the end of the war, Moholy made direct contact with Schwitters and helped him get food. Ironically, as Schwitters wrote to a friend: "Moholy starb anfang Oktober [*sic*; *i.e.*, November 24] und sandte mir vorher über Kopenhagen ein Dänisches food parcel. Marvelous."[730] [Moholy died . . . {on November 24} and sent to me beforehand a Danish "food parcel."]

One of Moholy's English friends, Jack Pritchard, visited Chicago in December, 1944, just before Christmas, having arrived earlier that month on the ocean liner "Queen Elizabeth."[731] He had traveled under wartime conditions because he was on official business for the British Ministry of Fuel and Power with a mission to study domestic heating in America for information that could help in post-War planning.[732] In Chicago he was taken by Moholy to visit the I.D. as well as Sears, Roebuck. At Sears Pritchard was interested in the study of whole-house heating and was struck by the stress the firm

---

[726] Sibyl Moholy-Nagy to Lucia Moholy, May 8th, 1946.

[727] László Moholy-Nagy to Jenő Nagy, June 23rd, 1946, Levente and Edith Nagy files, Budapest; the letter appears, in English translation, in: Passuth, *Moholy-Nagy*, 409.

[728] Myron Kozman to László Moholy-Nagy, carbon copy of TLS. May 28th, 1944; copies are in my files and in those of Hattula Moholy-Nagy.

[729] László Moholy-Nagy to Myron Kozman, TLS, August 25th, 1945; copies are in my files and in those of Hattula Moholy-Nagy.

[730] Kurt Schwitters to Carl Buchheister, December 18th, 1946; published in: Kurt Schwitters, *Wir Spielen, bis uns der Tod abholt: Briefe aus fünf Jahrzehnten*, gesammelt, ausgewählt und kommentiert von Ernst Nündel (Frankfurt am Main: Verlag Ullstein GmbH, 1974), 252-253.

[731] Jack Pritchard, *View from a Long Chair: the Memoirs of Jack Ptritchard* (London: Routledge & Kegan Paul, 1984), 135-136.

[732] Pritchard, *View from a Long Chair*, 132-140.

placed on testing all of its fuel-burning appliances before they were advertised for sale.[733]
The entré to Sears was through E. Penn Brooks, the firm's Vice President, who had
joined the board of the I.D. earlier that year. (DVD figure 476) Pritchard noticed that
Brooks was impressed by the "drive and energy" that Moholy put into his work at the
I.D.[734]

Herbert Read presented two lectures at the I.D. in April, 1946,[735] and wrote a lively
account of his visits to I.D. classes.[736] On April 1st and 2nd he visited the Paepcke farm at
Somonauk, where Moholy photographed him and Walter Paepcke together.[737] (DVD
figure 516)

Life in Chicago: Political and Social

On July 31st, 1937, Moholy made a three and one-half hour visit to the Art Institute of
Chicago, and described it in a letter to his wife:

> gestern nachmittag besuchte ich das art-institute (museum). eine ganz
> aussergewöhnliche sammlung von porzellan, ton, glas, möbel,
> plastikund bildern. china und japan [sich] als sonderliche
> amerikanische undeuropäische malerei. [unread–werke?] vom
> mittelaltern bis zum picasso mit ausgezeichneten franz. impressionisten.
> nach 3 ½ stunden studium (ich wollte sehen, was man dann für
> [unread—unsere?] schule verwenden kann) kam ich—von der kunst
> invalid—mit kopfschmerzen nach hause.[738] [Yesterday afternoon I
> visited the Art Institute (museum). An entirely extraordinary collection
> of porcelain, ceramics, glass, furniture, sculpture and pictures. China
> and Japan and remarkable American and European paintings. {Works?}

---

[733] Pritchard, *View from a Long Chair*, 126 and 137; and Jack Pritchard to E. Penn Brooks, carbon
copy of TLS, February 6th, 1947, Pritchard Papers, Library of the University of East Anglia,
Norwich.

[734] Jack Pritchard to J.M. Richards, carbon copy of TLS, December 4th, 1946, Pritchard Papers,
Library of the University of East Anglia, Norwich.

[735] Sibyl Moholy-Nagy to Lucia Moholy, TLS, May 8th, 1946, Lucia Moholy papers, Bauhaus-
Archiv, Berlin; and Findeli, *Le Bauhaus de Chicago*, 66.

[736] Herbert Read to David Stevens, TLS, October 18th, 1946, copy appended to a memorandum
from Walter Paepcke to the Board of Directors, Institute of Design, Institute of Design Paperes,
University of Illinois Library, Chicago; see also reel 948, frames 0702-0703, Moholy-Nagy files,
Archives of American Art, Washington, D.C.

[737] Jeannine Fiedler and Hattula Moholy-Nagy, editors, *Laszlo Moholy-Nagy: Color in
Transparency*, 166-167.

[738] László Moholy-Nagy to Sibyl Moholy-Nagy, ALS, August 1st, 1937, reel 951, frame 0244,
Moholy-Nagy files, Archives of American Art, Washington, D.C.

from the Middle Ages to Picasso, with splendid French
Impressionists. After 3 ½ hours of study (I wanted to see what could be
useful for {our?} school) I went home with a headache, disabled by
art.]

The direct participation of Moholy with a major activity of the Art Institute, on a later occasion, was related by his daughter, Hattula, who recalled that her father, along with other Chicago artists, had been invited to hang one of his paintings at a kind of artists' open house at the Art Institute, and that he and the other artists stood near their works to answer questions asked by museum visitors. She is no longer certain which painting Moholy chose for the occasion.[739]

Moholy himself provided an indication of his understanding of the English language in his letter to his wife about attending a play shortly after arriving in Chicago. The play, referred to in note 198, was a Pulitzer-Prize winning comedy, *You Can't Take It with You,* written by Moss Hart and George S. Kaufman. Moholy wrote: ". . . ich war froh das zu sehen und zu verstehen," but added, parenthically, "nicht alles." [I was glad to see it and to understand it {but not all}.] Since this was the evening following his three and one-half hour visit to the Art Institute, perhaps his headache made it hard to concentrate on spoken English!

Three years later it was Sibyl who was assessing her husband's English. She recalled that when they had taken an automobile trip to Mills College in the summer of 1940:

By the time we arrived at Mills College, Moholy had lost most of his
English vocabulary. During the trip he had insisted on speaking only
German, which he loved.[740]

Sibyl drove their 1937 gray Ford four-door sedan to Oakland; Moholy never learned to drive.[741] Claudia and Hattula Moholy-Nagy stayed behind in Illinois; during the early part of the summer a German "nanny" took care of them, and during the latter part of the summer they were enrolled in a six-week summer camp at Somonauk for children aged four to ten, organized by Claudia's and Hattula's teacher at Miss Marston's Private School in Chicago, Marjorie Marston.[742]

---

[739]Hattula Moholy-Nagy, interviewed by Lloyd C. Engelbrecht, Zurich, June, 1976. She recalled that her mother had brought her and her sister to the Art Institute for the occasion; see Hattula Moholy-Nagy, "Chicago Memories," Appendix E, page 727.

[740]Sibyl Moholy-Nagy, *Moholy-Nagy: Experiment in Totality*, 180.

[741]The 1937 Ford sedan was replaced with the 1946 model not long before Moholy died; the information is from an exchange of E-mail messages between Hattula Moholy-Nagy and me in July, 2007.

[742]Hattula Moholy-Nagy, interviewed by Lloyd C. Engelbrecht, Ann Arbor, Michigan, November, 1995 (with subsequent clarifications); Sibyl Moholy-Nagy to Walter P. Paepcke, TLS, February 7th, 1940; László Moholy-Nagy to Walter P. Paepcke, TLS, March 1st, 1940; and Walter P.

(continued...)

In addition to being his principal supporter in Chicago, Walter Paepcke shared with Moholy, and their families, many social contacts with each other. These contacts did not mean that they were really part of the same social circle; in actuality they took place in spite of the fact that the Moholys and the Paepckes belonged to separate social circles. Once, in a dejected mood, Sibyl wrote to her husband, after visiting the Paepcke's at their summer home near Somonauk, that she had the impression that Mrs. Paepcke felt that they were just *Schnorrers*, which could be translated, in this context, as parasites.[743]

Walter Paepcke's wife, Elizabeth ("Pussy") Paepcke, related to me (in December, 1967, in Aspen, Colorado), and also separately to Hattula Moholy-Nagy, that during the summer sessions at Somonauk the Moholys would sometimes be invited to visit the Paepckes at their summer house, which was located about two to three miles from the farmhouse and other buildings that housed the school. Hattula Moholy-Nagy remembers that several times Walter Paepcke rode to the school on his horse, and that he and Moholy would then play chess outdoors at the school.

Many social contacts between the Paepckes and the Moholys would be hard to document now because they no doubt were arranged during in-person or telephone conversations. Nevertheless there are written references to shared meals[744] and to other social occasions.[745] Moholy and Walter Paepcke often met for games of chess, at

---

[742](...continued)
Paepcke to László Moholy-Nagy, carbon copy of typed letter, March 5th, 1940; all three letters are in the Institute of Design Papers, University of Illinois Library, Chicago.

[743] Sibyl Moholy-Nagy to László Moholy-Nagy, June 8th, 1942.

[744] "Perhaps we could have dinner together as I am alone at the apartment and I believe you are also alone these days while your family is still in the county," Walter P. Paepcke to László Moholy-Nagy, carbon copy of TLS, August 10th, 1942; a luncheon is referred to in a letter of December 31st, 1943, László Moholy-Nagy to Walter P. Paepcke, TLS; "He [Moholy] and Sibyl had dinner with us last Saturday evening," Walter P. Paepcke to Walter Gropius, carbon copy of TLS, December 17th, 1945; "I am expecting you for dinner [at Somonauk] at about 6:30 Wednesday evening, August 7," Walter P. Paepcke to László Moholy-Nagy, carbon copy of TLS, August 5th, 1946; these are all in the Institute of Design Papers, University of Illinois Library, Chicago.

[745] ". . . we are thinking of having a sort of interesting group of people over some time soon, and Pussy and I will hope very much that you and Sibyl can be there too." Walter P. Paepcke to László Moholy-Nagy, carbon copy of typed letter, March 5th, 1940, Institute of Design Papers, University of Illinois Library, Chicago; and "Donnerstag, den 5. Februar . . . Von 4.30 bis 7 Uhr geben die Paepckes, die hier so etwa cream of society, ein Empfang fuer Euch. . . . Sie sind uebrigens intime Freunde der Charles Swift's die auch da sein werden." [Thursday, February 4, from 4:30 until 7, the Paepckes, who here, as it were, are the cream of society, have extended an invitation to you {Ise and Walter Griopius}. . . . In addition they are intimate friends of Charles Swift's, who will also be there.], Sibyl Moholy-Nagy to Ise Gropius, photographic copy of TLS, January 21st, 1942, Bauhaus-Archiv, Berlin. Charles Henry Swift (1872-1948) was a wealthy meat packer and philanthropist.

Somonauk, as noted above, or in Chicago.[746] In a letter, Moholy made an interesting proposal to Paepcke: "I thought that next time we should play some few games of great chess players, with a third person sitting beside us. We would make the steps first, by our own thinking, then the kibitzer would give us the master's moves."[747] Perhaps this suggestion was made because Moholy was the better player; Hattula Moholy-Nagy recalls her mother describing him as much the better player.[748] In sum, as Moholy wrote about their relationship in a letter thanking Walter Paepcke for his support: ". . . our life here in America would have been sometimes very dark without your and Pussy's friendship."[749]

Hattula Moholy-Nagy recalls accompanying her parents for lunch or dinner engagements in the homes of people who supported Moholy's schools. She also remembers many dinner parties at 2622 North Lakeview Avenue, where she and her family lived on the third storey of a three-storey apartment building dating from around 1900.[750] Some of the guests were members of the Chicago business community or faculty members of the University of Chicago.[751] One such party, held in 1942, is documented by a letter inviting Walter and Ise Gropius to a dinner party of twelve

---

[746]"I especially enjoy Somonauk, where we miss you very much, especially in the chess tournaments," László Moholy-Nagy to Walter Paepcke, TLS, July 15th, 1942, Institute of Design Papers, University of Illinois Library, Chicago; "I hope to see you and play chess with you one day in Somonauk or in the city," László Moholy-Nagy to Walter P. Paepcke, TLS, June 24th, 1943; "I enjoyed our chess last night," Walter Paepcke to László Moholy-Nagy, carbon copy of typed letter, August 2nd, 1945; "Last night I read a most interesting analysis of Black Mountain College—its purpose, teaching plan, and practice. I would like to discuss it with you some day, I hope no less enjoyable than our chess playing," László Moholy-Nagy to Walter P. Paepcke, TLS, August 3rd, 1945; all in the Institute of Design Papers, University of Illinois Library, Chicago.

[747]Moholy added: "I also thought one could publish such a chess book in which the new steps are always on the other side of the page, so that one could play alone with such a book and use his wit—then be able to check his moves with the master's moves. I have two different solutions for such a book—one which saves paper—and one which wastes paper." (This seems like a premonition of some chess computer software.) László Moholy-Nagy to Walter P. Paepcke, TLS, undated, probably 1941, Institute of Design Papers, University of Illinois Library, Chicago.

[748]Hattula Moholy-Nagy, "Chicago Memories," Appendix E, page 730.

[749]László Moholy-Nagy to Walter P. Paepcke, TLS, August 5th, 1942, Institute of Design Papers, University of Illinois Library, Chicago.

[750]This building and its neighbors were demolished and replaced in 1968 with a forty-two storey apartment building with the address of 2626 North Lakeview Avenue. In front of this building a Chicago Tribute marker in honor or Moholy was erected in November, 1999.

[751]Hattula Moholy-Nagy, "Chicago Memories," Appendix E, pages 730-731.

people, in the Moholys' apartment, where the men were to wear black ties and the women evening dress.[752]

The building designated as 2622 North Lakeview Avenue did not actually face Lakeview Avenue but instead was part of a group of similar buildings lining a grassy court that faced Chicago's lakefront gem, Lincoln Park. The furniture in the Moholy-Nagy apartment included several Breuer-designed pieces: an Isokon long chair (DVD figure 286), a pair of armchairs, and a round dining-table and chairs. The long chair was acquired in England, the other items were acquired by László and Lucia in Dessau, and visible in two of Lucia's photographs of the interiors of their duplex there. (DVD figures 157 and 162). There was also some mahogany-veneer art-deco furniture that Sibyl had acquired as part of her divorce settlement with Carl Dreyfuß. The dining room and living room faced north. The apartment was smaller than the one on Astor Street so Moholy did not have a room set aside as his studio but rather located his large brown paint-speckled easel near the living-room window. It was in the kitchen oven that he bent his Plexiglas sculpture, as noted above.

The move to the the apartment at 2622 North Lakeview Avenue took place before the end of 1940,[753] but the decoration was not finished until the end of summer, 1941,[754] and the earliest letter I have seen written on printed stationery with that address is dated September 2nd, 1941.[755] Hattula remembers that "the walls were covered in pale gray, featureless wallpaper" that provided a suitable background for the hanging of Moholy's paintings.[756] Carpeting was of neutral colors but by way of contrast window draperies were of school designed-fabrics.

---

[752]"Sonnabend, den 7. Februar abends 7.00 eine kleine Dinner party bei uns zu Hause, 12 Leute, wo wir so die besseren Koepfchen zu haben hoffen. Wir muessen leider black tie und Abendkleid machen da das hier in der duesteren Provinz so Etikette ist." [Sunday, February 7t, 7:00 p.m. a small dinner party at our place, 12 people, where we hope to have the best minds. Unfortunately we must wear black tie and evening clothes, since that is etiquette here in the melancholy provinces.] Sibyl Moholy-Nagy to Ise Gropius, January 21st, 1942. Later Sibyl Moholy-Nagy wrote of the party that: "Die 'Party' war glaube ich ein grosser Erfolg fuer Chicago's unverwoente Leute die so selten mit 'Intellect' gefuettert werden." [The "Party" was, I believe, a big success for Chicago's unspoiled people who so seldom dine with intellectuals.] Sibyl Moholy-Nagy to Ise Gropius, photographic copy of TLS, February 12th, 1942, Bauhaus-Achiv, Berlin.

[753]Sibyl Moholy-Nagy to Lucia Moholy, TLS, January 10th, 1941, Bauhaus-Archiv, Berlin. This is the earliest letter I have found sent from the Lakeview address, which is typed on the first sheet *in lieu* of printed stationery, indicating a recent move since nearly all of Sibyl's letters sent from a home address are on printed stationery.

[754]Sibyl Moholy-Nagy to Ise Gropius, photographic copy of TLS, October 15th, 1941, Bauhaus-Archiv, Berlin.

[755]Sibyl Moholy-Nagy to László Moholy-Nagy, September 2nd, 1941, TLS, microfilm reel 951, frames 0366-0367, Moholy-Nagy Papers, Archives of American Art, Washington, D.C.

[756]From an E-mail message, Hattula Moholy-Nagy to Lloyd C. Engelbrecht, July, 2007.

László and Sibyl greeted the arrival of 1940 with a second visit to "Fallingwater" on Bear Run, Pennsylvania. This time they were holiday guests from December 27th, 1939, until January 3rd, 1940, in the famous house designed for Edgar J. Kaufmann, junior, and his parents by Frank Lloyd Wright.[757] In *Vision in Motion* Moholy described the house, as "one of the masterpieces of contemporary architecture," and added, "To live in such a house creates the sensation of being in an airplane, giving an emotionally freer relationship to the surroundings."[758]

MOHOLY REMAINED FASCINATED WITH HUNGARY and enjoyed the friendship of fellow Hungarians. Two of these were Margit Varró, a concert pianist, and her husband István; Hattula remembers that they were especially close friends.[759] Other Hungarians included a skilled carpenter, Kálmán Tomaniczka (also spelled Tomanicka),[760] sometimes known as Kálmán Toman, and his wife, Katica. Hattula Moholy-Nagy remembers a visit to their apartment on the Far West Side of Chicago. Toman and Moholy once spent a summer afternoon making sauerkraut on a porch of the house used for the summer school at Somonauk. They split the results, and Toman stored and cured his portion in the Tomans' house while Moholy stored and cured his portion in the storage area of the apartment house in which the Moholy-Nagy family was then living. Hattula Moholy-Nagy still remembers the pungent odor![761] Toman, trained in traditional crafts as a peasant in Hungary, provided various services for the School of Design in Chicago, including helping the students with the wooden bedsprings project, described above. He also got the old house at the school's farm at Somonauk ready for the summer sessions there with projects such as building porches, making cabinets and laying linoleum.[762]

The first involvement of Moholy with the Hungarian-American community as a group was service in a morale program of the Office of Civilian Defense during World War II. Moholy described his role: "I am among the people who try to unify the Hungarian language groups for the war efforts."[763] Nothing further is known about Moholy's work in this capacity.

---

[757]László Moholy-Nagy to Alfred Neumeyer, TLS, December 22nd, 1939, Institute of Design Papers, University of Illinois Library, Chicago.

[758]László Moholy-Nagy, *Vision in Motion*, 257.

[759]Hattula Moholy-Nagy, "Chicago Memories," Appendix E, pages 731-732.

[760]Sibyl Moholy-Nagy, *Moholy-Nagy; Experiment in Totality*, 186, 237 and 239.

[761]Hattula Moholy-Nagy, "Chicago Memories," Appendix E, 732.

[762]Sibyl Moholy-Nagy, *Moholy-Nagy; Experiment in Totality*, 237 and 239; and Sibyl Moholy-Nagy to László Moholy-Nagy, June 8th, 1942.

[763]László Moholy-Nagy to Immigration & Naturalization Service, carbon copy of TLS, May 29t, 1942, microfilm reel 949, frame 0706, Moholy-Nagy papers, Archives of American Art, Washington, D.C.

In contrast, Moholy's involvement with the the Hungarian-American Council for Democracy [*Amerikai Magyar Demokratikus Tanács*][764] is very well documented. The Council had been started in 1943 by supporters of former Hungarian Premier Count Mihály [Michael] Károlyi, who was then living in London.[765] Actor Béla Lugosi was national president and head of the Hollywood branch of the Council; Count Károlyi was honorary president; and Moholy headed the Chicago Chapter. The Council's short-term (but unrealized) goal was to bring Károlyi to the United States;[766] its longer-term goal was to install him as leader of a post-War, democratic Hungary.[767] Sibyl Moholy-Nagy remembers the group as ". . . a curious assembly of doctors, lawyers, shopkeepers, artisans and workmen, who had no more in common than their Hungarian nationality and their devotion to Moholy."[768] She also recalled a visit her husband had with Eleanor Roosevelt in connection with the Council's activities: "Moholy kam gerade aeussert animiert von Washington zurueck wo er eine halbe Stunde im White House bei Mrs. Roosevelt war und sonst noch Gott und die Welt gesehen hat." [Moholy, appearing very excited, just returned from Washington, where he spent a half hour in the White House with Mrs. Roosevelt, and where, besides her, he had seen absolutely everyone who was anybody.][769]

Most of Moholy's work for the Council was less dramatic than the visit to the White House. Sibyl Moholy-Nagy recalled the time, energy and travel expended by Moholy on behalf of the group's aims:

> Moholy spoke before steel-mill workers in Gary and coal miners in
> Pennsylvania; he sat through endless amateur shows which are the
> peculiar obsession of all foreign language groups . . . and he spent hours
> on the telephone, trying to pacify the fiercely individualistic tempers of
> his followers.[770]

---

[764]Evidently due to a simple error, Sibyl Moholy-Nagy referred to it as "The American Federation of Democratic Hungarians (Sibyl-Moholy-Nagy, *Moholy-Nagy; Experiment in Totality*, 189.) Moholy, too, often ignored the official name of the group and sometimes referred to it in English as the "Hungarian Democratic Council."

[765]Nandor F. Dreisziger, "Émigré Artists and Wartime Politics: 1939-45," *Hungarian Studies Review*, volume XXI, numbers 1-2 (Spring-Fall, 1994), 43-61, here 51-53.

[766]*Ibid.*, 53-55.

[767]László Moholy-Nagy to Garrett R. Foley, January 17th, 1946, microfilm reel 951, frames 0458 and 0459, Moholy-Nagy papers, Archives of American Art, Washington, D.C.; printed in *Hungarian Studies Review*, volume XXI, numbers 1-2 (Spring-Fall, 1994), 100-[102].

[768]Sibyl-Moholy-Nagy, *Moholy-Nagy; Experiment in Totality*, 189.

[769]Sibyl Moholy-Nagy to Ise Gropius, January 21st, 1942. See also: Sibyl-Moholy-Nagy, *Moholy-Nagy; Experiment in Totality*, 189.

[770]Sibyl-Moholy-Nagy, *Moholy-Nagy; Experiment in Totality*, 189.

Károlyi wrote about the movement in his memoirs. He recalled that: "In Chicago a mass meeting was organized on the basis of my programme. . . ."[771]

Károlyi also recalled the roles of "Moholyi Nagy [sic] the artist" and "the well-known actor Bela Lugosi" in his movement,[772] as well as his visit to Hollywood in 1928 when he met Lugosi.[773] In the end the most visible political job Károlyi filled after his return to Hungary in 1945 was as ambassador to France, beginning in 1947.[774]

Oliver Botar interviewed Zita Schwarcz (née Strauss), a Budapest native, about the Council, for which she served as "Chairman of Entertainment." She described Moholy's growing realization that Károlyi was unlikely to head a post-War Hungarian government, and also that some members of the Council were Communists.[775]

Moholy himself once described his work with the Council:

> The Hungarian Democratic Council [sic] worked for two purposes: it supported Count Michael Karolyi in London as a potential leader for a liberated and thoroughly liberalized Hungary, and it spread democratic information and better understanding of Allied war aims among the Hungarian-born population. When I was asked to become chairman of this group in Chicago I accepted in spite of my heavy commitments because I saw a chance to win my new country more loyal citizens. It never occurred to me that my intentions could be so dangerously misinterpreted. When Hungary had been liberated and Count Károlyi had been asked by the Russian Government to return to Hungary, I saw my mission fulfilled and I resigned from the Hungarian Democratic Council on May 23, 1945.[776]

There was a long-standing delay in getting United States citizenship for Moholy and his wife, and Moholy wrote a letter to Garrett R. Foley on January 17th, 1946, evidently

---

[771] Mihály Károlyi, *Memoirs of Michael Karolyi: Faith without Illusion*, translated by Catherine Karolyi (London: Jonathan Cape, 1956), 301.

[772] Károlyi, *Memoirs*, note 50 on page 381.

[773] Károlyi, *Memoirs*, 245.

[774] In his *Memoirs* Károlyi summed up his political activities at the end of the war, beginning with his election to the Hungarian House of Deputies in December, 1945, "as a non-party member for the City of Budapest." See: Károlyi, *Memoirs*, 310-359.

[775] Oliver Botar, "Documents on László Moholy-Nagy . . . Excerpts from an Interview with Zita Schwarcz on László Moholy-Nagy (Hamilton, Ontario, 22nd May 1988, by Oliver Botar, Jr.)," *Hungarian Studies Review*, volume XV, number 1 (Spring, 1988), 79-81.

[776] László Moholy-Nagy to Garrett R. Foley, January 17th, 1946.

in the hope that he could help with their citizenship applications.[777] It is not clear what if any action Foley took. Not much is known about Garrett R. Foley. He lived in Foley, Alabama, a small planned community organized by John Burton Foley. The latter was a Chicago businessman who commissioned a design from Moholy (DVD figures 490 and 491), was briefly a student in the School of Design[778] and also briefly a member of the board of the I.D.[779] Evidently Moholy had access to Garrett R. Foley through John Burton Foley. In any case by 1963 John Burton Foley, who owned two of Moholy's "plexiglas pieces," also lived in Foley, Alabama.[780]

Moholy must have had reason to believe that Garrett R. Foley could help in some way with his application for citizenship. Whether Foley had any official governmental position is not clear from the correspondence, because Moholy wrote to him at his home address and no letters he may have written to Moholy or in his behalf have come to light.

Shortly after writing to Garrett R. Foley, Moholy wrote about the problem in a letter of February 14th, 1946, to William Benton (1900-1973),[781] an Assistant Secretary of State in Washington whom he had earlier known in Chicago.[782] Moholy wrote that he feared that "his connection with the Democratic American-Hungarian Council [*sic*] might be under scrutiny" by the FBI (Federal Bureau of Investigation), and pointed out that he had

---

[777]*Ibid.*.

[778]László Moholy-Nagy, *Vision in Motion*, 173.

[779]"Minutes of the Board of Directors' Meeting of the Institute of Design," mimeographed, June 10 and September 10, 1946, respectively, Institute of Design Papers, University of Illinois Library, Chicago).

[780]John Burton Foley to Sibyl Moholy-Nagy, TLS, July 6th, 1963, microfilm reel 946, frame 0707, Archives of American Art, Washington, D.C.

[781]On Benton, see: "Benton, William (Burnett)," *Britannica Online*, available via the Internet as of July 6th, 1996. Benton was a close friend of Robert M. Hutchins, who in turn was a close friend of Walter Paepcke. Hutchins was an influential president of the University of Chicago while Benton served as vice president there from 1937 to 1945, which was during the time Moholy was engaging University faculty members to teach part time for him.

[782]László Moholy-Nagy to William Benton, February 14th, 1946, carbon copy of TLS, Moholy-Nagy reel 951, frames 0460 and 0461, Moholy-Nagy papers, Archives of American Art, Washington, D.C.; the letter also appears in *Hungarian Studies Review*, volume XV, number 1 (Spring, 1988), 81-82. Moholy began his letter with a reminder of their association in Chicago: "I remember with great pleasure the luncheon I had with you . . . at my arrival in this country in 1937, and our subsequent meetings during your work at the University of Chicago. At that time you made me feel that my ideas on art and education which I had come to teach in this country were well received by you; and I therefore hope you will understand why I turn to you in the following matter."

resigned from the Council and went on to downplay his role in it.[783] Moholy began his letter with a reminder of their association in Chicago:

> I remember with great pleasure the luncheon I had with you . . . at my arrival in this country in 1937, and our subsequent meetings during your work at the University of Chicago. At that time you made me feel that my ideas on art and education which I had come to teach in this country were well received by you; and I therefore hope you will understand why I turn to you in the following matter.

Shortly after the letter was sent, on April 10th, 1946, the Moholys were granted United States citizenship.[784] Benton acknowledged Moholy's gratitude, and his own role, in a brief note of April 20th, 1946: "If I've been of small help—I'm most happy."[785]

The original "Declaration of Intention" by Moholy and his wife had been dated February 9th, 1942, and the actual application for citizenship was dated May 29th, 1942.[786] Before writing to Benton, Moholy wrote at least four letters to others trying to advance the proceedings.[787] Moholy had also engaged an attorney, Joseph Edelman, of the Chicago firm of Abbell, Edelman, Portes and Abbell, who reported on March 23rd, 1945, that the Immigration and Nationalization Service could do nothing until the FBI had completed its report, and added that he would try to speed things up.[788] Moholy's

---

[783]László Moholy-Nagy to William Benton, February 14th, 1946.

[784]The certificate of citizenship, dated April 10, 1946, is on microfilm reel 951, frame 0472.

[785]William Benton to László Moholy-Nagy, April 20th, 1946, TLS, microfilm reel 951, frame 0462, Moholy-Nagy papers, Archives of American Art, Washington, D.C.

[786]László Moholy-Nagy to Immigration & Naturalization Service, May 29th, 1942.

[787]Laszlo Moholy-Nagy to Garrett R. Foley, January 17th, 1946, has already been cited; the other three letters are: Laszlo Moholy-Nagy to Andrew Jordan, August 28th, 1945, reel 951, frame 0451; Laszlo Moholy-Nagy to Andrew Jordan, November 12th, 1945, reel 951, frames 0453 and 0454; and Laszlo Moholy-Nagy to Emily Taft-Douglas, November 12th, 1945, reel 951, frame 0452. All of these letters are in the Moholy-Nagy papers, Archives of American Art, Washington, D.C.

The letters to Andrew Jordan and Emily Taft-Douglas are printed in *Hungarian Studies Review*, Volume XXI, numbers 1-2 (Spring-Fall, 1994), 98-99 and 99-100, respectively.

There is a note of irony in Moholy's decision to write to Emily Taft-Douglas (1899-1994), who was then serving as United States congresswoman-at-large for Illinois. She was the daughter of sculptor Lorado Taft (1860-1936) who, like Moholy, was one of Chicago's best-known artists, although with totally different artistic aims and approaches.

No correspondence among these figures in connection with Moholy's application for citizenship have come to light.

[788]Joseph Edelman to Laszlo Moholy-Nagy, carbon copy of TLS March 23rd, 1945, reel 951, frame

(continued...)

frustration with the process is clearly conveyed in a letter of November 12th , 1945, recalling a hearing held on July 27th, 1945:

> All in all I tried to do my best as a loyal and useful citizen, and I feel most bewildered and deeply hurt by the treatment meted out to me by the Immigration and Naturalization service. From time to time I have heard wild rumors of slanderous accusations brought against me. The hearing granted me in July was a quick-fire succession of questions concerning the past and present history of Hungary of which I have no detailed knowledge since I left that country twenty-five years ago. It is my deep conviction that what I did for the Hungarian Democratic Council [*sic*] was in the interest of the Allied cause for the shortening of the war. But this was treated ironically by the investigator. I was given to understand that my support of a democratic movement in Hungary was either too naive or too subversive to be credible. I may tell you,Sir, that I left this hearing deeply depressed, and with a feeling of frustration about the apparent inability of a civil servant to understand the motives of an artist and educator for freedom, democracy and peace.[789]

Following the hearing on July 27th, 1945, Moholy was asked to supply copies of his correspondence with Count Károlyi, which he did.[790] Moholy was probably not aware that the Count, a democratic socialist in spite of his inherited wealth and noble title, had not always been well received in the United States, and two of his visits to the United States had caused a great deal of controversy.[791] On his second visit, in 1924, Károlyi was admitted on the condition that he ". . . would not deliver any public speeches, give interviews or write articles." The Count quickly accepted the conditions because his wife was already in the United States and was seriously ill with typhoid fever. Roger Baldwin, president of the American Civil Liberties Union, protested, and on Károlyi's third and last visit to the United States, in 1928, the conditions were not re-imposed.[792] But some American officials might have had long memories.

In summary, Moholy applied for citizenship for himself and Sibyl on February 9th, 1942, and they were granted citizenship on April 10th, 1946. The reasons for the delay are not fully known, but it is evident that there was concern about his activities in the

---

[788](...continued)
0449, Moholy-Nagy papers, Archives of American Art, Washington, D.C.; printed in *Hungarian Studies Review*, volume XXI, numbers 1-2 (Spring-Fall, 1994), 97.

[789]László Moholy-Nagy to Andrew Jordan, November 12th, 1945. Jordan served in the Chicago office of the United States Immigration and Naturalization Service.

[790]László Moholy-Nagy to Andrew Jordan, August 28th, 1945. The correspondence between Moholy and Count Károlyi cannot now be located.

[791]Károlyi, *Memoirs*, 209-212 and 241-248; and Catherine Andrássy Károlyi, *A Life Together; the Memoirs of Catherine Károlyi* (London: George Allen & Unwin, Ltd., 1966), "Lecturing in the USA," 234-251.

[792]Károlyi, *Memoirs*, 209-212 and 241-248.

Hungarian-American Council for Democracy and especially his relationship with Mihály Károlyi.

Zita Schwarcz, as noted above, was interviewed by Oliver Botar, an interview that was conducted, in part, on tape. Schwarcz, who was married, nevertheless described a growing personal relationship between herself and Moholy during their participation in the activities of the Hungarian-American Council for Democracy. She recalled that they tried to avoid any overt romantic involvement because they feared it would damage the Institute of Design. She also recalled that they considered returning together to Hungary after the war, where Moholy could establish a school.[793]

HATTULA MOHOLY-NAGY RECALLS her mother's jealousy of Schwarcz.[794] By contrast, Sibyl was merely amused by the attraction that she had noticed her husband often felt toward younger women. In that regard, she commented to Kepes on how much Moholy would have enjoyed talking with Hannah Weitemeier (born 1942; later Hannah Weitemeier-Steckel) who interviewed Sibyl during her research trip to the United States in 1968: "I was very grateful that you saw Hannah Weitemeier, that young German art historian who is doing her PHD [dissertation] on Moholy. She is so young and enthusiastic and clean. God, how Moholy would have delighted in the idea that a beautiful girl has accepted him as her hero."[795]

Perhaps Moholy's last political interest was his leadership role in the *Amerikai Magyar Roosevelt Bizottság* [American-Hungarian Roosevelt Committee], an organization seeking to promote the re-election of Franklin D. Roosevelt in 1944.[796] He wrote an essay in Hungarian for a brochure supporting the re-election of Roosevelt.[797]

---

[793]From an interview of 1988; see note 579.

[794]Hattula Moholy-Nagy interviewed by Lloyd C. Engelbrecht, Ann Arbor, Michigan, September, 1993.

[795]Sibyl Moholy-Nagy to György Kepes, TLS, February 16th, 1968, microfilm reel 944, frame 099, Archives of American Art, Washington, D.C.; and Hannah Weitemeier Steckel, "László Moholy-Nagy: 1895 -1946, Entwurf seiner Wahrnehmungslehre" [Lászlò Moholy Nagy: 1895 -1946: An Outline of His Teachings on Perception] (Ph D. dissertation, Freie Universität, Berlin, 1974).

[796]Oliver Botar, "Documents on László Moholy-Nagy . . . Introduction" volume XV, number 1 (Spring, 1988), 78-79 and 84; and *idem*, "László Moholy-Nagy and Hungarian-American Politics II," *Hungarian Studies Review*, volume XXI, numbers 1-2 (Spring-Fall, 1994), 91-[94], here 93. See also: "Events of Campaign as Candidates Near the Date of Decision," *Chicago Tribune*, November 2, 1944, 10.

[797]Published in an English translation by Oliver Botar, in: "Why Every Hungarian-American Should Vote for Roosevelt," *Hungarian Studies Review*, volume XXX, numbers 1-2 (Spring-Fall, 1994), 96.

Also, a sound recording was made of one of his speeches in support of Roosevelt's re-election.[798] (sound clip 3)

As noted above, Moholy died on November 24th, 1946 and there were two memorial events in Chicago. The first took place at the Institute of Design on Wednesday, November 27th, at 2:30 p.m. Gropius estimated that more than 1,000 people were there.[799] Eulogies were offered by Walter Paepcke, by Moholy's former Bauhaus student Xanti Schawinsky, by Moholy's physician, Dr. Hugo Rony,[800] and by Gropius. Songs by Béla Bartók were sung by Andor Földi,[801] baritone, accompanied by Margit Varró at the piano.[802] Katharine Kuh recalled that: ". . . a crowded auditorium in his own school was touchingly decorated with his latest works, all of which breathed an optimism and health totally unrelated to the sick body which had produced them."[803]

The second memorial event for Moholy was held Monday, December 2nd, 1946, at 8:30 p.m. in the Walnut Room of the Midland Hotel (now a hotel called W Chicago City Center), 172 West Adams Street. It was staged by the Hungarian community in Chicago[804] under the banner of the Chicago chapter of the *Amerikai Magyar Demokratikus Tanács*. The memorial was organized by the group's treasurer, George Striker,[805] who announced the event by means of a handwritten mimeographed announcement. (DVD figures 531 and 532) Speakers included photographer Steve Deutsh (also called Stephen Deutch) of the Council, Kálmán Tomaniczka, György Kepes

---

[798] The recording is on the DVD disc accompanying *Moholy-Nagy: Mentor to Modernism*.

[799] Walter Gropius to Lucia Moholy, December 12th, 1946, TLS, Bauhaus-Archiv, Berlin.

[800] On Rony, see: György Litván, *A Twentieth-Century Prophet: Oscar Jászi, 1875-1957* (Budapest: Central European University Press, 2006), 428.

[801] Földi was then a student at the University of Chicago. Later he was known professionally as Andrew Foldi.

[802] Leslie L. Lewis to Members of the Board, Institute of Design, December 9, 1946, mimeographed, Institute of Design Papers, University of Illinois Library, Chicago.

[803] Katharine Kuh, "Moholy in Chicago," in: Kuh and Schniewind, *L. Moholy=Nagy; an Exhibition Sponsored by the Society for Contemporary American Art*, 4.

[804] On the Hungarian community in Chicago, see: Zoltán Fejős, *A Chicagói Magyarok Két Nemzedéke, 1890-1940: az Etnikai Örökség Megőrzése és Változása* (Budapest: Közép-Európa Intézet, 1993).

[805] Striker's name does not appear on the invitation, but his widow, Barbara, gave a copy to Hattula Moholy-Nagy in Budapest and informed her that the invitation had been hand-lettered by her late husband.

and István Varró. Poems were read that had been written by two poets who had been an inspiration during Moholy's early life, Endre Ady and Sándor Petőfi.[806]

It was Gropius who had known Moholy longer than anyone else present at the November 27th memorial. Thus his eulogy there, based on nearly a quarter of a century of close collaboration and friendship, is especially poignant:

> When I try to appraise the weight and scope of our dead friend for this gathering to bid him farewell—of Moholy, the man and his work—my whole respect and admiration for him have still greatly gained; for when a friend you have loved irrevocably disappears into silence, it happens that the sudden loss enlightens our consciousness in a flash.
>
> A life of tremendous vitality, will-power and love has been cut short in its zenith. What we shall miss most—all of his friends—is the exuberant warmth of his generous, passionate heart and the faithfulness of his friendship.
>
> It seems almost too vast a field for one man to till but this abundant versatility was uniquely his. With a strong power of imagination he kept this tremendous variety of interests in creative activities in balance. His creative vision took brilliant short-cuts to synchronize his observations into a consistant [*sic*] whole. He felt the danger of over-specialization leading to fallacies. He constantly developed new ideas, managing to keep himself in a stage of unbiased curiosity from where a fresh point of view might originate. Many of us will remember his peculiar freshness when faced with a new problem. With the attitude of a deeply interested child at play he surprised us by the directness of his intuitive approach. Here, I believe, was the source of his priceless quality as an educator, namely his never-ceasing power to stimulate and to carry away the other fellow with his own enthusiasm. What else can true education achieve than setting the student's mind in motion by that contagious magic? With curiosity and a shrewd sense of observation he investigated everything in his stride, taking nothing for granted. Every time when I had a discussion with him personally about our artistic problems I left him feeling deeply refreshed and satisfied. We always covered much ground in rapid speed because of his deep and genuine interest in another guy's work and ideas. This was typical for the broadness and generousness of this man's character.[807]

---

[806] A photocopy of the handwritten, two-sided mimeographed announcement by George Striker is the Hattula Moholy-Nagy files, Ann Arbor, Michigan.

[807] Carbon copy of typed manuscript, Bauhaus-Archiv, Berlin.

Moholy's body was laid to rest in Graceland Cemetery, located a short distance northwest of the Lakeview Avenue apartment.[808]

---

[808] Graceland Cemetery (Swain Nelson, Horace W.S. Cleveland and Ossian Cole Simonds, begun 1861) is one of the best examples of American landscape design influenced by the same English landscape tradition that had been a strong influence on two of the landscapes that Moholy experienced in Europe: the park in the Ilm River valley in Weimar (DVD figure 131) and the park at Wörlitz, near Dessau.

Moholy's interment in Graceland Cemetery is appropriate for another reason: many of the people who are mentioned in this Chapter are also buried there, including Ludwig Mies van der Rohe. In fact, Graceland has long been known as the cemetery of architects, and not only was Louis H. Sullivan buried there but he also designed two of the cemetery's tombs.

Chapter Six: Moholy and the Future

". . . the pioneer of the new light image, Moholy-Nagy . . ."
—Walter Benjamin, 1928

Since Moholy was just 51 years old when he died, it is tempting to think about the role he might have played had he lived another two decades or longer. Would his innate optimism have carried into the troubled post-War years?

SUFFICIENT TO SHAKE anyone's optimism had been the emergence of atomic weapons in the bombings of Hiroshima and Nagasaki in the summer of 1945. In the wake of these epic catastrophes, Moholy read through the complete Smyth Report on the development of the atomic bomb.[1] His concerns found their way into his paintings, especially *Nuclear I, CH*, of 1946 (oil on canvas, Art Institute of Chicago), a depiction of an atomic blast in terms of intense colors, superimposed on a grid that resembled Chicago as seen from the air. (DVD figure 533) The grid in this painting was probably suggested to him by his memories of flying over Chicago, shortly after the entry of the United States into World War II, when Mayor Edward J. Kelly appointed Moholy to an official city committee charged with investigating the possibility of camouflaging landmarks and key targets in Chicago (as noted in Chapter Five).[2] In fact, Chicago's grid had impressed him on his arrival there, as seen in a drawing of 1938. (DVD figure 534) *Nuclear I, CH* can now be seen in context thanks to the recent research of Stephen Petersen on the compelling reactions to nuclear weapons by artists ranging from Salvador Dali to Jackson Pollock and Jean Tinguely.[3] Moreover, Petersen reminded us that Wassily Kandinsky had pointed to the news of the divisibility of the atom as clearing the way for his turn to abstraction.[4]

A variation on *Nuclear I, CH*, without the urban grid, and without the "CH" suggestive of Chicago in its title, was known as *Nuclear II* (oil on canvas, Milwaukee Art Museum). (DVD figure 535) Both paintings were shown together at an exhibition

---

[1] Sibyl Moholy-Nagy, *Moholy-Nagy, Experiment in Totality*, second edition (Cambridge: The M.I.T. Press, 1969), 229; and Henry De Wolf Smyth, *Atomic Energy for Military Purposes: the Official Report on the Development of the Atomic Bomb under the Auspices of the United States Government, 1940-1945* (Princeton, New Jersey: Princeton University Press, 1945).

[2] See Chapter Five, page 612, and Sibyl Moholy-Nagy, *Moholy-Nagy: Experiment in Totality*, 183-184.

[3] Stephen Petersen, "Explosive Propositions: Artists React to the Atomic Age," *Science in Context*, volume XVII, number 4 (December, 2004), [579]-609. Moholy is not mentioned in the article.

[4] *Ibid.*, 580; and Wassily Kandinsky, "Reminiscences," in: Robert L. Herbert, editor, *Modern Artists on Art: Ten Unabridged Essays* (Englewood Cliffs, New Jersey: Prentice-Hall, Inc., 1964), 20-44, here 27.

seen in Springfield, Illinois, and in Chicago in 1990 and 1991.[5] Since *Nuclear II* was originally owned by his close friend Kenneth Parker,[6] and before that hung on Moholy's office wall (DVD figure 536), one can easily imagine that the two spoke about the painting and its meaning and significance, even if there was no indication of that when Parker wrote about his fondness for the painting:

> I have always loved that picture, for personal reasons, and objectively. Perhaps I have structured this opinion in my own mind: anyway I have always thought this particular painting—a splitting atom—showed the depth and breadth of Moholy's wonderful thinking and vision better than anything else I have seen of his.[7]

During his last years Moholy had retreated from his usual aloofness from political activism, so that, had he lived longer, surely his concerns about atomic weapons would have led him to take an active role of some kind in attempts to abolish them, or to avoid major-power confrontations making use of them. He had already joined with other artists in trying to cope with these life-and-death concerns through artistic expression.

Turning to something less overpowering, in my view one of Moholy's most important legacies for the future is the foundation course. As we have seen in Chapter Three, he did not originate the Bauhaus foundation course, but rather taught it after the departure of Johannes Itten, who had originated it in 1919. Josef Albers also taught the foundation course at the Bauhaus, first sharing it with Moholy during the same semester, then by teaching during alternating semesters, and, after Moholy left the Bauhaus, becoming its sole teacher at the school. But Moholy was the first to publish an in-depth discussion of his foundation-course teaching methods. Itten wrote only a few brief statements about the course while at the Bauhaus, published a short periodical article in 1930[8] and brought out a book about the course only late in his life, in 1963[9] along with a 1961 book about color, described in Chapter Three. Albers published a brief article in

---

[5] Terry Suhre, editor, *Moholy-Nagy: a New Vision for Chicago* (Chicago: University of Illinois Press and the Illinois State Museum, 1990), 97-99.

[6] *Ibid.*, 99.

[7] Kenneth Parker to Sibyl Moholy-Nagy, TLS, July 5th, 1963, microfilm reel 944, frames 0705 and 0706, Moholy-Nagy papers, Archives of American Art, Washington, D.C.

[8] Johannes Itten, "Pädagogische Fragments einer Formlehre; aus dem Unterricht der Ittenschule," *Die Form*, volume V, number 6 (April 15, 1930), 141-161.

[9] Johannes Itten, *Mein Vorkurs am Bauhaus* (Ravensburg, Germany: Otto Maier, 1963). The first edition in English was: *idem, Design and Form; the Basic Course at the Bauhaus* (New York: Reinhold Publishing Corporation, 1964).

1928,[10] and late in his life he published a book about his teaching of color in the course,[11] and a more general book based on three lectures about it.[12] As seen in tables three and four in Chapter Five (pages 558-559), in 1937 Moholy had hoped that Albers might be coaxed to write a book about the foundation course, but no such book ever materialized.

Thus, over the years, the only available published materials on the foundation course were Moholy's *Von Material zu Architektur* of 1929,[13] the first English-language edition of 1932 as *The New Vision*,[14] the 1938 edition (described in Chapter Five), and the third edition.[15] Moreover, each edition included slightly different but clear statements of teaching methods and examples of student work; these could be, and were, used by teachers of art, architecture, design and planning, both in high-school and university-level classes.

As outlined in Chapter Three, one reason the foundation course garnered so much attention among those teaching art is that it was a significant alternative to the academic practices used at the École des Beaux-Arts in Paris, and the many schools around the world that reflected its teaching practices.[16] Based on methods derived from the academic instruction that originated in Italy in the late-Renaissance/early-Baroque period, these academic practices in the early twentieth century still centered around the ideals of Classic art, from antiquity and the Italian Renaissance. One central exercise involved sketching from casts of ancient sculpture—in effect presenting an ideal for the students to emulate. The foundation course was more open-ended, and seemed to many teachers to be more attuned to the twentieth century. Basically, the foundation-course teachers sought to nurture the creative powers of each individual student: a phrase that sounds like it might have come from a slick brochure for an art school. But foundation-course teachers really meant it.

---

[10] See note 182 in Chapter Three.

[11] Josef Albers, *Interaction of Color* (New Haven: Yale University Press, 1963).

[12] Josef Albers, *Search Versus Re-Search: Three Lectures by Joseph Albers at Trinity College, April 1965* (Hartford: Trinity College Press, 1969).

[13] See: Appendix F, "Notes for Notes," page 734-735.

[14] László Moholy-Nagy, *The New Vision: from Material to Architecture*, translated by Daphne M. Hoffman (New York: Brewer, Warren & Putnam Inc., 1932). See also: Appendix F, pages 733-734

[15] László Moholy-Nagy, *The New Vision 1928 third revised edition, 1946, and Abstract of an Artist*, The documents of modern art, director: Robert Motherwell (New York: Wittenborn and Company, 1946). *Abstract of an Artist*, which appears on pages [65] through 87, is a short biographical note that does not appear in any of the earlier editions. A poor-quality reprint of the third edition with the same pagination, a new edition in name only, was issued the following year. See: Appendix F, "Notes for Notes," page 735.

[16] See, *e.g.*: Albert Boime, *The Academy and French Painting in the Nineteenth Century* (London: Phaidon; New York: Praeger Publishers, 1971), *passim*.

P ART OF THE REASON for the influence of Moholy's foundation course lay in the timing: many of his students in Chicago decided to become teachers, some in high schools, some in independent art schools, and many in colleges and universities. This was just at the time, following World War II, when college and university offerings in art, design, architecture and planning rapidly expanded.[17] Many of Moholy's former students, along with students from the I.D. who studied there later, and along with I.D. faculty members, were appointed to college and university jobs in many parts of the country because of these expanding opportunities. Influenced by the presentation of the I.D. foundation course,[18] they went on to teach their own versions of it elsewhere: Richard Filipowski (1923-2008) at Harvard University[19] and later at the Massachusetts Institute of Technology; also at M.I.T. was Robert Preusser (1919-1992);[20] Hin Bredendieck at the Georgia Institute of Technology; Jesse Reichek (1916-2005) at the University of California in Berkeley; and John Walley (1910-1974) at the University of Illinois in Chicago, to give just a few examples.

In 1991, cultural critic Richard Kostelanetz argued for the contemporary relevance of Moholy's last book, *Vision in Motion*, asserting that it is ". . . among the masterpieces of conceptual art,"[21] and also in the same year wrote of *Vision in Motion*:

> Asked to identify a single work that epitomizes his achievement, that
> represents the sum of his imagination and intelligence, I would choose,
> without intending to deprecate anything else, not a work of primarily
> visual art but the big book written in Chicago. . . .[22]

Critic Christopher Knight, writing in the mid-1990s, has analyzed the relevance of Moholy's work for a later generation. He pointed out that Sigmar Polke, Cindy Sherman and John Baldessari had simultaneously ". . . sidestepped the narrow preciousness of

---

[17]This is one of the most important developments in the arts in American history, yet, to my knowledge, no study of it has been carried out.

[18]On the foundation course as taught in Chicago, see: Lloyd C. Engelbrecht, "Grundkurs," in: Peter Hahn and Lloyd C. Engelbrecht, editors, *50 Jahre New Bauhaus; Bauhausnachfolge in Chicago* (Berlin: Argon Verlag, 1987), 121-135.

[19]Jill Pearlman, *Inventing American Modernism: Joseph Hudnut, Walter Gropius, and the Bauhaus Legacy at Harvard* (Charlottesville: University of Virginia Press, 2007), 218-228.

[20]See: Robert Preusser, "Visual Education for Science and Engineering Students," in: *Education of Vision*, Vision+Value Series, ed. by György Kepes (New York: George Braziller, 1965), 208-219. Preusser pioneered in teaching the foundation course as an element in the education of students outside the arts disciplines; his students were "engaged in the artist's visual-thought process without the barrier of competitive professional considerations . . ."; see *ibid.*, 213.

[21]Richard Kostelanetz, "A Contemporary Appreciation of Moholy-Nagy," in: Suhre, editor, *Moholy-Nagy: a New Vision for Chicago*, [102]-113, here 113.

[22]Richard Kostelanetz, "Laszlo Moholy-Nagy (1895-1946), *Vision in Motion* (1946)," in: Colin Naylor, editor, *Contemporary Masterworks* (Chicago: St. James Press, 1991), 844-845, here 845.

traditional 'art Photography' . . ." and ". . . supplanted the cloud of visual numbness created by the ubiquity of photographs in the modern world."[23]

Polke, Sherman and Baldessari were influenced by Moholy's photography, which might lead one to ask: what influence did Moholy have on painters who came after him. His watercolor, *Space Construction,* 1945 (DVD figures 537 and 538), published on the cover of *Art News* of its June, 1947, issue, leads one to wonder what affect he had on the development of Abstract Expressionism, sometimes referred to as the New York School, that was starting to emerge at that time. The artistic, as well as the social and political origins, of Abstract Expressionism were complex, but this painting, brought to the forceful and timely attention of New York artists by appearing on the cover of *Art News* in 1947, with its complex interweaving of curving lines around two loosely-defined spheres, punctuated with patches of color, seems to have anticipated much that transpired in the years immediately following. It should also be kept in mind that the painters who were to be identified with Abstract Expressionism, evidently with only a single exception (from 1944), were not to have their work illustrated on the pages of *Art News* until well after June, 1947.[24]

I T SHOULD BE NOTED that the lines in *Space Construction* were applied to the paper with rubber cement, and then painted over. Then the rubber cement was scraped off to reveal the white paper underneath. Those who saw Space Construction in *Art News* and who lived in or visited New York were, of course, able to see the original work in the Moholy-Nagy Memorial Exhibition at the Museum of Non-Objective Painting and read about its method of creation in the review of the exhibition by Thomas Hess.[25]

One aspect of Moholy's *Space Construction* of 1945, however, seems to have had little direct effect on other painters: it is signed twice, suggesting two possible orientations.

At the time of his death, in 1946, Moholy was well positioned to interact with members of the New York School since one of its most influential members, Robert Motherwell (1915-1991), had a role in bringing out the third edition of Moholy's *The New Vision*, which appeared in that year.[26] This was part of a series, "The Documents of

---

[23] Christopher Knight, "An Artist of Many Inventions; Moholy-Nagy Pushes the Limits of Photography," *Los Angeles Times*, July 1, 1995, pages F1 and F6.

[24] See the "Selected Bibliography," in: Henry Geldzahler, editor, *New York Painting and Sculpture: 1940-1970* (New York: E.P. Dutton & Co., Inc., 1969), 455-483.

[25] Thomas Hess, "Moholy-Nagy: Memorial to a Many-Sided Non-Objectivist," *Art News*, volume XLIV, number 4 (June, 1947), [1; *i.e.*, front cover], 5, 22-23 and 49-50.

[26] As in note 15.

Modern Art," of which Motherwell was director.[27] He also edited the fourth edition of 1947.[28]

Aside from Motherwell's work as editor of two editions of *The New Vision*, there is not much documentation of interaction between these two artists. But what there is, two brief mentions of Motherwell in letters written by Moholy to Robert J. Wolff in May[29] and July, 1944,[30] suggests other contacts between Moholy and Motherwell and surely some correspondence even if it cannot now be located. A possible trip to Chicago, presumably for a lecture or an exhibition or both, had to be postponed because Motherwell had unexpectedly been persuaded to have large single-artist exhibition at Peggy Guggenheim's Art of This Century Gallery in New York, to open on October 15th, 1944.[31] This exhibition marked a turning point in Motherwell's career because it was his first major showing in the United States and was favorably reviewed[32] and also because he was showing, among other works, his earliest collages, made while working side by side with Jackson Pollock in the latter's studio.[33] Had Moholy lived longer, he surely would have been involved with the artists active in a movement that was gaining momentum, as Motherwell's exhibition demonstrated, and thus would have met with other artists in the movement, likely including Pollock.

Moreover, Moholy's renewed contacts with Robert J. Wolff, who had been his faculty colleague at the School of Design in Chicago, would have led to still further involvement with the Abstract Expressionists. In the last year of his life Moholy had met with Wolff in New York three times.[34] Wolff had begun teaching at Brooklyn College

---

[27] László Moholy-Nagy, *The New Vision 1928 third revised edition, 1946, and Abstract of an Artist*, [3; *i.e.*, title page] and 82.

[28] László Moholy-Nagy, *The New Vision 1928 fourth revised edition, 1947, and Abstract of an Artist*, [3; *i.e.*, title page].

[29] László Moholy-Nagy to Robert J. Wolff, MLS, May 31st, 1944, Archives of American Art, Washington, D.C., microfilm reel 69-73, frames 0361 and 0362.

[30] László Moholy-Nagy to Robert J. Wolff, TLS, July 25th, 1944, Archives of American Art, Washington, D.C, microfilm reel 69-73, frame 0363.

[31] Robert Saltonstall Mattison, *Robert Motherwell: the Formative Years* (Ann Arbor, Michigan: UMI Research Press, 1987), 125.

[32] See, *e.g.*: Clement Greenberg, "Art," *The Nation*, November 11, 1944, 598-599.

[33] Frank O'Hara, *Robert Motherwell, with Selections from the Artist's Writings* (New York: The Museum of Modern Art, 1965), 74.

[34] Robert J. Wolff to John Thwaites, TLS, December 2nd, 1946, Archives of American Art, Washington, D. C., microfilm reel 69-73, frames 0372 and 0273.

on February 1st, 1946;[35] his colleagues there were to include two key Abstract
Expressionists: Ad Reinhardt, who began teaching at Brooklyn College September 1st,
1947,[36] and Mark Rothko, who began teaching there on February 1st, 1951.[37]

Christopher Knight's observations about photographers, specifically Moholy's
possible influence on and interaction with younger painters, leads one to wonder what
role Moholy would have played in some of the rhetoric about the arts that developed in
the years since he died. A portent can be glimpsed from his early entry into the debate
over Post-Modernism.

Charles Jencks (born 1939) has been a leader in framing the debate about
Post-Modernism, beginning in 1975. Jencks, however, credits a 1945 *Architectural
Record* article by Joseph Hudnut (1886-1968),[38] dean of the Graduate School of Design
at Harvard University, and until 1944 a member of the Sponsors Committee of the
School of Design in Chicago, with introducing the term "Post-Modernism," as Jencks put
it, "into the architectural subconscious."[39]

Jencks went on to point out that Hudnut used the term only in the title of his article,
"The Post-Modern House," and added that in the article Hudnut did not "define it
polemically." Nevertheless, Hudnut did anticipate much of the content of later debates.
He expressed surprise at "the vehemence with which architects assert the scientific
nature of their activities." Hudnut went on to praise "that search for expression which
transforms the science of building into the art of architecture," and ended with the hope
that: "houses will still be built out of human hearts."[40]

Architectural Record solicited responses from Moholy and others and published
some of them in its August, 1945, edition. However, Moholy's response, dated July 6th,
1945, was late, for reasons he explained in his letter to the magazine, and was not
published until many years later. Moholy wrote:

> Thank you for your little note concerning Dean Hudnut's article on the
> post-modern house. I was not able to comment on it until now, as I left
> town and in the meantime we moved to a new location [1009 North
> State Street] (which, by the way, looks very promising).

----

[35] Mona Hadler and Jerome Viola, editors, *Brooklyn College Art Department, Past and Present,
1942-1977* (New York: Brooklyn Collee Art Department, 1977), 104.

[36] Hadler and Viola, editors, *Brooklyn College Art Department,* 82.

[37] Hadler and Viola, editors, *Brooklyn College Art Department,* 86.

[38] Joseph Hudnut, "The Post-Modern House," *Architectural Record*, volume XCVII, number 5
(May 1945), 70-75.

[39] Charles Jencks, *What is Post-Modernism?* (New York: Academy Editions, 1986), 14.

[40] Pearlman, *Inventing American Modernism*, 6 and 172-173.

I admire Hudnut and observe with great interest his educational policy at Harvard. Reading his article, however, I was somewhat worried by his wavering back and forth between the "engineered house" and the architecture of the "heart." For instance, here in the Mid-west, one hardly sees anything which could be called contemporary architecture. One has not to be afraid of science. One has not to be afraid of "function". They are the tools of a conception, but this conception itself is partly the result of their influence. We have today the unimaginable luck that, through the efforts of a great number of creative scientists we can use science in many places where formerly intuition directed us.

The criticism of some people is (and I think this is what makes Dean Hudnut restless) that we only conquered technicalities, but did not translate them as yet into our emotions and into our culture. Modern architecture and contemporary arts try to do exactly that. They need all encouragement and wise explanation of their goal to carry on the work.

Contemporary architecture is not yet a fact, it is only an attempt. In the present state of global changes we should not retreat or we will be destroyed. What we need from the pen of such an eloquent writer as Hudnut is the summarization of the positive values of the pioneers, as he did in some part of his article, where he speaks of space and light.[41]

Walter Gropius read Moholy's letter and commented: "I fully agree with you re Hudnut's article. I think that such a version at present is bringing confusion instead of clarification."[42]

THE DEBATE ABOUT Post-Modernism had more or less disappeared by the end of the 1980s, but still alive in the early twenty-first century is interest in an essay by philosopher and cultural critic Walter Benjamin (1892-1940), the title of which, "The Work of Art in the Age of Mechanical Reproduction," has become a catchphrase; Adam Kirsch recently described the essay itself as "now a canonical text in art history, film studies and related fields."[43] More recently, Frances Richard wrote that the essay "remains a touchstone for techno-ethical visual criticism."[44] Benjamin's essay is sometimes known as "The Work of Art in the Age of Its Technological

---

[41]László Moholy-Nagy to Kenneth K. Stowell, *Architectural Record*, July 6th, 1945, carbon copy of TLS, Bauhaus-Archiv, Berlin; first published in Engelbrecht, "László Moholy-Nagy in Chicago," in: Suhre, editor, *Moholy-Nagy: a New Vision for Chicago*, 53-54. Moholy sent a copy to Gropius, with a note stating that: "I doubt that Stowell [will] print it since I let it go many weeks" (László Moholy-Nagy to Walter Gropius, TLS, July 6th, 1945, Bauhaus-Archiv, Berlin).

[42]Walter Gropius to László Moholy-Nagy, TLS, July 12th, 1945, Bauhaus-Archiv, Berlin.

[43]Adam Kirsch, "The Philosopher Stoned: What Drugs Taught Walter Benjamin," *The New Yorker*, August 21, 2006, 79-84, here 81. (The title of Kirsch's essay has no direct bearing on his discussion of "The Work of Art in the Age of Mechanical Reproduction.")

[44]Frances Richard, "Photography's Ghosts," *The Nation*, March 16, 2009, 30-36, here 34.

Reproducibility."[45] As Krisztina Passuth has pointed out, Moholy's factory-produced enamel images of 1923, first exhibited in 1924 (DVD figures 203 and 204), as discussed in Chapter Three, seem, in retrospect, as quintessential works of art in an age of mechanical reproduction.[46] She argued that Moholy provides one of the rare cases in which an artist has influenced philosophical theory instead of the other way around. Benjamin pointed to the example of a photographic plate from which "one can make any number of prints" as the basis for his statement that ". . . the work of art produced becomes the work of art designed for reproducibility."[47] That description applies perfectly to the enamel images, each of which could have been produced in an endless series of identical images once the parameters had been given to foreman at the Stark & Riese sign factory in Tannroda, Thuringia.

If Moholy and Benjamin ever met, that occasion has not been documented,[48] but in his writings Benjamin directly cited Moholy in two instances,[49] and, as related in Chapter

---

[45] Walter Benjamin, "The Work of Art in the Age of Its Technological Reproducibility," in: *idem*, *The Work of Art in the Age of Its Technological Reproducibility and Other Writings on Media*, edited by Michael W. Jennings, Brigid Doherty and Thomas Y. Levin (Cambridge: The Belknap Press of Harvard University Press, 2008), 19-55.

[46] Krisztina Passuth, "Moholy-Nagy et Walter Benjamin; un Rencontre," *Cahiers du Musée National d'Art Moderne*, number 5 (1980), 398-409, here 398 and 401.

[47] Benjamin, "The Work of Art in the Age of Its Technological Reproducibility," 24-25; and *idem*, "The Work of Art in the Age of Mechanical Reproduction," in *idem*, *Illuminations*, edited and with an introduction by Hannah Arendt, translated by Harry Zohn (New York: Schocken Books, 1969), 217-251, here 224.

[48] Walter Benjamin and Sibyl Moholy-Nagy were briefly associated in Frankfort am Main and in Berlin, but that was before Sibyl and László knew each other; see Appendix D, 723-724.

[49] Walter Benjamin, "Kleine Geschichte der Photographie (Schluß)," *Die Literarische Welt*, volume VII, number 40 (October 2, 1931), 7-8, here 8; this was the conclusion of a three-part article. The citation is to: László Moholy-Nagy, *Malerei, Photographie, Film*, Bauhausbücher 8 (Munich: Albert Langen Verlag, 1925), 21. The same passage appears in the 1927 edition (*Malerei, Fotografie, Film*) on pages 25-26; and in: *idem*, *Painting, Photography, Film*, with a note by Hans M. Wingler and a postscript by Otto Stelzer; translated by Janet Seligman (Cambridge: The MIT Press, 1969), on pages 27-28.

Benjamin's essay on photographic history was reprinted in his *Gesammelte Schriften*, [Band] II, [Teil] 1, edited by Rolf Tiedemann and Hermann Schweppenhäuser (Frankfurt am Main: Suhrkamp Verlag, 1980), 368-385. It appeared in translation as "Little History of Photography" in his *The Work of Art in the Age of Its Technological Reproducibility and Other Writings*, 274-298; the cited passage appeared on page 290.

The other time Benjamin cited Moholy was in a 1928 book review (the book under review did not mention Moholy) in *Die literarische Welt*, but although the cited text by Moholy cannot be identified, it refers to ideas Moholy did write about. Benjamin's review was reprinted in: Walter Benjamin, *Gesammelte Schriften*, [Band III] (Frankfurt am Main: Suhrkamp Verlag, 1972), 151-

(continued...)

Three, as a known fan of Berlin's Kroll Opera[50] he probably saw at least one of Moholy's three productions there. Thus Benjamin was aware of Moholy's work, might easily have known about the enamel images, and surely knew about his contention, in a book from which he (Benjamin) had quoted, ". . . that painterly methods of representation suggestive merely of past times and past ideologies shall disappear and their place be taken by mechanical means of representation and their as yet unpredictable possibilities of extension."[51] On the other hand, surely Moholy never was aware of Benjamin's essay, "The Work of Art in the Age of Mechanical Reproduction." Its only appearance in print during Benjamin's lifetime was in 1936 in a French translation in a German émigré journal;[52] editions in German, English and Hungarian appeared only after both men had died.[53] Nevertheless, Benjamin's essay, along with Moholy's *Room of Our Own Time* project of 1930 for the *Landesmuseum* in Hanover (discussed in Chapter Four), have recently been cited by Erkki Huhtamo, a leading historian of innovative media, as influential precursors of virtual museum presentations that began in the 1990s.[54] I would argue that it is especially fitting that the DVD disc accompanying the paper volumes of *Moholy-Nagy: Mentor to Modernism* can be considered a virtual-museum presentation.

Just as Huhtamo saw Moholy as a crucial figure in the development of the virtual museum, an idea that coalesced in the 1990s, when Moholy had been deceased for more than four decades, one is tempted to imagine which of Moholy's creative works or ideas

---

[49](...continued)
153; it appeared in English translation in Benajmin's *The Work of Art in the Age of Its Technological Reproducibility and Other Writings*, 271-273.

[50]See Chapter Four, note 37.

[51]László Moholy-Nagy, *Painting, Photography, Film*, (1969), 15. The corresponding passages in the German editions are: *Malerei, Photographie, Film* (1925), 11, and *Malerei, Photographie, Film* (1927), 13.

[52]Walter Benjamin, "L'Œuvre d'Art à l'Époque de sa Reproduction Méchanisée," *Zeitschrift für Sozialforschung*, volume 5, number 1 (April, 1936), 40-66. *Zeitschrift für Sozialforschung* had been begun in Frankfurt am Main, but by 1936 it had been moved to New York.

[53]Momme Brodersen, *Walter Benjamin, ein kommentierte Bibliographie* (Morsum/Sylt, Germany: Cicero Presse, 1995), 90, 141 and 222-223.

[54]Erkki Huhtamo, "On the Origins of the Virtual Museum," in: Nobel Symposium 120, "Virtual Museums and Public Understanding of Science and Culture," May 26-29, 2002, Stockholm, Sweden (accessed July 11, 2006, on the Internet at nobelprize.org/nobelfoundation/symposia/interdisciplinary/ns120/lectures/huhtamo.pdf), [1]-14, here 3-7.

While Moholy's *Room of Our Own Time* was never completed, the project was discussed at length by Alexander Dorner's biographer; see: Samuel Cauman, *The Living Museum; Experiences of an Art Historian and Museum Director, Alexander Dorner*, with an introduction by Walter Gropius (New York: New York University Press, 1958), 102-103 and 109-111.

will spawn future developments that presently are not yet anticipated. In other words, I think of Moholy as not just a mentor to the Modernists of his own time, I also think of him as a mentor to future generations of innovators.

Appendix A: Letter from László Moholy-Nagy to Iván Hevesy, April 5th, 1920

The letter transcribed and translated below will give valuable background to the brief references to this letter in Chapter Two, and also serves as a model of cooperation among Moholy scholars both within and outside the artist's family circle.

An important letter, László Moholy-Nagy to Iván Hevesy, April 5th, 1920, Documentation Center of the Art History Research Group, Hungarian Academy of Sciences, Budapest (MKC-c-T-52/53), has not been published in its entirety before, either in the original Hungarian or in translation in other languages. What follows is a complete transcription of the Hungarian original, and a translation into English. The transcription into Hungarian was made by Hattula Moholy-Nagy on July 13th, 2000; corrections were made by Edith Nagy and Oliver Botar in August, 2000. The English translation was made by Oliver Botar in August, 2000.

Kedves Ivánom

elég rég írtam neked, hogy most beszámolhassuk a közben történtekrÅl. Megbettem volna ezt más előbb is, de spanyolt kaptam tüdÅgyulladással, míg most is. Köhögök belé is ez bizony kis telhette a beszámolós. Bécsben kb. 6 hétig voltam. Rothadtam tulajdonképpen, mert úgy rémlik, nem is tudott mást cselékedni senki. Most már az egész **Ma** ott van. Ők terveztek állandóan családi alapon művészetet (kiadni a lapot), de nem volt hajlandó senki a magáért (pénzt) "richirozni," így tán most is húzódik az ügy. Tegnap hallottam egy itteni tehetséges fiútól, Pór Nándortól (novellát írt valamikor abba a számba, amelyikban Kmetty rajz önarcképe volt), hogy már Bartáné (U. E.) [probably Újházi Erzsi, according to Edit Nagy] is jönni van is Kemény is megérkezett. Kassák igen magához tartozónak számitott újabban, de *timeo Danaos* alapon örülök itt lenni és nem az ő közelében. Bécsben Tihanyi volt drága jó emberem. Sokat együtt voltam vele, igazán és mélyen megszerettem. Múzeumok kevés meglepetést hoztak, néhány nagy magán gyűtemény azonban gyönyörű volt. Van Gogh, Cézanne, Manet, Renoir, Greco, Tintoretto, Kokoschka képek seregszámok. Leveledben (mikor Mariáék utaztak kaptani) azt írtad, szakítani minden eddigi rothadt stb. Azt hiszem, a centrális probléma az, különb embernek lenni, mint az eddigiek. A kifejezés is **más** lesz e révén. Van Gogh, Kokoschka, Picasso (nálunk Tihanyi) pl. külön rendszerek (őrültek), de ki mondhatja, hogy az őrültségük rosszabb őrültség (rendszer) a mi kollektiv őrültségünknél (rendszerünknél). Ezek épen, hogy nincsenek a fejlödés vonalában. Ezek cask ingerelhetnek, izgathatnak, felfokozott más idegélekkel, de úgy, mint Cézanne pl. nem hathatnak. Gondolod, hogy Cézanne-t el lehet hajítani? Vagy kell? Vagy érdemes? A kubisták, futuristák eredményei (a mindent eldobás sem volt valójában az) most az epigonok kezén kétségbeesett tehetetlenséggé züllött. A Sturm legújabb kiállításán egy Kurt Schwitters nevű ember újságcikkekből és vasúti bárcákból, szőrökől meg abroncsokból csinál képeket. Minek? Festői problémák ezek? Azonkivül hogy nem is új. 10-12 évvel ezelőtt a Salon des Indépendants kiállításán seregszámra voltak az ilyenek. Igazán teljes lecsúszás ez és nem újrakezdés. Igen, azt én is érzem, hogy **mást** kell adni, mint amit eddig adtak, de ez úgysem lehetséges másképp, csak ha én is **más** lettem, mint az eddigiek.

Bécsben együtt voltam sok régi és új ösmerössel. Teljes nyomor és tönkrement gyomor-falak. Tanulni oly kevesen tanulunk. Néha beáll valaki rikkancsnak, úgy szerez pénzt – ezt aztán megbeszélik s tovább – rothadás. Néhányan ügyért dolgoznak, ezek meg szentélyt és tabut csinálnak munkájukból, magukból. Balázs Béla Halálos fiatalságát adták közben elö. A premiéren minden magyar jelen volt. Kitarthatatlan unalom volt a darab és dühito. A II. felvonás után eljöttem. A darab megbukott és legnagyobb meglepetéseruve más napon összes lapok agybe-főbe dicsérték a Neue Wiener Bühne premiért. Jól szervezett klakk. Az íródalom más is irányban is ütögette a fejét. Az emberen kivül a vörújság és most egy vasárnap cimü hetilap indult meg, talán már a ma is. Ennyi honfitárs van ott, hogy üzletnek lehet szerkeszteni belőle, látod. Mielött eljöttem rendezte Tihanyi a kiállítását, azota – úgy hallom – meg is nyilt. Utána ez a terv – Berlinben, Münchenben, Drezdaban fog kiállítani. Egy képést 30-40,000 k-t kér. Gondolom, itt jól is fog menni neki, mert Kokoschkán kivül, aki bálvány már, egyetlen rendes festőjük sincs a németeknek. Az expresszionizmus meg, amely közben [akadémia lett és technika és recept kérdése, most kezd igazán hatni, hogy megbukott. Képzelheted, ha a Leipziger Illustrierte Zeitung expresszionista jubileumi különszámot ad ki!

A képzőművészeti [helyet] itt is klikkszerű. A Sturm szervezöje Herwarth Walden milliomos lett, pazar képgyáteménye van – ingyen kapta őket – s ehhez fejedelmi allűrjei. Csak titkárral bejelentve lehet beszélni vele, a képgyűteménye megszemlélésénél hangosan – lákájszerűen – bemondják a nevedet stb. stb., ahogy egy dadaista lap mondja: üzleti zsenijét rablott szellemi rongyokkal ékesíti és gazdagítja és a művészet csak álarc neki a pénzszerzésre. Hogy pénzt szerzett, megvált (anyagilag) a Sturmtól és a Sturm még úgy sem fizet, mint eddig. A kiállítások legyengültek. Itt is új, meglepö is sose látott legyen! dominál. És ostoba kis férctrujukok illitgatnak ki, most meg ez a ragasztós ember. (Kurt Schwitters)

Itt másik klikk a Cassireré. Ott megvesznek egy műveszt szőröstül-bőröstül olcsón, ki adnak róla pár könyvet és zsebelik a hasznot. Most a 8-ak egyike Czóbel Béla állitott ki nála. Meglepöen önállátlan és keves. Matisse és Rousseau (Henri) hatás. Pedig azt mondták, ő Czóbel az kemény legény! (otthon hallottam így.) Ennek nem volt megszervesve az újság kritikája. Nem láttam kritikátat róla. Lehet, mert közben volt a sztrájk, vagy elkerülte figyelmemet. Németül olvasok néha újságot, könyvet, gyakrabban. Magyar újság ritkán kerül a kisember s csak akkor látni innen messziröl – milyen keserű cik játozodnak le otthon. Mi benne ül, talán észre se veszi. Itt a spartakuszok új taktíkát kezdenek. Sztrájkot, sabotaget és ennek fegyveres védelmét. Ti. a strájktöröt ők maguk lövik agyon. Harcokba agyáltalán nem bocsátkoznak. Elkerülik így a tőmegharcot és kimélik a vért. Kis megbizhat csapatokat alkotnak, amelyek a föntebbi módon védik a sztrájk és szabotage eredményéit. Ezeket a csapatokat könnyen tologatják aztán ide-oda. Igy remélik, hogy katoni diktatúra nélkül elkövetkezik az ő idejük. A nyugatinknál biztosan így számítják – Ti. áll a nagy fegyveres védelem ……. alka…. Felé a házak gépfegyverrel, ágyúval az utca, és nincs, aki ellen használják.

Álljanak csak – mondják sp-ék, mi tudományos alapon vezetjük a mozgalmat, úgyis ide kell adnotok a gy….tokat, mindenetek, mert mi nem dolgozunk. Végére járt a papíros – még pár szót. Pénzem nincs. Kopenhágába ugyan eladtam egy dán írónönak egy festményt 1000 M-ért, 500 M-t kaptam már érte, a másik 500-t postán várom. De most ott is forradalom van, vagy mi a szösz. Egyébként dolgozom. Nagy tájkép kompoziciót csináltam, rajzokat, litográfiakat, portrét festek (nem rendelés). A pensioért (szoba, ellátás) havonta 600 M-t kell fizetem. Szobám gyönyör. Nagy, világos. Koszt? Na jó. De nem túl jó. És nem sok. Írj te is kimeritón.

Ölel Lacid

Itt Lampérthtal találkozom gyakran. Sokat kiüldött. Most megy valahogy neki is. Imre [Bach] jön holnap Leipzigböl ide. Sürgönyözött ő ott dolgozik egy klinikán.

My dear Iván,

It's been sufficiently long since I wrote you that I should now report on happenings in the meantime. I would have done this earlier, but I caught Spanish flu with pneumonia. I am coughing into it and this slowed down my report. I was in Vienna for about six weeks. As a matter of fact I was rotting there, since it seems to me that nobody was able to do anything else but the same. By now the whole Ma circle is there. They were planning (to publish a journal) on a family basis, but nobody was willing to risk his own (money), so perhaps now it is postponed. Yesterday I heard from a local, talented youth, Nándor Pór (he wrote a short story in that issue in which was Kmetty's self-portrait drawing), that Mrs. Barta (Erzsi Újházi) will also come, Kemény has also arrived. Lately Kassák regards me as someone strongly attached to him, however, on the basis of the *timeo Danaos* principle, I am just glad to be here and not around him. In Vienna Tihanyi was my dear good man. I was together with him a lot and I came to love him deeply. The museums brought few surprises, however, some large private collections were beautiful. Legions of Van Gogh, Cézanne, Manet, Renoir, Greco, Tintoretto, Kokoschka pictures. In your letter (which I received when Maria and those around her traveled), you wrote to break away from everything rotten up to this point, etc. I think the central problem is that you have to be a better person than those that came before you. Through this, the expression will also be **different**. For example, there are Van Gogh, Kokoschka, Picasso (Tihanyi in our case) with their individual systems (they are insane), but who can say that their insanities are worse insanities (systems) than our collective insanities (our systems)? It is precisely these who are not in the line of development. With their different, more intensive nerves, they can only irritate and excite us, but they cannot influence us the way, for example, Cézanne did. Do you think it is possible to throw away Cézanne? Or do we need him? Or is it worth it? The results of the Cubists, Futurists (their tossing out of everything was not really that) were degraded into a desperate incompetence in the hands of the epigones. In the latest Sturm exhibition, a man named Kurt Schwitters is showing pictures made of newspaper articles, railroad tags, hair, and hoops. What for? Are these painterly problems? Aside from this it is not even new. Ten-twelve years earlier, in the exhibition of the Salon des Indépendants, there were innumerable similar things. This is a total decline and not a new beginning. Yes, I also feel that one has to offer something **other**, other than that offered untli now, but this is only possible if I became **other** than those until now.

In Vienna I was together with many old and new acquaintances. Total misery and ruined stomach-walls. So few of us learn anything. Sometimes someone takes on work as a courier, thus earns money this way – later they discuss this further – rotting further. There are few who work for a cause, but these make a sacrament and a taboo out of their work and out of themselves, too. They staged Béla Balász's "*Halálos Fiatalság*" ("*Tödliche Jugend*"). Every Hungarian was present at the opening. Insufferably boring and infuriating. I left after the second act. The piece failed and, most surprisingly, the next day all the newspapers heaped extravagant praise on the Neue Wiener Bühne's premiere. A well-organized claque. Literature has come up against a brick wall in other areas as well. Besides *Az Ember* (*Mankind*, OB), now *Vörös Újság* (*Red Newspaper*), and a weekly entitled "*Sunday*" were launched, too, perhaps now also *Ma*. You see, so many fellow countrymen are there that editing a journal has become a going concern. Before I left, Tihanyi organized an exhibition, since then – I heard – it has opened. Afterwards the plan is to exhibit in Berlin, Munich, Dresden. He asks 30 – 40,000 Crowns for a picture. I think he is going to make good here, because, with the exception of Kokoschka, who is already an idol, the Germans do not have a single decent painter. Expressionism, which meanwhile [has become academic and] a question of technique and recipe, has now truly begun to exert influence, now that it is bankrupt. Imagine if the *Leipziger Illustrierte Zeitung* were to publish an Expressionist jubilee special number.

The fine arts [situation] here is cliquish, too. [The head of Der Sturm] Herwarth Walden has become a millionaire, he has a splendid picture collection, which he got free, and to this he affects the airs of a prince. If you want to talk to him, you have to be announced by his secretary, and while you are visiting his picture collection, they announce your name as though by a lackey, etc. etc. As a Dadaist journal said: he is enriching and decorating his financial genius with plundered spiritual rags and art serves him as a disguise for making money. Now that he obtained money, he divorced himself (materially) from Sturm and thus Sturm pays less than before. The exhibitions are weaker. Here, too, the new, the surprising, the never-seen-before dominates! And foolish, little, bunglers frequent it, and now this glueing person. (Kurt Schwitters)

There is another clique at Cassierer's. There they cheaply buy out an artist lock, stock, and barrel, publish a couple of books about him/her, and pocket the proceeds. Now one of the Eight, Béla Czóbel, exhibited with them. Surprisingly derivative and sparse. Influenced by Matisse and Rousseau (Henri). Although they say that Czóbel is a tough young man! (at home I heard such) Newspaper reviews were not organized for him. I didn't see a review about him. possibly because of the strike or it escaped my notice. Sometimes I read German newspapers, books more often. A Hungarian newspaper rarely gets into my hands, and then I only see here from afar – what kind of bitterness plays itself out at home. Whoever sits in the thick of it may not even notice. Here the Spartacists begin new tactics. Strikes, sabotage, and armed defense for themselves. That is, they themselves shoot down strikebreakers. They don't thoughtlessly engage in battle. Thus they avoid mass combat and spare blood. They form small, trustworthy units, who defend the successes of the strikes and sabotage. These troops are then shifted here and there. Thus they hope their time will come without a military dictatorship. [Oliver Botar was not able to make sense of this sentence either, according to Hatttula Moholy-Nagy] — because, you know, the great armed defense stands. Machine guns in the houses, cannons in the street, and no one to use them against. "Wait," say the Spartacists, "we lead the movement on a scientific basis, anyway you will have to give up all the [illegible plural noun], because we won't work." The paper comes to an end – still a couple of words. I have no money. I sold a painting to a Danish woman writer for 1000 Marks. I already received 500 Marks on account, the other 500 I await by mail. But now they also have a revolution there, or whatever! Otherwise I work. I made a large landscape composition, drawings, lithographs, painted portraits (unsolicited). I must pay 600 Marks a month for the pension (room, supplies). My room is beautiful. Large, light. Food? Well, good. But not especially good. And not much. Write me in detail too.

Embraces,

Your Laci

Here I often encounter Lampérth. Very much worn out. Now it is somehow going all right for him as well. Tomorrow Imre [Bach] comes here from Leipzig. He telegraphed that he works in a clinic there.

Appendix B: Ákos Nagy

Chronology for Ákos Nagy compiled by Erwin Nagy,
translated from German by Hattula Moholy-Nagy, October, 2006.

1897
March 19 Ákos Nagy is born to Lipót Weisz and Karolin Stern in Borsód (later Bácsborsód). Hungary. He is the youngest of their five children, who were Jenô (31 January 1891-30 March 1986), Elza (28 July 1892, died at the age of 2 years), Sándor (23 August 1893-19 September 1895), and László (20 July 1895-24 November 1946).

1898
Lipót abandons the family. Karolin's brother, Gusztáv Nagy, a lawyer, becomes the children's guardian.

1898-1906
Karolin and her children move several times between the home of her mother, Rozália Engelmann, in Ada and her brother, Gusztáv Nagy, in Mohol (Moholy, now Mol).

1906
Karolin moves to Szeged with Laszlo and Ákos. Jenő already there since 1904. Ákos attends gymnasium [secondary school].

1910
During this year the three boys change their family name to Nagy.

1911
Death of Gusztáv Nagy.

1914
Outbreak of World War I. Ákos moves to Budapest to study medicine.

1915
Ákos drafted into the army.

1916 June 4-August 13
1.5 million soldiers, including Ákos Nagy, are taken prisoner by the Russians during the Brusilov Offensive, and many Austro-Hungarian soldiers, including Ákos Nagy, are taken prisoner by the Russians during it.

Ákos Nagy writes in his autobiography that he was taken as war prisoner on the first day of the Brusilov Offensive – June 4.

This event took a place at the Lemberg (now L'vov), in the Przemyśl area.

Till December Ákos was in Ukraina near Kiev and in Mordovia near Saransk (it is in the eastern part of European Russia).

On **December 2 1916** Ákos was moved to East Siberia near Ulan-Ude. There was a camp for Hungarian war prisoners. Whole year 1917 Ákos Nagy worked as chemical-bacteriological assistant for Hungarian professor Shuster.

1917
Abdication of the Tsar, Nicholas II. Rise and fall of the Kerensky government, overthrown by the Communists.

Ákos Nagy writes in his autobiography, he was taken as war prisoner at the first day of the Brusilov Offensive – June 4.

At the beginning of year 1918 the first influence of October Revolution and communist ideology at East Siberia and Far East could be seen. In March of this year this camp for Hungarian war prisoners begins to receive communist materials in the Hungarian language. Ákos was fascinated with these ideas, and thus he begins his revolutionary activities.

1918-1919
Political chaos in Eastern Siberia and the Far East.

1920
Ákos joins the Communist Party. Japan attacks Vladivostok and occupies the southern part of the Primorsky Region. Ákos, as a foreign medical technician, is in charge of the medical personnel in the occupied zone.

1922 November 15
The occupied zone is freed and the Communists seize power.

The newspaper *Red Banner* (Red Flag) was founded in Vladivostok at 1922. Ákos took a part in this event, and he was appointed as a chief of editorial office's department in Nikolsk-Ussyrisky. In 1923 he was moved into central editorial office in Vladivostok.

1924
Ákos Nagy becomes a citizen of the Soviet Union. From then on, he is called Alexei Lvovich Nagy. In the same year he is promoted to chief representative of the editor-in-chief of *Krasnoe Znamja*. By this time he has a wife, Dora Wilenskaya, and a son, Gusztáv, who is three years old.

1926
In Moscow Alexei Nagy works for TASS, the Soviet news-wire agency. In the same year he makes business trips to Moscow and Shanghai; he remains in the latter city for six months .

1927
Alexei Nagy and Dora Wilenskaya file for divorce.

1929
Alexei Nagy meets Fanya Zak from Kharkov at a workers' resort near Soschi. Their life together begins at the end of the year.

1930 November 7
Their son, Erwin Nagy, is born.

1931
In June, 1931, Alexei Nagy, accompanied by his family, moves to Japan on business and remains there until November, 1937. On July 3 he starts his work as chief correspondent of the Japanese office of TASS.

1935 May 5 - September 3
Alexei Nagy is on a business trip to Moscow for TASS. He is also in Kislowodsk for treatment for asthma, and visits Fanya's relatives in Kharkov and Voroshilovgrad, now Lugansk.

1937 November 5
The family is notified that they will have to move, and they all leave Tokyo.

November 24 they return to Moscow. From November 25 Alexei Nagy and his wife undergo an examination by the Party Examination Commission of the Central Committee of the Communist Party.

1938 April 9
Alexei Nagy and his wife receive notice that they passed the examination and that Alexei Nagy can resume his work at TASS.

April 29
Alexei Nagy is arrested. In autumn Alexei's wife Fanya Zak receives a notice from the NKVD (the Peoples' Commission [Ministry] of the Interior) that Alexei Nagy has been sentenced to 10 (ten) years' imprisonment by the Military Commission of the Supreme Court of the USSR. Correspondence with him is forbidden.

Many years later Fanya Zak and Erwin Nagy learned that Alexei Nagy was charged as a spy for Japan and as a member of a group that aspired to overthrow the Communist Government.

During the Stalin time it was not necessary to have any real charges. As General Prosecutor of USSR Vyshinsky said: "The most important evidence is a confession of the prisoner at the bar." There were many ways to receive required confessions: torture, threats of destruction of family, etc., etc.

After this Alexei Nagy's wife, Fanya, and his son, Erwin, hear nothing more of his fate.

1938 Summer
The only meeting of Erwin and his half-brother Gusztáv in the city of Babuschkin.

1941 August
Gusztáv Nagy has perished at the front not so far from Moscow

*   *   *

1953 March 5
Death of Stalin and the beginning of "Thaw"-time.

1955 February 24
Erwin receives a notice that Alexei Nagy died at home of cancer of the liver.

September 20
Erwin petitions the Military Commission of the Supreme Court to re-examine the case.

1956 July 25
The Military Commission of the Supreme Court of the Soviet Union issues a certificate that Alexei Nagy was entirely innocent and was fully rehabilitated.

*   *   *

1985 "Perestroika"

1988 December 2
Erwin Nagy again petitions the Military Commission of the Supreme Court for more information about his father.

That same year, the Military Commission of the Supreme Court of the Soviet Union sends Erwin a letter in which it is confirmed that on 7 September 1938 Alexei Nagy was sentenced to be shot. The sentence was carried out on the same day that he was sentenced.

*   *   *

1991 Soviet Union disintegrates.

1992
Erwin Nagy receives permission to examine personal data in the archives of the FSB/KGB and Party Examination Commission. Furthermore, it was possible to get copies of some of the documents.

2002 April 10
A list of Hungarians who belonged to the Communist Party is published in the newspaper *Vetshernaya Moskva* [Moscow at Evening]. This list describes the place where this group was shot and buried. Among many others is also the name of Alexei Nagy. This happened on the grounds of an NKVD country house. It is called "Kommunarka" and is near the settlement of Butovo, 25 km south of Moscow.

Appendix C: Lucia Moholy: Some Notes on Her Life

Lucia (née Schulz) Moholy (DVD figure 541) was born January 18th, 1894, in the Prague suburb of Karolinenthal, or Praha-Karlin, in the Kingdom of Bohemia, then part of the Austro-Hungarian Empire; Prague is now the capital of the Czech Republic. She died in Zurich on May 17th, 1989.

This appendix provides background to the numerous passages in my text that relate to Lucia Moholy. I have already provided as much relevant detail as I could about her relationships with the two loves of her life, Theodor Neubauer, murdered in 1945, and László Moholy-Nagy, who died of leukemia the following year. She had had no contact with Theodor after 1933, and no contact with László, whom she divorced in 1934 but with whom she remained friendly, after 1937, except through letters. As far as I know, she did not have a romantic relationship with any other men.

There is very little documentation about Lucia's contacts, as an adult, with her parents and siblings. Her brother, sometimes known as Franz Spencer (1897-1971), published two autobiographical books that did not mention Lucia or their sister Gisa.[1] Franz, a screenwriter,[2] lived for many years in Los Angeles, but Lucia, although she once attempted to move to America, in the end did not, as related in Chapter Five; nevertheless, as related on page 597, Franz aided her effort by supplying needed documents. Franz's efforts on behalf of Lucia's attempt to immigrate to American suggest contacts with her brother that cannot be documented. Six of Lucia's portraits of Gisa, dating from about 1929, are in the Bauhaus-Archiv in Berlin, along with one portrait of their mother, Waleska, dating from 1936.[3]

Much biographical information appears in Lucia's bi-lingual book-length publication,[4] *Moholy-Nagy, Marginal Notes: Documentary Absurdities*, of 1972. Appalled by the large amount of erroneous information that had by been published about her one-time husband, in her book she concentrated on correcting misinformation, but nevertheless ended up supplying a lot of biographical information about herself and her relationship with her husband, including a description of the intellectual help she offered him.

---

[1] Franz Spencer, *Battles of a Bystander* (New York: Liveright Publishing Corporation, 1941); *idem*, *Candide 19 oder das miese Jahrhundert* (Munich: Rütten + Loening, 1966); and *idem*, *Candide 19 oder das miese Jahrhundert* . . . [new edition] mit einem Nachwort von G[inny] G. von Bülow (Berlin: Aufbau-Taschenbuch-Verlag, 1994).

[2] "Franz Schulz (Franz Spencer," in: Rudolf Ulrichm, *Österreicher in Hollywood* (Vienna: Verlag Filmarchiv Austria, 2004), 456-458. See also: Ginny G. Bülow, *Franz Schulz: ein Autor zwischen Prag und Hollywood* (Prague: Vitalic, 1997), 59-219 *passim*.

[3] Rolf Sachsse and Sabine Hartmann, *Lucia Moholy; Bauhaus Fotografin* (Berlin: Bauhaus-Archiv, 1995), 121-122.

[4] Lucia Moholy, *Moholy-Nagy, Marginal Notes: Documentary Absurdities* (Krefeld, Germany: Scherpe Verlag, 1972) *(Marginal Notes* is bi-lingual, and carries an alternate German title: *Marginalien zu Moholy-Nagy: Dokumentarische Umgereimtheiten).*

Appendix C, page 714

Two publications supplement each other as the chief sources of information about Lucia Moholy, and both have appeared only in German. The first was a monograph of 1985, written by Rolf Sachsse.[5] The other was a catalogue of 1995 documenting the holdings of Lucia's photographs in the Bauhaus-Archiv in Berlin, put together by Rolf Sachsse and Sabine Hartmann; included in this publication were biographical information, letters and selections from Lucia's writings.[6]

Oliver Botar has supplemented the information available in these three publications by providing a good summary of the early years of Lucia Moholy in an article he published in 2007; what he wrote about Lucia Moholy includes these passages:[7]

> Lucia Schulz was both intellectual and very interested in art from an early age. She had been educated at the German University in Prague, where she remembers having studied art history, as well as science and philosophy. Already as a teenager she had visited relatives in Berlin, where she prowled the museums, enthralled by what she saw. She recorded her reactions in her diaries, the precocious documents of a deep thinker. As soon as she could, she left Prague for Germany. In 1914, while working at her first job for a newspaper in Wiesbaden, near Frankfurt/Main, she read [Ernst] Haeckel, which imbued her thinking with monism. Her response to Rhenish religious art was ecstatically *Ideenphilosophisch*: "Life, Life is their highest Art . . . Art for Life! Life for Art!"

> Schulz's acceptance of a job with B.G. Teubner publishers in 1918 proved to be decisive for her. As she later put it, "Leipzig was meaningful through personal contacts . . . that led to lifelong friendships," including friendships with Youth Movement activists Paul Vogler (1899-1969) and Friedrich Vorwerk (1898-1969).
> . . . .

> Before the end of 1918, Lucia Schulz had quit her job with Teubner to join [Friedrich] Vorwerk at the Barkenhoff [commune at the Worpswede artists' colony near Bremen]. By 1919 Vorwerk felt himself to be with "the most radical leftist group of workers." Given this and Worpswede's proximity to Bremen, there is little doubt that he took an active part in the Bremen Soviet Republic between January 10 and February 4, 1919, especially since his [Vorwerk's] friend [Ludwig] Bäumer was a member of the Revolutionary Council. We know for certain that like Vorwerk and [Heinrich] Vogeler, Schulz was a staunch anarcho-Communist at the time and she resisted the suppression of the Soviet on February 4, 1919. Vogeler recalls that Schulz and her "active Communist" friend Klara Möller assisted the wounded in the battles. Vogeler also suggests that they were engaged in intelligence operations among the radical groups: "They were in the midst of the battle and they were able to shelter some threatened and many wounded comrades in the Bremen City Hall. They became hardworking Party workers."
> . . . .

---

[5]Rolf Sachsse, *Lucia Moholy* (Dusseldorf: Edition Marzona, 1985).

[6]As in note 3.

[7]Oliver Botar, "The Origins of László Moholy-Nagy's Biocentric Constructivism," in: Eduardo Kac, editor, *Signs of Life: Bio Art and Beyond* (Cambridge: The MIT Press, 2007), [315]-344, here 321,325-327 and 329.

Schulz also participated in the commune's intellectual life, through her contributions under the pseudonym "Ulrich Steffen" to the single issue of *Neubau*, the Barkenhoff newsletter that appeared in June 1919. . . . The motto of this journal, Nietsche's "I beseech you my brothers to again love the earth," was as biocentric a text as one could find in the philosopher's oeuvre. Her own contributions display her radical, if naive, Communist beliefs, in line with [Heinrich] Vogeler's and Vorwerk's. Probably through Vorwerk's contacts, Schulz published "Symbole" [Symbols], her only philosophical text of the period, in the October, 1919 issue of *Freideutsche Jugend*. In this ecstatic articulation of Nietzschean antitranscendentalism, she argued for an antireligious, Haeckelian monism in harmony with Vogeler's nature mysticism: "In the cosmos of unity, the body is no longer the temple of the Godhead, but is, rather, its very body. Body and soul . . . are one . . . There is no cult other than Life. All of Life is cult, or none is , , , God is no longer in us, God is. We are God."[8]

Botar's narrative continues with events described in my Chapter Two, specifically that Friedrich Vorwerk was the person who brought László and Lucia together in Berlin, and goes on to discuss changes in Lucia's life:

> . . . Schulz arrived at Vorwerk's boarding house around April, 1920. By this time she was tiring of the ecstatic radicalism of the *Freideutsche Jugend* and was looking for a new direction in her life. She was impressed by what she felt to be Moholy-Nagy's level-headedness. Her arrival in Berlin forced her into a choice between Vorwerk, whom she termed a *Pathetiker* [an elevated or exalted romantic], and Moholy-Nagy, whom she characterized as a *Pragmatiker*. "Thus it became clear to me, that I had left the time of the pragmatic behind me, but had not yet taken up a new attitude. And so I was thoroughly open to new impressions." Moholy-Nagy and Schulz soon found a place together, and by June 1, when she began her job with the prominent Berlin publisher Ernst Rowalt, she was able to provide their basic needs.

Lucia Moholy continued as a writer on various topics after leaving Germany, including a short article on the German Bauhaus and its influence that briefly described, among other topics, the educational endeavors of László Moholy-Nagy in Chicago.[9] Her most ambitious publication, aside from *Marginal Notes*, was *A Hundred Years of Photography, 1839-1939*,[10] a book marking the first hundred years of activity in that medium. This important book emphasizes the social significance of photography.

Most of the book is devoted to the nineteenth century, and perhaps as a result Lucia Moholy mentioned her former husband only once in her *A Hundred Years of Photography*, and that was in connection with the photogram:

> Photography . . . has been adopted by a few abstract painters as a new medium by means of which they tried to give shape to their feelings of balance. They are Man

---

[8] Excerpts from "Symbole" appear in Sachsse and Hartmann. *Lucia Moholy, Bauhaus Fotografin*, 71.

[9] Lucia Moholy, "Der Bauhausgedanke," *Blick in die Welt*, "Erscheint monatlich [*sic*: it was irregular in its appearance]," number 10 (undated: [April 1947?]), 30-31.

[10] Lucia Moholy, *A Hundred Years of Photography, 1839-1939* (Harmondsworth, England: Penguin Books, Limited, 1939).

Ray, living in France, and Moholy-Nagy, living in the U.S.A. They took up the method of "Photogenic drawing," discovered by Schulze in 1727 and familiar to Fox Talbot before 1834, and applied it in their own way. The results are abstract pictures called "Rayographs" —" Rayograms" — "Photograms" — "Shadowgrams" — "Skiagrams" and other names.[11]

She modestly refrained from referring to her own role in the development of photograms, described above in Chapter Two, but she did refer to her own portrait photographs, and even reproduced an example,[12] although none of her former husband's photographs was illustrated.

Many of Lucia's publications relate to her role as a pioneer in the use of microfilms in documentation, beginning with her years in England during World War II. While the United States was still neutral, as related in Chapter Four, she was denied a visa by American consular authorities in part because of nitpicking as to her professional qualities as a photographer; she summed up her efforts to counter this nitpicking in a letter to these authorities on November 27th, 1940.[13] Ironically, early in the next year, 1941, she began her key role as a photographer in planning and carrying out a project funded by the American Council of Learned Societies: the microfilming of manuscripts and early printed books in British repositories.[14] Later the same year, with some of the funding coming from the Rockefeller Foundation (based in New York), she directed a project initiated by the Association of Special Libraries and Information Bureaux (ASLIB) to make available in Britain and in some allied and neutral countries microfilm copies of scientific and technical journals published in enemy and enemy-controlled countries. In the case of China, for example, the microfilm reels were delivered by air mail.[15] The leadership role of Lucia was evident because it was she who wrote the lengthy treatise summing up all this activity shortly after the war ended.[16]

She went on play a key role in the United Nations Educational, Scientific and Cultural Organization (UNESCO), beginning with an August, 1945, memorandum to its London-based preparatory commission, "Microfilm Services and Their Application to Scholarly Study, Scientific

---

[11]*Ibid.*, 162.

[12]*Ibid.*, 166 and illustration facing page 97.

[13]Lucia Moholy to The American Consulate General, carbon copy of TLS, November 27th, 1940, Bauhaus-Archiv, Berlin.

[14]Lucia Moholy, "The ASLIB Microfilm Service: the Story of its Wartime Activities," *The Journal of Documentation*, volume I, number 3 (December, 1946), [147]-173, here 158; and Lester K. Born, Editor, *British Manuscripts Project; a Checklist of the Microfilms Prepared in England and Wales for the American Council of Learned Societies, 1941-1945* (New York: Greenwood Press, 1968).

[15]Lucia Moholy, "Das Kleinbild im Dienste der Dokumtarphotographie," *Blick in die Welt*, "Erscheint monatlich [*sic*: it was irregular in its appearance]," number 8 (undated: [January, 1947?]), 42-43, here 43.

[16]Lucia Moholy, "The ASLIB Microfilm Service: the Story of its Wartime Activities."

Research, Education and Re-Education in the Post-War Period."[17] Not long afterward she began work for UNESCO on microfilm projects in Czechoslovakia, Iran, Iraq and Turkey.[18]

In 1946, when the possibilities opened up by microfilms were not widely realized, she wrote a letter to a newspaper pointing to the advantages of microfilms in making available the texts of out-of-print books, and also enabling libraries to lend out microfilm copies while retaining the original book.[19] In 1946, in her first article published in Germany after she had fled that country in 1933, she summed up the history of microphotography and pointed to the possibilities opened up through use of microfilms.[20] Shortly after these two items were published she began planning a book on documentary reproduction, but was unable to obtain funding for a task that she estimated would take a year.[21]

In terms of László's 1926 essay, "directness of the mind—detours of technology,"[22] which Lucia might have helped to write and almost certainly edited, microfilming was by no means a detour of technology. In fact this technology, which she so presciently promoted, is finding new life in the early twenty-first century, when the microphotographs of texts can be converted into digital files by means of optical-character-recognition computer software, and the illustrations can also be converted into digital files and edited with appropriate computer software.[23] Of course these digital files can be made available over the Internet. In other words, far from engaging in a detour of technology, her foresight and expertise in promoting and preparing microfilms will continue to provide valuable intellectual resources far into the future. All of this is less obvious than the legacy of marvelous photographs that constituted her creative work, but in assessing the impact of Lucia Moholy's career her documentary work with microfilms should be borne in mind.

While working for UNESCO, Lucia Moholy lived in Istanbul in 1952 and 1953 and in Ankara in 1955 and 1956;[24] she moved to Zurich in 1959. I visited her in Zurich in 1976.

---

[17]Portions quoted in German translation in: Sachsse and Hartmann, *Lucia Moholy; Bauhaus Fotografin*, 84-85; the original text is in the Bauhaus-Archiv, Berlin. On the UNESCO Preparatory Commission see: United Nations Educational, Scientific and Cultural Organization, A Chronology of UNESCO, 19945-1987: Facts and Events ion UNESCO's History with References to Documentary Sources in the UNESCO Archives . . . (Paris: UNESCO, 1987), 4-5.

[18]Sachsse, *Lucia Moholy*, 63.

[19]Lucia Moholy, "Shortage of Books," *The Times* (London), November 2, 1946, 5.

[20]Lucia Moholy, "Das Kleinbild im Dienste der Dokumtarphotographie."

[21]Lucia Moholy to Allan Nevins, carbon copy of TLS, July 6th, 1947, Bauhaus-Archiv, Berlin.

[22]See Chapter Three, 264-265.

[23]Sachsse and Hartmann, *Lucia Moholy; Bauhaus Fotografin*, 163.

[24]Sachsse, *Lucia Moholy*, 63.

Appendix D: Sibyl Moholy-Nagy: Some Notes
on Her Life

Sibyl Moholy-Nagy (DVD figures 535 and 542) was a multi-talented woman who lived an intriguing life during which she was able to re-invent herself several times. Her unique set of qualities made her a fitting companion to László Moholy-Nagy. Sibyl was an acclaimed actress on stage and screen; a pioneer in running a script office in a major Berlin motion-picture company during the transition years from silent to sound films; a valued assistant to her second husband, Láazló Moholy-Nagy, during his early years as a film-maker; a writer who was fluent in two languages and who began her writing career by using her family's fascinating history as raw material for semi-autobiographical narratives, only one of which, *Children's Children* of 1945,[1] has thus far has made its way into print; an educator who began that aspect of her career in Chicago along with her husband as the manager of a bucolic summer school and who also taught humanities and served as the librarian of the I.D.; a professor who taught at Bradley University in Peoria and Pratt Institute in Brooklyn and other schools; and toward the end of her career enjoyed much success as a prolific writer and lecturer on design, architecture, planning and other topics. Her delight in being the mother of two lively girls was caught in photographs made by their father. (DVD figure 511)

Much information about Sibyl Moholy-Nagy is presented in context in many parts of *Moholy-Nagy: Mentor to Modernism*, and the information in this appendix is intended to supplement that information with things that have seemed out of context if presented above.

Sibyl played a role in documenting her own achievements as a writer by compiling a bibliography of her published writings in 1966, "The Architectural Writings of Sibyl Moholy-Nagy, January, 1944 to March, 1965,"[2] an impressive summary of her achievements to that point in her career, but an endeavor that thus far has added little to her reputation.

A dearth of writing about Sibyl was attended to by Judith Paine in 1975 in an astute and informed article that seemed, nevertheless, to invoke no sustained interest in Sibyl as a writer.[3] This gap is now being filled by Hilde Heynen, who in 2002 published a major

---

[1]Sibyl Moholy-Nagy (as S.D. Peech), *Children's Children* (New York: H. Bittner and Company, 1945).

[2]Sibyl Moholy-Nagy, "The Architectural Writings of Sibyl Moholy-Nagy, January, 1944 to March, 1965, compiled by Sibyl Moholy-Nagy," in: William B. O'Neal, editor, *Papers [of] The American Association of Architectural Bibliographers,* volume II (1966) (Charlottesville: The University Press of Virginia, 1966), [1]-9.

[3]Judith Paine, "Sibyl Moholy-Nagy: a Complete Life," *Archives of American Art Journal*, volume XV, number 4 (1975), 11-16.

article on Sibyl in the form of a book review of her masterwork, *Matrix of Man,*[4] originally issued in 1968,[5] as well as an earlier article on Sibyl and the American landscape.[6] Heynen, who has written of Sibyl, "As a critic and a historian she was sharp, witty and polemical,"[7] is at work on a book-length study, emphasizing the intellectual achievements of her later years.

Meanwhile, the first book-length study of Sibyl Moholy-Nagy, written by Hannelore Rüttgens-Pohlmann, has recently been published in Germany.[8] It is an attempt to give a balanced account of her subject's entire life, and was based on Rüttgens-Pohlmann's doctoral dissertation.[9]

Following are comments by Hattula Moholy-Nagy on Rüttgens-Pohlmann's dissertation, comments that Rüttgens-Pohlmann did not see until after the book based on her dissertation was published:

> "Es muss gelingen, das grosses Kunstwerk meines Lebens…"
> Doctoral dissertation by Hannelore Rüttgens-Pohlmann, 2006
>
> Comments for Hannelore Rüttgens-Pohlmann by Hattula Moholy-Nagy,
> 15 October 2008
>
> p. 66, Claudia's birth date was 25 March 1936.
>
> p. 66, my impression is that SMN left the Institute of Design in April 1948.
>
> p. 67, SMN also taught, or at least lectured, at the University of California in Berkeley. I remember this because she had to sign a "loyalty oath" (this was the

---

[4]Hilde Heynen, "'Matrix of Man'," *Harvard Design Magazine*, number 16 (Winter/Spring, 2002), 28-33.

[5]Sibyl Moholy-Nagy, *Matrix of Man: an Illustrated History of the Urban Environment* (New York: Frederick A. Praeger, Publishers, 1968).

[6]Hilde Heynen, "Navigating the Self: Sibyl Moholy-Nagy's Exploration of American Architecture," in: Michelle A. Rinehart, editor, *Oriental-Occidental Geography, Identity, Space: Proceedings, 2001 ACSA International Conference, June 15-19, 2001, Istanbul, Turkey* (Washington, D.C.: Association of Collegiate Schools of Architecture, 2001), 151-155.

[7]Heynen, "Navigating the Self," 151.

[8]Hannelore Rüttgens-Pohlmann, *Kunstwerk eines Lebens: Sibyl Moholy-Nagy, Rekonstruktion des biographischen Verlaufs einer deutschen Emigrantin* (Oldenburg: BIS-Verlag der Carl von Ossietzky Universität, 2008).

[9]Hannelore Rüttgens-Pohlmann, "'Es muss gelingen, das grosse Kunstwerk meines Lebens' Krisenprozesse- Identitätsentwicklung-Streben nach Grösse; Rekonstruktion des biographischen Verlaufs einer deutschen Emigrantin im Nationalsozialismus" (Ph. D. dissertation, Mainz Universität, 2007).

time of anti-Communist hysteria). She protested this oath vigorously at home, but she did sign it.

p. 67, SMN was not exactly ill in June, 1954. She had to have a hysterectomy, which was a great blow to her self-esteem.

p. 77, Hertha died perhaps 6 months before Eva or some time in 1980.
Eva died at the beginning of 1981.
Footnote 11, the child that died in infancy was a boy born after SMN.

p. 78, Onkel Hans Strauch in Braunschweig was a physician.

p. 79, ftnt 17, Herbert Pietzsch emigrated to the USA, married an American, and had three daughters: Hildegard, Martha, and Vera.

p. 143, as far as I know, as an adult SMN did not have any women friends. I had the impression that she felt women (including herself) were inferior to men, therefore men were the only people worthwhile making friends with.

p. 210, I got 34 hits for "Curtis Melnitz" on Google 12/12/2007, so he is not entirely obscure.

p. 220, ftnt 39, there is a great deal of documentation available to show that Ellen Frank was indeed one of Ise Frank Gropius's younger sisters.

p. 225, Mädchenschicksale

p. 230, July-August 1928, Walter Hasenclever

pp. 286-287, I feel it is not quite fair to judge SMN to be anti-Semitic because she didn't keep Carl Dreyfuss's family name. SMN told me how deeply hurt she was by Carl's infidelity, so it would have been expected that she would want to distance herself from him for personal reasons. Most of the important men in her life were, in fact, Jewish: besides Melnitz, Dreyfuss, and Moholy, also Metal, Rowan, and Arno.

p. 308, it is unlikely that Lipót Weisz ever left Hungary. László Moholy-Nagy (LMN) was as ready to obfuscate his autobiographical data as SMN was.
There were 3 surviving brothers: Jenö (1891-1986), László (1895-1946), and Ákos (1897-1938).
László's convalescence was mainly in Budapest. He visited Odessa in 1918 after he recovered, probably to look for Ákos who had been taken prisoner by the Russians.

pp. 310, 322, *Dynamik der Grossstadt* was never filmed by LMN. It was first published in 1924 as a script in Hungarian in *Ma*.

p. 324, Jeanpaul Goergen put together some good data on LMN's early films in 1995.
Gross-Stadt Zigeuner has a sequence featuring Ellen Frank.

SMN writes of filming *Berliner Stilleben* with LMN, which would have had to be after Nov. 1931.

p. 325, it's true that SMN's writing and statements are not always reliable. I think there are several reasons: she was bored with looking up facts, she liked to make things interesting, she liked to impose her own version on events, and she really enjoyed fooling people.

pp. 336, 357-358, "Hattula" was LMN's pet name for Sibyl (and possibly also for Ellen who was with LMN in Finland in 1931) until it was given to me. It is a Finnish place-name and also occurs as a family name. I believe I am unique in having it as a first name.

p. 343, SMN always told us that having children was her idea over LMN's objections, and that she had to fool him into having me.

p. 357, SMN told me that my second middle name, Carola, was after Carola Giedion, with whom my father was close in the 1930s.

p. 358, Abb. 32 depicts Claudia not Hattula. It is also misidentified in *Experiment in Totality*.

p. 358, the 1926 painting's title should be *Al 2*, aka *The Great Aluminum Painting*.

pp. 361-362, 365, ftnt 155, in my opinion, one of the great tragedies of the Holocaust is that in pre-World War II Germany, social class and national origin were more important to many Jews than their ethnicity, so they did not pull together enough to vigorously protest the genocide.

Hattula Moholy-Nagy had learned about her father's one-time Calvinism from her parents; she also knew from an early age that her great-great grandfather on her mother's side, Moritz Hermann Strahl (1800-1860), had been Jewish. (Her great-great grandfather had been known, before his conversion to Christianity, as Moritz Schlesinger.) But she was not aware, until I had discussed with her my bibliographic search utilizing Internet resources, that Strahl, a medical doctor, had been a prolific author, writing mostly on various aspects of medicine,[10] but his works also include poems and an autobiography.[11] Hattula was not fully aware, until after the death of both of her parents, of her father's Jewish background. All she learned from her mother, after her father had died, was that she suspected Moholy was Jewish but that they had never discussed this together. Nevertheless, I would like to point out that Sibyl's *Children's Children*, along with her related unpublished semi-autobiographical narratives,[12] constitutes a strong condemnation of anti-Semitism as it narrates examples of how the deeply rooted anti-Semitism present in her own family took hold of some family members (but not Sibyl and her maternal grandfather, who married Moritz Strahl's daughter) during the period covered by her narrative, stretching back into the early nineteenth century.[13]

It should also be noted that the mixture of facts and imagined events that characterize Sibyl's semi-autobiographical writings result in passages that are nevertheless revealing, and this is by no means a rare feature in autobiographical writings. In fact there is a large body of writings concerning autobiographies; see, *e.g.*, Paul John Eakin's thoughtful and well-documented study of 1992,

---

[10]Hattula Moholy-Nagy has discussed her great-great grandfather with me on several occasions over a period of years. She had been told that Strahl had converted to Lutheranism, that he was a physician and a *Sanitätsrat*, or member of the Berlin Board of Health. His official title was *Königlicher Kreis-Physikus*; see: E.G. [*i.e.*, E. Geddings], "Der Alp, sein Wesen und Heilung. . . .," *The American Journal of the Medical Sciences,* volume X, number 36 (August, 1836), 393-407, here 393.

The article in *The American Journal of the Medical Sciences* was a review of Strahl's book on a malady that he himself suffered from, nightmares: *Der Alp, seim Wesen und seine Heilung: Eine Monographie* (Berlin: Enslin, 1833). His work on this subject makes him a precursor to Sigmund Freud's discussions of the interpretation of dreams.

[11]Moritz Hermann Strahl, *Aus dem Leben eines Berliner Arztes* (Breslau: Schletter, 1835).

[12]See Chapter Four, note 424.

[13]*Children's Children* is loosely based on Sibyl Moholy-Nagy's own family and on her experience with her confirmation pastor in Dresden, who was to become her lifelong friend; see the documents on reel 946, frame 0567 and reel 945, frame 3148, Moholy-Nagy Papers, Archives of American Art, Washington, D.C. *Children's Children* details an anti-Semitic strain among some members of the family as they reacted to the fact that Moritz Hermann Strahl was one of their ancestors; the character of Jarni Dallmann, based to some extent on Sibyl Moholy-Nagy, is presented as a fierce opponent of anti-Semitism.

See also: Moholy-Nagy, Sibyl (as Sibyl Peach), "My Life in Germany - Two Years Before and Two Years After the Start of the Hitler Regime," microfilm copy of carbon copy of typed manuscript, pages 1-181 on microfilm reel 946, frames 0628-0814, Moholy-Nagy Papers, Archives of American Art, Washington, D.C. This unpublished manuscript contains passages describing the author's strong opposition to anti-Semitism; see, *e.g.*, pages 101-102, frames 0733-0744,

Touching the World: Reference in Autobiography.[14] See also note 71 in my
Chapter Five.

Sibyl attracted much acclaim as an actress using the name of Sibyl Peach.
She was especially successful as Lena in a 1928 film, *Mädchenschicksale*,
directed by Richard Loewenbein. One critic compared her to that delicate but
determined film pioneer, American actress Lillian Gish (1893-1993): "Sybill
Peach [*sic*], ein Lilian [*sic*] Gish-Typ, nimmt durch ihr feines, kultiviertes Spiel
gefangen." [Sibyl Peach, a Lillian Gish type, captivates through her fine,
cultivated performance.][15] (DVD figure 542) However, Sibyl's main
contribution to the development of motion pictures was less glamorous but
should not be overlooked; she once wrote: "*Madame Butterfly* was still playing
at the Kroll Opera House when I took over the scenario office of a large motion-
picture company in Berlin,"[16] and went on to identify the company as Tobis.
The full name of the company was Tonbild-Syndikat AG, formed in 1928, a
pioneer in the production of sound films.[17] Her recollection would put her
involvement in the company as beginning before July, 1931.[18] Since sound films
were relatively new, Sibyl, as director of a scenario office, was clearly a pioneer
in that aspect of the industry.

Besides her first husband, Carl Dreyfuß, the Frankfurt intellectual Sibyl was
closest to was Walter Benjamin. They spent some time together in Frankfort am
Main and later in Berlin during a brief period late in 1931 and early in 1932.
Sibyl later recalled, in a letter to Hannah Arendt:

> Nach meiner Scheidung sah ich Benjamin einen Winter durch sehr viel
> in Berlin - ohne ihm in seiner zunehmenden Verinsamung helfen zu
> können. Aus sehr komplizierten Urgründen kam ich zu dieser
> unkongruenten Freundschaft die mich, als ich etwas heller sah, für
> immer von der Frankfurtern entfremdete. Als ich im New Yorker las,

---

[14]Paul John Eakin, *Touching the World: Reference in Autobiography* (Princeton, New Jersey:
Princeton University Press, 1992).

[15]Friedrich Karl Kaul, "Mädchenschicksale: Uraufführung . . .," unidentified German newspaper,
November 8, 1928; a photograph of a clipping is on microfilm reel 944, frame 1180, Moholy-Nagy
Papers, Archives of American Art, Washington, D.C.

Sibyl Moholy-Nagy once made an indirect reference to herself as a sort of German Lillian Gish
in her novel *Children's Children*, in which the character of Jarni Dallmann is to some extent based
on herself; see: Sibyl Moholy-Nagy, *Children's Children*, 331.

[16]Sibyl Moholy-Nagy, *Moholy-Nagy, Experiment in Totality*, 57.

[17]Hans-Michael Bock, Wiebke Annkatrin Mosel and Ingrun Spazier, editors, *Die Tobis 1928-
1945; eine kommentierte Filmografie* (Munich: Edition Text + Kritik, 2003).

[18]As noted above in Chapter Four, the last performance of *Madame Butterfly* at the Kroll was July
2, 1931.

dass Teddy Wiesengrund jetzt Benjamin herausgegebn hat, konnte ich
es fast nicht glauben. Die Grausamkeit seiner (und [Max]
Horkheimer's) totaler Kälte gegen Benjamin's abgründige
Lebensverwicklung war zu rege in meine Erinnerung. Heute ist
Benjamin eine reinere Gegenwart als Teddy und Grete Wiesengrund![19]
[After my separation {and pending divorce from Carl Dreyfuß} I saw
Benjamin very often one winter in Berlin—without being able to help
him in his increasing isolation. For very complicated reasons, I came to
this incongruous friendship, which, with clearer insight, estranged me
forever from the Frankfurt group. I could scarcely believe it when I
read in *The New Yorker* that Teddy Wiesengrund [now better known as
Theodor W. Adorno] has now published Benjamin's works. The
cruelty of his (and [Max] Horkheimer's) extreme coldness towards
Benjamin's deep involvement with life was too vivid in my memory.
Today Benjamin has a clearer presence than Teddy and Grete
{Margarethe née Karplus (1902-1993)} Wiesengrund!]

The background to the passage quoted above is in another part of the letter: it
was through Dreyfuß that Sibyl was acquainted with leading figures of the
Frankfurters, a group of intellectuals interested in philosophy and sociology who
were active in the *Institut für Sozialforschung* [Institute for Social Research].
Sibyl recalled gatherings of *Frankfurters* in her living room in Frankfurt, which
would have been prior to mid-1931:

Viele der Debatten zwischen ihm [Benjamin] und der Gründern des Instituts für
Sozialforschung (Weill [*sic*.; *i.e.*, Felix Weil], Horkheimer, Wiesengrund und
mein damaliger Mann, Carl Dreyfuss) haben sich in mein Wohnzimmer in der
Ulmenstrasse in Frankfurt abgespielt. Der sterile Marxismus der wirklichkeits-
unfähigen Dreieinigkeit Weill-Horkheimer-Wiesengrund und Benjamin's [*sic*]
verzweifelte Abwehr sind mir noch heute ganz scharf in Erinnerung . . .[20]
[Many of the debates between him [*i.e.*, Benjamin] and the Founders of
the *Institut für Sozialforschung* (Weill [*sic*; *i.e.*, Felix Weil], [Max]
Horkheimer, Wiesengrund and my husband at the time, Carl Dreyfuss)
took place in my living room on Ulmenstrasse in Frankfurt. The sterile
Marxism of the divorced-from-reality trinity Weil-Horkheimer-
Wiesengrund and Benjamin's desperate defense are even today quite
sharp in my memory . . .]

---

[19] Sibyl Moholy-Nagy to Hannah Arendt, TLS, November 23, 1968, microfilm reel 944, frame
1180, Moholy-Nagy Papers, Archives of American Art, Washington, D.C.

[20] *Ibid.* The differences between Benjamin and other members of the Frankfurt School are summed
up in: Hannah Arendt, "Introduction," in: Walter Benjamin, *Illuminations*, edited and with an
introduction by Hannah Arendt, translated by Harry Zohn (New York: Schocken Books, 1969),
[1]-55, here 10-11.

Appendix E: "Chicago Memories," an Essay of 1995 by Hattula Moholy-Nagy

The text of Chicago Memories" has never been published before in its original English text. It first appeared in an exhibition catalogue in a Hungarian translation by Magdolna Kolta as: "Chicagói emlékek" in: Károly Kincses and Miklós Tarján, editors, *Moholy-Nagy László:100 Fotó* (Kecskemét and Budapest: Magyar Fotográfiai Múzeum and Pelikán, 1995), 7-15.

Since writing the essay for the Kecskemét exhibition, Hattula Moholy-Nagy has learned more about her father's work in color photography; see: Jeannine Fiedler and Hattula Moholy-Nagy, editors, *Laszlo Moholy-Nagy: Color in Transparency; Photographic Experiments in Color, 1934-1946=Fotografische Experimente in Farbe, 1934-1946* [exhibition catalogue, Bauhaus-Archiv, Berlin, June 21 to September 4, 2006] (Göttingen: Steidl Publishers, 2006).

"Chicago Memories"
by Hattula Moholy-Nagy
March 2, 1995 (revised March 20, 1995)

My Father

My father was 38 years old when I was born and so my clearest memories of him are as a middle-aged man, already portly, always well-groomed and neatly dressed. He had a full head of dark hair with a remarkable white streak down the center and a wide smile that showed many teeth. His left thumb was permanently bent and thickened from a wound he had received as an artillery officer in World War I. After that happened, his left hand never appears in photographs of him.

My father came to the United States in July, 1937, to become director of the New Bauhaus in Chicago. My mother, my sister, Claudia, and I followed in September. We came by ship and, like millions of European immigrants before us, we entered the United States at Ellis Island. Our very first home in Chicago was the Knickerbocker Hotel near Michigan Avenue. But after a few weeks we moved to a grand apartment at the corner of Astor and Division Streets, where we were to live for approximately two years.

I remember this apartment as huge, with large windows in the front rooms from which one could see Lake Michigan. The window drapes in the living room were of heavy, hand-woven, nubby fabric that started each winter as white and gradually acquired the same color as the soft, sooty coal that was used for heating in those days. The walls were covered with the palest and most boring wallpaper my father could find, which would not compete with his paintings. The floors were carpeted with Japanese tatami mats, elegant to look at but slippery disasters for little girls who needed to have the tiny splinters removed from their knees.

Most of the furniture in the sparsely-furnished living and dining rooms had been acquired by Father and his first wife, Lucia Moholy, in the 1920s when they had been at the Dessau Bauhaus. Some of it can be seen in the series of photographs Lucia made of their *Meisterhaus*. But our bedrooms were furnished with a luxurious set of Art Deco mahogany veneer furnishings, a legacy of my mother's first marriage to a wealthy businessman.

In late 1939 or early 1940 we moved from Astor Street to Lakeview Avenue, where we lived until June of 1949, when my mother, sister, and I moved to San Francisco. Although it had as many rooms as the apartment on Astor Street, our Lakeview Avenue home was smaller, farther away from the center of town, and considerably less expensive. By this time Father was putting all of his personal resources into his new effort, the School of Design, and our move was an economy measure.

As the years went by the assemblage of Bauhaus household furnishings brought from Europe underwent attrition, a material metaphor for the diminishing influence of Germany and the Bauhaus on my parents' lives. In the Lakeview Avenue apartment, the pure style only survived in the dining room with white wooden cabinets for the china, silver, and stemware, a stack of Marcel Breuer's black lacquered nesting chairs, a big round white table on a pedestal base, and—best of all—a stainless steel lazy susan that sat in the middle of the table. Mother's Art Deco furniture had been allowed into the living room and the tatami matting had been replaced by more conventional dark gray carpeting. By the time my mother had moved to California and then New York, only a pair of graceful, uncomfortable Breuer steel tube armchairs and a set of four steel and lacquered wood end tables survived.

By the time we moved to Lakeview Avenue Father was extremely busy with his school and he did not spend much time at home. I cannot say that I knew him well. I recall him as a remote and kindly presence. Yet he did try to spend some time with me and my sister as we got older. By the time I was nine or ten, we had established a weekly routine. One side of Lakeview Avenue bordered Lincoln Park and an entrance to the park was only half a block from our apartment. On Sunday mornings Father would take the two of us for a walk in the park, usually around a small artificial lake that we called the Lagoon. We would amble along and Father would tell us another episode of a long story about a Green-Checkered Pig. This animal had many adventures, all of them in brilliantly colored settings. Many years later my uncle, Jenő, who was four years older than my father, said that he had told my father stories about the Green-Checkered Pig when they were young. I was pleased to discover that the Pig was a family tradition.

By the time we had circumambulated the Lagoon and arrived back home, my mother had dinner on the table. The food was always the same, baked chicken with sour cream gravy, and it was always delicious. Years later I asked my mother, who was an inventive and versatile cook, why we invariably had chicken for Sunday dinner. She replied, "I asked him, wouldn't you like me to fix something else sometimes—veal chops? a pork roast? But he said always no, he wanted chicken. So I made chicken."

My Father the Artist

I remember Father occasionally working at home in both the Astor Street and Lakeview Avenue apartments. On Astor Street he worked in a room he had converted into a studio. On Lakeview Avenue, he worked in the living room.

My Astor Street memories of Father painting probably date to the period between after the New Bauhaus school closed in June, 1938, and before the School of Design opened in February, 1939. I recall watching him painstakingly incise Plexiglas sheets with a steel point and steel straight-edge. One of these, subsequently named "Iridescent Space Modulator," had an oblong figure painted on it in a beautiful shade of bluish green, made iridescent by many incised horizontal lines. On another sheet of incised Plexiglas he painted many orange and black dots. I was charmed to see that the colors matched those of the black fire escape directly outside the window, which had been painted with patches of bright orange rust-proofing paint.

On Lakeview Avenue our living room had a large window that faced north. Father set up a large, brown, paint-speckled wooden easel near it. My sister and I were strictly forbidden to get within six feet of the easel, whether there was a canvas on it or not. But if we kept our distance he would let us watch him work. Watching him was always deeply interesting. When he began a canvas, he would sketch the composition on it in pencil. We marveled at his ability to draw perfect circles with one great sweep of his hand. It was also fun to watch him paint textured backgrounds. He would take a broad, straight-edged paintbrush and pat the surface of the canvas with thick dabs of color, lifting tiny peaks in the paint. Once, when I was about twelve years old, and he was working on the canvas, "Leuk I," he actually gave me the paintbrush and guided my hand as I patted in a square inch or so of textured background. But this only happened once.

In the late 1930s and early 1940s Americans in general, and Chicagoans in particular, had little appreciation of abstract art. Father had few exhibitions in the United States. In Chicago, as far as I know, only one courageous gallerist, Katharine Kuh, showed his works. One of her objectives was to acquaint Americans with the work of European avant-garde artists and she gave a number of exhibitions until World War II made it impossible. During his lifetime Father never had a major show at the Art Institute of Chicago, the most prestigious art museum in the city and one of the most important in the country.

On at least one occasion, however, he showed a painting at the Art Institute. My mother, sister, and I went downtown to meet him there. We looked for Father and found him in front of a small crowd gathered around one of his large canvases, engaged in earnest discussion with a male spectator. My father, in his heavy accent, was trying to explain his painting and abstract art in general. But the man's reaction was the standard objection of that time: "Is that supposed to be art? Why, my eight-year-old can do better than that!" Far from being hurt that the man did not like his beautiful painting, my father enjoyed the opportunity to educate him.

It is certainly not his fault that neither my sister nor I became artists. He always encouraged us to paint and draw. We made all of our greeting cards and we were expected to design our own paper-dolls. For years both of us attended Saturday morning children's classes at the School of Design. For our artistic efforts at home, we had plasticene, pencils, crayons, and paint, the latter always water soluble. Our first paints were black metal boxes of Prang watercolors, but by the mid-1940s we were upgraded to Shiva casein paints in tubes. I loved these for their pungent odor as much as for their beautiful colors. One of our favorite Sunday afternoon activities was to draw and paint while listening to the radio. Father, ever the teacher, would sometimes look in on what we were doing. I remember two things he told me. One was always to leave some white spaces in the picture to set off the composition. The other was how to clean a brush with soap and water.

As I child I loved to draw. I still enjoy it, although I am not gifted. One day, after I had entered a phase when I was drawing nothing but impossibly slender young women, instead of nothing but horses, my father gave me a project. He wanted me to make a series of women figures, starting with a typical slender one and then gradually reversing the proportions so that if the first drawing was, let's say, 4:1, the last one would be 1:4. I found this project difficult and spent quite a while on it, but when I gave him the drawing he seemed satisfied with it. A couple of years later I was surprised to see it in his last book, *Vision in Motion*.

On at least a couple of occasions when we lived on Lakeview Avenue he made Plexiglas sculptures in the kitchen. We had a gas range that stood off the floor on four legs. Our cat lived under it. Father brought home from the school sheets of Plexiglas that had already been perforated, incised, and sawn, heated them in the oven until they were soft, and then, working rapidly with a lot of grimaces because the plastic sheets were hot, he bent them into the desired forms.

My clearest memories, however, are of his photography: his movies, photograms, and camera pictures.

He kept a 16 mm. movie projector in the hall closet of the Lakeview apartment and it was a special occasion for my sister and me when he would give us a movie show. Most likely, at one time or another, we saw all of his films, but the only ones I can recall with certainty are *A Lightplay Black White Gray* and the two films he made of us from the time we were newborn babies to about 1938 when we were living on Astor Street.

Although *A Lightplay Black White Gray* has no soundtrack, it seemed to me that the whirring and clanking of our old projector was a perfect mechanical accompaniment to the stately movements of the Light Machine. The two children films are both a joy and a frustration to me. A joy because there we all are, in settings and surrounded by objects that in many cases I can still recall. I can see my father, my mother, my sister, myself, and a couple of the young women who helped care for us. I can glimpse the large garden of the house in which we lived in London, the front rooms of the Astor Street apartment, Oak Street Beach and the Chicago skyline of 1938. But the films are a frustration as well because it was not Father's style to establish a panoramic setting for filmed action. I think to myself, Oh, if only he had shifted the camera—just for a moment—from that fat little girl and let us see the rest of the room! If only he had shown us the artwork and furniture in our London living room, or the paintings along the corridor on Astor Street!

I have a more interactive reminiscence about photograms. I remember Father making them outdoors with his students at the summer school in Somonauk. Usually my sister and I were sent away to camp so that we would not be underfoot. But one summer my father showed me how to put objects on photosensitive paper and expose the paper to the bright sun. I would watch with interest as the paper turned lavender and then brown. He once gave me a coiled metal bedspring with a sheet of paper wrapped around it and told me to hold it in the sunlight. After a while we unwrapped it, but the result disappointed both of us. I made more satisfying compositions with leaves and flowers. Floris Neusüss has pointed out that Father never lost interest in photograms. Of his activity in photography after he came to Chicago, only his photograms have survived in significant number.

Nevertheless, it seemed that he took his favorite camera, a Leica, everywhere we went. He must have taken hundreds of photographs but the only ones I have been able to locate are the many shots he made of my sister and me, and a few 35mm. Kodachrome slides, some of great beauty. Beaumont Newhall has suggested that after he came to the United States, Father's interest shifted to color photography. This may be a possible explanation for the virtual absence of published photographs from that period. On the other hand, Nathan Lerner recalls that Father kept his negatives at the school. Perhaps my mother left them there when we moved to California in 1949 and they did not survive the Institute of Design's move to the Illinois Institute of Technology. So my father's latest-known black/white camera photographs are of his family, images never meant to be shown to the public. Nevertheless, they incorporate all of the elements of his distinctive style including bird's-eye views, worm's-eye views, extreme close-ups, asymmetrical compositions, clipped heads and torsos, emphasized shadows, and so on.

Posing for him was tedious. As far as I know, my father never did his own darkroom work. In Chicago this was mostly done at the school, which is probably why he kept his negatives there. As is well-known, his first wife, Lucia Moholy, developed his photographs in Germany during their marriage, and according to my mother, occasionally afterwards when they all lived in London. I also have a number of paper folders from commercial printers in German cities, the equivalents of our One-Hour Photo shops, which indicate that Father also sent his photos out, just like the ordinary tourist.

Probably because he did not print his own photographs, Father composed them in the camera view-finder and this could take a long time. He generally took pictures of us indoors using daylight. I do not recall that he used a tripod for these shots. However, I do have a series of 35mm. Kodachrome portraits of us where spotlights and a tripod were used. But for daylight photo sessions, I remember he would seat me near a window holding his favorite photographic accessory, a large sheet of white construction paper, while he would determine its optimum position for reflecting light on my face. I had a better opportunity to see how this worked when he had me hold the paper as he photographed my mother or my sister.

Although Father did some color photography before he came to the United States, as far as I can tell he did not work with Kodachrome before then. I have deep admiration for the quality of Kodak's color film of that time. Of the few images I still have, the colors appear to be as bright and true now as they were half a century ago.

Friends, Colleagues, and the School

My father knew a lot of people and maintained a surprisingly large correspondence. As in the case of his black/white photography, copies of the letters he wrote and the replies he received are gone. My mother kept only the letters he wrote to her. But, fortunately, other people are not as thorough in their housekeeping and a good deal of Father's correspondence is coming to light in other archives.

We had many visitors, both in Chicago and at the summer school in Somonauk. Furthermore, my sister and I sometimes accompanied our parents on luncheon and afternoon visits to other people's homes. Sometimes these visits were to wealthy businessmen, whose support Father was trying to win for the school. Usually we were the only children there. After the meal we were expected to entertain ourselves unobtrusively. I remember timidly exploring, like cats, large, silent North Shore mansions, keeping two strict rules: not to open any doors and not to touch anything. This was my introduction to the fascinating pastime of seeing how other people live.

The businessman who figured most importantly in Father's efforts to maintain and run his school was Walter Paepcke. It is generally known that Paepcke's contacts and personal support were directly responsible for the survival of this enterprise. Paepcke owned the property in Somonauk that was used for the summer school and he generously rented it to Father for the sum of $1.00 a year. My earliest memories of the Paepcke family are from Somonauk, although we were also in their Chicago apartment on Lake Shore Drive.

The Paepcke country house, complete with stables, tennis court, and swimming pool, was perhaps a mile and a half, cross-country, from the summer school. My sister and I were over at the house sometimes to visit with the three beautiful blonde Paepcke daughters, Nina, Paula, and Toni. Toni was closest to us in age and we saw the most of her. However, either Paula or Nina taught me card tricks. At that time I was still in the phase of drawing nothing but horses and Paula showed me how enlarging their ears would greatly improve my compositions. Mrs. Paepcke, whom adults addressed as Pussy, was a very attractive woman with wonderful coloring. She had a pink complexion and light blue eyes and, although she was then only in her late thirties, she had beautiful silver hair.

I recall only Walter Paepcke at the summer school. He was a robust man with a very energetic manner. Occasionally he would ride over on one of his horses. He and Father played chess on the terrace in front of the house. Father must have been a very good chess player. He taught both me and my sister to play. But one day he checkmated me in only two moves and I lost my enthusiasm for the game. But my sister was not as easily intimidated and became a skillful player. I once asked my mother if Mr. Paepcke had been good at chess. She smiled and said, "Well, Laci would say, Paepcke is coming over to play chess this afternoon. Remind me to let him win this time."

My mother gave dinner parties to facilitate my father's contacts with the Chicago business community and with the University of Chicago faculty. After we moved to Lakeview Avenue and we no longer had a cook and a nanny, my sister and I sometimes helped by setting the table and making place cards for the guests. When we got bigger we would clear the table and do the dishes. At least once Walter and Ise Gropius came to lunch on Lakeview. They unexpectedly came into the kitchen where my sister and I were washing dishes, in order to say good-bye to us. "Good-bye, Mr. Gropius," I said to him politely. "But you must call me Pius," he replied. "And you must call me Pia," Ise chimed in. My sister and I just stared at them, struck dumb by the unthinkable audacity of addressing these two distinguished persons by their nicknames.

Ise could do something wonderful. "Watch my eyes," she told me. As I looked at her brown irises they began to rotate, first a couple of slow turns and then two or three fast ones. I was entranced.

I do not think I ever met Alexander Archipenko, who spent some years in Chicago during the 1940s, but his friendship with Father led to my first lesson in art appreciation. One day my father brought home a sculpture that Archipenko had either given him or exchanged with him. I watched as Father set the piece on the dining room table. "What do you see?" he asked me. At first only I saw a tall black stone about half a meter in height with smooth, wavy surfaces, a shallow grooved line, and a small round perforation through one edge. "Look," said Father. "It is a woman. This grooved line, it could be her hair, or the kind of caps that nuns wear. See how it continues down to become her arm. And the hole—it is her eye." And so I saw that it was a statue of a seated woman.

And there were the Hungarians. I knew that my mother was German and my father was Hungarian. I grew up with the thought that, while Germans were everywhere, particularly in the Midwest, Hungarians were special, and that this half of my heritage was to be treasured. When I was in the fifth or sixth grade, I discovered a book in the school library and brought it home to show Father. It was called *The Good Master*, and it was written and illustrated by a woman with a Hungarian name, Kate Seredy. The story was about a young boy, János, nicknamed Jancsi, who lived on a farm on the Great Hungarian Plain at the time of the First World War. Father was pleased at my interest in Seredy's book. He said that he, too, had lived on a farm on the Great Hungarian Plain, thereby leaving me with the impression that he had been a farmer's son, rather like the farmers we knew in Somonauk. I was well into middle-age before I discovered this was not the case.

But other than mentioning that he had once lived on a farm, Father never spoke about his childhood or his family. In fact the families of both my parents seemed remote and unreal to us. We knew they lived in Europe, but the War had cut off all communication with them after 1940. I had seen photographs only of my father's mother, his handsome younger brother, Ákos, and his nephew, Levente, the son of his older brother, Jenő. My parents referred to my father's mother as "Vilmosné," which I naturally, but mistakenly, assumed was her first name. She had once visited us in London when I was very young and my dim recollection of her is a very broad old lady dressed in long, dark clothes. Hungary seemed like a mythical place and I imagined that it looked like the world Kate Seredy depicted in her books, well ordered, rural, and inhabited by people who wore elaborate costumes as everyday clothes.

My father took up contact with many of the Hungarians living in Chicago. One person whom I remember most vividly was Madame Varro. Margit Varró had been a

famous pianist in Europe, but she, her husband, and her son had to flee to the United
States. Her husband, Stefan, whom we were permitted to address as Pista Bácsi, a
mellow elderly gentleman with a beautiful mustache, was a bookbinder. Madame Varro
had been reduced to giving piano lessons in other people's homes to unmusical children
like me. I see now, fifty years later, how difficult this must have been for her and I can
sympathize. But back then her impatience terrified me. I was happier when I began to
take lessons from Mrs. Jonas, a cheery Viennese who did not take my shortcomings to
heart.

Another Hungarian we saw a good deal of was a carpenter, whom we referred to as
Kálman Toman, but whose name was actually Kálman Tomaniczka. In my memory he
looks like Pista Bácsi. He built the white shadowbox frames for my father's paintings
and he also worked out in Somonauk. One summer, working alone, he added a screened
porch onto the front of the house. It took him all day, but to us it seemed like an
astonishing achievement.

It was probably towards the end of the same summer that Father and Kálman Toman
made sauerkraut. They spent the afternoon on the new porch carefully shredding the
cabbage and packing it into large pottery crocks. According to my mother, they ate
almost as much raw cabbage as they put into the crocks: "Laci called me to the porch,
and I fell to the floor—gassed!" We brought the crocks back to Chicago and put them in
our basement storeroom. I don't remember actually eating the sauerkraut. What I do
remember is the way the basement of our building smelled as the sauerkraut fermented in
it all winter long.

Once we all visited Kálman and his wife at home. They lived far out on the west
side. This circumstance alone was exciting because, at my age, anywhere west of Clark
Street was *terra incognita*. My sister and I were immediately captivated by a large
wooden chest standing by the living room window. Kálman had built it himself, of
course, and then covered every square inch of its exterior with intarsia inlay. There was
one medallion after another, each depicting a figure or a scene composed of several kinds
of beautiful wood. The largest medallion in the center of the lid showed a large female
nude that looked as though it had been worked in ivory. We thought the inlaid chest was
one of the most gorgeous things we had ever seen. On the drive back home we continued
to praise it. My parents said very little, and we were nearly home before I realized that
they actually considered Kálman Toman's chest a good example of *kitsch*.

One hundred years after his birth and nearly fifty years after his death there is a
growing recognition of my father's achievements. By now the main events of his life and
career are generally known. These reminiscences are offered as details that can be added
to the overall picture.

Appendix F: Notes for Notes

1.) There are numerous references in the footnotes to day-book entries kept in German by Ise Gropius. These are available in her English translation on microfilm in the Archives of American Art in two forms: handwritten English translation (reel 4130), and typed transcript of English translation (reel 2393). The original German text is available at the Bauhaus-Archiv, Berlin.

2.) Numerous letters are cited in the footnotes. Whenever the information is available I have included the abbreviation ALS for autograph letter signed, indicating a signed letter in longhand. Likewise, I have used the abbreviation TLS for typed letter signed.

3.) Moholy's best-known book, *The New Vision*, has a complex publishing history. Before publication Moholy planned to call it *von leben zu kunst*, or from life to art.[1] Just prior to publication he had decided on *von material zu architektur*, or from material to architecture.[2] The first edition was published by Albert Langen Verlag in 1929, with a preface dated September, 1928, as one of the Bauhaus Books.[3] The original title was kept for the Japanese edition of 1931 (DVD figures 370, 371, 372, 373, 374 375 and 376). Facsimile reprints of the 1929 edition appeared in 1968 and 2001.[4]

For the first American edition, published in New York by Brewer, Warren & Putnam in 1932, the original title had become the subtitle: *The New Vision: from Material to Architecture.*[5] Also, for no discernable reason, the 1932 edition spawned a phantom 1930 American edition, often cited and discussed as if it really existed. However, the

---

[1] *bauhaus; zeitschrift für gestaltung*, volume II, numbers 2-3 (July 1, 1928), [2].

[2] *bauhaus; zeitschrift für gestaltung*, volume III, number 4 (October-December, 1929), [2]; the publication date of that issue of *bauhaus* is listed as November 15, 1929 (*ibid.*, 31).

[3] László Moholy-Nagy, *von material zu architektur*, bauhausbücher 14, schriftleitung Walter Gropius [und] Moholy-Nagy (Munich: Albert Langen Verlag, 1929).

[4] László Moholy-Nagy, *Von Material zu Architektur*. Faksimile der 1929 erschienenen Erstausgabe, mit einem Aufsatz von Otto Stelzer und einem Beitrag des Herausgebers, Hans M. Wingler (Mainz: Florian Kupferberg, 1968); and *idem, Von Material zu Architektur*. Faksimile der 1929 erschienenen Erstausgabe, mit einem Aufsatz von Otto Stelzer und einem Beitrag des Herausgebers, Hans M. Wingler, 2. Auflage (Berlin: Gebr. Mann, 2001).

Neither reprint includes Moholy's innovative double-page title "page."

[5] László Moholy-Nagy, *The New Vision: from Material to Architecture*, translated by Daphne M. Hoffman (New York: Brewer, Warren & Putnam Inc., 1932).

publication date of 1932 for the of Brewer, Warren & Putnam edition is well documented and it, unlike its phantom twin, is actually the first American edition and the first in the English language.[6]

The second American edition was published by W.W. Norton in 1938; the illustrations had been revised to include a number devoted to the work of Moholy's Chicago students.[7] This was followed by the third (text figure 17, DVD figure 543) and fourth revised editions of 1946 and 1947, respectively, published by Wittenborn,[8] which had the added feature of a new autobiographical essay that was an ironic play on words: "Abstract of an Artist."[9] Actually, the only difference between the third and fourth editions is a slight change in the sequence and selection of illustrations for "Abstract of an Artist," as well as an "Obituary note" by Walter Gropius and the addition of a frontispiece in the 1947 edition. There is also a curious circumstance in which an illustration appears with its caption in the 1946 edition but only the caption appears in the 1947 edition. (text figure 17, DVD figure 543)

---

[6] See, *e.g.*: "Books Scheduled to Appear During the Autumn Months; a Selected List of Volumes That Are Promised for Publication Before Christmas," *The New York Times Book Review*, September 18, 1932, 10-11, 23, 25, 27 and 31, here 27.

[7] László Moholy-Nagy, *The New Vision: Fundamentals of Design, Painting, Sculpture, Architecture,* translated by Daphne M. Hoffmann, revised and enlarged edition, The New Bauhaus Books, no. 1, editors Walter Gropius, L. Moholy-Nagy (New York: W.W. Norton & Company, Inc, 1938). This edition was also published in London in 1939 by Faber & Faber.

[8] László Moholy-Nagy, *The New Vision 1928 third revised edition, 1946, and Abstract of an Artist,* The documents of modern art, director: Robert Motherwell (New York: Wittenborn and Company, 1946); and *idem, The New Vision, 1928, fourth revised edition 1947 and Abstract of an Artist,* The documents of modern art, director: Robert Motherwell (New York: George Wittenborn, Inc., 1947).

The only difference in these two editions is in the frontispiece and in the selection and order of illustrations in "Abstract of an Artist." This section of the book was based on a lecture given by Moholy in 1944; a recording of this talk is on sound clip two on the DVD accompanying *Moholy-Nagy: Mentor to Modernism.*

Although these editions were designed by Paul Rand, an accomplished graphic designer and an admirer of Moholy's work, the illustrations are much less well printed than in the 1938 edition.

[9] The reader should remember that abstract art was still a matter of some controversy in 1946, and Moholy no doubt felt that since most of his works of fine art were abstract his career as a painter and sculptor had been hindered. Also, it should be borne in mind that Moholy was fascinated by the writings of James Joyce, and he might have considered his "Abstract of an Artist" as a play on words on the title of Joyce's *Portrait of the Artist as a Young Man* of 1914.

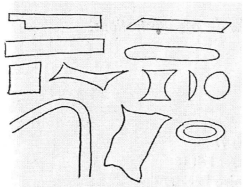

All the shapes which I used in
the last twenty-five years surprised me
one day as being variations of a ribbon
(strip).

All the shapes which I used in
the last twenty-five years surprised me
one day as being variations of a ribbon
(strip).

left: illustration and caption from page 77 of the third edition of *The New Vision, 1946*

right: caption without illustration as it appeared on page 86 of the fourth edition of *The New Vision, 1947*

text figure 17, DVD figure 543

Finally, the handsome edition of *The New Vision* issued by Dover Press in 2005 would be the edition that serves most readers best.[10] On the verso of the title page is this bibliographical note:

---

[10] László Moholy-Nagy, *The New Vision: Fundamentals of Bauhaus Design, Painting, Sculpture, and Archiecture, with Abstract of an Artist* (Mineola, New York: Dover Publications, Inc., 2005).

Because it has become *The New Vision* of record, as it were, two mistakes in pictures and captions in the 2005 edition should be noted. On page 188, reference is made to a Wright building in figure 203 on page [189]; in this edition a photograph of a bathing pier in Berlin was substituted for a photograph of Frank Lloyd Wright's Robie house in Chicago. This error also appears in the 1929 and 1932 editions; the Robie house appears in its proper place in the 1946 and 1947 editions. The other error occurs on page 230 of the 2005 edition (and on page 86 in the 1947 edition): a caption appears without its illustration. The illustration and the caption appear together on page 77 in the 1946 edition (DVD figure 543).

> This Dover edition, first published in 2005, is an unabridged
> republication of the revised and enlarged edition of *The New Vision:*
> *Fundamentals of Design, Painting, Sculpture, Architecture*, as
> published by W.W. Norton & Company, Inc., New York, in 1938.
> Included in this Dover edition is "Abstract of an Artist," excerpted from
> the fourth edition of *The New Vision*, published by George Wittenborn,
> Inc., New York, in 1947. Walter Gropius's Preface to that edition has
> been included as well. Thirty-five of the original half-tone illustrations
> from "Abstract of an Artist" have been replaced in this Dover edition
> with comparable images of better quality.

4.) Moholy's last book, *Vision in Motion*, was published posthumously in 1947, with editorial assistance from Sibyl Moholy-Nagy. There was only one edition, but it was reprinted numerous times, with slight changes in the illustrations in the second printing that were carried over into later printings. There is no reference to the specific printing in citations in *Moholy-Nagy: Mentor to Modernism* unless there is a reference to an illustration that does not exist in both the original printing and the second printing.

5.) Sibyl Moholy-Nagy's biography of her husband, *Moholy-Nagy: Experiment in Totality*, was first published by Harper & Brothers in 1950.[11] Included was an introduction by Walter Gropius. A second edition was published by the M.I.T. Press in 1969.[12] It included the introduction by Walter Gropius, and in addition had an introduction to the second edition by the author herself, and as an epilogue a letter from Robert Jay Wolff to the author, dated May 2nd, 1949. The text of the main body of the book is unchanged, but there were some changes in the illustrations. In *Moholy-Nagy: Mentor to Modernism*, the 1969 edition is cited unless there is a reference to an illustration that appears only in the 1950 edition.

---

[11] Sibyl Moholy-Nagy, *Moholy-Nagy, Experiment in Totality* (New York: Harper & Brothers, 1950).

[12] Sibyl Moholy-Nagy, *Moholy-Nagy, Experiment in Totality* (Cambridge: The M.I.T. Press, 1969).

Appendix G: Original German Texts for Passages That Appear Above Only in English Translation

German-language text number one:

(In Chapter One a facsimile of the original newspaper article appears on page 46 and an English translation appears on page 47.)

"Die amtlicher Berichte von Sontag," *Pester Lloyd, Abendblatt* [Budapest], July 2, 1917, 2.

Die amtlicher Berichte von Sontag. Bericht unseres Generalstabes.

Das Ungarische Telegraphen-Korrespondenzbureau meldet: Amtlicher Bericht. Ausgegeben am 1. Juli.

Oestlicher Kriegsschauplatz.

In Ostgalizien ist bei der Heeresgruppe des Generalobersten v. Böhm die Abwehrschlacht in vollem Gange.

Noch mehrtägiger sichtlicher Zunahme des Artilleriefeuers entwicklte sich gestern die Artillerieschlacht zu größter Heftigkeit. Auch schwerste Geschütze haben eingegriffen.

Nachmittags setzen sich südlich und südöstlich Brzezany und bei Koniuchy starkte inanterieangriffe ein, die überall vollkommen abgewiesen wurden. Wo sich Teile der feindlichen Infanterie in unserem Vernichtsfeuer überhaupt erheben konnte, blieben sie im Sperrfeuer liegen.

Ein in späten Nachmittagsstunden nordwestlich Zalosce angesetzter, sehr starker Angriff brach im vorzüglich vereinigten Artilleriefeuer zusammen.

Gegen Mitternacht versuchte der Feind südlich Brzezany ohne Artillerievorbereiten vorzubrechen. Er wurde abgewiesen.

Nachtsüber flaute das Artilleriefeuer ab. Um in den Morgenstudnen wieder aufzuleben.

German-language text number two:

(An English translation of this review appears on page 152 of Chapter Two.)

Ludwig Hilberseimer, "Bildende Kunst," *Sozialistische Monatshefte*, volume XXVIII, number [4] (March 6, 1922), 242-243.

Moholy-Nagy, von dem Der Sturm eine Ausstellung in Berlin veranstaltete, verrät schon durch die Bezeichnung seiner Bilder seine konstruktiven Absichten. Er versucht das Unpersönlich-Kollektive unserer technischen Zivilisation, des Industrialismus, synthetisch zu formen. Er ist völlig unromantisch. Während etwa Kurt Schwitters bei seinen Merzbildern die von ihm verwandten verschiedenen Materialen durch übermalung aufhebt, eine malerische Wirkung erstrebt, verwendet Moholy-Nagy seine Gestaltungsmittel mit asketischer Nacktheit, läßt sie vollkomen in ihrer Materialität bestehen. Bei seinen Reliefs aus Holz, Glas, Metall, Porzellan, Stoff und Papier vereinigt er fertige Gegenstände oder geformte Materialen zu einer Konstruktion, bei der Farbflächen und -streifen nicht übersondern völlig gleichgeordnet sind, das konstruktive Prinzep ledeglich unterstüzen. In seinen Bildern dient die ungedeckte graue Leinwand den geometrischen Konstruktionen als Untergrund. Reine Formen: geometrische Figuren, Kreise, Räder, typographische Elemente, streng liniiert, ohne Willkür, geometrisch geordnet, präzisierte Formen, äußerste Exaktheit. Entsprechende Farben: weiß, gelb, rot, blau, schwarz. Ungebrochene Töne von technischer Klarheit. Moholy-Nagys Materialartistik zeigt sich vor allem bei seinen Plastiken. So bei seiner Nickelplastik mit Feder, deren strahlender Glanz und Spiegelung die Exaktheit vielfach bricht und variiert. Oder bei seiner Holzskulptur, deren stumpfes Material einzig durch die Spannung der Formen belebt wird.

German-language text number three:

(An English translation of this text appears in Chapter Two, pages 167 and 168.)

[Max Burchartz?], "Stijl-und Dada- Abend im Jenaer Kunstverein, 1922," as in Chapter Two, note 327.

Chapter Two, note 360: [Max Burchartz?], "Stijl-und Dada- Abend im Jenaer Kunstverein, 1922," Theo van Doesburg files, Rijksbureau voor Kunsthistorische Dokumentie, the Hague, also available on microfiche (*Theo van Doesburg Archive*, Leiden: IDC, 1991), sheet 373.

This document is evidently an essay submitted to van Doesburg for publication in *De Stijl* that never appeared there. It is typed, with handwritten editorial corrections. The author remains unknown, but it is possible that he was Max Burchartz (1887-1961).

Im Kunstverein war der Saal mit einer äusserst misstrauisch und feindlich blickenden Zuschauerschar gefüllt, als Doesburg mit schwarzen Hemd und weisser Kravatte, bleich, aber gefasst, zum Rednerpult schritt. Schwitters sah eine kleine Katastrophe voraus und kam seinem Freund vorbeugend zu Hilfe. Er trat unversehens vor und erklärte mit eindringlicher Stimme:

"Jena ist die einzige Stadt in Europa, in der es vorgekommen ist, dass jemand es wagte bei einem Vortrage van Doesburgs zu pfeifen. Dass dergleichen nicht wieder passiert! Bleiben Sie gefälligst ganz still und hören Sie schön zu!" (Womit er Does das Wort erteilte.)

Schwitters schrach hier wie der Lehrer zu ungezogen Schulkindern. Und so unglaublich das ist: der Bann heilt wirklich über den Vortrags Doesburgs an, der ohne Zweifel gut war, aber extrem und

agressive, wie es in Doesburgs Art lag, [five unread handwritten words] sah.

Und dann schritt Nelly zum Flügel und liess den "Elephantenmarsch" los. Da gab es dann bald kein Halten mehr. Man zischte und pfiff, während Nelly unbeirrt weiterspielte, die grossen blauen Augen erstaunt-belustigt aufs Publikum gerichtet. Bei Schwitters' Gedichten herrschte dann wieder einige Ruhe, da der alte Magier die Leute in Bann schlug. Dafür brach bei Hans Arps Vorlesung plötzlich ein Höllenlärm los. Das Publikum fühlte sich verspottet. Anderseits hatte der Lärm im Publikum die unerwartete Wirkung, dass nun der Maler Peter Röhl (Schüler van Doesburgs) aufsprang und eine seiner phantastichen Ansprachen hielt, die zwar nicht für logischen Aufbau, dafür aber der überraschenden Wendungen wegen bekannt waren. Diesmal hieß es unter anderem: ". . . Da sich aber der deutsche Puffkismus hier wieder einmal deutlich gezeigt hat, so stehen wir drei junge Burschen hier auf (der nicht gerade junge Soester Kunstkritiker Will Frieg und ich waren geistesgegenwärtig genug uns rasch zu erheben) und rufen: Theo van Doesburg lebe hoch (hoch, hoch riefen wir aus vollen Halse), ungeachtet, dass die Rede in diesem Moment keinen erkennbaren Sinn hatte. Die Versammlung grübelte noch ein wenig über Peters Worte nach die ihr ebenso unverständlich erschien wie alles, was auf dem Podium vorging, und begab sich, erregt diskutierend, nach hause.

German-language text number four:

(An English translation of this text appears on pages 359 and 360 of Chapter Four.)

Max Marschalk, "'Hoffmanns Erzählungen,' 'Absage' an Jacques Offenbach," *Vossische Zeitung; Berlinische Zeitung von Staats- und gelehrten Sachen*, Post Ausgabe, February 14, 1929, [11].

"Hoffmanns Erzählungen," "Absage" an Jacques Offenbach

Als ich gestern die Staatsoper am Platz der Republik verließ, fragte ich mich: waren das "Hoffmanns Erzälungen," die da vor sich gingen, war das die phantastische Oper Jacques Offenbachs? Und ich fragte mich weiter: wenn nun schon Bühnengestalter und Spielleiter so absurd sich gebärden, so stilwidrig, wenn sie so ein frivoles Spiel treiben mit einem immerhin illustren Kunstwerk: warum lassen sie sich nicht einen neuen Text schreiben und warum zu dem neuen Text nicht eine neue Musik? Mögen sie auf die "kommenden Autoren" warten, wenn ihnen "das schöpferische Erlassen der wahren und nicht der vorgestellten (scheinbaren) Bedürfnisse" Aufgabe zu sein scheint? Mögen sie das alte nicht frevlerisch antasten und in Grund und Boden "erfassen." Es geht nicht an, daß eine unserer klassischen Opern nach der anderen, monumentale Meisterwerke, beim Spieltriebe unklarer Phantaste verfallen.

Alle Phantastik dieser phantastischen Oper ist durch den "Bühnengestalter" L. Moholy-Nagy gründlich zerstört worden. Er will neu sein um jeden Preis; als ob es beim Vorstotzen ins Neuland auf das Wollen ankäme und nicht vielmehr auf das Müssen; auf das Müssen wirklich schöpferischer Geister.

Aber handelt es sich hier wirklich um einem Vorstoß? Ist das, was dieser Maler-Mathematiker herausrechnet, nicht von den Produktiven längst aufgegebene, von den Rezeption längst preisgebene Kunst von gestern und vorgestern? Müssen wir unter den Hartnäckigen leiden, die sich immer noch nicht entschliessen können, aufzugeben und preiszugeben? Hätte der Intendant Ernst Legal nicht dem Regisseur Ernst Legal das Handwerk legen müssen? Oder, wenn der Intendant versagte: Gibt es nicht einen General-Intendanten, dazu eingesetzt, ein Machtwort zu sprechen, zu verhindern, daß der Anfang vom Ende uns so gefährlich nahe rückt.

Ich will nicht weiter auf die verdrießlichen Details dieser Bühnengestaltung eingehen. Anfangs dachte ich noch, daß aus der Verneinung alles dessen, was uns bisher Phantastik war, eine neue Art von Phantastik erstehen könnte. Aber der nicht ungünstige Eindruck schwächte sich schnell genug ab, und schließlich hinterliessen die furchtbare Selbstgesölligkeit der Bühnenbilder und der Bühnengeschehnisse und die nicht minder furchtbare Aufdringlichkeit, die den "wahren Bedürfnissen" des Werkes Hohn sprachen und seine Verehrer brüstieren, eine tiefe Verstimmung in mir; und, was beinahe noch schlimmer ist, ich langweilte mich.

Was ist nun noch viel zu sagen? Das Werk verschwindet hinter dem Aufführungsrummel — welche ein Venedig-Bild: ein ridicüle Varieté-Szene mit drei papageienhaft aufgeputzten Frauen, die auf Trapezen sitzen und aus dem Hintergrund immer gegen das Orchester geschleudert werden, mit Lazarett-Betten, fünf Monden und sonstigen unergründlichen Detail — und es bleibt eigentlich nur übrig festzustellen, das Alexander von Zemlinsky, der musikalische Leiter, seine Sache sehr gut machte, aber doch vergeblich versuchte, dit Aufmerksamkeit auf die immer noch schöne und in Schönheit lebendig Musik zu lenken. Im übrigen scheint mir die Staatsoper am Platz der Republik ihre Experimentierlüsternheit auch auf die Sänger und Sängerinnen auszudehnen. Da gab es einen vielleicht nicht unbegabten, aber gefangstechnisch noch vollkommen unfertigen, wenn nicht gar in die Irre geführten Tenor sehr kleinen Kalibers, der erst einmal lernten und ich sich auf einer kleinen Provinzbühne die nötige Routine holen sollte. Nicht unbegabt ist auch die Vertreterin der Olympia, doch bat sie nicht mehr als eine Konservatoriumsleistung: mit welchem Urteil ich den Konservatorien nicht zu nahe treten möchte. Karl Hammes ragte durch gefanglich und schauspielerisch kräftige Gestaltung als Lindorf, als Coppelius-Dapertutto-Mirakel hervor. Sodann fiel noch Käthe Heidersbach als Antonia auf, wenn sie auch in allem zu gesund ist. Sonst gab es — leider! — nur mittelmässige Leistungen. Es wurde viel geklaticht: es wollte mir aber so scheinen, als ob das Gros des Publikums nicht gerade erbaut war.

Man stelle sich vor, daß unser ganzer Reichtum an klassischen und romantische Oper auf die von L. Moholy-Nagy in "Hoffmanns Erzählungen" angewohnte sachliche und abstrakte Manier — Ewald Dülberg ist ein zahmer Reaktionär gegen diesen Bauhäusler! — inszeniert würde: es wäre nicht auszuhalten. Aber diese Manier ist eine Krankheit, die sich austoben wird. Einstweilen philosophiert in den "Blätter der Staats und der Städtischen Oper" der am Platz der Republik amtierende Hausphilosoph von einer "Absage an falschen Theater-Naturalismus, Absage an falsche Schönheit und Echtheit des Kostüms, Absage an die falsche Pathetik der Gebärde"; und das, was in diesem Falle beim Philosophieren und Experimentieren hervorkommt, ist doch weiter nicht als eine Absage an Jacques Offenbach.

German-language text number five:

(An English translation of this text appears on pages 366 and 367 of Chapter Four.)

Oscar Bie, [review], *Berlin Börsen-Courier; Tagezeitung für alle Gebiete*, February 24, 1931; reprinted in Curjel, *Experiment Krolloper*, 309-310.

Die wartende Butterfly konnte überhaupt nicht ganz gelingen, weil die Geschlossenheit des Raumes fehlt, die Moholy-Nagy bei seinem Dekorationssystem nicht brauchen konnte. Der Meister am Bauhaus, abstrakt und konstructiv veranlangt, fand in dem Schema des japanischen Hauses Reizmomente für seine Phantasie. Er stellt das Haus offen in der Luft, läßt die Wände hin und her schieben, dreht es vom ersten zum zweiten Akt nur ein wenig nach nach der andere Seite, betont überall die reine Mathematik seiner Konstruktionen, läßt zur Erhöhung der Dekorative Wirkung über die halbe Bühne von eine Reihe japanischer Stäbe herabhängen, befiehlt der Drehbühne die verschiedenen Partien des Hauses und seiner Umgebung nebeneinander zu entwickeln, entwirft als Hintergrund eine reizende Gebirgslandschaft mit weitvorgestrecken Landzungen ins Meer hinein, so wir wie sie von der japanischen Kunst her kennen. Eine einartige Form des Bühnenenprospekts, die von der gewohnten kitschigen Art des japanischen Landschaft ebensoweit entfernt ist, als sie sich hütet, bei einer realistischen Oper in die reine Abstraktion aufzugehen.

German-language text number six:

(An English translation of a portion of this text appears on page 437 of Chapter Four.)

Siegfried Kracauer's review, "Abstrakte Kunst," discusses two of Moholy's films: *Lichtspiel Schwarz Grau* [A Lightplay Black White Gray] and *Impressionen vom alten Marseiller Hafen* [Impressions of the Old Port of Marseilles]. The review originally appeared in the *Frankfurter Zeitung*, March 19, 1932; it was reprinted in: Siegfried Kracauer, *Kleine Schriften zum Film*, in: idem, *Werke*, Band 6, [Teil] 3, 1932-1961, edited by Inka Mülder-Bach (Frankfurt am Main: Suhrkamp Verlag, 2004), 37-38.

Moholy-Nagy ist, wie seine beiden in *der Kamera* gezeigten Filmchen wieder einmal beweisen, ein außerordentlicher Photograph. Am liebsten unterdrückte er alles Gegenständliche, um noch Kontrastwirkungen, Licht- und Schatteneffekte usw. übrig zu lassen. So jedenfalls verfährt er in dem einen der Filme, der sich darauf beschränkt, verschiedene Konstruktionselemente wie Kugeln, Spiralen, gestanzte Bleche, polierte Röhren und Teile komplizierter Apparaturen in photographisch günstige Situationen zu bringen. Es ist nicht zu leugnen, daß hierbei wunderschöne Formspiele enstehen. Glanzlichter und Schraubenschatten durchbringen einander, und das ganze mechanische Getriebe bildet, vom Zwang der statischen Gesetze befreit, eine Folge sehenswerter Ornamente, die den imaginären Raum in stetem Wechsel erfüllen. Allerdings fehlt ihnen Zweck und Sinn. Ihres stofflichen Untergrundes enthoben, sind sie nur bedeutungslos schön, ohne sonst die geringste Funktion auszuüben; es sei denn die, durch ihr bloßes Dasein die Fülle der Chancen auszudeuten, die unsere helldunkle Welt dem Filmoperateur bietet. Das ist von großem artistischen Interesse, aber eine Werkstattangelegenheit, deren öffentliche Vorführung unter Umständen Verwirrung stiftet. Denn diese abstrakte Kunstübung kann ebenso gut als Studie des Avantgarde-Künstlers aufgefaßt werden wie als Flucht vor der Auseinandersetzung mit dem Gegenständen und Sachproblemen, die uns bedrängen. Der epigonale deutsche Idealismus z.B. ist kaum noch etwas anderes als eine solche Flucht ins Abstrakte und verhält sich sich denn auch der Wirklichkeit gegeüber reaktionär. Zum Glück scheint sich Moholy-Nagy der mit rein formalen Kunstbetätigung verbunden Gafahren bewußt zu sein. Sein anderer Film behandelt das Thema *Marseille*. Und zwar durchschweift er die Stadt nicht wie ein Genießer, sondern nummt sich vor, das soziale Elend in ihr zu beleuchten. Eine Menge von Aufnahmen aus dem Hafenverteil sind aneinandergereiht, und finstere Gassenperspektiven, verwüstete Gesichter und zerlumpte Figuren häufen sich dicht. Der Eindruck ist um so stärker, als auch der Gegenschatz zwischen der menschlichen Not und dem Naturzauber des Südens offenbar wird. Wenn die Bilder ihre Absicht doch nicht erreichen, so ist der Grund hierfür der, daß weniger Gewicht auf die Verdeutlichung des Elends als auf die Auswertung seiner malerischen Wirkungen gelegt wird. Das Mosaik spult sich auch so rasch ab, daß nichts recht haften bleibt. Totalbilder hätten öfters die zahlreichen kleinen Ausschnitte unterbrechen müssen, und eie zeitweilige Verlangsamung des Tempos wäre entschieden zweckdienlich gewesen.

Appendix H: "Virtually Moholy"
by Regan Brown

The main goal of this particular "old meets new media" combination of book and DVD (Digital Versatile Disc) is a simplicity of form and ease of use mediated by contemporary technologies, one that I would hope does justice to both the legacy of László Moholy-Nagy and to the work of his innovative biographer, Lloyd C. Engelbrecht.

By convening an age-old form of publishing with a current one in the presentation of Moholy-Nagy's work, we hope to reach beyond those already somewhat familiar with his work to bring this "mentor to Modernism" to the attention of twenty-first century artists and art historians struggling to come to grips with work created from an ever-expanding welter of media, message and material. For Moholy-Nagy this creative process appeared to be a seamless and effortless alchemy, but was in fact a momentous and focused evolution, one thoroughly documented in this new tome.

I met Lloyd during the finalization of the text portion of the project, but Lloyd, much in the spirit of Moholy-Nagy, wanted to push the envelope a bit by introducing the recent technological advances of the digital realm to the presentation of the book. After a few meetings together, discussing all the various alternatives available, we decided on a straightforward approach that would "triangulate" the needs of a wide-ranging audience by committing images, audio and video to a standard play DVD, a disc which would also carry an all-encompassing PDF file, the two encoded together to be slipped succinctly into a sleeve at the back of the first volume of the printed book. This DVD will allow the user to view Moholy-Nagy's work in a virtual museum of her or his own making, whether they chose to sit back in a comfy chair with book in lap, perusing images with their DVD remote control on a TV, or sidled up to a computer in some corner of a library, hyper-linking to images, sound or film clips embedded in a PDF (Portable Document Format) file.

Whichever way you choose, I thank you, the reader, for your participation in this unique and interactive approach to the work of one of the twentieth century's most versatile artists. I would also like to thank Lloyd Engelbrecht for including me in this wonderful project and commend him for being a biographer well up to the task of presenting Moholy-Nagy's work in a contemporary format worthy of this twentieth-century renaissance man.

Appendix I: Addenda and Corrigenda

Chapter One, pages 19-21:

The evidence available to me at the time I wrote pages 19 through 21 led me to conflate two men known as János Horváth. In fact Moholy's teacher in Szeged called János Horváth is different from the man of the same name who taught at the University of Budapest. Although no exact dates could be found by me for the Szeged János Horváth, he was of approximately the same age as the Budapest János Horváth (1878-1961). It is possible the two might have been related, perhaps as cousins, but at least as teachers of literature they may well have known each other, and surely the Szeged Horváth was aware of the Budapest Horváth because of the latter's publications.

I first made the mistake of conflating these two figures in an article I published in 2004,[1] and carried it over into the text of *Moholy-Nagy: Mentor to Modernism.* Nevertheless, my main points, as they relate to Moholy, are still valid. Moholy received an excellent literary education at his *gimnázium* in Szeged. He became aware of the poetry of Endre Ady at an early age, and he surely was aware that the Budapest Horváth received criticism from conservatives for his book on Ady and that Horváth stood his ground and went on to have a very successful career.

Thanks to research carried out by Márton Orosz of Budapest, at my request, I now have the information that János Horváth of Szeged taught at the school Moholy attended, now known as the *Radnóti Miklós Kísérleti Gimnázium*, from 1905 to 1935.[2]

Chapter One, page 50:

With reference to Moholy's visit to Székesfehérvár early in 1918, it is known that he was sent by a hospital in that city to a hospital in Budapest for treatment for his injured thumb on February 7th.[3]

---

[1] Lloyd C. Engelbrecht, "The Formation of a Renaissance Man: László Moholy-Nagy's Secondary Schooling in Hungary," *Hungarian Studies Review*, volume XXXI, numbers 1-2 (Spring-Fall, 2004), [1]-[14], here 5-6.

[2] Ferenc Tóth and István Udvari-Nagy, editors, *Centenáriumi Emlékkönyv: Iskolánk Száz Éve* (Szeged:Radnóti Miklós Kísérleti Gimnázium, 1998), 2:284.

[3] See: Attila Bonhardt to Csilla Markója, TLS, December 15, 2001, available in Vienna from the Ständige Ungarische Archivdelegation beim Österreichischen Kriegsarchiv/Az Osztrák Hadilevéltár Mellett Működö Állandó Magyar Levéltári Kirandeltség [The Permanent Hungarian Archive Delegation to the Austrian War Archive].

Chapter Three, pages 201-202:

Concerning the history of the Bauhaus, the catalogue of a recent exhibition provides a good introduction. See: Barry Bergdoll and Leah Dickerman, editors, *Bauhaus 1919-1933: Workshops for Modernity* (New York: Museum of Modern Art, 2009)

after Chapter Three, page 332:

The following sentence appears with slight errors. The corrected sentence should read:

Sound Clips: Enter the Sound Clips section by scrolling down until the blue line appears beneath the Sound Clip section heading, and then press enter.

Chapter Five, page 614:

In connection with a quotation by Conrad Sommer, excerpted from his full statement in Moholy's *Vision in Motion* and beginning with these words, "The Institute of Design's method of group therapy can be likened to psychoanalysis in that it reaches down into the unconscious," and evidently written in 1943,[4] earlier evidence of Moholy's continuing interest in psychoanalysis and its relevance for his school should be noted. On January 16, 1941, Thomas M. French (1892-1974), Associate Director of the Institute for Psychoanalysis, delivered a lecture at the School of Design in Chicago called: "Dreams, Day Dreams and Creative Fantasy." French discussed: "Dream as wish fulfillment—dream as the expression of the social attitude and the artistic fantasy—the mechanic of inspiration and creative work."[5]

---

[4] László Moholy-Nagy, *Vision in Motion* (Chicago: Paul Theobald, 1947), 72.

[5] The information is from an announcement designed and printed as a postcard by Frank Barr; a copy is in the Chicago Historical Society.

Chronological Index

Chronological Index, page 748

Chronological Index, page 750

Chronological Index, page 752

Chronological Index, page 754

Chronological Index, page 758

Chronological Index, page 760

Chronological Index, page 762

Chronological Index, page 764

Chronological Index, page 766

General Index

A II, painting of 1924 by Moholy, 323, 329-330, front cover of Volume One, DVD figures 215, 216 and 218

Aabenraa, Denmark, 195

Aalto, Aino, designer and architect, wife of Alvar Aalto, 400-401, 419-420, 528, 610, DVD figures 55 and 298

Aalto, Alvar, designer and architect, husband of Aino Aalto, 400-401, 419-420, 610 and 647

Aaron, David, architect, 651

Abbot, Berenice, photographer, 460, 625 and 628

Abbott, Jere, museum curator, 275

A.B.C. in Sound, film, 428-431 and 500

Abraham Lincoln High School, Brooklyn, 608-609

Abstract Expressionism, 697-699

Abstract of an Artist, essay by Moholy written in 1944, 183-184, 307-308, 671-672 and sound clip 2

Abstraction-Création, Paris, 515

Abstraction-Création, Paris, Moholy's one-artist exhibition at, 1934, 497-498

Abstraction-Création, Paris, Moholy's paintings illustrated in its annuals, 1932-1936, 497-498

Abstrakte und Surrealistische Malerei und Plastik, Zurich, 1929, 493

Achenbach, Ado von, theatre director and photographer, 417-418, DVD figures 291 left, 292 and 293 left

Ada, Serbia (Ada was in Hungary when Moholy lived there), 6-7, 11-12 and DVD figure 5

Adachi, Kazumi, architect, 651

Adams, Ansel, photographer, 606-607 and 615-616

Addams, Jane, pacifist and social reformer, 538-539

Adorno, Theodor W., writer and social critic, 360, 413-414 and Appendix D, 723-724

Ady, Endre, poet, 19-21, 63, 69-71, 73, 89, 691 and DVD figure 35

AGFA, German camera-film company, 480-481

General Index, page 770

General Index, page 786

General Index, page 796

General Index, page 798

General Index, page 800

General Index, page 810

General Index, page 814

Museum of Modern Art, San Francisco, see: San Francisco Museum of Modern Art

General Index, page 830

Spanish Flu, see: Influenza pandemic

Spanish Lady, see: Influenza pandemic

Spaarnestad, Dutch magazine publisher, 397-398 and 402-403

Speight, Sadie, architect, 469

Spencer, Franz (né Schulz), writer and brother of Lucia Moholy, 382, 595 and Appendix C, 713

Spencer, Robert C., architect and designer, text figure 13 and DVD figure 406

Spiegel, Fred, mail-order merchandising executive, 636

Spiegel, Inc., mail merchandising firm, 576 and 635-637

Spiegel, M.J. ("Modie"), mail-order merchandising executive, 636-637

Sponsors Committee of the School of Design in Chicago, 590-591 and 598

Sprague, Paul, art historian and architectural preservationist, xv

Springfield, Illinois, 693-694

Staatliche Akademie für graphische Künste und Buchgewerbe zu Leipzig, 289-290, 336-337 and 339-340

Staatliche Bauhochschule Weimar, successor school to the Weimar Bauhaus, 242

Staatliche Kunstbibliothek, Berlin, 386

Staatsoper am Platz der Republik, see: Kroll Opera, Berlin

Staatsoper on *Unter den Linden*, 341, 367 and 369

Städtische Kunsthalle, Mannheim, 508-509

Stahle, Norma K., artist, designer and good-design advocate, 532, 546-549, 566, 574, 576-577, 583, 588 and DVD figure 441

Stark & Riese, porcelain-enamel sign factory in Tannroda, Thuringia, 317-318, 322 and DVD figures 203-204 and 206-210

State Academy for Graphic and Book Arts in Leipzig, see: *Staatliche Akademie für graphische Künste und Buchgewerbe zu Leipzig*

State Opera on the Plaza of the Republic, see: Kroll Opera, Berlin

State Street, 2009 North, Chicago, 624, DVD figures 401 and 477

Stedelijk Museum, Amsterdam, 180, 288-289 and 488-489

General Index, page 834

General Index, page 836

General Index, page 838

Colophon

The type faces used in this book are Cooper Light for the colophon, covers, title pages and versos of title pages, and Times New Roman for the text faces.

Cooper type faces, originated by Chicago designer Oswald ("Oz") Bruce Cooper (1879-1940), with their subtly-rounded serifs, were widely used as display type faces in the Windy City while Moholy lived there.

Times New Roman is a face originated by Stanley Morison (1889-1967) for *The Times* (London), where Moholy would have encountered it. While Moholy lived in London, Times New Roman was emerging as a widely-used type face for books and magazines, and Morison was probably the most widely-known designer in England. Nevertheless there is no indication that Morison and Moholy ever met.

The Flying Trapeze Press, located in Cincinnati, was formed to publish scholarly books in art history and other fields in which images, films and sound clips on a DVD disk supplement the paper text. The name of the Press refers to a highlight of the long tradition of printing and publishing in Cincinnati when, during the heyday of the traveling circus, many American circus posters were printed by the Strobridge Lithographing Company. It also refers to a colorful passage in the first book published by The Flying Trapeze Press, *Moholy-Nagy: Mentor to Modernism*, describing Moholy's 1929 Berlin production of Jacques Offenbach's *The Tales of Hoffmann*, when, during the singing of the opera's famed "Barcarolle," three female trapeze artists swung from the stage over the orchestra pit and out over the audience.

The publisher's logo, seen on the back cover of each volume, is based on a detail of a Strobridge lithograph dating from the nineteenth century.

This is copy number 24 of 300 copies.

Lloyd C. Engelbrecht

works written or co-written by Lloyd C. Engelbrecht and not cited in *Moholy-Nagy: Mentor to Modernism*

"Adler & Sullivan's Pueblo Opera House: City Status for a New Town in the Rockies," *Art Bulletin*, volume LXVII, number 2 (June, 1985), [277]-295

"Eames, Charles [and Ray]" and "Martin, Noel," *Contemporary Designers*, second edition (Chicago: St. James Press, 1990), [150]-151 and 370-371, respectively

"Fire-Proof and Decorative: Metalwork by Henry Trost in the Lafayette Square Opera House," *The Decorative Arts Society Newsletter*, volume XII, number 2 (June 1986), 3

"Henry Trost: the Prairie School in the Southwest," *The Prairie School Review*, volume VI, number 4 (fourth quarter, 1969) [entire issue]

"Marie-Zoe Greene-Mercier: the Polyplane Collages," *Art International*, volume XXII, number 6 (October, 1978), 21-23 and 52

"The Second Owls Club, Tucson, Arizona, Restored," *Triglyph; a Southwestern Journal of Architecture and Environmental Design*, number 7 (Winter, 1988-1989) [published by the College of Architecture and Environmental Design, Arizona State University], 26-27

"Trost in Tucson," *Triglyph; a Journal of Architecture and Environmental Design* number 2 (Spring, 1985), ii and 25-31

in preparation: *Rudolph Wseissenborn: Pioneer of Modernist Painting in Chicago* (Cincinnati: Flying Trapeze Press, date to be announced)

with June F. Engelbrecht:

Henry C. Trost: Architect of the Southwest (El Paso: El Paso Public Library Association, 1981) [reviewed in: *Journal of the Society of Architectural Historians*, volume XLI, number 4 (December, 1982), 351-352, and in: *Essays and Monographs in Colorado History* (Colorado Historical Society), 1984, 81-91]

"Henry C. Trost as Draftsman," *Library Chronicle* [published by the Humanities Research Center, University of Texas at Austin], new series, number 16 (1981), 78-92

"Prairie School Architect: Henry C. Trost," *Texas Homes*, volume II, number 4 (November/December), 1978, 26-30

"The Trost Touch: Henry Trost & the Bhutanese Architecture," *NOVA; the University of Texas at El Paso Magazine*, volume XVI, number 1 (December, 1980), 3-5 and 16

in press: "Trost, Henry Charles," *Grove Encyclopedia of American Art* (Oxford University Press)